TENNIS

DO NOT TAKE AWAY!

TENNIS

A Cultural History

Heiner Gillmeister

LEICESTER UNIVERSITY PRESS

LONDON

Leicester University Press
A Cassell imprint
Wellington House, 125 Strand, London WC2R 0BB, England

First published 1997. Reprinted in paperback 1998

Originally published in German as *Kulturgeschichte des Tennis* © Wilhelm Fink Verlag 1990.
This translation © Heiner Gillmeister 1997.

British Library Cataloguing-in-Publication Data
A catalogue record for this book is available from the British Library.

ISBN 0 7185 0147 0 Hardback
 0 7185 0195 0 Paperback

Typeset by Ben Cracknell Studios

Printed and bound in Great Britain by Redwood Books, Trowbridge, Wiltshire

Contents

◇

List of plates

◇

List of figures

◇

Preface

⬦

The more superficial beholder of the book's cover (a magnificent piece of artistry by the Venetian painter Gabriel Bella) will have failed to notice, on its continuation overleaf, the employee of an ancient *jeu de paume* who, having scaled the slanting roof of the gallery, is busily retrieving from the dusty recesses of the window-sill the stray tennis balls from below. Many thousand times, it may be said with some justification, I have made efforts similar to his in order to collect the stray tennis balls of more than eight hundred years of tennis history; this in order to secure for the reader, on the pages following, a game that is both instructive and enjoyable.

In this work, I have brought to a conclusion my long preoccupation with the game's history. Its various manifestations are described from the beginnings in the twelfth century to the dawn of modern lawn tennis, the first decades of the All England Championships in Wimbledon, the Davis Cup, Olympic lawn tennis tournaments, sporting events which today claim the attention of millions of people world-wide.

Generally speaking, books on the history of sport, and the history of tennis in particular, have hardly ever been works of scholarship. Systematic research into original sources has never been undertaken, nor have writers cared to name their sources with any precision. The special feature of this book is that it is not only based on a vast amount of original data, but also that all the sources used are stated accurately. This holds good for the history of the ancient game of tennis as well as for its modern offshoot, lawn tennis. In my opinion, my own original contribution lies in the investigation of the medieval varieties of tennis. The origins of the game and its evolution over a period of many centuries have always been the weakest point in existing history books which are anecdotal at best. More than fifteen years have elapsed since I for the first time advanced the theory that the competitive ball games of Europe (including tennis) took as a model the medieval tournament. In this book, an attempt has been made to substantiate this claim. In addition, peculiarities of the ancient game which have survived in modern tennis such as its curious counting method, its often strange terminology (all inherited from its medieval ancestor) and the history of its implements and rules are explained in detail.

The history of modern lawn tennis is by far better documented than that of its predecessor. In recent years, many useful books have appeared on the subject, and the sections dealing with the beginnings of lawn tennis in the more important tennis nations such as England, the USA and France are to a great extent based on them. Not infrequently, however, original research has shown that even some of the most accepted truths of tennis history are in need of revision, and here the misconceived view of the origin of the Davis Cup may be quoted as a case in point. As for Germany, existing literature (which I had consulted for the original German edition of this book) turned out to be more or less useless on closer inspection. That is why for the present edition a new evaluation of primary sources has been inevitable. In particular, the role played by English and American players and officials in breaking the stolid subjects of the Kaiser into the routine of the game had never been dealt with. It is to this task that I, not least because of my professional background, have set my hand with great enthusiasm.

I would like to express most sincere thanks to Anja Roesinger and Bert Ventzki for help with the typescript and illustrations, the staff of Bonn University Library for their ceaseless help over the years, and Janet Joyce and Cassell/Leicester University Press for presenting the work in such an attractive form. Cassell have a long tradition in sporting books; their *Cassell's Book of Sports and Pastimes* came out in 1893, and I hope to be a worthy continuator of it.

    For help of various kinds, I owe a debt of gratitude to the following: The Rt. Hon. The Lord Aberdare, London; Sir Ralph Anstruther, Balcaskie, Pittenweem, Fife; Don Anthony, Sidcup, Kent; Giovanni Bagaglia, Rome; Cees de Bondt, The Hague; Guy Bonhomme, Paris; Rolf Bremmer, Leiden; Pieter Breuker, Groningen; P. Cutts, Leamington Spa; Sigrid Gaertner, Heidelberg; Manfred Groten, Cologne; Gerald N. Gurney, Great Bromley; Eerke U. Hamer, Dassel; Andreas Höfer, Cologne; Charles Hoey, Elizabeth, PA; Judith Joseph, Edgbaston; Ferenc Krasovec, Budapest; Béatrice Leroy, Pau; Alan Longbottom, Pudsey, West Yorks; R. Mattausch, Bad Homburg v.d. Höhe; Roger Morgan, Cambridge; Vicente Navarro Adelantado, Las Palmas de Gran Canaria; Frank van Rensselaer Phelps, King of Prussia, PA; Heino Rose, Hamburg; Ditta Sikorski, Hanover; Hannes Strohmeyer, Vienna; Eric Taladoire, Paris; A.J. Tinkel, Reading; Erik de Vroede, Louvain; Annemie Weiss, Saarlouis.

Heiner Gillmeister
Bonn, Spring 1997

ONE

The origins of tennis: the monks' racket

◇

TENNIS AND THE DEVIL

However much its many followers may paint it in glowing colours, the origins of tennis are rather sinister. The first record of the game, at least, comes from a dark and evil establishment, hell itself. There once was in medieval Paris a young clerk in holy orders who, because of his extremely short memory, was called an 'idiot' by his comrades.[1] One day the devil approached him and showed him a magic stone: 'As long as you hold this in your hand', the fiend said, 'you will know everything.' The student accepted the gift and soon became a perfect scholar. Not long after, however, he was struck by an illness and fell down dead (or so it was thought). A band of demons snatched his soul from his body and rushed it to a horrible valley steaming with sulphurous vapours. Here the devils divided into two teams, each taking a position at one end of the valley, and began to play. 'And those standing at the one end hit the poor soul after the fashion of the game at ball, and those at the other end caught it in mid-air with their hands.' To make things worse, the devils' claws had the sharpness of iron nails, and so tortured was the poor soul that no martyrdom imaginable could compare.

This story has been passed down to us by Caesarius of Heisterbach, a monk of the order of St Bernard. Caesarius incorporated it in his *Dialogus Miraculorum* written between AD 1219 and 1223.[2] His informant had been a certain Hermann, the Abbot of Marienstatt, a monastery not far from his native town of Heisterbach. Hermann, in turn, had heard the story from the victim himself, the Paris student who, having survived the ordeal after all, had entered the Cistercian order and later become Abbot of Morimond, an important monastery in the diocese of Langres in France. In this capacity, he had told Brother Hermann about the devilish pastime from which he had had to suffer.

Although the enlightened modern reader may wish to banish the whole story into the realm of fantasy, Hermann is quite real and by no means an invention. He was the first Abbot of Marienstatt (Place of the Virgin Mary), so called because the Blessed

Virgin had instructed him where to build.[3] And the spiritual head of Morimond is not an invention either. He, too, is authentic and even had a name. He was called Pierre, and is known to have been Abbot of Morimond twice: first from 1183 to 1193 as Petrus I; then after an interval of two years and eight months until his death (on 14 September 1198) as Petrus II.[4] If we consider thirty to forty years to be the time a novice needed to reach the position of an abbot, we find ourselves back in the middle of the twelfth century. This then was the time when we first hear of the existence of the game tennis. Apparently, it was so well known that an author could afford to give it no specific name. He simply referred to it as 'the ball game'. Of course, the game was at the time hardly the preserve of the underworld. Despite the mists swirling around him, the student had been able to identify it mainly because he had, as a young clerk in holy orders, played it a lot himself.

As has been said, Caesarius did not call the game by any of the many names under which it became known later. But there can hardly be any doubt that it was tennis all the same. There is, for one, the fact that two teams were picked and, for another, the fact that in order to strike the ball the players used the palms of their hands. These are the most characteristic features of the later *jeu de la paume*,[5] the ball game played with the palm of the hand, from which modern tennis evolved.

Before the discovery of Caesarius' story, another source had been considered the earliest record of our game. This was John Beleth's *Summa de ecclesiasticis officiis*, a book written before 1165 and dealing with the history and meaning of religious customs.[6] Here, the question is raised why in some French churches even bishops and archbishops had taken to playing games, and why some had even condescended to playing ball games. Beleth believes that the origins of such amusements should be sought in ancient pagan harvest customs. He nevertheless has to admit that the games in question were a feature of even the more important churches such as Rheims, although his own belief is that it would be more decorous for the clergy not to play at all. One important detail in Beleth's account is his reference to the venue of these games, the cloisters. This feature, together with the evidence provided by Caesarius, is likely to dispel some of the doubts that have been expressed about Beleth's testimony.[7]

TENNIS CHEZ GADDAFI

A whole century elapsed before tennis emerged from Lucifer's realm. If we are to believe the *Ystoire de Appollonius roy de Thir*, a courtly novel written in northern France during the second half of the thirteenth century, the first earthly tennis match was held in North Africa, in that part now under the sway of Colonel Gaddafi. The first champion was, of course, not a European, but a man from the orient, Apollonius of Tyre, a citizen of Lebanon. He can be said to be the oldest (albeit fictional) tennis player on record. In addition, he is an early example of the 'from rags to riches' story, that of the lucky beggar who becomes a millionaire. In the Middle Ages, the most successful method of becoming a millionaire was to marry a princess. This is exactly what Apollonius did, apart from playing tennis.

Trying to escape from the incestuous ruler of his native country, King Antiochus, Apollonius got shipwrecked in northern Africa where he was washed ashore near the city of Cyrene. The city was at that time ruled by a certain Archistrates who was known for his fondness for staging games of the type known in contemporary Greece as the Olympics. In marked contrast to the latter, however, the programme of these African Olympics provided for the ball game of tennis. The event took place on a square in the centre of the city. Apollonius, in a threadbare garment which a charitable fisherman had given him, had decided to compete. By his formidable return, he impressed everybody, including the ruler of the city, Archistrates, and, even more so, his daughter. Invited by the king to play against him, he well held his own, although he afterwards stood no chance against the charms of his daughter. He married her on the spot.[8]

THE DILIGENT ROMANS AS INVENTORS OF TENNIS

That in ancient Tyre the sons of kings were instructed in the art of tennis is, of course, a gross anachronism, although this is exactly what the anonymous French author tells us. In the Middle Ages, the idea that all things were the result of a long evolutionary process would have occurred to nobody. According to general belief, when he had created the world, God had, at the same time, invented our games. Shakespeare, in this respect very much a child of the Middle Ages, has Cleopatra take off for a game of billiards, her eunuch, Mardian, at her heels.[9] In much the same way the author of the *Ystoire* could depict his hero as a tennis champion. What the Frenchman's story proves is that during the second half of the thirteenth century tennis was played, after the fashion attributed to the prince of Tyre, in the market squares of Artois, in Picardy, and in French Flanders. About the game itself, we learn hardly anything. Apart from pointing out the traditional venue for such a game, an open square or yard somewhere in the middle of the town, the author only informs us that the ball had to be returned from many a difficult position into which the player had been forced by his opponent, and that in order to do so great speed and agility were required. About the origin of what was apparently the favourite pursuit of the sporting youth of France, the author is silent.

The one thing which becomes clear from the story, however, is that medieval tennis was not handed down from ancient Rome, as many a historian would make us believe. This appears from a comparison with the Latin original on which the French author based his story. This original goes back to the fifth century AD. It featured a ball game in which Archistrates and Apollonius tossed to each other a ball and in which the players were not allowed to let it fall to the ground. Failing to do this meant that one's opponent was credited with the points.[10] This was perhaps, although only two players seem to be involved, the Roman game of skill called *pila trigonalis* described in a well-known Latin poem, the so-called *Laus Pisonis*.[11] As its Greek name implies, the players positioned themselves in a triangle and then played the ball to each other, the point being to catch one's opponents unaware.

WAS IT ISIS OR THE INGENIOUS ARABS WHO SET THE BALL ROLLING?

In early accounts, ball games often appear in conjunction with wedding ceremonies. By this fact, William Henderson, librarian of the New York public library, was led to believe that the origin of ball games – and therefore of tennis – should be sought in some ancient fertility rite. This highly speculative idea had already been expressed, in fairly flowery language, by H.J. Massingham, in his book *The Heritage of Man* (1929).[12] After World War II, Henderson made the idea explicit, in a book with the highly suggestive title *Ball, Bat and Bishop*. This work was uncritically received, especially in English-speaking countries,[13] and its theses have hardly ever been questioned.[14] According to Henderson, it was the gods of ancient Egypt who, as it were, set the ball rolling, gods who were not on speaking terms with each other. On the one hand, there were the deities Isis and Osiris and their son, Horus, who symbolized fertility and shooting sprouts, and, opposing them, the evil god Seth, who nursed a deep-seated grudge against the green cult. Henderson's argument went something like this: the ancient Egyptians devised a ball game in which the two opposing parties represented the above-mentioned gods and in which the ball represented the human head, that part of the body in which, if we are to accept Henderson's view, the people of the Nile believed fertility to be housed. The team with the green shirts would walk off as victors every time, and this 'charm of analogy' would instil new confidence in the well-meaning and fertility-bringing gods while demoralizing the evil god, Seth. Henderson then went on to describe the further development of events as follows: gradually, the ritual character of the game, in which the defeat of Seth's team was, as it were, a foregone conclusion, became completely lost. The ritual was transformed into a truly competitive game which then spread eastwards as well as westwards. In the East, and via the polo-playing Persians, it reached those Mongolian tribes who later crossed the Bering Straits into the American continent. In the West, meanwhile, the Arabs had been transporting the traditional game of ancient Egypt to their cousins, the Spanish Moors, from where it was usurped by the pleasure-seeking French.[15] These then passed it on to those fanatic gamesters, the English, who were quick to ship it over the Atlantic, on the *Mayflower* with the Pilgrim Fathers, at the first best opportunity. Finally in Canada, the Eastern and Western branches of the ancient Egyptian ball rite met in a kind of family reunion after a journey around the globe and after several millennia, and lacrosse was born, the Canadian national sport, a game in which both European and Indian elements are said to have coalesced.

It is unfortunate, especially on account of the wealth of material which Henderson so diligently gathered together, that his fantastic vision of ball games which overcame oceans and continents does not bear closer examination. Egyptologists have been at pains to discover in the land of the Pharaohs a ball game that could be described as a fertility rite, but have not found one shred of evidence.[16] Even the well-meaning attempts by the American Davis Cup player Malcolm D. Whitman to come to the rescue of his friend Henderson proved abortive,[17] as will be shown. In his book *Tennis: Origins and Mysteries*,[18] Whitman tried to credit the Arabs with the invention of the game, by bringing into play the name of the ancient town of Tinnis in the Nile Delta and the Arabic word for hands, *rahat*. He claimed that the cloth of which medieval tennis balls were made was woven in Tinnis, and that *rahat* – compare the French term *jeu de la paume*, 'ball game played with the palm of the hand' – gave the racket its name. Of course, the medieval cloth manufacturing monopoly was to be found in Northern Europe, in Flanders, whence the products were exported to the Mediterranean.[19] If, therefore, French tennis players had felt the urge to have their tennis balls sewn in cloth rather than in leather as was their wont,[20] they would no doubt have gone to the local dealers. The racket was not elected protector of the tennis players' hands before the sixteenth century. Those crusaders whom Whitman envisaged in the role of early capitalist tennis entrepreneurs would therefore have carried away from Northern Africa an invention which would have become meaningful only to their great-grandchildren. They are, perhaps, the most dreadful anachronism in tennis history.

BATTLING KNIGHTS AND BRAWLING FOOTBALLERS

Nevertheless, the simultaneous occurrence of ball games and wedding ceremonies by which Henderson was led to set out on his misguided tour to Ancient Egypt and its religious practices, might still provide a clue to the mystery in which the origin of European ball games is shrouded. In his book *Language in Thought and Action*, the American sociologist and linguist S.I. Hayakawa enlarged on the function of sports and games accompanying nuptial vows. According to him, the games were meant to make an indelible imprint on the memories of those concerned, and thus served as a safeguard for what had been stipulated in the marriage contract, for the benefit of the community.[21]

If we consider the games which accompanied wedding ceremonies in former times, there were remarkable differences among them depending on the social status of those pledging their troth. Duke Gowther, for example, whose marriage is described in a fourteenth-century English romance of chivalry, decided to celebrate the event with a fashionable tournament. This turned out to be a fairly violent affair in which the bridegroom himself was not exactly a pleasant customer to deal with:[22]

> *Knyghtus of honour tho furst day*
> *justyd gently hom to pley ...*
> *Tho duke hymselfe wan stedys ten*
> *and bare don full doghty men,*
> *And mony a cron con crake.*

(Honourable knights on that first day
Jousted nobly to disport themselves …
The duke captured ten steeds
And laid out very courageous men
And cracked many a skull.)

Other examples of such aristocratic wedding amusements, if they may be so called, could be enumerated at pleasure. If we turn to the nuptials of simple people, however, there is a marked difference. Here, the tournament of the aristocrats has been replaced by a ball game. R. Carew, for instance, gave the following account of a football match in Cornwall at the beginning of the seventeenth century.[23] 'Some indifferent person throweth up a ball, the which whosoever can catch, and carry through his adversaries goale hath wonne the game … these hurling matches are mostly used at weddings, where commonly the ghests undertake to encounter all comers'.

The intriguing parallel between knightly tournaments and the ball games of commoners suggests that they served the same purpose. The heavy blows which Duke Gowther rained on the heads of his noble guests had the same function as the pokes and kicks which peasants and craftsmen doled out to each other in a football match: all this violence was intended literally to hammer the marriage contract into the memories of those concerned. The fights and brawls without which medieval football is simply unthinkable indicate that football was a deliberate copy of the tournament, as it were, a 'people's tournament', and it looks as if contemporaries were well aware of this. This appears from *Li gieus de Robin et Marion*, a pastoral play by Adam de la Halle, a poet from Arras who flourished in the second half of the thirteenth century. In it, a beautiful shepherdess called Marion is the object of attention of a knight and a shepherd called Robin. In order to win her favour, the two rivals try to impress her by their sporting prowess, but go about their task very differently.

If the rake of today may be seen casually driving around in his sports car, with a couple of expensive tennis rackets or a set of golf clubs, the knight of yesteryear had to appear on his steed and to parade his hunting falcon, and this is exactly what the knight of Adam de la Halle's invention does. On his way to his sweetheart, he merrily sings a song in which he informs all those who care to listen that he is just returning from a tournament, and this is important for the issue at hand. A little later, Robin drops by, without a horse and, of course, on foot, tired and very hungry because he has, he says, exhausted himself playing football with the lads.[24]

GATEWAYS TO THE SPORTSMAN'S PLEASURE

The medieval tournament was the continuation of war, and, at least in the beginning, it would have been difficult to tell the difference between the two. There are early witnesses, such as the English chronicler William of Newburgh, who greet the tournament – he calls it a festive preamble to war – as an opportunity for the feudal warring caste to practise the various disciplines of contemporary warfare.[25]

The chief medieval authority on warfare was the Roman author Vegetius. His work was at an early date incorporated into the ubiquitous *De regimine principum*, a treatise written around 1280 by an Augustinian hermit, Giles of Rome. As early as the thirteenth century, the book was translated into French, under the title *Li livres du Gouvernement des Rois*, and here four types of war were distinguished.[26] One is, the author says with remarkable simplicity, whenever one party and another party line up on the battlefield and fight; another, whenever a castle is attacked; another, whenever the inmates of a castle defend themselves; another still, whenever the fight is on water or at sea.

There can be no doubt that the first three types of warfare are reflected in the main disciplines of the medieval tournament:

1.   the tournament proper (Old French: *tornei*), a mounted skirmish;

2.   the joust, the clash at full speed of two riders armed with a lance;

3.   the passage of arms.

The tournament and the joust were clearly the stylized versions of the encounter on the battlefield.[27] The so-called passage of arms represented a battle for the control of a castle in the course of which a strategically important bottleneck, usually the castle gate, was attacked or defended.[28] All of them, but notably the passage of arms, can be said to have inspired the inventors of ball games.

It may be noted in passing that the only authentic report of a knightly competition which, in the heyday of chivalry in the twelfth and thirteenth centuries, was expressly called a passage of arms, appears in conjunction with a wedding ceremony. It was held at the marriage of the Picardian knight Mellion, the champion of an Old French *lai* named after him,[29] and lasted no fewer than fifteen days. This event helps to explain how later, on a different social level, football matches used to accompany wedding festivities.

The main difference between the tournament and football was that, instead of the knight in his pinching armour, a leather pouch stuffed with hay had to penetrate through some narrow passage. The remainder was the same. The ball was kicked and poked as had been its human predecessor before. And so were the two teams who either propelled or tried to stop it. On illustrations that have survived of the Italian game of *calcio*, a near relative of the medieval ball game first mentioned in the *Roman de Renart* (c. 1200),[30] the origin of early football goals is clearly visible. In Andrea Scoto's *Itinerario* of 1642 (**Figure 1**), for example, we have before us two goals which could be described as descendants of the thirteenth-century French Porte d'Ardon in Laon (**Figure 2**), a typical medieval city gate. A pennant blowing merrily in the wind on either goal is all that has remained of the two towers on either side of the gothic archway which in the Middle Ages were adorned in a similar way.[31]

Medieval tennis, too, was played in front of Gothic arches. At some point in the twelfth century, the clergy, banned by the authorities of the church from the public riots called football, thought of ways to improve their situation. What they wanted

LVDVS QVEM ITALI APPELLANT IL CALCIO

FIGURE 1   One of the rare depictions
of early football (Padua, Italy, 1642).
The goals are still reminiscent of the
medieval city or castle gate.

FIGURE 2   A typical medieval gate, the
Porte d'Ardon in Laon, France (13th
century). The gate not only played an
important role in the chivalric
tournament, but also became a
characteristic feature of competitive
ballgames.

was to avoid the worst excesses of the game, its violence, and to preserve the excitement of shots at goal and brilliant saves.

A characteristic feature of the medieval monastery was its inner courtyard, the so-called cloisters. It was surrounded by an arcaded walk covered by a slanting roof. It is not known who first noticed the similarity between these arcades and the goals used in contemporary football, but it must have occurred at a very early date. In addition, there was another circumstance which made the cloisters an almost ideal venue for the staging of matches (**Figure 3**). Because of the seclusion of the place, no rumours could spread outside the monastery about its inmates' worldly activities. Under these circumstances, even the bishop might be persuaded to turn a blind eye to them.[32]

VESTIGES OF FOOTBALL IN GOTLANDIC TENNIS

The fact that tennis is an offshoot of football has been obscured by the changes the two games have undergone in the course of many centuries. A survey of modern popular ball games, however, would bring to light many a clue confirming their original relationship. We shall return to this matter later on in this book. For the present it will be sufficient to call attention to the ancient game of tennis which has survived over many hundreds of years on the Swedish island of Gotland. In this game,

FIGURE 3   The cloisters of medieval monasteries became the venue for a variety of football played by the clergy. It is from this game that *jeu de la paume* evolved.

called *pärkspel*, the ball is not only hit with the palm of the hand (**Figure 4**), but is also given an almighty kick whenever this seems expedient (**Figure 5**). Such behaviour, shocking to the mind of the tennis aesthete, is, however, in absolute accordance with the rules of tennis prevailing on Gotland.[33] From a historical point of view, *pärkspel* is in all probability one of the oldest forms of tennis. In particular, the kicking of the ball, the *pärkspel* player's delight, goes back to a time when tennis had not yet emancipated itself from the father of the whole ball game family: football.

PROBING INTO THE MINDS OF TENNIS-PLAYING MONASTICS

The divided monasterial courtyard, where the arches at one end would be the goal from the opposite end, thus became the first tennis court. It has retained its rectangular shape until today. The cloisters of the monastery of Moissac give a fairly realistic picture of what an early tennis court may have looked like. If, in addition, we wish to think ourselves back into the minds of those tennis players who had been assigned the roles of goal defenders in this monasterial game, two wood-carvings on the sides of a chest now in the possession of the Musée de Cluny (*c.* 1300) might be a great help. On the sides and front of the chest, the anonymous woodcarver availed himself of a motif well known in the Middle Ages. It was a passage of arms contested between Richard the Lionheart and his eleven noble companions and the Muslim Saladin and his host.[34] Legend has it that it took place in the course of the Third Crusade,[35] and

FIGURE 4   Service in the Gotlandic *pärkspel* (1886). Traditional games descended from the ancient game of the cloisters often preserve original features of the latter.

FIGURE 5   One feature in *pärkspel* is the rule which allows the player to kick the ball.

it may well be that famous clashes such as this helped to give shape to the knightly tournament discipline as well to medieval football. On the one side, Saladin, who can be identified by the dragonsnake adorning his shield and standard,[36] leads his armoured riders against the pass. Ahead of him, on look-out, Saladin's scout Tornevent can be seen. Tornevent, who knew the Christians' coats of arms well, is trying to spy on them. With his head turned, he reports to his master with whom he will be doing battle (**Figure 6**). On the front side of the chest, we then see the defenders of the pass, the Christian knights, as Tornevent would have seen them. Here a knight is arranging his helmet, elsewhere another is drawing his sword. Most of them, however, are ready for action, with their shields under their chins, their swords or lances at the ready. They occupy carefully designed archways which closely resemble those in the cloisters at Moissac. One can easily imagine how the peaceable novice guarding his tennis goal at some forlorn place in France fancied himself as this very Richard Lionheart, the defender of Christianity, second from right and with three leopards on his shield (**Figure 7**).[37] However, unlike his model, he was not smashing back a swarthy heathen, but a fair-skinned ball.

In European goal games, at least, the young monk's vision has lingered on, most notably in billiards and cricket, which are both related to tennis. In Charles Cotton's *The Compleat Gamester* of 1674, a depiction of contemporary billiards (which featured a little gate through which the ball had to run) received the following comment (**Figure 8**):[38]

FIGURE 6   Carved images of an
authentic medieval passage of
arms, the so-called *Pas Saladin*.
It took place during the Third
Crusade and pitted the Sultan
Saladin (on the picture
advancing to the pass) against
the Christian knights under
Richard Lion-Heart.

FIGURE 7   The defenders of the pass. The pass is depicted in the form of the arched openings in
the gallery of the cloisters. King Richard is the second from right flaunting in his coat of arms on
his shield three leopards.

FIGURE 8   The game of billards is the most recent form which, in the evolutionary process of ballgames, the chivalric attack on the castle gate eventually adopted.

> *Billiards from Spain at first deriv'd its name,*
> *Both an ingenious, and a cleanly game.*
> *One gamester leads (the table green as grass)*
> *And each like warriers strive to gain the pass.*
> *But in the contest, e're the pass be won,*
> *Hazzards are many into which they run.*
> *Thus while we play on this terrestrial stage,*
> *Nothing but Hazzard doth attend each age.*

In a French children's book, the following moral was appended to a pictorial representation of cricket as late as the beginning of the nineteenth century (**Figure 9**):[39]

> *D'un coup d'œil just et sûr faisant sans cesse usage,*
> *Sachez à l'ennemi défendre le passage.*
>
> (*By using a quick look accurately and surely at all times*
> *Know how to defend the passage against the enemy.*)

It is, perhaps, not a mere whim of cricket history that in England the 'passage' here referred to should go by the name of *wicket*. It is a term which, ultimately of northern French origin, was applied to a little door within the fortified city or castle gate,[40] and it seems only natural that cricketers should eventually have availed themselves of it.

FIGURE 9   Cricket also preserves the element of the defence of the gate. In this French children's game, the walls of the gate (*wicket* meant 'little door') had degenerated into two stones.

When, in the evolution of goal games, the element of physical strength gave way to skill and goals were reduced in size as a result of it, they adopted, very appropriately, the expression used for the miniature gate within the gate. Cotton's work and the French children's book, it should be noted in passing, are late offshoots of the emblem book, a poetic genre which will claim our attention in a later chapter.

THE FIRST ILLUSTRATION OF A COMPLETE MEDIEVAL TENNIS COURT

The earliest picture of a complete medieval tennis court – with slanting roof, gallery, and a player defending it – comes from the *Factorum et dictorum memorabilium libri IX*, a work by Valerius Maximus, or rather, from a fourteenth-century French translation of it. It is preserved in a mid-fifteenth-century manuscript in the collection of the British Library (**Plate 4**).

The picture introduces a chapter dealing with man's hours of leisure in which Valerius praised the commanders Scipio and Laelius, who, inseparable friends at play and at work, like children enjoyed collecting mussels when they went for a stroll by the river. He commended the Pontifex Maximus Publius Mucius Scaevola who, an excellent player at ball, after his speeches at the forum would relax by playing his favourite games. At the same time, Scaevola was a lawyer, who, after the strain of a day at the bar, would divert himself with a game of chess or draughts.

Despite the explicit details of the text before him, its medieval illustrator was nevertheless led astray. Instead of Scaevola, he had the mussel collectors Scipio and Laelius engage in a game of chess. However, he did justice to Scaevola, the ball-player, although he transformed him (as had been Apollonius of ancient Tyre before him) into a typical medieval tennis athlete. Scaevola is depicted as if he were in the process of defending the gallery at his back, while an opponent who has not been given a name at all is aiming at it. As we shall see, there is one fundamental error in this obvious description of the picture, but for the time being, we will be satisfied with having an authentic example of a tennis player who, as a substitute of the armed knight, defends a gallery. At least in this respect, the picture is correct.

THE ORIGINS OF THE PICTORIAL TENNIS TRADITION: THE BOOK OF HOURS

The most popular medieval tennis motif was that which combined service and return in a single picture. It was used by the artist of the oldest tennis picture to have come down to us,[41] who can therefore be said to be the founder of a long pictorial tradition. The tradition originated in the medieval book of hours. It is the only genre of the medieval illustrated book in which representations of sports and games occur with some regularity. The book of hours was a kind of layman's breviary. As such, it was not subject to church control, and miniaturists felt free to choose for their illustrations motifs which were not necessarily of a religious nature; hence the sporting scenes which occasionally adorn its pages.[42]

The source of the oldest tennis picture is a book of hours which, to judge from its calendar and its office for the dead, originated in the workshops of Cambrai around the year AD 1300 (**Figures 10 and 11**).[43] If the identification of the place of origin is correct, it would confirm the belief expressed elsewhere in this book that the origin of tennis should be sought in the north of France. As has been said, the picture combines the actions of service and return. The server (who, significantly, occupies a position on the left) has just completed his underarm swing. The ball has just reached the highest point of its trajectory and will soon descend to the opposing party expecting it with their hands raised high above their shoulders. The opponents, surprisingly, both belong to the somewhat rarer species of the 'southpaw'. The fact that one server has been matched with two opponents does not mean that we have before us, as in ice hockey, an early instance of a short-handed team with one player in the 'sin bin'. Rather, the two players are a kind of artistic shorthand for 'team'. Medieval tennis, at least in the beginning, was above all a team game. It is very likely that the server was backed by a number of team-mates who, for the reasons given, do not make an appearance in the picture.[44] What should be noted is the size of the ball. It is a rather unwieldy affair, and this is sufficient proof that the picture must be very old.

Until well into the sixteenth century, medieval miniaturists doggedly followed the pattern here described. There are several reasons for their apparent lack of variation. One is the typical medieval belief in authority, an attitude characteristic not only of the medieval writer, but also of the medieval artist. Another is the commercialization which took place in the late medieval book trade. A motif which had found favour with customers once was copied again and again, above all by the less talented and the mere copyists. These continued to reproduce the models before them and even failed to notice that under the very window of their *scriptorium* the game had in the meantime undergone considerable changes.

The *Heures a l'usage de Romme* (1498) by the Parisian printer Philippe Pigouchet and again used by Simon Vostre a decade later show the basic elements of its model of two hundred years before (**Figure 12**). Here, the tennis picture has been set apart for the calendar, where it illustrates the feasts of November. Of course, there are more details in the picture. The returning player stands in front of a solid wall with a small rectangular opening indicated by hatching. The side gallery is populated by spectators, and provision has been made for an entrance in its middle. The gallery offers shelter to a groundsman or caretaker who, ignoring the balls whizzing past his ears, is placing a marker, a flat brick, on the edge of the court. (We shall in due course return to the question of this marker.) A ball boy, even less impressed by the balls, scurries to and fro between the opponents, whilst a supporter swings his purse over the balustrade. This is a clear hint that in those days money was bet on tennis hand over fist, a feature of medieval tennis which in modern times is most conspicuous in Basque pelota. The match is played on a tiled floor, smooth and perfectly even, an innovation which had come into existence in Belgium and France early in the sixteenth century, if we are to believe the testimony of the Spaniard Juán Luis Vives.[45]

A still later miniature is an example of the thoughtlessness with which the traditional motif was copied (**Figure 13**). The manuscript also originated in France, where, by

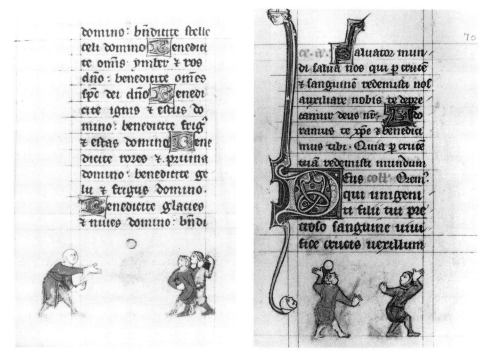

FIGURE 10   This may well be the oldest picture of *jeu de la paume*. It shows the characteristic underhand service for which a sort of gauntlet protecting the hand was used. The balls are rather large sized, which proves their close relationship to their unwieldy brother, the medieval football.

FIGURE 11   The returning party, it seems, was not allowed to wear gloves.

FIGURE 12 Woodcut from a late 15th-century book of hours. The purse of one of the spectators indicates that, much as in modern Basque pelota games, a lot of betting went on during matches.

the time of its execution (the second quarter of the sixteenth century), some sort of tennis racket had been introduced. In his *Recherches de la France*, Estienne Pasquier quoted an old *paume* player called Gastelier, who claimed to have played with the flat, unprotected hand when he was young.[46] Gastelier was 76 at the time, and since Pasquier's work was published from 1560 onwards, tennis rackets must have come into being around the turn of the sixteenth century. Yet the artist of the miniature before us seems ignorant of this interesting new equipment which was to revolutionize the game. In contrast to Pigouchet, however, he depicted two goal apertures in the rear wall. This feature has a remarkable parallel in the traditional tennis court of Falkland Castle in the county of Fife. Designed after a French model and built in 1539, this is nearly contemporary (**Figures 14 and 15**).[47]

WAS TENNIS REALLY THE GAME OF KINGS?

In its infancy, tennis was the game of the people, although many historians would like to make us believe that it used to be the 'Game of Kings'. The reason for such misconception is not hard to find. It is the dire predicaments in which the members of royalty found themselves by their passion for tennis. Numerous indeed are the tragedies which have come to pass on princely tennis courts. The first to meet his fate because of his love for tennis was Louis X of France, known as Hutin, the Quarrelsome. His is therefore the honour of being the first tennis player whom we know by name.

According to the chronicle of Jean Paris,[48] Louis had on 5 June 1316, in a grove near Vincennes, contracted a very serious illness. After a heated match the young man –

		Nouember	d	Ioānis epiſ·
		habet dies.	ıx e	Eucharıı epī
xxx.	Luna xxıx.		f	Anıanı epiſco:
	d	Oīm ſanctorᴜ.	xvıı g	Hubertı epī
xııı	e	Cōmēo. aīarᴜ	vı A	Helızabeth re:
ıı	f	Hılarıonıs epī	b	Stephanı cōſeſ.
	g	Vıtalı martırıs	xıııı c	Oblatıo vırḡ
x	A	Zacharıe. paıo.	ııı d	Cecılıe vırḡıs.
	b	Leonardı conf:	e	Clemētıs ꝑpe
xvııı	c	Proſdoamı epī	xı f	Grıſogonı mr̄.
vıı	d	Coronatı mrıs	xıx g	Katherıne ·:
	e	Dedıcatıo ſalua	A	Petrı Alexādrı
xv	f	Trıphoīs. mrıs	vııı b	Iacobı mrıs.
ıııı	g	Martını epī	c	Proſperı epī.
	A	Martını pape.	xvı d	Vigilıa.
xıı	b	Brıcıı epıſco.	v e	Andree aplī:
ı	c	Felıcıs epī.		

FIGURE 13 This miniature from a 16th-century book of hours is rather disappointing because it shows no trace of the racket which by this time had been introduced in the game in France.

FIGURE 14   The tennis court of Falkland Castle, after Hampton Court the second oldest in existence.

FIGURE 15   Falkland Castle. This court belongs to the type of the so-called *jeu carré*, the characteristic feature of which was the missing *dedans* – openings in the wall were substituted.

at the time Louis had seen 26 summers and eight months – had in a state of complete exhaustion unwisely succumbed to a natural urge for refreshment and allowed himself to be led into an cool grotto. There he gulped down large quantities of chilled wine which froze him to the bone. He sank into a slumber which caused his death on the eve of Trinity Sunday.

A rather irreverent report on his death is given in a rhyme chronicle by Geoffrey of Paris. Geoffrey, if indeed he was the author of this crude piece of verse, painted a rather unflattering picture of the ruler of France. He likened him to a cock among barnyard fowl which had lost its feathers, but he is the only author who expressly blames tennis for having been the king's ruin. Other writers vaguely mentioned only a ball game:[49]

> *En cel temps qu'estoit ceste chose,*
> *Au rois Loys la vie esclose*
> *Fu, droit au boys de Viciennes:*
> *Là perdi-il plumes et pennes.*
> *Disoit-on qu'en ceste manière*
> *Mourust de maladie ague,*
> *Qui les saines genz souvent tue.*
> *Li autres dient qu'il avoit*
> *Joué à 1 gieu qu'il savoit,*
> *A la paume, si s'eschaufa,*
> *Et son conseil, qui le bifa,*
> *L'en a mené en une cave*
> *Froide; et à 1 hanap plein d'iave*
> *Si but trop, et froit se bouta,*
> *Et li sitost si se coucha*
> *Qu'au lit acouchier le convint,*
> *Et de ce cèle mort li vint.*

> *(At the time when this thing happened,*
> *The life of King Louis was put to an end*
> *Right in the middle of the Forest of Vincennes:*
> *There he lost plumage and feathers.*
> *It has been said that the kind of illness*
> *From which he died was a stroke*
> *Which often kills healthy people as well.*
> *Others claim that he played a game*
> *Which he knew well,*
> *Namely tennis; he became so heated at it,*
> *And his better judgement which betrayed him*
> *Led him away to a cold cave,*
> *And from a jug full of water*
> *He drank too much; cold, he laid himself down,*

And as soon as he had lain down,
He remained bound to the bed,
And out of this jug death came to him.)

Louis is the first member of royalty whose death was caused by playing tennis, even though rumour had it that his passing away had had less to do with a large measure of tennis than with a goodly dose of poison measured out to him.[50]

In the night of 20 February 1437, James I, King of Scotland, died, not because of his enthusiasm for tennis, but because of the anger it had caused him. This at least is what John Shirley would have us believe in his *Full Lamentable Cronycle of James Stewarde, Kyng of Scotys.*[51] Having been surprised by conspirators shortly before bedtime, James managed to dive into a privy by pulling up a board in the floor. He then made for a small square aperture used for cleaning the privy, only to find that it had been bricked up three days previously on his own express orders. On the other side of the hole, that side which would have been James' salvation, lay his beautiful tennis arena, and the king had been constantly annoyed by the frequency with which his right royal tennis balls used to roll into the smelly pit.

The death of Charles VIII of France (1498) was caused by different reasons. Intent on showing his consort, Anne, an exciting match in the moats of his royal palace at Amboise,[52] Charles crashed his forehead into a lintel. This tragic episode is passed down to us in the memoirs of a contemporary, Philippe de Commynes.[53] Philippe, as he says himself, was not an eye witness to the tragic incident, but he had a most trustworthy testimony from the Bishop of Angers who was the King's confessor.

Their passion for games did not always cost monarchs as much as their lives, but it often made enormous inroads in their coffers. To the private purses was, as it were, assigned the task of compensating for their masters' lack of talent. One of the first to spend much money on lost games seems to have been John II of France. His epithet was The Good, but this was hardly owing to his aptitude for tennis. In 1355 he had to settle a bill of 144 crowns, a princely sum indeed:[54]

> for two long lengths of Brussels cloth which His Majesty purchased in order to have made four robes bordered with the exquisite fur of the grey squirrel to be presented to certain personages to whom he had lost at tennis.

The private account book of King Henry VII of England also makes highly illuminating reading:[55]

> 13th June 1494: To a Spaynyard the tenes pleyer, £ 4.[56]

> for the Kinges losse at tenes, to Sir Robert 14th August 1494: At Windesor. . . . To Sir Charles Somerset Curson, with the balls, £ 1. 7s. 8d.[57]

> 8th March 1495: (At Shene.) To Hugh Denes for the Kinges losse at tenes, 14s. and for the silke girdle, 6s. 8d. – £ 1. 0s. 8d.[58]

> 29th March 1495: For the Kinges losse at the paune [*sic*] pley 7s. 8d.[59]

5th July 1496: At Waltham 5. July 5. To a new pleyer at tenes, £ 4.[60]

30th August 1497: To Jakes Haute for the tenes playe, £10.[61]

6th June 1499: For the Kinges losse at tenes, 8s.[62]

According to this list Henry not only treated himself to home-bred opponents such as the Lords Somerset and Curson, and domestics such as Hugh and Jack when he wanted to quench his thirst for tennis, but also occasionally allowed himself a young, up-and-coming star from the provinces or even some exotic from southernly Spain.[63] It is not known whether this Spaniard is identical with the mysterious 'Biscayen' who is said to have received for his excellent performance in tennis no less than £100.[64] At any rate, Henry's losses indicate that there cannot have been much of a difference between English and Basque or Spanish tennis in those days. In addition, these payments are the first reference to the existence of the famous Basque pelota games which in most tennis histories are credited with an almost biblical age.[65] The first picture showing a pelota player is to be found much later still, in 1629, on one of the picturesque disc-shaped tombstones in the cemetery of Garris, a small village in the Pays de Mixe in what is now the French Département of Basses-Pyrénées (**Figure 16**).[66]

ROYAL TENNIS ADDICTS IN MEDIEVAL FICTION

As time went by, medieval men of letters, too, must have been persuaded that extravagances such as tennis belonged to the basic necessities of a royal lifestyle. One purely fictional tennis hero of royal blood has already been mentioned, Apollonius, the King of Tyre. He was able to out-play at tennis the young Cyrenaics against whom

FIGURE 16   The oldest pictorial representation of Basque pelota, a game which has often (albeit wrongly) been considered the prototype of the tennis games, but it is not older than the 17th century (1629).

he was pitted, because in his youth he had been instructed in all things befitting a future king, including sports. Of all the sports, however, the thing he understood best was tennis, a game in which nobody was his equal anywhere.[67]

The fifteenth-century romance *The Three Kings' Sons*, a translation from the French, must have had a special appeal to the medieval reader, especially if he was French. It deals above all with the exploits of Philip, the son of the King of France, whom the French author made the handsomest of all. Despite his many assets, Philip chose to call himself 'The Destitute' (*le despurveu*) when he set out to woo Jolante, the beautiful daughter of King Alfours of Sicily. Sicily in those days was located uncomfortably close to the bloodthirsty Saracens, a fact which makes it easy to predict the task which eventually awaited the young prince. However, before he was allowed to lash out against the poor infidels, he was subjected to a kind of aptitude and endurance test. The various contests arranged on his behalf by King Alfours include, besides jousts and tournaments, a tennis event in which, of course, Philip excelled.[68]

TENNIS LESSONS FOR ROYAL TEENS

Perhaps not unaware of the role tennis played in romances idealizing kings and princes, medieval educators were soon led to grant the sport a place in their educational treatises. Giles of Rome was the first to recommend, besides wrestling, ball games as a sporting activity suitable for royal children between the ages of 7 and 14. In so doing, he gained support from no less an authority than Aristotle, who was known throughout the Middle Ages as 'the Philosopher' *par excellence*: 'Dont li philosophes dit que leutier et jouer a la pelote sont propres travaus as enfanz'.[69] We may doubt whether Giles, the tutor of Philip the Fair, was referring to tennis with his phrase *jouer a la pelote*. Later authors, however, clearly interpreted him that way. One of these was Philippe de Mézières, Chancellor to the King of Cyprus and later educator of the King of France, Charles VI. He allowed his royal charge an occasional game or two of *jeu de la paume*, but only as long as it did not last too long and was held at a secret venue.[70]

Christine de Pisan's educational book, *Li livres du corps de policie*, written between 1404 and 1407, was meant to be a guidebook for the French Dauphin, Louis de Guienne.[71] In a chapter titled 'Exhortations Which Should Be Given To Young Princes' and much indebted to Giles, Christine also drew on Aristotle, and then went on to expressly mention the game of tennis. Aristotle, she wrote, declared that no one would become wise unless he had heard a little of everything. It would therefore be a good thing if even the child of a king occasionally embarked upon some strenuous task and played at games such as tennis to a state of exhaustion. Since virtue lay in moderation, however, care should be taken in order never to overdo things. If this advice were heeded, the body would neither become too flabby, nor, because of too much rest, heavy and ungainly, and a reservoir of superfluous humours.[72] The author's opinion that in tennis moderation should be observed had its origin in Greek philosophy. The principles of modern competitive sport would have appeared to her and her contemporaries very strange indeed.

Sir Thomas Elyot's *The Boke Named the Governour*, an educational primer for the personal use of the ruler, appeared more than a hundred years later – in 1531. It well illustrates the fact that the medieval writer was not particularly keen on innovation, but as a rule preferred to be in agreement with the authorities. Tennis, to Elyot's mind, played but rarely and for short periods of time, was a good exercise, especially for young men. But it was a more violent sport than, for instance, archery. The latter, in addition, had the advantage of serving a good purpose: the defence of one's beloved country, whereas tennis had a decided disadvantage: its reprehensible pace which resulted from the fact that it took two to tennis:[73]

> Tenese/seldome vsed/and for a litle space/is good exercise for yonge men/but it is more violent than shoting: by reason that two men do play. wherfore neither of them is at his owne libertie to measure the exercise. For if the one stryke the balle harde/the other that intendeth to receyue him/is than constrained to vse semblable violence/if he wyll retourne the balle from whens it came to him. If it trille fast on the grounde/& he entendeth to stoppe; or if it rebounde a great distaunce from hym/and he wolde eftesones retourne it: he can nat than kepe any measure in swiftnesse of mocion.

Today, no tennis player will deny the truth of this, but at a time so very favourably disposed towards exercise of all kinds he certainly will not blame his favourite pastime for it. In the Middle Ages, running and sweating, at least for a person of high rank, was the biggest bugbear imaginable.

Shortly before the turn of the century, in 1598, a king reached for the quill himself in order to admonish his own flesh and blood. The *Basilicon Doron* by James I of England was written for Prince Henry, his eldest son, who was 4 years old when the book was written. Despite his tender age, his father expected him not only to understand, but also to take to heart the following piece of advice:[74]

> amang all unnecessaire things that are laufull & expedient I thinke exercises of the boddie maist commendable to be used be a young prince, in sicc honest games or pastymes as maye further habilitie & mainteine health, for albeit I graunt it be maist requisite for a king to exercise his engyne (quhilke suirlie uith ydilnes uill rouste & becum blunte) yet certainlie bodilie exercises & ghames are uerrie comendable, als ueill for banishing of ydilnes (the mother of all uyces) as for making his boddie abill & durabill for trauell [= work] quhilke is uerrie necessaire for a king, but from this compte I debarre all rumling uiolent exercises as the fitball meitter for laming nor making able the useris thairof, as lykeuayes sicc tumbling trikkis as onlie seruis for comoedians & gysairis to uinne thaire breade uith, but the exercises that I uolde haue you to use (althoch but moderatlie not making a crafte of thaime) are rinning, leaping, urestling, fensing, dansing, & playing at the cache [= Scots for tennis].

By 1698, the educational truism that its low degree of 'motion' made tennis the ideal sport for personages of royal blood, had at last found its way into Germany. In his *Abbildung der Gemein-Nützlichen Haupt-Stände* (Description of the Chief Callings Useful to Society), Christoff Weigel tried to give a description of all professions. One of these was that of a *Ballmeister* (literally, a ball master, the name for the tennis professional in Renaissance Germany), and Weigel painted a gloomy picture of all those who refused to call upon the services of a member of this craft.[75] The text is accompanied by a fine picture of a ball master which, Weigel claimed, had been taken from life,[76] but which he had obtained from Caspar Luyken,[77] his Dutch partner in the late seventeenth-century pre-capitalist book trade (**Figure 17**).[78]

Das Wasser/so sonder Bewegung still stehet/gehet endlich in eine Fäulung/und wird stinckend; und der Menschen Cörper/so sonder benöthigte Bewegung und Regung/zeigt einen trägen Umlauff des Geblüts/daher rührende Verstopffungen/wodurch die verhaltene Feuchtigkeiten gleichsam in Fäulung und Schärffe gehen/und eine Kranckheit nach der anderen/ja endlich gar ein frühes Sterben verursachen. Solchen besorglichen Übeln vorzubeugen/hat man einige belustigende Bewegungen vor die jenige Personen ersonnen/deren Würde und Stand in vielfältiger Ruhe und weniger Motion bestehet/unter solchen Bewegungen ist das Ballen-Spiel eines der edelsten und ergötzlichsten/und auch nützlichsten. Heut zu Tag ist uns auch noch der so genannte Ballon/so mit den Pila magna und inani der Griechen/wie auch dem Folli der Römer übereinstimmt/gewöhnlich/wird aber nur von schlechten Personen geübet. In denen besondern Ball-Häusern aber/so theils in allen Fürstlichen Residenzen/theils auch in großen Städten befindlich/wird mit dem kleinen Ballen/vermittelst des Racquet, so den Alten unbekannt gewesen/gespielt/und darinnen von hohen Personen öffters ein sonderes Vergnügen geschöpffet. . . . Dieses dient noch dem geneigten Leser zu wissen/daß das Ball-Spiel nicht nur ergötze/sondern/wann man sich dessen mässig bediene/herrlichen Nutzen zu Erhaltung der Gesundheit schaffe/welches dann den trefflichen Artzt Galenum veranlasset/seinen Wercken eines/von Nutzbarkeit des kleinen Ballens/einzuverleiben/woselbst der geneigte Leser sich Raths erholen kan.

(Water which stands without any movement finally transmutes into putrescence and begins to stink; and the human body without its required movement and motion shows a slow circulation of the blood resulting in constipation, whereby residual fluids turn putrid and pungent and thus cause illness after illness and finally even lead to an early death. In order to forestall such worrisome evils, some amusing movements have been devised for such personages whose nobility and rank consist in all manner of stillness and but little motion. Of such exercises, the game at ball is one of the noblest and most pleasurable as well as the most useful. Nowadays, the so-called balloon, with which the *Pila magna et inanis* [the large, empty ball] of the Greeks as well as the *Follis* [Latin *follis*, the bellows] of the Romans compare, is commonly used. However, these are only practised by the populace. In special ballhouses, however, found in part in the palaces of lords and in part in the larger towns, they play with a small ball and a racket, which was unknown to our forefathers, and from this game high personages often derive a special pleasure . . . It is useful for the gentle reader to know that this game not only gives pleasure, but also is, if moderately used, highly beneficial to the maintenance of one's health, a fact which inspired that great physician, Galenus, to include in his works one on the usefulness of the small ball which the gentle reader may consult for advice.)

FIGURE 17   The German engraver and book-trader Christoff Weigel from Regensburg claimed to have executed this engraving from a live model. The sieve which was only used in the tennis variety of *kaatsen* in the Low Countries gives him away: the picture was appropriated from the work of his Dutch colleague Casper Luyken.

As we have seen, references to tennis-playing royalty are numerous. Why, then, is it wrong to claim, as so many tennis historians have done, that the medieval game was the preserve of kings and princes? Until very recently, historians have focused their attention on the lives and circumstances of those whom they regarded as the great characters of history, emperors and kings, and on what they considered their great achievements, battles and military campaigns. In so doing, they could hardly fail to discover the more trifling matters with which some noble personage happened to be preoccupied. Tennis was one of them, and that is why our histories of tennis literally abound with tennis-mad kings, but are generally silent about the common people, who, throughout the Middle Ages, played and loved this game just as much as their masters did.

The fact that the everyday lives of ordinary people have largely been ignored by historians until very recently has been of consequence also in other areas of research. This is particularly true for the field of literary studies. In the so-called Corpus Christi cycle, a series of religious plays performed in Wakefield, a small town in Yorkshire, a particularly charming one is the *Secunda Pastorum*. It has a cast which features five humans and one animal, namely three shepherds, a disreputable individual called Mak, Mak's wife Gyll, and a fat ram. Mak steals the ram and, knowing that he will be suspected of the crime and that the shepherds will soon be on his heels, hides it in a cradle. When the shepherds enter Mak's cottage, Gyll begins to moan aloud as if she had only just given birth to a child. At first, the shepherds are effectively fooled. But after they have left, it occurs to one of them that the baby should be given a present. When they return, Mak's game is up. The baby's long muzzle and splendid horns simply cannot be explained away. According to medieval popular justice the thief is then tossed in a blanket,[79] but the punishment of so capital a sinner leaves the three shepherds completely exhausted, and so it is that they fall into a deep sleep. They awake only after an angel has called them. On his instructions they set off for Bethlehem, where they find a real child at last, Jesus Christ. Again they offer their modest gifts. The first shepherd comes forward with a bunch of cherries; the second gives the baby a bird; the third, however, has brought little Jesus something very special. He says:[80]

> *Put forth thy dall!*
> *I bryng the bot a ball:*
> *Haue and play the withall.*
> *And go to the tenys.*

> (*Stretch out your hand*
> *I'm bringing you only a ball:*
> *Take it and play with it*
> *And go to the tennis.*)

Instead of enjoying the Yorkshire Bard's amusing idea of making little Jesus an early addict of tennis, critics go on and attach some deep and symbolic meaning to the third shepherd's gift. Since traditional historians had sworn that tennis was the 'game of kings', it occurred to none of them that the Wakefield Master was here simply passing on to posterity a record of the everyday life of ordinary people. Instead, they were deeply convinced that the Lord Jesus was here receiving a present befitting his rank: a royal tennis ball.[81]

Pastoral plays such as the *Secunda Pastorum* formed part of medieval mystery plays, so named after the 'mysteries', the craftmen's guilds in charge of performing them. Of course, mysteries including pastoral plays were popular not only in England, but also in France, and the fact that a tennis ball as one of the traditional shepherds' presents has not cropped up in any of the French plays must be ascribed to pure chance and the incompleteness of our literary records. That the motif of the tennis ball was there is almost proven by the French *noël*, a literary genre which may be called an offshoot of the mystery play.[82] In a fifteenth-century *noël* from Poitou, which is thus fairly contemporary with the *Secunda Pastorum*, the shepherds' journey to the crib and their gifts are treated in much the same way as in the pastoral plays. It is by no means surprising, therefore, that here, too, Jesus should have been given a ball (*pelotte*).[83] It is true that the ball is not a tennis ball, but rather a billiard ball, because it is supplemented by the forerunner of the cue, the curved shepherd's crook (*billiard*). Nevertheless, it is more than likely that there had been precedents for the motif of the ball in medieval France. In addition, the idea positively suggests itself that tennis was one of the traditional shepherds' games as, indeed, was billiards,[84] which in those days was played, in the company of grazing sheep, on the village green of which the green baize of the billiards table is the only reminder today.

'REAL' IS NOT 'ROYAL'

Real tennis, a game which in England has a small, but select following, is a direct descendant of the medieval monastic game. Not only in England, but also in America (where it is called *Court Tennis*) and in Australia (where it goes by the name of *Royal Tennis*), it possesses a not inconsiderable amount of snob appeal, and not infrequently a real lord presides over the Real tennis club. In the opinion of the Real tennis player this is as it should be, since, at least to his mind, the obvious meaning of 'Real' is 'Royal'. Yet the term 'Real tennis' is merely a hundred years old.[85] It first appeared in the 1870s, when the followers of Real tennis, in view of the overwhelming success of the new-fangled lawn tennis, felt the threat of extinction. In much the same way as the advertisers of a certain caffeinated soft drink who called their product 'the real thing' when a competitor promised more pep, they claimed to play the Real tennis. The popular fallacy, however, that 'real' should be equated with 'royal' has its roots in the belief that in the Middle Ages, tennis had been the monopoly of kings.

The unearthing of tennis-playing aristocrats from medieval sources presents no difficulty, but the discovery of tennis-playing monastics is not an easy task. The tennis historian's chief informant is the medieval prelate who objected to a clergy addicted to ball games such as tennis, and therefore banned the game in the form of edicts and statutes. Cardinal Louis de Bar, the Bishop of Langres, was one of them. In 1404, Louis issued a statute for his diocese, an independent bishopric in a little corner between Burgundy and Lorraine, in which he made a clean sweep of the games of the day. The bishop's writ is of great value to sports historians, since it constitutes a catalogue of virtually all sports current at the time.[86] Most prominent among the games so roundly berated is tennis. It is especially denied to clergymen and monks, and introduced under its Latin name, *stophus*, which is explained by the French phrase *à la paume*, so that the poor monk – who may have had a good command of returns, but whose command of Latin was rather poor – could not fail to understand what he must not play under any circumstances. The fact that only *stophus* was found to be in want of a translation suggests that this game in particular was the biblical thorn in the Cardinal's flesh, and that the trespassers against his tennis ban were so many that misunderstandings had to be ruled out once and for all.

It is in the nature of prohibitions that they are rarely specific about the thing prohibited. The implication of Louis de Bar's statute is merely that monks may have succumbed to the temptations of tennis. However, we are not told whether they in so doing profaned the cloisters with their boisterous game.

In this connection, a remarkable record has survived in the papers of John Shillingford, Mayor of Exeter. The papers cover the period between 1447 and 1450 and contain the minutes of a law suit between the mayor and his community and the Dean and chapter of Exeter Cathedral. The minutes of the law suit are in two parts: the complaint by His Worship, the Mayor, and the reply by His Reverence, the Dean.

In his complaint, the mayor began by describing the situation as it had existed before the quarrel. The Dean and chapter of St Peter's, Exeter, were the masters not only of the cathedral, but also of the cloisters adjacent to it; there was an open area in the square of these cloisters known as *the Praiell*; this had served as a cemetery whenever the municipal one was flooded; in addition, there was a public access to the cathedral which led through the cloisters and for which the mayor and his community owned the right of way. Only recently, however, the Mayor continued with growing testiness, the dean and his chapter had locked and bolted the doors to the afore-mentioned cloisters against the good custom of the entire Holy Church and in defiance of the King's laws.[87]

To the clergymen, the situation presented itself very differently. First, the Dean and chapter observed, the afore-mentioned access had never been a public one, nor had it ever been under the jurisdiction of said mayor and his community either. Second, there were people in the said community, and especially young people, who showed extremely bad manners and who, especially during divine services, played unlawful games in the said cloisters, and most notably tennis. In so doing, the walls of said cloisters had become badly soiled, and all the windows had been smashed to smithereens, as anyone who cared might see himself, and such behaviour was against all spiritual goodness and good citizenship.[88]

> atte which tymes and in especiall in tyme of dyvyne service, ungoodly ruled peple most custumably yong peple of the saide Comminalte within the saide cloistre have exercised unlawfull games as the toppe, queke, penny prykke and most atte tenys, by the which the walles of the saide Cloistre have been defowled and the glas wyndowes all to brost, as it openly sheweth, contrarie to all good and goostly godenesse and directly ayens all good policy.

Nothing is known about the outcome of this strife. From Shillingford's papers it becomes evident, however, that the cloisters of medieval monasteries could well serve as tennis courts, and that, in particular, those of Exeter Cathedral *did* serve this purpose in the fifteenth century. Unfortunately, these cloisters have not survived, and that is why we have to complain at the loss of what would have been an authentic medieval tennis venue.

Another piece of evidence for tennis in the cloisters comes from a very different corner in the sixteenth century. We owe it to the vanity of two patricians from Augsburg, Matthew and Veit Konrad Schwarz, who had pictures painted of virtually every episode in their lives. It is only natural therefore that from one of the pictures contained in the so-called *Schwarzsche Trachtenbücher* young Veit Konrad Schwarz should have emerged in contemporary tennis outfit (**Figure 18**). To this picture, and perhaps dictated by Schwarz himself, the following captions were assigned. Upper margin: In March 1556 striking the ball was my pleasure. I bandied it then with the Italians either in the cloisters of the church, called domo, or in the piazza del potesta. My clothing was as shown below with the cuts and colours. The trousers were made of rash [a smooth silk or worsted fabric]. Below: I was fourteen years and five months old.[89] Here we may be surprised at Veit's tennis garb – shorts made of rash and displaying three slit bulges running all around his legs – which made a mockery of the old saying that tennis is a running sport. But Veit's statement is presumably correct that in Italy, or, to be more precise, in Verona where Veit attended a school of trade and commerce, tennis balls were chased about in the cloisters of a church. The artist, well aware of the fact, accordingly sketched the rough outlines of their colonnades in the background.

The documents so far all have certain shortcomings. Louis de Bar's statutes indicated that medieval clerics were involved in the game, but failed to tell us where they played it. From Shillingford's papers and the *Schwarzsche Trachtenbücher* we learn that youngsters availed themselves of the cloisters in order to play their game. Yet there is no evidence that they were at least occasionally joined by young novices in the process. Fortunately, there are two contemporary testimonies in which the highly desirable combination of cloisters, on the one hand, and of tennis-playing monks, on the other, is to be found. The first takes us back to Merry Old England, and again to the neighbourhood of that notorious tennis stronghold, Exeter. In August

FIGURE 18 Veit Konrad Schwarz, the son of a wealthy citizen from Augsburg, testifies to the fact that in 16th-century Italy the preferred venue for a tennis match was the cloisters of a church.

1451, a series of rather unpleasant incidents in the parish of Ottery St Mary caused the Bishop of Exeter, Edmund Lacy, to take immediate and drastic action. The canons of the local collegiate church had, together with some accomplices from the laity, organized a kind of tennis league within the precincts of the church. In the course of their regular competitions they had given the lie to the prevailing view that tennis was a disciplined and courteous game. Because of the importance of this historical document, we will reproduce in full the charges which the angered bishop levelled against the pitiable warden, and which today make the connoisseur smile because of an intriguing linguistic detail: the English word *Tenys* (with a capital *T*!) amidst Bishop Edmund Lacy's convoluted Latin:[90]

> nonnulli tam clerici quam laici quorum nomina ignoramus pariter et personas, prout ex fidedignorum testimonio et fama publica accepimus, in cimiterio ecclesie beate Marie collegii predicti, pro sepultura christiana inibi consecrato . . . ad ludum pile vulgariter nuncupatum *Tenys* diebus festivis sepissime et aliis tanquam in loco prophano seu theatro ludere quin verius illudere, atque vanis fedis et prophanis colloquiis et iuramentis inaniter et vanis et sepissime periuriis illicitis insistere, atque exinde sepius rixas, contenciones movere et conclamaciones erigere . . . in cimiterio predicto non formidant, honorem et devocionem populi christiani in eodem loco pro salute animarum defunctorum Deum exorare volentis nequiter et dampnabiliter perturbando pariter et tanquam per spectacula prohibita subtrahendo, in animarum suarum periculum ac divine magestatis offensam . . . . Et ut libencius suis huiusmodi nephandis ludis insistere vellent, cumulando mala malis, quoddam opus meremiatum ad prestandum obstaculum ludentibus huiusmodi super tectum cuiusdam domus in cimiterio predicto situate, ubi huiusmodi ludum prohibitum exercere vellent, clanculo a tecto domus huiusmodi violenter diversis vicibus separaverunt, ruperunt, deposuerunt, fregerunt et eiecerunt, iura ecclesiastica perperam et inique violando, sentenciam excommunicacionis maioris in sanctorum patrum constitucionibus . . . incurrendo.

Some members of the clergy, as well as of the laity, of whom we neither know name nor personality, about whom we are informed, however, by reliable witnesses and vociferous complaints, apparently have no scruples about playing a game, or rather, an evil game called *tennis* in the vernacular, in the churchyard of the above-mentioned collegiate church of St Mary, consecrated for Christian burials, and they play it on feast-days as well as on other days, and in the manner of a fair ground or theatre. In so doing they inveterately voice vain, heinous and blasphemous words and utter senseless curses, which, as a consequence, all too often give rise to squabbles, disputes, brawls and battles of words. By their unlawful games they distract in a thoughtless and reprehensible manner those Christians who come here to plead for the salvation of the deceased, from saying their prayers reverently and with devotion, thus making light of the terrible peril in which their souls find themselves, and of the insults to God's majesty. What is more, so that they might continue with their dastardly games even more unashamedly, these individuals, by piling up more disgraceful deeds onto the old ones, have clandestinely and on several occasions forcibly loosened, pulled down, thrown aside, broken and slung out of the courtyard a certain wooden construction erected upon a house in the churchyard where they would play their unlawful games: all this because the wooden construction proved to be an obstacle to those trying to play on to the roof according to the rules of the game. They have thus infringed upon the rights of the Church in a most unlawful manner, and inflicted on themselves the sentence prescribed by the laws of the Church Fathers, namely that of strict excommunication.

Although the spiritual inmates of Ottery St Mary and their worldly confederates may have entertained a rather different opinion here, the tennis historian is much indebted to Edmund Lacy for the explicitness of his condemnation. He learns that not only was the world full of frocked John McEnroes even then, but also that 'aggravated behaviour' on court did not entail a mere fine, but excommunication. More important for the matter at hand, however, is the fact that members of the clergy were indeed playing tennis within the precincts of a monastery-like institution, a collegiate church, even if the term *coemeterium* does not necessarily refer to the cloisters, but rather to any enclosed burial place within a monastery. We will at a later stage return to the house which seems to have formed the lateral confines of the playing area, and to the question of what role its roof played in the canons' game.

The second testimony, a much earlier one, comes from the statutes of a college established in Paris in 1329 by the Benedictine abbey of Marmoutier near Tours for members of the order.[91] The statutes were published in the third volume of the *Histoire de la Ville de Paris* by the Benedictine Michel Félibien.[92]

Out in the provinces, it had been rumoured that other things besides diligent studying were prospering in the Parisian college. That is why two commissioners were appointed by the worthy Abbot of Marmoutier, Elias, who were to make inquiries into the matter at the Parisian outpost itself, and who were not to spare the rod where necessary. Armed with powers of attorney signed by Elias himself and dated 1 June 1390, the two commissioners made their way to Paris. Their visit amply confirmed the old saying that where there is smoke, there most certainly is fire. From the numerous articles of the statutes which the commissioners imposed upon the college, it is not difficult to infer that the poor clerks in holy orders were roundly berated indeed. Not only were they from that moment on to converse with one another only in Latin, they were also to get rid of their dogs, birds and other pets, to abandon playing on the rebec (or fiddle), and to ban notorious women from their sleeping quarters. In accordance with the content and form of the mother house's statutes and the punishments provided by these, Article XVI forbade them from playing any board or dice games, as well as tennis. And if it should happen that the clerks were occasionally allowed to play after all, they were to do it only after express permission had been given by their Master, without making any noise, and in such a manner that others were not disturbed, and only as long as the monastery gates remained locked, so that no other players from outside could be smuggled in.

The statutes of the college of Marmoutier strongly resemble those imposed a decade earlier, in 1379, on the Collegium Narbonae by Archbishop John. In this foundation, which had been in existence since 1317 for the benefit of poor clerks from the province of Narbonne, playing ball games (which may have included tennis) was also forbidden.[93]

From a historical perspective, the two statutes, taken together, shed light on the question of the origin of tennis in general. It looks as if a leisure time activity which had prevailed in the monasteries of the province was eventually taken up by the students of their Parisian colleges. Such a view gains support by the story told by Caesarius of Heisterbach. The Parisian student Pierre, as will be remembered, could only have had his tennis vision if he had engaged in the game himself, and a personal experience of the hardness of the blows characteristic of it. While it is true that the Cistercian order founded a college of their own, the Collège du Chardonnet in 1246,[94] much too late for Pierre to have studied there, he might well have attended one of the schools of theology which flourished, precursors of the University of Paris and her colleges, near Notre Dame and on the hill of St Geneviève in the twelfth century.[95]

MONKS AS TENNIS INSTRUCTORS

By analysing medieval sources we come to the conclusion that tennis had its home in the seclusion of the cloisters and that the laity, especially the young, tried to share the cloisters' natural facilities. These youngsters were, so to speak, the first to jump on to the bandwagon of the monastic tennis monopoly. The fact that tennis was played behind monastery walls would also explain why the aristocracy was able to usurp the game then still in its infancy. It was the monastery to which the rulers of the feudal world entrusted the education of their children,[96] and there can be hardly any doubt that it was within its walls that the sons of kings, dukes and earls first became acquainted with the tennis ball. Upon their return to the parental estate, castle or palace, these young gentlemen at once decided to have built a tennis complex of their own in which to continue a pastime which had become dear to them. So it was that, probably as early as in the thirteenth century, a kind of religious fever broke out, however misdirected it was. It resulted in the foundation of new 'monasteries', the building of which was discontinued as soon as half of the cloisters had been completed. Only that much was needed for the devotional activity for which it catered: tennis. These fragmentary cloisters nevertheless featured all the necessary details. There were three colonnaded walks encompassing the playing area which were covered, as in the classical monasteries of France, by a slanting roof. In addition, great importance was attached to the inclusion of a detail from which the tonsured teams must have derived a highly frivolous pleasure: the so-called *grill*. Originally, the word *claustrum*, 'cloisters', referred to that area within the monastic building complex to which laymen had no access. Whenever these wanted to communicate with a relative inside the only way to do so was via a barred window. In Church Latin this window was called *craticula*, whence the Medieval French term *grille*, English *grill*.[97] Apart from the normal openings in the gallery, this *grille* must have become the favourite target for shots at goal, and by the irreverent act of hitting it decisive points might be won. It is hardly surprising that the intriguing device of the grill should later have been adopted into the aristocratic tennis court. The grill is perhaps the most conclusive piece of evidence that tennis was hatched behind monastery walls.

TWO

The tennis games of the Middle Ages

◇

In the beginning, the private courts of the aristocracy were more or less close copies of the cloisters. However, a particular nuisance made itself felt soon enough. It was the fact that balls had constantly to be retrieved from the vast territory beyond the fourth open side of the court. That is why a fourth wall was erected which extended well above the gallery. Henceforth, balls came ricocheting off the walls from all sides, which severely tested the reflexes of the players. In addition, a player who tried to play a ball skimming along this fourth wall had to risk crushing his hand. It was a feature which the medieval game shared with the modern Basque game of pelota called *la mano desnuda*, the naked hand.[1]

After the addition of a fourth wall, other innovations followed soon.[2] One of the shorter galleries was bricked up, with the exception of the *grill* which survived in the form of a rectangular opening close to the side wall. At some distance from it, on the side wall, the *tambour* was contrived, a slanting surface which deflected the ball into the court even more unpredictably. For the gallery to the rear of the server a simple wall with much smaller openings might be substituted. Courts which kept the goal-gallery went by the name of *jeu à dedans*, 'inside game', whereas the type without a gallery was called *jeu carré*. (As we have seen, the court at Falkland Castle belonged to this type.)

In the *jeu carré* points could also be scored by hitting hazards called *ais* and *trou*. The *ais* was a recess in the wall adjacent to the long gallery. A wooden plank, 6 foot high and 1 foot wide, was suspended in front of it. Balls hit it with a bang which made the ancient game a rather noisy affair. The *trou* was located opposite the *grill* at the far end of the court, but at ground level.

A player could collect as many as four points, enough to win an entire game, by hitting the ball into the *lune*, a round opening (as the name implied) high up on the wall. Generally speaking, no player expected to find *trou*, *lune* and their ilk in the same place in every court. In marked contrast to the architect of modern sports arenas, his medieval predecessor did not aim at standardization. Johann Georg Bender, a seventeenth-century German tennis professional, when trying to explain the function of the *ais* remarked that tennis courts only rarely featured the plank, since no court was like another.³ In Jacob van der Heyden's *Speculum Cornelianum* of 1618, for example, it is easy to identify the *lune* (see **Figure 62** on p. 159). The black square, however, at which one player is aiming his forehand shot, because of its position at ground level, can only be the *trou*. According to Garsault's description, however, one would expect it in the opposite corner where we see another aperture not easily explained. It is hardly an *ais*, since it obviously is not protected by a plank. The court of Falkland Castle possesses a *grill*, but has no *tambour*: the *jeu carré* type of the tennis court never had one. The *tambour* was the characteristic of the *jeu à dedans* (**Figure 19**), and the first on record was to be found in the Louvre in Paris. We know of its existence from a plan in Antonio Scaino's *Trattato del Giuoco della Palla* of 1555.⁴ Nevertheless there were also exceptions to this rule. The frontispiece in Charles Hulpeau's *Le jeu Royal de la paume* of 1612 (**Figure 20**), although it showed a *grill*, and apparently represents the *jeu à dedans*-type, lacked a *tambour* altogether (the picture is side-inverted).

The court depicted on one of the folios of the Duke of Brunswick's *Stammbuch* (**Plate 8**), if the painter was not guilty of a capital error, presents a real puzzle. The court is that of the Collegium Illustre in Tübingen, and here, in the year 1597, the tennis universe seems out of joint. In this *jeu carré* two 'moons' shone on opposite walls, or rather, they did not shine at all, since the illustrator chose an even darker shade for them than he did for the surrounding walls. In addition, it would be tempting to speculate about the black square on the left-hand wall (and the one opposite it), if other pictures which have survived of the same court did not help to

FIGURE 19 The real tennis court in Leamington Spa. Through the strings of the racket the grill is faintly visible, and looking past the right edge of the racket frame we can see the so-called tambour.

FIGURE 20   The frontispiece of Charles Hulpeau's *Le jev royal de la Paulme* (1632) has by some error of the printer been side-inverted. That is why we see, in marked contrast to the photograph from Leamington Spa, the grill in the 'wrong' corner.

solve the problem. On an engraving by Ludwig Ditzinger in Johann Christoph Neyffer's *Illustrissimi Wirtembergici Ducalis novi Collegii ... Accurata delineatio* (*c.* 1589) (see **Figure 61** on p. 158), the court is viewed from the opposite direction, and here the bar and two cross-bars prove that we have before us a grill, although it definitely is not where it should be. The opening on the opposite wall would then have to be similar to that in the Falkland court. As in the Falkland court, it would have had a counterpart to the right of the moon. It is invisible here because Ditzinger omitted that part of the wall where it was to be found. That this conjecture is correct is proved by another *Stammbuch* picture of 1598 on which the artist marked both, although he, for a change, forgot to indicate the two moons (**Plate 9**).

The Tübingen court demonstrates why from the sixteenth century onwards theoreticians of the game had no longer reason to examine the question of how to rule a ball which was struck over the wall and was either, after landing in a cart, given an unvoluntary lift, or thrown back into the court by some over-eager passer-by after a new ball had already been introduced into the match. Such questions were in all seriousness discussed by Antonio Scaino and Johann Georg Bender, the seventeenth-century professional from Nuremberg already mentioned[5] to whom we will return in a later chapter. A roof over the court prevented such escapades of the ball and academic discussions resulting from them. The roof also made tennis players independent of wind, weather and season. A clerestory made sure that there was sufficient light, and curtains protected the court against undesirable sunlight. In addition, rather than paint their balls bright, players preferred painting the walls of their courts infernally black, and this is a feature still characteristic of Real tennis. As late as towards the end of the eighteenth century, in 1767, François Alexandre de Garsault handed down to us the recipe for the wall paint used for tennis courts.[6] 'Take half a hogshead of ox's blood, fourteen bushels of lamp-black, ten galls of oxen to dilute the lamp-black, and a bucket of urine in order to give a sheen to the composition; mix it all cold.'

THE MEDIEVAL CHASE RULE

What did the game look like which was played in these rather funny courts? If we believe that the service was the same as in modern Real tennis, medieval tennis may at first have been played in the following way: a player from the team defending the gallery served the ball onto the slanting roof of the cloisters to his left from where it dropped onto the playing area of the opposing team. This team tried to hit the gallery in front of them, a strike being worth one or more points.[7] The defenders of the gallery (who fancied themselves as sentinels of a castle gate) did their best to prevent this, by hitting back, either on the volley or on the rebound, every ball that would have entered the gallery. The attacking side renewed their efforts to sink the ball into the gallery, and for them, too, every ball was playable which could be hit on the volley or on the rebound. The rally continued until either the gallery was hit (or the grill, for that matter), or the ball bounced a second time. In that case, the point was not automatically lost for the side which had allowed the ball to do so. Rather, and in marked contrast to modern tennis, the ball rolling along the ground had to be stopped as soon as possible. The spot where the ball had been blocked was marked and referred to as a chase (French *chasse*).[8] After every chase, the teams changed ends, and in the rally which followed both teams were obliged to win the chase. This meant that the team attacking the chase had to play the ball in such a way as to force it (again, after its second bounce) beyond the mark of the previous chase. If they succeeded, the point was theirs, if not, their opponents were credited with it. After the battle for the chase, the former attackers had to take over the goal position until another chase had been achieved and contended. The game lasted until one side had accumulated as many points, by hitting the gallery and by chases conquered, as had been stipulated for the final victory before the match. Later, in *jeu de la paume* as well as in the vast majority of tennis games in which the system of counting by fifteens was applied, a chase was contended whenever the score had run up to 45, game point, or whenever two chases had occurred. For the battle of the chase, the teams had to change ends.

The chase rule made it imperative for the players to give their balls good length, much more so in fact than in modern tennis. For if a ball was too short, the opponent would not make the slightest effort to play it. Rather, he would with a sneer let it bounce a second time, and then stop it at once. From the earliest days, therefore, the most cherished thing in the game was a long chase, and one of the earliest known sources testifies to this fact. In the *Roman du Comte d'Anjou* of 1316, three burgesses' sons from Orleans have met on a fine summer day in order to play at tennis, a game here called *jeu de bonde*, 'the bouncing game':[9]

> *Le gieu de bonde commencierent.*
> *L'un fiert l'estuef, l'autre rachace,*
> *Chascun pour faire bonne chace.*
>
> (*They began with 'the bounce game':*
> *One hits the ball, the other chases it back,*
> *Each in order to make a good chase.*)

This indeed was the quintessence of the medieval game: a serve here, a return there, followed by a rally in which each player was eager to achieve a long chase.

The measuring of the chases was a deadly serious matter. Teams would haggle and squabble over every single inch, and their differing views on the length, or lack of it, of a chase often made them hurl insults at one another, and not infrequently they came to blows over it at last. A letter of remission issued by King John of France in 1354 is very specific about a dispute over a chase in the town of Corbie four years earlier. After a certain Regnaut and his partner, Fremin de Beaumont, had been disputing with their opponents over a chase, a certain Jehan Hunaut was appointed to act as umpire. Unfortunately, Jehan was the uncle of Mahieu and the cousin of Pierre and Thiebaut, who in this match had apparently been the opposing side. That

is why both Regnaut and his team-mates called Jehan's decision partisan, and 'foolish'
into the bargain. After Fremin de Beaumont and his nephew, Huc de Beaumont, had
added a few more insults, the insulted, in a fit of rage, dealt Huc a severe blow and
he, in turn and together with some accomplices, then and there started beating the
living daylights out of poor old Jehan.[10]

Since in medieval tennis the long chase was the thing most sought after, tennis
players hardly ever might, as it were, rest on their rackets with the smug self-
complacency of the tennis disciple Nicolas who in the *Colloquia familiaria* of Erasmus
exclaimed: 'We have two sufficiently long chases!' (Habemus duos terminos satis
longinquos).[11] The chase rule obliged players not so much to strain their muscles,
but to use their brains, and this may be one of the reasons for its disappearance from
the boom-boom tennis which now rules the day. Not least because of it, the old game
has been called 'chess in motion', and it is not difficult to see why such a game should
so have fascinated the intellectuals of the Middle Ages – the monks.

The necessity of putting a stop to the runaway ball is mirrored in the poem *In
Praise of Peace*, a eulogy on King Henry IV which the English poet John Gower
composed in 1400. At first sight, Gower's lines seem to be a truism, and yet they
contain a valuable piece of information:[12]

> *Off the Tenetz to winne or lese a chace*
> *Mai no lif wite er that the bal be ronne.*
>
> *(Whether a chase is won or lost at tennis,*
> *Nobody can know until the ball has run.)*

These lines reveal the fact that, before a chase could be made, the ball had first to
'run' (after its second bounce). Only then had it to be stopped, and it becomes clear
at once that in medieval tennis the term *stop* had a meaning completely different
from that in modern tennis. When, for instance, Charles d'Orléans in his famous
tennis poem of 1439 complained about the fact that one of his opponents, Worry,
stopped even his best shots – 'va estouppant Les cops'[13] – we should not imagine
Worry as a player who nonchalantly makes the ball drop dead behind the net. Rather,
we should imagine him as a kind of goal-keeper who, cat-like, diving left, right and
centre, manages to stop the ball at once.

The fact that medieval tennis players were earthbound moles, at least in England,
until well into the sixteenth century appears, at least by implication, from Sir Thomas
Elyot's *The Boke Named the Governour*: 'If (the balle) trille fast on the grounde, and
he entendeth to stoppe'.[14] In 1522, Henry VIII, reputedly an excellent player, and
Emperor Charles V sided in a team against the Prince of Orange and the Marquis
of Brandenburg. In this match, the old custom of stopping the ball was still adhered
to, although this rather lowly job was not for their Royal and Imperial Highnesses. This
part in the game was played by Lord Edmund and the Earl of Devonshire who may

have recommended themselves for the task by their extremely deep bows at court. The parts which the two 'lower' aristocrats played in their respective threesomes were termed accordingly: they were called 'stoppers'.[15]

Whilst in England King Henry and his compatriots continued to stop each other's tennis balls assiduously, the French had invented a different way of assessing a chase. In his *Exercitatio linguae latinae* of 1539 Juán Luis Vives has his spokesman, young Scintilla, explain the new rule to his Spanish friends and team-mates. On the other side of the Pyrenees, in Paris, Scintilla says, the game had of late been played in the following manner: the ball was either returned on the volley (*ex volatu*) or after the first bounce (*ex primo resultu*). A stroke after the second bounce was invalid, and the chase was marked where the ball had bounced: 'ex secundo enim ictus est invalidus, et ibi fit signum ubi pila est percussa'.[16] The new method was soon adopted everywhere in Europe. Today, the rule is observed in Real tennis, whereas in traditional games such as Frisian *keatsen* players continue to go down headlong in order to stop the ball.

At the beginning of the sixteenth century it is again Erasmus' young Nicolas who informs us about how the chases were marked. He does so in Latin, the language the true humanist considered to be the most convenient for conversations during a tennis match. Nicolas and his like would use a shard or a piece of mortar, or, if preferred, a felt cap for the purpose.[17] The Spaniard Vives confirms that these felt caps, with a ribbon under the chin to keep them in place, were a necessary piece of equipment for anybody with a professional attitude towards the game.[18] Jan van den Berghe, the author of the *Kaetspel Ghemoralizeert* (1431), names stones and fragments of brick as well as wooden chips as markers; if need be, even spittle would do the job, as indeed would any other object that the players managed to scrounge before the match.[19] Of this hotch-potch of markers, strangely enough, spittle has proved the most durable, for even today such is the substance with which the *arbitro*, or umpire, in the traditional Tuscan ball game of *palla* marks the spot where he has espied the second bounce of the ball. The bottle of wine which he swings in his right hand and from which he occasionally takes a great gulp ensures that even prolonged battles with the ball under the southern sun need not be abandoned simply because the umpire's mouth has run dry and the chases can no longer be marked effectively.[20]

From Ditzinger's engraving of the ducal ballhouse in Tübingen, it appears that the gentleman player had every reason to sneer at the humble contrivances of the Flemish and Tuscan yokels. Of course, he did not do the marking job himself. He could afford to employ a marker, and on Christoph Neyffer's picture such an individual can be seen near the entrance to the court, on the point of marking a chase which is hopelessly short. The man is using a long-handled piece of equipment and therefore does not need to take the trouble of bending low (see **Figure 61** on p. 158).

TENNIS BEFORE THE ADVENT OF THE NET

The chase rule also promoted togetherness, but at least the team defending the *dedans* cannot have regarded such intimacy very favourably. If we assume a situation where the defenders had been guilty of an extremely weak return, the attackers might, of course, advance to where they were literally stepping on their toes. They might either stop the ball even closer to the *dedans* and so achieve an extraordinarily short chase, or they might avail themselves of the short range and cannon the ball under the roof of the goal. In a game of this description, nothing was more superfluous than a net. However, so firmly has the idea of a net become imprinted in the consciousness of the contemporary tennis player that he finds it difficult to imagine a time when tennis was played without it. Julian Marshall, for example, one of the few tennis historians deserving the name, was intrigued by the idea that at least some precursor of the net might have been hinted at in one of the two oldest pictorial representations of the game. On the beautifully illuminated page of a manuscript (*c.* 1300) of the Arthurian romance of *Lancelot du Lac* (**Plate 1**), a damsel delivers to King Arthur and Queen Gwynevere a message from Lancelot. At the same time, a game of doubles is in progress on the lower margin of the folio page. The miniaturist, who perhaps wanted to give an impression of what life was like at the court of King Arthur, chose to separate the two players on the left from those on the right by means of a decorative border. This border first and foremost served the purpose of marking the division of the text into two columns, but to the mind of Julian Marshall it represented, if not necessarily a net, a string spanning the court, or at least a line drawn on the ground dividing the court into two camps.[21]

   To assume the existence of a line in those early days is certainly intriguing. From the viewpoint of the Church, such a line would have been most welcome, since it would have been a check on those clergymen who, oblivious to the Christian virtue of charity, and not unlike those notorious fighting cocks, the footballers, were on the point of getting into a tussle. However, on medieval tennis pictures, more than half a dozen if we include the late fifteenth-century and early sixteenth-century books of hours, line or net are conspicuous by their absence. Not even in an emblem-book as late as that by Guillaume de la Perrière (1539) is there any trace of it (see **Figure 56** on p. 136), even though the two grim representatives of the tennis-playing fraternity would seem desperately in need of one. The two may be swinging their primitive, short-handled, and catgut-strung rackets, they may be slithering about on the elegant tiled floor – innovations which the Spaniard Vives claimed to have witnessed in Paris in the very same year – but of the line which Vives mentioned in the same breath we do not see an inch.[22] An explanation for its omission may be that Guillaume, the author of the *Théâtre des Bons Engins*, lived way out in the provinces, in Toulouse, and had not the slightest idea of what was going on in the tennis metropolis of the day, Paris.

DAVID AND BATHSHEBA AND THE CHRONOLOGY OF THE NET

Very helpful to anyone wishing to determine the advent of the net is a series of paintings all of which originated in Flanders and have for a subject King David's affair with Bathsheba.[23] Presumably because of the somewhat risqué subject, the pictures enjoyed an immense popularity which, in turn, accounts for the great number of copies which have survived.

A peculiarity of these paintings is that they all tell the different episodes of Bathsheba's seduction in a single picture. We see how, from the balcony of his palace, the old sinner David espied Bathsheba sitting on the edge of her lavish bath, how he handed over to Uriah the letter which was to send the captain of his army on a mission without return and how Bathsheba, Uriah's wife, succumbed to temptation with unladylike haste – along with her lady-in-waiting she is already on her way to the king's palace.

What must have sent the owners of the paintings into raptures was the setting in which the artists allowed old David to savour the fruits of the world, permitted and illicit ones. There is a truly royal palace, and this included sporting facilities befitting a king's rank. In the background we see a fashionable maze, and, before it, a shooting range with two archery butts. In the left-hand corner, and betraying the Flemish origin of the paintings, there is a game still popular in Flanders called *beugelen* (in medieval England it was known as closh). A must for any Renaissance ruler, however, was a private tennis court, and it is only natural that a particularly fashionable one should have occupied the very centre of the paintings.

The many artists who tried their hand at the story of David and Bathsheba, and who were inveterate plagiarists all of them, of course did their best to out-rival each other. Although they were reluctant to deviate too much from the pattern which had found so much favour with their customers, some of them nevertheless tried to introduce into David's tennis arena the novelties they had noticed in the tennis courts of their time.

The paintings all belong to the second third of the sixteenth century when written sources began to report that touch of sophistication which had of late been added to the tennis of Paris: the line. An appearance of it, in fact its first pictorial representation, might therefore be suspected on one of them. And indeed, while in Guillaume de la Perrière's emblem-book of 1539 not even an inch of it could be discovered (see **Figure 56** on p. 136), the whole length of the rope swings nonchalantly in a court in a painting signed L[ucas] G[assel] and executed only one year later, in 1540 (**Figure 22**).[24] However, it should cause no surprise if on paintings of a considerably later date the line is still missing. A 'David and Bathsheba' owned by Lord Aberdare, an almost exact copy of Gassel's, is signed R.A. [Ruhl, Andreas?] and dated 'Año 1559', and yet there is not a trace of a line or net (**Plate 5**). At the same time, there are paintings of exactly the same type which have a line, and that is why they should be considered refurbished versions of the Aberdare specimen.[25]

In marked contrast to the Aberdare type, a new prototype of the painting displayed the line from the very beginning. By a stroke of luck, what may well be its first draft has been preserved in a drawing from the Louvre (**Figure 21**). Here it looks as if the line had in the meantime become firmly established. No longer is it hung across the court in some makeshift way. A solid post and a clamp in the wall opposite it have been devised in order to fasten it securely. At least five more pictures were executed after this model, two of which have again been ascribed to Lucas Gassel. Of these, one now adorns the Members' Pavilion at the Marylebone Cricket Club in London, whereas the other belongs to the collection of the Wadsworth Atheneum in Hartford, Connecticut. Generally speaking, Gassel's versions of 'David and Bathsheba' are characterized by a steady progress and refinement in the artist's handling of the tennis motif. In what was presumably his last treatment of the subject, the one from the Wadsworth Atheneum, he painted the most complete picture of the game, which even included a marker of the chases. As in Pigouchet's book of hours, he is busily placing a flat tile on the spot where a rather mediocre chase has only just been laid (**Figure 22**).

The painting at the Marylebone Cricket Club is a very successful piece artistically. It is unique in that it displays an inscription. It adorns the wall butting out onto the

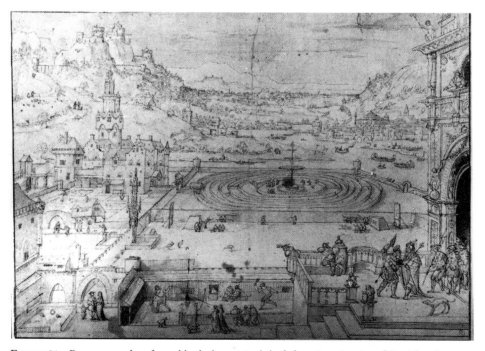

FIGURE 21 By some stroke of good luck the original draft for a 'new' series of David and Bathsheba paintings has been preserved. As opposed to an older generation of paintings using the same subject, it shows a significant innovation: a line dividing the tennis court into two halves.

FIGURE 22   After having added a few finishing touches, the painter Lucas Gassel presented a tennis court with all the trimmings: a sagging line, a large basket for the balls, and a marker preoccupied with marking a chase and presumably charged with umpiring the match and keeping the score.

terrace, and a negligent palace administration has apparently failed to wipe it out In Latin, it denounces the machinations of the ruler of the palace: 'DAVID . CVM . BAR/ SABAEA . ADVLTERIO/COMISE . . . VRIAM/AB . HOSTIBVS/OCCIDENDIVM IN . /PRAELIV(M) MITTIT. /ANNO 15..4' (after having committed adultery with Bathsheba, David sends Uriah into battle in order to have him killed by the enemies. In 15..4.). Here the most intriguing question is what digit the writer of these lines had once inserted between the numbers 5 and 4. Julian Marshall, from whom the painting descended to the Marylebone Cricket Club, and who gave it a somewhat misguided interpretation in an article in *The Field* in 1895, had not the slightest of doubts that it was a three.[26] If this were true, the club would have inherited from him the oldest illustration of the line or net, which was to revolutionize the game.

Our findings on the Bathsheba paintings are in a way confirmed by contemporary views of Flemish cities. There are two such views of the city of Bruges. One of them is fairly contemporary with the 'David and Bathsheba's under consideration (1562) (**Figure 23**),[27] the second is from 1641 (**Figure 24**),[28] and both show, for a change, the palace of the Counts of Flanders. The palace precincts exhibit two tennis courts facing Moerstrate, but whereas in the earlier picture there is no indication of a line whatsoever, this lack has been effectively amended in the second picture executed some eighty years later. Here the line suspended across the square court to the right even shows the extravaganza of tassels attached to it. And this is not owing to the engraver's greater love for detail.[29] By 1641, the line had become simply indispensable. On the other hand, its absence in the earlier picture indicates that as late as the middle of the sixteenth century it did not necessarily belong to the equipment of a tennis court, not even a nobleman's.

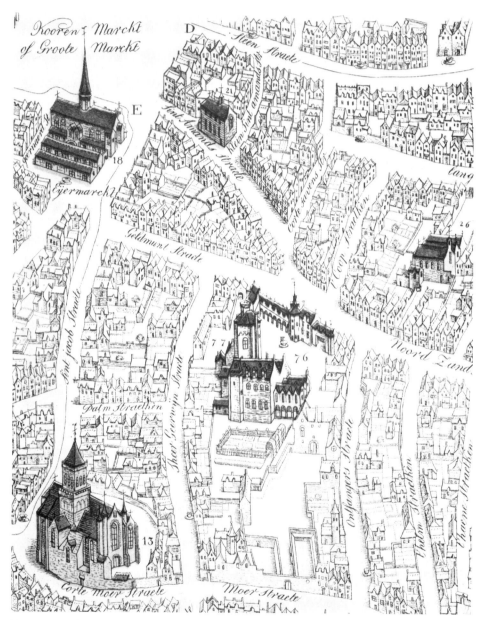

FIGURE 23   The tennis courts of the Counts of Flanders in Bruges (centre bottom) before the introduction of the line (1562)

We will end our exposition on the tennis lines of Flanders with a story gleaned from a letter of pardon, that genre of source material by which light is shed on the seamier side of medieval sport,[30] quarrel and strife. Not exactly commendable for the reader addicted to the principles of fair play, the letter of pardon is nevertheless an indispensable tool in the hands of the sports historian because of the graphic detail with which sports and games, the cause of some conflict, are often described. The letter of pardon under consideration was issued by King Philip II in 1567, and was written in response to a petition for mercy by a certain Franchois Pieterssen.[31] In his petition, Pieterssen referred back to 25 January of the same year, the day on which he met, 'in our city of Antwerp', at the 'Wynshuys' (winehouse) of Hans Croppe (the individual who at the same time ran the tennis court (*caetspel*) adjacent to it) a certain Jan van Scherus and his junior journeyman. Van Scherus had struck a ball under the line (which therefore had been introduced in Antwerp by 1567), upon which (presumably because van Scherus refused to admit it) he, Pieterssen, had snatched it and thrown it (outside) over the wall. Van Scherus, in an outburst of rage (because he had paid for the balls), insisted on getting paid for the loss; if not, he threatened to stab the life out of good old Pieterssen with his dagger. Pieterssen retaliated by offering to try out his racket on van Scherus's pate. After this exchange of kindnesses the two hotheads ('quereleux') left the winehouse and made for Meir Bridge where, opposite the 'Iron Cross', they drew their knives. Van Scherus lost his life, and the City of Antwerp what must have been an able tennis player.

FIGURE 24   The tennis courts of the Counts of Flanders (top) after the introduction of the line (1641).

THE LINE'S PROGRESS

A line dividing tennis balls into high and low is also featured in the *Emblemata* of Zsámboky János (**Figure 25**). The fact that the author's first name appears to be his last reveals his nationality. János was a Hungarian, and called himself by a Latin name, Johannes Sambucus, whenever he was writing in a scholarly vein. His emblems were printed in Antwerp in 1564, but the inspiration for this particular emblem had presumably come from tennis matches in Paris where János studied in the 1550s and the beginning of the 1560s and where he may himself have developed a taste for the game.[32] In so doing, he perhaps also tried to avail himself of two rackets at a time in much the same way as the player on the left (who may, however, be a coach). The ball which the players here have to master has more of the shape of an egg, and has to travel across an unusually taut line.

A satisfactory answer to the question of how the most common reason for strife and argument might be banned from Renaissance tennis courts was found only towards the end of the century. If players are today likely to pick a quarrel about whether a ball was 'in' or 'out', those of old found fault with each other – as we saw earlier in this chapter – about balls that were 'above' or 'below' the line. This intolerable situation was remedied by the introduction of longish fringes which, by heftily swinging to and fro, were expected to put an end to never-ending altercations. Whether these fringes met these expectations cannot be said with any certainty. Dangling from a decidedly sagging rope, they were, however, not abandoned before the next century, although they could also be completely missing as late as the middle of the seventeenth century, in a court depicted by Johannes Amos Comenius in his *Orbis sensualium pictus* of 1658 (**Figure 26**).

FIGURE 25   In the tennis court of an emblem book by Johannes Sambucus (1564), the taut line is as unusual as the player wielding two rackets. He is either a coach, or has discovered a method to circumvent the backhand stroke.

FIGURE 26   In his *Orbis sensualium pictus* (The Visible World in Pictures) (1658) Comenius tried to stimulate the use of Latin by means of pictures which illustrated Latin sentences. The text ran: 'In the tennis court (1) you strike a ball (2) which the one serves, and the other strikes back with a racket (3).'

The Spaniard Vives is generally believed to have been the first to mention the line in writing. In his tennis dialogue of 1539, he had young Scintilla inform his Spanish compatriots about the existence of such a line in the courts of Paris. To have struck the ball under the line, Scintilla says, is regarded as a vice or a sin in Paris (sub funem misisse globulum, vitium est, seu peccatum).[33] The credit of having been the first to testify to the sin-line goes either to François Rabelais, the author of the famous novel *Gargantua* (1534), or to John Frith, an Englishman and the author of *An other boke against Rastel …* (*c.* 1533),[34] a book not otherwise remarkable. At the very end of *Gargantua*, the Monk considers the prophecy discovered at the erection of the Abbey of Thélème to be a description of a contemporary tennis match couched in a somewhat obscure terminology. One of the tennis truths he is convinced to have discovered in the text is this.[35] 'On croyt le premier qui dict si l'esteuf est sus ou soubz la chorde' (He is believed who first said the ball was over or under the line).[36] In Frith's book, Rastel is accused of having placed the ball clearly below the line, 'Here Rastell hath smyte the ball quyte under the corde'. Frith's acquaintance with this new obstacle must have been a fairly recent one, for otherwise he would scarcely have employed the French term *corde* instead of line, which became the generally accepted term hereafter. The same degree of unfamiliarity also appears from Pieter van Afferden's Latin–Dutch phrase-booklet *Tyrocinium linguae latinae* which, according to its preface, was ready for the printer in 1545. Here the line is first tentatively referred to by Dutch *rouwe* (a misprint for *touwe*, 'rope'), before the author made a final decision in favour of the loan-word from French, *coorde*, which occurs three times.[37] Vives, Rabelais, Frith, and van Afferden, however, all lend support to the opinion expressed above that in the 1530s and 1540s painters began to think in earnest about embellishing King David's ball courts with a fashionable line.

WHEN FIRST COURSES WERE SERVED ON THE ROOF:
OR, THE MOST UNUSUAL WAY OF SERVING A BALL

The capricious little hops with which tennis balls frolicked along the slanting roofs of the gallery constituted a not inconsiderable part of the pleasure which the monks derived from their game. The roof, however, was not merely an elevated stage for the prancing tennis ball. It had a highly important function. It was the target aimed at by the server and in this capacity it was virtually indispensable.

Why the attackers should have been deprived of their privilege to open fire on the defenders' broadside is not easy to see. It is certain, though, that the right of opening the game was exercised by the defenders, and the procedure was roughly the following. From any point in the defenders' half, the ball was served onto the roof of the long gallery. After a hop, skip, and jump it would slowly descend into the territory of the attackers who had, as it were, been lying in ambush there and whose impatience is well illustrated by a picturesque saying in Spanish denoting a question that has not yet been decided: *Aun esta la pelota en el tejado*, literally, 'the ball is still on the roof'.[38]

Why the ball had to be served onto the roof is not known. One reason for this strange service rule may have been that the returning party was thus kept at a considerable distance from the goal. In addition, the returners' task was made all the more difficult since they were kept guessing for a long time as to what kind of serve they would have to return, and from precisely what part of their court they would be able to aim the ball at the gallery.

This medieval service rule was later to become a characteristic feature of the *jeu de la paume*, and it is still valid for Real tennis. Its existence is attested in very early sources. From Jan van den Berghe's *Kaetspel Ghemoralizeert* (1431) we learn that tennis players first had to look for a suitable venue with a sufficiently high roof, convenient for striking the ball up onto it, and equally convenient for returning the ball back in.[39] 'Daer een goet hooghe dack sij daert schoone es omme uut te slane ende schoone es weder in keren'.

Bishop Lacy's fulminating against the canons of Ottery St Mary proves that the rule mentioned by the author of the *Kaetspel* was indeed adhered to in practice. The wooden ridge turret on the side wing of the collegiate church was pulled down several times, not out of sheer wilfulness, but because it constantly stood in the way of a service according to the rules of the game.

The *Kaetspel* and the episcopal register cause a great deal of confusion, because they are completely unambiguous: a crucial role in any attempt at reconstructing medieval tennis must be assigned to the picture depicting the match between the Roman citizen Scaevola and his anonymous opponent in the French Valerius Maximus manuscript (**Plate 4**). It looks as if Scaevola's opponent had been playing truant whenever teacher broached the subject of tennis rules, since he apparently has not the slightest qualms about aiming his serves directly at Scaevola's gallery, while it apparently does not occur to the latter to initiate a rally by sending the first ball onto the roof.

Still, from Scaevola's point of view, the service roof is not where it should be. Had he wished to deliver his service ball correctly, he would have needed a roof to his left rather than to his right. There is, therefore, the intriguing question of whether as late as in the fifteenth century two distinct types of tennis existed: one in which the servers attacked the gallery without much ado, and another in which the horn was sounded for the attack on the gallery only after an overture on the roof.

HOW OLD IS THE SERVICE TO THE ROOF?
THE TELL-TALE 'ADVICE FOR KINGS'

In the spring of 1946, an exhibition was opened at the Pierpont Morgan Library in New York. It was devoted to sports and pastimes from the fourteenth to the eighteenth century, and in addition to other exhibits, a picture was shown to the curious post-war visitor which carried the highly misleading label 'A Game of Hand Ball'.[40] The picture, a beautiful miniature from a mid-fourteenth-century French manuscript (**Plate 2**), was returned to the treasure vaults of the library soon after the exhibition had closed, and all that remained was the entry in the exhibition catalogue, which, however, was committed to the endless bookshelves of the library and so became almost as inaccessible as the manuscript itself. That is why the miniature has not had the ghost of a chance to solve, as well it might, the puzzle of Scaevola's irregular service.

The miniature had been gleaned from a book entitled *Avis aus Roys* where it illustrates the first page of a chapter on how to educate the offspring of kings. In the portion of text we are considering, the first two phases in the life of the crown prince are discussed. Each phase is said to last seven years, which suggests that Giles of Rome had been influential here, and for the second phase, from 7 to 14 years of age, the guidebook for kings has the following advice to offer: princes should be accustomed to certain honourable games and physical exercise, albeit in moderation (an idea also well known from other 'mirrors for magistrates'), and to enduring heat and cold so that they would under no circumstances become too delicate and soft. (Item es autres sept ans enseuguens on les doit acconstumer a aucuns Jeus honestes et exercitations de corps attempres et a suffrir froit et chaud si quil ne soient mie trop tendre ne trop doillet.)[41]

At this point, the decorative artists of the book apparently thought it proper to provide the user of the manual with an illustration showing how these rather vague instructions might be put into practice. In a charming miniature issuing from the letter I of the initial, the baby prince is first subjected to a thorough rub-in-a-tub by his mother and a wet nurse (upper left-hand corner). Having grown too big for the tub, the little prince, now distinguished by a coronet, is then sent to school. Sitting at his teacher's feet, he is now playing the role of a first-year schoolboy (upper right-hand corner). Finally, and in order to show the reader what was meant by an honourable game for aristocratic 7 to 14 year-olds, the miniaturist sacrificed the whole lower space of the initial for the depiction of a medieval tennis match. In the opinion of the artist, this game required two basic skills which had to be clearly distinguished from one another: the service, and the return. The royal house, of course, can afford to treat itself to two tennis tutors, one for each of these skills, and that is why we find, on the left-hand side, the service specialist, and, on the right-hand side, the coach entrusted with breaking his royal pupil into the routine of the return.

The pictures leave no doubt as to their meaning. On the left, the royal pupil is weighing the little tennis ball, in a manner with which we are familiar, in his left hand, in order to carefully place it with his right hand exactly where his instructor is pointing: onto the roof of a small house, which may well be a chapel in an inner courtyard surrounded by high walls. On the right-hand side, the pupil and his coach have swapped their roles, for here the tennis instructor is showing his pupil how to force the server to duck by a mighty return. The prince has turned his head and seems to be inquiring whether the ball should in all earnest be returned to where, after all, the cunning opponent could easily get it.

This early tennis illustration from the *Avis aus Roys*, the third oldest we know of, proves that well before the fifteenth century medieval tennis players were indeed obliged to give the slanting roof the benefit of the ball's first bounce. There is, however, more to it than that. It also suggests that, in the even earlier picture from *Lancelot du Lac* (**Plate 1**), the cowled tennis instructor is not pointing to the Lord Above watching over man's tennis here below. The strikingly similar picture from the *Avis* tell us that he is pointing to an imaginary roof onto which, hopefully, his pupil will be landing his ball the next minute. Most importantly, however, the *Avis* also solves the puzzle of the match between the Roman Scaevola and his nameless opponent. In all probability, Scaevola is not playing against a mystery man. He is not engaged in any match at all. The intriguing feature that his alleged opponent is the only person to have remained without a name ceases to be a mystery if we conceive of the picture as an attempt on the artist's part to show Scaevola as the perfect master of the two basic strokes. On the left, we see him as a shrewd server, and on the right the very same Scaevola is defending his gallery against a powerful return. The miniaturist has, as it were, telescoped into one picture what should in reality have been depicted in two.

One serious objection may nevertheless be raised against the view that Scaevola is, so to speak, a double Scaevola. In the original manuscript in the British Library, the two opponents are after all clearly distinguished and their likeness is more seeming than real. This fact is likely to escape tennis historians for the simple reason that the picture in question, although incorporated into almost every account of the early history of tennis, has only very rarely been inspected in the original. On the usual black-and-white reproductions, it looks as if the two players were indeed completely identical. As far as the cut and design of their tennis-outfits are concerned this is perfectly true. With regard to the colours of fifteenth-century tennis fashion, however, tastes were as diversified then as they are now. Whereas the Scaevola on the right would insist on his favourite mauve jerkin, worn over a blue undershirt, the Scaevola on the left would prefer the unobtrusive grey overall, with a striking orange undershirt to go with it. Scaevola I seems to consider orange the colour suited for his footwear only, whilst Scaevola II can only really get his game together when he is wearing his lucky green shoes. The colour white seems to have been obligatory only for the players' shorts, and for the fashionable tennis glove, of which, it seems, the medieval tennis player needed only one, and which he used to wear on his right hand.

Of course, even the different colours in which the two medieval tennis aces strut about on the folios of the Valerius Maximus are not altogether conclusive evidence that they had two identities. Just as the miniaturist might have been willing to give a demonstration of the two basic medieval tennis strokes, he might also have depicted the very same player in different garbs.

THE NECESSITY OF THE ROOF

Exeter's youngsters who boisterously swarmed into the cloisters of the canons had no intention to commit a sacrilege. They were simply attracted by the slanting roof which there awaited them. Without it, a tennis match was simply impossible. Unfortunately, they found it difficult to convince the clergymen of the healthy effect of games on the upbringing of the city's young. That is why they tried to find the support of non-clerical sponsors, by launching a campaign under the motto: 'Citizens, sacrifice your gables!'

One of the well-meaning citizens willing to sacrifice the front wall of his house, a draper called Jacobyn de Schot (Jamie Scot), lived in the city of Antwerp.[42] On 8 November 1494, he and Mihiel Wateble (Michael Wastewheat) concluded a contract by which Wateble was permitted to exploit forty feet of that part of Jacobyn's wall which from the end of the little wall of Mihiel's tennis court headed towards the street.[43] Mihiel was to exercise the privilege of executing carpentry and masonry, and of fixing clamps,[44] provided the roof of the tennis court would hang on the wall the way it now hung ('alsoe dat nu hanckt'). To put it up, or fix it, higher was not allowed, nor was Jacobyn's permission going to be for Mihiel and his father-in-law, Jan de Cuyper (John the Cooper) a vested right. Rather, it would have to be considered an expression of good neighbourliness, and last only as long as the tennis court was owned by the aforementioned.[45]

Gables giving support to a tennis roof can also be found in medieval book illustration. A remarkable instance is that in a book of hours owned by Adélaïde of Savoy, the Duchess of Burgundy (**Plate 3**). The book is a very important document for the early history of many games in general, and a learned article of some length and an entire monograph have been devoted to its illustrations dealing with games. Strangely enough, however, its remarkable tennis picture has not even been mentioned in either of them.[46] To judge from the saints' names prominent in its calendar, the book was manufactured in the workshops of northern France around the middle of the fifteenth century. About the artist who painted the picture nothing is known.[47]

The picture of a tennis roof is to be found at the bottom of an illustration of the month of June, a hint that in the Middle Ages, too, the season of the tennis players was the summer. The miniature gives a good idea of how in those days a tennis match was staged in this part of the European continent in a small market square and on a warm summer evening. Three players on either side are involved as seems to have been the rule in the fifteenth century. On the left-hand side the poker-faced server is about to strike the white ball in the familiar manner onto the few square metres of a sloping roof. It has been attached to the gable of a wealthy citizen who perhaps was the local patron of the game. He and his goodly wife have taken their seats in the medieval VIP box, a window on the first floor and above the roof construction from where the couple is watching the match. The match is also watched a number of gentlemen whose furred coat-tails document their wealth and who, by sitting comfortably on a bench under the tennis roof, demonstrate that besides receiving the serves the roof also served as a kind of grandstand.

Entrenched on the right-hand side is the returning squad with their right hands raised above their shoulders and in anticipation of the ball which will soon come down from the roof to their right. The server's team-mates, by way of contrast, do not seem very keen on the match at all. They are fooling around behind their team-mate's back. Perhaps they are trying to work up courage by slapping each other's hands, thus anticipating a ritual well known from modern ball games such as volleyball and basketball.

With regard to contemporary tennis fashion, the taste of the players here seems to have been very similar to that of the tennis star of Roman antiquity, Scaevola. This proves that the two pictures are fairly contemporary. The players wear decent tights even in summer, a doublet, a felt cap, and the pointed, turned-up tennis mocassins called *poulaines*, 'shoes from Poland', which were so very characteristic of the age.

Adélaïde's book, because of its richness of detail, is surely impressive, but it is by no means unique. There are another two of which one is by the same artist and the other at least from the same school or workshops. They have never been mentioned in connection with Adélaïde's book, and, as might have been expected, never in connection with its tennis picture either.

The first is part of the collection of the Gulbenkian Foundation in Lisbon (**Figure 27**). It was presumably written some time after that owned by Adélaïde. Here, the tennis roof, which in the latter showed traces of improvisation, seems to have at last been constructed much more professionally. The wooden posts which once supported it have now been replaced by a solid, tiered brick wall, and the attempt by the former court architects to stop the server's ball at the rear end of the roof, and to direct it onto the playing area, by means of a narrow wall has been not been repeated. Instead, a simple but highly functional plank set on its edge, and extending over the whole

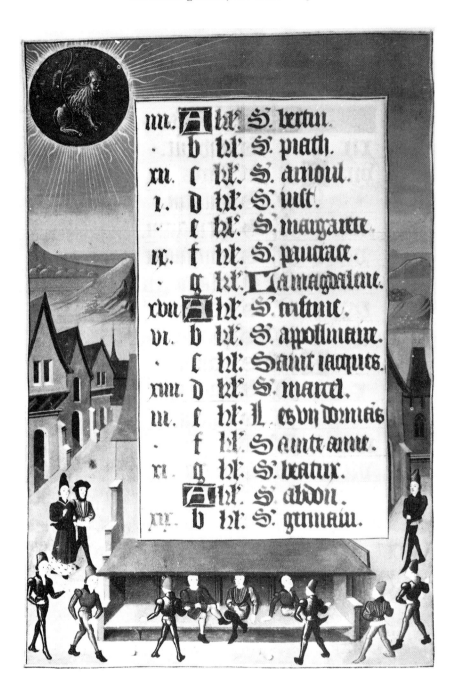

FIGURE 27 A book of hours later than that of the Duchess of Burgundy (*c.* 1450) (see PLATE 3). The miniature by the same artist shows two significant alterations: two balls in court, which indicate that two chases are being contended; and a plank at the end of the tennis roof, which forced the served ball to descend to where it belonged, the tennis court.

width of the roof, has effectively diminished the servers' chances of hitting their balls into no-man's land.

The match in progress shows a higher degree of sophistication, too. Whereas in Adélaïde's book the artist had contented himself with the traditional service scene which we know from earlier pictures, he has now tried his hand at the most dramatic phase of the game, the moment when the two chases had to be contended. This is probably the message of the two tennis balls, which hardly adorn the pitch because Mrs Slipshod reigned supreme on the courts of medieval France, but because they served as markers of the chases. As will be remembered, every time when the score had run up to two chases, the players were obliged to change ends in order to decide the battle over these chases.

The second is part of the collections of the Biblioteca Nacional in Madrid (**Figure 28**). It may well be the latest of the three because it combines two motifs gleaned from each of the others separately. From Adélaïde's book of hours it has borrowed the motif of the team-mates slapping each others' hands, from its Portuguese cousin it appropriated that of the two balls marking the chases. Another indicator of its comparative lateness might be the reduced size of the roof: extensive experiments with tennis roofs may in the meantime have led to the conclusion that only a certain portion of a roof was really needed for a regular match. The idea to regulate the course of the ball by a transverse plank has also been discarded, in a match which, for a change, takes place in the month of August rather than in June.

If in the Middle Ages the plank held in check the servers' tennis balls, in more recent times it is suited to clarify a much debated question in art history. The plank had a near cousin which makes an appearance roughly a hundred years later in an etching by Barthélemy de Momper showing the ducal tennis court in Brussels (see **Figure 30** on p. 59).[48] Barthélemy's picture proves that transverse planks were a prominent feature of Flemish tennis roofs, and at the same time lends support to the view that Adélaïde's book of hours and its Iberian companions originated in the north: no such planks have, in fact, ever been seen on the tennis roofs of Paris.

It is by no means clear according to what rules the matches here depicted were played, since galleries, walls and all seem to have fallen prey to late medieval economy measures. The absence of a line at least indicates that the antagonists were prepared to make a dive in order to prevent a long chase of the opponent. The role of the gallery goals was presumably taken over by some imaginary line behind the server's team, and the score was fifteen-love as soon as the ball had travelled beyond it.[49]

Tennis roofs continued to be attached to the gables of generous citizens for more than two hundred years, as is evidenced by three pictures which have been preserved by a stroke of good luck. The first is from the Cabinet d'Estampes of the Bibliothèque Nationale in Paris (**Figure 29**). The rough wooden battoirs with which the ball is sent onto a miniature type of roof prove that we are in the sixteenth century now, and that the era of the tennis racket has begun. There is, to be sure, no trace of a line here either.

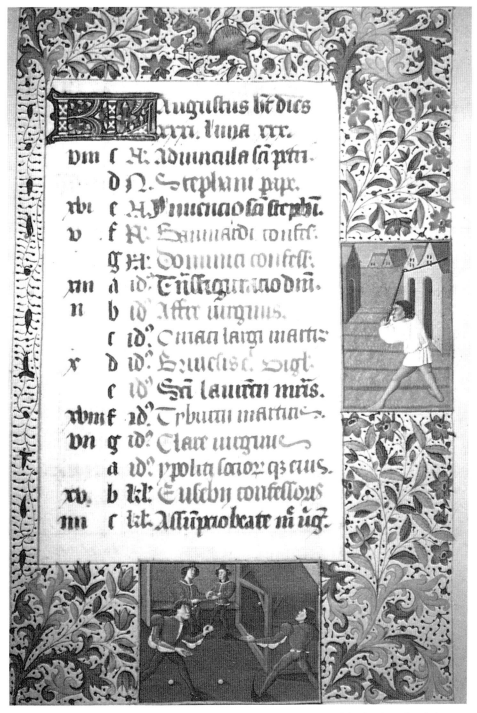

FIGURE 28   A miniature from the same Franco-Flemish school as Adélaïde's hour book (*c.* 1460). It also emphasized the battle for the chases, and chose to incorporate two fellow-players slapping each other's hand for encouragement.

Sauter dans le cerceau,& autres ieux.

Sans efpargner l'adreffe de leurs corps,   Autres qui font d'ingenieux cerueau,
Ceux-cy gaillards,iouënt à la boutte hors,   A qui mieux,faultent dans le cerceau,
Deffus ce toiƈ; Autres,aux Dames iouënt: Et ce plaifir merueilleufement louënt.   x·ij.

FIGURE 29   Engraving from a series illustrating French children's games (16th century).
Wooden bats are used, and barely a single square metre attached to the wall of a house has
remained of the longish roofed gallery of the cloisters.

Just as in this picture, a line is also missing in Barthélemy de Momper's etching
which has already claimed our attention (**Figure 30**).[50] Against the backdrop of the
Duke of Brabant's palace, we see a fashionable joust in progress – we have before us
one of the many revivals of the medieval tournament. The joust takes place on a large
square surrounded by a high wall and several adjacent buildings, and amidst the vivid
scene a tennis roof supported by four wooden posts might easily escape the viewer's
notice, had not Jean van de Velde, who made an almost exact copy of Barthélemy's
picture in 1645 (**Figure 31**),[51] chosen to explain it by means of the letter 'H' which,
in turn, refers to a caption at the bottom of his picture which reads: 'Het Kaets Spel',
the tennis court.[52]

   Unfortunately, Barthélemy for his picture picked a day when, because of the
tournament, there were no tennis fixtures. Because of the absence of the tennis players,
however, the tourneying knights could avail themselves of the tennis roof for the

FIGURE 30   For the Duke of Brabant a tennis court simply was a must. In this etching by de Momper (1535–1590) the tennis players had their day off because of a tournament.

storage of their tournament lances. Along with the spectators in front of them, these lances give a fairly good idea of the height and proportions of the roof.

Barthélemy's picture not only inspired van de Velde, it also served as the model for a contemporary painting signed 'Lucas Van Velen [Van Uden?] 1635' (**Figure 32**). The painting has been assigned to the middle of the sixteenth century, erroneously it seems.[53] For not only do the citizens of Brussels depicted in it wear clothes after the fashion of the seventeenth century,[54] the wooden tennis roof, too, after having braved the rains and storms of Flanders for almost a century, apparently had to be replaced by a new one. This one no longer rests on four wooden posts, but is supported by a dozen odd struts protruding from the wall. Another indicator of the picture's age is the disappearance of the 'tilt' or barrier which in Barthélemy's version served the purpose of preventing a clash of the tourneying champions. It has disappeared under a layer of paint, and the lists have been converted into a rectangular pitch on which the citizens of Brussels are hitting about the hefty balls used in pallone, for which wooden cuffs protecting the arm (Italian *bracchiale*) were required.[55] By the middle of the seventeenth century, the tournament had clearly become an

Tennis: a cultural history

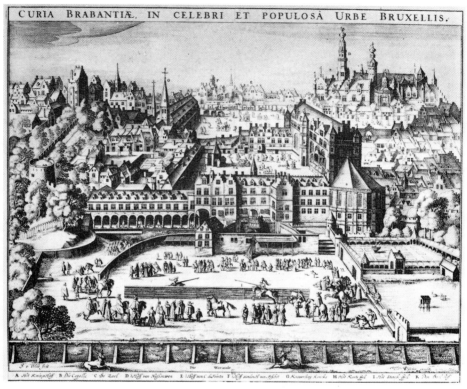

FIGURE 31   This 17th-century copy of de Momper's picture (FIGURE 30) was, with its tournament, clearly an anachronism.

anachronism. Tennis and pallone matches continued to be staged in front of the ducal palace of Brabant (later to become the residence of the Governor General of the Low Countries) until 1731. In that year the palace, which once occupied part of the Place Royale of today, was destroyed by a great fire.[56]

The third picture is by Jacques Stella (1596-1657) (**Figure 33**), a painter and draughtsman whose family also originated in Belgium, their real Flemish name being Stellaert. It was on his drawings that his cousin, Claudine Bouzonnet-Stella, based the engravings for her children's book *Les jeux et plaisirs de l'enfance*, published in 1667. Claudine's chubby little tennis imps are so innocent that they would have been tolerated even by the moralist Scaino who in his treatise on ball games referred to the wrestlers of Greek antiquity who competed oiled and naked and warned against similar practices in tennis which to him would present an ugly and highly indecent spectacle: '(un) spettacolo schifo, & troppo sconueneuole'.[57] Irrespective of Scaino, Stella's tennis toddlers clearly demonstrate that in France tennis continued to be played after the manner of Adélaïde of Savoy's book of hours for more than two hundred years.

FIGURE 32 More in keeping with contemporary customs was a 17th-century painting which also took de Momper as a model. Here the artist substituted a more civilized pastime, the game of *pallone*, for the obsolete tournament.

FIGURE 33 Youngsters' game under a miniature roof in 17th-century France.

Fairly contemporary with van de Velde's and Claudine Stella's engravings is a coloured pen-and-ink drawing by the Dutchman Lambert Doomer (**Figure 34**). It testifies to a significant change which must have occurred in the construction of tennis roofs while the traditional practice was still being adhered to. The picture was drawn, as the artist himself informs us on the reverse of the sheet, while he was travelling through France in 1646, and it shows the castle of Saumur on the river Loire: 'De veste van Samuers/Doomer f[ecit].A[nno] 1646'.

FIGURE 34 The game of the cloisters eventually moved into the open. The picture disproves the assertion that a game played in the open preceded that in the cloisters.

Facing the ruins of the old castle and the turreted wall down on the left, the beholder looks (the artist's stance was the Montée de la Petite Genève) down into a narrow valley, perhaps the extension of the moat.[58] And here he sees a rather curious example of how an age-honoured custom has transmuted into something new. Whatever the motivation of the players may have been to abandon the streets and squares of the town and to make the open country the venue for their game, even here the roof seems indispensable.

The long-handled rackets employed by the players indicate that balls had to be hit much harder, for the distances from one team to the other had become greater, and consequently more leverage was required. Nevertheless, the roof still dominated the field, and Lambert Doomer did not fail to capture the critical moment when the 'centre forward' of the attacking team lunged out forward to strike the ball, a tiny brown ink spot below the middle of the roof, descending from it after the opposing threesome's serve. For the sake of completeness it should be noted that this pastime of simple country folk, after the roof had eventually been discarded, evolved into *longue paume*, the game called 'alla distesa' by Scaino.[59] The overly long racket handle remained a characteristic of this game, which continued to flourish in France where in more recent times its stronghold has been the Jardin du Luxembourg.[60] Appropriately enough, it appeared on the programme of the Olympic Games in Paris in 1900.

Roofs in the countryside resting on four posts may have ensured a quick tennis match at any time, but the immobility of the construction turned out to be a serious drawback as time went on. Flexibility was needed when, for instance, the village centre court with its permanent roof happened to be occupied and the second team wanted to play a match all the same. The solution here was a corn sieve mounted on three legs, a wooden block underneath one of the legs resulting in a slanting surface for the sieve, and here you had your miniature roof.[61]

This new invention had much to recommend it. First, at least one such sieve belonged to the inventory of even the most run-down farmstead. Second, it could be taken anywhere with ease and be set up in a matter of seconds. Of course, the idea of doing away with the roof and its substitutes completely occurred to no one at the time, which proves that giving up old habits is difficult even in sports.

The invention of the mobile roof barely affected the game as such, the only difference being that it now was the servers who had to come to terms with a ball which, after having banged onto the slanting surface of the sieve, rebounded from it in a rather capricious manner.[62]

That variant of tennis for which a sieve (French *tamis* or *sas*) was needed is first recorded from the vicinity of Boulogne-sur-Mer on the north-western coast of France in 1498,[63] and from the sixteenth century onwards engravers and draughtsmen with a bent for the homely folk scene give us an idea of how this *jeu de tamis* may have been played. On an engraving by Perelle it is a game which looks like a compromise between a *jeu de tamis* pure and simple and the game Lambert Doomer had watched in the moats of Saumur (**Figure 35**). The long handles terminating in solid heads

FIGURE 35   In this form of 'Open' tennis, the role of the slanting service roof has been taken
over by what may well have been a washboard resting on a tub turned upside down.

seem to predict the kind of racket which was to be used in the game of *longue paume*
later on. The server, or rather, his assistant, is about to flick off a little ball onto a
board which is hardly a roof, but not yet a sieve either, and which rests on the edge
of a tub turned upside down.

A wealth of details of the *jeu de tamis* can be seen on a view of the Abbey of
Beaumont in the *Description particulaire de tout le Pais et Comté de Hainaut* of 1598
(**Plate 6**), where the adjective *particulaire* does not apply to the description of the
county of Hainaut only, but also to the pictorial representation of the 'sieve game'
which in this part of Belgium has always been extremely popular.[64] For his illustration,
the artist has again selected that phase of a match when the first of two chases is
being contended. Both chases have been marked on the court by small tiles. After
the ball has bounced back from the sieve, the server has only just delivered it into
the half of the opposing team, from where it is returned immediately. The player
nearest to the viewer has gone down on his knees in order to stop the ball. It is the
first and only portrait of a player to whom the humble job of stopping the ball has been
assigned, and it was not before the twentieth century that a similar scene was depicted
on a sketch illustrating the Picardian *jeu de tamis*.[65]

For a rather funny picture of the *jeu de tamis* we are indebted to a student at the
faculty of arts in the university of Louvain (**Figure 36**). His name is Jan Wouters. Jan
attended the lectures of the erudite professors Mennekens and Joannes Pauli van

FIGURE 36   The Pig's College in Louvain on the playground of which a tennis match is being contested by three-a-side teams recruited from the students. A corn-sieve mounted on three legs has for the first time and in an ingenious way been substituted for the roof. The same sieve is clearly visible towards the end of the 17th century in Weigel's estate book (FIGURE 17).

Virton between the years 1648 and 1650, but apparently found the subject of these lectures, Aristotelian logic, rather insipid. Leaving Aristotle to the Aristotelians, he devoted himself to the fine arts, and, not unlike students in more recent times, he adorned his desktop and his writing pad with funny pictures. Among these was a real masterpiece, a coloured drawing of his students' hostel, called the Paedagogium Porci, Pig's College, and on it, with a pedantry which might have been expected from his academic teachers, he recorded in the vast architectural complex the spot where, above the rear gate (*posticum*), Professor Mennekens was lodged. And that is why we are today in a position to form an idea about what Mijnheer Mennekens would have seen if he deigned to abandon his books for a moment in order to look down onto the open space under his window. There was, for one, a large cobble-stone courtyard, *area lapidea*, bearing the number 17, and, for another, an equally large college green bearing the number 18, and described in the caption as an 'earthen area or playing field for physical education (*area terrea siue lusoria pro physicis* [add: *exercitiis*]).

It was on this vast area that Jan and his fellows, instead of devoting their labours to the logic of Aristotle, chose to belabour mid-seventeenth-century tennis balls. After having picked three-a-side teams after the manner of the games played on Perelle's engraving and in front of Beaumont Abbey, the players on either side have positioned themselves in a kind of triangle – two forwards or wingers are backed by a player behind. The latter plays the role of the server whenever it is his team's turn. Jan Wouters has captured the moment when the ball has just been released from the server's hand and is about to drop onto the sieve.

That monkeying around on a tennis court is not a feature of the twentieth century is proved, in a literal sense, by a print designed by Peter van der Borcht and cut by Justus Sadeler (**Figure 37**). It is entitled 'Playing Monkeys', and is, so to speak, a zoological equivalent of Breughel's encyclopaedic composition 'Playing Children'.[66]

The pictures showing the *jeu de tamis* and discussed on these pages originate from the north of France and the southern parts of the Low Countries. This gives the lie to Christoff Weigel who in his book of 1698 claimed that the tennis professional (*ballenmeister*) had been 'drawn from life and brought onto copper', as indeed all

FIGURE 37 Even monkeys in this counterpart of Bruegel's famous painting 'Children at Play' did not fail to see the advantages of the portable roof of the humans and used it in their own game.

FIGURE 38   *Kaatsen* in Flanders. The underhand service is essentially the same as that on the first known picture of the game (*c.* 1300) (FIGURE 10), the only difference being that in the modern game the server is not allowed to wear a glove. Only the returning party is.

the other representatives of the various contemporary trades in his work. If we did not know of his business contacts with the Dutch engraver Casper Luyken, the conspicuous sieve in the tennis game of his picture would give him away.[67]

It should be noted in passing that the old *jeu de tamis* has survived in the south of Belgium among the Walloons and the Flemings where the game is known as *jeu de pelote à main* and *kaatsen* respectively. In the Dender Valley to the west of Brussels, in particular, the game is still extremely popular (**Figure 38**), and league matches are held regularly by five-a-side teams. Balls are no longer sewn by hand, but are synthetic, and the picturesque sieve has long disappeared. All that has remained of it is a rectangle painted onto the asphalt and still referred to as the *zeef* or *zift*,[68] but why this should be so is a question which in the age of the combine harvester only the oldest villagers and adepts of the game can answer.

THE SIEVE ON ITS WAY TO THE NORTH

A question much disputed among experts of Frisian *keatsen* is whether this variety of medieval tennis in days of old also featured a sieve (**Figures 39 and 40**). The expression *de stuit*, literally meaning 'the bounce', by which players refer to the two rectangles on the pitch from which the ball is brought into play,[69] seems to presuppose

FIGURE 39   *Keatsen* in Friesland. Again the service is that exemplified by the medieval book of hours.

FIGURE 40   *Keatsen* in Friesland: the return, again, is an exact copy of that of the medieval book of hours. In the modern game, the glove ('want') has been reinforced by a solid insert called a 'nap' or 'talon' imported from Belgium. It covers the palm of the hand and makes the return highly efficient.

its existence. Of course, such an expression seems justified only if a surface of some kind to which the server committed his ball once occupied the spot. However, since there is not the slightest hint in the vast literature on the sport that a sieve has ever been used,[70] experts have now begun to doubt that it ever existed, despite the telling name *de stuit*.[71]

As in other doubtful cases of tennis history as well, an answer to this question can be found by the comparative study of games. A close relative of Frisian *keatsen*, not least because it was played by the Frisians' former cousins, was the Saterlandic game popular among its practitioners till around the 1850s, but now extinct.[72] It had some very archaic features, and one of these is the so-called *steute* (compare *de stuit*),[73] 'a trunk of a tree of hard wood smoothed on its top and dug into the ground' from which the server had to make the ball rebound (a ball of wool sewn in leather and 8 centimeters in diameter) before he hit it into the opposing half (*pork*) 'with the palm of the hand, after a wide back-swing, at an angle of approximately 45 degrees'. That the trunk here described is but one of the many transformations the sieve has undergone can hardly be doubted. In the closely related Frisian and Gotlandic games, the trunk (or whatever served as a substitute of the sieve) is only remembered by the name *de stuit* or *ståitu* (variant *stötu*) respectively.

THE SIEVE ON ITS WAY TO THE SOUTH

Before long, the peoples of the south also thought of ways to get rid of the rigid roof. Unlike their cousins in the north, they apparently never considered the resilient surface of a sieve as a suitable ersatz. Instead, from the start they opted for a slanting surface which was smooth and perfectly solid.

Among the games availing themselves of a surface of such description is the so-called *jo de paumo* which has for many generations and with much enthusiasm been played in the streets and alleys of Provence. In this game, the server (*boundaire*) employs, as a trampoline for his ball, a stone or iron platform, the latter not infrequently being a fender divorced from its original purpose. The apparatus is aptly referred to by the term *boundadou*.[74] The Provençal game is a kind of missing link in the question of how the *tamis* games of the north were transmitted to the south where they must have reached Upper Italy by the end of the sixteenth century at the latest. In 1610, the Austrian physician Hippolytus Guarinonius with a great deal of self-irony testified to the existence of a game in which for the service a stone slab was used:[75]

> The other ball game is that of a somewhat bigger (and) harder leather ball which you
> hit with the hand, and hit back, used in all Italy and, coming from there, in many places
> in Germany, for the most part by uncouth, strong workmen rather than by noblemen,
> because for such a game a good strong hand and not a delicate one is needed. Since
> the players' hands swell from such a game, those from among the delicate and the tender
> who enter upon such a game will clandestinely have to blow their hands because of the

pain, or hush it up, and will be an object of derision, too. For he who wants to use a glove might not as quickly and aptly send the ball where he had wanted to, and even a flexible glove would be of little use. I for my part have often nibbled at the bait and wanted to try it, but to me it has never appeared other than when my instructors, long ago, occasionally hit my hand with the wooden ferula, or rod. And since there is little pleasure in this game because of the punishment for the hand which accompanies it, I have cared little for it. The service is made onto a stone slab onto which you throw the ball, and the self-same ball, bouncing back, is thrown with the free hand far into the air of the other team, and by this back, and this with all sorts of running and jumping on either side as well as bending low, stretching, hitting, etc., and this until the ball comes to the ground where the mark is set, and the place or position is changed. It is, all things considered, a good, strong and lively exercise for students, but not by any means suitable for organists, lute players, etc., for it makes for rough, thick and heavy hands, etc.

This game, which, according to Guarinonius, even found its way into the German south, does not seem to have survived in Italy, nor, for that matter, in Germany either. On its way to the Iberian peninsula, the *jeu de tamis* left its traces in the oldest varieties of Basque pelota, *bote luzea* and *lachoa*.[76] The service disk does not seem to have been known from the very beginning. At first, the ball was apparently thrown onto a slanting, roof-like piece of masonry supported by the wall of a house.[77] At a later date, the technical innovation of the mobile service disk (French *butoir*; Spanish *botadera*; Basque *bota barri*) was introduced. In villages it consisted of a simple stone slab, whereas in the towns a more refined contrivance was used, a wooden disk mounted on a tripod.[78] Today, *bote luzea* and *lachoa* have disappeared almost completely and are not even known among pelota experts. The former can still be seen in some places in Zuberoa; *lachoa*, a variant type played with gloves and on a larger pitch, has been preserved in the Aldudes.[79] In the highly spectacular Basque pelota game *jai alai*, the fact that the ball has to be bounced onto the floor before the service may well be a reminder of the custom of serving it onto some slanting surface in the days of yore.

On the Iberian peninsula, offshoots of medieval tennis have survived in the area around Valencia only.[80] Among the many varieties practised in streets and alleys and in elaborate ball-courts (*trinquetes*) there is one, *a rebote*, in which a tilted stool is required for the service. If there is none available, the server may for a change make the ball rebound from the naked floor or even from his own arm.[81]

Another offshoot of the *jeu de tamis* has survived in the solitudes of the Canary Islands where it leads a rather unobtrusive life.[82] Here, too, the progress of the game seems to have been one 'by instalments', in much the same way as in the Basque country. It is mentioned in a written source rather late, in 1616, when it was referred to in a document relating to a property sale in the village of Teguise on the island of Lanzarote. In the document it is stated that the houses sold faced the local *juego de la pelota*.[83] A Calle Pelota appears much later still, in 1686, on a map of Las Palmas, Gran Canaria. The street name may be much older, though, since the street to which it refers is located in the oldest part of the city.[84] Of course, the bare names tell us nothing about what kind of pelota was indulged in by the islanders in those early days. It may well be, however, that these early references make an allusion to a game in which the server had to send his ball onto a slanting stone slab on top of a wall. Later, a wooden surface (Spanish *bote*) resting on three, then four legs was imported from the mainland (**Figure 41**).[85] Both devices, the wall and the implement mounted on legs, lead a life of peaceful coexistence in only a few out-of-the-way villages of Lanzarote.[86] The game goes by the name of *pelotamano*.

THE SIEVE'S BIG LEAP ACROSS THE ATLANTIC

A disk onto which the server bounces his ball and called *botadera* is also the characteristic feature of a game played by Mestizos and pure-blooded Indians in Xoxocotlán in the State of Oaxaca (**Figure 42**).[87] The many x's in the names indicate that we have moved from Europe to Mexico, a country proud of her ancient culture which flourished long before the Spaniards set foot in it. This fact persuaded two Mexican anthropologists, Jorge R. Acosta and Hugo Moedano Koer, to discover vestiges of an ancient, pre-Colombian Mexican game in the ball game of Oaxaca known as *pelota mixteca*. Their views were readily accepted by Mexican politicians who welcomed *pelota mixteca* in their attempt to reject US influence and at the same time to give a boost to Mexico's indigenous sporting culture.[88] It is rather odd that in their attempt the service disk used in *pelota mixteca* had to carry the burden of proving

FIGURE 41 *Pelotamano*, 'handball', as played on the island of Lanzarote. A slanting board mounted on four legs ('bote') is used for the service. In this picture, the 'bote' is hidden behind the centre players.

FIGURE 42 *Pelota mixteca*, a descendant of the medieval tennis game of Europe. The stone slab employed for the service has, albeit wrongly, been associated with the circular boundary markers in indigenous Indian ball courts.

that the game of the Mixtecs and Zapotecs was of Old Mexican extraction.[89] The disk was compared with the border stones in the ritual ball courts of the Maya.

Modest objections were made against such a view by the American Theodore Stern,[90] but these have recently been brushed aside by William R. Swezey who, in his sweeping article, combined sarcasm with an amazing ignorance of European ball games.[91] Despite Swezey's assertions to the contrary, there can hardly be any doubt that *pelota mixteca* is in fact a very close relative of some Franco-Flemish game which after long migrations through the south of France and the Iberian peninsula eventually reached the New World. The many features the game shares with the Basque pelota games of *bote luzea* and *lochoa*, and the Canarian game make such a conclusion simply inevitable. As has been noted by Stern, the leather ball stuffed with wool,[92] the leather gloves strapped onto the players' hands and studded with ornamental nails (**Figure 43**),[93] the chase rule and the manner of scoring all prove the European origin of *pelota mixteca*. The strongest argument against Acosta's and Koer's view is the complicated chase rule. It could hardly have been invented a second time and independently from its European model.[94]

The sieve underwent a significant transformation in another game of the Americas either simply called *pelota*, or, more significantly because of the presence of the traditional chase rule, *juego de la chaza*. Perhaps introduced by Spanish conquistadors as early as the sixteenth century, it is played by the Indian part of the population of Southern Colombia and Northern Ecuador (**Figure 44**). In this game, none of the

FIGURE 43 Glove studded with ornamental nails. It is used in the variety of *pelota mixteca* played with the heavier rubber ball.

players seems to object to a strange stumbling-block in the very centre of their court, a stone which seems to serve no other purpose than that of marking the service point.[95] It is, of course, what has remained of a stone slab by which in former times the ball was brought into play.

Those who still refuse to believe that this *juego de la chaza* is a cousin of the *jeu de tamis* as played in the borderland between Belgium and France are perhaps convinced by the little word *cuerda* which in the Indian game denotes the lateral boundary. Of course, the inquisitive gringo trying to find an explanation for this expression will in vain look for ropes, *cuerdas*, marking off the court, but will perceive a furrow, or a line of pebbles or shells instead.[96] From an article in the French sporting journal *La vie au grand air*,[97] it appears that at the turn of this century in the *jeu de tamis* the same lateral boundaries went by the name of *cordes*. Similarities like these prove, on the one hand, the close relationship of the South American and the European game, and, on the other hand, the basic correctness of the claim made by modern folklorists that the Middle Ages survived in the rural areas of Europe until shortly before the Second World War.[98]

FIGURE 44 *Pelota de mano* on the Plaza de Ponchos in Otavalo, North Ecuador. There are several varieties of the game in the border regions of Colombia and Ecuador which are played with a glove (*guante*), a racket (*tabla*) or, as in this scene, the unprotected hand.

TWO PRECOCIOUS RACKET OWNERS:
TROILUS OF TROY AND MARGOT OF HAINAUT

In 1385, Geoffrey Chaucer, the Father of English Poetry, had the hero of his courtly novel *Troilus and Criseyde* ask an intriguing question:[99] 'But kanstow playen raket, to and fro?', Troilus asks his friend Pandarus, who had suggested to him to look for another paramour after Criseyde had sneaked off to the enemy's camp.

We have heard from the *paume* player Gastelier that the tennis racket began its battle with the tennis ball hardly before the beginning of the sixteenth century. It is plausible, therefore, that Troilus cannot have had a tennis racket in mind when he spoke of 'pleyen raket'. That he was nevertheless referring to the game of tennis cannot, however, be ruled out completely, since the eternal back and forth (compare the phrase *to and fro*) has been a characteristic of it from its very beginnings. The meaning of Troilus' question seems clear enough. It is an instance of what rhetoricians call an impossibility topos, and what the Trojan knight wants to say is something like: 'It is as impossible for me to find another sweetheart as it is impossible for you to play "raket to and fro".' But why should good old Troilus not have been able to play tennis? We will delay the answer to this question until the next chapter. Here it shall suffice to point out that the term *raket* cannot have referred to the tennis implement which clearly belongs to a later age, but that it can well have something to do with the game as such. It may be noted in passing that at the sight of Chaucer's *raket* the editors of the *Oxford English Dictionary* threw up their rackets completely, and, following the explanation offered by DuCange's Medieval Latin dictionary, turned the Trojan racket into a medieval dice game.[100]

Another premature reference to the racket has been suspected in a piece of historical writing titled the *Journal d'un bourgeois de Paris*. The *Journal* is remarkable because its author, a member of the University of Paris, in marked contrast to other historians of his time, rather than deal with important matters of state, described the everyday life of ordinary people. The *Journal* covers the period from 1405 to 1449, and since the unknown author started to work on it rather late in life, he may have died at some time around the middle of the century.

Under the year 1427, the *Journal* records a sports event which must have aroused the curiosity of contemporaries.[101] A woman called Margot – Maggie – had come to Paris, who was, in the author's opinion, fairly young, between 28 and 30 perhaps. She had come from Hainaut and played tennis, better in fact than anyone had seen it played before. She played with her forehand (*devant main*) and her backhand (*derrière main*) as powerfully, cunningly, and adroitly as any man, and of the men who came to play against her it was only the most powerful players who would not be beaten. The author of the *Journal* concluded his account by saying that the best tennis court in Paris was in the Rue Grenier-Saint-Lazare called the Little Temple (Petit Temple).

The passage contains two valuable pieces of information. First, we learn where the best tennis court in fifteenth-century Paris was to be found. (There were, incidentally, another four which we know by name and which, strangely enough, were for the most part located in plaster or clay pits.)[102] Second, we are given the name of Margot (in fact the only female player in over half a millennium of male-dominated tennis history), a player who is said to have struck the hard leather ball not only with the forehand, but also with the backhand. This latter was something the tennis historians' guild, also a male-dominated body, found extremely difficult to swallow. And that is why the representative of the fair sex was generously conceded the use of a racket.

Of the pain which the Basques call the nail and the martyrdom of Saint Francis Xavier

An English romance of the fifteenth century is likely to cast some doubt on the existence of a powerful backhand stroke, be it male or female. It deals with a Turk of diminutive stature and that colossus among King Arthur's knights, the courageous Gawain.[103] The two set sail for the castle of the King of Man who, it turns out, is a rather unpleasant fellow. He makes sport of Gawain, Arthur and his chivalry, and he takes special delight in deriding the pious clergy, and in challenging King Arthur's knights to rather gruesome competitions.[104] Among these is a nice little tennis match, since the King of Man correctly assumes that tennis belongs to the pastimes of Arthur's court, and that, as a consequence, Gawain knows how to play it.

In more than one sense, the game Gawain has to face is not cricket. Upon the King's orders, a troop of incredibly hideous giants – seventeen of them – throng in onto the court, eagerly dragging in behind them their master's ball. It is made of brass and so heavy that nobody in England can even carry it, but it is virtually ideal for the giants' massive maulers, and the monsters are confident that they will knock the brains out of Gawain's head with it.[105]

Unfortunately, nothing is known about the run of play or the result of the match, for that half of the page which would have informed us about them was torn out of the only manuscript to relate this story, the so-called Percy Folio – presumably by some medieval tennis fan. The fact that Gawain, on the pages which follow, is engaged in other competitions proves, however, that he has at least survived the ordeal.

The story of Gawain and the Turk belongs to the medieval genre of the romance which in England, as opposed to France, was of a more homely nature, a characteristic being its frequently indulging in rather grotesque exaggeration. Every exaggeration has a grain of truth to it, though, and the truth of the giants' little toy is that even hitting a normal tennis ball with the palm of one's hand could be a rather painful experience. The pain, which the physician Guarinonius chose to compare with the pangs occasioned by the rod, had a most revealing name among Basque pelotaris when they still played their traditional games with the naked, unprotected hand. It was called *itzia*, 'the nail'.[106] One who most certainly had to suffer a lot from it was St Francis Xavier (1506–1552), the pelotari's patron saint. When in 1945 an autopsy was performed on his mortal remains the deformation of the right hand typical of the pelota player came to light. It proved that the saint had not only taken upon himself the toils of his many missions to the Far East, but that he had also for many years endured the martyrdom of his fellow pelotaris.[107]

Adepts of the old tennis game less given to self-sacrifice must at an early date have found the nail simply intolerable and looked for something by which its effects might be alleviated. The curious reader will not have failed to notice that not only in the much-quoted illustration from Valerius Maximus (**Plate 4**), but also in what may well be the oldest tennis picture to have come down to us, medieval tennis players protected their hands by means of a glove (**Figure 10**). Whereas on the first Scaevola seems to have put on a rather elegant kid glove, the unknown player on the second seems to prefer a somewhat rustic gauntlet glove.

The glove is the forerunner of the racket, which in the beginning was a round board fixed to a handle (French *palet*). At last, and from the sixteenth century onwards, according to the testimony of both pictorial representations and written sources, a gut-strung frame took on the hard tennis balls.

The first author to allude to the catgut racket is Erasmus of Rotterdam. In his *Colloquia familiaria* (Basle 1522) his two interlocutors, the young clerks Nicolas and Jerome, inform us not only about the advantage the racket gave its user (that of sweating less), but also, by means of an ingenious play upon words, about what it looked like. After Nicolas has suggested to Jerome to avail himself of the wooden implement, Jerome flatly refuses to do so. He for his part prefers the more elegant form of the game (we would call it the more sportsmanlike one), namely, that in which the palm of the hand is used. The racket, referred to by the Latin term *reticulum*, should be left to fishermen.[108] Since the principal meaning of *reticulum* is 'fishing net', Jerome's remark only makes sense if the rackets with which Erasmus was familiar strongly resembled a net.

The second reference to the strung racket is to be found in the *Exercitatio linguae latinae*, written by the Spaniard Vives in the vein of Erasmus's dialogues and published in 1539. Vives also tried to make a little pun when he had one of his interlocutors, young Borgia, query: 'How do they strike the ball in Paris? Is it with the fist as in fist-ball?' 'Nay,' Scintilla, the Paris expert, says, 'they use a *reticulum*.' 'Made of knotted string?', Borgia wants to know. (He is a kind of sixteenth-century Dr Watson who fails to see the obvious and seems to think of a fishing net.) 'No,' Scintilla replies, 'it is made of fairly thick catgut, about as thick as the bass string of a lute.'[109]

<h2 style="text-align:center">SMOOTH WITHOUT AND ROUGH WITHIN: THE MEDIEVAL TENNIS BALL</h2>

What did the medieval tennis ball look like? The author who gave us deep insights into the human soul, also lets us catch a glimpse of the inner life of tennis balls. In his comedy *Much Ado about Nothing* (1598), Shakespeare said of the die-hard bachelor Benedick that the full growth of his beard had often served the purpose of filling tennis balls.[110] Much less known is a passage from Thomas Dekker's *The Guls Horn-Booke* (1609) in which the author pokes fun at the exuberant tresses with which the fops of his day strutted about. This wealth of hair, prerequisite of any man *à la mode*, caused so much envy among the Turks that whenever they took prisoner a Christian they at once as a token of slavery sheared him clean. An instance of Muslim cruelty it was, therefore, to stuff breeches and tennis balls with something which, once lost, all the hare-hunters of the world (a clever pun on *hare/hair*) would not be able to catch even if they sweated their heart-blood.[111]

The French, who apparently could not avail themselves of this type of English wool, had to use dogs' hair instead if we are to believe again our chief informant Vives.[112] It was sewn into white leather which in Flanders, according to the *Kaetspel Ghemoralizeert*, was cut into eight patches.[113] Spanish ball-makers had adopted a different method. Rather than with human and canine hair they stuffed their tennis balls with scraps torn from a woollen cloth, and this custom seems to be still adhered to in the Mixtecan ball-game.[114] French tennis balls apparently were much harder than Spanish ones, because in France the game was, again according to Vives, only rarely played with the palm of the hand.[115]

<h2 style="text-align:center">THARSIA'S RIDDLE</h2>

The custom of stuffing tennis balls with hair is as old as the game itself. This becomes evident from the story of the earliest tennis player we know, Apollonius of Tyre. Before the story has its happy ending, Apollonius has to recover his daughter Tharsia

who had been abducted by pirates. In pursuit of them, his ship gets caught in one of
those sea storms by which the whole novel is infested and is driven to the city of
Mytilene, the very sea-port where Tharsia had been sold to the keeper of a brothel.
In this establishment, Tharsia had made herself a name as a lute-player and a singer,
and it is in this capacity that she is sent to Apollonius, who is moping in the hull of
his ship, in order to cheer him up. Unlike Scheherazade, the heroine of *A Thousand
and One Nights*, she does not entertain Apollonius with tales, but with riddles. One
of these is as follows:

> *A grant plente ay de chevaulx*
> *Autelz comme une vacque ou veaulx*
> *Mais nulz ne les voit ilz sont dedens*
> *De mains aux autres ce sachiez*
> *Suis en lair boute et saciez*
> *Et aussi tost court pres que vent.*

> *(Of hair have I plenty,*
> *Such as a cow or calves;*
> *But no one can see it, it is inside.*
> *From hands to other hands, hear what I say,*
> *Am I struck into the air and hustled*
> *And almost as swiflty as the wind it runs.)*

Of course, this riddle presents no difficulty to Apollonius, the tennis ace who had
held his own against Archistrates, the King of Cyrene. 'Ha!', he exclaimed, 'that I
should know, for this fellow did me a lot of good when I played against Archistrates.
A ball has no hair on the outside, but plenty of it inside; and it is struck into the air
with the palm of the hand'.[116] Tharsia's riddle reveals that whenever tennis balls had
to be stuffed in the north of France cows and calves had to be called upon. Cows
and calves are still the chief suppliers of ball stuffings in Friesland which is yet another
proof of the antiquity of the Frisian game.

TENNIS, THE MANY-HANDED GAME

The question of how many hands on either side were dealing out boxes to the little
bald heads from Tharsia's riddle is a complex one. In the *Ystoire de Appollonius*,
King Archistrates is pitted against the whole lot of his servants, before he invites
Apollonius to a singles match.[117] A similarly ill-balanced match is that of King Arthur's
knight Gawain against the King of Man's hideous team in which the ratio was
one to seventeen. But whereas the superior numbers in the case of Archistrates were
meant to show the King's superiority, in the case of Gawain they clearly showed the
magnitude of the offence against the ethics of fair play. The rules of the South
American *juego de la chaza* provide for the possibility of superior numbers on one
side. Although a match of one against one, two against two, and so on, is the normal

procedure, it is also possible for one team to be short of one player, and this special form of the game is referred to by term *chuspilla*,[118] a loan word from Ketschua meaning 'little purse'.[119] Perhaps the game was so called because betting gains might be boosted by betting on the team playing with one player less.

In the course of the fifteenth century three players on either side seem to have become the standard formation. In his famous allegorical poem of 1439, Charles d'Orléans sides with Hope (*Espoir*) and Good Fortune (*Bon Eur*) against invincible Old Age (*Aage* or *Vieillesse*) and her fierce confederates Fickle Fortune (*Fortune*) and Worry (*Soussy*).[120] In the miniature from Adélaïde's book of hours and its variant from Lisbon the same formation is adhered to, and such is also the case in the match between Henry VIII and the Emperor and the Prince of Orange and the Margrave of Brandenburgh in 1522, in which both sides availed themselves of one 'stopper' each, namely Lord Edmund and the Earl of Devonshire.

In the *jeu de tamis* played against the backdrop of Beaumont Abbey (**Plate 6**) and on the sacred lawn of Jan Wouter's Pig's College (**Figure 36**) we also encounter three-a-side teams, and the Frisian game of *keatsen* is played by threesomes, too, although here the idea seems to have been born in the twentieth century only. Alternatively, Provençal *jou de poumo* is performed by a quartet,[121] and the Flemish game of *kaatsen* and Franco-Walloon *jeu de pelote à main* by quintets.[122] The last also applies to the Tuscan ball game of *palla* played on Sunday afternoons in Vetulonia and some neighbouring villages,[123] and indeed to all the southern offshoots of the medieval game. In *longue paume* there are six players on either side (at least in the so-called *partie terrée*),[124] in the *pärkspel* of Gotland as many as seven,[125] and in what seems to be the oldest of all, the Saterlandic ball-game, the number of players was virtually indefinite.[126] If we were to judge from these modern popular outgrowths of the game, medieval tennis appears to have been a rather populous affair.

THE FRIGHTFUL CHALLENGE MATCH

In Jan van den Berghe's *Kaetspel Ghemoralizeert* of 1431 there is the earliest reference to a tennis threesome. Here three respectable gentlemen, John, James, and Peter, have it out with three blackguards whose bad character is reflected in their telling names Willekin (Wilfulness), Reynkin (Deception), and Desier (Cupidity).

The match is arranged in the following way: 'Three tennis players,' the author says, 'had heralded a match and said that they would hold their own against all those coming up against them in equal number'.[127]

At this point it is worth remembering that medieval ball games were modelled after the tournament, and the passage of arms in particular. The passage of arms was, of course, also preceded by a formal challenge, and it is certainly rewarding to compare an instance of it with that of the three Flemish tennis players which has just claimed our attention. In 1493, ten knights had gathered at the castle of Sandricourt, and had sounded the following message all around the place:

> the said knights and squires who are inside the said castle of Sandricourt are resolved, all ten of them, to appear at the perilous barrier of the said place, … and shall appear there on the fifteenth day of September, afoot, armed as it is fitting, … to defend the said perilous barrier against the first ten to present themselves there.[128]

The similarities between the tournament and the tennis challenges are indeed striking, so much so, in fact, that a close relationship between the two sports can hardly be denied.

In geographically isolated areas to which innovations gain access only with difficulty, the age-honoured rites of the formal challenge have long been preserved. On the island of Gotland, for instance, the medieval custom of challenging an opponent to a tournament by means of a formal letter couched in the most flowery rhetoric seems to have survived in the ball-game of *pärk*.[129] In the *juego de la chaza* of Colombia and Ecuador the rather aggressive challenge is not unknown either, and the Spanish term used for it is *desafiar*.[130] In the Low Countries, and especially in Friesland, many subtypes of the challenge have been developed. As late as the seventeenth century, Antonin van Torre showed in his *Dialogi familiares* (1657) that very little had changed since the appearance of the *Kaetspel Ghemoralizeert*. Antonin's book is one of the traditional language-teaching books in which the characters speak Latin and Dutch in everyday situations. One such everyday situation is a tennis match in which after the manner of the *kaetspel* three are pitted against three in fictional competition, the names of the players being Arnold, Peter and William on the one hand, and Lawrence, Charles and Martin on the other. 'I challenge every one of you who so desires' ('quemlibet vestrum provoco'), Lawrence throws out his chest at the beginning of the match, or, in Lawrence's own language:[131] 'Ick beroepe den besten van ulieden.' This rendering may not be quite literal, but the closeness of Lawrence's challenge to that of the *Kaetspel Ghemoralizeert* two centuries earlier is indeed striking.

In Friesland the formal challenge survived until about the turn of this century. It could either be made by words of mouth for which the term *uitdagen* was used;[132] or by some symbolic act of which there existed a real wealth. One was the so-called *balopsteken*, the public exhibition of a ball. This was done by either squeezing it into a joint in the bricked wall of the player's favourite pub, or by fixing it to an iron clamp (Dutch *beugel*) especially designed for the purpose and hung up outside the players' haunt. The clamp occasionally took the shape of a bird of prey's claw, and a specimen of such a stylish device can be found among the exhibits of the museum in Franeker (**Figure 45**). Alternatively, the ball could be deposited inside the pub itself, ideally between the genever bottles on the shelf. This had the advantage that the players could have a watchful eye on it while working up a Frisian courage before the coming fight.

According to Le Franq van Berkhey, who left an account of Dutch *kaatsen* in 1776, the ball was, not unlike the throwing down of a gauntlet, flung onto the pitch after as many scraps of leather had been cut from it as there were challengers. By a curious coincidence we know from an allegorical poem written by the Dutch poet Anthonis de Roovere that this custom is an ancient one going back to the fifteenth century. The

FIGURE 45   In Friesland this claw of a bird of prey made of brass served the purpose of the challenge. It was hung up outside a tavern, and a *keatsball* stuck in it signalled to the passer-by that somebody inside was very keen on a match.

poem is titled 'Gheestelijck den Bal te Slane' (Striking the Ball Spiritually), and the reader, knowing about the lack of interest exhibited by the literary scholar for so trivial a matter as sports and games, will scarcely be surprised at the dreadful blunders committed by these academics when trying to assess the poem. One of them even wants to make us believe that the game described by Anthonis is an instance of medieval hockey (Dutch *kolven*).[133] The relevant portion of Anthonis de Roovere's poem runs thus:[134]

> De hertheyt des bals bediet gedooghsaemicheyt
> Want hemel ende aerde is in zijn ghewelt
> Binnen vol haers dats de almachticheydt
> Sijnder grondelooser ontfaermicheyt onghetelt
> Van desen drijen heeft een ghevelt
> Ons lijden door zijn ontfaermen groot
> Recht als een Bal int aerdtsche velt ghestelt
> Sijn menschelijckheyt ghecruyst ghedoodt
> Figueren zign hier af tsbals plecxskens roodt
> ...
> Den Bal die zijn veel stucxkens ghesneden of
> Waer by de stucxkens verwe ontfaen

(The hardness of the ball denotes Patience,
For heaven and earth are in His power.
Full of hair inside, it is the Omnipotence
Of His infinite, indescribable Mercifulness.
Of these three things, he has cast down one,
For us humans: through his great Mercy
He has laid it onto the earthly field just like a ball.
His humanity, crucified and murdered,
Is hinted at by the ball's red spots.

...

Many little scraps are cut from the ball,
By which these spots obtain their colour.)

Instead of calling poor Anthonis a rather muddle-headed poetaster, critics would have done well to become better informed about the subtleties of their indigenous game of *kaatsen*. If they were, they would soon have realized how intelligently the peculiarities of the game have been put to good use for Anthonis's well-conceived simile of man's salvation. Of the three Divine Virtues, Patience, Omnipotence and Mercy, the Lord had sent one into this vale of tears, Jesus Christ. The Son is, as it were, a challenge to sinful mankind. His Mercy Personified is bleeding to death on the Cross, and such is the figurative sense of the *kaats*-ball into the white skin of which little holes have been cut so that its filling, the red hair of a cow, becomes visible. After this fascinating example of medieval allegorical poetry we will conclude this chapter with something more prosaic, a challenge printed in a Frisian daily newspaper of 25 September 1802:[135]

FIGURE 46   Purported to be the oldest pictorial representation of Frisian *keatsen* (1824), this picture on closer inspection turns out to be an adaptation of Caspar Luyken's 17th-century engraving which was also used by Christoff Weigel (FIGURE 17) and in the work of Abraham a Sancta Clara (1711).

De liefhebbers van kaatsen van Vrouwenparochie verzoeken aan de Liefhebbers van Buiten, zes of negen man uit een dorp, tegen haar te kaatsen. Ieder partuur om een zillveren bal. Zondag 3 oct. percys de klok 3 uur.

(Amateurs of *keatsen* from Vrouwenparochie invite enthusiasts of the game from elsewhere, namely six or nine from each village, to a game of *keatsen* against them. Each game will be played for a silver ball. Sunday, 3 October, at three o'clock sharp.)

If almost half a millennium ago John, James and Peter had in the *Kaetspel Ghemoralizeert* formulated a challenge according to the usage of the medieval passage of arms, we have here before us an almost exact copy of it. The medium may have changed, and the press may have usurped the role of the medieval herald, but both the form and the contents of the message have remained the same. As in the chivalric challenge the venue and time of the competition are given, and the prize is named as well as the number of competitors – the exuberant number of nine players on either side appears to have been quite normal in the Frisian game in those days (**Figure 46**).[136] The example shows how the spirit of the chivalric tournament lingered on in the ball games descended from it, and we begin to realize why the tennis novice should be given such a scare by the prospect of a challenge match. Perhaps the collective unconscious recalls to his memory those by-gone days when one of his tourneying forebears was sent sprawling into the dust by a merciless opponent.

THREE

The language of tennis

◇

THE LANGUAGE OF TENNIS AND MILITARY JARGON

The most reliable route to the origins of tennis is its language. It has been our contention that tennis (as indeed a great many of medieval ball games) was based on the principles of the knightly tournament. If this is true, it would seem plausible that the fact should be reflected in the game's language.

The tournament was, as we have heard, itself an outgrowth of medieval warfare, and that is why an analysis of tournament language is best begun by having a look at medieval military jargon first. Giles of Rome's treatise on the education of princes has already been mentioned. Not surprisingly, it includes a manual for the future army leader, and here the pious ecclesiastic's guidelines for the siege and eventual capture of a castle are of particular interest. Three methods are recommended to attain the objective: The first is to cut off the water supply; the second to starve out the besieged; the third to scale the castle walls.[1] A particularly elegant solution is suggested for the second type. If by any chance those without (*cil de hors*) managed to capture some of those within (*de ceus de denz*), the prisoners should not be executed on the spot, but have some limbs hacked off by which they would be rendered invalid and completely useless to those still within (*a ceus de denz*). The poor wretches should then be sent back to the castle where they would make further inroads on the dwindling provisions of those within so that want and misery would befall them all the sooner.[2] What is important here is the terminology used for the besiegers and the besieged. Whereas those attacking the castle are referrred to by the term *those without* (in modern French something like *ceux de dehors*), their opponents are called *those within* (*ceux de dedans*).

As might have been expected, the distinction made between *within* and *without* also was a characteristic of the tournament as becomes evident from the description of a tournament by Thomas Malory. In his famous *Morte d'Arthur*, Malory narrates with great effect the story of a battle in front of a castle gate, the *locus classicus* of the passage of arms, which has all the features of a deadly serious encounter, but is nevertheless termed a tournament by the author. Sent into this fray is the Arthurian champion Sir Galahad, who just happened to be passing by and apparently needed no second asking to help the defenders, who by the time of his arrival had got themselves into dire straits indeed (emphasis by the present writer):[3]

> Than he [Galahad] toke hys way to the see; and on a day, as hit befelle, as he passed by a castell there was wondir *turnemente*. But they *withoute* had done so much that they *within* were put to the worse, and yet were they *within* good knightes ynow.

> So whan Galahad saw tho *within* were at so grete myschyff that men slew hem at the *entre of the castell*, than he thought to helpe them, and put a speare furthe, and smote the firste, that he flowe to the erthe and the speare yode in pecis. Than he drew hys swerde and smote thereas they were thyckyst; and so he dud wondirfull dedys of armys, that all they mervayled.

Not long after this, when the numbers of the attackers had been reduced considerably thanks to the activities of Galahad, the reason for the inner team's initial difficulties becomes evident. The opposing team is supported by no less a man than Gawayne, King Arthur's famous knight errant, who, it seems, also just happened to be passing by, but who, in contrast to Galahad, had felt immediate sympathy for the attacking team and therefore championed their cause. This he lives to regret. Galahad lands him a blow which sets his ears ringing and sweeps him off his steed. This breaks the resistance of *those from without*, who, after the defenders have mustered their courage for a counter-attack, are scattered to the four winds at last. When Galahad sees that nobody really feels like continuing the skirmish, he slinks off (emphasis by the author):[4]

> Thus thorow hy hardynesse he [Galahad] bete abacke alle the knyghtes *withoute*, and than they *within* cam oute and *chaced* them all aboute. But whan sir Galahad saw there wolde none turne agayne, he stale away prevaly, and no man wyste where he was becom.

Malory's description is a good example for how the language of war was adopted for the tournament in general, and its relation, the passage of arms, in particular, but it also presents a difficulty. Malory's work was completed in 1470, and the passages of arms so-called and on record belong to the fifteenth century,[5] and this would seem much too late for them to have given rise to ball games. As has been shown in the previous chapter, tennis 'tournaments' were held as early as the twelfth century. Thomas Malory, on the other hand, is known to have drawn on older sources for his tournament descriptions, some of which go back to the thirteenth century.[6] It is not impossible therefore that some day a text will turn up in which a similar distinction is made between an inside and an outside team and which can be shown to have been used by the English author. Such a discovery, however, is hardly necessary. More recent research has shown that the distinction between an inside and an outside team was perhaps as old as the tournament itself.[7] In Chrétien's romance *Perceval* (*Li contes del Graal*), which was finished before 1190, the knight errant Gawain meets by chance a knight called Meliant de Liz who is the leader of a small army. A squire informs him that Meliant is on his way to the castle of a certain Tiebaut de Tintaguel and that the knight is a suitor of Tiebaut's eldest daughter who had promised to accept him if he showed great prowess and feats of arms. That is why Meliant had challenged Tiebaut to a tournament. Following the squire's suggestion, Gawain decides to help Tiebaut and his men (emphasis by the author):[8]

> *Et vos i iroiz ja mon vuel*
> *El chastel contre caus defors*
> > *(lines 4836f.)*

> *(My wish is that you go there.*
> *To help those of the castle against those from*
> > *without.)*

Tiebaut has misgivings that the sporting event in front of his castle gate might get out of control and result in an attack on his castle outright. That is why he has barricaded himself in. An old campaigner, however, dispels his fears. If the enemies' arrogance should lead them to capture the whole castle, the defenders would still gain the upper hand because of their greater number and their archers. To the aggressor would be left ignominious defeat (emphasis by the author):

> *Et je sai bien que il vandront*
> *Tornoiier devant ceste porte.*
> *Se lor orgiauz les i aporte,*
> *Nos avromes le gaaing,*
> *Et il la perte et le mehaing.*
> > *(lines 4944–4948)*

> *(And I know well that they will come,*
> *In order to tourney in front of this gate.*
> *If their arrogance brings them here,*
> *Then we will win the day*
> *And they will carry the loss and the damage.)*

The tournament takes place on a plain in front of the gate and continues until the evening.

> *Tote jor jusqu'a l'anserir*
> *Fu li tornoiz devant la porte.*
> > *(lines 5110f.)*

> *(The whole day long until the evening*
> *The tourney lasted in front of the gate.)*

Those from without carry off the tournament prize, but those within cannot really complain either, and finally when the two sides after the manner of true sportsmen shake gauntlets, both teams agree to play the return match the following day:

S'an orent cil defors *le pris,*
Et cil dedanz *i gaeignerent*
Et au partir refiancierent
Que l'andemain rasanbleroient
El chanp et si tornoieront.
    (lines 5160–5164)

(Those from without had gained the prize,
But those from within had won as well;
And when they parted, they ensured each other,
That they would meet the very next day
On the field in order to do battle again.)

At this point, Tiebaut's youngest daughter, the 'Maiden with the Green Sleeves', had heard enough of the praises sung by her sister on behalf of Meliant. At her instigation, Gawain takes up the cudgels for the inside team, and from this point Meliant sees his success rate slump.

The passage from Chrétien substantiates the claim that from the early days of the tournament a distinction was made between those within and those without. This fact has, of course, been pointed out before. In his book *Les sports et jeux d'exercice dans l'ancienne France*, the French diplomat and sports historian Jean Jules Jusserand not only referred to the passage of arms held at Sandricourt Castle in 1493, but also tried to assess the terminology of this kind of the tournament. He confirms that the defenders of the passage went by the name of *ceux de dedans*, their opponents by that of *ceux de dehors*, but at the same time he brings to our attention two other terms which apparently functioned as synonyms: the term *tenants*, 'holders' for the defenders, because their task was to hold the pass (French: *tenir le pas*), and the term *venants*, 'comers', for the attacking side.[9] Incidentally, the term *tenant* occurs in the very first of the passages of arms mentioned by Victor Gay in his *Glossaire archéologique*. It took place near Saint-Omer in 1449 and in it the role of the 'holder' was played, along with five like-minded companions, by Jean, Bastard of Saint-Pol, Lord of Hautbourdin.[10]

UPS AND DOWNS IN THE PARK: THE *ROMAN DU HEM*

In the absence of a reliable account of the language of the tournament, our analysis will have to be completed by an inspection of another important medieval source, the *Roman du Hem*. Written in the last third of the year 1278 by the Picardian trouvère Sarrasin, the *Roman* is perhaps the most lavish account of a medieval tournament. As a work of literary art it may not exactly be a masterpiece, but it is a historical document of the first order and for any lexicographer a mine of information.[11] According to Albert Henry, to whom we owe an excellent critical edition, the *Roman* belongs to the genre of the versified medieval (sports) commentary of which it is perhaps the only representative.[12]

The work was modelled on a tournament which was actually held by two Picardian lords, Huart de Basentin and Aubert de Longueval, and the venue of which was Le Hem, a hamlet between Bray and Péronne. Especially noteworthy is the fact that as late as the 1930s visitors to the place were able to get a clear picture of what the scene was like in the days of old. To quote from Albert Henry:[13]

> in the thirteenth century the local situation was as follows: the river, a castle at some distance from it, and, between the two, a little plain. Was not this a rather ideal venue for staging a tournament? ... A little plain, bordered on one side by a forest or a river, and by the walls of a town or castle on the other; on the two remaining sides you put up wooden barriers and, beyond these, the pavilions of the tournament champions were pitched. All this was gathered together at Le Hem.

In the poem proper, there are many reminiscences of the original venue. There are constant reminders of its location in front of a castle gate (*porte*),[14] and, as might have been expected, repeated references to an inside and an outside team.[15] But there are other technical terms of a more elusive nature which seem to have escaped the notice of historians dealing with the tournament. In a remarkable way Sarrasin divided the tournament topography into an upwards (*amont*) and a downwards (*aval*) section. The two adverbs of place function as synonyms of *within/tenant* and *without/venant*, and apparently reflected the fact that the castle had a slightly elevated position.[16]

Perhaps the most significant term is mentioned last. Because there was a huge number of competitors – no fewer than 180 in all – the tournament had to be continued until well into the night, and that is why Keu, King Arthur's seneschal,[17] had torches lit all over the place:[18]

> *Kex li senescaus devant cort,*
> *Et fait tant alumer tortis*
> *Que il sanloit que tous espris*
> *Fust et li castiaus et li pars [= parcs].*
>
> (Keu the Seneschal rushes forward
> And has so many torches lit
> That entirely illuminated seemed
> The castle and the lists.)

Here the term *parc*, ' lists',[19] as we shall see, is a very intriguing one. It was derived from a Latin noun *parricus* which, in turn, was formed on the basis of a reconstructed form **parra*, meaning 'stick'.[20] Conceivably, *parc* denoted an area enclosed by a barrier of sticks to be removed as soon as the tournament was over. That the convention of confining the tournament pitch by means of a wooden barrier was a firmly established one is borne out by a synonym for *parc*, Old French *lice* (whence English *list*),[21] and by the term *bourdis*, 'tilting'.[22] If we are to believe the lexicographical authorities, *lice* was derived from Frankish *listja*, 'lath', whereas *bourdis* went back to Germanic **bihordôn*, 'to fence in'.[23]

CHASING AND RECHASING

The next question is how the encounters which were staged on the venue just described were put into words. An answer to this question is given in the second half of the twelfth century by two French poets, Gautier d'Arras and Benoit de Sainte-Maure. In Gautier's romance *Ille et Galeron*, Gille, the Duke of Brittany's seneschal, and his men from a hiding place watch how their allies, the Romans, are forced to retreat into their castle by their enemies, the Greeks.[24] The very next moment, however, the Greeks, who had just launched a vicious attack, have to defend themselves against a fierce sortie by the Romans. The terms here used for attack and counter-attack are truly remarkable. The Greeks' attack is described by the verb *chaser* ('to chase'), whereas the counter-attack of the Romans is referred to by the verb *rachaser* ('to chase back'). For both actions, attack and counter-attack, the noun *chase* is used.

In English, the noun *chase* long retained its military meaning. As late as 1627, Michael Drayton used it skilfully in his epic on the battle of Agincourt (*The Battaile of Agincourt*) (emphasis by the present writer):[25]

> *The men of Harflew rough excursions make*
> *Upon the English watchful in their Tent,*
> *Whose courages they to their cost awake,*
> *With many a wound that often back them sent,*
> *So proud a Sally that durst undertake,*
> *And in the* Chase *pell mell amongst them went,*
> *For on the way such ground of them they win,*
> *That some French are shut out, some English in.*

As has been said, the subject of an attack on a castle gate was also expoited by Benoit de Sainte-Maure in his *Roman de Troie*. As is indicated by the title of his romance, the action takes place in Ancient Troy, but since we are by this time sufficiently familiar with the medieval poet's methods, we know that we will be treated to a typical medieval battle scene. Under the leadership of their valiant 'knight' Polybetes the Greeks rush to one of the gates of Troy. There, they are met by the courageous 'knight' Deiphebos and his men. Deiphebos with a barbed arrow hits Polybetes in the thigh, and the protagonist of the Greeks, in order to staunch the blood running from his wound, is forced to retreat from the frontline. Seeing this, the Trojans pluck up courage, enough to risk a counter-attack, and this is described in the following way: 'And those within (*cil dedenz*) drove the Greeks back to their tents (*rechacierent*)'.[26]

In the choice of his words Benoit is in complete agreement with both Giles of Rome and his fellow-poet Gautier: whereas the former invariably called the defenders *ceux de dedans*, the latter used the verbs *chasser* and *rachasser* in order to describe attack and counter-attack. This latter usage is still reflected in the passage from Thomas Malory quoted above in which the verb *to chase* describes the back-lash of Sir Galahad's inside team.

THE PASSAGE OF ARMS IN MEDIEVAL ART

Occasionally, the battle for the castle became a subject in medieval art, for example in a series of ivory caskets which originated in the first half of the fourteenth century. The lids of these caskets invariably show the attack on a very particular stronghold: the Castle of Love. Here, the subject is treated with a great deal of good humour. From the battlements of the fortress Cupid showers his arrows upon the courageous attackers. He is supported by noble ladies 'hailing' roses onto the scaling enemy. The dramatic highlight of the pictures, however, is the clash of two jousting knights either in front of (**Figure 47**), or virtually inside the castle gate (**Figure 48**).[27] All these pictures are classic examples of the passage of arms, although the fact escaped the notice of experts in the field of medieval iconography.[28] Another picture combining the subject of the conquest of a castle and that of the passage of arms belongs to the thirteenth century. It is a miniature illustrating Chrétien de Troye's courtly novel *Yvain* (**Figure 49**). Here the miniaturist tried to capture the critical moment when the knight Calogrenant frivolously poured water into the Knight of the Fountain's (hollow) emerald stone.[29] On the realistic plane, this symbolic act must be viewed as a downright attack on the knight's forest and castle,[30] and that such is indeed the case soon appears from the latter's reaction: the Knight of the Fountain immediately comes dashing out of his castle in order to lift the aggressor, Calogrenant, out of his saddle.[31] Their fight has all the characteristics of the joust, since the victor, in accordance with medieval tournament rules, keeps the courser of the defeated as a prize.[32] The miniaturist grasped the symbolic meaning of Chrétien's text admirably, even though he may have

FIGURE 47   A typical tournament scene in front of a medieval castle gate.

FigURE 48 The tournament sub-discipline called Passage of Arms, emphasizing the storming of the castle gate, on a medieval ivory mirror case.

substituted swords for the competitors' lances.[33] Calogrenant is represented twice, once as the cheeky water-pourer, and once as the impudent intruder into the castle of the Knight of the Fountain. The hollow stone clearly stands for the masonry of the castle gate, which in the picture is occupied, ready to defend it, by Calogrenant's antagonist.

THE LANGUAGE OF BALL GAMES

Did medieval ball-players fancy themselves as defenders of a pass? An intriguing piece of evidence for such a hypothesis comes from one of the oldest varieties of Basque pelota. In the so-called *bote luzea* a point is scored whenever the ball is driven across the base line of the server's team. This line is drawn at the very spot where in the days of old the arched openings of the cloisters were to be found. And it is in *bote luzea* – and in this game only – that this boundary is called *paso*, 'pass'.[34] Of course, this may be a mere coincidence, and that is why we would do well to look somewhat deeper into this matter.

THE GAMES OF THE FRISIANS

In the first chapter, football was described as a kind of tournament ersatz of the common people, and tennis was said to have been a variety of football originally

FIGURE 49   In this miniature from a manuscript of Chrètien de Troyes' *Yvain*, the Knight of the Fountain occupies the *dedans* position.

played by monks in the cloisters of their monasteries. If such was indeed the case, it would seem not altogether impossible that at least a few traces of this former relationship may still be discovered in the language of games. The most likely source where such traces could be found are the games of the Frisians, for the ball games of northern France must have reached them at a very early date, a fact which should cause hardly any surprise.[35] In the Middle Ages, the territory of the Frisians, a marsh fringe some twenty miles broad along the coast of the North Sea, extended from the estuary of the river Weser south to near the city of Bruges. The strip of land occupied by the Frisians should not be imagined as the continuous coastal area of today. In those days it consisted rather of a string of islands interrupted by numerous inlets of the sea, canals and swamps. Not infrequently, the Frisians were forced to settle on artificial mounds (Old Frisian *therp*), the only viable approach to them being that by means of small boats with a very shallow draught. As early as in the time of their missionary, St Boniface, it was said that the Frisians lived like fish in the water which encompassed them on all sides. Into the civilized world they could hardly venture except aboard a ship, and the seclusion of their homes was, according to the same source, the reason for their stand-offish and barbarian nature.[36]

From their French neighbours in the south, the Frisians inherited the prototype of a game which in the centuries to follow proliferated into three subtypes, namely Frisian *keatsen*, the *pärkspel* of Gotland[37] and a game which was played in the so-called Saterland in the south-western part of the former duchy of Oldenbourg in Germany until about the turn of the century. Comparison with the other two suggests that the Saterlandic game is closest to the game's prototype (see **Figure 50**).[38] It seems to present itself in the shape it had taken by the second half of the thirteenth century. This was the time when, as a result of famine and war, many Frisians left their coastal homes.[39] Some of them, coming from the Emsland, settled in the Saterland.[40] Others got as far as Gotland where they introduced the so-called *pärkspel*, the Frisian origin of which can hardly be doubted and which has already been referred to in the first chapter. This must have happened before 1280 when the city of Lübeck dealt Frisian and Flemish seafaring a fatal blow. So many Frisian vessels had cruised in the Baltic Sea (in an attempt to load grain for their starving kindred at home, or as carriers of merchandise from Flanders) that the outpost of the Hanse, eager to safeguard her trading monopoly, forbade Frisians and Flemings to set sail for Gotland through the Baltic Sea ('per mare orientale versus Gothlandiam') once and for all.[41]

If the practitioners of the original game had led a rather solitary life in the coastal regions of the North Sea, this can be said with even more justification of their cousins on the island of Gotland and in the Saterland which, owing to the moor surrounding it, was virtually inaccessible for the greater part of the year, with the exception of the winter when the moor was frozen. In addition to geographical isolation, the inhabitants of the Saterland were separated from their neighbours on ethnic and religious grounds.[42] It is hardly surprising, therefore, that the Frisian games, and especially the Saterlandic game, should have preserved some particularly archaic features. This will become evident, if we now turn to an inspection of their terminology.

The Frisian games are unique in that they adopted (and indeed preserved) the expression used in the tournament of medieval France for the venue, namely *parc*; for this reason they can be united under the label 'park games'.[43] Medieval French *parc* became *pork* in Saterlandic Frisian, *perk* in West Frisian,[44] and *pärk* in the Swedish as spoken on Gotland. The Gotlandic *pärkspel* exhibits the most peculiar reminder of the Frisian game's origin. Its rules stipulate that for marking out the *pärk* sticks or wooden laths or the branches of trees ('Stänger och stickor av träribbor') have to be used.[45] Of course, the lathes marking the *pärk* are, although none of the players is any longer aware of it, all that has remained of the wooden barriers which once

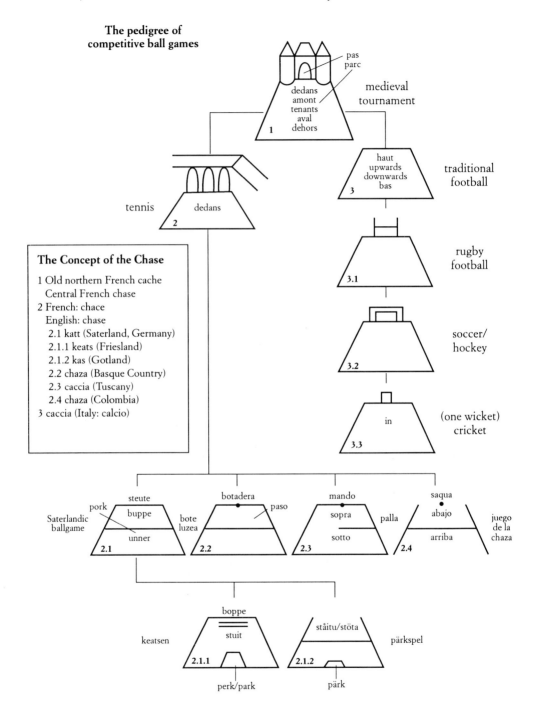

The pedigree of competitive ball games

pas
parc

dedans
amont
tenants
aval
dehors
1

medieval
tournament

haut
upwards
downwards
bas
3

traditional
football

tennis   dedans
2

The Concept of the Chase

1 Old northern French cache
    Central French chase
2 French: chace
    English: chase
    2.1 katt (Saterland, Germany)
    2.1.1 keats (Friesland)
    2.1.2 kas (Gotland)
    2.2 chaza (Basque Country)
    2.3 caccia (Tuscany)
    2.4 chaza (Colombia)
3 caccia (Italy: calcio)

3.1   rugby
football

3.2   soccer/
hockey

in
3.3   (one wicket)
cricket

steute   botadera   mando   saqua
pork   buppe   paso   sopra   palla   abajo
Saterlandic   bote   juego
ballgame   luzea   de la
unner   sotto   arriba   chaza
2.1   **2.2**   **2.3**   **2.4**

boppe
stuit   ståitu/stöta
keatsen   pärkspel
2.1.1   **2.1.2**
perk/park   pärk

FIGURE 50   Tree diagram documenting the survival of tournament expressions in various ball games.

confined the venue of the tournament (**Figure 51**). They are, perhaps, the most convincing example of the conservatism of traditional ball games, and prove that the term *pärkspel* actually meant 'tournament game'.

A similar reminder of the medieval tournament enclosure may be the custom in Frisian *keatsen* to mark the *perk* with tape where chalk would serve the purpose equally well. In the Middle Ages, as we have seen, strings might occasionally be substituted for the wooden construction, and the fact that in French and South American varieties of tennis the lateral boundaries of the pitch went, or still go by the names of *cordes* or *cuerdas* supports the view that many centuries ago the forebears of Frisian players were deliberately enacting a tournament whenever they staged their games of ball.[46]

Another feature of the Saterlandic game is that it also reflects the distinction made by the French *trouvère* Sarrasin who divided the tilting ground into up and down. In the Saterlandic game, the French adverbs *amont* and *aval* appear in the form of *buppe* and *unner*: whereas the attacking side attempt to drive the ball – ideally – back across the service line (*buppe*), the defending side, by trying to lay a good chase, aim at driving their opponents back into the recesses of the park (*unner*).[47] It is significant that the distinction between up and down should not only have been preserved in the late seventeenth-century German ballhouse game,[48] but also be made in the ball game of Tuscany and in the *juego de la chaza* of Colombia.[49] By the very same

FIGURE 51   The Gotlandic *pärkspel* and its *pärk* marked by small wooden laths painted white.

distinction a link can be established between the large family of the tennis games and the varieties of traditional football. In the football game of la Mayenne and Ille-et-Villaine in the Canton de Mellé, France, the terms *haut* and *bas* are used,[50] and in the British Isles the traditional Shrovetide football in Ashbourne in Derbyshire, as well as the games of Workington and Kirkwall, show a strikingly similar usage. In Workington, the terms are *up'ards* and *down'ards* or *Uppies and Downies*,[51] in Kirkwall *Uppies* and *Doonies;* or *Up-the-Gates* and *Down-the-Gates* (!) respectively.[52]

THOSE WITHIN AND THOSE WITHOUT

The differentiation between a team which plays within and another which must play outside was not only a characteristic of the tournament. From the earliest days, the same distinction must have been made in tennis, even though, because of the general lack of explicitness of early sources, we hear about it rather late. In the *Kaetspel Ghemoralizeert* it is stated that the medieval tennis player, before a match, had first to look for a place where a good, high roof made it possible to strike the ball elegantly outside, and to return it back in as elegantly: 'daer een goet hooghe dack sij daert schoone es omme uut te slane/ende schoone es weder in keeren'.[53]

From Dutch sources above all it emerges that throughout the early phases of tennis history the distinction between inside and outside was of prime importance, and it may well be that in the two examples which follow both authors were still acutely aware of the relationship which once existed between tennis and the attack on a castle.

The first example has again been gleaned from the *Kaetspel Ghemoralizeert*. In the passage under consideration the author tries to cope with the difficult task of finding a suitable allegorical interpretation of the complicated chase rule. He is, of course, familiar with the rule which said that whenever two chases had occurred the teams had to change ends, or, in the language of contemporary tennis, that those players who had been inside had to go outside, and vice versa (emphasis by the author):[54]

> Ende als twee kaetsen ghemaect sijn / zo gaen *buten* diere *binnen* waren / ende die *buten* waren gaen *binnen* spelen / omme die twee kaetsen diere ghemaect sijn te winnene.

On the allegorical plane, the author referred to a famous heroine in the Old Testament, the beautiful widow Judith. After having left the city of Bethulia, as it were the 'dedans', Judith had gone out into the camp of the Assyrians, the 'dehors'. Once there, she cut off the head of Holofernes, the commander of the enemy's army, with two slashes (*Judith*, 13,8;[55] wordplay on *kaetse* meaning 'chase' and 'stroke'), and after this 'victory' she returned back inside her native city in triumph.

The story of the powerful besieger Holofernes and the beautiful defender of the city, Judith, is not only a remarkable example of medieval allegorizing, but also a subtle hint at the origin of tennis. The author may not be conscious of the fact that in the medieval tournament, and hence in games such as football or tennis, the conquest of a town was imitated, but his curiosity was apparently aroused by the terminological parallels between the warlike and leisure time activities. In both, a distinction was made between an inside and an outside team, and it was this similarity, and, of course, his familiarity with Holy Scripture, which made him associate the ball game with the story of Judith and Holofernes.

The same could be said of a poem on an attack on the city of Antwerp in 1583. The poem is titled *Tcaetspel der Franchoysen*, and this title is deliberately ambiguous, since the term *caetsspel* in the language of the time denoted the game as well as the facility, the tennis court. The poet, Jeronimus van der Voort, a rhetorician from Lier, wanted to make a point of the fact that the unsuspecting Antwerpers had shortly before the attack presented to the Duke of Anjou, for the disport of his courtiers, the gift of a tennis court within St Michiel's Abbey.[56] The Frenchmen, however, whom the Antwerpers had considered their friends and the protectors of the new faith, rather than enjoying the generous gift were keen on a very different little match. Not satisfied with a small tennis court, they had plotted to win the whole big city.

The attack of Anjou's troops started at one of the city gates, the Kipdorppoort, which, owing to the activities of some conniving conspirator within the city-walls, had been left open. At first this helped the French to achieve, in the language of tennis, a long chase, a strategic advantage. In the end, however, the French failed to win the match, because they had failed to win the decisive chase, marked in a rather unusual way with corpses. In a quite literal sense, the Antwerpers had in this match occupied the *dedans* position as the poet informs his readers by means of another ingenious pun ('Wy stonden int Spel binnen' – in this match we were playing inside).[57]

In Antonin van Torres's tennis dialogue of 1657, Laurence wants to draw lots in order to decide who will play inside and who outside. Charles, however, would like his opponents to take up the inside position first because, he says, they play better. Charles's arguments seem to imply that if you played outside you had a slight advantage:[58]

> *Laur.* Laet ons loten wat partije datter sal binnen zijn / ofte buyten.
> *Car.* Ghy-lieden speelt beter: zijt ghylieden eerst binnen.

The distinction between inside and outside is also made in Johann Georg Bender's tennis textbook of 1680,[59] and it is still valid for the Gotlandic *pärkspel*, where the teams are called *innelag* (inside team) and *utelag* (outside team) alternately.[60] Comparison with the more archaic Saterlandic game reveals that, strictly speaking, the Gotlandic terms should be reversed, and the same holds good for Frisian *keatsen*, where the team in possession of the *perk* are called the *útslaggers*, literally 'the strikers out'.[61] Here, too, the original situation mirrored in the quotation from the *Kaetspel Ghemoralizeert* (compare *uut te slane*) had become obscured after the *perk* had degenerated into a small rectangle on the ground. In the absence of an opening in the wall, this was apparently reinterpreted as the goal.

The Frisian term *útslagger* has a long tradition and can be traced back to fourteenth-century French. Here (as in the *Kaetspel*), it correctly referred to the service. Eventually, it even became one of the names for the game as such. The French term was *boute-hors*, literally 'strike outward', a word formation in which an imperative, in this case *boute!* from *bouter*, 'to hit', 'to strike', is compounded with an adverb, *hors*, 'outside' or 'outwards'. The caption of a sixteenth-century copper engraving is accurate in that it calls the game shown on it the game of *boute-hors*: 'Ceux-cy gaillards, iouent à la boutte hors, Dessus ce toict.' (These lads here are playing 'strike-out' onto this roof.) The name *boute-hors* appears early in a document of 1387,[62] but in contrast to most other names this one has a fair chance of being the oldest because of the intriguing adverb *hors*. At the end of this paragraph it remains to be said that the gallery defended in Real tennis still goes by the French name of *dedans*.

CHASING AFTER THE CHASE

We will now turn to an inspection of the ramifications of the term *chasse*, the expression for the attack. In the famous Florentine football game of *calcio* the defensive line which, as we have heard, in pelota goes by the name of *paso* was known as *caccia*, an obvious loan translation into Italian of the French term.[63]

However, *chasse* not only found its way into the terminology of medieval football, it also became the earliest known name for tennis. This is again illustrated by the *Ystoire de Appollonius*. In a significant way, the name of the game played by Apollonius and Archistrates in the city of Cyrene is not *jeu de la paume,* which in all the history books appears, not only as the father, but as the terminological great-grandfather of the entire family. Its name is *chasse*, and the whole passage in which it occurs illustrates perfectly how in this game the attack on, and the defence of, a medieval castle gate was re-enacted. Archistrates steps into the arena expressing his wish to play tennis (*à le cache*), this being the Northern French variant for what would have been *a la chace* in the French as spoken in contemporary Paris.[64] Position yourselves, he tells his opponents, as you please. I want to play alone against you all. And then, the text continues, they began their match, and the King held his own (*se tenoit*) against all who wanted to come up against him (*venir*).[65] Here we have no fewer than three of the characteristic terms for the passage of arms, namely *tenir, venir,* and *chasse*!

Its name *chasse* is one of the most archaic features of the whole game. Many members of its large family the world over have retained it in one way or another up to the present day. From northern France, *chasse* at an early date found its way into the southern parts of the Low Countries. As early as 1338 it appears in the town regulations (the so-called Keurboeken) of the Flemish town of Oudenaarde. 'Men verbiet,' the local magistrates warned their citizens, 'de kache to speelne op t Kerkhof op XX schel. te mesdade. Ende die sine mesdaet niet ghelden en mach,' the text continued in the most beautiful Flemish town officialese, 'men sal hem de Poert verbieden tes hi sine mesdat bringt'.[66] In equally bureaucratic English this would have been something like: Herewith the game of *cache* is prohibited in the churchyard, a 20 shilling fine [having to be paid] by the offender. He who cannot pay the fine will be denied access to the Gate until he comes up with the fine. (It may be noted in passing that the defilers of Flemish churchyards later on somehow managed to introduce their form of the game into the Rhineland under the name of *caeche*.)

Tennis, either the French or the Flemish game, was also at an early date imported into Scotland where it seems to have been welcomed by the young, but hardly by parents intent on imposing severe discipline on their children. It was one such parent who doled out a proper dressing down to young Scottish boys between the ages of 7 and 15, in a versified treatise with the incomprehensible title *Ratis Raving* (1475):[67]

> *For resone than is yong and wak*
> *And may nocht lat that eild to laik,*
> *   ... now at the killis,*
> *Now at the prop, and vthir-quhillis*
> *Ryne at baris and at the ball*
> *And at the caich play with-all,*
> *Now at the tablis, now at the ches*
> *Weill oft, and seldin at the mes,*
> *And mekile with playing at the dyce*
> *That werk yhit hald I maist unwyß,*
> *For thar is aithis set at nocht,*
> *And infortunne to mekil socht*
>
> *...*
>
> *My sone, Set nocht thi happynes*
> *In na syk plays mar na les.*
>
> *(Since reason is then immature and weak*
> *And this age cannot refrain from playing*
> *   ... [it is] now at skittles,*
> *Then at the [archery] butts, another time*
> *At running at the bars and at football*
> *And especially at tennis;*
> *Sometimes at backgammon, then very often*
> *At chess, but only seldom at holy mass;*
> *And much time at dice.*
> *Such conduct I consider most foolish,*
> *For there curses are considered a trifle,*
> *And misfortune is virtually beckoned.*
>
> *...*
>
> *My son, do not seek your fortune*
> *In any such games neither more nor less.)*

Among the immoral games listed, there is the game of tennis, a fact slightly obscured because of the Scots name it has adopted, namely *caich*. It clearly shows whence the ruin for Scotland's young had come, the north of France or Flanders.[68]

The warning expressed by the author of *Ratis Raving* seems to have been of little avail. The tennis plague spread all over Scotland and had soon not only infested the feeble young, but also the pillars of society. This appears from a humourous passage in Sir David Lindsay's morality play *Ane Pleasant Satyre of the Thrie Estaitis* of 1540 in which two representatives of the clergy have to justify themselves before the royal court. The first defendant is an Abbot; he is followed by a Parson:[69]

SCRIBE

My Lords how haue ye keipit your thrie vows?

ABBOT

Indeid richt weill till I gat hame my bows.
In my Abbay quhen I was sure professour,
Then did I leife as did my predecessour.
My paramours is baith als fat and fair,
As ony wench into the toun of Air.
I send my sons to Pareis to the scullis,
I traiste in God that they salbe na fuillis.
And all my douchters I haue weill providit,
Now iudge ye gif my office be weill gydit.

SCRIBE

Maister Person schaw vs gif ye can preich?

PERSONE

Thocht I preich not i can play at the caiche:
I wait thair is nocht ane amang yow all,
Mair ferilie can play at the fut-ball:
And for the carts, the tabils and the dyse,
Aboue all persouns I may beir the pryse.

In modern English the Scribe's cross-examination is something like this:

SCRIBE

My Lords, how have you kept your three vows?

ABBOT

Indeed, quite well until I received my benefice.
However, when I was sure of my position in my abbey
I lived as my predecessor had done.
My concubines are as ample and fair
As any wenches in the town of Ayr.
I send my sons to the university in Paris
And for all my daughters I have provided well.
Now judge yourself whether I have held my office well.

SCRIBE

Master Parson, show us whether you can preach.

PARSON

Although I do not preach, I can play tennis;
I know that there is not one among you all here
Who can play football better than I.
And as for cards, backgammon and dice
Before all parsons I would carry off the prize.

Whilst the Abbot has managed to score time and again in his love life, the Reverend turns out to be an all-round sportsman. Not only does he always come out on top in the games of fortune, he is also no mean player in either football or tennis. Again the name for tennis, *caiche*,[70] shows that it was Scottish ball arenas which were the favourite haunt of this early example of Don Camillo. The term *caiche* was used in Scotland throughout the Middle Ages, and in this respect as in so many others the Scots differed from their southern neighbours very markedly. This is confirmed by the *Basilicon Doron*, the small educational treatise which James I wrote on behalf of his little son Henry. When he completed the first draft of this work, he was still James VI of Scotland. That is why he used the Scots term *caiche* when he recommended to his son the aristocrats' pastime, tennis. Later, in 1603 when the second revised edition of the book appeared, the King's attitude had changed. In his new capacity as the first Stuart on the English throne, he was eager to please his new subjects by paying tribute to their use of the English language. He therefore encouraged young Henry to play at 'the caitche or tennise'![71]

With the exception of the north, the term *chasse* does not seem to have been used for the whole game in France either. As was shown by the *Roman du comte d'Anjou* and by John Gower's poem, England and France, with a rare degree of unanimity, only used it to denote the spot where the ball came to a stop after its second bounce. On the other hand, the chase rule was such an important feature of the medieval game that it could be named after it later at virtually any time. This is well born out by the *juego de la chaza* of Colombia. The French term *chasse*, after having found its way into Spain, was first changed into a pseudo-Spanish word, *chaza*.[72] In South America where it had been taken by Spanish conquistadors, the meaning of the word was then extended, so that in the Colombian *juego de la chaza* it came to refer to the game as a whole.

THE INVENTORS OF THE RACKET

In the earlier part of the fourteenth century, the author of the *Roman du Comte d'Anjou* described the first two strokes in a medieval tennis match. One of the players in the city of Orleans strikes the ball, the other strikes it back, or, to quote the French text: 'L'un fiert l'estuef, l'autre rachace.' Here the word used for the return, the verb *rachacier*, is of particular interest. In due course, the simple, unprefixed form, *chacier* (northern French *cachier*) had together with the game reached the Low Countries where it took the form of *caetsen*.[73] This term, an infinitive in more recent times spelt *kaatsen*, is in the Dutch-Flemish language area still used to denote the traditional form of tennis. In the Middle Ages, a decidedly Flemish dialect variant, *ketsen*,[74] developed alongside *caetsen*. In his dictionary of 1574, the *Etymologicum teutonicae linguae sive dictionarium teutonico-latinum*,[75] Cornelius Kilian mentioned it, but it is also to be found much earlier in a glossary called *Gemmula vocabulorum* which was published in Antwerp in 1490. In fact, it looks as if Kilian copied it from the *Gemmula*, for the entries in both dictionaries are virtually identical: 'kaetsen/ketsen. Sectari pilam, ludere pila palmaria', 'chasing after the ball, playing hand tennis', the definitions read in both.[76]

There are good reasons for focusing our attention on the Flemish variant *ketsen* as will be seen if we now return to the term for the backstroke in the *Roman du Comte d'Anjou*, namely *rachacier*. If the simple French verb *chacier* took the form *ketsen* in Flemish, the composite verb would inevitably have resulted in **raketsen*.[77] If this was indeed the case, we would first be given a clue as to what to make of the *raket* in Chaucer's *Troilus and Criseyde* which, it will be remembered, had been a real puzzle indeed. It looks as if *raket* was an early loan from Flemish meaning 'to strike a ball back', and when Troilus asked his friend Pandarus whether he could 'pleyen raket to and fro', the implication was that *raket* could only be played 'fro' (back), and not 'to' (forth).

However, there is more to it than that. If we accept the existence of a verb **raketsen*, we would be able to solve one of the greatest mysteries in tennis history, namely that of the origin of the term *racket*. The first thing we would have to explain is how the Flemish verb, **raketsen*, became a noun.[78] This may have occurred by a process referred to by linguists as back-formation, by which the verb was shortened to **raketse*, a noun which at first denoted the return, and later was used for the implement with which such a stroke was accomplished. That such a process actually took place is exemplified by the term *racache*, 'racket', in the children's language of Picardy which was derived from the verb *racachier*.[79] In eighteenth-century Danish there existed the noun *ketse*, 'racket', a word apparently loaned from Flemish.[80] It is true that it lacked the prefix *ra-*, but the noun as such is hardly anything else but an instance of back-formation on the basis of the Flemish verb *ketsen,* and this lends support to the view that racket evolved in a similar way. How Flemish **raketse* got rid of its final *s* is easily explained. The English dropped it in much the same way as they had done in the case of final *s* in the northern French noun *cherise*, which was misconceived as a plural and became English *cherry*.[81]

In England, the term *racket*, 'bat used in ball games', is first instanced in a manuscript in the British Library. The passage in question deals with a tennis match which took place in 1505 and in which Philip, the King of Castile, played against the Marquis of Dorset with the English King Henry VII simply watching them, his arms akimbo. The King of Castile, the text says, played with a racket and under a handicap of fifteen:[82] 'the kynge of Castelle played wth the Rackete and gave the marques xv.' The implication of the passage is that Philip's opponent did not avail himself of this implement, and a situation in which one player was without it must be considered a not unusual one in these early days of the racket.

The French treated the Flemish word very differently, by adding to its root a suffix used in their language for tools of all kinds, namely *-ette*,[83] hence *raquette*. Generally speaking, it is perhaps worth pointing out that in modern Flemish *kaatsen* as well as in Frisian *keatsen* only the returning team is allowed to wear gloves whereas the server is not. This regulation may well go back to a time when only the returners were conceded the use of the racket.

We will finish this discussion on the transformations the French terms *chacier* and *rachacier* underwent in the dialects of the Low Countries by calling to the reader's attention an investigation carried out by the Belgian dialectologist Willy Bal. Shortly before the Second World War, Bal tried to assess the language of the traditional Walloon *jeu de pelote à main*, a direct descendant of the *jeu de tamis*. In the course of his field work, he recorded the following sentence in the Walloon patois which he had heard from one of the players:[84] 'èl bale a stî bin cassiye mes èle a co stî mieu r'cassiye'. Translated into English, it is something like: the ball has been served well, but it has been returned even better. Here we not only have before us a notable instance of the survival of the term *rachacier* from the *Roman du Comte d'Anjou*, but also of the two key terms of the medieval tournament, Old French *chacier* and *rachacier*.

THAT DURABLE CATGUT: AN ESPECIALLY DURABLE AND RESILIENT ERROR

As early as the fifteenth century, a compound *caetsspel* was coined, the first element of which was the root *caets-* and the second the Middle Dutch noun *spel*, 'game'. The term, which first appeared in the title of the *Kaetspel Ghemoralizeert* of 1431, was adopted into Scots where it is instanced in 1526 as *cachpuyll* or *cachepuyle*.[85]

Despite the corruption of its second element, the word suggests that the Scots did not owe the blessings of tennis to the French, but to the Low Countries, and the spelling of the first element indicates that the game had come to them from the Flemings rather than from the Dutch. On the other hand, there can hardly be any doubt that a game with the rather misleading name *katzenspil* in sixteenth-century Germany for the same reason was introduced from Holland, the north of the Low Countries, since the first element of this word reflected Dutch *caetse*. Of course, and although the Germans may have thought otherwise, the term had nothing to do with cats (German *Katzen*, plural of *Katze*, 'cat').[86] This rather funny instance of a popular etymology helps to correct a widespread error by which above all the English speaking tennis community is still beset. It is the belief that tennis rackets are strung with cats' gut.

In his book *Tennis: Origins and Mysteries*, Malcolm D. Whitman naturally tried to unravel this mystery. He suspected that it must have something to do with the saying that cats have nine lives, hence the longevity of the durable and resilient catgut. And Whitman remembered well a tennis banquet in New York in 1929 when twenty tennis experts had stated that from their childhood they had been convinced that the strings of their rackets were made of the intestines of *Felis domestica*. Of course, even Whitman (as, indeed, every child) knew that catgut was not in fact 'cat' gut, but 'sheep' gut. As early as 1533, the Frenchman Rabelais had made a statement to this effect.[87]

Before we move on to solve Whitman's catgut mystery, it should be noted that the tennis champion's own attempts to come to grips with the problem were highly inadequate, and that as late as the 1970s the president of the Fédération Française de Longue Paume, Monsieur Pierre Buffard, could with much confidence claim the following about rackets in the sixteenth century: 'After the wooden rackets which had been used at first, rackets which had been strung with cat or sheep gut came into general use'.[88] The reader who has up to this point followed this discussion on the language of tennis will realize that the German term *katzenspil* was not cats' play. The origin of the word must be sought in the Dutch equivalent of the French word *chasse*, namely *caetse*, even though the doyen of German tennis history, the Alsatian Baron von Fichard, would by no means rule out the possibility that German cats had had a paw or two in it.[89]

It would seem only natural that Dutch racket manufacturers early in the sixteenth century, when they began to thread specially twisted sheep gut through wooden racket frames, called their material **caetsdarm*, 'tennis gut'. The word *darm* (gut) was unintelligible in England as well as in France, where the new-fangled implement was enthusiastically received, and a translation was needed. As for the first element, *caets-*, a translation could be dispensed with, for both Englishmen and Frenchmen believed to have before them a word which existed in their own language. The English naturally identified *caets-* with the possessive of *cat*, *cat's* (the apostrophe was not obligatory in those days),[90] and turned *caetsdarm* into *catsgut,* whereas the French conceived of it as the equivalent of *cat*,[91] the northern French dialect variant of Central French *chat*, 'cat',[92] and coined something like *boyau de cat* or *boyau de chat*. This closes the file on Whitman's 'catgut mystery'. It only remains to be said that the etymology of *catgut* proves that the gut strung racket was invented in the Netherlands.

A NEVER-ENDING STORY: THE ORIGIN OF THE WORD TENNIS

Before attempting to answer the question of the origin of the term tennis itself, a glance at yet another old name for the game is perhaps not altogether out of place. It is the term *jeu de bonde*. It first occurs in a medieval play, the *Miracle de Nostre-Dame*, in a passage where the heroine of the play tries to explain how evilly she and her child have been treated by a merciless mother-in-law. The *Miracle* was modelled on a romance by the thirteenth-century *trouvère* Philippe de Reimes. It was a rather long-winded piece, and that is why the unknown author tried to improve on it by highlighting his own text with lively images. In a reunion scene in which the Queen of Scotland had to describe to her husband how she and her child had been set adrift in a rudderless boat on the wild ocean, he for a change used a simile taken from tennis:[93]

> *Et puis, quant je fu respitée*
> *Et que je fu en mer boutée*
> *Sanz avoir qui me gouvernast,*
> *Cuidez-vous que point me grevast?*
> *Car souvent la mer par mainte onde*
> *Jouoit de moy comme à la bonde*
> *Et me jettoit puis ça, puis là.*

> (And then when I had been saved from instant
>   death,
> And had been thrown out onto the ocean
> Without having a helmsman
> Do you think this caused me no anguish?
> For the sea with its innumerable waves often
> Played with me as with a tennis ball,
> And cast me first here, then there.)

In this passage, the term *jeu de bonde*, the bouncing ball game, in the penultimate line proves the great antiquity of a variety of tennis, in which a sieve or some solid slanting surface was used onto which the ball was bounced before each rally. The French term *bonde*, which is reflected in the Provençal word for the service slab, *boundadou*, corresponds almost exactly to the term *steute* in the Saterlandic ball game which we considered to be the most archaic of all. Since the *Miracle* was written at some time around 1300, this seems to be the earliest known occurrence of this name for the game. At any rate, it pre-dates the instance in the *Roman du Comte d'Anjou*

(1316), and is certainly older than the famous *jeu de la paume*, the 'game played with the palm of the hand', which in existing histories of tennis is unanimously allotted the role of the father of all tennis games, but is first recorded in the chronicle attributed to Geoffrey of Paris which relates the death of Louis X, the Quarrelsome (1316).[94] In a document of 1395, extracts of which were printed in Gay,[95] it is asserted that the *jeu de la paume* was called *jeu de bonde* in Lisieux, which suggests that the Département of Calvados in Normandy was its ultimate home. If this is true, not only its oldest name, *cache*, but also its second oldest, *jeu de bonde*, would point to the north of France.

Tennis was referred to as *jeu de la paume* mainly in fashionable Paris, the city which as a result of the rise of the Capetians had since the middle of the thirteenth century become the cultural centre of Europe. England at the time mainly followed the fashion of the French capital, and that is why it is hardly surprising that England's upper classes should have opted for the Parisian form of the game rather than for that played in the French provinces. This explains why in 1440 John Shirley should have described the sporting activity which caused (albeit indirectly) the death of James I of Scotland as playing 'at the pawme'.[96] For the man in the street, however, the game had only one name, and that was tennis. Shortly before the turn of the century, in 1396, a certain William Terrey (who was, perhaps, the landlord of some inn or pub) was summoned before the burghmote of the city of Canterbury because he had allowed certain people to play on his premises 'le Closhe' and 'le Tenesse'.[97] It was the first time that the game was recorded in England. Its being referred to in a legal document proves that action was taken at last in order to enforce laws which had been passed, first by Edward III and then by Richard II, by which ordinary people were enjoined not to engage in ball games.[98] William Terrey appears to be the first and only person known to have come into conflict with them.

It is somewhat surprising that England was by no means the only country where tennis was called tennis. In Italy, Donato Velluti, in his chronicle written between 1367 and 1370, sang the praises of a countryman, Tammaso di Lipaccio, who had returned from France and played games at ball with five hundred French knights who came to Florence in order to help the Republic in her fight against Castruccio Castracani. These were the days when a game called *tenes* began to be played there: 'e in quello tempo si cominciò di qua a giucare a tenes'.[99] The implication of Velluti's statement seems to be that his compatriots had been taught a game called tennis by some French knights and that this game retained its name and was played in the vicinity of Florence from about 1325 (the *terminus a quo* being the battle of Altopascio on 23 September 1325 in which all the French knights lost their lives) until at least the end of the 1360s when Donato wrote his chronicle.

Apart from England and Upper Italy, there is yet another candidate who can lay claim to the authorship of the term tennis. In 1401, the city council of Utrecht in their 'Buurtspraakboek' drew up a ban which forbade people to play with hockey sticks and to 'tennis' on Oudwijk Field ('nochte met kolven en spelen nochte en teneyzen tot Oudwijker velt'). Here, the existence of the verb *teneyzen* implies that of a noun **teneys.*[100]

What, however, do these *tenesse*, *tenes*, and *teneys* (to which must be added the *tenetz* from John Gower's poem) all mean? This is a question over which the learned world has racked its brains for a very long time.

As early as 1671, Stephen Skinner, in his dictionary *Etymologicon Linguae Anglicanae*, gave a typical example of medieval etymologizing which, in order to discover the true meaning of a word, associated it with another which sounded similar. Tennis, Skinner proposed, should be derived from the French noun *tente*, because tennis, to his mind, was played in tents.

In much the same vein, Isidoro del Lungo and Gugliolmo Volpi, the editors of Velluti's chronicle, and others, tended to give the ancient Germans the credit of inventing the game. They pointed to Old High German *tenni* (Modern German *Tenne*), 'threshing floor', on which, for a change, tennis balls rather than corn got a good thrashing.

Whitman's suggestion which would connect *tennis* with the name of the sunken Nile metropolis, Tinnis, has already been mentioned. It should be added here that this fairy tale worthy of a place in the famous *Arabian Nights* was retold by Philip Khûri Hitti in his book *The Arabs*.[101] By constant repetition it gained so much persuasive power that it was eventually given the status of an academic fact when Sahira Abdul Hamid Al-Sayed, an Arabic linguist, included it in her *A Lexicon and Analysis of English Words of Arabic Origins*.[102]

In 1890, in his contribution to *The Badminton Library of Sports and Games*, John Moyer Heathcote reviewed existing opinions and mentioned a rather strange derivation in the process. Tennis might have been derived 'from Tennois or Sennois in the district of Champagne in France, where it was said that the game was played'.[103]

In 1902, a German gymnastics magazine, after investigating the matter with German thoroughness, came up with the following findings.[104] Some etymologists, the journal said, consider tennis to be derived from *tamis* (French: sieve), an expression used in some games to describe the sieve-like racket (!). Others derive tennis from *tainía* (tape), that is, from the tape which separates the players. An old game always involved ten players; tennis might therefore also be derived from ten.

The reader who has up to this point played the game diligently will know what to think of the existence of sieve-like rackets when the players were looking for a name for their game. The second explanation goes back to Walter Skeat,[105] a lexicographer whom undergraduates are told never to trust. It will be swallowed only by those who are still convinced that when tennis was invented, a line was part of the invention.

That tennis was a game frequently played by two five-a-side teams cannot be denied. What can be dismissed out of hand, however, is that the word owes its existence to the English numeral ten. Those French knights involved in the tennis of Italy in the fourteenth century would hardly have resorted to an English word if they had tried to give the game a name, and even if they did, and even if teams of five were their favourite formation, it is difficult to see why they should not have called it fives.

As early as 1617 an etymology was put forward which had much to recommend it. In his *Ductor in linguas*, a rather ambitious dictionary which covered no fewer than eleven languages, John Minshew expressed the belief that a French word was at the root of tennis. Tennis, Minshew said, is the word 'which … the Frenchmen, the onely [= singular, outstanding] tennis players, vse to speake when they strike the ball, at tennis'.[106] Considering the fact that the game originated in France, and that the form *Tenetz* in the five-beat iambus of John Gower's poem was stressed on the last syllable, this was not a bad idea at all. What did leave a few twinges of doubt was the fact that the game should have been called by a French name in Italy, in England and in the Netherlands, but not in France itself. This puzzle certainly is in need of an explanation. And there is another awkwardness still. There is, so far, no tennis player on record who is known to have actually cried *tenez!* before sending the first ball, as indeed he must, onto the slanting roof of the gallery.

WARNING CRIES, LIVING AND DEAD

In medieval sport, cries of warning were by no means unusual. In archery, for instance, the marksman had to warn others by shouting *fast!* Indeed, this little word might save him from a charge of murder brought up against him, if by some misfortune somebody was hit by his missile all the same.[107] In golf, the cry of *fore!* serves as a warning to poeple who may be crossing the fairway. In chess, *check!* signals an attack on the king.

In ball games, many traces are left that similar cries existed. When in 1946 and 1947 documentation of the *tamis* games which had survived the War appeared in the *Bulletin folklorique d'Ile-de-France*, it contained a delightful drawing of a Picardian version of the game in which the server (*tireur*) cried 'à vous, balle!' The cry is answered by an 'entendu!' from the mouth of the centre player (*fort du jeu*) of the opposing team, who is supported by two team-mates who, by calling 'à nous!', seem to say that the server's message has been understood by everybody (**Figure 52**).[108]

FIGURE 52   The Picardian *jeu de tamis* which in recent years seems to have been discontinued. The word balloons indicate that some sort of servers' cry existed.

In the Tuscan ball game (**Figure 53**), the server announces the arrival of the ball by means of a cry 'eccola!' (here it is!).[109] That in Italy announcements of this kind had a long tradition is evidenced by a picture which has already claimed our attention. In the fashion book of Veit Konrad Schwarz (**Figure 18**), commentators have failed to come to grips with the inscription found in the scroll above young Schwarz's head. The text reads: 'O mi – rebuzo – zuge',[110] which in English is something like: 'O play (the ball to me), I will strike it back!' and where *zugar* is an Old Italian word for 'to play'.[111]

Juego, 'I play', is what the server in the Colombian *juego de la chaza* has to say before striking the ball, upon which his opponents are obliged to answer either by *llego*, or by *jugarà*. The former means 'I am coming', or 'I am ready', and the latter, which is used when the players are not ready, 'you will play (later)'.[112] In the *Colloquia familiaria* Jerome urges his partners to start playing: 'Send the ball onto the roof', he says, adding, 'Whoever sends it without having said anything will have sent it in vain' ('Mittite pilam in tectum. Qui miserit nihil praefatus, frustra miserit'). Nicolas, who is a member of the opposing team, accepts the challenge by saying: 'Hem, accipe igitur', 'All right, here take (the ball)!'[113] In so doing, this Nicolas did not only take on the job of coming to terms with Jerome's formidable returns. Since the learned Erasmus's Latin *accipe!* might well have been a translation of French *tenez!*, poor Nicolas has been under the burden of proving that English tennis went back to a French *tenez!* ever since.

FIGURE 53   Extensive use is made of the roofs adjacent to the market square in the Tuscan game of *palla*. *Palla* also features a servers' warning cry ('Eccola!').

KING HENRY VS. FRANCE

Even though the ordinary tennis player may not find the subtleties of literary art particularly attractive, he may nevertheless be familiar with a famous scene in Shakespeare's history play *Henry V*. After Henry had claimed territories in France, emissaries arrive at the English court bringing with them a large barrel. It is a gift of the French Dauphin, and a spokesman (with his tongue in his cheek) explains what it means. If Harry must sow his wild oats, French duchies could still not be won by drinking bouts. His master was therefore sending him a 'treasure' more befitting his youthful temperament. 'What treasure?' Henry, whose curiosity has by this time been sufficiently aroused, wants to know. 'Tennis-balls, my liege', his uncle Exeter replies.[114] Of course, this insult is impossible to swallow. Henry, foaming with rage, swears to change the French tennis balls into English cannonballs and then to play one hell of a match with the French.

Tennis 'histories' have been (and continue to be) the preserve of the ex-tennis player of note rather than the noted historian. That is why this amusing anecdote has been incorporated into most of them. The origin of the story has, however, never been explored. More than eighty years ago, Oskar Emmerig, a German man of letters, demonstrated in a doctoral thesis that this episode from Henry V's life had no historical foundation whatsoever.[115] In Greek antiquity, a similar anecdote had been associated with young Alexander the Great. To him, the gift of a whip, a ball and a casket full of gold had been presented by the Persian King Darius. As in the case of the Dauphin's gift, this one had also been accompanied by a message full of scorn. Alexander, not known for his stupidity, had given it a different interpretation, humiliating, in turn, the sender. At the beginning of the fifteenth century, the very same story was adapted to suit two other enemy rulers, young Henry and the French Dauphin. This becomes evident, as Emmerig noted, from *The Famous Victories* (1598), a forerunner to Shakespeare's play where the same story is told. *The Famous Victories* has two presents rather than three, a carpet and the barrel filled with balls. Henry's delighted exclamation, 'What a guilded Tunne?',[116] however, not only shows that in this later version the French had attached greater importance to the quality of the packing. It also betrays the origin of the story. Shimmering through the high-carat plating of the vessel is the Alexandrian version of the tale: in the course of many centuries, the casket full of gold from the Persian king's gift collection had transmogrified into the gilt barrel presented by the French.

Obviously, Shakespeare had no idea of the tripartite gift in the ultimate source of the story. This detail formed part of the literary rather than the historical tradition on which Shakespeare based his account. From a modern point of view, it is nevertheless strange that in commentaries on Shakespeare's work no mention should have been made of the origin of the story in English historiography. That such information should be absent from traditional tennis histories, however, might, despite the intriguing nature of the story, have been expected.

The first occurrence of the Dauphin's ball gift is to be found in a genre of historical writing following in the wake of Geoffrey of Monmouth's highly influential *Historia Regum Britanniae*. Geoffrey, who has been described as 'a romance writer masquerading as a historian', was the source of inspiration to a real host of historiographers who, from the late twelfth century onwards and in much the same vein, created chronicles in verse and prose which are aptly described as *Brut* chronicles after Geoffrey's legendary founder of Britain, Brutus. Of these, there appeared in the fourteenth century a prose version in the English language to which, in the course of the fifteenth century, several continuations were appended. In the continuation taking the work up to the year 1419,[117] and thus comprising Henry's campaign in France, we hear of an English embassy sent to the King of France (a notable difference to the story as told by Shakespeare) in order to make known to him the claims of their King to the duchies of Normandy, Gascony, and Guyenne. If, they say rather bluntly, the King of France did not comply with Henry's wishes, he would win his duchies back by dint of his sword and within a short time, with the help of Jesus. Rather than the King of France himself, who did not condescend to honour the English with his presence, it is the Dauphin who deals with Henry's request. His answer is, perhaps, less blunt, but a great deal more mischievous: 'thanne the Dolfynne of Fraunce answeryd to our ambassetours, & sayde yn this manere: that the King was ouyr yonge & tendir of age to make eny warre ayens hym, and was not like yette to be no gede [sic] warryor to make such a conqueste there vpon hym'. And then he sent him 'yn scorne & despite [...] a tonne fulle of teneys-ballis', not failing to explain the gift himself. He was sending the tennis balls, he said, 'be-cause he schulde haue sumwhat to play with-alle, for hym & for his lordes; and that would 'become hym bettir thanne to mayntayne eny warre'.[118]

Back to their island went the ambassadors and told Henry and his council about 'the vngodely answere' they had received from the Dauphin, and about the present they had brought with them. And when Henry had heard their words, and the Dauphin's answer, he was sick of the French and the Dauphin beyond all measure ('wondir sore agrevyd, & ryght evil payed towarde the Frenschmen'), and he decided to avenge himself on them as soon as God would send him the grace and the power. And at once he 'lette make tenysballis for the Dolfyn in alle the haste that thay myhte be maad, & that thei were harde & grete gune-stonys, for the Dolfyn to play with-alle'.[119]

Up to here, the story is basically the same as in Shakespeare's historical play. But whereas Shakespeare forgot about the incident later on in his play, the author of the English prose *Brut* did not. On the contrary, he contrived a truly remarkable continuation. In it, he described how Henry took his armada to France, sailing into the Seine estuary on 'Ladies Evyn, the Assumpcion', and how he then proceeded to the town of Harfleur with his army and ordnance. There he at once besieged it 'by londe and by watir', and summoned the captain of the place to surrender ('delyuer the towne'). The captain, not abashed in the least, answered pertly that he had not delivered him anybody, and would not deliver him anybody, and then asked him to try his best. (He saide, 'non he delyuerd hym, ne non he wolde to hym delyuer, but bade hym do his beste.')[120]

> And than the Kinge leyde his ordynaunce vnto the toun, that is for to saye, Gunnes, Engynes, Trigettis [catapults] schet and cast vnto the wallis & eke yn the toun, and caste doun both toures and toun, & layde ham vnto the grounde: & there he played at tenys [variants of MSS T and R: 'at the t.'] with his harde gune stones that were withynne the toune. Whan thai schulde plai, thai songen 'welawaye and allas that eny suche tenyes ballis were made,' and cursed al tho that warre beganne, & the tyme that thei were born.

This ingenious continuation of the story which depicts the barrage of Harfleur in terms of a medieval tennis match, not only provides some of the earliest instances of the terms tennis and tennis balls in the English language, it also, if indirectly, has led to the discovery of other important elements of tennis vocabulary and ultimately to the solution of the greatest puzzle, the origin of the term tennis itself. Without it, in all likelihood it would have remained shrouded in mystery forever.

The unknown chronicler's continuation of the English prose *Brut* inspired, presumably shortly after 1419, another unknown contemporary who was a professional poet and singer, or a minstrel, to use the terminology of the time. In a ballad titled *The Bataile of Agyncourt*,[121] he retold the story, in four-beat couplets, not infrequently echoing the language of his source, but embellishing it in a truly remarkable way, much to the delight of the tennis historian.

The poem survived in several versions. We will first quote from the version of MS. Harley 565 of the British Library, which we will call the B-version. Here, the Dauphin opens the dialogue in flawless English, even though his brand of the language would still seem a far cry from the English of today:[122]

> *And than answerde the Dolfyn bold …*
> *'Me thinke youre Kyng he is nought old,*
> *No werrys for to maynteyn;*
> *Grete well youre Kyng,' he seyde, 'so yonge*
> *That is bothe gentill and small,*
> *A tonne of tenys ballys I shall hym sende*
> *For to pleye hym with all.'*

As in his source, the insult so angers Henry that he promises a counter-present which will score a real knock-out:

> *'Swyche tenys ballys I schal hym sende*
> *As schall tere the roof all of his all [= hall].'*

In the expedition to France, the first detail treated with a great deal of care is the array of the Royal Artillery. In what may well be the oldest version of the Agincourt ballad – we will call it the A-version – the English king is first given an opportunity to show off his skills as a battle planner:[123]

'My Gonnes schall lye up on thys grene,
For they schall play with Harflete
A Game at the tenys, as Y wene.
Myne Engynes, that be of Tre so clene,
They schall be set by syde thys hylle
Over all Harflete that they may see,
To marke the chase whan they play well.'

...

'My chyldren ben redy everichone.'

After Henry has declared that the English side is ready – as a fatherly coach he calls his 'players' his children – the fight might start at once. The minstrel, however, first captures the attention of his audience by means of a formula very characteristic of the oral poetry of the time (the somewhat idiosyncratic spelling has been slightly amended):[124]

Lestenyth Lordys al a bowt,
Of Pamplys schall ye here.

At first sight, the minstrel here seems to be guilty of a terminological *faux pas*. Instead of tennis, the term employed up to this point, he used *palmplay* (this, apparently, is the meaning of *Pamplys* in the text). The term is very appropriate, though. In the language of the defenders, tennis was always called *jeu de la paume*, 'palm game'. The use of palmplay here is therefore superbly ironic. What the poet wants to insinuate is the fact that his countrymen were on the point of playing with the enemy a match 'à la française'. The appearance of palmplay at this point, more than a hundred years before the first instance of this word recorded in the *Oxford English Dictionary*, illustrates very well the linguistic habits of the time. *Tenys* was as much the English word as *jeu de la paume* was the French.

After the call for attention the game is started immediately, a moment for which we have been waiting with our ears pricked. Would one of the cannons indeed come forward with a *tenez!* as we expected? The first piece to 'raise her voice' answers to the amiable name of Good Grace:[125]

'Have I do Felowys, go we to game.'
A monng the Howses the balles ren,
And mad many a Frenche men lame.
'XU be fore', than sayd London, 'in same,'
Hys ball foull fayre he gan throwe
A gayne the stepyll of stone roue.
The Bellys they rowng up a rawe.
'XXX his myne', sayd messyn gere,
'I woll hit wyn yif that I may.'
The wall, that was y mad fule seure,
He brake hyt doune, the sothe to say.

The Kynge's doughter sayd, 'harke how they play.
Helpe my maydonys at this tyde
XLU, that nys no naye.'

...

The Frenche men sayd, 'Now be we schent.

...

But the Dolfyn rescu us in thys cace.
Thys Towne delywer will we.'

Because of its colourfulness and attention to detail, this medieval tennis report is very likely to send any connoisseur into raptures. In the issue under consideration, however, it is rather disappointing. Good Grace simply denies us the confounded *tenez!* Instead, she voices a rather unspecific exhortation with which to rally her companions: 'Have do!'

The report nevertheless has its precious moments, which, at least for the time being, somewhat compensate for its shortcomings, the missing *tenez!* The term *palmplay* has already led us to surmise that the minstrel was using contemporary tennis terminology with subtle irony. This strategy is also adhered to here. When Henry threatens the Dauphin with a very special brand of balls making the roof of his hall come tumbling down, the audience is invited to imagine a service *in tectum*, a service onto the roof of the gallery. However, in marked contrast to a 'normal' game of tennis, these balls will not roll down from the roof obediently. They will cause it to go to rack and ruin.

Henry, as we have seen, had placed his cannons and catapults at vantage points, from where they commanded a perfect view of the court, Harfleur, and could clearly see the chases, the impact of the cannon balls. For the match against Harfleur, the English king had picked a four-a-side team, and the nominated players, Good Grace, London, Messenger and The King's Daughter reveal a detail which should be difficult to recover from any other historical document: the names of the big guns which at the time formed part of the Royal Artillery. They prove that guns had been nicknamed long before Big Bertha and her like thundered onto modern battlefields.

After the rather colourless 'have do' from the muzzle of Good Grace, the first balls begin to fly in between the houses of Harfleur. Again it should be noted how intelligently the literal and the allegorical planes of his poem are linked to one another. Whistling in between the houses – 'A monng the Howses the balles ren' – is what in medieval tennis balls did in an almost literal sense. In medieval French, the gallery encompassing the monastery courtyard on all four sides was called *apendeis*. The term originally referred to an annexe with a sloping roof which was supported by the walls of another building. Out of *apendeis*, derived from Latin *appendo*, 'to append', the English, with their usual disregard for foreign linguistic structures created a penthouse.[126] This word, in Real tennis still used to designate the crossway as well as the broadside galleries, was at an early time shortened to the much more convenient word *house*. This appears from John Florio's *Second Frutes*, an Anglo-

Italian tennis dialogue published in 1591 and in many respects similar to that of Erasmus. Here, Sir Thomas, Sir John and Sir Henry and their servant Piccinino are talking shop on the subject of tennis.[127] The point at issue is the service:[128]

> T[homas]. Whose lot is it to plaie?
> H[enry]. Mine, for you are at the house.

John Florio, a language teacher and lexicographer, here gives the first instance of this usage in the English language. It is truly remarkable, therefore, that in the *Batayle of Agyncourt* there is evidence that in the sloppy everyday conversation of tennis players the term *house* had been substituted for the clumsier *penthouse* some two hundred years earlier.

Another characteristic of the ballad worthy of note is the fact that, after the second bull's eye by London, the church bells of Harfleur should have begun to ring hideously. In Real tennis the last gallery opening on the returners' side is also a point-winning goal. As is the case with all gallery openings, it is normally protected by a net, but unlike the others it has a bell fastened to it which rings whenever this gallery is hit. Did such winning galleries with a net and a bell already exist at the time when the *Batayle* poet set pen to paper? This is certainly a most intriguing question.

The second stroke is played by Messenger who for his shrewd rebound play avails himself of the town wall. The ball, which shows every quality of the giants' toy employed in Sir Gawain's match, does not rebound off it, however, but goes crashing right through it.

The last point scored by the English team takes the game into its decisive phase. The defenders of Harfleur are threatened by humiliating defeat if the Dauphin does not arrive with relief soon. Apparently, the besieged requested of their master (as was the wont at the score of forty-five) that he play out the chase with the English King. Some later copyist, however, no longer familiar with the rules of tennis, failed to understand. Ignoring the author's subtle use of contemporary tennis terms here as elsewhere, he possibly sacrificed the meaningful *chace* at this point, substituting for it an everyday word, *case*.

As has already been pointed out, the Agincourt ballad has survived in several versions. In the A-version, Good Grace, by not initiating a rally by the cry of *tenez!*, proved highly uncooperative. In the B-version, however, another big gun has taken over which does not even have a name but which otherwise behaves perfectly. At exactly the same point where Good Grace voiced her unimaginative 'have do' in version A, this gun produces a truly remarkable text in version B. It runs like this:[129]

> *Tenys seyde the grete gonne,*
> *How felawes go we to game.*

This is definitive proof that as late as the beginning of the fifteenth century a rally used to be announced by the call of *tenez!* This *tenys*, in turn, did represent the plural imperative of the French verb *tenir*, 'to hold', as becomes evident from another version of the Agincourt ballad, preserved in an early printing from the Bodleian

Library, entitled *The Batayll of Egyne Court, and the Great Sege of Rone.* Imp. by John Skot. We will call it the C-version:[130]

B-version:

> *Tenys seyde the grete gonne,*
> *How felawes go we to game.*

C-version:

> *Than sayd the greate gunne,*
> *Holde felowes we go to game.*

Here *holde*, the remainder of the two texts being almost identical, must be the literal translation of *tenys* in the B-version.[131]

    Apart from the bits and pieces of different versions of the Agincourt ballad, there is yet another possibility of unravelling the tennis mystery. There is a carol by the English poet John Audelay, who as chaplain of Richard Lestrange, Lord of Knockin, led a drab existence in Haughmond Abbey near Shrewesbury.[132] English carols were originally sung at Christmas,[133] but the portion reproduced from this one clearly shows that carol poets occasionally turned to other subjects than the birth of Christ. The addressee of the carol is King Henry VI, who succeeded to the throne at the tender age of 8 months. Since there was hardly anything praiseworthy in so young a boy – Audelay's song originated in the 1420s[134] – the poet apparently felt obliged to take advantage of the chivalrous deeds of his progenitor, Henry V. Of these, however, we have already heard, as we shall see presently:[135]

> *His fader fore loue of mayd Kateryn,*
> *In Fraunce he wroht turment and tene;*
> *His loue hee* [the Dauphin] *sayd hit schuld not ben,*
> *And sent him ballis him with to play.*
>
> *Then was he wyse in wars with alle,*
> *And taht Franchemen to plaie at the balle*
> *With tenes hold he ferd ham halle;*
> *To castelles and setis thi floyn away.*
>
> *To Harflete a sege he layd anon,*
> *And cast a bal unto the towne;*
> *The Franchemen swere be se and sun,*
> *Hit was the fynd that mad that fray.*

In the Agincourt ballad we were compelled to piece together the service call of *tenez!* and the translation belonging to it from two different texts. The patriotic John Audelay has spared us this game of hide and seek. Not only has the singing chaplain from Shropshire here served up another authentic example of the service cry *tenez!*, he has at the same time, by way of a dessert as it were, presented us with an English translation of it.

We have thus provided sufficient proof that the origins of the name of the game should be sought in an old warning cry on the part of the serving party. However, about how the opposition in the other half of the court reacted, we know next to nothing. In this respect, the texts which we have consulted so far leave us completely in the dark. In all of them, the returners invariably remain as silent as posts, and if the matter had been left up to them, no rallies would probably ever have got off the ground, since none of them apparently cared to give the server a sign to launch his first ball.

In the course of this study, we have time and again been able to complement our knowledge of medieval tennis by taking a look at traditional folk games which, although still keenly played today by minorities, are virtually unknown to the larger part of the sporting public. In so doing, we were guided by the following principle. Many of the sources available to us point to the north of France as the cradle of tennis. From there, the game spread in all directions over a period spanning many centuries. Bearing this in mind, it would seem only logical that the oldest forms of the game should be encountered, not at their original starting-point, but where on their long journey they arrived last, the outer fringes of their diffusion where the innovations which meanwhile might have occurred at the place of origin are least likely to have penetrated. In other words, a game like *juego de la chaza* played by American Indians in the loneliness of Colombian mountains, is among those furthest removed from the modern international tennis circuit, which, thanks to the invention of Major Walter Clopton Wingfield, began to swing in late nineteenth-century England.[136] At least theoretically, it therefore constitutes the type of game on which to base a reconstruction of medieval tennis.

In addition to games geographically remote, there is another type which can also be called 'remote', albeit in a different sense: children's games. It is generally accepted that children's games, although they reflect activities in the adult world, are rather conservative, because the child, as it were, lives in a society within society with class rules of its own and separated from the adult world by what has been called a 'social distance'. This becomes evident above all from children's games. Windmills may long have disappeared from our landscapes, and also the games of tilts from our sports arenas, yet they have both survived in children's toys and games.[137]

After what has been said, it is hardly surprising that medieval tennis should also have survived in the form of a children's game. It would seem plausible that when in France, several hundred years ago, fathers, uncles and elder brothers went out to teach the team of the neighbouring village a lesson in a match of tennis, little Maurice and little Jean-Jacques were watching and listening most attentively. Of course, it did not escape their notice what answer would be given to every cheeky *tenez!* voiced from the other camp. The next thing was to introduce it, along with the service cry, into a game of their own. This was played with somewhat poor equipment, but according to rules very similar to those prevailing in the tennis played by their seniors. The characteristic feature of this game was an oblong piece of wood tapering at the ends which had to serve as a substitute for the ball. This piece of wood was hit with a stick on one of its pointed ends and was thus sent spinning through the air. A team of catchers tried to catch and to throw it back into a circle drawn around the spot from which the service had been made. This circle was, at least in principle, the point-winning 'opening', the *dedans*, peculiar to the tennis of the time. If the catchers missed the 'ball', the distance between the service spot and the spot where the 'ball' had landed was measured, and the next server had to try to surpass this mark. This was what in the children's game had remained of the chase.

Of course, the children's game also preserved the traditional language of tennis. This becomes evident from the writings of Jens Christian Svabo, an inhabitant of the Faeroes who seems to have been the first to consider the game worth recording. When in 1781/1782 he watched it on his native islands, his curiosity was at least sufficiently aroused by the cries he overheard from the serving as well as the returning players of which he carefully took a note. From the servers he had heard something like *exebiti* or *exaksebiti*, from the returners something like *roti*.

At first sight, the meaning of these calls escapes us, but if we assume for a moment that they might represent something the young Faroese had picked up in their Latin lessons, their meaning is no longer difficult to ascertain. *Exebiti* is, of course, the *accipite!* from Erasmus's *Colloquia familiaria* and the variant *exaksebiti* turns out to be *ecce, accipite!*, 'look here, accept the ball!' *Roti*, in turn, is what teacher had been driving into the pupils' heads in the form of *parati sumus*, 'we are ready'.[138]

The children's stick tennis did not only preserve the Latin terms of the humanists, though. In one of its many varieties, the old French terms for which these served as substitutes have survived as well, and it is here again that a significant contribution to the history of tennis is made by the Germans. In the Rhineland Palatinate, where the children's stick game remained popular until after the Second World War, the servers, before sending the little piece of wood soaring into the air, would literally call *tenee, tenees*, and even *tenis*.[139] And in the Rhineland Palatinate only there was an answer to this cry: it was either *ui* or *wuplee*.[140]

These two little words answer the question what in medieval tennis returners were expected to retort on hearing the server's *tenez!* Their answer was either *oui*, 'yes', or, for those who preferred a little rhetorical flourish, *s'il vous plaît*, 'yes, if you please'. It seems likely that the young players from the Rhineland learnt the game, together with its language, from their peers across the French border at some time during the Napoleonic Wars, or even earlier.

In the Rhineland Palatinate, the stick game went by the name of *tenee-ui* after its two characteristic calls, although it was never so called in France. This has a remarkable parallel in the Middle Ages when tennis was called tennis in England, Italy and The Netherlands of all places, but never so in the country of its origin. The

German children's game offers an explanation for why this should have been so. If a French boy could not be persuaded to use the imperative of a verb as a noun, a mature and language-conscious Frenchman could be least of all. Only people who did not see through the structure of these words could be guilty of a solecism of this magnitude: the barbaric British, the infernal Italians and the dampish Dutch. If we ignore for a moment the proud Frenchman's indignation, however, this must also mean that wherever tennis became known as tennis, the game had been usurped by simple, uneducated people who did not understand foreign languages. The word tennis itself proves that at the very outset the game was the sport of ordinary people.

FOOTBALL IN HELL AND TENNIS ON EARTH: TENEZ!

If it is true that tennis was a milder form of medieval football sanctioned by the church, the fact should be borne out by the language of the two games. So far we have noted parallels in the use of the terms *upwards* and *downwards* in various traditional or folk games of tennis and football. At the same time, we noted the fact that hardly anything is known about the terminology of medieval football, and unless such information becomes available, further investigation would, at least for the time being, seem almost impossible. There is, however, at least one highly attractive example of how in medieval France, where football was called *mellat* or *soule*,[141] the adepts of football and tennis behaved very similarly in a remarkable way. In the *Mystère de la passion*, a fifteenth-century Passion play written in 1448 by Arnoul Gréban, Canon at St Julian's in Le Mans, the audience is treated to a spectacle which was rather unusual even for the medieval stage: a veritable football match. The match has been devised as a punishment for the arch-traitor Judas, and the implication is that football in the north-west of France was in those days a pretty violent affair. After Judas has been escorted to Hell by Despair personified (*Deseperance*) and the devil Berich, he stands before Hell's supremo, Lucifer, awaiting his sentence. The Archfiend is ready to gobble him down then and there, but, at the request of Astaroth, he is willing to part with his prey for a little while. He gives his underlings permission to play a little football match in which the wretched Judas's role will be that of the ball. According to the old proverb slightly revamped as 'first come, first kick' (*Qui premier y vient, premier solle*),[142] Berich, Judas's jailer, enjoys the privilege of the kick-off. But a cue must be given before the shaggy lot is unleashed, and that is why Lucifer shouts:[143]

> *Tenez, mes petiz dragonneaulx,*
> *mes jeunes disciples d'escolle;*
> *jouez en ung peu a la solle*
> *au lieu de croupir ou fumier.*

> (*Tenez!, my little dragonlets,*
> *Young pupils of my school,*
> *Play a little football with him,*
> *Instead of lounging around on the dung heap.*)

It looks as if not only in tennis, but also in football the game was opened by the cry *tenez!,* although only this singular instance of such a usage seems to exist. Here as elsewhere in medieval sources *tenez!* occurs independently which seems to confirm the hypothesis that we have before us an instance of ellipsis, a linguistic form in which something is omitted or tacitly understood, namely, either the word for football, Old French *soule,* or that for the tennis ball, Old French *esteuf.* It is highly doubtful, however, whether *tenez!* ever meant 'here, hold the ball!' If we bear in mind that in the tournament the team representing the town or castle were called *tenants,* 'holders', it would seem plausible to assume that the original meaning of *tenez!* was something like 'hold (your positions)!' Into tennis the term was adopted rather thoughtlessly, because it would seem more logical to hear it from the lips of those attacking the *dedans.* But, as we have heard, this is not the case.

15:0! The Lord supplies the points

The Agincourt ballad, written shortly after 1415, is the first to testify to a generosity otherwise unheard of among ball players. With the possible exception of flashing pinball machines, there is hardly anyone willing to concede, as do the tennis players, fifteen bonus points for a single strike. In his tennis allegory, Jan van den Berghe also seemed a little mystified by the fact that the rules of tennis bless a player with no fewer than fifteen points for a single lucky stroke:[144]

> Voren es gheseyt hoe dat tkaetsspel ghewonnen es met vier kaetsen / maer daer en es niet gheseyt hoe dat de speelders winnen met eenen slaghe / XV. Ende dit es een ghedeelkin vreemde dat sy meer rekenen of winnen / dan een / met eenre kaetse ...

> (Earlier the manner in which a tennis match could be won with four winning strokes was explained. What was not explained was how players can win fifteen points for a single stroke. It is, after all, a little curious that they count or win more than one point for a single stroke.)

'Why,' he goes on to ask, 'is not one point given for one stroke, and two for two strokes?' As was typical of his time, Jan seeks the answer to a mystery of this magnitude with the Almighty in heaven:[145]

> ghelike dat de kaetsere wint / met eenen slaghe ... XV. Also winnen sy in loone de ghene die recht ende iusticie voorderen / voor een ducht ... XV. voud loons of meer / ... Ende int ghelike dat de eerde / in wien dat men zayt zaed / ute gheeft ... vann eenen zade / menichvoudich zaet / ... so eist wel recht dat God menichvoudich loont / ... ghelike den kaetspeelders.

> (In much the same way as a tennis player wins fifteen points for a single stroke, those who support and further righteousness and justice are also awarded fifteen times or more than normal for their good deed. For, if the earth, into which man sows his seed,

yields for one seed manifold, it behoves the Lord to award manifold in the same manner as the tennis players.)

The only thing that is clear about Jan's explanation is that he will not be receiving fifteen points for doing justice to the counting problem in tennis, and that even in those early days nothing was known about the origin of the curious scoring method.

The scholar Erasmus of Rotterdam also seems to be acutely aware of the problem, but even he cannot think of a plausible explanation with which to adorn the dialogue of his tennis freshmen Jerome and Nicolas. When in the *Colloquia familiaria* Nicolas celebrates his points, thirty and forty-five, the tennis greenhorn Jerome asks his partner whether he is rejoicing over the prospect of money, sesterces. 'No,' Nicolas explains. 'Then what else?' Jerome asks doggedly. 'Numbers,' Nicolas answers. 'What's the use of numbers if you don't count anything with them?' Jerome insists. 'That's just the way of the game,' Nicolas states laconically and so brings about a rather one-sided end to the discussion.[146]

In 1555, Scaino, indulging in garrulous prolixity here as elsewhere in his book, is confident of cracking the tough nut of why tennis-players score by fifteens. He begins by elaborating upon the question of how victories were scored in Italy. Apparently, Scaino's countrymen were not content with simply winning a game for which, in much the same way as today, an advantage of two points was needed. Such a victory, in the mind of the passionate Southerner at least, was stale and devoid of all interest. That is why a 'double victory' was cherished, one in which the opponent was not conceded a single point. The ultimate achievement, however, was the 'triple victory', also called the rabid or frenzied victory (*vittoria triplice, o rabbiosa*): this required that the player, after trailing love-forty, and almost hopelessly behind, score five consecutive points to snatch the game after all. Only utter bitterness at the sight of one's own deficit, and the prospect of ignominious defeat would lend one the wings to such a triumph, worth, according to Scaino, a triple reward.[147]

The five consecutive points necessary for the *vittoria rabbiosa*, and the threefold reward this victory held in store for the player, inspired Scaino to a highly speculative explanation which at the same time gave him the opportunity to show off his learning. Although words, he argued, had been assigned to things in a rather arbitrary fashion, a close relationship might still exist between a word and the nature of the thing it denoted. The Italian word for man, for example, *l'huomo*, was derived from Latin *ex humo*, 'of earth',[148] and why should not similar equations be possible in the case of the vocabulary of tennis? What would be more natural than linking the counting method in tennis with the supreme form of the game, the rabid victory? Indeed, the most sensible explanation of the number fifteen would be to regard it as the product of the five successive points and the triple reward of the *vittoria rabbiosa*:[149]

> For it is manifest that any player who wins five consecutive chases also wins the three degrees of reward; & whosoever aspires to reach such degree of honour must, travelling the arduous and difficult road of five chases, tire himself & sweat. What more fitting name then, what more suitable number could be chosen from the Arithmetical art than

the number fifteen which contains all the activities, all the being, form & perfection of that art with which the Ball game has been devised?

Apart from the frenzy conducive to the *vittoria rabbiosa*,[150] the division of the hour into sixty minutes, and the division of the circle into six segments of sixty have been considered as possible models for the counting method in tennis.[151]

As for the first, it was assumed that one hour was the time needed to win a game. This explanation will not hold even if we regard medieval tennis as a geriatric exercise in which the ball is hit to and fro in high arches from one baseline to the other in order to kill time. The circle argument was brought forward as early as the sixteenth century by the French tennis theoretician Gosselin who, however, discarded it at once, a fact which seems to have escaped tennis historians who have mentioned him. Gosselin himself, rather than subscribing to the circle theory, advanced one of his own, and this must have so impressed his contemporaries that in the century to follow it was deemed worthy of being incorporated in a learned encyclopaedia, *La Maison Académique,* 'The Edifice of Science'.

Gosselin's little treatise is titled: 'Explanation of the two doubtful facts found in the counting of the tennis game which deserve to be understood by cultured people.'[152] The first is this:[153] Why do people count in tennis by augmenting the number of points by 15, to wit: 15, 30, 45, and, finally, game (which would be worth 60), instead of counting by means of some other number, either larger or smaller? The second is:[154] What kind of measure do these numbers 15, 30, and the others stand for? Those familiar with the principles of astronomy, Gosselin goes on, know very well that a physical unit (*vn Signe Physic*) which is the sixth part of a circle is subdivided into sixty degrees. If one was inclined to follow this argument of the sixties, it could be said that the way of counting in tennis was in accordance with it, in imitation of the physical unit, since fifteen degrees times four have the same value as a physical unit, in exactly the same way as four times fifteen make up a game in tennis.[155]

But as for the application of the physical unit to the language of tennis, Gosselin does have his doubts. In France, a tennis match is played for four winning games. Since four times sixty is enough to win a match, but is not sufficient to complement a full circle, and since Gosselin seems unwilling to accept any model other than the tennis customs of France, the whole astronomical argument collapses. In addition, it is difficult to see, Gosselin concludes, how those toiling in a match of tennis, by striking or driving the ball, or returning it, should derive much pleasure from contemplating the sky in the process.[156]

Of course, a scholar of Gosselin's learning will know of ways to deal with minor problems such as the tennis players' scoring. In the writings of Varro, Pliny and others he had encountered measures such as the *climat* and the *iugerum* which may not have been exactly the type of measure with which the inventors of tennis had been familiar, but nevertheless served his purpose passing well. The former was a measure of length of sixty feet, the latter a square measure of 240 times 120 feet (an acre). That the counting system in tennis was inspired by these two was, to the mind of Gosselin, beyond all doubt. The number sixty in tennis represented the four parts of the *climat*, since the numbers in tennis were based on feet, a unit with which the chases were measured. Likewise, the *iugerum* must needs be the model for the match, since it was only the length which mattered, and chases and strokes were assessed, not with regard to their breadth, but with regard to their length.[157]

Despite the ingenious solution offered by Gosselin, the only thing which can be taken for granted in the much disputed question is this: the number sixty which formed the basis of the curious scoring by fifteens in all likelihood originated in France. This was the place where sixty (rather than one hundred) was considered to be a major numerical unit. This fact is reflected in the French language which has no single word for seventy, but has to use a compound of sixty plus ten (*soixante-dix*) instead.

At this point, the purse-swinging fan from Philippe Pigouchet's book of hours reminds us of the fact that in the Middle Ages tennis was always played for money, and Lance St John Butler has only recently brought to light a most intriguing example of how in medieval racket games obsessive betting was the rule. On a misericord in Barcelona cathedral, a ball game involving two players with rackets is in progress while two spectators 'are exchanging coins in what clearly is a bet'.[158] This was also true of most other games, and as late as the seventeenth century, Francis Quarles in one of his emblematic poems envisaged the biblical Mammon as an English bowls player with a bulging purse tied to his belt.[159] From a fifteenth-century English carol in which the idol money is worshipped we learn that money was virtually indispensable also in tennis:[160]

> *Money, money, now hay goode day!*
> *Money, where haste thow be?*
> *Money, money, thow goste away*
> *and wylt not byde with me.*
>
> *At cardes and dyce yt bereth the pryce*
> *As kyng and emperoure*
> *At tables, tennes, and othere games*
> *Money hath euer the floure.* [= Money always
>   takes the cream.]

In Jan van den Berghe's *Kaetspel*, it is expressly stated that after the players have put off their clothes and are ready for the match, they have to be agreed as to how expensive their match will be and how much they may win or lose at it. This done, it was the custom, in order to be quite safe, to deposit the money or some security.[161] Towards the end of the sixteenth century, John Florio in his *Second Frutes* tells us where the negotiated purse was stored. It is a regulation which might well be recommended to the top earners in the tennis of today for the storage of their money belts:[162]

T. Let vs keepe the lawes of the court.

G. That is, stake money vnder the line, is it not so?

T. Yea, sir, you hitt it right.

H. Here is my monie, now stake you.

The question of what Jan van den Berghe's players did with their stakes in the days before the advent of the line or net must remain open, but both Jan and John Florio suggest that the method of scoring in tennis was based on some monetary unit, and that it was a unit used in ancient France, where the sixty was not only used for counting eggs, but also for counting money, in a way which resembled the old English measure of threescore. The first to entertain this idea was an Englishman, A.E. Crawley,[163] who regarded the *double royal d'or* as the coin in question, a gold coin minted in 1340 and worth sixty *sous*. But Crawley's calculation, ingenious though it is, has two major flaws. On the one hand, he does not answer the question why the sixty *sous* should have been divided into four times fifteen *sous*. On the other hand, a game in which it was possible to win, or, for that matter, to lose, a gold piece after four poor strokes and in a matter of seconds was by far too expensive. Crawley, it seems, was also beset by the idea that medieval tennis was the game of kings and peers, who could afford such extravagant pastimes. Crawley nevertheless pointed in the right direction. There was a coin which did not have the disadvantages of the *double royal d'or*, and which made tennis a game which was within the means even of ordinary people. This coin was the so-called *gros denier tournois*, the Great Penny of Tours.[164] At the beginning of the fourteenth century it was valued at fifteen pence (called *deniers*).[165]

A different question is whether there is any evidence that this French coin ever served as a stake in medieval games. In order to answer it, it would be worth knowing something about the stakes which could be laid on the outcome of a medieval game. With regard to tennis, we have to admit that, at least for the time being, we do not have the slightest idea. This does not mean, however, that we are not better informed about other games. In the game of dice, the game with 'the bicched bones two',[166] as Chaucer called it, rules existed as early as the Third Crusade. They had been laid down by Philip II of France, and Richard the Lionheart who, of course, felt themselves to be unaffected by any limitations there may have been. The knights and consorts, on the other hand, were obliged not to lose more than twenty *sous* during the period of one day and one night, failing which, the not inconsiderable fine of one hundred *sous* awaited these gentlemen. Workers and sailors were not allowed to roll the dice at all. If they could not resist the temptation, they risked corporal punishment.[167] The following centuries seem to have been a little more liberal, especially with regard to the games of simple folk. Two sets of regulations are known, one from the end of the thirteenth century and one from the fourteenth century, in which dice and board games are permitted to commoners as long as they, regarding the margin of the stakes, subject themselves to a kind of voluntary self-control. By the first set of regulations from Nuremberg commoners are enjoined not to play for more than sixty 'haller' and for no object or possession valued at over sixty 'pfennige'.[168] In the second, the city regulations from Munich of 1365, the stakes are also limited to sixty 'denare' (*deniers!*).[169] Even though the regulations mentioned above originated in Germany and not in France, they do without doubt prove one thing: by at least the end of the thirteenth century and during the fourteenth century, the time when *sous* worth fifteen *deniers* were in circulation, games played for stakes of over sixty *deniers* were forbidden. Who can tell if other games (besides those played with dice) where money was at stake were not also affected by this law? And why should tennis not have been one of them? At any rate, the depositing of stakes in tennis so graphically described by John Florio is a feature taken over from dice games, where the money had to be placed, under the wary eyes of a neutral counter, between the players (**Figure 54**). And this parallel again suggests that tennis could indeed have been subjected to the same regulations as dice.[170]

ADVANTAGE IS BETTER THAN DEUCE

In the Agincourt ballad, three counting terms are conspicuous by their very absence, namely *deuce*, *advantage* and *love*. That the first two are missing is perfectly understandable. Unabashed patriotism prevented the poet to credit the enemy with enough courage and skill to take the fabulous English side to *deuce* and *advantage*. On the other hand, he might well have put to good use the third in an attempt to heap ridicule on the utterly unsuccessful French. But perhaps, the term *love* had not yet been invented.

FIGURE 54   A characteristic feature of medieval dicing was the so-called counter (German *Pfandner* or *Rechner*) who supervised the game. Here he is seated between the two players with his hand resting on the wagers protectively.

Despite the poet's silence, *advantage* and *deuce* must have existed. Only a few decades after the Agincourt poem, Jan van Berghe translated the French *avantage* into his native Dutch, in the course of a rather long-winded explanation of how, after the score of *deuce*, play is continued. If, he says, the players reach a stage where those who have been collecting the least number of points start playing so well and assiduously that they also reach forty-five points, two chases must be played. And if it then happens that one of the sides wins the first chase, this side calls out as loudly as possible *tvoordeel/tvoordeel* ('advantage, advantage').[171] Eight years later, Charles d'Orléans in his famous birthday poem came forward with the French term which must have served as a model for Jan's *tvoordeel*. Worry (Soussy), the Duke says, discourages me to play on, because she will stop the strokes which will give me advantage:[172]

> *Car Soussy tant me descourage*
> *De jouer, et va estouppant*
> *Les cops que fiers a l'avantage.*

In John Florio's *Second Frutes* (1591), *advantage* and *deuce* for the first time put in an appearance together:[173]

> *H. You haue fortie then, goe to, plaie.*
> *T. And I a dewes then.*
> *H. I haue advantage.*

In Florio's lines we notice two things. By the end of the sixteenth century, the English had, albeit wrongly, substituted the Latin prefix *ad-* for the French *a-* in *avantage* and shortened the usual *forty-five* to *forty*, a short cut which seems to have been discovered by lazy continental schoolboys even earlier.[174] The passage from Florio also shows that the English had given a very special treatment to *deuce*. If in ancient France two tennis players had played an evenly balanced game up to forty-five each, they were, as it were, separated from winning the game by two points (as in modern tennis). They were, in other words, two points away from the game, a fact which in modern French would be expressed by the phrase *à deux (points) du jeu*. In England where French had ceased to be a spoken language since about the beginning of the fifteenth century this *à deux* (*a deus* in Old French, from *duos*, the accusative of the Latin plural *duo*, 'two') was considered a noun preceded by an indefinite article. That is why Sir Henry and his countrymen eventually were convinced to have won *a deuce* whenever they had reached the score of forty each: 'I have a deuce!' Later, the indefinite article was regarded as superfluous and dropped altogether.

A PARTICULAR BAD EGG: ENGLISH LOVE

Perhaps the best known example of English sports lingo is *love*, meaning 'nothing'. The normal explanation is that it goes back to French *l'œuf*, 'egg', a word which at least to the mind of the layman sounds fairly similar. Perhaps *l'œuf* would never have been associated with *love*, had not in the English national pastime cricket a veritable *duck's egg* (a *duck* for short) been used for a similar purpose. The derivation is, of course, impossible as a simple equation will show. If the Latin accusative *bovem* – via French *bœuf* – resulted in English *beef*, *illud ovum* – via French *l'œuf* – would naturally have become **leef*, but not *love*.

It has been said that the curious scoring by fifteens originated in a French coin. It could therefore be argued that the player scoring the winning points might have been considered the one playing for money, whereas his opponent (by way of euphemism) was regarded as the one playing for fun, or for the love of the game only. In the English language, the expression *neither for love nor money* existed in the Middle Ages, and that is why this explanation of *love* is perhaps not completely unjustified.

At this point the political song written by Jeronimus van der Voort in 1583 is worth remembering.[175] It describes a battle between the citizens of Antwerp and the French in terms of a tennis match, a match in the course of which the latter turn out to be contemptible breakers of the rules. The rules stipulated, for instance, that before a match wagers had to be placed, and these might be, according to Jeronimus, of three different kinds. People played either for money, for pledges, or simply for the honour. From the palace of the Duke of Anjou, the poet says, nothing of the kind had been laid at all. All that had been coming from the French were unwieldy balls and weeds (*kruit*), a punning reference to lead bullets and gunpowder (Dutch *buskruit*):[176]

> *Ghelt/Pant noch loff//wt s'Hertochs Hoff/*
> *En sachmen haer by-setten:*
> *Maer Ballen groff//fijn Cruydt als stoff/*
> *Daer moesten wy op letten.*

> (No money, pledge nor honour from the Duke's
>   palace
> Did we see being staked here:
> But of unwieldy balls and quality powder for
>   loading [guns]
> We had to take care there.)

Of course, in the issue under consideration, the most remarkable item in these lines is the Dutch or Flemish equivalent of English 'honour', *lof*. It looks as if the English expression for a player's failure to score a point owes its existence to an expression used in the Low Countries, *omme lof spelen*, 'to play for the honour'. Love would then be one of a real host of sporting terms adopted from the continent, for example *blot* (from backgammon),[177] *closh*,[178] *cricket*,[179] *golf*,[180] *kayles*,[181] *luck*,[182] *poker*,[183] *putt*,[184] and *set*. It is interesting that of these *set* should also be represented (in the form of the verb *by-setten*, 'to stake') in Jeronimus's lines. As a sporting term, the noun *set* seems to occur for the first time in John Florio's *Second Frutes*, where Piccinino, the servant, asks his masters whether they wanted to play for money: 'Will you plaie in set?'[185] What is really strange here is the pronoun *in*, which is easily explained, however, if we conceive of it as the prefix of an underlying Flemish noun *inzet*, meaning 'stake'. How *lof*, which was re-interpreted as *love*, reached England is not difficult to see. At the beginning of the sixteenth century Jeronimus's Antwerp was the centre of Protestantism, and the social unrest following the introduction of the new creed led the most enterprising citizens to move north (resulting in Antwerp's decline, and the rise of Amsterdam), or to emigrate to England.[186]

FOUR

Tennis in Renaissance literature

◇

On the preceding pages, medieval and Renaissance literature has time and again been consulted in order to shed light on the evolution of the game. In this chapter, however, works of literary art in which the subject is dealt with will be examined for their own sake.

From the fifteenth century onwards, tennis has exercised considerable influence on creative writers, especially on playwrights, and on poets writing in a didactic vein. Of these, the latter will claim our attention first. The didactic poet's preferred method was one he had inherited from the Middle Ages: the allegorical.[1] Saying something allegorically meant, according to the Greek term, giving one's words a different meaning. A poet may have been writing about a tennis match, but this was not what his poem was really about. As well as its surface meaning, the poem had a figurative one which was used by the poet as a means for moral instruction. Of course, a straightforward sermon might have served the purpose equally well, but a poem on a fascinating subject, in this case a favourite pastime, was not infrequently considered more suitable still in order to drive a moral message home. In the Renaissance, the allegorical method of the Middle Ages became even more sophisticated by the use of a special device, the so-called conceit (from Italian *concetto*), which is, perhaps, best described as an ingenious comparison by which two otherwise completely unrelated subjects such as tennis and man, or God and the hereafter were in a startling way brought together. The conceit was the delight of the wits of the age, especially in the sixteenth and seventeenth centuries.

CHARLES D'ORLÉANS

The first to employ the allegorical method in a tennis poem was Charles d'Orléans, famous prisoner of the battle of Agincourt and the last of the courtly poets. Charles's poem was composed on a special occasion, his forty-fifth birthday on 24 November 1439. The Duke's overlong exile in England, until November 1440, may have contributed to the melancholy pervading it, but (if we are to believe the author of *The Waning of the Middle Ages*, Jan Huizinga) it was the melancholy of the whole age. In the very middle of his life, the poet finds himself in a situation where the monotony of everyday life is interrupted by an 'exceptional' birthday. All of a sudden, the *trouvère* realizes how life has been running out stealthily and how much of a threat Old Age has become to him. It is here that he is struck by an intriguing analogy: the number of his own years and the number referring to the critical stage in a game which must have belonged to his favourite pastimes. This resulted in an ingenious poem in which, after the principles of the allegorical method, life is described in terms of a tennis match in which Old Age (*Aage* or *Vieillesse*), fickle Fortune (*Fortune*), and gnawing Worry (*Soussy*) are turned into very real opponents. As was characteristic of medieval tennis, these three had formed a three-a-side team by which the Poetic I is put under agonizing pressure:[2]

> *J'ay tant joué avercques Aage*
> *A la paulme que maintenant*
> *J'ay quarante cinq; sur bon gage*
> *Nous jouons, non pas pour neant.*
> *Assez me sens fort et puissant*
> *De garder mon jeu jusqu'a cy.*
> *Ne je ne crains riens que Soussy.*
>
> *Car Soussy tant me descourage*
> *De jouer, et va estouppant*
> *Les cops que fiers a l'avantage.*
> *Trop seurement est rachassant;*
> *Fortune si lui est aidant:*
> *Mais Espoir est mon bon amy.*
> *Ne je ne crains riens que Soussy.*
>
> *Viellesse de douleur enrage*
> *De ce que le jeu dure tant,*
> *Et dit, en son felon langage,*
> *Que les chasses dorenavant*
> *Merchera, pour m'estre nuisant;*
> *Mais ne m'en chault, je la deffy,*
> *Ne je ne crains riens que Soussy.*
>
> *Se Bon Eur me tient convenant,*
> *Je ne doubte, ne tant ne quant,*
> *Tout mon adversaire party,*
> *Ne je ne crains riens que Soussy.*
>
> (*I have played tennis with age*
> *So long that now I am*
> *At forty-five: for high stakes*
> *We play, never for nothing.*
> *I feel strong and vigorous*

To determine the course of the game till now.
I fear nothing but Worry.

For Worry takes all my courage
To play and already He stops
The strokes I strike to gain advantage.
He returns too well;
Fickle Fortune also comes to help Him.
But Hope is my good friend.
I fear nothing but Worry.

Age is livid with pain,
Since the match lasts so long,
And says in his traitor's language,
That He will from now on
Mark the chases to do me harm;
But I do not care, I defy him.
I fear nothing but Worry.

If Good Fortune remains true to me,
I am not afraid in any way
Of the whole opposing team.
I fear nothing but Worry.)

Charles's poem is a ballad, a poetic form the poet chose with deliberation. The Poetic I and his two teammates, Good Fortune and Hope, have taken up Age's challenge, and the match is played in complete accordance with the conventions of medieval tennis. Naturally, stakes are involved, and playing without one (which, as late as the end of the seventeenth century used to be announced by a call *pour néant*, 'for nothing')[3] is ruled out from the start: 'sur bon gage Nous jouons, non pas pour neant'. In this match the stake is the highest imaginable: life itself. According to contemporary tennis rules, the chases are contested when forty-five points have been accumulated, and in such a situation the long chase – on the allegorical plane, a long life – is the thing most sought after. Worry, however, in the other half of the court, by stopping the ball soon is shortening the chase of life mercilessly. Age is another evil antagonist who does not even shrink back from unfair practices by measuring the chases of life to his own advantage.[4] The worst enemy, however, is Worry. Not only are his retrieving qualities simply unfailing ('Trop seurement est rachassant'), the fact that the poet employed the ballad-typical refrain to introduce him again and again suggests that he will be the Poetic I's discomfiture at last.

That the game of life could last longer than sixty 'points' is shown by a conversation recorded by Georges Chastellain, chronicler of the Dukes of Burgundy.[5] On 1 August 1456, one day after his sixtieth birthday, Philip the Good, the Duke of Burgundy, was having lunch with his nephew, the Duke of Cleves, when, perhaps alluding to Charles's poem, he is said to have remarked: 'I have played tennis. I've lost a game which I shall "write off". I lost it yesterday, but today I will begin a new game.' The Duke of Cleves, not exactly a connoisseur of contemporary poetry, did not understand a word, and that is why Philip, turning to his chronicler, went on to explain. He hoped, he said, that he might be saved by the Almighty from having to play this new game to the very end. For, as he knew well, man at this age became altogether decrepit and a nuisance to himself as well as to others. He wished to live for only as long as Nature granted him to be of some use and to serve his people.

THÉOPHILE DE VIAU

The counting system of tennis in particular often seems to have tickled the poets' fancy, and sometimes a real good-for-nothing was among them. Théophile de Viau, for instance, despite his Christian name, was the very opposite of the pious Duke of Burgundy. To a publication titled *Parnasse satyrique* (it appeared in 1622 and contained much that normally defies publication),[6] he contributed a notable instance of number symbolism, to the delight of his readers, but very much to the dismay of the moral umpires of the time who disqualified him at once. A ban was imposed on him and, after a two years' sentence, he had to leave Paris altogether:[7]

> *Si vous la baisés comptés quinze*
> *Si vous touchés le tetin trente*
> *Si vous auées la motte prinse*
> *Quarante cinq lors se presente*
> *Mais si vous metés en la fente*
> *Ce de quoy la dame a mestier*
> *Notés bien ce que ie vous chante*
> *Vous gaignés le Jeu tout entier.*

> *(If you kiss her, count fifteen,*
> *If you touch the buds, thirty,*
> *If you capture the hill,*
> *Forty-five comes up.*
> *But if you enter the breach*
> *With what the lady needs,*
> *Remember well what I sing to you,*
> *You will win the game outright.)*

Although to many readers Théophile's piece of verse may seem rather unsavoury, it nevertheless testifies to the fact that in seventeenth-century France, in marked contrast to England, tennis players continued to be credited forty-five points rather than a mere forty.[8]

Guillaume de la Perrière

The allegorical approach is also a characteristic of emblematic poetry, a poetic genre especially popular in the sixteenth and seventeenth centuries. An emblematic poem typically consisted of a motto, a picture – the emblem – which illustrated the motto, and a poem in which the picture was given an allegorical interpretation. The inclusion of a picture emphasized the medieval conviction that even the material world, the world of things, and even so trivial a thing as a tennis court and the equipment needed for a match was fraught with meaning, and to unravel this was the poet's task.[9] The poet's message, in turn, was not conceived of as some clever aphorism, but as a fundamental truth. This will above all become evident from an emblematic poem by Francis Quarles where a deeply religious meaning is hidden in almost every detail of the game.

The first two poems are to be found in *Le Théâtre des Bons Engins*, an emblem book by Guillaume de la Perrière published by the Parisian printer Denis Janot in 1539. There are two woodcuts – perhaps the work of Jean Cousins – of which the first shows a tennis player armed with a short-handled racket and bending his knees down in an exemplary manner in order to play a forehand volley (**Figure 55**). He is turning his back to the rear wall of a *jeu carré* characterized by an exceptionally low and extremely wide opening immediately above the tiled floor. Especially noteworthy in this pictorial representation of sixteenth-century tennis is the rather voluminous ball sent (against the backdrop of a side gallery covered with a shingled roof) into the opposite court in a high arch and with a good deal of cut. The tennis balls used clearly belong to the type manufactured in contemporary Paris, the characteristic of which was a leather cover and a pattern of the seam which in a significant way deviated from the dumbbell-shaped one of modern tennis balls.[10] The latter seems to have been inspired by English cricket balls of which the first exhibiting this pattern appears to be that on a portrait painted by Daniel Gardner in 1778, and showing an English gentleman cricketer, Frederick Francis Barker.[11]

Guillaume's emblem seems to illustrate the first two lines of his poem (number V in his collection) which appear to function as the motto which, at least in this version of the poem,[12] appears to be missing:

> *Qui pour le bond delaisse la vollée,*
> *Ne fut iamais tenu ferme ioueur.*
> *Qui prent le mont & laisse la valée,*
> *Ne sera pas tenu pour bon coureur.*
> *C'est grand folye à laisser son honneur*
>
> *Pour vng abus, de promesse incertaine.*
> *De vouloir prendre vng vieil chat sans mateine,*
> *Ce n'est pas faict de saige entendement:*
> *Aussi folye, & gloire trop haultaine,*
> *Font tomber l'homme en maint encombrement.*

FIGURE 55   This is how the 16th-century tennis player played the volley.

(Whoever prefers the bounce to the volley
Has never been considered a good player.
Whoever takes the mountain route and ignores the
   valley,
Will never be considered a good runner.
It is great folly to lose one's honour

Due to wrong use, an uncertain promise.
Wanting to take an old cat without a tomcat
Is not a thing done with true insight:
Folly and too much glory
Both often impose a burden on man.)

In his poem, Guillaume has more sympathy for the more resolute player who prefers the volleying game. He has less time, it is true, and his is the more difficult task, but he knows what to expect. The player waiting for the ball to bounce is playing the riskier game, since in Renaissance courts the bounce was not infrequently untrue, and there was, in addition, the *tambour* against which the player had to be on his guard. In much the same way, the runner using the certain, albeit longer, valley route is much safer than the one trying the mountain route in the uncertain hope of a short cut. On the allegorical plane, wrong tactics in Renaissance tennis (*abus*) as well as in Renaissance track and field (*promesse incertaine*) are both the cause of Man's losing his honour.

The final couplet points to another allegorical interpretation of defensive play and foolish cross-country clambering over mountains: the one is pure folly, the other, in a literal sense, too high presumption, and Man gets himself into trouble by both.

Guillaume's second poem (number XLI in his collection) elaborates on a woodcut showing two tennis players facing each other grimly (**Figure 56**). Here the motto is contained in the first quatrain. It is the paraphrase of an old proverbial expression still in use in both Dutch and Frisian.[13] It has even survived in some German dialects of the Lower Rhine.[14] The Dutch version runs 'wie kaatst, moet de bal verwachten', and there is a nice engraving in a Frisian almanac of 1824 illustrating it.[15] In English it would be something like: he who serves must also be wary of the return, or, in other words, he who gives should also be prepared to take.

Si tu te metz à iouer à la paulme,
En te voulant pour passe temps esbastre:
Ne pense pas que ton compaignon chaulme:
Car de sa part l'esteuf uouldra rabatre.
Penser außi doit tout homme folastre,
Que si par ieu quelque broquart prononce,

Par ieu recoit la semblable response,
Ne pour cela se doit fort trauailler:
Car en bon poix on uend once pour once,
Pire ieu n'est que mocquer ou railler.

FIGURE 56   The proverbial expression 'Who strikes the ball must be on his guard against the return' is illustrated by these tennis players in Guillaume de la Perrière's emblem book (1539).

(Whenever you are about to play tennis,
In order to take pleasure in such pastime,
Do not think that your partner will be twiddling
   his thumbs,
For he will want to return the ball.
Every person with a bent for folly should remember
   that
When he jokingly utters some snide remark,
He might receive one back, by way of a joke.
Therefore he should not become annoyed,
For well-balanced [everything] is sold ounce for
   ounce.
There is no worse game than mocking or teasing.)

In this example, the server trying to make life difficult for his opponent is compared with somebody poking fun at somebody else.

HENRY PEACHAM

A motto extremely popular among poets was the Latin aphorism *concussus surgo*, 'cast to the ground, I rise again'. It is first instanced in the *Devises Heroïques* (1557) where it appears – above the emblem of an air-filled ball – as the *devise* of Admiral de Chabot.[16] In 1612, it was used by Henry Peacham in his *Minerva Britanna*:[17]

The tennis-ball, *when strucken to the ground,*
With Racket, or with gentle Schoole-boies hand,
With greater force, doth back againe rebound,
His fate, (though senceless) seeming to withstand:
Yea, at the instant of his forced fall,
With might redoubled, mountes the highest of all.

So when the Gods aboue, haue struck us low,
(For men as balls, within their handes are said,)
We chiefly then, should manly courage show,
And not for every trifle be afraid:
For when of Fortune, *most we stand in feare,*
Then Tyrant-like, *she most will domineere.*

It is interesting that in the first stanza, a distinction is made between the brand of tennis played by grown-up people and the one played by children. The former use a racket, whereas the latter strike the ball with their hands.[18] The ball smashed onto the ground, be it by man or boy, lends itself to allegorical interpretation: in much the same manner as the unfeeling tennis ball, man would do well to suffer the blows of the capricious gods as well as of Dame Fortune, and to exhibit most courage when their strokes are hardest. It is again interesting that, if we assume that the poet handled his imagery consistently, the racket swinging grown-ups of the first stanza should have been equated with the gods above, and that the machinations of Dame Fortune should have been likened to the doings of naughty little boys. In the emblem matched up with the poem, a hand emerges from the clouds and strikes a ball which, to make the meaning doubly clear, is hovering above the tiled floor of a tennis court. An English country house in the left-hand background provides a clue to the picture: the world is a tennis court on which the gods indulge in playing tennis, man being the ball.[19]

GEORGE WITHER

The motto *concussus surgo* received a much more elaborate treatment at the hands of the English poet George Wither. In his *A Collection of Emblemes* of 1635, he for one reworked the Latin dictum into an English couplet:[20]

> *When to suppresse us, Men intend,*
> *They make us higher to ascend.*

In the poem proper, the poet clearly had in mind a tennis match as he would often have seen it in his native England, played in a court surrounded by high walls, divided into two halves by means of a line and featuring all sorts of hazards. But the reader trying to discover the things described in the poem in the emblem illustrating it will be greatly surprised. Instead of being shown a tennis court, he sees a match of Dutch *kaatsen* in progress (**Figure 57**). At a time when the art of copper engraving was little developed in England, English emblematists often borrowed the copper-plates of their Dutch colleagues. In the case before us, George Wither had no qualms about buying second-hand an engraving by a member of the renowned engravers' dynasty van de Passe, presumably of Crispijn van de Passe (the Older),[21] which had previously been put to good use in Gabriel Rollenhagen's *Nucleus Emblematum Selectissimorum* (1611–1613).[22] Apparently, Wither was not aware of the fact that the same artist had also created a fully fledged tennis court with walls, roof and all which would, of course, have been much better suited for his poem:[23]

> *When we observe the* Ball, *how to and fro*
> *The* Gamesters *force it; we may ponder thus:*
> *That whil'st we live we shall be playd with so,*
> *And that the* World *will make her* Game *of us.*
> Adversities, *one while our hearts constraine*
> *To stoope, and knock the Pavemants of* Despaire;
> Hope, *like a Whirle-wind mounts us up againe,*
> *Till oft it lose us in the empty ayre.*
> *Sometimes, above the* Battlements *we looke;*
> *Sometimes, we quite below the* Line *are tost:*
> *Another-while, against the* Hazard *strooke,*

Then to suppresse us, Men intend,
They make us higher to ascend.

I L L V S T R .   X V I .   *Book.* I.

Hen we obferve the *Ball*, how to and fro
The *Gamefters* force it ; we may ponder thus :
That whil'ft we live we fhall be playd with fo,
And that the *World* will make her *Game* of us.

FIGURE 57   *Kaatsen* in the streets of a Dutch town (1635).

We, but a little want, of being lost.
Detraction, Envie, Mischief, *and* Despight,
One Partie make, and watchfully attend
To catch us when we rise to any Height;
Lest we above their hatred should ascend.
Good Fortune, Praises, Hope, *and* Industries,
Doe side-together, and make Play *to please us;*
But, when by them we thinke more high to rise,
More great they make our Fall; *and more disease*
    us.
Yea, they that seeke our Losse, *advance our* Gaine;
And to our Wishes, *bring us oft the nigher:*
For, we that else upon the Ground had laine,
Are, by their striking of us lifted higher.
When Balls *against the Stones are hardest throwne,*
Then highest up into the Aire they fly;
So, when men hurle us (with most fury) downe,
Wee hopefull are to be advanc'd thereby:
And, when they smite us quite unto the Ground,
Then, up to Heav'n, we trust, we shall rebound.

It becomes clear at once that George Wither, when he composed his version of the *concussus*-theme, tried to give more thought to detail, but the result of his preoccupations is a rather dull poem bedevilled by redundancy and an imagery both inadequate and contradictory. In contrast to Peacham, Wither does not put the blame for man's misfortunes on the gods, but rather on his fellow human beings. There are those, he says, who begrudge him his well-being, the vices personified Slander, Envy, Mischief and Spite, and those who appear to help him, Good Luck, Praise, Hope and Diligence, but who make him fall all the more deeply. There were, contrary to what Wither seems to have believed, hardly any four-a-side teams in the tennis of his day, nor did the situation occur when the ball was struck 'above the battlements', or into 'the empty ayre' so that it got lost, or, for that matter, rebounded 'up to Heav'n'. No tennis ball was in danger of getting lost when driven into a hazard, and that the tennis players active in Wither's time ever attempted a smash – 'when men hurle us (with most fury) downe', to use Wither's language – is equally a myth. How the imagery of a tennis court and a match could be used much more consistently is shown by Francis Quarles, in a poem to which we now turn.

FRANCIS QUARLES

In this poem from *Divine Fancies* of 1632, the microcosm of a tennis court serves as a simile for the macrocosm of the universe in which God and Satan battle for the human soul. A characteristic of the best-known English emblematist in general is his meticulousness. Literary critics may feel inclined to call it pedantry, but in the case of his tennis poem we accept Quarles' alleged weakness with gratitude. Quarles indeed singled out every detail of a contemporary tennis court in order to give it an allegorical interpretation. Nevertheless, it is somewhat unfortunate that for reasons unknown his poem lacks a pictorial representation of tennis, for which reason 'On a Tenis-court' has been called a 'naked emblematic poem'.[24]

> *Man is a* Tenniscourt: *His Flesh, the Wall:*
> *The Gamster's* God, *and* Sathan: *Th' heart's the*
>   Ball:
> *The higher and the lower* Hazzards *are*
> *Too bold* Presumption, *and too base* Despaire:
> *The* Rackets, *which our restlesse* Balls *make flye.*
> Adversity, *and sweet* Prosperity:
> *The Angels keepe the* Court, *and marke the place,*
> *Where the* Ball *fals, and chaulks out ev'ry* Chace:
> *The* Line's *a Civill life, we often crosse,*
> *Ore which, the* Ball *not flying, makes a* Losse:
> Detractors *are like* Standers-by, *that bett*
> *With Charitable men: Our* Life's *the Sett:*
> *Lord, in this* Conflict, *in these fierce* Assaults,
> *Laborious* Sathan *makes a world of* Faults;
> *Forgive them Lord, although he nere implore*
> *For favour: They'l be set upon our* score:
> *O, take the* Ball, *before it come to th' ground,*
> *For this base* Court *has many a* false Rebound:
> *Strike, and strike hard, but strike above the* Line:
> *Strike where thou please, so as the* Sett *be thine.*

Of the two allegorical principles of transforming abstract concepts into objects of the material world, and of turning objects of the material world into abstract concepts, Francis Quarles used both. *Presumption* and *despaire* become facilities of the tennis court such as higher or lower hazards, and rackets and the line transmute into *adversity, prosperity* and *civill life*. A special feature of Quarles' poetry is the way in which words are made to work on both the real *and* the allegorical level. The verb *crosse*, for example, refers to the tennis ball which crosses the line on the literal plane, and then to the transgression of the rules of social conduct by the human heart on the allegorical plane.

   Again on the literal plane, the ball drops into the court, and the Lord is implored not to let it bounce, but to play it on the volley: 'take the *Ball*, before it come to th' ground'. On the allegorical level, however, *Ground* refers to the grave, that little piece of earth in which humans find their last peace. Seen in this way, the Poetic I is now asking the Lord to take him unto Himself when his sands are running out. Finally, God is requested to win the *sett*, and here we have before us another ingenious example of Quarles' playing upon words. It is a pun on the two meanings of the word *set* which (as we have seen in the previous chapter) in seventeenth-century English referred to the stakes in a game, and to the set as well. Quarles availed himself of both. Of course, the Lord, as befitting a keen tennis player, should be intent on winning the set. At the same time, however, he will naturally want the prize. And since earlier in the poem it was said that the stakes were, in fact, nothing less than a human life, the Poetic I would be granted life eternal, if the Lord were to carry away the prize.

TENNIS ON THE STAGE

Tennis, as we have seen, had been a subject suitable enough for the medieval mystery play. The game also proved sufficiently attractive for the Renaissance stage,[25] although dramatists' reasons for using it were somewhat different from those of earlier poets. Whereas the latter strove to conquer the hearts of the faithless, they, by availing themselves of this popular motif, wanted to capture, faithless or not, their fellows' purses.

It was especially the fashion foibles of the time with which the wits of the stage tried to amuse and to attract the crowds. For the tennis historian, their dialogues are interesting mainly because they contain, couched in some flippant remark, many a detail of the game about which other sources are silent.

In the sixteenth and seventeenth centuries, tennis was, if we are to believe the comedy writers of the time, above all a game for gallants, pompous fops, upstarts and would-be greats. This becomes evident from the opening scene of *Eastward Ho* (1605), one of the best-known English Renaissance comedies and an early example of a 'co-production' involving three of the most renowned playwrights of the time, George Chapman, Ben Jonson and John Marston. In the play, the protagonists are Master Touchstone, a respectable goldsmith, and his two journeymen, Golding and Quicksilver, all of whom have been given telling names. The name Touchstone refers to a tool used to test the quality of precious metals; Golding is a hard-working and modest journeyman truly worth his weight in gold; but Quicksilver is a false and loud-mouthed rake.

When the curtain opens, Touchstone and Quicksilver enter the scene through different doors. The stage direction here is intended to show early in the play their different characters. Touchstone seems to be dressed in his modest craftsman's outfit. By contrast, Quicksilver parades hat, coat and 'pumps', the shoes worn by dancers, fencers, acrobats – and tennis players! The manner in which his journeyman has dressed up warns the wary Touchstone that the quicksilver in his employ has once again left the straight and narrow. Consequently, he carries out, as befitting his name, a thorough test: by frisking the young man from top to toe. He lifts Quicksilver's cape, and lo and behold, he finds, sticking out of his servant's belt like a sore thumb, a sword pommel and – at a time when the tennis bag was as yet unknown – a tennis racket. 'Ruffin's Hall! Sword, pumps, here's a racket indeed!',[26] good old Touchstone exclaims. Here 'Ruffin's Hall!' refers to an ill-reputed place in West Smithfield, the favourite haunt of duellists and ruffians, and the fact that Touchstone let slip the name meant that Quicksilver was heading for it in order to gamble away his money in a tennis match, and later perhaps to regain its possession by some nice little sword-play. Later on, Touchstone holds out to Quicksilver the virtually shining example of Golding: 'But does he pump it, or racket it?'[27] To this remarkable example of how in the language of the time a noun could be used as a verb the obvious answer is: certainly not, but, as might have been expected, Touchstone's well-meaning efforts are all in vain, and Quicksilver's life takes a course which a life spent in tennis sneakers inevitably must: *Jailward Ho!*

Tennis shoes are also assigned a leading part in Ben Jonson's comedy *Epicoene, or The Silent Woman* (1609–1610). The play is about the old bachelor Morose, who has a neurotic aversion to any kind of noise. Ridiculed because of it by his nephew, Sir Dauphine Eugenie, Morose is determined to disinherit him, and in order to do so he wants to be married and to beget offspring himself. His problem is to find a silent bride (hence the title of the play). Predictably, the silent woman in the end turns out to be the very opposite, an inveterate scold, but besides this, there are minor noises in Morose's household which are sure to amuse the audience. One of them is caused by a pair of creaking servant's boots made of brand-new leather. From Clerimont, a friend of Sir Dauphine's, we learn that they have very nearly led to the poor servant being given the boot, if the poor fellow had not decided to do his daily routine in tennis-court socks, slippers with a woollen sole: 'And this fellow waits on him, now, in tennis-court socks, or slippers sol'd with wooll'.[28] English tennis players, it seems, at the time of King James skated about majestically on tiled floors and on woollen soles.

Not unlike today, sporting prowess was above all exhibited in order to impress the fairer sex. Strangely enough, certain proof of tennis heroism was not the number of matches won, but the number of tennis shirts soaked with sweat in the process. In Ben Jonson's allegorical comedy *Cynthia's Revels* (1600), the playwright's target are the vices of the court. One of his victims is the courtier Hedon representing (as the name implies) the vice of lust. How philandering Hedon manages to win the ladies' favour is revealed by Mercury, the messenger of the gods. Sometimes he boasts of how many fiery horses he has ridden in the morning, or how the week before he vaulted wholly, or only half, over the pommel of his horse's saddle. At other times, however, over-confident in the power of his pomander (= 'an apple filled with amber, an aromatic mixture'), he tells the ladies how many shirts he has during the week soaked with sweat. Very wisely, Hedon is silent about a different number, that of how many dozen balls he had to pay for.[29] (It was the loser in a match who inevitably had to face the bill for the balls.)

Ben Jonson's reference to the sweat lost in Renaissance tennis courts may have inspired his compatriot Thomas Dekker who in *The Guls Horn-Booke* published in 1609 wrote a manual of how to make a fool of oneself. In it, the following piece of advice is given to the courtier: Pontificate on how this or that lady sent her coach for you and on how often, in the company of some important lordship, you have sweated on the tennis court. To have sweated together in 'France' (this was apparently an elegant expression for 'in the tennis club') is a great topic, and well received even when the aristocrat converses with the lowly husbandman. From the same source, the dandy might glean an important piece of information as to where to parade his stylish outfit. The recommended places are, in this order, St Paul's Cathedral,[30] the theatre and the tennis court. If that was not enough, and if an even greater number of admirers was desired, the *soirée* was the solution. Pick from among those attending a poorly dressed person, and (by discussing with him or her any topic you may think of) strut about in the main hall proudly and noisily.[31]

One year before Ben Jonson's courtier Hedon we find, in George Chapman's comedy *A Humorous Day's Mirth* (1599), his fellow Catalian who, because he had given his rival Besant fifteen, has been sweating his guts out. Nevertheless, the idea of taking a shower would not have occurred to him. However, he did use a *course napkin*, a rough towel, and he also treated himself to what seems to have been the Elizabethan tennis drink *par excellence*, a beverage composed of three parts of water and one part of wine from the Canary Islands.[32]

During the 1984 US Championships in Flushing Meadow – rather unsuccessful ones by his standards – Ivan Lendl is said to have remarked: 'I keep swearing until I hit the ball properly again.' A comment such as this may be considered further proof of the excesses of modern competitive sport, but it is hardly as modern as might be thought. This appears from one of the highlights of John Webster's play *The White Devil* (1609, published 1612). Here the scene is set in Italy, a country which was, even in those early days, firmly in the clutches of the Mafia, if we are to judge from the plans of Francisco, Lodovico, Antonelli and Gasparo, conspirators determined to murder Brachiano, the adulterous Duke of Florence. The spokesman of this foursome is Lodovico, a brilliant preparer of poisons, who has been racking his brains how best to administer his stuff to the prospective victim. Prayer book, rosary, saddle pommel and hand mirror are one by one rejected as carriers. But then Lodovico's criminal eyes light up in triumph:[33]

> *Or th'handle of his racket – o that, that!*
> *That while he had bin bandying at Tennis,*
> *He might have sworn himselfe to hell, and strooke*
> *His soule into the hazzard! O my lord!*
> *I would have our plot be ingenious,*
> *And have it hereafter recorded for example*
> *Rather than borrow example.*

In Mediterranean tennis arenas above all, blasphemous swearing was a sure bet. Even today, the unwary player is warned against it in Spain, where inscriptions on the wall such as 'proibido blasfemar', 'swearing prohibited', are proof that cursing and swearing continued despite them.[34] If Lodovico managed to transport Brachiano into the hereafter by means of a poisoned racket handle, he could be sure that the Duke would die with an oath on his lips, to the ruin (after that of his body) also of his soul. Webster employed another tennis metaphor again later, in the second of his major works, *The Tragedy of the Duchesse of Malfy*, where it aptly sums up a series of reckless murders and atrocities in the fifth act. 'We are meerely the Starres tennys-balls (strooke, and banded Which way please them)',[35] says Bosola, a former galley-slave in the pay of the Duke of Calabria, to the dying Antonio whom he had mistaken for the criminal Cardinal and whom he had to inform, after dealing him the fatal blow, that his beloved wife and two children have also been murdered.

We will conclude this chapter with a somewhat different example, demonstrating that the courts of the dramatic guild could at times be as slippery as those of the poets. In Henry Porter's comedy *The Pleasant Historie of the Two Angrie Women of Abington* (1599), Philip, the son, tries to explain to his father how two estranged wives might be reconciled. Of all things, the one that would do the trick would be, Philip says, a match. When the father fails to understand (because of the *double entendre* of *match*, meaning both 'marriage' and 'sporting competition'), the son explains:[36]

> *How a match? Ile warrant ye a match.*
> *My sister's faire, Frank Goursie he is rich,*
> *His dowrie too will be sufficient,*
> *Franke's young, and youth is apt to loue,*
> *And by my troth my sisters maiden head*
> *Stands like a game at tennis, if the ball*
> *Hit into the hole or hazard, fare well all.*

Where the French rhymester Théophile de Viau exploited the curious counting system of the game systematically, Henry Porter, for a similar effect, cleverly used the tennis court metaphor.

FIVE

Tennis in the German ballhouse

◇

When everywhere in Europe the tennis race began, the Germans showed little interest. They may have produced the first chronicler of the game, Caesarius of Heisterbach, but one looks in vain for somebody actually practising it. Neither is there among their poets a Charles d'Orléans. Their courtly poet, Walther von der Vogelweide, may be widely known for his jubilant outcry of '*tandaradei!*' This, however, in marked contrast to the Frenchmen's *tenez!*, did not signal the beginning of a rally, but the end of a *rendez-vous*.

There is no reference to any game at ball prior to the fourteenth century. Then we hear of a match said to have taken place in Stuttgart in which a certain Hans Bernhard Rugger was trounced by a certain Rudolf Werner of Weissenburg. Because Rugger's sweetheart, the beautiful Hilde Loselin, had thrown herself at the victor's head afterwards, Rugger had, on St Servace's Day (13 May) 1339, stabbed the unfortunate Weissenburg. Although the heinous crime, reported in a local chronicle, may be a fact, there is no evidence that the game mentioned here was indeed tennis.[1] At a time when tennis balls were struck around almost everywhere in Europe, the Germans, at best, indulged in playing a rather rustic game of their own invention and one apparently better suited to their Teutonic physique: the game of skittles. Tennis, the favourite pastime of the nimble French, was for a long time clearly not for them.

The first to take to playing tennis was a tribe partaking least of the Germans' somewhat stolid nature: the merry Rhinelanders. In 1475, Gerhard van der Schueren, Chancellor of the Dukes of Cleves and imperial notary from Xanten, compiled a dictionary entitled *Teuthonista of Duytschlender*. It has come down to us in an edition printed in Cologne in 1477. The dictionary has the entries *catze*, *meta* (the Latin word for the chase), *catzen mit den bal* (to play at ball), *catzenteyker*, *metarius* (marker of the chases), and *catzer*, *pilator* (tennis or ball player). These expressions indicate that on the Lower Rhine tennis was at least not completely unknown.[2] However, in those days the dialect of Cleves could easily pass for a variety of Dutch, and that is why it is doubtful whether Gerhard's dictionary should be considered an early reference to tennis in Germany at all.

A quarter of a century before the *Teuthonista*, in 1450, a friar from Cologne put the finishing touches to a book which can justly claim to be the first proof of the existence of tennis in this country. For this book, a translation into the Cologne dialect of the *Kaetspel Ghemoralizeert*, a somewhat awkward title was adopted: *Eyn suuerlich boich van bedudynge des kaetschens* ('A Weighty Book on the Meaning of Tennis'). Underneath its title, there is, in a different hand, the following *ex libris*: 'Ind yt zobehoirt den Cruitzbroederen bynnen Coelnen', 'and it belongs to the Crutched Friars in Cologne'.[3]

The Community of the Crutched Friars, also known as the Order of the Holy Cross, lived according to the Rule of St Augustine. In 1309, it had acquired property in Streitzeuggasse (Armourers' Alley), on which the friars soon built their monastery.[4] Today, the name of another alley, Kreuzgasse (Cross Alley), still testifies to its existence. In former times, the alley led past its very gates, and on an engraving by Mercator of 1571 a long roofed annexe to the stately church (the latter having been completed in 1399) can be seen facing Streitzeuggasse.[5] It is conceivable that the friars, in order to initiate a rally in the street tennis of the day, sent their balls onto this very roof.

On the title page of *Eyn suuerlich boich*, an explanation in Latin says what the book was written for. It is a moral exposition of the game of tennis by which all judges, members of the jury and others at the bar are instructed by way of an allegory how to administer the law and how to deal with lawsuits in general. This moral subject was the main reason why the brethren had it translated into their local dialect. Another reason was, of course, the fact that tennis (which had its roots in the medieval monastery) was their favourite pastime, and that moral instruction could be obtained by contemplating something very pleasant.

We do not know which of the Crutched Friars took the task of the translation upon himself. He may have been an expert on Flemish, but whether he knew enough about tennis is somewhat doubtful. According to him, the tennis players of Cologne at times arrived at the highly unusual score of 45:35, and this is explained in the following way: Sometimes it happens, the translator says, that only one chase is contended rather than two. Such is the case whenever one party has scored 45 and the other no more than 30 or, believe it or not, 35 points![6] The curious counting method in tennis must have caused problems even in Cologne.

The name given to the game in Cologne, namely *caetschen* or *kaetschen*, shows the same phonology as the type of tennis played one hundred years previously in the churchyard of the Flemish town of Oudenaarde, namely *cache*.[7] It therefore must have come from Flanders, and we may safely assume that it closely resembled the game which appeared on the miniature in Adélaïde's famous and fairly contemporary book of hours.

Some details of the book have been mentioned in the previous chapters whenever its Flemish predecessor was discussed, but a few others, most precious testimonies of the game in this country, are perhaps not altogether out of place here. As has been pointed out, tennis players in those early days hardly ever possessed a permanent court. Whenever they felt like playing a match, they first had to look for a suitable venue. The next thing to do was to look for 'servants' (German *diener*) who served two purposes. The first was to mark well and truly the chases (as it was bad manners to mark them unfairly, more to the advantage of one party than to that of the other).[8] The second purpose was to retrieve balls hit too far away, or having disappeared in a gutter, a cellar, a window,[9] or elsewhere and therefore not ready for use.[10] These servants also had to carry lots of balls with them. If one ball was not ready for play, they had to provide another to play with while its fellow was being sought; for the players must not be without one, nor wait for the unplayable ball.[11] The institution of the ballboy, it seems, was thus clearly established by the middle of the fifteenth century, even in the somewhat primitive tennis played in the provinces.

If in the previous chapter, we discussed examples from late medieval and Renaissance poetry in which the allegorical method was applied, the Rhenish version of the *Kaetspel* offers many examples of the same method in a work of prose. As we have heard, medieval tennis players, before starting a match, had to agree on how much money they would bet on their game. This done, their wager, cash money or some pledge, was deposited openly. The deposit served as a security and made it impossible for the loser to take to his heels after the match without having paid anything.[12]

Even such a rather down-to-earth procedure lent itself to some superb allegorization. Allegorically speaking, the wager represented the human soul. This becomes clear, to anybody with enough imagination and understanding, from an *exemplum* found in the famous *Legenda Aurea* which reported a miracle which had taken place in the French city of Langres. There, a heathen prince from days of yore had been discovered in a coffin. He had ruled his country with exceptional justice, but was not allowed to die in peace, because even the souls of the just (although they cannot be condemned) cannot be redeemed without baptism. The soul of the poor Prince had, in other words, been a sort of wager in a cosmic tennis match between God and Satan. After being baptized at last by the bishop of Langres, the soul's body crumbled into ashes, definitive proof that its case had at last been decided in God's favour. It looks as if this exemplum from the Rhenish *Kaetspel* was an early version of Francis Quarles' famous emblematic poem.

THE SECOND PHASE: TENNIS IMPORTED FROM THE NETHERLANDS

After this early instance of tennis in the Rhineland, a second phase saw the advent of the commercially run tennis court in the German north where the game was introduced from the Low Countries. Evidence for this development can be found in the so-called *Bursprake* books,[13] the minutes of town-council sessions in which citizens (Low German *bur*) involved in some litigation were allowed to have their say.

In the Hanseatic town of Lübeck, for instance, a certain Hans Mülich had in the yard of his house put up a 'Katzenspiel' in 1483 which was a real grievance to a distinguished neighbour of his, Heinrich Brömse, an alderman who was to become mayor later on, a 'vir grandis, doctus et eloquens'. Brömse was eventually persuaded to tolerate playing on his neighbour's premises until St Martin's Day of the same year, 'if illness did not befall his house', but he would not allow matches to be played thereafter without a special permit by either himself or future owners of his house.[14]

The existence of another commercial court in the town of Jever is attested by the death of a certain junker Christopher who breathed his last in 1517 after a strenuous match and a drinking bout following it.[15] Then Cologne seems to be again in the vanguard of the tennis movement, although whether one should call this a merit is a matter of some doubt. On 6 August 1562, Antony Hersbach, Clerk of the City Council, faithfully recorded a lawsuit which had arisen from a complaint filed with the local authorities about a tennis court in St Gereon Street:[16]

> After there have been many complaints about the tennis court in St Gereon Street next to Nazareth Convent because the place is notorious for the many blasphemies committed there as well as for all sorts of scandalous writings said to be thrown over the wall into the convent by which persons in holy orders are greatly annoyed, [Nicolas of] Mors, [Euerhart] Suderman and the two City Gaolers have received orders to inquire into the matter and also to visit the place and to report on it without delay.

That medieval tennis players were not altogether innocent of swearing we have heard in previous chapters. To this bad habit, the players of Cologne seem to have added a new facet by committing their filthy language to writing. Goodness knows what those 'fly-leaves' contained which kept sailing from the tennis court onto the premises of the pious nuns of Nazareth Convent.[17] Because of the atrocity of the crime, immediate action was taken. The City Gaolers investigated the matter and, more quickly than even the most callous of delinquents would have thought possible, submitted their report. In the very same month of August, the tennis players of Cologne were, so to speak, without a roof over their heads, albeit not in a literal sense. The very nature of their crime makes it clear that the court in St Gereon Street, not unlike the one possessed by King David in sixteenth-century Flemish paintings, was without a roof, for if it had had one, its customers would have been unable to keep their utterly depraved correspondence aloft. At any rate, on 14 August 1562, Antony Hersbach, the town clerk, was able to put an end to the scandalous affair when, under the rubric 'Tennis Court Abolished', he wrote:[18]

> Milords Liskirchen, Treasurer, Clas of Moers, Everhart Suderman and the two Gaolers have reported on how Their Graces [literally: *Their Charities*, polite form of address corresponding to *Vestra Caritas* in Latin writings], as a consequence of the many complaints by the Father [Confessor] of Nazareth, inspected the place, and how they encountered much despicable filth there which is an utter vexation to the spiritual children, and greatly obnoxious to others. That is why it was finally agreed that the Gaolers should soon notify and severely enjoin Landskron to demolish the tennis court on the next workday, to wit on Monday before noon. If no action is taken, the bailiffs together with milords' workmen shall go there and break down and destroy the tennis

court. In addition, the inmates will be forbidden to hold any tennis matches there on the two holidays, tomorrow and the day after tomorrow, upon pain of imprisonment in the tower.

The Landskrons were a family of patricians from Cologne, and a black sheep of this honourable clan was perhaps the owner of the sporting facility, which may not have enjoyed the best of reputations, but certainly was a prospering enterprise. Its name *kaetsbane* was now, after the lapse of one century, clearly indicative of the Dutch provenance of the institution, and the same applies to the courts in Lübeck and Jever mentioned earlier in this chapter. This testifies to the cultural pre-eminence of the northern Low Countries in the sixteenth century which made itself felt not only in France and England, but also in the Rhineland.[19]

The game as played in the *kaetsbane* of Cologne must have strongly resembled the one described by Pieter van Afferden in his Latin–Dutch tennis dialogue.[20] The players wielded a *raket*, the balls travelled to and fro between three-a-side teams and across a line (called *touwe* or *coorde*). But it had no longer to be stopped after its second bounce. Whereas Pieter still envisaged the stopping action (his rendering of Latin *sistere, retinere pilam* is, correctly, *houden*, 'to hold'), a glaring mistranslation has won the day in a German translation which appeared in Cologne in 1575. Here, '*sistere, retinere pilam*' has become 'Den ball kheren', 'to return the ball',[21] and this blunder proves that the old chase rule had fallen into disuse completely, and that tennis players of Cologne had long begun to direct their attention to the second impact of the ball only.

Despite this mistake, the High German version of the *Tyrocinium* is a precious early document of German tennis history. It contains the first references in the German language to a challenge match ('Jemanden furderen/außheischen mit dem ball zu spielen') and the racket (spelt *ranckett*),[22] and a verb for the service, *außschlahn* (= *ausschlagen*, 'to strike out') which latter reminds us of the important distinction in medieval tennis of an inside and an outside team. The terms *khatzen*, 'to play tennis',[23] and *katzbahn*, 'tennis court', together with the almost complete absence of French ones, again reveal that the teachers of the unruly players from St Gereon Street were Dutchmen. In the second half of the sixteenth century Dutch influence began to give way to French tennis customs, even in the Rhineland. In 1595, a ten-year monopoly for a new commercial tennis court near St Apostles was granted to a certain Nicolas Steinweg.[24] In the minutes of the City Council relating to the fact, the term 'katzban' is glossed, by a different hand, 'oder ballhauß' ('or ballhouse'). This latter is a term characteristic of the German south, where the game had in the meanwhile been introduced from France. Here, the term *ballhaus* is conclusive evidence that playing tennis the French way had also become fashionable in Cologne.[25] Before turning to the south, however, mention might be made of another two attempts to establish tennis in the north, although both turned out to be abortive.

In 1556, the *Bursprake* book of the city of Hamburg recorded the fact that the city council had heard rumours about some highly suspicious goings-on outside the city wall. There, a rather strange game ('ein ungwontlich speel') called *katzespeel* was being installed in the yards of farmsteads ('up den hoeven'). And because this game, in the opinion of the authorities, threatened to be the ruin of the city's young, the council insisted on the game's being completely abolished and forbidden. Those who still dared indulging in it were to be fined ten Joachimsthaler, the sixteenth-century German currency and an early forerunner of the modern dollar, as often as they were caught racket-handed![26]

When in 1567 citizens again came forward with the idea of putting up tennis facilities in their houses, the council remained adamant. Those who still wanted to have tennis courts built in the backyards of their houses were liable to having them broken down by municipal housebreakers, and to being fined the tidy sum of five hundred 'dalers'.[27] It is interesting, in view of this flat refusal of any ball-games, that Hamburg should in the nineteenth-century have become the cradle of German lawn tennis.

THE BALLHOUSE IN SOUTHERN GERMANY

The Dutch game which had set its foot in the north must be distinguished from that played in the ballhouse. The ballhouse derived its name, not from swinging fancy dress balls held in it, but from the balls set flying there by the swing of the racket. The ballhouse was a predominantly southern institution imported from France. It owed its success mainly to Huguenots who, at a time when the *jeu de la paume* was at its peak, had turned their backs on their native country. These Huguenots became this country's first tennis instructors called *ballenmeister* ('master of balls', a singular as well as a plural noun) as well as, in fact, its fencing-, dancing- and riding-masters. Their task was to wean the Germans away from their unsophisticated skittle matches, and to break them into the routine of the capricious white ball.

The first examples of the southern courts are to be found (if we consider Austria as part of the Holy Roman Empire) in Vienna where the Emperor Ferdinand I had built one as early as 1525.[28] It was built beside his castle, on a site which later became known as 'Ballhausplatz', and when it fell prey to a fire in the first year of its existence, a second was put up almost immediately, in 1526, on Michaelerplatz, only a few yards from the first.[29] When the castle was refurbished between 1536 and 1552, a very handsome new tennis court was provided, number three, again on Michaelerplatz and opposite the second.[30] The keepers of the imperial tennis court, or professionals in the language of today, seem to have been Italians rather than Frenchmen, which may mean that tennis found its way into Austria (and possibly also into Bohemia where an imperial court was erected in Prague as early as 1568)[31] from Italy. The first Viennese tennis court keeper to be known by name was a certain Giovani Taberino who, in 1583, wanted his contract to pass down to his son Maximilian after his death, for the period of six years. His petition was granted by Emperor Rudolf II.[32] The first Frenchman to be employed was a certain Urban Pantin in 1651. He was paid 300 florins annually.[33] Speaking of Austria, mention may at last be made of the ballhouse in Salzburg designed for archbishop Paris Count Lodron and his family by the famous court architect Santino Saleri.[34] It may have been completed as early as the 1620s, although the proof of its existence comes from a view of Salzburg executed by Philipp Harpff in 1643. In the same year, the name of a princely court keeper, a certain Bartholomä Harrath, then 27 years old, appears in a local document. He had a predecessor about whose identity nothing is known, although one might speculate about whether he was, like the architect of the building, an Italian.

The first courts on German territory were in Augsburg, Frankfurt, Nuremberg, Halle, and Heidelberg. From the second half of the 16th century until shortly after the turn of the century, quite a few were added to the list, e.g. in Munich, Kassel, Tübingen, Ingolstadt, Strasbourg (priding herself on two),[35] Ziegenhain, Basle, Marburg, Darmstadt, Butzbach, Giessen and Heidelberg which latter outstripped the others with a total of three.[36] The ballhouse in Augsburg was put up, according to the City's oldest printed Chronicle of 1595,[37] in the month of April 1548 on the occasion of the Diet convening there after the Emperor Charles V's victory over the Protestants at Mühlberg which put an end to the Schmalkaldic War. It was built for the entertainment of the Spaniards and Charles's courtiers, but especially for the Bishop of Arras that he might, by watching the game, enjoy himself and dispel melancholy. Unfortunately, the ballhouse collapsed shortly after its completion, on the last day of March, killing three people in the process,[38] after which Master Bernhart Zwitzel who had been commissioned to build it was enjoined, according to the minutes of the Town Council under the date of 1 May 1548, to restore it at his own cost.[39] Having received a more solid foundation, the ballhouse (which was located 'at St Anna's Church close to the Library'), is said to have served its purpose well for many years. About the Heidelberg courts not much is known except that one of them, presumably the 'old ballhouse' near the dungeon Seltenleer ('Seldom Empty'!),[40] prevented John Casimir Count Palatine of Zweibrücken from delivering, in his capacity as Rector of the University, his rector's address on 21 January 1606, and from enjoying a banquet given in his honour afterwards: a tennis ball which had hit him in the eye the day before made it impossible.[41] A 'new ballhouse' was put up in 1618, in connection with the exuberant Palace Garden ('Hortus Palatinus') with which the Elector Frederick V had commissioned the French architect Salomon de Caus when he married Elizabeth, the daughter of King James I of England (**Figure 58**).[42] Frederick had become acquainted with de Caus in England, and it is perhaps due to this 'English connection' that his new ballhouse should have so closely resembled the royal tennis court at Hampton Court said to have been rebuilt on the foundations of the old one by Charles I in 1625.[43]

The dimensions of the Ingolstadt ballhouse, put up in 1593/4 for the entertainment and suitable exercise of the students ('zur Unterhaltung und zweckmäßigen Leibesübung'), must have been very impressive. So impressive, in fact, that Gustavus Adolphus, the Swedish king, at one time expressed the wish of playing there with his officers. The citizens of Ingolstadt, however, were rather unsympathetic and refused to surrender to the Swedish army.[44]

Although the ballhouse in Tübingen was especially devised for students, the ballhouses of the south owed their existence mainly to the desire of German rulers

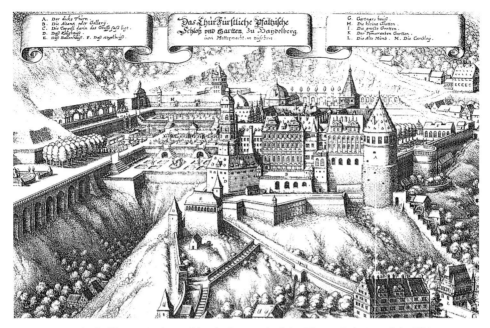

FIGURE 58   The ballhouse (indicated by the letter E) of the Elector Palatine of the Rhine, Frederick V, later and for a short spell (1619–1620) King of Bohemia, in Heidelberg. Frederick's English connections (he had married Elizabeth, James I's daughter, in 1613) may be the reason why it so closely resembled the court at Hampton Court.

to emulate, and possibly to outdo, the trendsetters of the time, their cousins in France. These local potentates were next emulated by the bourgeoisie. This led to the erection of ballhouses in towns and cities as well. The ballhouse of Basle, for instance, was built at the instigation of the mayor's wife.[45]

Simple folk had neither the time nor the money to indulge in the ball-hitting pastime. Popular varieties of tennis such as *kaatsen* never prospered in Germany, and that is why the depiction of a game played in the open and resembling tennis by the so-called Petrarch Master is very difficult to explain (**Figure 59**).[46] Generally speaking, the ballhouses of the south outnumbered those in the north by far. Apart from those mentioned earlier from Lübeck, Jever and Cologne (1595) we only know of two others in Oldenburg and Bückeburg.[47]

TENNIS, A FAVOURITE PASTIME OF GERMAN STUDENTS

An institution unique to Germany was the so-called Knights' Academy (*Ritterakademie*). Established by German rulers from the sixteenth century onwards, it served the purpose of training the future courtier after the model of the French *galant homme*. There had been an early forerunner of it in the city of Mantua, the 'Casa Gioconda', of which Vittorino da Feltre (1378–1446) had been appointed headmaster by the house of Gonzaga.[48] As a remarkable novelty, the school had

FIGURE 59 A *kaats* match illustrating a discussion in Petrarch's *De remediis utriusque fortunae* on whether walking or playing at ball is the healthier exercise. Aristotle and two of his pupils (upper left hand corner) are shown as advocates of the former; Dionysius of Syracuse (with sword and turban), Augustus, Scaevola (with lawyer's beret) and Mark Antony the latter.

introduced to its curriculum physical education.[49] This was to become a feature characteristic of German Knights' Academies as well.

All German Knights' Academies, the majority of which were founded after the Thirty Years' War, were modelled after that of Tübingen, the 'Collegium Illustre'. Several abortive attempts, the earliest of which went back to the year 1559,[50] had been made to build it. Then, in 1588, Duke Lewis erected a four-winged building on the premises of a dismantled monastery of the order of St Francis to which a ballhouse was annexed on the site of the former municipal arsenal.[51] The completion of the complex was celebrated on 27 November 1592,[52] and on 25 April 1594 the new college was put into operation under Lewis's successor, Duke Frederick.

Above the front porch of the stately Renaissance building, an inscription had been mounted at Lewis's behest by which the Duke wanted to make known to his subjects that his college also accepted students who were not the sons of noblemen: 'Hie sollin studiern zu jederzeit, Herrn von Adel und ander Leut', it read.[53] (Here shall study at all times, noblemen and other people.) Only one year later, under Lewis's successor, the off-spring of ordinary people were with a sneer locked out, and the new statutes, passed in 1596, gave sanction to this act of despotism. Henceforth, only princes and their equals, counts, lords and noblemen ('Fürsten und Fürstenmessige, Graven, Herrn und Adels Persohnen') were admitted.[54]

The curriculum of the Knights' Academy provided for scholarly disciplines such as mathematics, history, languages and political sciences, but the study of these seems to have been optional whereas for the future courtier the so-called *exercitia* were compulsory. From the statutes issued by Duke John Frederick of Württemberg for his academy in Tübingen in 1609 we learn what these exercises looked like.[55] In order that within our ducal college young scholars of noble birth may be furthered, it said, and be given the opportunity of training themselves in knightly and courtly exercises such as riding, fencing, playing at ball, and dancing besides the customary rifle and crossbow shooting, riding, fencing, ball and dancing masters have been agreed upon and appointed. Play at ball thus had a place among the collegians' exercises, and a ball master had to be employed by the local sovereign accordingly.[56]

Duke Albrecht of Saxe-Coburg who received his education at the Collegium together with his brother Ernest from 1666 to 1668, has left an accurate account of the institution, its tutors and the daily routine of its aristocratic clientele.[57] In Albrecht's days, three professors and three instructors in charge of the knightly exercises were in the Duke's pay. Whereas the professors taught politics and history, feudal and civil law and the French and Italian languages, the instructors had to divide among themselves the following tasks: that of a horse trainer (or breaker-in of the ducal mounts), a fencing master (who also had to direct the vaulting, flag-waving and other military exercises), and a dancing and ballmaster. This meant that the dancing demonstrator and tennis tutor were the same person.

What were, we may ask, the Duke's expenditures for someone who could handsomely demonstrate the pirouette, and competently teach the long chase? He was paid: '162 fl. [florins = guilders] cash, 1 bushel of rye, 6 bushel of grain and two pails of wine in kind'. In his capacity as ballmaster he was entitled to an extra of 1 bushel of rye and 4 bushel of grain. In addition, the statutes stipulated the following: 'The inmates of the college have free exercises [which meant that tennis lessons were free of charge, too], and shall give to the masters of the exercise only a present of their own choice every year or on their leave.' All others had to pay a tuition fee for tennis amounting to one and a half reichstaler for a month. It is interesting to compare this with the annual payments to the remainder of the college staff. The highest official, the Oberhofmeister, received 200 guilders, the professors occupying the history and law chairs 150 each, the language teacher, 'a Frenchman of noble birth', 234, the riding master 100, the fencing master 85, the combined dancing and ballmaster – as has been said – 162. It looks as if, apart from being an Oberhofmeister, administering language lessons and tennis tactics were the most profitable teaching jobs.

The Duke's expenditures for his entire staff ran into 10,860 guilders per annum, the students' fees not included. Little wonder, therefore, that to support his Knights' Academy the revenues of the confiscated monastery of Einsiedel had to be drawn upon. The result of this was quite amusing as the ducal tennis instructor (and indeed the Oberhofmeister, the professors and all the inmates of the college), had to do their jobs in long violet-blue coats with blue lapels, without sleeves, and with long wings dangling down from behind the shoulders. These clothes were a reminder of the monks, who had worn a similar outfit, and were, in fact, the Duke's only tribute to the former owners.[58]

There is a ducal curriculum of 1596 which specified the following:[59] 'Wednesday, from 4 to 5 o'clock: French dancing; after that, ball hitting, "crossbow shooting"; Thursday, from 4 to 5 o'clock: "riding, German and French dancing, the circle ball game"'. Whereas the circle ball game was a German game,[60] the term ball hitting (*Ballschlagen*) in contemporary usage referred to tennis. The description of the Collegium and the information given by the curriculum, if taken together, lead us to conclude that morning and early afternoon lectures served the exercise of the brains, whereas the late afternoon was devoted to the exercise of the body.[61]

Owing to the decline of the 'Collegium Illustre', its famous ballhouse eventually fell into disuse, too. In 1790, the decayed building was at the cost of 8000 guilders converted into an institution of the church. Then in 1817, it was demolished and a Catholic church was erected on the spot.[62]

Only the sons of peers were admitted to the Knights' Academies, and that is why the offspring of the wealthy bourgeoisie had to appeal to the universities (institutions open to them for the training of their brains as well as their bodies) for ballhouses in which to disport themselves. The universities not infrequently complied with their wishes, although deans and vice-chancellors often had to take drastic steps against carousing students whose cups had been filled by the ballmaster himself, the latter being seldom without a licence to provide alcohol. Geiler of Kaisersberg is one of the authors who fulminate against mylords the young scholars who neglect the study of the liberal arts in favour of the art of tennis: 'On the Foolish Freshman [*Studiernarr*] ... or they set themselves to work after lunch in honest disciplines such as ball hitting, fencing, dancing and leaping ... and there is not one found among a hundred who would attend the lectures ... [in the evening] they will again boast about what they have studied during the day, namely how much he has won at the ball play'.[63]

Today we have no reason to complain about German students' tennis mania. It is to their chronic addiction to the game that we owe, almost without exception, all the pictorial representations of the German ballhouse that have come down to us. As a rule, they are to be found in the so-called *Stammbuch*, in Latin contexts of the time referred to as *album amicorum*, 'friends' album'. The *Stammbuch* was a collection of sheets, each of which was the gift of a student attending a Knights' Academy or university to a fellow student before parting company. The sheets depicted scenes from the students' life and could be purchased in the form of existing prints. Alternatively, some specialist might be commissioned to paint them. Before it was made a farewell present, the print or commisioned work (the latter painted in body colours or in watercolours and made durable with white of egg or rubber) would be adorned with the donor's coat of arms. This, in turn, would be accompanied by some piece of verse the donor thought memorable (*memorabilia*).[64]

Because of its truly European reputation,[65] there is among the *Stammbuch* illustrations the amazing number of four depicting the Collegium Illustre in Tübingen: one exterior (**Figure 60**) and three interior views (**Figure 61** and **Plates 8 and 9**). In addition, there is another interior view from the workshop of Crispijn van de Passe (**Figure 62**). It is presumably the work of one of his pupils and may show the favourite haunt of the students of Leiden, one of the local ballhouses.[66] Apart from these pictures, there are only two outside the *Stammbuch* tradition. These are an engraving by Peter Aubry (**Figure 63**) and an exterior view of the Coburg covered court from the Thirty Years' War (**Figure 64**).

HIPPOLYTUS GUARINONIUS: GERMANY'S FIRST PHYSIOTHERAPIST

The first to leave a detailed account of the healthy effects of tennis is a doctor of medicine from Trento, Hippolytus Guarinonius. Before he was appointed resident doctor of the royal foundation in Hall in the Inn valley, a position which he was to keep all his life, he had been a student in Prague, where he attended the Latin school of the Jesuits, and in Padua, where he had earned a twofold doctor's degree 'medicina et artibus'.[67]

FIGURE 60   Exterior view of the Tübingen ballhouse. The curtains in the clerestory are quite a feature. A student of the Knights' Academy is, racket in hand, on his way either from or to the tennis court.

7. Hæc PŸTHI domus est qui primus in äere palmis | Quia pilas mélius palmis ↄue tractat Honoris
     dicitur inuentas exagitaſse pilas | Palmam uel uicto judice Victor habet

FIGURE 61   Interior of the Tübingen ballhouse. The marker placing a long-handled marking implement on the tiled floor is perhaps the same as the umpire referred to thus: 'This is the house of Pythus said to have been the first to invent the whirling round in the air of balls with the hands; whoever here treats the balls with his hands better, after the umpire has been convinced, the victor has the palm of honour.'

It was Guarinonius' conviction that exercise was the prerequisite for a healthy life, and he tried to impart it to his contemporaries by means of a mnemonic device, an acrostic which gave prominence to the word *gesondt*, 'healthy':[68]

> G ott
> E ssen und Trinken
> S chlaffen und Wachen
> O ede oder Ringerung des Überflusses
> N utzung oder Übung des Leibs
> D auglich Lufft
> T rost des Gemüths.
>
> (God
> Eating and Drinking
> Sleeping and Waking
> Fasting or Lessening of Superfluity
> Use or Exercise of the Body
> Healthy Air
> Consolation of the Mind.)

'Exercise of the body', to use Hippolytus' phrase, can be achieved best by playing games of ball, of which Guarinonius distinguished seven different kinds, in a book entitled *Die Grewel der Verwüstung Menschlichen Geschlechts* ('The Atrocities of the Ruin of the Human Race').[69] The book was published in Ingolstadt in 1610.

At the very beginning of his discussion of games, Hippolytus confirms a fact with which we are already familiar, namely that in the more important towns and places the rulers of Christianity maintained huge buildings for what he calls 'the chief game of all games'. Well provided with all things necessary and with ballmasters, these institutions served the purpose of training the young, but especially those of noble birth.[70]

Hippolytus knew well what he was talking about. He had himself been one of some two hundred freshmen who, at the Jesuits' convent in Prague, had not only received an education in all the scholarly disciplines, but also undergone a thorough training in the knightly exercises of fencing, riding, poetry writing and painting.[71] Naturally, those knightly exercises would also have included tennis. Guarinonius

Retia dum pilulam faciunt hinc inde volantem,   *Nam pila reſtaurat maleſano in corpore vires,*
Exercet iuuenis corpus, et ingenium .   *Torpet at aſsiduis obruta mens ſtudijs.*

FIGURE 62   Tennis court in Leiden (1612) by the Dutch engraver Crispijn de Passe. The verse underneath reads: 'The rackets, while they make the little ball fly to and fro, train the young man's body and spirit, for the ball restores energy to the body of poor health, whereas the brains overburdened with assiduous studies are paralysed.'

FIGURE 63   Picture of a 17th-century German tennis court which has come to light only recently. The caption reads: 'Playing at ball with a racket according to the art is such a thing as you would not completely deny to youth if only it is no misuse'.

mentions the ballhouse in Prague, and he also refers to the five ball courts which at the time existed in Padua.

The authority admired most by Hippolytus was the Greek physician Galenus[72] who considered the game at ball the best of all games. Unlike the hunt which necessitated much work and labour and high costs, for which reason it was the prerogative of the rich and powerful, in a word, the aristocracy, ball games were within the reach of many, even the poor, provided they could buy a ball, or make one themselves. In addition, it was possible to derive much pleasure from them, and to achieve a healthy fatigue, even though one had to do without a partner. If only the ball was hit high up, or against a wall, the ball would itself make a formidable opponent, rebounding behind and before the player, to the side of him and into every corner.[73]

Historically speaking, this is, to be sure, the first reference to the usefulness of a wall for practising shots.

The first game to claim Hippolytus' attention is that 'with the little ball, or racket game' (*Raggetenspiel*); to his mind, it is the most important of all. In the opinion of many people it was this game on which Galenus enlarged in his little book. In the variety practised among the ancients, players threw the ball to each other from a short distance. This variety was still played in the same manner in some places of Italy. Meanwhile, however, the highly distinguished racket game had become fashionable there, but also in France and in Germany. Who started it, and at what time people began to play it, is a question Hippolytus had never wanted to go into, because such was devoid of interest. However, this game was a magnificent workout for the whole individual and all his limbs:[74]

> Suffice it to say that such a game is the best exercise for the whole man and all his limbs, since the head and neck as well as the eyes have to bend and turn into all corners and directions, after which the feet have to quickly carry the body to and fro after the flying ball. There you run, jump and swing up the masonry and the wall, bend low, rise again, turn back and to the fore, and to all directions, and, lifting the racket, you agitate the hand, and turning it, the fingers in all manners this way and that way, since at one time

FIGURE 64   The princely ballhouse in Coburg in 1632. A peculiarity are the weather vanes in the shape of tennis players. In the left-hand corner of the yard, a game of closh (Flemish *beugelen*) is in progress. A covered shooting range, access to which is gained by three steps (on the left) adds a finishing touch to this fashionable Renaissance sporting complex.

you have to receive and hit the ball overhead, then besides your feet, a third time straight,
a fourth time with cut.

The idea that tennis constituted the most complete workout for the body, and was
therefore of the greatest therapeutic value, found favour with other writers as well.
G. Gumpelzhaimer, in his *Gymnasma de exercitiis academicorum* of 1621, went one
step further. He not only ascribed to it the capability to enhance the agility of the
body, to obviate obesity and to stimulate defecation, but also that of developing the
brains, especially those of young students.[75]

But let us return to Guarinonius. Apart from its healthy contortions for the benefit
of the whole body, tennis, to him, was capable of yielding a not inconsiderable profit
for the soul as well, provided it was not taken too seriously, and those indulging in it,
instead of using a racket, wielded a slipper, a shoe, a cup or some drinking vessel.[76]
As we shall see, this piece of advice was before long taken to heart by the players
who make an appearance in the tennis dialogue of Daniel Martin, the language teacher
from Strasbourg.

Generally speaking, tennis is a pastime beneficial to the younger generation,
especially the nobility, from the tender age of 14 until the age of 31. During this
period of life, when movements of the body are swiftest and most supple, the game
is a harmless one, provided it was not pursued with too much ambition, as when
high stakes are involved. These are the ruin of the whole game, and the reason why
it ceases to be fun altogether.[77]

Tennis is a game suited best for those who, while desirous of some exercise for the
benefit of their body, yet want it the soft way and without too much physical strain.
It is therefore the favourite pastime of young princes, rulers, and overlords.[78] In order
to prevent these high gentlemen from being laid most urgently low, 'ballhouses have
tiled floors so that the feet of the practitioner may have a firm grip'.[79] Tennis was thus
clearly a rather exclusive sport, a view which would certainly have been shared by a
contemporary such as Guarinonius's compatriot Johann Michael Weckherlin when
he had himself portrayed as a tennis player in his *Wappenbuch* (Book of Arms) (**Figure
65**).[80] Nevertheless, the game might well overcome social barriers at times. Hippolytus
at least knows of many a prince or lord in Italy as well as in Germany who had no
qualms at all about playing 'with a lowly, base fellow' if only he was 'well versed in
such a game'.

Despite such goodwill and condescension exhibited by those in power, there were,
according to Guarinonius, certain individuals who criticized their social betters'
healthy urge to play at ball in the ballhouse, and who, in the form of anonymous and
insidious diatribes, even had the effrontery to make their criticism public. Against
these impertinent slanderers the respectable doctor advanced some truly striking
arguments. To an especially 'dishonest, blasphemous writer of pasquinades',[81] he
offered nothing less than 'a blow with the racket on his foul snout'.[82] This individual
had dared to blacken the reputation of a highly virtuous lord who, however much
he may have indulged in the game of the ballhouse, had still only done so on the

advice of his physicians.[83] Should the afore-mentioned sovereign have practised guzzling and similar vices as valiantly as other princes and indeed the pasquinader himself? This ball would herewith be returned to his (the pasquinader's) court, and not secretly, but in public. The game of ball, however, was a public, honest, praiseworthy and noble game, and even an indispensable one for some people.[84]

Guarinonius concluded his chapter in praise of the ballhouse game with a rather sombre note, by relating, as a warning to all, the sad story of the son of a noble patrician from Padua. When he had been a student in that city, this fellow had so 'long and intensively exercised and grown so hot' ('lang vnd starck gevbt vnd erhitzt') that he, after having swallowed a large gulp of water, had swollen the next day, contracted dropsy and died. Obviously, he had shared the dire fate of Louis the Quarrelsome, the King of France.

Apart from Guarinonius's discussion, German seventeenth-century tennis is well illustrated by two pieces of writing composed for the benefit of those attending the Knights' Academies and for the promising offspring of the bourgeoisie. These were the *Parlement Nouveau* (1637) by Daniel Martin, a language teacher from Strasbourg, and the *Kurzer Unterricht deß lobwuerdigen … Exercitii deß Ballen–Spiels* (1680) by Georg Bender, a tennis professional from Nuremburg. We will first examine Daniel's language book, but before doing so cast a look at the tennis industry of Strasbourg which, owing to the meticulous work of August Herrmann,[85] a local historian, is the

FIGURE 65 Representatives of fashionable Renaissance sports – fencing, tennis, pallone, and equestrian sports – are united in one picture in Michael Weckherlin's *Wappenbuch* (Coat of Arms Book) (1603).

best researched of any place in this country. What we learn from this author about seventeenth-century tennis in Strasbourg is in many ways representative of Germany as a whole.

TENNIS IN STRASBOURG AT THE TURN OF THE SEVENTEENTH CENTURY

On 23 December 1601, the Great Council of the city of Strasbourg granted a petition presented by members of the nobility and the mayor (Ammeister). The Council consented to the erection of a ballhouse, on the condition that the local building commission and other people concerned with the project were notified. To these the decision was left 'where to put it up, what steps to take and what regulations to enforce'.[86]

This judicial act had been preceded by a long bureaucratic tug-of-war. As early as in May of the same year, John Klapp, citizen, had begged the Great Council to grant the following: that he, willing to earn a living for himself and his children and intent on building a ballhouse in the city, might be allowed to show the members of the building commission what he considered a suitable site for it, and that he would come to terms with them should they think of a different place. A shrewd entrepreneur, he had at the same time been able to produce two letters of recommendation which he had read aloud to the assembly: one by Margrave John George of Brandenburg, the bishop, the other by Duke Francis of Luneburg. Of his two supporters, the first was the Lord Administrator who had been promoted to the see of Strasbourg by Protestant electors.[87] Klapp's presentation had not failed to make an impression on the councillors. They had advised the building commission to inspect the place where John wanted to have his ballhouse put up.

The report of the building commission, dated 6 August, had proved far less enthusiastic, though, than Klapp had hoped:[88]

> The Building Commissioners and [Dreyer vom Pfenningthurn] have journeyed to the place and back, especially, because John Klapp, tumbler and dancer and ball-player, had presented a petition to the Council and the Twenty One for granting him leave to build a ballhouse. Having then been enjoined to look for an appropriate site, and intent on having it put up in the court of the cathedral chapter, he had frequently asked mylords to inspect it. That is why mylords went there, to this old court, formerly owned by Palsgrave Duke Reichert, which nearly collapses at every end, to find that the space would be sufficient for such [a ballhouse] if only the old long stable were pulled down … after inquiries, since it was to be in the chapter's court, and it might not be approved by the lords of the chapter, and mylords might be blamed, because in such a match between counts and lordships strife and manslaughter and the like may occur, he has therefore been denied such, some place elsewhere in the city of the commoners being more commendable. However, it has for the time being been decided to grant him permission, but still to bring his case before mylords since as a citizen the applicant could well be subjected to all kinds of restrictions.

The commissioners, obviously, had turned up their noses at the place and had mixed feelings about the feuds that would be stirred up amongst Klapp's noble tennis customers. Their recommendation to establish the ballhouse elsewhere, in the commoners' city, demonstrates their reluctance. On the other hand, they cannot make up their minds to flatly refuse Klapp's wishes then and there. His request will be granted for the time being, but still be brought before the Council where all kinds of conditions could be imposed on the 'tumbler, dancer and ball player'.

The Council, however, are made of a sterner stuff than the commissioners. On 24 August they make a decision, short and sweet: his plea is to be rejected.[89] Nevertheless, the cause was decided in Klapp's favour at last. Strasbourg's aristocrats had argued that a ballhouse should be put up and maintained on behalf of all students. There had been an academy in Strasbourg since 1566,[90] and if a ballhouse were erected for the students attending it, this would have added greatly to its reputation. The bishop had recommended Klapp's plans because the inhabitants of Strasbourg, threatened with inertia, might be prevented from it if there was an opportunity for exercise.[91] What eventually persuaded the Council to comply with Klapp's wishes, however, were hardly the aristocrats' idealistic arguments, but the prospect of money for the Common Purse, if only Klapp managed to whet the bishop's and his courtiers' appetite for tennis.

The Council's expectations were by no means unrealistic. The bishop was only 26, and in his sporting prime, and at first, he and other noble customers from his entourage turned Klapp's ballhouse into a thriving business indeed. Only one year later, in October 1602, John Klapp, 'ball player of Crutenaw', was granted the privilege of executing the carpentry of a roof on a new ballhouse.[92] Klapp's noble customers must have been so many in the first year, and their rackets must have become entangled so frequently in his truly singular establishment, that Klapp, in an early capitalist spirit, had quickly built a second one. These twin Strasbourg ballhouses were to be alluded to in years to come whenever in the Alsatian metropolis the subject of tennis came under discussion.

In the autumn of 1604 firing tennis balls at the hazards of Klapp's ballhouses must still have had a very strong appeal to Strasbourg's citizens. Klapp was rolling in money, or so at least the Council of the Twenty-One thought. So firmly convinced were they of the huge revenues Klapp collected from his tennis facilities that even the rather steep annual tax of a hundred guilders imposed on him was considered to be in need of upward revision.[93] One year earlier, however, an incident had occurred which eventually was to lead to Klapp's discomfiture. Bishop John resigned from his see after he had inherited an estate in Silesia. As a result of the treaty of Hagenau (on 22 November 1604), Cardinal Charles of Lorraine, the Bishop of Metz and candidate of the Catholic faction, was promoted to the vacancy.[94] Whether or not the Catholic indifference towards sport was at the root of Klapp's demise is not clear: in April 1605 he placed a petition before the Twenty-One in which he complained about his annual dues of a hundred guilders which he considered exorbitant.[95] Since the Lord Administrator and other princes were no longer there, he argued, he had ceased to make a profit altogether, and was compelled to eke out his income from private sources. He asked to waive the payment due or to reduce it in such a way as to enable him to subsist. Soon enough, in June, the Council pinned Klapp down to the annual sum of fifty guilders, payable to the Common Purse,[96] but another petition was presented by Klapp in August in which he remonstrated against the fifty guilders, the annual payment to the city for his tennis courts. He said that tennis had not been played at all, or but little, since mylord the Administrator had left the city, and that he was unable to pay.[97] The Council, however, proved adamant and declared that Klapp should either foot the bill of fifty guilders annually, or have his ballhouse closed.[98] Apparently, the ballmaster then tried to tap other resources in order to meet the magistrate's exactions. In April 1608, the Council of the Twenty-One was sitting on the following issue:[99]

> Item, that in the ballhouse not only a lot of money is being squandered by young people, but also, that the ball master has kept two beds for lords and esquires to 'cool down' in and to stay out there over night, and for women, even respectable women whom one would not suspect of anything like it, to be brought to them.

It is not known how the case was eventually decided. In 1612, Nicolas Pennier, a new ballmaster – poor Klapp seems in the meantime to have passed away – even had to be on his guard against being kicked out of Strasbourg altogether, on grounds that he was not a citizen, for which reason he should quit the city after the fair (either the St John's, Christmas or Summer Fair) and spend his money elsewhere. This, however, was impossible for him, Pennier protested, since he had put his whole money into the repair work for the ballhouse so that it might sustain him for a while and the Councillors might be paid their annual one hundred guilders. He had four children and had suffered hardship of many kinds. If he were compelled to leave the city he would be deprived of all his poor belongings.[100] The Council wanted to inquire 'who leased the house to him, how he deported himself there, whether he also sold wine and if prostitution was engaged in'.[101] In November, 1612, Klapp's widow apologized for then having no money at all; she was willing to pay by Christmas, and the next tax-payment would be made by the proprietor of the house.[102] Apparently, she was referring to the new owner of the ballhouses, a certain Salomon Maclet, of whom Pennier was either an employee, or a renter of his houses.[103]

After the ballhouses of Strasbourg had had to serve other purposes during the Thirty Years' War, tennis nevertheless seems to have been resumed. At least, ballmaster Salomon Maclet, who ran a silk goods business besides, and his annual contributions of then twenty-five guilders, to be paid at Christmas, continue to be referred to in the tax-rolls of the city from 1652 to 1672.[104] The ever diminishing payments, however, are indicators of the general decline of tennis in the ballhouse. So reduced had enthusiasm for tennis become in Strasbourg in the century to follow that the city's ballhouses were divorced from their original purpose and, like the Imperial ballhouse in Vienna, turned into playhouses. All that remains of their former glory was the name of a Strasbourg alley: Ballhausgasse.

DANIEL MARTIN AND GEORG BENDER ON
THE ART OF TENNIS TALK AND THE TENNIS TUSSLE

The seventeenth-century Strasbourg tennis world here described is, so to speak, the backdrop against which a tennis dialogue in a language primer by Daniel Martin should be viewed. At the beginning of the dialogue, two tennis players keen on a match meet each other in some Strasbourg alley:[105]

> X: Is there a ballhouse in this city?
> Y: Yes, certainly, there are two of them, one beside the other like the barges that come down from Basle. Let us go there in order to hit a dozen balls about.

Of course, the two ballhouses resembling two barges drifting down the Rhine alongside each other on their way from Basle are the two tennis facilities run by the notorious ballmaster Klapp of whom we have heard.[106]

By means of a flowery sub-title the author of the book explains what kind of help the reader will be offered in his *Parlement Nouveau* in his attempt to learn either the German or the French language. Under the names of the individual professions, the book contained all those words and phrases necessary for a conversation; thus serving extremely well the purpose of a dictionary and word-list for all amateurs of the German and French languages: 'comprenans sous les Tiltres de Professions … tous les mots & phrases necessaires en la conversation humaine, & par ainsi servant de Dictionaire & Nomenclature aux amateurs de deux langues Françoise & Allemande.'[107] Of course, the seventeenth-century person intent on expressing himself or herself did well to converse in French rather than in German, above all on the tennis court, but if for some reason resort to German had to be made all the same, the *Parlement Nouveau* in which each chapter in unsurpassed French had an equivalent in German was a great help, although in the case of talking about tennis there was hardly any difference between German and French. As we shall see from the following passage from a chapter 'On the Ball Master', the language of tennis in this country was completely Frenchified:[108]

> wer in dreyen mahlen kein rechtmessigen *serviss* geben kann / *quinze* verlieren soll. … Jetzt gilts. *Quinze.* … *Trante. trantins. Karantcinq a trante. Schasse morte* oder ist kein *schass* da? Es ist keine da. Spielt über die *corde. A dö.* Verzeihet mir. Er hat die *corde* angerühret. Ja wohl, aber unterwartz.

> (he who cannot serve correctly in three attempts shall lose fifteen. Now it counts. Fifteen. Thirty. Thirty all. Forty-five to thirty. Is the chase dead, or is there not any? There is not any. Play over the line. Deuce. Excuse me. It has touched the line. Yes, surely, but from below.)

Rather than a double fault, the German 'Serviss' (French *service*; the German term is now *Aufschlag*) seems to have been a triple fault, whereas the German counting was accomplished in a way reminiscent of Roland Garros, the venue of the French Open: 'Quinze', 'Trante', 'Trantins' (the latter being the mystifying modern French *trentains*, 'thirty all'), 'Karantcinq a trante' (modern French *quarantecinq à trente*, or *avantage*, to use the modern French tennis term), 'a dö' ('deuce', modern French *à deux*, now *égalité*). Whenever the players had reached forty-five, the question which had to be asked in Daniel's German was 'Schass morte?' (French *est la chasse morte?*, 'have we contended the chase?', or, literally, 'is the chase dead?'). Chase or no chase, the ball had always to travel over the 'Corde', although there was a real host of German terms which might have been substituted for this French word, namely *Strick*, *Seil*, *Schnur*, *Tau*, or, for that matter, *Kordel*.

The marker of the chases, perhaps an employee of the keeper of the court, seems to have been a rather humble creature, to judge from the arrogant instructions he is given by his juvenile customers:[109]

> Marckirer / bring vns ein paar guter racketen, / vnd ein dutzet newe oder partey ballen / spielschuch / vnd sägmal vnder die Corden / vnsere hände / vnd das hefft an vnsern racketen / wann wir schwitzen werden / ab zu wischen vnd zu trücknen.

> (Marker, bring us some good rackets and a dozen new or 'party' balls, tennis shoes and sawdust [to be placed] under the line so that we may wipe and dry our hands and the handle of our rackets with it when we perspire.)

At last, they order a tankard of ale to help them to cool them off in the heat of the match, and, after this order has been duly executed, they want the poor drudge to mark their chases, and to umpire their match.[110] New balls (which in those days consisted of a lump of lead around which stocking wool was wound which then received a cover of leather)[111] were apparently referred to as 'party balls', because for a competitve match (= partey) where money was at stake new balls were needed. Large quantities of them (at least a dozen) were necessary, possibly because the rate of loss was exceptionally high. This is at least suggested by the scene depicted by Crispijn van de Passe (see **Figure 62** on p. 159) where the tennis-playing students in their bulging trousers may have had difficulties in moving about the court, but where there was certainly no shortage of balls. In case of excessive perspiration, which should hardly cause any surprise in view of the elaborate collars, doublets and baggy trousers, sawdust was required to wipe one's hands. It was heaped up under the line rather than carried around in one's pocket. The perspiring tennis player in the German ballhouse finally needed a large mug of beer, and the expression used for it (*maass*) indicates to initiates of the Oktoberfest that in Daniel's language book we are on our way to the German south.

Despite his lowly social status, the marker was entrusted with the brainwork in this game, that of marking the chases and of keeping the score. Daniel had his tennis players, whose verbal exchanges at least are flawless, start their match on even terms, without a handicap ('gleich vnnd gleich'). In much the same way as today they had to spin round their rackets in order to choose sides,[112] and the decision depended on which side of the racket head came up, the 'rough' or the 'smooth' side. The 'rough' side was referred to as 'Knöpffle' ('little knots') in seventeenth-century German,[113] because of the old custom of winding the transverse strings of the racket round the longitudinal ones.[114]

In Daniel's exemplary tennis match the gods have willed it that the less expert player also has to suffer from the misfortune of losing the toss for sides: his will be the 'upward' position ('Ihr must oben stehen'),[115] i.e. the more difficult task of defending the *dedans*-gallery. After the match, his opponent can well afford to be generous:[116] 'Mr Loser', he is heard to offer the underdog a new chance, 'what handicap are you willing to give me? I will play you with a beetle, a basket, or a laundry battledore, or from underneath the thigh.' Such is his superiority that he thinks he can hold his own against an opponent, owing him, perhaps, no less than fifteen, with a rather unusual bat, or under the obligation of playing every stroke through his legs.[117]

His opponent, who even before the match began had misgivings that his part in it would be that of a greenhorn recruit on the drill-ground,[118] rejects this offer with thanks. To have to pay for balls, tennis slippers, drinks, the marker's fee, fuel and all,[119] in this uneven match is quite enough for him, and from the last item on the bill it appears that the place had been made hot for him not only by his opponent's shots, but also by the ballmaster whose duty it was to keep ablaze some round iron stove.

Why there was such a demand for balls in German ballhouses becomes clear only at the end. The tennis athletes of Strasbourg have to deplore the loss of no fewer than two dozen, and the defeated player who had to 'pay the piper' at last suspects that his opponent had played a nasty prank on him, by deliberately volleying them into the grill and hazard holes for good.

But then it looks as if there had been in the ballhouses of the German *beau monde*, despite their exclusiveness, individuals who fell a long way short of the ideal of the *galant homme*. It could well be, the victor says trying to free himself from blame, that the boys lurking in the gallery for that very purpose had slipped some into their boxes or thieves' bags.[120]

Apart from these juvenile delinquents, there were apparently other criminal elements who belonged to the establishment itself. We are informed about them by Georg Paul Hönn who, at the beginning of the eighteenth century, was councillor and bailiff of the Dukes of Saxe-Gotha. In his capacity as High Sheriff of Coburg, he was familiar with the seamier side of life and thus able to write a book titled *Kurtzeingerichtetes Betrugs-Lexicon* (*Dictionary of Cheating, Briefly Devised*; first edition of 1721). The book had for its motto the rhyme 'Der Welt Wagen und Pflug ist nur Lug und Betrug' (The World's Chariot and Plough is only Lying and Cheating). It is about the evil practices of the various trades which are listed in alphabetical order. The method applied by Hönn is that of the medieval penitential in which the vices were contrasted with their appropriate remedies. Accordingly, Hönn first enlarged on the unethical practices of a trade, and then offered his readers an antidote against them. Since he arranged his 'dictionary' alphabetically, his readers arrived at the entry relating to the ballmaster's craft soon enough:[121]

Ballmasters cheat, firstly, if they charge more balls, and are paid for them, than they have handed out, or than have been lost; secondly, if, when marking, they consider who the persons are, and count more than they justifiably may in favour of those whom they wish well, but in so doing greatly deceive the others; thirdly, if they ask of strangers (knowing that they will not be their customers again) more for a match or a dozen balls than their employers have allowed them to; fourthly, if they, travelling to where they are not known, keep to themselves their profession, pretending not to be good ball-players at first, only to deprive this or that partner of his money; fifthly, if they, when playing a serious match, toss the ball to the advantage of those whom they support.

Against such sharp practices, Hönn recommended the following:

> *Remedy*: That there shall be printed a special regulation for ballhouses and a price-list, to be put up publicly for the notification of everybody; secondly, that everybody should be well on his guard against playing with ballmasters for money.

Hönn's book belongs to the genre of the medieval estates satire, and as such it is a caricature of Christoff Weigel's book with its portrait of the highly respectable ballmaster. A notable example of the latter type was the honourable Georg Bender, author of the first tennis manual in the German language who will claim our attention next.

GEORG BENDER'S BRIEF INSTRUCTION OF THE PRAISEWORTHY GAME AT BALL
(1680)

A single copy of Johann Georg Bender's tennis primer has by a stroke of good luck been preserved in the Palace Library of Ansbach.[122] Not unlike Daniel Martin's language book, Bender's book was written with a noble readership in mind. This is not least proved by the numerous verbal bows and genuflections of its author in his Preface to the Most Benevolent Reader. Tennis, Johann Georg explains, highly popular among both high and low, is a rather complicated game. Yet it is most certainly one which can be learnt, albeit by some people sooner than by others.[123] What Bender wants to say is fairly clear, but the way he says it proves that the honourable ballmaster from Nuremberg may have wielded his racket competently, but that in the art of mastering the goose-quill championship honours must have been denied to him.[124]

Nevertheless, his work, in his opinion at least, filled a gap. Because of its simple and unstilted language, he said, reading it would lead to success in a short time.[125] Three hundred years later Baron von Fichard would recommend young Friedrich Adolf Traun, who was to become Olympic doubles champion in 1896, to read with care his tournament reports in the journal *Spiel und Sport* in order to improve his game!

> Although now sundry exercises and liberal arts are to be found in printed books according to which those who list to understand them may rule themselves, there has as yet never been anything devised on the game at ball famous and worthy of praise,

nor has anything been put into print. Neither has there been anybody willing to devote himself to accomplishing such. That is why I have considered it a good thing to gather together its nature in the briefest manner, not with high-flown and precious terms, but with intelligible and clear ones, so that every amateur who may read it will grasp and learn it with but little effort, and in a short time.

Books in those days were unthinkable without a dedication to some Maecenas or patron of rank, and in this respect Georg Bender's little treatise is no exception. Addressed to a patrician and merchant from Nuremberg, Georg Winter, the dedication comes at the end of the preface, and is a good example of how, even in those early days, to bend one's knees low was an important part of any ballmaster's daily routine:[126]

> I have wished to address the dedication to mylord the honourable and very noble Georg Winter, citizen and merchant here, my most benevolent patron, as to someone highly expert in this art and exercise, asking with my utmost devotion his favour not to reject this puny effort, but to accept it most generously and to sense in it my goodwill to be of the most serviceable assiduousness. Besides recommending you to God's care, I remain herewith, yours, honest, steadfast and most serviceable, Johann Georg Bender [a name, it seems, befitting its bearer], ballmaster in Nuremberg.

On the pages which follow, the ballmaster from Nuremberg comments on those points which in the course of a match may give rise to questions, from the tossing for sides to the footing of the bill. The game at ball is for anybody having enough enthusiasm and love for the exercise of the body, for enjoying himself and for being of good cheer, provided it is engaged in without a great deal of swearing and blasphemy.[127] Rule Number One is to grasp the racket in such a way as to make sure that the smooth side points towards the body which means that (for reasons not known) the forehand stroke was accomplished with the smooth, the backhand with the rough side imparting more backspin on the ball.[128] Next in importance is having good judgement of the ball (the German term is *judiciren*), and in order to acquire this, the player had to bandy the ball to and fro before the match (German *ballutiren*, a loan from French *peloter*).[129]

When tossing for sides, one is obliged to ask one's opponent whether he wants to have the inner or outer side of the racket (rough or smooth?), upon which the racket must be spun round in one's hand once, and then dropped.[130] After this, the ball is thrown (by hand!) onto the roof. It is a kind of test service, and in order to tell the opponent not to take this ball seriously, a call in elegant French is necessary. It is either *pour neant* (this is for nothing, it does not count), or, more elegantly still, albeit somewhat debatable in more recent times as a term for something which did not count, *pour les dames* (this is for the ladies).[131] There was a minor difference here between the tennis customs of Nuremberg and Strasbourg: whereas the tennis addicts of Nuremberg seem to have paid homage to more mature womenhood, those of Strasbourg dedicated their invalid services to the young and pretty ones. Hence their cry of *Voilà vos demoiselles*, at least in the French part of the text. In the German version of Daniel's dialogue, the girls' mothers were given their due as in Bender's book ('Das ist für die Damen').[132]

He who won the first game could claim, at least for the time being, the prize or money at stake. As a rule, however, the wager was deposited under the line.[133] For hanging up the line, flexibility was required. Its height was not measured (as in the era of lawn tennis) by means of a racket, but was relative to the height of the competitors; to be more precise, it depended on the height of the one who had been allotted the upwards position, the defence of the *dedans*:[134] It is also convenient, the rule said, that the line should be no higher than that the one standing upwards might see, when looking down the length of the ballhouse in the middle and over the line, the feet of the one standing at the other end of the court.

The line very much lent itself to malpractice of many sorts, and Johann Georg Bender especially took to task those rascals who, in pursuit of his ball, lifted up the cord or line, an act he considered impolite and discourteous (*unhoeflich*).[135] The punishment of these delinquents was part of the duties of the marker, or umpire, and the German ballmaster has a lot to say about their importance in seventeenth-century sporting life. With a clear voice, they were to tell the players where the ball had bounced for the first and the second time.[136] They then had to mark chases and other bounces of the ball assiduously, failing which they were in danger of losing their markers' fee, or of having, because of their slackness, others substituted in their place, thus becoming an object of derision. Finally, they were to decide which party was in the right and which was not, the guideline for their ruling being the opinion of those standing by, namely which party was supported by them most. Having made their decision, they were to make it known without the least fear and without respect of persons, whoever they may be.[137] The rule that a point should be awarded to the party supported by the majority of the crowd prevailed throughout the Middle Ages. It might, democratic as it is, with no small margin of profit be reintroduced in the big tournaments of today.

In the seventeenth century a set ('Partie') consisted of either four or six games. A two set match, once begun, had to be played to its bitter end. There was no bluffing one's way out:[138]

> If two sets are played you must not slip away unless your reasons are important ones,
> e.g. if you are driven away by the imminent night or a thunderstorm, in which case the
> same match will have to be played off and completed on the days following.

If the match had to be interrupted, the player trailing behind had to advance both the stake and half of the costs, whereas his opponent got off cheaply. He had only to pay for the other half.[139] It looks as if in those early days the players' self-confidence was not marked. Nobody expected to be able to pull back after going behind.

A long paragraph is devoted to the odds which could be given in the game, and which must have been the craze of the German ballhouse gambler. In the ballhouse of Nuremberg they could be excessive, the highest being 'halb quarante Cinque avantage', an advantage of thirty and forty-five alternatively for every game of the set.[140] A peculiarity of seventeenth-century tennis was the so-called *Biscaye* (or *Bisque*).[141] It was a point which could be collected at any time during a match. There must have been many a shrewd tennis player who kept their *Biscayes* in cold storage until match-point, a fact of which Bender seems to have been well aware![142]

The final passage of Johann Georg Bender's little treatise is devoted to the stuff by which the tennis world has been ruled since time immemorial: money. According to Bender, a player playing for money did well to make sure that as much cash as was staked was deposited under the line or cord by the competitors; for it often happened that, since nothing had been laid down, somebody who had won a lot, eventually got little or nothing at all (as quite a few must have realized to their own cost). In this respect, a player should by no means feel abashed and insist on it since one party was entitled to it as much as the other, and payment would thus be safest.[143] It looks as if in Germany the question of how a profit might be made in tennis was discussed long before the advent of Ion Tiriac.

SIX

Lawn tennis:
the sturdy bastard

◇

The eighteenth and nineteenth centuries had witnessed the steady decline of the ancient game of tennis.[1] What had remained of the pastime of the aristocrats, was at last swept away by the insurgent populace of the French Revolution.[2] In this situation there appeared, on 7 March 1874, in the London *Court Journal*, the favourite reading of English court circles, a truly remarkable note. Sandwiched between notable instances of a fisherman's yarn and a report about top-flight hunts that had gone to rack and ruin because of some uninvited second fox, the following announcement caught the curious reader's eye:[3]

> We hear of a new and interesting game coming out, which is likely to attract public notice, now blasé with croquet and on the *qui cire* for novelty. It has been patented under the name of 'Sphairistike or lawn tennis'. It has been tested at several country houses, and has been found full of healthy excitement, besides being capable of much scientific play. The game is in a box not much larger than a double gun case, and contains, besides bats and balls, a portable court, which can be erected on any ordinary lawn, and is ornamental as well as useful.

The publication of this item was of service to a man the court considered to be a friend. The author of these lines, Major Walter Clopton Wingfield, was a personal acquaintance of the Prince of Wales, later to become Edward VII.[4] Only a few days previously, on 23 February 1874, he had obtained a provisional patent on a 'New and Improved Court for Playing the Ancient Game of Tennis'.[5] In June, the patent became valid. Six months had elapsed during which it might have been challenged, but nobody had cared to.[6]

In the patent itself it was stated that the purpose of the invention was to create a portable court by which the game of old might be played in a 'much simplified' manner, in the open air, and with complete disregard for special courts which had always been considered an indispensable requisite. In principle, the inventor argued, only two posts were needed, to be erected at a distance of about twenty-one feet, and an oblong net, stretched between them and dividing the court into two halves. By means of paint, a coloured line or tape, an in-court and out-court had to be marked, a right and left service-court (at the base-line of the out-court), a service crease and the side boundaries. In this way, the ancient game of tennis, a pastime requiring covered courts and therefore, because of the high costs, the preserve of a privileged few, would be within the means of everybody; a highly democratic view, no doubt. Such a court could be erected within a few minutes, on any appropriate surface, indoors as well as outdoors, and even on ice.[7]

On 25 February 1874, two days after the patent had been granted, Wingfield's Rules of the Game appeared in print.[8] In this pamphlet, the Major proudly referred to the legal document in his possession. It was the last piece to be added to the boxed tennis sets that had been ready for delivery at Messrs French and Co. in Churton Street, London, from where they were now dispatched in large numbers. French and Co. were the sole distributors of the Wingfieldian monopoly.

On the title page of the small booklet (no more than eight printed pages) the game was referred to (as in the *Court Journal*) as '*Sphairistikè* or Lawn Tennis' (**Figure 66**). The Greek name appeared in Greek letters on top of the page whereas Lawn Tennis was printed onto a Wingfieldian tennis net running diagonally across it in the form of a band.[9]

Inside, the game was called 'The Major's Game of Lawn Tennis', and it was dedicated to the members of the glorious party which had gathered, in December

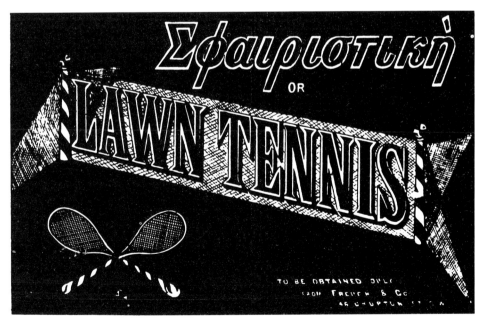

FIGURE 66   The cover of Major Wingfield's rule booklet, which came out in February 1874.

1873, at Nantclwyd, a stately mansion in Wales.[10] A short description of the court, said to measure twenty by ten yards, was then given, and an illustration showed, against the background of an English country-house park, a mixed doubles 'à la Wingfield' in progress (**Figure 67**). Two more pages contained the rules, six in all. Of the complex rules of the tennis game of old (which, as we have seen, Wingfield expressly mentioned), only two had been allowed to stay: the ball had to be played over the net, and hit either on the volley or after its first bounce (Rule III).[11] Another relic of the past was the rule envisaging a service from one side of the court only. In Wingfield's system, however, there was an additional constraint in that it had to be executed from a fixed point, a diamond-shaped service crease. Curiously enough, the server's camp was still referred to as the 'in-side', although there was no longer a *dedans* which had to be defended. Goals were notably absent from Wingfield's invention, and, of course, the age-honoured chase rule had also been abandoned at last. Points (called *aces*) could be scored by the serving party only, and, as in modern volleyball, their opponents (Wingfield provides for a singles as well as a doubles

FIGURE 67 The Wingfieldian lawn tennis court, its characteristic being, above all, its hour-glass shape and its service crease.

game) could score only after the right to serve had been wrenched from them. Fifteen aces were needed to win a game.

TENNIS CONQUERS THE CROQUET WASTES

The English Major had launched his game at the best of times. England's sporting public virtually craved, as Wingfield rightly observed in his *Court Journal* note, some newfangledness. Croquet which had boasted of a vast following only a few years before had for some become too complicated by the introduction of new complex rules; to others, it was either too simple or too sissy, a girls' pastime at best. Nevertheless there were, as a consequence of the croquet mania, vast areas of well-trimmed croquet lawns available throughout the country. Such spare land, from a sportsman's point of view, was badly in need of exploitation.[12] It has often been claimed that lawn tennis owes its existence to the invention of the lawn mower,[13] but this is only partly true. Before England, Ireland, and, to a less degree, Scotland, could become 'white with lines of lawn-tennis courts' (as H.W.W. Wilberforce at the beginning of the 1890s once put it),[14] the lawn mower had earlier produced surfaces that allowed the smooth run of croquet bowls. Lawn tennis courts were the by-product of the croquet lawn.

As a result of another invention, the discovery of vulcanization by Charles Goodyear, it had been possible for some time to manufacture rubber balls filled with air which proved to be real bouncing bombs even on turf. It was therefore not only the solid walls encompassing the ancient tennis court, and the shelter of its roof that could be dispensed with, but also its hard tiled floor which alone had prompted a reaction from the stuffed tennis-balls of old. Those who had learned Goodyear's lesson best were the Germans. Little wonder, therefore, that Wingfield ordered his first assortments of balls from Germany. They were naked little featherweights, greyish or red and without the flannel cover which was later to become their hallmark.[15]

The huge success which the Major's game enjoyed, at least in the beginning, was the result of careful planning. Apart from the note in the *Court Journal*, there had been eulogies in advance in the *Army and Navy Gazette* as well as in the journal *The Field*,[16] of which the former had recommended the new game for no less than every barrack square in the entire United Kingdom. *The Field*, the country gentleman's journal the English-speaking world over, had gone so far as to print Wingfield's rule book almost in full in its sporting section.[17] As a result, the journal in the months to follow abounded with contributions devoted to the new game.[18] In this manner, lawn tennis managed to command the attention of a large readership for a long time.

THE PELOTA GAME OF HARRY GEM

The publicity which the Major's game received did much to boost sales figures. In their first year, French and Company sold more than one thousand boxed sets.[19] On the other hand, it stirred up rivalry of various kinds. The first to raise their voices were

English sportsmen claiming to have played some form of lawn tennis long before Wingfield. One of them was Harry Gem who, in a letter to the editor of *The Field*, told of a game which he and a Spanish friend of his, Augurio Pereira, had begun to play in the city of Birmingham in 1860, and which they had continued to play, after having changed their place of residence, in Leamington Spa. Gem's statement was perfectly true, although he blandly refused to be called the originator of lawn tennis.[20]

Thomas Henry Gem was born in Birmingham on 21 May 1819, the son of a solicitor.[21] Educated under the famous Dr Martin at King's College, London, 'Harry' Gem, as he was invariably called to the day of his death, was articled to a Birmingham solicitor in 1835, in whose office he began to study law.[22] At the age of 22, he became a solicitor himself, assisting his father in his duties as clerk to the magistrates of the City of Birmingham. Jean (Juán) Batista Augurio Pereira, to use his full Spanish name, had come to England at the age of 17 and become a wealthy man as a trader in Spanish merchandise. Both men were all-round sportsmen of note. In the summer of 1859 they had begun to experiment with a version of lawn tennis on the croquet lawn of Pereira's manor 'Fairlight', in Ampton Road, Edgbaston.[23] They were later to refer to it as pelota, and it is truly remarkable how again it was descendants of the medieval game which helped to inaugurate the new game: Gem and Pereira were both excellent rackets players,[24] and whereas the Englishman was also a devotee of Real tennis, Pereira is likely to have grown up with some variant of the Basque pelota game – hence the name of honour given to the new game, pelota.[25] In 1872, Gem and Pereira moved to Leamington Spa, and, being without a suitable greensward at the back of their own houses, they appropriated the lawns of the Manor House Hotel, in Park Avenue, opposite Pereira's home, for their favourite pastime.[26] Here their opponents were two physicians, Dr Frederick Harry Haynes and Dr Arthur Wellesley Tomkins,[27] and this foursome were to become the founders of the world's first lawn tennis club, the Leamington Lawn Tennis Club.[28] The club flourished some fifteen years, holding (apparently since 1874 and according to rules of which two printed versions have survived)[29] an annual tournament every summer.[30] As time went on, however, and perhaps inadvertently, the game of one Major (Harry Gem, too, had been raised to the rank of Major in The Birmingham Rifle Volunteer Corps)[31] seems to have been replaced by that of the other, Wingfield's. At any rate, in the 1880s, lawn tennis tournaments were held in Leamington which were repeatedly honoured by the presence of Ernest Renshaw, the Wimbledon star and a native of Leamington.[32] This, perhaps, suggests that by this time the hosts of the tournament, the Leamington Lawn Tennis Club, no longer adhered to the rules as laid down by Harry Gem, its founder.

When the end of the tennis season of 1874 was drawing near, Major Harry Gem for his friends and himself composed a tennis poem. It is a piece both captivating and highly artistic, and it could be sung to the tune of the famous Irish song 'The Wearing of the Green'.[33] It is a poem full of melancholy and brimming with superb self-irony. The imagery Gem chose is ingenious and not unlike that employed by his fellow-poet Charles d'Orléans. Falling leaves and the green grass turning fallow, harbingers of the tennis season's close, remind the poet that his own days are waning.

He and his friend Pereira have long passed their fifties. Now they can be seen panting painfully, battling against their friends Haynes and Tomkins, younger than they by almost three decades, as well as against their own age. At times, the subtle Pereira twist may well be helpful against the youthful hero Haynes. But what remedy will there be against old age? An intriguing feature of the poem is Gem's use of the term *list* to denote the tennis lawn, as if the poet were entertaining thoughts of the days of yore with their splendour of knightly tournaments.[34] The poem is, perhaps, the best testimony a man could offer to posterity about his most unusual talents: Gem was not only a gifted actor, cartoonist, composer, but also an excellent all-round sportsman who eventually became the bard of his favourite sport, lawn tennis. Introducing himself as Homer may not demonstrate a talent for unpretentiousness, but it is hardly inappropriate either. His use of onomatopoeic verbs as a means of showing how lawn tennis, then in its infancy, might send its worshippers into raptures as well as plunge them into utter despair is truly remarkable:[35]

> The Manor House is moaning, there's a sigh in every breeze,
> And the Leam is flowing sadly by the leaf-forsaken trees,
> And the green grass that we've trodden now is darker in its woe,
> As the tread of the Pelota boys it must no longer know.
> > As we tripped about the green,
> > As they slipped about the green,
> > As they fumbled, and they stumbled,
> > and they tumbled o'er the green.
>
> Oh remember, let's remember, we were merry when the sun
> Shone o'er us bright and cheery in the days when we begun,
> But the eyes that looked upon us were more bright and cheery still
> And urged us on to desp'rate deeds of nimbleness and skill.
> > As we jumped about the green,
> > As we thumped about the green,
> > As we rattled, and we prattled,
> > and we battled o'er the green.
>
> Let all our deeds be written on the lasting roll of fame,
> How Homer bet the shilling, and Tomkins won the game,
> How Haynes' youthful vigour placed him high upon the list,
> And baffled all who hadn't got the great Pereira twist.
> > As we stuck about the green,
> > As we struck about the green,
> > As we betted, and we sweated,
> > and we fretted o'er the green.
>
> 'Twas sad to see age vie with youth, it brought the heavy sigh,
> To hear some old one saying, 'good bye, sweet youth, good bye'.
> To see them limp, and hear them puff, and learn how idly vain

It was to wish for eyes and limbs that won't come back again.
  As they waddled o'er the green,
  As they straddled o'er the green,
  As they muffled it, and they puffed it,
  and enough'd it o'er the green.

Farewell the turf, the bounding ball and nets are in the box,
The rackets on the shelf are laid to wait next season's knocks;
Then let us now pass round the wine, a brimming bumper fill,
And drink the great Pelota game, Lawn Tennis if you will.
  Yes! we'll toast it o'er the green,
  And we'll boast it o'er the green,
  And we'll chink it, and we'll clink it,
  and we'll drink it o'er the green.

WHERE EXACTLY DID LAWN TENNIS BALLS BEGIN TO BOUNCE?

The variety of tennis inaugurated by Harry Gem, in marked contrast to Wingfield's brand of tennis, had never managed to become popular outside the inner circle of his friends. Nevertheless, the remonstrances of Gem and others led to debates about the origins of lawn tennis and to inquiries about where Wingfield first practised his game during the latter's life-time. The question still captures the attention of lawn tennis annalists.

In the note which appeared in the *Court Journal*, it was claimed that the Major had tested his game at various country houses, and this statement was repeated in the first edition of his Rules. However, where exactly the Major launched his game and when is a matter which still remains to be determined. Many an expert, in order to settle the question for good, went out on a pilgrimage to Rhysnant Hall, an old estate of the Wingfield family in Llandysilio, a small village in faraway Montgomeryshire, Wales. Rhysnant Hall boasted a croquet lawn, a must for the nineteenth-century well-to-do, of which photographs were duly taken by those who claimed to have detected the true Wingfieldian testing ground.[36] However, there also existed an anecdote told by no less a personage than a member of the English peerage, Lord Lansdowne. According to the testimony of his lordship, a 'Major Wingfield' had introduced himself to him in the summer of 1869 and offered to give a display of some newly invented game in the garden of his London residence south of Berkeley Square. His lordship had accepted the offer, and he and those of his friends who had taken part in the experiment had thoroughly enjoyed the new game and played it three or four times a week ever since.[37] As there seemed to be no reason why a real lord should be distrusted, the stately mansion off Berkeley Square became the leading candidate for having first seen the Major at play. Still there was that most mysterious evening party at Nantclwyd to which the Major had dedicated his invention. That Wingfield had availed himself of an event such as this splendid gathering of Welsh glitterati in order to stage his new game most effectively seemed obvious. On the croquet lawns of Nantclwyd, the conclusion was inevitable: about five miles from the Welsh market town of Ruthin,[38] *sphairistikè* would have begun its unparalleled career. Sceptics, however, had some doubts as to whether a fashionable evening party might easily have been persuaded to engage in a new summer pastime in the month of December.[39]

All these theories about the original site of Wingfield's lawn tennis experiments have only recently been sufficiently demolished by the meticulous research of George E. Alexander. Only for a short period of time, in 1864, did Wingfield reside at Rhysnant Hall.[40] At that time, he had not given a thought to his new game, and, as a consequence, the pastures around Rhysnant Hall are not likely to have been the place where the Major would have pitched his *sphairistikè* nets. It may well be that Lord Lansdowne enjoyed the privilege of playing lawn tennis with Wingfield, but the date of his alleged tennis matches is hardly accurate. His 'Major Wingfield' had been raised to the rank of Major of the Montgomeryshire Yeomanry in May 1873, and that is why the tennis party at Berkeley Square cannot have been arranged prior to that date.[41] Finally, the mysterious countryside gathering at Nantclwyd did not feature Wingfield as the inventor of a new game, but in his capacity as a gifted actor. The owners of Nantclwyd Hall, Major Naylor-Leyland and his wife, celebrated a housewarming which was highlighted by the performance of two contemporary plays. Wingfield had taken a leading part in both, accompanied in one of them by 'Patsy' Cornwallis-West, a celebrated beauty of the time. It may well be that the very same Patsy was the hidden cause for the gallant Major's dedication. There is not a shred of evidence among the activities at Nantclwyd that the Naylor-Leylands and their guests, besides having a shot at the theatre, were also practising lawn tennis shots.[42] The only thing that can now be taken for granted is this. On 8 December 1874, Wingfield, in a letter to the congenial Harry Gem, actor and inventor of lawn tennis like himself, stated that he had been experimenting with his version of lawn tennis for a year and a half. According to the Major's own testimony, therefore, lawn tennis à la Wingfield was played not earlier than in the spring of 1873.[43] The only place to have so far been identified as Wingfield's *sphairistikè* testing ground is the parental home of his cousin, Constance Delicia Combe. It is located in the hamlet of Earnshill in Somerset.[44]

WHAT A NAME! SPHAIRISTIKÈ

Why of all names Wingfield hit on *sphairistikè* is a matter difficult to explain. It was simply unpronounceable for the uneducated who soon enough viciously corrupted it into *sticky*,[45] a word which evoked the idea of something unpleasantly gluey. For the learned it constituted a blunder as glaring as the one the Major had committed at the age of 17 when he, in the geography part of his entry test for the 18th Light Dragoon Guards at Sandhurst, had located Toronto in Spain – one of the reasons why he failed in the test the first time.[46] *Sphairistikè*, the feminine gender of the Greek adjective *sphairistikós*, 'belonging to the game at ball', made no sense if used independently and without some appropriate noun such as *tékhne*, 'art', for example.[47]

The name's only asset was its being rather exceptional, and it was perhaps this quality which highly commended it to the inventor.

The simple fact that the question of the origin of lawn tennis was being discussed by the British sporting public had given rise to a legal uncertainty, a circumstance not altogether favourable to the Major's cause. Very soon, rival manufacturers began to unload on the market lawn tennis sets of their own, counterfeited after the Wingfieldian best-seller. Wingfield seems to have anticipated this. Knowing that his game, despite the patent in his possession, had not a single characteristic that would prove to be irrefutably his own invention in future lawsuits, the Major had set his heart on this rather exotic name from the very beginning. This name, at least, would be his property completely and unmistakably, something that might come in handy as a bogey for competitors if need be.

That the Major soon began to play this card becomes evident from the title page of his rules book. When, in the autumn of the same year, the brisk sales made a second print necessary, it carried the sole name of *sphairistikè*, ostentatiously and in big letters.[48] Little impressed by the Major's stratagem, however, the competitors continued to turn out their imitations by the thousand.

Detractors at work

In this situation, the honourable Major is said to have resorted to dishonest practices. This, at least, is how the late Tom Todd would have it, the lawn tennis historian and author of *The Tennis Players*, a book written with a truly remarkable love for detail. The book appeared in 1979, in the wake of the hundredth anniversary of the All England Championships at Wimbledon, and as a result of Todd's presentation of the facts Wingfield acquired the reputation of a money-raking rogue. His major part in the evolution of lawn tennis was denied to him almost completely.[49]

According to Todd, guardian of the Wimbledon Lawn Tennis Museum and a historian of great merits, the sketch of a *sphairistikè*-court which Wingfield included in his rules had created among his customers the impression that the court was narrower at the net than at the baseline. Wingfield, said to have been a mere dabbler at drawing pictures in perspective, was held responsible for this error.

The rules, however, had envisaged a court perfectly rectangular and measuring 20 by 10 yards. Now a particularly inquisitive *sphairistikè* fan making the sketch his guideline rather than the rules is said to have approached *The Field*, asking the journal about the width of the court at the net.[50] Wingfield, who realized at once that his game was being credited with something for which his original plan made no provision at all, grabbed the opportunity with determination.

The simple-minded author of the letter had bestowed on him a precious gift, something he had long been looking for, and in vain. Here it was, the distinctive feature by which his game could be said to differ from the tennis of old: the hour-glass shaped court. Wingfield, according to Todd, with a haste that gave him away, had posted a letter to *The Field*.[51] It was dated 11 April 1874, and foisted upon the public the piece of information that the waistline of his mistress *sphairistikè* measured seven yards as opposed to the ten yards he had previously envisaged for the baselines. Not satisfied with this, he had declared in all subsequent editions of his Rules that the hour-glass shaped court was his property exclusively, and that he had bequeathed the right to use it to the Marylebone Cricket Club (MCC), henceforth the sole body to wield authority. All distributors of games called lawn tennis had therefore to employ the traditional (and now outmoded) rectangular tennis court, if they did not want to infringe upon his own 'improved-shaped' and portable one.[52] In making such a claim, Wingfield was said to have deliberately told a lie.

Only recently Wingfield has been cleared of the charge – also trumped up against him by Todd – of not having possessed a patent.[53] Here an attempt will be made to exculpate him from that of not having invented the hour-glass shaped court. That Wingfield in his Rules gave the measurements of his *sphairistikè* lawn as being 20 by 10 yards is perfectly true. From the very beginning, however, he must have had an hour-glass shaped court in mind, presumably for patent reasons. This becomes evident from the measure he had specified (as has been outlined above) in his application for a patent of February 1874, a fact which apparently escaped Todd's notice. Trying to describe the function of his new portable court, Wingfield had stated the following:[54] 'The manner by which I propose to accomplish the above object is as follows: – I insert two standards in the ground at about twenty-one feet from each other; between these two standards a large oblong net is stretched.' Of course, the twenty-one feet mentioned here are those seven yards Wingfield is said to have invented, in his letter to *The Field*, after his invention, and that is why Wingfield can no longer be accused of any monkey business whatsoever. The hour-glass shaped court is his invention well and truly.[55] How to judge the Major's assertion that the whole art of his brand of open-air tennis consisted in using a court narrower at the net than at the baseline, is a completely different question.[56] To claim this was, of course, completely silly, and the return to the original rectangular shape of the tennis court has proved ever since that Wingfield's hour-glass shaped specimen was but an ill-constructed bugbear.

WINGFIELD, AN EDWARDIAN GENTLEMAN AGAIN

On closer inspection, therefore, of all the accusations and allegations nothing remains. It is, above all, by the untiring efforts of his biographer, George E. Alexander, that Wingfield has been vindicated completely, and that the former rascally entrepreneur has been turned into a flawless Edwardian gentleman again. He not only commands our respect, but is very likely, because of the many tragic moments in his life, to arouse our sympathy (**Figure 68**).

Wingfield belonged to a family which was one of the oldest in England and traced itself back to a time well before the Norman Conquest.[57] One of his ancestors, John Wingfield, fought in the major battles of the Hundred Years' War, and Wingfield Castle in Suffolk, where Charles d'Orléans, taken prisoner in the battle of Agincourt, lived in exile, has been claimed (albeit wrongly) to have been a family estate.[58] That

FIGURE 68   One of the few portraits of
Walter Clopton Wingfield.

branch of the family from which Walter Clopton Wingfield was descended had, early
in the seventeenth century, been dispersed to Shropshire.[59] That is why the inventor
of lawn tennis first saw the light in nearby Wales. He was born the son of a captain
serving in Canada, Clopton Lewis Wingfield, on 16 October 1833, in the house of his
grandfather, the vicar of Ruabon (Welsh Rhiwabon) in the county of Denbigh. On
1 November, Walter received baptism from his grandfather in the local St Mary's
Church.[60] His middle name, Clopton, was that of his grandmother's family: the
Cloptons had come to England in the company of William the Conqueror and had
afterwards exchanged their French name of de Grandcourt for an English one.[61]
Walter's parents died early, so that the boy, from the age of 13, was under the tutelage
of his grandfather's brother and his uncle.[62] His grandfather's brother, a retired colonel,
was influential in his being admitted, after having succeeded in his second attempt
to pass the entrance examination at Sandhurst, to the prestigious 1st Dragoon
Guards.[63] He served in India, where he met Alice Lydia Cleveland, the daughter of
his general, who was later to become his wife, and he took part in the China campaign
of 1860 and the capture of Peking.[64] Wingfield returned to England in 1861, and
together with his family moved from Wales to London six years later.[65] In the spring
of 1874, when he presented to the public his game of *sphairistikè*, his residence was
112 Belgrave Road in Pimlico.[66] It was the time of his success, overshadowed already
by the mental illness of his wife which grew worse as time went on. But Wingfield

was destined to suffer even harder blows. His three sons all died young and under rather tragic circumstances.[67] Wingfield lost all interest in his game of lawn tennis and in 1877 did not even care to have his patent renewed.[68] He had entrusted the much respected Marylebone Cricket Club with it before that date, in a letter to *The Field* in which, at the same time, he bade tennis farewell for good, and with much decorum.[69] In the 1890s, Wingfield again gained prominence as an inventor. After experimenting with bicycles, he constructed a new improved prototype which he christened 'Butterfly'. For this, he devised rides for single cyclists and teams, to be executed to music.[70] At the same time, he founded, after he had for a whole decade been vice-president of 'The Universal Cookery and Food Association', a Culinary Society, called 'Le Cordon Rouge'. It had espoused the idea, as its adepts put it, of furthering the advancements of the Sciences of Cookery,[71] a not altogether pointless undertaking in England, to be sure.

Wingfield passed away on 18 April 1912 at 33 St George's Square, London.[72] His sick wife, Alice, survived him by many years. She died, aged 92, in an asylum in November 1934.[73] The couple are buried at Kensal Green Cemetery near Harrow Road in the northwest of London. Surprisingly, at a time of an unprecedented tennis boom, Wingfield's grave had to be re-discovered by his biographer, George E. Alexander, under a huge overgrowth of grass and vine in 1974.[74] It was restored in 1980 after an initiative taken by The Major Wingfield Club, a club which constituted itself in the United States, proving once again that a prophet counts least in his own country. Nevertheless, the grave is now maintained by The Wimbledon Lawn Tennis Museum.[75]

TENNIS IS MONOPOLIZED BY THE ATHLETE

'Hit your ball gently': these were the words with which Major Wingfield began his 'Useful Hints' which he prefixed to his Rules.[76] They were consciously addressed to the Real tennis player of his day who, performing in a court surrounded by walls, had never before given a thought to the question of whether his ball landed within his court or not.[77] It was he above all to whom the Major intended to teach a lesson of how that most erratic lawn tennis ball might be brought under control. In so doing, however, he could hardly foresee the most unfortunate side-effect which this piece of advice was to entail. Rather than enabling the Real tennis player to tame the tennis ball, he disabled the game. Real tennis players heeded the Major's advice, and, in view of the shortness of the court and the bogey of a disproportionately high net in front of them (it measured five feet at the posts and a still remarkable four feet in the middle), they made every effort to place their ball in the opposite court slowly and delicately, and in high arches. And so did all others who regarded these gentlemen as the new sport's undisputed experts. The real sportsmen of the day, however, and above all, the cricket players, treated the rival with utter contempt. Commander George W. Hillyard, a first-class athlete and a county cricketer,[78] and himself one of the lawn tennis protagonists before and after the turn of the century, had rather strange recollections of how he became acquainted with the Major's game:[79]

> My earliest recollections of lawn tennis are somewhere about the middle 'seventies, when, on coming home from school one summer, I found that an uncle who was staying with us had marked out the lawn with a figure shaped like a gigantic hour-glass. He told us it was a lawn tennis court. The net was about five feet high at the posts and four feet or so in the centre. There was a centre tape, and the posts were not the heavy firm ones of modern times, but thin attenuated affairs with little flags stuck on the top, and held by guy ropes, which latter were always slipping and constantly needing adjustment. ...
>
> My uncle appeared to think there were great possibilities in the game, and prophesied a world-wide future for it. Now, this was curious ... a dozen years or so later, when I took up the game myself, I found great prejudice against it amongst my cricketing friends. They nearly all condemned it as fit only for women and quite unworthy of the attention of a man, certainly of a cricketer! ... we youngsters would have none of it. Cricket for us every time and at all time. ... the other seemed pat-ball, and *was* pat-ball at that period. Players had small skill, nor was it possible to play anything but a comparatively slow sort of shot, because of the height of the net ...

Pat-ball, or *patters*, to use the terms current among students for such inordinate caressing of a ball,[80] had first and foremost to get rid of the bad reputation it held among university sportsmen (the most innovative and influential element in contemporary sporting life), if it was to achieve a permanent success.[81]

The acceptance of a new idea is not only dependent on some new technology, but also on a change of mentality. The new way to play tennis was a case in point. As a result of industrialization, and owing to the wealth of its colonies, England had become a prosperous country. Most members of the English upper classes could afford to spend hours either doing nothing at all, or applying their energies to that typical outgrowth of idleness, sport. Curiously enough, however, the leisure time preoccupation was governed by the very spirit which had brought about the advance of the nation's economy.

The new concept of sport was inseparably linked to that of the record, and both had their roots in the philosophy of nineteenth-century industrial society. At a time when capitalist entrepreneurs strove for the manufacture of ever better products in even less time, sportsmen began to measure, not the output of a machine, but the efficiency of the human body, by comparing their performances with earlier ones, with a view to improving them. Such experimenting is borne out by the appearance of records: the keeping of times and the results of matches. Neither the Middle Ages nor the Renaissance have handed down to us any such records. The insistence on the comparability of performance is one of the reasons why the immeasurably complicated rules of medieval tennis were so dramatically curtailed even by Wingfield. Even though the shrewd Major may have had in mind a highly entertaining five o'clock pastime for the rich, as well as one offering a young lady an opportunity of becoming acquainted with a promising young man, the transmutation of tennis into a sport became inevitable when, significantly, a cricket club, the famous Marylebone Cricket Club, laid hands upon Wingfield's *sphairistikè*. What was going to happen to the game became clear at once. A simpler, standardized tennis court was inaugurated which left no doubt as to who was the fitter player, able, in a truly Darwinist sense, to outlast his opponent on the other side of the net. Standardization was the magic word: not only had the measures of the court to be definitely settled, but the ball, too, its make-up and weight had to be regulated with the utmost precision.[82] The rules were no exception. They also had to be adapted in such a way as to enhance athleticism and speed.[83] From the very moment the first tennis players appeared on court pertly wearing cricket-style caps, tennis was no longer in danger of ever degenerating to a 'girls' game'.[84] These players did away with absurdities such as the one advanced as late as 1892 by a German expert who had, far off in the lawn tennis hinterland, preserved the mentality of the peaceful five o'clock pastime of yore:[85]

> Recommendation for Learning the Game of L.T. ... Make sure to hit all balls, to throw them correctly, to keep rigorously within the boundary lines and, last but not least, to play balls to the opponent in such a way as to make the return difficult, nay impossible for him, so that he makes mistakes. This you achieve by playing your balls low over the net, or to where the opponent does not expect them, but in so doing every exaggeration or nasty trick should be avoided, in the interest of the game.

Clearly, the author of these lines was not abreast with the changes that had taken place in the country of the game's origin, England. Here, every lawn tennis player had passionately embraced the exaggerated play and saw to it that not a single nasty trick was spared.[86]

TENNIS BECOMES ORGANIZED

At the instigation of John Moyer Heathcote, a real tennis champion and as such a much respected authority,[87] a meeting was held on the premises of Marylebone Cricket Club on 3 March 1875. It was meant to put to the test the various forms of lawn tennis then in use in order to establish a set of rules which could be universally accepted. An invitation had also been extended to Wingfield who stated his opinion and succeeded in having his hour-glass-shaped court accepted by the MCC commission. It was incorporated in the rules which were published shortly afterwards, in May 1875. Important innovations, however, became apparent at once. In marked contrast to Wingfield's original plan, the court had been extended to the length of 78 feet, the measurement still valid today. The service courts had been shifted from the baseline to the net, Wingfield's service diamond had been abandoned and the server banished to the baseline. He was enjoined to have at least one foot behind it when serving.[88] As might have been expected in view of the popularity of lawn tennis and the vast following it could claim, the MCC rules were subject to criticism. It was levelled above all at the height of the net and the absurdity of the hour-glass shape, and it was in this situation that a club gained prominence which was destined to become the most important institution in the history of lawn tennis: the All England Croquet Club. Founded on 23 July 1868,[89] it demonstrated by its very name that it had an almost ideal predisposition to become the cradle of the game then in its infancy. On the extensive site of its three-terraced croquet lawns between Worple Road and the track of the London and Southampton Railway (later to become the South Western),[90] in the vicinity of Wimbledon Station, lawn tennis had been played for some time.[91] In April 1877, the managing committee of the club, following a suggestion by its founder member and honorary secretary, John Walsh (he was at the same time editor of *The Field*), decided to acknowledge the fact by incorporating in its name the word *lawn tennis*.[92] Not satisfied with this, the new All England Croquet and Lawn Tennis Club had made up its mind to become the stronghold of lawn tennis in the entire United Kingdom. As a first step on its way to future glory, the club announced a grand-scale lawn tennis tournament, to be held in the same year in the month of June.[93] This necessitated having a fresh look at the rules. As was suggested by the All England Club, a triumvirate was substituted for the old MCC commission, consisting of Henry Jones of the All England Club and, in order not to break the continuity, two members of the MCC, Julian Marshall and J.M. Heathcote.

Heathcote had, to begin with, been a member of the MCC commission. He had done the young sport an immeasurable service by laying, as it were, a golden egg on the question of the most important prerequisite of the game: the tennis ball. It was he who had suggested enshrining it in a white flannel cover.[94] As becomes evident from a note advertising Wingfieldian tennis balls in 1882,[95] they no longer enjoyed their primeval state *au naturel* so characteristic of good old *sphairistikè*. Of late, they had been clad in a stout cloth made in Melton Mowbray in Leicestershire, which now revived dear memories of the times before Heathcote's invention when it led a more peaceful, albeit somewhat uninteresting, life as a material for men's wear.

Julian Marshall was the son of a manufacturer from Leeds, an art collector and a connoisseur of music,[96] and a man of means throughout his lifetime. He had codified the rules of real tennis in 1872, a factor which strongly recommended him for the task.

Last, but not least, came Jones. He was a physician who had resigned from his job and worked for *The Field* under the *nom de plume* Cavendish. He had become the journal's self-elected authority on games, especially on the popular game of whist, the forerunner of bridge.[97]

The three commissioners in the weeks to come achieved something truly remarkable. When the first ball at a Wimbledon tournament was served on Monday, 9 July 1877, they had laid down rules which have been allowed to stand until the present day, and with hardly any exception. It was through their efforts that the All England Club, which in 1882 reversed the order of the words *croquet* and *lawn tennis* in its title in order to signal a change of emphasis,[98] established itself as the supreme court of appeal on the question of rules.

Under the scrutiny of the commission, the time for Wingfield's hour-glass court had at last run out. The commission decreed a return to the traditional rectangular court, for which Heathcote had opted before in a thoughtful letter to *The Field*.[99]

Wingfield's counting method also had to bow out. The commission, following a recommendation by Cavendish, abandoned the rackets scoring and restored to its rights the old tennis counting by fifteens.[100] The lawn tennis court for the future was to measure 78 by 27 feet.

Within the next three years, the height of the net was gradually reduced, and in 1880, by a unanimous decision of the MCC and the All England Club, it was eventually set at four feet at the posts,[101] and three feet in the middle. Since the lowering of the net was thought to give undue advantage to the server, the service line was moved closer to the net. A distance of 21 feet was finally considered satisfactory. Not before 1882, however, did the confederate pundits of the MCC and the All England Club hit on the glorious idea of extending the outer boundaries of the service courts to the baseline for the doubles. Before that date, the unfortunate English groundsman had been compelled to mark singles and doubles courts separately, at a time when the acquisition of suitable acreage apparently did not present a problem to English lawn tennis clubs.[102] Henceforth, a doubles court could also be used as a singles court, and vice versa (**Figure 69**).

CHERCHEZ LA FEMME,
OR, THE FOUNDATION OF THE LAWN TENNIS ASSOCIATION

The first attempts to set up an English tennis organization go back to the year 1883.[103] Since that time there had been an informal annual meeting of club secretaries, but when during the first of these it was moved that an association should be founded, the assembly, strangely enough, had voted against it. The plan was taken up again in January 1888, and prospects were more promising this time.[104] The initiative had presumably been taken by Harry Scrivener, president of the Oxford University LTC, and a friend of his, George Hillyard. The two men disliked the way lawn tennis was monopolized by the All England Club and the high-handed attitude of Julian Marshall, the club's secretary since 1880. In addition, Hillyard bore the All England Club a very personal grudge. The club had refused to give up the privilege of holding the ladies' championships which in the past four years had yielded a handsome profit. Blanche Bingley, the All England champion and of late Hillyard's wife, had played a prominent part in them. Her brilliant performance in front of the large excited crowd, however, had sent her husband into fits of jealousy, and he insisted on having the venue for this exhibitionism removed to the provinces.

Scrivener and Hillyard had been in charge of sending invitations for the meeting in January, but, by some inadvertency, the All England Club had not been invited. Naturally, the All England Club considered this an act of wilful disregard.[105] A schism of the lawn tennis universe into an All England Club and an Association seemed inevitable. However, with Daniel Jones, president of the Hyde Park LTC and at the same time a member of the All England Club, acting as an intermediary, the split could be avoided.[106] Because it had been so easily reconciled, the All England Club was granted the perpetual right of holding the championships. The club reciprocated

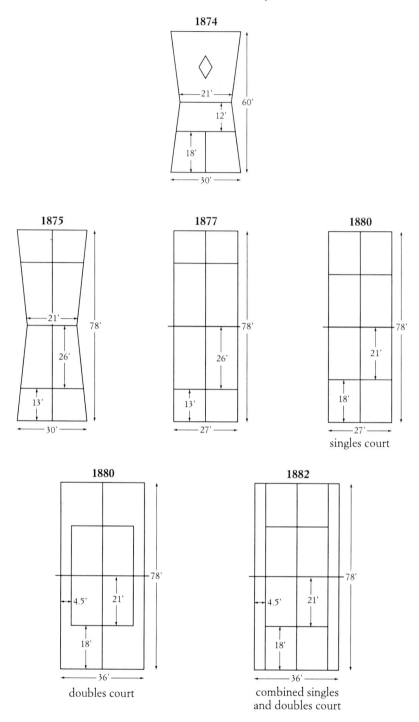

FIGURE 69 The evolution of the lawn tennis court. It is interesting that for a comparatively long time, singles and doubles courts should have been kept strictly separate.

by entrusting the rules to the guardianship of the newly-founded Lawn Tennis Association (LTA).[107] Herbert Chipp was unanimously elected secretary of a board that was to reign supreme in European lawn tennis for decades to come, and the presidency was gained by the outstanding tennis player of the time, William Renshaw. By calling their new organization the Lawn Tennis Association pure and simple, the founders showed little interest in what was going on outside their own country. No true Englishman at the time really cared. The fact that there had been in existence another organization of the same name since 1881, the United States National Lawn Tennis Association (USNLTA), did not bother them in the least.

THE INTERNATIONAL LAWN TENNIS FEDERATION:
CONTINUATOR OF THE WINGFIELDIAN HERITAGE

As is generally believed,[108] the suggestion to form an international umbrella organization for lawn tennis was made by Duane Williams, an American citizen who lived in Geneva. What exactly Williams suggested is not altogether clear. According to one version, Williams approached the secretary of the Swiss Lawn Tennis Federation, Charles Barde.[109] The Swiss official, in view of the magnitude of the task, sought the help of a more influential person and was fortunate to meet Henry Wallet, a Frenchman who happened to be on holiday on Lake Geneva and whom he informed about Williams' proposal. Wallet was the president of the Commission Centrale de Lawn-Tennis which, within the Union des Sociétés Françaises de Sports Athlétiques, and prior to the foundation of the French Lawn Tennis Federation, was in charge of lawn tennis.[110]

According to another version, Williams' plan reached Wallet through a different channel, a letter which Williams wrote to him in October 1911, and in which the American proposed, not the inauguration of an international federation, but the introduction of world championships on clay courts.[111] It was this proposal which found favour with Wallet. In order to organize these championships, an international committee was set up. It was from this organizing committee that the International Lawn Tennis Federation eventually evolved.[112]

The inaugural meeting of the ILTF eventually took place on 1 March 1913, at 34 Rue de Provence, in the headquarters of the USFSA (**Figure 70**).[113] The location was described by one of the participants as 'not exactly splendid'.[114] One of the more unfortunate aspects of the meeting, in which the representatives of thirteen nations participated, was the absence of the United States,[115] while the initiator of the organization, Duane Williams, did not live to see the day. He had been among the casualties in the wreck of the *Titanic* in the previous year.[116] Every nation was conceded a contingent of delegates according to its supposed importance in the tennis world of the time. Acknowledging England's pioneering role in the evolution of the sport, the ILTF was willing to confer upon the LTA the maximum of six votes and the exclusive right of holding lawn tennis world championships;[117] these were identical with the All England Championships in Wimbledon.[118] The Americans, unwilling to brook such extravagance on behalf of the English, refused to join the organization.

FIGURE 70   The founding members of the International Lawn Tennis Federation. Back row, standing: B. Sabelli, E.R. Clarke, C. Barde, P. Gillou, Chevalier P. de Borman, A.E.M. Taylor, Allan H. Muhr; middle row: E. Gambs, R. Gallay, G. Inglis, R.J. McNair, Dr H.O. Behrens, H. Wallet, H.H. Monckton, M.J. Feith; front row: Dr E. Larsen, K. Zetterberg, Dr O. Nirrnheim, Dr A. Zborzil, Dr W. Lümann.

In their opinion, only one world championship existed which deserved that name: the Davis Cup, inaugurated in 1900.[119] Following a sugggestion by the English delegate R.J. McNair, the Paris assembly elected the German Dr Hans Oskar Behrens chairman of the first meeting.[120] The versatile German, who had a perfect command of English and French, acquitted himself well, and praises were lavished on him for the excellence of his performance afterwards. The first general assembly of the ILTF abstained from creating the office of a president.[121]

Only in 1923, and after considerable wrangling, could the Americans be persuaded to become members. England had to jettison her sixth vote, and to relinquish the prerogative of calling her All England Championships world championships. In order to satisfy everybody, the ILTF raised to the rank of offical championships the championships of four of its members, England, France, Australia and America. At the same time, the English LTA transferred the rules it had inherited from the All England Club to the custody of the ILTF, after stipulating that they should be printed for all time in the English language,[122] the very language in which Major Wingfield's rules, six in all, had gone to the printers almost exactly half a century before.

WIMBLEDON, PRESERVE OF THE AMATEUR

The credit for having launched the first Wimbledon tournament must be given to Henry Jones who had presented the proposal to the managing committee of the All England Club.[123] On the question of what led 'Cavendish' to make the suggestion, opinions are divided. According to one, the croquet club's pony roller was in need of repair, and it was hoped that the revenues would cover the expenses.[124] According to another, the initiative taken by 'Cavendish' was not altogether unselfish. Knowing that championships had to be earned by the sweat of the players' brows, he had a changing-room set up at his own costs, fees being payable to Mr Jones.[125]

On the other hand, 'Cavendish' was not the man to flinch from unpleasant duties. It was by no means a foregone conclusion that the championships would indeed be staged on the lawns of the All England Club (**Figure 71**). Well before the idea of holding a tournament materialized, Henry Jones had inspected a real host of possible venues, but had found none worthier of the task.[126] That is why on 9 June 1877, and, of course, in *The Field*, an announcement could be made intimating to the honourable readership of the journal the intention of the All England Club to hold a lawn tennis tournament precisely one month later, on 9 July 1877 and the days following. At the same time, invitations were circulated to prospective participants.[127] In both announcements, the entry fees for competitors had been specified: one pound and one shilling, or, as the authors put it, one guinea. The guinea was long the monetary unit used for pricing works of art or landed property. It had a tinge of exclusiveness.

The expenditure of one guinea might, of course, repay. When on the opening day the elegant visitors had arrived in Worple Road, either by coach or the London and Southampton Railway, had paid the entrance fee of sixpence,[128] and another sixpence

FIGURE 71   The first All England Championships on the courts at Worple Road, Wimbledon. The courts are viewed from the West. Worple Road is on the left, the track of the London and Southampton Railway on the right-hand side.

for the first issue of the printed programmes (these appeared daily with the last results entered), they might read the following about the prizes to be awarded to the victors. The winner could expect a gold prize worth twelve guineas and a silver cup, presented by *The Field*, worth twenty-five guineas. The runner-up and the third-placed might still await prizes valuing seven and three guineas respectively.[129]

What might have caused surprise, at least in view of the prize money, were the restrictions placed on the competitors. Only amateurs were eligible.[130] By their insistence on a competitor's amateur status, the hosts of a tournament did not, however, envisage an amateur in the modern sense of the term. What seemed desirable was the competitor's allegiance to a particular class. Since the foundation of the London Amateur Athletic Club in 1866 – it had, significantly, its roots in university circles – the term *amateur* had become a synonym of gentleman.[131] Its semantic opposite was *professional*. The term *professional*, though also referring to sportsmen who made a living out of their sport,[132] had the stigma of the manual labourer. Craftsmen, petty shopkeepers, workers and servants went by the name of *professional*. They were normally excluded from membership in amateur clubs. Those, however, who, in the eyes of society, had acquired the status of a gentleman amateur, could earn as much money as they wanted to, and even by practising a sport. Dr W.G. Grace, for example, physician, gentleman, and the outstanding cricketer of the time, accepted cheques for fifteen hundred and nine thousand pounds, a real fortune in those days.[133] The gentleman who would turn out victorious in the first Wimbledon tournament would therefore collect the prize money offered without the slightest scruple.

The obligatory reference in the programme to the amateur status of the competitors indicated within what social layers lawn tennis had taken its roots in the 1870s. The concept of the amateur was part of the ideology of the well-to-do who had enlisted the help of a voluble spokesman, just when the first All England Championships were running their course, in the person of an Irishman, John P. Mahaffy.[134] Mahaffy, whose favourite ambience was the British nobility, was convinced he had discovered the prototype of the English amateur in the Olympic athletes of Greek antiquity. A third-rate historian himself, and not realizing that he was merely grafting onto the sporting heroes of Ancient Greece the preconceived notions of his social betters, he created the myth of the Olympic amateur. It was this myth which was to cause considerable damage to lawn tennis.

THE FIRST ALL ENGLAND CHAMPIONSHIPS

The programmes also listed the names of the twenty-two competitors, and they daily bore witness to the grim progress of a certain Spencer W. Gore, a rackets specialist, who steadily worked his way through a phalanx of Real tennis players.[135] Since nobody had informed 'Mr Bye' (later to become so extremely popular with tennis players as an opponent) to make an appearance in the first round,[136] a rather curious configuration (from a modern point of view) presented itself when the tournament came to a close. There were three semi-finalists. A drawing of lots (or, to put it differently, a belated 'Mr Bye') helped a Real tennis player, W. Marshall, to reach the final, whereas Gore and the third semi-finalist, C.G. Heathcote, had to fight for the chance of winning the prize money and the cup. The Real tennis players had entertained the belief that the battle of the ball could be decided in their favour by imparting much cut (or 'stoof') on the ball and sending it, by turns and with a clean stroke, into the right and left corner of the opposite court. Gore, the brother of the Bishop of Birmingham,[137] demonstrated clearly that this belief was an erroneous one. He put an end to their nice little game by strutting forward to the net, raising his racket and distributing, with a deft forward movement, right and left, all balls which came sailing in across the middle of the net, considerably lower here than near the posts. For Gore's opponents, this meant a great deal of running, and with distances on court simply not negotiable, one of them in fact confessed that he 'was ready to drop'.[138] And yet, the idea of outmanoeuvring Gore who, close to the net, kept brandishing his racket, by punching the ball down the line, occurred to none of them, despite their dire predicament. They had been taught that such a shot was by far too risky because of the height of the net at the posts.[139] They were still calculating the risks after Gore had long made a fool of all of them.

The Real tennis players, it seemed, were incapable of learning a lesson, but their stubbornness is easily accounted for. The easy victory of a man who by his intuition alone had adopted the right tactics, proved beyond any doubt that the new game required a new style peculiar to it. The Real tennis players were unable to develop it. They were all of an age at which improvement had its limitations, and change was impossible. As Gore, the champion, writing down his recollections fifteen years later, wisely put it,[140] lawn tennis was waiting for the advent of a completely new race, young players who had grown up with it. For the time being, however, the sport suffered a set-back, in an almost literal sense. At the next All England championships, an event occurred which sounded the bold volleyer's retreat, and persuaded Real tennis players to cling to their traditional way of playing, come hell or high water.

THE COFFEE PLANTER WHO SOWED RETROGRESSION

A novelty was introduced in the championships of 1878 (**Figure 72**). The competition became divided into an All Comers' Round and a Challenge Round.[141] In the latter, the champion of the previous year had to defend his title against the winner of the All Comers' Round – he did not have to fight his way, as the modern champion must, through the whole seven rounds again. The first All Comers' Round saw the victory of a certain Patrick Francis Hadow, a coffee planter from Ceylon.[142] Hadow had come to England for a holiday and, rather than playing some cricket as he had intended to do, the former captain of the Harrow cricket team and county player for Middlesex, resolved to try his hand at lawn tennis. He first came into contact with a tennis ball in the famous Maida Vale Club, and then played a few matches on the lawns of Wimbledon where the future champion H.F. Lawford was his partner.[143] A friend of his family, L.R. Erskine, suggested to him that he should enter for the Wimbledon

FIGURE 72   Popular illustration of the All England Championships in their second year, 1878, from the *Illustrated Sporting and Dramatic News*.

tournament. Hadow accepted the invitation with gratitude, but proved far less grateful to his mentor Erskine later on, by beating him in the final of the All Comers' Round. Now he was facing the long-legged and long-armed Gore who, spider-like, again and again took up a position close to the net. 'It was not easy to drive down the side lines', Hadow remembered much later, at the age of 71,[144] 'with the net sagging to the centre from the posts and fastened below the top of each post, instead of being level … My attempts to pass Gore, … with a low hard stroke, when he was at the net, usually failed.' Rather desperately, he resorted to a stroke which neither he nor anybody else had ever tried before: the lob.[145] It compelled Gore to scurry back from his position near the net to the baseline.[146] It was, considering the hot sun of July, not a fortuitous turn the match was taking for the champion. The victor in this frolicsome chase was Hadow, even though he was taken to two sets with 'advantage games', the first to be played in Wimbledon's history.[147] Hadow's ingenious stratagem against the net-rusher Gore, however, had fateful consequences for the game in the years to come. Hadow discouraged all those who had been willing to throw in their lot with Gore and his pioneering tactics. The Real tennis players and their deadly monotonous way of playing it safe from the baseline had won the day. Their method of playing the game was to hold sway for the next three years.

'Safest of all safety players' would have been the epithet befitting a clergyman from Yorkshire, the Reverend J.T. Hartley. A participant in the 1878 championships called Tabor had persuaded him to make an appearance in the next,[148] and, hardly expecting to survive the initial rounds, he was prepared to return to his parish before the weekend in order to hold the service on Sunday. He lived to regret his lack of faith. Victorious even in the quarter-finals on Friday, he had to embark on a long journey back to Yorkshire on Saturday. On the morning of the Monday following, Hartley was back on the train to Wimbledon again and, reaching his destination early in the afternoon, just made it for the semi-final. After his train ride, he could hold his own only with difficulty, but the next day, after a good night's sleep, he won easily against V. Goold, the Irish champion.

In the tournament, the spirited Irishman, who had entered under the pseudonym 'St Leger',[149] had been among the few who resorted to the volley more frequently, but against Hartley he did not stand the ghost of a chance. The result of the match evoked a rather sarcastic comment from one of the London daily newspapers. 'Safety is the first requisite in lawn tennis, and brilliancy the second,' it said.[150] After rallies in which the ball was allowed to cross the net between forty to fifty times, critics of this style (including the former champion Gore) began to draw a gloomy picture of what might still have happened, if in the Challenge Round the indefatigable Reverend had met the invincible coffee planter Hadow.[151] Hadow, however, had, thank goodness, returned to his plantation, and that is why the championship could be awarded to the Reverend without further ado – and much time be saved.

In the following year, the excellent baseliner H.F. Lawford, after a four-set struggle, had to yield to the unsurpassed baseliner Hartley in the Challenge Round. It was in this match, however, that Lawford demonstrated a skill which was to make him one of the greatest players of the time. Rather than placing his ball (as the Real tennis players did) with a great deal of under-cut, he tried to hit it hard with the flat of his racket-head. This technique greatly surprised the old strategist Gore. Spin and cut, Gore realized, made the ball travel more slowly as soon as it made contact with the court, and thus returns were much easier. From around 1881, therefore, the best lawn tennis players had begun to develop a stroke of their own. They hit the ball with the flat face of their rackets, and harder and harder ever since from year to year. Was it not short of a miracle, Gore was heard to exclaim, that so light a ball can be hit so hard, within such limited space, without being driven out of court?[152] Lawford was well on his way to bringing this stroke to perfection,[153] although the final of 1880 was still dominated by the perfect placer, Hartley.

THE REVOLUTION: THE RENSHAW TWINS

The protagonists of the 'new race', the twin brothers William and Ernest Renshaw (**Figures 73 and 74**), were born in the cradle of lawn tennis, Leamington Spa, on 23 January 1861.[154] William was the older of the twins by fifteen minutes and, because of his greater power, determination and coolness,[155] the better tennis player. Ernest

FIGURE 73   William Renshaw, the unrivalled All England champion of the 1880s.

FIGURE 74   Ernest Renshaw, William's twin brother, whose game was somewhat less consistent. He became All England Champion once, in 1888.

was a fine stylist with excellent footwork. However, as much as for his lightfootedness he was known for his lightheartedness. At the Fitzwilliam Club in Dublin, a club famous for its cheerful hospitality, he once let slip an Irish championship (coveted almost as much in those days as the English), because he chose to sacrifice the night before the final, not to Morpheus, the god of sleep, but to Terpsichore, the muse of the dance.[156] Not unlike the late French musketeer René Lacoste in the 1920s, the twins, while still in their teens, began to make notes of other players' style and kept analysing their own game in order to improve it.[157] They were lucky to be the offspring of a wealthy family who could afford to devote their whole time to lawn tennis. Even the greatest handicap of the tennis-playing Briton, the weather, was of but little concern to them. During the winter, they applied an extra polish to their repertoire of strokes on a private tennis court they had built for themselves at their own cost at a hotel on the French Riviera.[158] Among their strokes, two were utterly novel: the overhead service and the smash. Attempts at an overhead service had been made by a certain A.T. Myers as early as 1878, but, for the simple reason that Myers was not good enough at lawn tennis, his experiments with this stroke had been abortive. By 1881, however, all top players had adopted this method of initiating a rally. Lawford, who has already been mentioned, served in this manner with some precision. The Renshaws, however, had turned it into a real 'hammer' (as contemporaries called it). It was with this implement that they forged their success. It was something of a shock to their opponents, who resorted to abusive language and denounced the serving method of the twins as 'nothing but brute force and ignorance'.[159]

The smash was so revolutionary that it was named after the brothers. The crowds which came flocking to the gates of Wimbledon in 1881 – it was the beginning of the Renshaw Boom[160] – respectfully referred to it as 'the Renshaw Smash'. It was a pity to see how the Reverend Mr Hartley, who, with a heart full of misgivings, had watched the dreadful William sweep through the All Comers' Round, was unable to offer him any resistance in the Challenge Round. With an illness making things still worse for him,[161] he in three sets collected no more than two measly games. The score was 6:0, 6:1, 6:1, and the whole match lasted a mere 37 minutes. It was the shortest Wimbledon final ever to be played and conclusive evidence that a revolution had taken place.[162]

The revolution was followed by a long rule of the Renshaws which was never seriously challenged. It lasted till 1889 when William Renshaw again wrenched the title from his brother Ernest. It was his seventh, and another lasting record in which a revolutionary style again found expression.

William's ultimate victory had been preceded by a protracted absence from play. In the opinion of experts, the champion's cannon serves and smashing mania were here at last exacting their tribute. William Renshaw had contracted tennis elbow. It was the first time that this tennis player's plight, first mentioned in the journal *The Field* in 1881,[163] became known to the public at large. William's handicap paved the way for his fiercest antagonist for a whole decade, H.F. Lawford, the perpetual runner-up. Lawford won his one and only All England championship. Not as fast on court as the Renshaws and older than they by ten years, Lawford, an athlete with an almost stoic disposition,[164] had not missed a single championship since 1878. In marked contrast to the Renshaws, he passionately advocated playing from the baseline. He continued to assert that only by inadequate 'back-play' was the volleyer given a chance to score. The volleyer's success, in his opinion, ought not to be attributed to his superior method, but to the inadequate play of the baseliner. 'Learn to play better' was Lawford's motto.[165] True to his principles, Lawford never grew tired of making his drives as precise and powerful as possible. He was among the first to run round his backhand in order to use his forehand drive even more effectively. The fact that in 1882 the net had been lowered for the last time (it now measured three feet and six inches at the posts)[166] was to Lawford's advantage, and in 1887 his pertinacity was finally rewarded, even though in the following year he was in turn overthrown by William's brother Ernest. To Lawford must go the credit of having been the Renshaws' touchstone as long as their careers lasted. Only through his influence did they become exceptional players. He forced them not to have too much confidence in their volleying powers, and to improve their 'back-court' play considerably.[167] Only through the antagonism amd challenge of Lawford did they become all-court players, the type of player which in the history of lawn tennis was destined to outlast all others.[168]

TWINS: THE DOUBLES' INSPIRATION

The first club to hold, in 1879, a doubles championship was not the All England Club, but the Oxford University Club.[169] Interest in the competition soon flagged, however, and that is why the organizers had no regrets to pass on to the All England Club the cups nobody seemed to want. From 1884 onwards, therefore, the doubles championships also took place in Wimbledon. Once wedded to the idea of expansion, the All England Club, in the same year, resolved to hold a ladies' championship as well. In so doing, it followed the example of the Irish who, more favourably disposed towards sporting womanhood, had inaugurated ladies' championships as early as 1879.[170] In addition, the All England Club had thought it proper to introduce Challenge Rounds for both the ladies' singles and the gentlemen's doubles, starting in 1886.[171]

In the doubles matches of these early days, the protagonists were at first entrenched somewhere near the baseline until an attempt was made to put an end to never-ending rallies by sending a one-man vanguard patrol to the net with the order to kill weak returns. The success of this outpost cannot have been a brilliant one. In the rear, his partner continued to have a hell of a job to retrieve the balls that had passed his partner.[172] At the sight of such an apparent imbalance, the author of a book on lawn tennis was apparently led to recommend, in the 1880s, a strategy for the four-handed game resembling the working of 'two buckets in a well'. As soon as one player advanced to the net, he argued, his partner should beat a hasty retreat to the baseline, and vice versa. Needless to say, the Renshaw smash sent the two buckets violently to the bottom.

The Renshaws, after having followed up their service, occupied a position at the service line immediately from where they dispatched their volleys, conceding to the ball only a minimum of contacts with the ground before the point was scored.[173] This they did to the groundsman's delight, and much to the dismay of the former champion Gore who in the early 1890s was still insisting on a change of either the rules or the dimensions of the doubles court so as to prevent this method from becoming the only one to bode triumph to future doubles players.[174]

It is hardly surprising that the Renshaw twins were even more successful in the doubles than in the singles. With the exception of the year in which William suffered from tennis elbow, they were victorious at all times, and it is significant that in order to terminate the series of their wins, supernatural powers had to be called upon. The Renshaws were at last defeated by an Irishman, Willoughby James Hamilton, nicknamed 'The Ghost' on account of his appalling thinness. Hamilton took the title from William Renshaw in 1890 in the Challenge Round.[175] The Renshaws' method of worrying their opponents by volleying from mid-court was revised after their retirement, in the 1890s, by another set of twins, Herbert and Wilfred Baddeley.[176] According to them, the players partnering for the doubles had to pitch their tents, not on the service line, or at a short distance from it, but as close to the net as by any means possible. Only in this way might the ball be hit on the rise, and only in this way might the area which had to be covered be significantly reduced, and Wilfred Baddeley tried to make his view carry more conviction by adding at this point of his discussion a useful diagram. The tactics adopted by the Baddeleys marked the last phase in the evolution of the doubles game, a game which can thus be said to owe its present form to the ingenuity of twins.

TENNIS FOR THE LADIES

The first ladies' championship was won by Maud Watson, the local heroine of Birmingham, the very place where Augurio Pereira's lawn pelota had originated. Since she had competed in a public tournament in Edgbaston in 1881 she had not lost a single match.[177] Maud was the daughter of the vicar of Berkswell,[178] a village near Leamington Spa. Before winning the championship, she had played many a strenuous practice match against students from Cambridge who received private tuition in mathematics in her father's home, and lessons in lawn tennis on the adjacent vicarage lawn, perhaps the most important venue in the early days of the sport. Maud left a very interesting (and little known) account herself of how she learnt tennis when she talked shop with Helen Wills at Great Fosters, a small hotel in Surrey where her famous successor had taken up quarters during the All England Championships of 1935:[179]

> My sisters and I took up tennis in our garden, and I didn't find it very difficult because I had played squash racquets with an uncle who was a master at Harrow. This helped my strokes. When I began to play tennis, I hit balls against the wall in our garden. My father was a vicar and a very broadminded man for those days. He let me and my sisters play in a match at Hurlingham, which we won. People thought it scandalous that he should let us play in public! We enjoyed it, though!

Maud was 19 when she beat her sister Lilian to win the All England championship.

The trophy awarded to the first male champion was the silver cup presented by the journal *The Field*. It was, not unlike the majority of the species, a pot, plain and rather unpretentious artistically, and yet not entirely unsuited for the not too particular male. It was, and still is, worshipped as a precious relic, and William Renshaw took possession of it after three successive victories.[180] Maud Watson's prize was not a cup, but a silver-gilt Rosewater Dish worth twenty guineas.[181] It made visible to everybody that the organizers had very different ideas about the gentleman's lawn tennis and that of the ladies, ideas which, it may be said, still persist.

In 1890 John Moyer Heathcote had given a royal welcome to any lady wishing to honour a Real tennis court with her presence. However, it was only in the spectators' box to the rear of the *dedans* where her presence was approved. Her presence on court would have been simply unthinkable.[182] Lawn tennis took a different stance in this respect; it gave the ladies a chance, albeit very reluctantly. At first, the patriarchs of the English family had condoned their wives' and daughters' dalliance with Wingfield's *sphairistikè*, at least as long as they indulged in the new pastime in the seclusion of their country houses. Then the representatives of the fair sex had asked to be admitted to the lawn tennis club where the former pat-ball had of late been converted to an exacting sport. These activities began to be frowned upon. At last, women came forward with the frivolous request of showing their talent in a public tournament. Such impudence met with a rude rebuff. The All England Club above all would have none of it, and justly so, it was thought.[183] For a game imposing so much strain on the human brain as well as on the body, a woman was simply too weak. As to the brains required in the process, hardly any woman would be capable of even mastering the game's counting method. As to the body, no woman would be capable of playing a game which meant very hard work even to a man.

With smug complacency, the lords of creation nevertheless offered the sporting lady a helping hand. They proposed a smaller court, a lighter racket and a lighter ball in order to reduce the terrible pressure brought to bear on the tender wrist. A deep anguish was caused to them by the fact that the dastardly tennis ball might chance to hit the lady's eye. They advocated a much simplified set of rules. A lady should be allowed to serve from a special service point close to the net; she ought to be conceded the privilege of refusing to take the difficult service as often as she thought fit; and she might expect the gentleman to serve the ball always within her reach. They continued to have their doubts, however, whether lawn tennis suited a lady at all, and badminton was thought by many to be a sport more appropriate to her.

What also aroused the true gentleman's compassion was the frightful burden a woman had to carry in the form of her tennis outfit. Even to his mind it was 'such a drag'.[184] And a drag it was indeed. A tennis dress in the modern sense of the word was, of course, unknown (**Figure 75**).[185] For playing, the fashionable lady wore the costume which the conventions of the time prescribed for her everyday routine: long skirts which reached the ground; several starched petticoats underneath and the obligatory corset tightly laced. All this was given additional support by a girdle adorned by a silver clasp; it terminated in a stiff whalebone collar around which a necktie or scarf was slung. No dress was without long sleeves. An extravagant broad-brimmed felt hat dominated the lady's head, and a sturdy heeled, elegant boot was considered a must. Perhaps it was thought that a better outlook on the court might thus be obtained.

Under the handicaps of her dress, the lady had developed a lawn tennis style of her own. A 'lady player', writing before the turn of the century, might consider the game itself 'exciting', but this hardly applied to the brand of lawn tennis practised by her own sex:[186]

> The great fault I have to find with the members of my own sex is that they are, as a rule, far too lazy; and how, I should like to know, can they expect to get even the least bit excited over a game when they refuse to move about court at a faster pace than a walk, or, at best, a jogtrot?

FIGURE 75   A rarity of the first order: an original lawn tennis dress from the 1880s.

And yet: how could the lady tennis player have moved about court at all? The heeled boot made rapid moves to the net and back impossible, since her long skirts caught in it whenever she attempted a dash.[187] If, in order to circumvent this pitfall, she lifted the pendant profusion of cloth, this procedure was questionable from the view-point of contemporary morals. The lady, therefore, had no option other than to keep riveted to the baseline. There, the bulging waist of her dress stood in the way of any natural swing of the racket, and this, in turn, greatly promoted the pat-ball variety of lawn tennis. In addition, the lady's impressive broad-brimmed hat (which later was replaced by a flat straw-hat) dissuaded her for decades from using the overhead service.

Worse still, the lady scorned the volley. It was perhaps because she had been told from the very start that this stroke was, as it were, contrary to her very femininity. 'Do not try and volley much', the lady was instructed by Lieutenant Peile who, in 1884, wrote a tennis manual. The 'volley game is not made for ladies! It is too quick, and is too great a strain on the system,' he continued.[188] Abstention from the volleying game might be tolerated in the singles, but how did it affect the doubles game? Here, close to the baseline and in perfect sisterly harmony, the two ladies stood, indulging in rallies which seemed never to end. 'As a game of this description is played at the present time,' Wilfred Baddeley, the masterly representative of the men's doubles game, said full of melancholy in 1897,[189] 'there is but little excitement to be got out of it, either by the players themselves or the spectators; its only useful purpose apparently being the amount of good exercise which all the ladies are forced to take.' Since ladies refrained from volleying, they were in the mixed doubles assigned a role which (according to the philosophy of their gentleman partners) suited them best: that of a charlady. While the bold male, close to the net, was expected to score one splendid triumph after the other, the lady to his rear did the job of a maid of all work by scurrying up and down the baseline.[190] *Faire la femme de ménage* was what the frivolous French called this unattractive and rather humiliating scrounging together of any stray balls that came her way.[191] Because of their inferiority as a sport, the ladies' doubles and the mixed doubles became adopted into the Wimbledon canon only in 1913.[192]

The question why the ladies' utterly inappropriate tennis outfit was not soon replaced (as all 'lady players' hoped) by an improved and more functional one is surely intriguing. Lottie Dod wrote:

> Ladies' dress, too, is a matter for grave consideration; for how can they ever hope to play a sound game when their dresses impede the free movement of every limb? In many cases their very breathing is rendered difficult. A suitable dress is sorely needed, and hearty indeed would be the thanks of puzzled lady-players to the individual who invented an easy and pretty costume.[193]

(The last adjective shows that Lottie was, after all, a woman!)

But whose fault was it that such an individual could not be found? Certainly not the ladies', Lottie exclaimed, but that of their courteous protectors who, in journals such as *The Field*, kept voicing their male chauvinist opinion without ever receiving the slightest rebuke. The editor of the journal is very roundly berated because,[194] 'invested with the prerogative of an irresponsible despot', he had been 'made the ruler of the game as well as an arbiter of fashion, credited with the ability to regulate not only the weight of the lady's racket, but also the length of her skirt'. Lottie here lays bare the true motives of those who considered lawn tennis to be either too exacting or too dangerous for ladies, or who were resolved on confining her, by the introduction of sissy rules, to the secluded atmosphere of the garden party. Rather than conceding to the hated rival a glance at her ankle, these gentlemen would have much preferred seeing their bride or wife collapse under the burden of her tennis attire.

And yet, the ladies' revolt took place at last. 'Ladies should learn to run, and run their hardest, too, not merely stride.' Lottie Dod found fault with those ladies who, with an 'Oh! I can't' on their lips and in feigned despair, used to let pass a ball that might have been returned with a little effort, and who seemed willing to resign themselves to the role of the maid of all work for ever.[195] Shortly before the turn of the century, Herbert Chipp, secretary of the LTA and himself a tennis player of note, had to admit that ladies, and indeed a great many, had taken Lottie's advice to heart. On the time when ladies learnt how to run, which their grandmothers would have called a lapse back into 'pure heathenism', Chipp has to say the following:[196]

> Among the manifold changes and consequent uprootings of prejudices which the latter half of this century has witnessed, nothing has been more characteristic of the new order of things than the active participation of women in sports and pastimes. ... Lawn Tennis must claim a large share of the responsibility for the introduction of the new regime. But whether for better or worse, whether we disapprove with our grandmothers or approve with our daughters, times have changed, and we have to accept facts as we find them. And although the present movement may be (and undoubtedly is) often carried to excess, and the athleticism of the *fin-de-siècle* woman appears sometimes too pronounced, still it cannot be denied that on the whole the changes which have been brought about must ultimately prove beneficial to the race at large – at all events physically. Whether the benefit will be as great morally is a question which only time can settle. But we may surely venture to hope that our daughters will not be worse mothers because, instead of leading sedentary lives, a great portion of their young years has been spent on the river, the tennis lawn, the hockey field and the golf links – ay, even on the now ubiquitous bicycle itself.

Even in Germany, the opinions expressed by educators became less severe as time went on. As early as the 1890s, tennis was very strongly recommended for young ladies by August Hermann, a 'Turninspektor' from Brunswick,[197] provided the kitchen, the laundry and the nursery were not neglected. To Hermann's mind, tennis for the German lady was, above all, of considerable value for the German male. Since it was a game for both sexes, he argued, it might lure away young men from their notorious haunt, the *bierhaus*, and from alcohol, tobacco smoke and playing cards, evils to which they had succumbed in the decades past.

A last, but futile, attempt was made by the gentlemen to send the tennising ladies to Coventry, as it were. Having failed to deny them membership of sports clubs, they tried to assign to them the status of a club within the club. This was a practice much adhered to in the United States where, in clubs devoted to the manly game of cricket, for instance, tennis for a long time remained a game exclusively run by the club's womenfolk.[198] When the ladies finally requested to compete in public tournaments along with the gentlemen,[199] this right was, after some hesitation, granted to them, but they had to play their matches at a different venue. In 1879, the first Irish ladies' championships in Dublin (discontinued two years later, in 1881) did not take place in Fitzwilliam Square like the men's, but in Wilton Place,[200] significantly on one of the club's covered (and therefore secluded) asphalt courts.[201] At the first ladies' championships at Wimbledon, the staging of which had been rejected in 1879,[202] the gentlemen in charge of the organization were playing for time: the ladies were admitted to the courts only after the gentlemen had finished their singles championships.[203] To Commander Hillyard, the husband of the Wimbledon champion of 1886, that was not enough. He and others strongly advocated having the ladies' championships played elsewhere, in the provinces and away from gawping crowds.[204]

SEVEN

Lawn tennis in America

◇

In 1890, Richard Dudley Sears, in his contribution to *The Badminton Library*, told the story of the lawn tennis ball's first bounce in the United States, and of the two players who had lent a helping hand in the process, his elder brother, Fred R. Sears, and Dr James Dwight who has been called the Father of American Lawn Tennis.[1] Sears, seven-time US champion and record holder to date, could write with authority. Dick was the grandson of David Sears who had been left 'the largest fortune ever inherited in New England' and had then been 'the richest citizen of Boston'.[2] David Sears, an ardent admirer of Napoleon, had named his country place 'Longwood', after the house on St Helena in which his hero had died. On a corner of the 600-acre Sears estate, at what now is Brookline and Longwood Avenue, twenty-five cricket enthusiasts had in 1877 organized the Longwood Cricket Club. One year later, a tennis court had been laid out on the club's premises, and by 1890, the Longwood Cricket Club had become essentially a lawn tennis club.[3] Sears as well as his friend James Dwight were both members of the Longwood Cricket Club, and as a student Dwight had been in the habit of cycling over to Longwood several times a week in spring in order to play tennis. Early photographs show Sears and Dwight, tennis rackets in hand, in the cricket attire of the Longwood Cricket Club (**Figures 76 and 77**).[4]

The story told by Dick about his brother and his friend Dwight was this. Not far from the very place where English tea had been thrown into the sea by angry colonists a hundred years earlier, the two boys had greeted another British commodity with enthusiasm. It was an original box with Wingfield's *sphairistikè*. They had discovered it in the seaside summer house owned by a certain William Appleton at Nahant not far from Boston. Appleton's son-in-law, Mr J. Arthur Beebe, had only just brought the boxed set with him from London and had meant to present it to the Appletons themselves,[5] but Sears and Dwight, out of youthful curiosity, had taken the gift, and with the impatience of youth, had marked out a court in the side yard of the house some time in August, 1874.[6] After a few rallies they had become so enthusiastic about the new game that despite a pelting rain neither of them felt an urge to stop. Only after each of them had won a set did they abandon their game, having played in rubber boots and mackintoshes all the time.[7] This 'Boston Tennis Party' remained a singular

FIGURE 76   Richard Dudley Sears, seven-times US champion and record holder to date, in the outfit of Longwood Cricket Club but armed with a lawn tennis racket.

FIGURE 77   Dr James Dwight, like Sears a member of the Longwood Cricket Club. He was the first to play lawn tennis in the United States, was five times US doubles champion (partnered by Sears), and President of the USNLTA.

experience at the time. Only from the beginning of spring in the following year did lawn tennis begin to be played with any regularity – in Nahant, Newport and New York.

At the beginning of the 1930s, an attempt was made in the United States to deny to the two Nahant players their pioneering effort. In their place, a pioneering lady was enthroned, a certain Mary Ewing Outerbridge, who, equipped with an original set of Wingfield's *sphairistikè*, was said to have disembarked in New York on 2 February 1874, after a cruise aboard the S.S. *Canima* to Bermuda where she had picked up her tennis paraphernalia.[8] The campaign was conducted, among others, by Malcolm D. Whitman and by William Henderson who, as we have seen, had already advanced a highly speculative theory about the origin of tennis in the Old World.[9] Knowing that Wingfield had been granted a patent no earlier than 23 February 1874, the two were compelled, in order to vindicate their theory, to again accuse Wingfield of highly dubious methods. Since Mary Outerbridge would hardly have acquired her *sphairistikè* box without the rules, a rather indispensable prerequisite, the very same rules had, through rather mysterious agencies, to have reached the British dominion before her departure, on either 22 or 23 January 1874. That is why Whitman, the player, asserted that the booklet had appeared in print in December 1873. Henderson, the historian, who saw at once that even this early date was much too late, corrected him by opting for November 1873.[10] On poor Wingfield, however, again fell the blame of having deliberately told a lie when he claimed, on the first page of his rules, to own a royal patent. Since 25 February 1874 has now and beyond all doubt been established as the date of the first printing of Wingfield's rules, Whitman's and Henderson's attempts to rewrite tennis history have turned out to be yet another unfortunate mission to the Bermuda Triangle.[11] Mary Outerbridge,[12] however, is not entirely without merits. On one of her many excursions to Bermuda (presumably in the spring of 1875)[13] she actually bought a set of Wingfield's *sphairistikè*. Having obtained the permission of her brother A. Emilius Outerbridge, director of the Staten Island Cricket and Baseball Club, she rigged up the net in a remote corner of the cricket ground without much ado. It was thus for the first time that lawn tennis (in the States, at first, as much a game for private circles as in England) was given the attention of a sports club and thus attracted public notice.[14] Mary's efforts will have to be rated higher even than those of Sears and Dwight who played the inaugural match at Nahant, for, without her, there would scarcely have been the notorious Staten Island tennis tournament, the first major event of its kind,[15] which by an organizational scandal of the first order eventually set things going.

THE FIRST TOURNAMENT IN THE NEW WORLD

It was yet another Outerbridge, another of Mary's brothers, Eugenius H. Outerbridge, who came forward with the idea of holding, on the courts of the Staten Island Cricket and Baseball Club, a national championships. Eugenius Outerbridge was the club's secretary.[16] The local press heralded the sporting event in the following way: 'It will no doubt furnish quite a good deal of amusement to Staten Islanders', the *Richmond County Sentinel* observed, 'to see able bodied men playing this silly game.'[17]

The tournament began in fine weather on 1 September 1880, on a site very close to the bay and now buried under the parking lot of the ferry.[18] The reporters of the New York newspapers who chose to write about the event were enamoured of the scenic view, the sunset over the bay, the elegant ladies in their colourful dresses and the gentlemen, coaches and horses which had brought the visitors, and the handsome silver cup worth a hundred dollars showing, on one side, the engraving 'The Champion Lawn-Tennis Player of America' (**Figure 78**).[19] A nice sketch accompanying the report was meant to give the reader a visual impression of the ladies and gentlemen, the nearby bay and its sailing ships, and finally the game, lawn tennis. The papers were silent about results at first.[20]

The subject of scores was eventually broached by the players themselves and reporters of *The New York Times* and the *Richmond County Gazette* which harked back to the event a week later.[21] In the men's singles the victory had been carried off by an Englishman, O.E. Woodhouse. Woodhouse happened to be on a visit to the United States, and had learnt about the tournament from a Chicago daily newspaper.[22]

FIGURE 78   The first lawn tennis tournament in the United States on the courts of the Staten Island Cricket and Baseball Club, New York.

He won easily, a fact which caused no surprise. The Englishman had reached the final of the All Comers' event of the All England Championships in the same year, yielding to no less a player than the formidable Lawford.

In the doubles, R.D. Sears and Dr James Dwight gained prominence, though in a manner the two men from Boston (excellent players and members of the newly founded Beacon Park Athletic Association) had hardly anticipated. The organizers urged them to play with a brand of ball smaller by one-third than the one they were used to in Boston (and manufactured by Ayres of England) and much too light. Dwight later in life became a stickler for rules, enforcing them with a zeal little short of the obsessional. It must have been here that he experienced the traumatic shock that caused his obsession.[23] He voiced a vigorous protest, upon which the organizers, little impressed, brought to his notice the inscription 'Regulation' adorning the Staten Island ball, and nonchalantly suggested to him to pull out if a ball of such description did not please him.[24] Dwight and Sears swallowed the decision made by the Staten Island management, but refused to play in the singles, and received a sound drubbing by the team from Morristown, New Jersey, in the early rounds of the doubles.[25]

THE FOUNDATION OF THE UNITED STATES NATIONAL LAWN TENNIS ASSOCIATION AND THE FIRST OFFICIAL US CHAMPIONSHIPS

In the Staten Island tournament, three things had turned out to be a nuisance: the counting method up to fifteen points as employed in rackets, the height of the net, and, above all, the type of ball used. A supreme court of appeal, this had become clear to everybody, was badly needed. That is why, on 5 May 1881, a notice appeared in the journal *American Cricketer*, signed by Clarence M. Clark, president of the All-Philadelphia Lawn Tennis Committee, James Dwight, representative of the Beacon Park Athletic Association, Boston, and E.H. Outerbridge, who had perpetrated the Staten Island ball trick, but seemed to have learnt a lesson after all.[26] As a result, the inaugural meeting of the United States National Lawn Tennis Association (USNLTA) took place at the Fifth Avenue Hotel in New York on 21 May 1881.[27] The thirty-six delegates, representing nineteen clubs and having a proxy to vote for another sixteen, agreed to adopt the rules of the All England Club for one year. A commission of three was entrusted with the organization of tournaments and a representative of the Albany Tennis Club, Robert S. Oliver, was elected first President of the USNLTA.[28]

The assembly also resolved on holding an official championship, and as early as June the executive committee, on the question of the venue, decided in favour of the newly built Newport Casino, Rhode Island; the date for the event was set for 31 August 1881 (**Figure 79**).[29] This time the competitors from Boston were by far more successful, although the reason for their superiority was not so much the tennis ball that was now employed (the English Ayres' ball), but the tactics adopted by the first United States champion, Dick Sears. He, not unlike the English champion Gore, advanced to the net to a point well beyond the service line where his opponents' returns met his 16-oz-racket held rather short in the handle. The harder the balls were hit through the middle, the higher was the speed with which Sears sent them back, giving the right as well as the left side of his opponents' court a fair share. On the other side of the net, Sears' victims scrambled over the court in a manner resembling (to use Sears' own words) the course of the see-saw.[30]

After his triumph over the uncomprehending baseliner, Sears and his partner Dwight had taken it into their heads that the tactics Dick had adopted in the singles would pave the way for success also in the doubles. In unison the two advanced to the net, only to realize that their opponents from Philadelphia, rather than clinging to the baseline, had divided up into a player who occupied the rear and one who positioned himself close to the net. The men from Boston failed miserably. So weak were their volleys that the man at the net had no difficulty placing them right and left near the side-line.[31] Not until the following year did they succeed in seasoning their doubles game with the swift gracefulness of the Renshaw brothers whose method they had taken over, albeit inadvertently. Their play was now in a different class and simply too fast for the net man,[32] and they won their first (out of five) championships. Fifty years later, in a commemorative publication of the USNLTA, Sears gave these recollections of the first US championships:[33]

FIGURE 79   The first United States Championships at the Newport Casino (1881), today the site of the Tennis Hall of Fame.

A large number of the players wore knickerbockers, with blazers, belts, cravats, and woolen stockings in their club colors. Their shoes were rubber-soled and generally of white canvas or buckskin. None of their sleeves were cut off, and while the large majority rolled them up, a few left them at full length. They all wore caps or round hats with a rolling brim that could be turned down in front to ward off the glare of the sun. The rackets were generally lopsided slightly as in the old court tennis bats.

The winners in both singles and doubles in this first championship were given medals instead of the usual cups, and the conditions were the best two of three sets until the finals, which was the best of five. No 'vantage sets were played and the players changed courts only at the end of each set.

The second year the championship found all of the players serving overhand with more or less speed, mostly less, with everyone coming in to volley as soon as any good opening presented itself; but as both Dwight and I had taken up lobbing, a stroke, which, to be effective, requires a good deal of practice, a certain amount of discouragement appeared, and when these players also tried this stroke they generally lobbed much too short, giving us an easy kill. In addition, we no longer tapped our volleys, as in 1881, but hit them with a good deal of speed. I had discarded my 16 ounce racket and was using one of only 14 ounces.

Until 1915 the courts at Newport Casino where Sears and Dwight collected their numerous victories proudly hosted the US championships. Then they were transferred to Forest Hills in the Borough of Queens, New York. In 1978 they found a new home in Flushing Meadow,[34] also in Queens, which derives its name from the Dutch town of Vlissingen from where the first settlers – English Non-Conformists who had ended up in The Netherlands – had come in the seventeenth century. In Newport, the International Tennis Hall of Fame and an annual men's tournament on grass are today the only reminders of a glorious past.[35]

THE DAVIS CUP

The greatest achievement of American tennis is the creation of the Davis Cup. It has a typically American flavour. Very much like the so-called round robin[36] (in Europe simply referred to as the American method),[37] it is a test which does not offer the slightest chance to players of the gambling type who always hope to evade some unpleasant competitor by means of a lucky draw. The obligation to play against each of the opposing team's singles player, and the necessity to acquit oneself well in a doubles competition (which in many ways is a completely different game), reflects a truly American competitve spirit.

The method by which the Davis Cup is contested was, as it were, foreshadowed in the first semi-official tournaments which Dwight organized in the New World.[38] As early as 1878, the doctor had staged an international tournament in Newport which was played according to the same scheme.[39] He and his Boston men first played an Englishman and a Canadian in the singles, and then in the doubles. The competition had also involved players from abroad. It therefore may have given rise to the idea of having at some later date a grand-scale international competition which at that time, if it was to deserve the name, could only be contested between the leading lawn tennis nations, England and the United States.

At any rate, the first attempt to challenge the master, England, was made as early as 1883. In order to find the team worthy of putting up a fight against the English, a qualifying contest was arranged between the best doubles teams of the United States. Unfortunately, for Dwight at least, it was not he and his partner Sears who qualified, but two brothers from Philadelphia, C.M. and J.S. Clark. The Clarks duly set sail for England, but on the courts of the All England Club were badly defeated by the Renshaws.[40]

It was then that Dwight made up his mind to discover the secret of English superiority himself. In the autumn of the same year, he met William Renshaw on the covered court of the Maida Vale Club,[41] a former skating rink.[42] Recognizing the Englishman's genius at once, Dwight decided to seek the master's company.[43] A man in well-off circumstances, he had abandoned, in 1880 and only one year after qualifying, the practice of medicine in favour of lawn tennis.[44] It was not difficult for him, therefore, to follow the Renshaw twins to whatever place they chose to go. During the winter months, the favourite haunt of the equally affluent Renshaws was

Cannes on the French Riviera.[45] In the years to come, Dwight played his fill in the South of France in winter. He then spent the early part of the summer in England before returning to the States, just in time and in good shape for the US championships.[46]

As a result of his many stays in England, Dwight was on good terms with English officials. One of them was Herbert Chipp, the first secretary of the English LTA. Since Chipp was a good friend of his, the President of the American Association wrote him a rather personal letter in which he invited an English team to the United States. When Chipp received the letter in the summer of 1897, he had been succeeded in office by W.H. Collins. He therefore forwarded it to the LTA Council which, while approving of Dwight's proposal at least in principle, later that year seemed somewhat nettled by the American's offence against proprieties: he had failed to inform the honourable LTA about his plans officially. In addition, Dwight, in a second letter, had offered a remuneration to English players for their travelling expenses. This, too, was frowned upon by the LTA, imbued as it was with the principles of amateurism. Dwight's cordial invitation was declined.[47]

However, Dwight did not give up. In the following year, he proposed to come to England with an American team. This offer could hardly be rejected. The LTA with good grace granted the sum of £160 to treat the guests well. It was bad luck that the Americans had to call off the meet at the last minute.[48] The project then reached a deadlock, but after two years, in 1900, the LTA received another letter, a highly official one this time, in which Dwight told the new Secretary of the Association, G.R. Mewburn, about an unexpected turn which his old plan of an international team competition had taken. 'One of their players', Dwight wrote, not mentioning the player's name, had offered them 'a Cup, to be a sort of International Challenge Cup'.[49]

The idea of a Cup was both new and alluring, and it eventually persuaded the LTA to accept the challenge. An account of how the idea occurred to him comes from the originator himself, Dwight Filley Davis. He was over 40 and Governor-General of the Philippines when he told the story, and it was incorporated in a book with which the USNLTA celebrated, in 1931, the anniversary of its fiftieth birthday.[50] In 1899, in the month of August, a team consisting of the players Malcolm Whitman, Holcombe Ward and Dwight F. Davis, and of Beals Wright and his father, had accepted an invitation to California where they played a series of exhibition matches in Monterey, on the courts of the Hotel del Monte, the venue of the Pacific championships. Whitman was the US singles champion, whereas Davis and Ward had been victorious in the US championship's doubles. Young Beals, in turn, was the winner of the inter-scholastic championship. The overwhelming enthusiasm which had greeted the team in California, the success it had scored and the many tokens of friendship it had received, deeply impressed Davis. On his way back to the East, he read in a newspaper about the trials for the America's Cup, the international trophy contended by sailing crews. Still under the impression of the tour, and with the model of the America's Cup before him, he was struck by a glorious idea. If a competition between players from different parts of the same country aroused such an interest and created such goodwill, would not an even greater effect be produced by an international competition? The idea of the Davis Cup was born. After his return, he told Dr James Dwight about his plan, and, as we have seen, it was then that the wheels began to turn. We will see much later, when it comes to the never-before-written story of lawn tennis in Germany, that in 1931 Davis only told one half of the story, for reasons which in retrospect are quite understandable.

The original trophy donated by Davis was a silver punchbowl which later, when space became scarce for the engraving of the victors' names, was mounted on a silver base on which it revolves.[51] The bowl, gilt on the inside, bears the inscription 'International Lawn Tennis Challenge Trophy. Presented by Dwight D.F. Davis, 1900'.[52] The trophy, executed by the silversmiths Shreve, Crump and Low, of Boston, was at the time worth $1000. In 1985, its value was said to be more than $20,000. Davis, a millionaire's son from St Louis who could well afford the expenditure, is reported to have said, a few years after his donation, that, had he foreseen the success of the competition, he would have ordered a trophy made entirely of gold.[53]

THE FIRST DAVIS CUP MATCH

The two lawn tennis heroes most worthy of championing Albion's cause against the upstart challenger from beyond the Atlantic were the Doherty brothers. For some unknown reason, however, they were unable to come to the Empire's rescue. The LTA, with the firm conviction that even its second string was one too many for the Yankees, selected the players Arthur Wentworth Gore, Edmund D. Black and Herbert Roper Barrett. Of these, only Gore was an outstanding player. In 1899, he had yielded to none except Reggie Doherty who beat him in the Challenge Round; he was to become champion himself in 1901.[54] In England, to grace the occasion, a mock-heroic poem appeared in the journal *Lawn Tennis*. It was ingeniously contrived by a rhymester of whose name, unfortunately, only the initials, W.A.B., are known. The poem was a parody on 'Horatius', a ballad from the famous 'Lays of Ancient Rome' by the author of the famous *History of England*, Thomas Babington Macaulay.[55]

In W.A.B.'s parody, Horatius is transmuted into 'Goratius' who is supported (albeit inadequately) by Roper Barrett and another pseudo-Roman fighter 'Niger' (Black). This glorious threesome is sent out on a mission at least as hazardous as that of the valiant Romans. Beyond waters bigger than the Tiber of old, it has to defend the lawn tennis supremacy of the British Empire. It is unfortunate that space does not permit us to include the relevant passages from Macaulay as well; the reader unfamiliar with W.A.B.'s model would certainly derive much pleasure from a comparison:[56]

THE DAUNTLESS THREE

But the Council's brows were sad,
  And the Council's speech was low,
And darkly thought they of the team,
  And darkly of the foe.
'They'll surely sit upon us
  And surely wake us up:
For, since we lack the brothers twain [i.e. the Dohertys]*,*
  What hope to win the cup?'

Then out spake brave Goratius,
  The back court player great;
'Lo every man upon this earth
  Gets beaten soon or late;
And how can man play better
  Than facing fearful odds
For the honour of his country,
  And the old lawn tennis gods?'

'Look through the list, O Council,
  With all the speed ye may;
I, with two more to help me,
  Will hold the foe in play;
Tho' Whitman, Ward, and Davis
  Three mighty champions be.
Now, who will go, I want to know,
  To Newport town with me?'

Then out spake E. D. Niger,
  A Yorkshire man was he:
'Lo, I will be the second string,
  And Singles play with thee!'
And out spake Roper Barrett,
  Of Gipsy club was he:
'I will abide, at right hand side,
  In doubles with E. D.'

'Goratius,' quoth the Council,
  'As thou sayest, so let it be.'
And straight against America
  Forth went that gallant three.

At this point, the poem was, for the time being, discontinued, and the editors of the journal promised its readership that the remainder of it would, perhaps, be written when it could be seen how things turned out.[57]

Before the Dauntless Three boarded their ship they were banqueted in the London Cannon Street Hotel like the knights errant of King Arthur's time. Collins, the team captain, decorated them in a manner befitting true knights. They were given gilt-embroidered caps of white silk, adorned in colour with the royal standard. Tens of thousands greeted them on their way to the boat train to Liverpool, while two bands played 'God Save the Queen' and the 'Yankee-Doodle' simultaneously. The crowds waved their handkerchiefs and hats and cried hysterically.[58] Davis' vision of humanity united through the agency of his generous gift had to give way to harsh reality. To the beholder, the scene revealed unabashed chauvinism.

The arrival of the Dauntless Three in the United States was somewhat less spectacular than their departure from home. They were welcomed by the man-servant of Mr Richard Stevens, the treasurer of the USNLTA.[59] This, however, did not mar their happiness in the least. Not feeling the slightest doubt about their superiority, they did not give a thought to the match that was to be contended at the Longwood Avenue LTC, the hub of New England tennis, in three days' time. Instead, they thought it would be a good thing to go on a trip to Niagara Falls and to subject this miracle of nature to close inspection.[60] This done, they were cordially received in Boston.

The British, rather particular about how sporting events of this magnitude should be conducted, got a mild shock as Holcombe Ward, a member of the US team, proceeded with the draw for this battle of the continents. Mr Ward, standing on the veranda of the club's pavilion while performing the ceremony, availed himself of two straw hats.[61]

In open-mouthed bewilderment the English players then inspected the two courts. There were two tables at the sidelines each carrying the umpire's 'chair' and demonstrating the Americans' improvising talents. On the courts themselves the fastidious Britons fancied themselves in the Wild West. The grass was as high as in the rolling prairie, at least twice as high as at home, if one is inclined to believe the testimony of Roper Barrett. The nets had been fastened by means of guy ropes which constantly gave way and after every few games had to be pulled tight. The balls were something which the same Roper Barrett loathed to mention at all: 'They were awful – soft and mothery – and when served with the American (afterwards notorious) twist came at you like an animated egg-plum'.[62] All this took place in a scorching heat – 136 degrees Fahrenheit in the sun – the effects of which the Americans tried to assuage by adjourning to the clubhouse after every set for a seven-minute rest and a rubdown. Meanwhile, the English were kicking their heels on court.[63] The miserable British were, in a word, the first victims of a practice by which the history of the Davis Cup became a history of inequity, in the course of which trim indoor facilities would be turned into sand pits, or equipped with surfaces giving the lie to those who had called absurd Wingfield's idea of playing lawn tennis on ice. The advantage of playing at home was exploited rather shamelessly.

Gore and Black lost their singles and, on the following day in the doubles, Roper Barrett and Black were also routed by Davis and Ward. 'Where was Barrett's forehand drive, and where Black's splendid backhand return?', the British journal *The*

Sportsman screamed in utter despair.[64] 'Useless, absolutely useless, both of them,' it continued. 'Not only did the ball screw, but it rose about 4ft. high in the shape of an egg.' Lastly, Black found fault with the courts which, he said, were covered with worm holes, and with the balls which squashed flat in the hand, and he criticized American officials who would not call foot faults even though their players were 'halfway up the court when serving and at the net for the return of service'.[65]

Rain put an end to this first Davis Cup match when the English were 0:3 down and Gore, still with plenty of guts, was about to score at least a consolation point against Davis, the donor. It was then that W.A.B. thought proper to finish his ballad on the miserable Dauntless Three (the blank left in the last stanza indicates that this was the time of the so-called unmentionables) (**Figure 80**):[66]

FIGURE 80   The American Davis Cup team – victorious in their inaugural match against the British Isles in 1900: (from left to right) Malcolm D. Whitman, Dwight Davis, and Holcombe Ward.

But the Council's brows were sad,
  And the Council's speech was low,
And darkly looked they at the scores,
  And darkly at the foe.
'The Eagle was upon us,
  before we saw his flight;
When Gore is licked three sets to love
  why, then – well, blow us tight!'

  *   *   *   *   *

The Three watched, calm and silent,
  The practice of the foes,
And a great shout of wonder
  From all the British rose.
For three great chiefs were serving
  In quite a fearsome way;
With force they drove, their 'faults' were few,
With curious twist the white balls flew
  like swallows in their play;

Holcombe from green New England,
  Champion of East and West;
And Davis, whose tremendous drives
  Sicken the very best;
And Whitman, long to Larned,[67]
  Second in every game,
Who soon developed mighty powers;
With that grim calm which lasts for hours
The champion of the U.S. towers
  O'er all the men of fame.

Stout Niger lost to Davis,
  By three fierce sets to one:
And Barrett and the former,
  By Ward and D. were done:
From Whitman brave Goratius
  Took not one single set;
And the proud Queen's man's tennis friends
  Wished they had never bet.

And in the nights of winter,
  when ancient players score
With the long story of the times
  When they were to the fore;

When by the cheerful fireside
  Snores loud the pussy-cat,
And the contented pug-dog
  Snores louder (for he's fat);

When the goodman mends his racket,
  And (for fear of stoutness) bants;[68]
When the goodwife's needle merrily
  Sews patches on his ———
With weeping and with laughter
  Still is the story told,
How our Goratius lost the match
  In the brave days of old.

THIRSTING FOR REVENGE

The lawn tennis giant had been dwarfed, but wisely abstained from venturing another campaign in the following year, though he anxiously waited for the time when the Doherty brothers would be ready to strike back. That time arrived in 1902. But then, the LTA and its president, W.H. Collins, made a mistake when it came to nominating the third player. They picked an Irishman, the physician Dr Joshua Pim. Pim was a member of the Lansdowne Club in Dublin and there he had been taught tennis lessons by the most famous of professionals, Thomas Burke.[69] Pim had been All England champion in 1893 and 1894, and as late as 1903, he was said to be ranked by experts 'as the finest player the world [had] ever seen'.[70] But that he was now long past his prime became evident from the task he had to take on: he had to shed no less than thirty pounds in six weeks.[71]

The reason for Pim's nomination (he was sent after the Dohertys as the mysterious Mr X)[72] was, perhaps, a diplomatic one. It seemed only fair that a team crossing the Atlantic to represent the British Isles should include an Irishman.[73] Unfortunately, this principle of proportional representation still prevailed when the team had to be nominated at last. To Pim rather than Little Do (Laurie Doherty) (who as the reigning English champion was at the peak of his power) fell the lot of playing the singles. It was the first glaring blunder by a team captain in the history of the Davis Cup. Collins had perhaps been guided by the idea that a Laurie Doherty who had not played in the singles might be, completely fresh and with undiminished power, a decisive factor in the doubles. When, however, Laurie entered the fray (the venue being, for a change, the Crescent Athletic Club in Bay Bridge, New York),[74] ignominious defeat for the British Isles was again inevitable. It was a tragic irony that, contrary to normal procedure, the doubles took place only on the third day, after the singles had been played and the whole match lost.[75] The Dohertys' victory in the doubles, certain though it was, therefore was of no avail.[76] In the singles, not only Pim had duly lost twice, but also the invincible Reggie Doherty had been routed once, albeit under circumstances that bordered on the tragic. Because his first singles match had been interrupted by rain, it had to be continued the next morning, and this time in a blistering heat. Reggie Doherty, who throughout his life suffered from a feeble constitution, was unable to hold his own against Whitman in his second match in the afternoon of the same day. He went down in three straight sets.[77]

COLLINS IN A GAMBLING MOOD

Despite this second *débâcle*, the LTA kept its countenance. Collins stayed in office as the team captain, which was hardly surprising since he was at the same time the president of the LTA. He soon proved that he was worth his money, as by a great coup he pulled off the next Davis Cup battle.[78] The British Isles prepared carefully this time, and Collins, having learnt a lesson from the previous exploit, had nominated the Dohertys for the singles as well as for the doubles. The services of the self-imposed Irish handicap, in the person of Harold S. Mahony, were to be called upon only in case of emergency. The emergency arose two days before the match. Reggie Doherty had, in an invitation tournament at Nahant the day before, strained his shoulder, and the physician who had been consulted made a diagnosis to the effect that, if Reggie played his first match on the appointed day, he might be unable to play for a couple of weeks. He added a proviso, though, that Reggie might be fit again the next day, if he gave his arm a 24-hours' rest. Collins politely inquired whether Mahony might play the first singles in Reggie's place, upon which Larned, the American team captain, with equal politeness, but intransigently, said that he would be pleased if Mahony played the first singles, but that, if he played at one time, he would have to play at all times. At this point, Collins decided to play Davis Cup roulette. He took the injured Reggie out of the competition and generously conceded Reggie's point to the Americans. After this, Reggie's brother Laurie equalized by beating in three straight sets 'Battling Bob' Wrenn who – though not among the top ten on the American ranking for several years – had by some mysterious agency found his way into the American team.[79] At this point, the score being one all, the British Isles were rescued by what may be called the Miracle of Bay Bridge. Heaven, which on previous occasions had heaped scorn on British Davis Cup teams, all of a sudden was utterly benign. It rained for two days on end, which gave Reggie plenty of time to cure his arm injury. After the rain, in what may justly be called the Great Anglo-Saxon Fratricide, the Doherty brothers defeated the brothers Robert and George Wrenn in the doubles, and then, in two gruelling 5-setters on the following day, both Larned and again Robert Wrenn. Laurie Doherty's scoring England's third and decisive point against America's number one, Larned, was long held in suspense. It was in this match that Dr James Dwight, the initiator of the Davis Cup and here acting as the referee, earned for himself a monument for his sporting fairness. At four games all and 15:40 in the fifth set, Larned passed Laurie who had rushed to the net, upon which the Englishman politely asked the umpire whether his service had been a good one. Much to his surprise, the umpire, wanting to make sure of it by asking the linesman, realized that this gentleman's chair was empty. The linesman apparently had declared well beforehand that he had to leave at a certain point in order not to miss his boat, but in the general excitement his disappearance had escaped notice. When asked for a ruling, Dr Dwight, the mastermind on the question of rules, decided on having the point played again. Laurie afterwards won his service, two of the three games which followed and the whole match.[80]

The British Lion had snatched the Davis Cup from the lions' den itself and on native soil defended it in the years to come, thanks to the unparalleled Doherty brothers. The Davis Cup regulations, laid down by Dwight and amended by Collins, had come into force by 9 July 1900. On second thoughts, and apparently following a suggestion made by Collins, all nations having an official association were allowed to compete. That was why in the beginning only Australia (including New Zealand), the British Isles, South Africa (then British), Canada, India and the United States were eligible as potential challengers, but only the British Isles had taken up the gauntlet. In the following two years, Austria, Belgium, France, Germany, Holland, Norway, Sweden, and Switzerland were to fill the ranks of at least potential challengers.[81] Not before 1907, however, when Australasia assumed power, was the Anglo-American supremacy broken.[82]

EIGHT

Continental colonies: lawn tennis in France

◇

In the country in which tennis originated, the bastard (as lawn tennis was called, rather endearingly, by the French) was most cordially received from the very start. Without much ado, the love-child mounted the throne given up by its ancestor, the ancient *jeu de la paume*.[1] At a time when imperialism was at its peak, the ascension of lawn tennis was a particularly subtle form of colonialism, but, somewhat surprisingly, contemporaries do not seem to have been very much aware of it.[2]

That it was Major Wingfield's *sphairistikè* which conquered the European continent can hardly be doubted. This becomes evident from a fine collection of tradecards which forms part of the Racket Sports Heritage Museum in Elizabeth, Pennsylvania,[3] among which there is one issued by the French chocolate manufacturers Poulain. It is a charming picture of a match of lawn tennis by which the firm tried to attract the attention of their customers. Apart from presenting them with a picture, the firm provided a special service, by having printed on its reverse side a description of the game in French. This description is clearly the description of the Major's game. It envisages a court which has two service courts at the base-line, and a service box in the opposite court.[4] Since the commission of the Marylebone Cricket Club abolished these Wingfieldian oddities in May 1875, the tradecard proves that Wingfield's tennis sets must have appeared in France, and possibly in considerable numbers, prior to that date.

The Major's game had reached the European continent in one of two ways: either as the piece of luggage of some well-to-do British tourist, or in the form of sports equipment ordered by one of the many sports clubs which had begun to be founded by British residents in the 1870s.[5] Where exactly the first lawn tennis sets were unboxed will, perhaps, be forever impossible to determine.[6] No fewer than three clubs claim for themselves the honour of being the oldest lawn tennis club in the country: the Le Havre Athlétique Club, the Tennis-Club de Dinard and the Decimal Club de Paris.[7] In Le Havre lawn tennis is said to have been played as early as 1872, a rather brazen-faced allegation in view of what is known about the chronology of Wingfield's 'invention'. Nevertheless, the statutes of the club, which was founded by

Oxbridge graduates, list lawn tennis (besides football and cricket) among the athletic activities to which the club was willing to give special attention. The statutes, in turn, are said to go back to the time of the club's foundation.[8] However, even though the distance from England to Le Havre may have been the shortest of all, a healthy scepticism should still be maintained on this matter. Before the middle of the 1870s no lawn tennis match is likely to have taken place even in Le Havre.

Le Havre, too, may well have been the place where continentals discovered for the first time that the otherwise so very meticulous Major had been guilty of an oversight. He had forgotten to include in his boxed sets an ingredient of particular importance: the English weather. At first, continental players tried hard to do justice to the game's name, by constructing grass courts. These, however, had soon to be abandoned in favour of clay courts.[9]

The lawn tennis club which can perhaps justifiably claim to have been the first is the Decimal Club of Paris, now long extinct and so-called because it was founded by ten Englishmen who lived in the capital at the time; it was founded in 1877.[10] In the Breton sea resort of Dinard, Englishmen staying for a holiday first played lawn tennis, somewhat paradoxically, on sand. They simply used the hard surface of the beach. Later more permanent visitors from across the Channel decided to build more permanent facilities and to found a club: the Tennis-Club de Dinard. Although it must be said that the lawn tennis mania that was thus sweeping across the Channel did not please everybody – the famous French author Guy de Maupassant,[11] for instance, in 1887 fulminated against the infamous racket – by 1898, as many as seven clay courts had been laid out. Every year in September the Tennis-Club de Dinard hosted a most prestigious lawn tennis tournament.[12]

The most important clubs from the sportsman's point of view came into being in the 1880s in the metropolis, Paris, the most bizarre story being that of the origin of the famous Racing Club. In 1880, passengers intent on boarding a train at Saint-Lazare Station, were greatly annoyed with a pack of bustling youngsters who had made a game out of running, at the highest possible speed, to a wall at the far end of one of the platforms.[13] They were schoolboys from Condorcet public school who were soon joined by their like from the Ecole Monge and the Collège Rollin.[14] An innocent extravagance at first, the schoolboys' game within a short time had rather strange results. For their 'races', the boys presented themselves dressed as jockeys, adopted the names of racing horses, divided up into 'stables', and some scallywags even went so far as to literally whip themselves on for the finish. The yellow press gave the thing a welcome boost, and the gaudy scene soon had its bookmakers, stakes and dividends. Prize money could be won. The venue of the races had meanwhile been transferred to the Bois de Boulogne and in 1882 the runners united into a club. In an age of rampant anglomania, they called themselves the Racing Club de Paris.[15]

The year 1884 witnessed a change in the club's management. A certain Georges de Saint-Clair, who had received his education in England, advanced to the presidency. Determined to turn the club into an amateur club after the insular model, he put an end to the undignified masquerade. Runners who competed for money were no longer admitted. Henceforth, the club was to foster all sports which served physical education. That is why, among the activities adopted into the club's programme in 1885, express mention was also made of the game of lawn tennis.[16]

In 1886, the municipality of the metropolis placed at the club's disposal a plot for the laying of lawn tennis courts in the Bois de Boulogne and two grass courts were laid out at once.[17] By the turn of the century, their number had increased to seven, even though the designers of the Racing Club had soon made the discovery themselves that on the continent grass courts were impossible to maintain. They were accordingly transmuted into clay courts.

The club of Stade Français was founded one year after the Racing Club, in 1883. Like the latter, it was a racing club in the beginning. The players of Stade Français first knocked their lawn tennis balls about on the wooden floors of indoor courts (in existence since 1889;[18] they were the first of their kind in France). Then, in 1899, the club acquired an extensive area in the park of Saint-Cloud. This stadium, which still exists in the so-called Faisanderie, later hosted the world championships on hard courts, which eventually evolved into the International Championships of France.[19]

To be in paradise itself is what players must have felt when engaged in a match on the courts of the famous club of the Cercle des Sports de l'Ile de Puteaux. Founded in 1886, it was established on a plot of land for which its founder, the Vicomte Léon de Janzé, had paid the sum of 50,000 francs, money he had raised without the slightest difficulty from friends and patrons.[20] The club's ten courts – sand courts laid out on a bed of rubble – were situated on a beautiful island in the Seine not far from the Bois de Boulogne.[21] The same site, before the turn of the century the refuge of Europe's tennis-playing aristocracy, still harbours an important tennis centre run by the municipality of Puteaux in which today the sons and daughters of the bourgeoisie are initiated into lawn tennis, a visible expression of the changes that have since taken place.[22]

Monsieur Georges de Saint-Clair, secretary general of the Racing Club, had most ambitious plans. In 1887, the Racing Club and the Club Stade Français, on his instigation, formed a runners' union. It was the germ of the powerful Union des Sociétés Françaises des Sports Athlétiques (USFSA) founded in 1889.[23] For a long time, until 1920 when the French Tennis Federation was founded, the Union served as the supreme board also for lawn tennis. It saw to it that the rules of the game were translated into the French language and that a lawn tennis commission was appointed.[24]

The first French championship held under the auspices of the Union and called the 'Raquette de l'Union' was won by Briggs, an Englishman and a member of the Club Stade Français, in 1891.[25] In the years to come, the championships took place, by turns, on the courts of the Cercle des Sports de l'Ile de Puteaux (which had hosted the first) and those of the Racing Club. The Union also organized the doubles championships (for gentlemen, since 1891, the prize being a cup presented by an insurance company, 'La Mutuelle militaire'),[26] and the intercollegiate doubles (since 1891)[27] and singles championships (since 1893).[28] A championship for women was first organized in 1896 and won by A. Masson.[29]

A FRENCH INVENTION: OLYMPIC TENNIS

As from February 1890, the Union had a new secretary general. His name was Pierre de Fredi, Baron de Coubertin.[30] He was a foster child of the Jesuits and former cadet of the Military Academy of Saint-Cyr. During a stay in England, the Baron had become acquainted with the educational principles of Thomas Arnold, the famous headmaster of Rugby School. He had been particularly impressed by the great value the English educator attached to sport. Still feeling the shock of his country's defeat in the Franco-Prussian war in 1870, and thinking of ways of how the nation's morale might be raised, he had come to the conclusion that new confidence could be instilled in his countrymen if they engaged in sports. The best incentive, the Baron thought, would be some grand-scale international sporting event providing an opportunity for young Frenchmen to compete with athletes from other nations.[31] On 25 November 1892, at the third annual conference of the Union at the Sorbonne, he sprung a great surprise on this assembly of dukes and princes. He proposed to revive the Olympic Games of ancient Greece. At the same time, Coubertin, not unlike the founder of the Davis Cup, expressed the hope that by means of an international sporting event such as this peace and understanding might be promoted.[32]

In 1894 a congress was held at the Sorbonne to which Coubertin had invited sports clubs and associations from all over the world.[33] Somewhat surprisingly, this inaugural meeting occasioned the foundation of an International Olympic Committee,[34] of which the Greek delegate Demetrios Vikelas was elected president.[35] A man of quick decisions, Vikelas offered, on behalf of his country, to organize in Athens, and as early as 1896, the first Olympic Games of the modern era.

At this first congress at the Sorbonne, the leading bodies of organized lawn tennis were conspicuous by their very absence. There were neither representatives of the All England Club and the LTA, nor of the USNLTA. On close examination, the list of participants in the first issue of the *Bulletin du Comité International des Jeux Olympiques* yielded the name of a single lawn tennis club only, the Decimal Club, represented by Messrs Gaskett-James and J.-H. Le Cocq.[36] Since the Decimal Club dissolved only one year later, its chances to lend support to Olympic lawn tennis were soon reduced to nil. Nevertheless the congress moved that the programme of the Athens games should contain, under the heading 'Athletic Games' and besides soccer and the traditional tennis game of France, *paume*, the new-fangled game from England, lawn tennis.[37]

In the same year, in November, the Baron (who was himself a tennis player)[38] went to Athens, but, when he returned to Paris, he did not seem to have made any progress there. It is very likely that he left Vikelas to his own devices. The Greek, with the help of an organizing committee he had set up and which was presided over by Crown Prince Constantine, had to draw up a programme himself.[39] The last item adopted into this programme read: 'Athletic Games. Lawn Tennis. Singles and Doubles. ... Rules of the *All England Lawn Tennis Association* and the *Marylebone Cricket Club*.'[40]

Those who have read the preceding pages carefully, will see at once that Greek officials had rather vague ideas about the organization of contemporary lawn tennis.[41] Nevertheless, the organizing committee formed a sub-commission for athletic games. It was in charge of the preparation of both an Olympic cricket and a lawn tennis tournament. A member of the commission was a certain Konstantin Th. Manos.[42]

It would be an exaggeration to claim that the work of this commission was an overwhelming success. The commission somehow managed to see to the laying of three 'mud courts' in the oval of the newly built velodrome at Neo-Phaliron.[43] It also had a phalanx picked of ten Hellenic lawn tennis players eager to be crowned with the leaves of Olympic laurel, but there was a notable absence of those players who would have added lustre to the tournament – the much admired foreigners. In Germany, Count Voss, the German champion, had at one time contemplated honouring the tournament with his presence, but had then given preference to the spring tournaments on the French Riviera.[44] From France, a single lawn tennis player had found his way to faraway Athens, an otherwise completely unknown member of the Racing Club called Defert.[45] It is not known whether Coubertin's message ever reached the lawn tennis circles of England and the United States which alone exercised authority in those days. If it did, it certainly elicited no response.

In order to give their tournament at least an international flavour, the organizers at short notice decided to fill up the draw with athletes from other Olympic disciplines who had either been eliminated in the preliminary heats, or who hoped to reap even more medals. Among these were Tapavica, a weightlifting Serb competing for Hungary; Traun, the 800-metres runner from Germany; Robertson, an English hammer thrower; finally Flack the Australian, Olympic champion in the 800 and 1500 metres track events.[46] By a rather curious chance, the German Traun and John Pius Boland, a tourist from Ireland, became partners in the Olympic doubles event. About these two, a rather funny story has been circulated in encyclopedias the world over, according to which the two met in an Athens shop where Traun was buying a racket and then and there decided to throw in his lot with the Irishman.[47]

This story, sufficiently discredited in the present writer's monograph *Olympisches Tennis*, has now in a definitive way been shown to be a myth by a rather sensational find. Well before the centenary of the Olympic Games in Atlanta, in 1994, the British Olympic Association received a parcel containing 137 hand-written pages, Boland's diary which, the anonymous sender of the parcel wrote, 'Jack' had lent him many years before and which he had simply forgotten to return.[48]

Boland's diary, perhaps the most intriguing document in Olympic history, is a remarkable account, not only of the Athens games in general, but also of the first Olympic champion himself and the circumstances under which he undertook the journey to the Greek capital in the spring of 1896. A student of law at Christ Church in Oxford,[49] he had decided to study, in order to become acquainted with the German language and German university life, at the University of Bonn.[50] After arriving in Bonn early in October 1895, he soon found lodgings with Herr Borgass, a master at the local Beethoven Gymnasium, and became a member of the Catholic 'Bavaria' students' corporation. He duly attended, having plausibly been given the very name of Paddy,[51] the corporation's tri-weekly evening gatherings ('Kneipe'),[52] very wisely abstaining from its worst beer-drinking excesses, and attended lectures, mainly on commercial and sea law,[53] but on other subjects as well. As some sort of preparation for the Games, Paddy took part in three soccer matches against school teams,[54] one golf party in Wiesbaden,[55] but played no lawn tennis (which at the time was strictly a summer sport).[56] After having thoroughly enjoyed the costume balls of the famous Rhenish carnival in Cologne (where he also saw the famous procession)[57] and Bonn, Boland together with a young German, Alfred Pazolt, and with a cut over the eye from the last football match,[58] left Bonn for Athens:[59] 'Professor Semish [*sic*] simply put a plaster on it. With the bandage I have been accordingly masquerading as a duelling student + so may be said to have put the finishing touch to my student life.'

Several of his compatriots and even his brother Patrick had been unwilling to undertake the trip,[60] when John Pius Boland and his German friend set out on their journey to Athens on Saturday 14 March 1896.[61] It took them to Wiesbaden, Munich,[62] Salzburg, Vienna[63] (by means of the Semmering Railway, 'a wonderful feat of engineering'),[64] Graz,[65] Trieste (where they went over to Miramar Castle aboard a little steamer),[66] Brindisi, Santa Quaranta on the Albanian coast, Corfu (in a first-class berth on the Austrian Lloyd steamer *Hungaria*)[67] and Patras (where they failed to cross over to Missolonghi so that they were 'unable to see where Byron died'.[68] In Patras, they boarded the train to Athens where they had arrived by 31 March finding quarters at the Minerva Hotel in the Rue du Stade which Cook Travels had secured for them.[69]

The story of how Boland eventually found himself in the Olympic lawn tennis event is very different indeed from that found in the handbooks. In the evening of 6 April (a Monday) an English-speaking Greek from Alexandria called Kasdaglis sat opposite Boland at dinner, presumably at the Metropole, and, deploring the small number of contestants in the Olympic tennis event, suggested to him to go in for it.[70] The Irishman was delighted and offered to be Kasdaglis's partner in the doubles, and also to compete in the singles. The next morning, Kasdaglis went to the committee room and arrived just in time for the draw. Unfortunately, all Greeks were paired off with countrymen of theirs in the doubles, and that is why John Pius had to say farewell to his friend Kasdaglis, and to enter into a partnership with a German from Hamburg, Friedrich Adolf Traun. On Wednesday, Boland, since he was 'totally unprepared for tennis', spent the whole morning hunting up the various requisites, flannels, shoes, and a racket;[71] this in order to be ready for play in the afternoon. Desperately looking for a pair of flannels, he was helped by an Australian named Broughton whom he met in one of the shops and who took him to an Austrian tailor. A racket was bought next door at the Panhellenic Bazaar in the Rue du Stade, but tennis shoes were not available in the entire Greek metropolis, and Boland had to be content with leather-soled and -heeled ones. In the history of the Olympic Games, Delves Broughton, to use his full name, has so far distinguished himself as the butler of the British Ambassador who accompanied his countryman Edwin Flack in the marathon race on a bicycle.[72] Boland's diary now proves that he even paved the way to Olympic victory, by securing for the

Irishman a pair of ready-made ducks. It was probably he, too, who gave rise to the story about Boland and Traun having first met in an Athens shop.

The Olympic tennis event started on Wednesday, 8 April 1896, at 4.30 p.m. after the 100-kilometres bicycle race. Boland, after having collected in haste his equipment in the morning, had arrived at the courts in Phaliron at 3 o'clock in the afternoon, but had to kick his heels there in beastly weather until the race was over. As chance would have it, he had to play the opening singles match against no other than his doubles partner Traun. 'I had a fairly stiff game against him,' Boland wrote,[73] 'as I was awfully out of practice and condition. I won the two necessary sets however.'

The following morning, Boland had to be up at 7.15 in order to catch the 8.30 train to Phaliron. Once there, he and Traun, 'after a fairly good game', beat the two Akratopoulos brothers, and immediately afterwards Boland disposed of Rallis, in his opinion the best Greek player, in three sets, the score being 6:0; 2:6; 6:2.[74]

Play was resumed in the morning of 10 April. Boland had 'no difficulty' in eliminating another Greek, Paspatis, and since his friend Kasdaglis had meanwhile defeated one of the Akratopoulos brothers and a Hungarian whom Boland spelt Tapovicza, but who in reality was a Serb named Tapavica, a player 'who had only the most rudimentary notion of playing', Boland and Kasdaglis had qualified for the finals.[75]

These were played on Saturday, again in the afternoon after the cycling competition had been finished. It was almost 5 o'clock when the Irishman and his German partner took on (the doubles being played first) the Greeks Kasdaglis and Petrokokkinos (**Figure 81**).[76] At first, it looked as if the Irish–German combination was going to have an easy time. They were soon leading 5:1 in the first set when suddenly they 'fell off terribly', letting the Greeks capture the set by 7:5.[77] But then they tried hard to get their game together again:[78]

FIGURE 81   Before the doubles final in the first Olympic tennis event in 1896. The photograph was published in *Sport im Bild*, which printed the names Traun and Boland (left to right) under the somewhat taller players on the right side of the net.

the next two sets we won by 6 : 3, 6 : 3, mainly by Traun's net work. I let him do all the attacking and just backed him up, but played very badly. A fair number remained to see the game, but I fear they carried away a poor impression of Tennis as a game. Traun improved very much towards the end, but was too excitable to be a good partner. His delight at winning was tremendous.

After the doubles,[79] Boland met Kasdaglis again in the finals of the singles, and by half past six had beaten him in two straight sets 6:2; 6:2. 'It was very bad luck for Kasdaglis losing both,' Boland, incidentally the first to give us the correct results of the finals,[80] commented on this match,[81] 'as it was he who had induced me to go in, but I could not well scratch to him, as the game was of an international character'. To the end the match was watched by royalty, the three Greek Princes, and Boland had to go through a lot of handshaking with all the umpires and committee members afterwards.[82]

Well before the finals, Boland had highly commended the organizational side of the Olympic lawn tennis event, the excellent hard courts, the stop nets, the ball boys neatly clad in light grey uniforms, the committee men and lines umpires who all spoke English and decided points very well.[83] At the end, he gave a most graphic description of the closing ceremony and the distribution of prizes:[84]

> The Stadium was nearly as full as on the Marathon day ... In the absence of any direction, we winners stood about the entrance leading to the dressing rooms, each one dressed according to his fancy. It was a pity that no attempt was made to secure uniformity. It would have been better if all were in athletic dress. Mano marshalled us in two rows on each side of the platform erected in front of the royal seats, victors + non victors alike being there. The royal party came punctually as usual + when they had taken their seats, the Princes staying at the steps of the platform, Robertson was called on to recite his Pindaric Ode. This over, an officer probably deputed on account of his powerful voice, proceeded to read out the various events, their victors + their respective countries. Burke the American was the first man to go up, he having won the 100 + 500 [sic] metres. Each winner received a huge diploma in a large circular cardboard case, a medal in a case and a branch of olive a couple of feet long. These latter I believe had been brought specially from Olympia itself. Lawn Tennis was the last on the list, but as the Singles were read out first, it remained for Traun to be the last man to go up for his reward. On mounting the platform the King shook me by the hand, said in English, 'I congratulate you' + then handed me the two diplomas, two medals + two olive wreaths. So full were my hands that I forgot, as indeed did the majority, to descend the steps backward, but I made up for the omission by bowing when I got to the bottom.

On closer inspection, Boland's participation in the Olympic lawn tennis event was by no means as accidental as has always been thought. Boland had been a fellow-student of the Greek Konstantinos Manos, the very same who, as a member of the Athens lawn tennis sub-committee, had been trying, with the assistance of Boland, to recruit from among the sporting circles of Oxford University competitors for the Athens games.[85] Boland was, firstly, an excellent cricketer, but certainly not a mean tennis player either. In the 1880s when he attended Cardinal Newman's Oratory School in Birmingham, he had received intensive coaching by one of the outstanding sportmen of the time, the Reverend Edward Pereira (**Figure 82**),[86] a county cricketer who represented Warwickshire.[87] That Boland was by no means a novice in the game becomes evident, above all, from the fact that he beat his partner Traun in the singles.[88] This was not easy. Traun was one of the promising young tennis players from Hamburg who as early as 1893 had aroused the curiosity of Baron von Fichard, the lawn tennis correspondent of the Berlin journal *Spiel und Sport*.[89] When the Hamburg Uhlenhorst Club staged a tournament for young players, Traun, 'equipped with perhaps too favourable a handicap', was victorious both in the singles and in the doubles, and he would have captured the title in the mixed doubles as well had he not been guilty of an error often committed by the novice and which he, the Baron said, had often criticized: he had poached recklessly! He expressed the belief, however, that the young man might profit from reading carefully his reports on earlier tournaments! Traun's victory in Athens proved that he had ignored the Baron's advice completely.

FIGURE 82   The Oratory School Old Boys' cricket team in 1895 featuring the Reverend Edward Pereira, a county cricketer for Warwickshire (seated, second from left). Pereira, an outstanding sportsman, gave John Pius Boland (seated, fifth from left) private tennis lessons which paved the way for him to two Olympic championships.

Boland in his diary himself attributed his victory in the doubles to Traun's net-play. Later in the year of the first Olympics, Traun reached the third round at the Austrian championships in Prague and competed with considerable success in the famous Bad Homburg tournament.[90]

The Paris congress of 1894 had expressly declared that only amateurs should be eligible for the Olympic events.[91] This meant that, in the opinion of most people, only members of the 'upper class' would be allowed to compete; it was only they who could afford to engage in sports anyway.[92] The social norms set by the Paris Olympians were fulfilled by the Olympic lawn tennis champions with distinction. Both Boland and Traun were the sons of immensely wealthy parents; Boland's father was the owner of Boland's Bakeries, Ireland's biggest bakery chain,[93] whereas Traun was the son of a Hamburg senator, owner of a world-famous rubber company.[94] Both Boland and Traun also belonged to the intellectual élite. They were undergraduates of distinguished universities.[95] Because of their high qualifications, both social and intellectual, Boland and Traun must have been considered almost ideal competitors, and their participation in the games must have been approved of with enthusiasm by members of the organizing committee such as Konstantinos Manos – who is known to have been a staunch advocate of a status-orientated amateur principle.[96]

The Olympic lawn tennis event owed its existence to the initiative of Pierre de Coubertin, and must be considered a great contribution of the French to the cause of lawn tennis. After its rather humble beginnings, it rose to considerable importance, though not without suffering some serious setbacks. The Paris Olympic tournament of 1900, for instance, was preceded by organizational chaos, and those immediately following, the tournaments of St Louis (1904), London (1908) and Stockholm (1912), were second-rate with respect to the quality of the entries. And yet, the Paris tournament, held at Coubertin's own club and the venue of the first French championships, the exuberant Ile de Puteaux, could pride itself on the participation of the outstanding players of the time, the Doherty brothers, who naturally won the Olympic championship. It also has the merit of having paved the way for the participation of women in Olympic games:[97] Charlotte Cooper of England won the day in the women's singles. The Olympic Games of 1924, which, to pay tribute to the retiring Coubertin, again took place in Paris, were highlighted by the Olympic lawn tennis tournament, not least by the participation for the first time of a team from the United States and the Four Musketeers whose star had only just begun to rise. Unfortunately, the Olympic tennis event was discontinued when a bright future seemed to lie ahead of it. On the surface, its removal from the Olympic programme was brought about by organizational blunders on the part of the French national Olympic committee which infuriated the ITF, and the philosophy of the amateur, that historically questionable heritage from nineteenth-century England. The real reason, however, was the unwillingness of the powerful international federation to concede to the IOC the organization of an international tennis event which had the potential of outshining its own major events, the Grand Slam tournaments and the Davis Cup. The ITF (and above all its Anglo-French faction) had opposed the

Olympic tournament since its foundation in 1913. In 1924, the defects of the Paris event and the diverging views of the IOC and the ITF on amateurism were a welcome (albeit flimsy) pretext to kill the rival at last.[98]

Only after a lapse of 64 years, at the Games of Seoul in 1988, did it rise from the ashes, not least through the efforts of an energetic ITF president, Philippe Chatrier, and a congenial IOC president, Juan Antonio Samaranch. It has continued to be part of the Games ever since, one highlight being Steffi Graf's so-called Golden Slam in 1992 when she won the Olympic gold medal on top of her first and only Grand Slam victory, a feat which will take a lot to equal.

NINE

Lawn tennis under the Kaiser

◇

If the Germans had been somewhat slow in warming up to medieval tennis, they were very quick at picking up the new-fangled lawn tennis, or rather, English residents in Germany were. In Wingfield's Day book, preserved in the Wimbledon Lawn Tennis Museum, there is, among the entries of 13 July 1874, one relating to the delivery by the Major's business partners French & Company of a 'large set' worth £10.10s to Lord Petersham at the 'Viktoria Hotel' in 'Homburg Bains'.[1] Whether it reached its destination, and whether indeed it served its purpose afterwards has never been investigated.

Almost a quarter of a century later, in 1898, an interesting note appeared in the journal *Lawn Tennis and Croquet*, which contained a clue to this intriguing question and therefore deserves being quoted in full:[2]

> Among the veterans at Homburg was Mr H. Hankey, late of the Indian Civil Service, who can claim to have been one of the first to play lawn tennis at Homburg. Together with an English nobleman he, in the seventies, brought over what was then a new outdoor English pastime, and a court was marked out in the grounds of one of the hotels.

If it could be shown that Mr Hankey's partner, the 'English nobleman', was identical with the 'Lord Petersham' mentioned in the Day book, and that at the same time the aristocrat and Mr Hankey stayed at Homburg in the summer of 1874, this could be taken as evidence for the truth of the statement in the English journal. In addition, it would make necessary a major revision in German lawn tennis history, for it would then be a proven fact that the game was played there two years earlier than has always been thought.

Nineteenth century continental spas held their guests in high esteem. Visitors' lists were printed regularly in which the world was told about the noble and the rich gracing the place with their presence. Bad Homburg was no exception. Its visitors' lists ('Fremden-Listen') are all preserved in the municipal archive, and they are indeed very illuminating. The 'Rt Hon. The Viscount' and the 'Rt Hon. The Viscountess of Petersham' did arrive at the Royal Victoria Hotel between 30 June and 2 July 1874,[3] and Mr and Mrs Hankey, coming from London, in fact took up residence at G.F. Scheller's boarding house on Obere Promenade between 14 and 16 July 1874.[4] This proves that His Lordship and the veteran of the Indian Civil Service did indeed spend part of their holidays together at the German spa in the summer of 1874, and that, since the Hankeys had left by 5 August 1874, their inaugural lawn tennis match on the premises of the Royal Victoria Hotel in Bad Homburg must have taken place in the latter part of July 1874.

About the identity of Mr Hankey we are informed by the *India Office List of 1898* in the Oriental and India Office Collections of the British Library. After having been educated at Harrow and Haileybury, Herbert Hankey had been superintendent of transport during the famine of 1874, and inspector-general of the police in the Lower Province in 1876, before he retired in 1878.[5] The English nobleman seems to have presented difficulties to both French & Co. and even to the prestigious Royal Victoria Hotel, for neither of them got the title of the first lawn tennis player on German soil right. Viscount Petersham was the eldest son of the 7th Earl of Harrington, Charles Augustus Stanhope, who had adopted, as he was entitled to, the courtesy title of Viscount Petersham when his father succeeded to the title in 1866. The epithet 'Rt Hon.' devolved on him in 1881 when, after the death of his father, he became the 8th Earl of Harrington.[6]

ARTHUR WELLESLEY ANSTRUTHER, THE CHRONICLER
WHO WAS MISCONSTRUED

Because of the irrefutable evidence of Viscount Petersham and his partner, Herbert Hankey, a most precious document which has always been regarded as the first testimony of lawn tennis in Germany has now to be content with second place. It is a photograph from the Bad Homburg municipal archive, and perhaps the oldest lawn tennis photograph to have so far come to light (**Figure 83**).[7]

The picture is very remarkable because of an important detail. An individual apparently belonging to the inner circle of those represented on it left a message, in lucid English and in dark ink, on the upper and lower margin, about what exactly is shown on it. The intention of the writer seems clear enough. He wanted to pass down to posterity a piece of information he considered important. Unfortunately, and despite its explicit, his message has been grossly misunderstood. The scribbled note has not even been read correctly, and that is why, as we shall see, some rather grotesque blunders have crept into the works dealing with the beginnings of lawn tennis in Germany.

The unknown chronicler accomplished his task with great skill. He gave answers to all the points a professional writer of news items has to be mindful of: the Who?, the What?, the When? and the Where?

> Upper margin: 'The first Lawn Tennis at Homburg. 1876. Game
> introduced by Sir Robert Anstruther'

Lower margin: 'This side of Net L. A.W. Anstruther. R. Mr. Johnstone. At
Net-posts. L. Mr. Trelawny. R. The Kur-Director. Beyond Net. L. Miss
Johnstone. R. Sir Robert Anstruther'

On the evidence of these lines, one thing seems clear at once. No reminiscences of
Viscount Petersham's experiments on the lawns of the Royal Victoria Hotel two years
previously seem to have lingered on in 1876, for otherwise Sir Robert would not have
been credited with having played the role of a pioneer. Despite this fundamental
error, the remainder of the statement is perfectly true. This becomes evident from
yet another inspection of Bad Homburg's visitors' lists. The much neglected source
even makes it possible to tell with some precision when the photograph was taken.

Sir Robert Anstruther arrived, together with his wife and his son Arthur, in
Homburg between 13 and 20 May 1876. They found accommodation at Albion
House, a boarding house run by a certain J. Fuchs.[8] In what appears to have been
an annexe of the same building, or an adjacent building belonging to the same
complex, a Mr Clarence Trelawny had taken up residence at the same time.[9] Last

FIGURE 83   A lawn tennis photograph which may well be the oldest since it is still shows Major
Wingfield's hour-glass-shaped court.

came, between 28 June and 1 July 1876, Mr J.S. Johnstone, of London, who was
lodged at the Hotel de France first, but later also moved to a private boarding house.[10]
By 1 July 1876, the Anstruthers had said farewell to Bad Homburg, and that is why
there is only a very short period for the match on the intriguing photograph. It must
have been staged on the very last days of June in 1876!

Sir Robert Anstruther was a genuine Scotsman, fifth baronet of Anstruther,
descended from an ancient family of soldiers, himself a captain and later lieutenant
colonel, of Hamilton's Grenadier Guards, Lord Lieutenant and Sheriff Principal as
well as Member of Parliament for the County of Fife and the St Andrew's District
of Burghs (**Figure 84**). At the time of the Bad Homburg match, he was, at the age of
42, in the prime of his life.[11] Trelawny was a Bad Homburg *habitué* who in the 1870s
lived at the watering place more or less permanently throughout the year together
with his family and his servants, which indicates that he was a pensioner and a man
of means. Trelawny seems to have led a rather adventurous life.[12] Born in 1823, the
third son of Harry Brereton Trelawny of Shotwick entered the Austrian Hussars
Regiment No. 5 of Field Marshal Count Radetzky von Radetz in 1840. After having
been transferred to the Hussars Regiment No. 7, and promoted to the rank of second
lieutenant, he retired in the summer of 1847. He then married the former mistress of
the exiled Prince Charles Louis Napoleon who afterwards was elected, as Napoleon

FIGURE 84   Sir Robert
Anstruther, the Scottish baronet
who was until very recently
believed to have introduced lawn
tennis into Germany.

III, Emperor of France and, after having obtained a divorce in 1865, married a second time. Upon his leaving the Austrian army, Trelawny was attested as having good horsemanship skills, and a good command of German, Italian, and French, which he could read and write well, and even a fair command of Hungarian. He was in his mid-fifties when he engaged in the Bad Homburg lawn tennis match in which, to judge from the photograph on which he is resting his arm on one of the net posts, his role may have been that of a sitter-on-the fence only. The fact that he and the Anstruthers were virtually neighbours fully accounts for his presence in the picture.[13]

Since the second member of the Anstruther clan (initialled 'A.W.') appears to be shorter than Sir Robert by at least a head, Burghard von Reznicek, a well-known German tennis journalist of the 1930s, in his history of tennis in the German language, was led to put forward an explanation which well illustrates the nonchalance with which histories of tennis tend to be compiled. Von Reznicek had no doubts that the inaugural match at Bad Homburg was a mixed doubles, played according to the rules laid down by Major Wingfield, and under the auspices of Homburg's *Kurdirector* Ferdinand von Schoeler, who was to make a name for himself in the 1890s as the genial host of the spa's famous lawn tennis tournaments. Accordingly, Herr von Reznicek wrote the following.[14]

> Man erkennt deutlich die Wingfieldsche Sanduhrform. Es spielen Mixed: Lady Ansbruther [*sic*] mit Johnstone, jenseits des Netzes Frl. Johnstone mit Sir Ansbruther [*sic*]. Neben den Pfosten l. Trelawney [*sic*], r. Kurdir, [*sic*] v. Schoeler [...]

> (What can be seen clearly is Wingfield's hourglass shape. Playing a mixed doubles are: Lady Ansbruther [*sic*] with Johnstone, on the other side of the net Miss Johnstone with Sir Ansbruther [*sic*]. At the posts [left]. Trelawney [*sic*], r[ight]. Kurdir[ector], v. Schoeler [...])

Unfortunately, von Reznicek's explanation of the photograph is not exactly a model of accurary. His 'Lady Ansbruther' was not even a lady, but the fourth son of Sir Robert, Arthur Wellesley Anstruther who, at the time of the match, was only 12 years old – which explains his lack of height.[15] Nevertheless, he was a boy of remarkable astuteness: the notes on the margins are by his hand; his son Peter, at least, had no difficulties in recognizing at once the handwriting as that of his father.[16]

Again, the match in progress by no means followed the rules of Major Wingfield, for in that case the court would have featured a service crease which is notably absent from the picture. The match was played according to the rules established by a commission of the Marylebone Cricket Club and published on 24 May 1875.[17] The hour-glass-shaped court had been the only feature of Wingfield's original rules the commission had deigned to approve. The Anstruthers and their partners, in turn, obey the MCC rules in so unflinching a manner that the historian is tempted to apply a measuring tape in order to assess (assuming the height of the net at the posts at five feet) the height of Bad Homburg's *Kurdirector* in 1876. This, however, would still not be that of the famous Ferdinand von Schoeler, for, as the reader must have expected, von Reznicek went astray also in this case. It would have been that of his predecessor, the unfortunate Alexander Schultz-Leitershofen, the very first in a long succession of Bad Homburg *Kurdirectors*. He had attained his post in 1873, after his remuneration had been set at 2,400 talers annually and a 10 per cent share in the returns for the mineral water. In 1891, he was suddenly taken into custody on a charge of embezzlement. 'I am lost!' he is said to have exclaimed, and the discerning reader will know what caused his despair. It was the game that had been his foster child since he had seen the Scottish Anstruthers experimenting with it amongst the shrubberies of Bad Homburg's park. He was accused of having, from 1886 to 1890, misappropriated the revenues of the lawn tennis court, to the sum total of 13,000 marks. The criminal division of the District Court in Frankfurt found him guilty of the crime, and he was sentenced to nine months' imprisonment and the costs of the action. He was granted a pardon in the year following, though, but still had to resign from his post after he had apparently paid back the sum he had diverted to his own coffers.[18]

The photograph from Bad Homburg is also likely to cast some doubt on another established truth in German lawn tennis history. Baden-Baden has always been considered the place where, in 1881, the country's first lawn tennis club was founded. The white pennon fluttering merrily in the wind on one side of the Bad Homburg court and carrying the letters LTC (= Lawn Tennis Club) seems to indicate that the matches played here did not so much belong to the category of the occasional family *rencontre*, but rather to the programme of a fully fledged lawn tennis club. Of it, no trace has been left. Perhaps all of its members were Anglo-Saxons who took with them their membership lists as well as the minutes of committee meetings after having dismantled their trim lawn tennis pavilions and abandoned their courts.[19] As we shall see, there is still evidence that in Bad Homburg a lawn tennis club existed at least as early as 1879.

Sir Robert Anstruther, who was among the first to bring to the Germans the precious gift of lawn tennis, did not end his life as happily as they would have wished. He fell victim to a heart attack on the family estate of Balcaskie only nine years after his legendary match when he was on the point of throwing himself into an election campaign.[20]

TWO MONKEYS AND TWO IRISHMEN: FOUR EARLY WITNESSES OF LAWN TENNIS IN STUTTGART

Arthur Wellesley Anstruther was not the only person to claim for himself and his ilk the honour of having been the first to play lawn tennis in Germany. Harry Plunket Greene, an Irishman, wrote in 1924:[21]

> My brother and I were, I firmly believe, the first people to introduce lawn-tennis into Germany. There was an old Thiergarten (otherwise a Zoo) in Stuttgart which had two or three very mangy monkeys and about three-quarters of an eagle on a chain as its sole

stock-in-trade. But it had a skating rink approximately the size of a lawn-tennis court, and we rigged up an apology for a net, marked out the lines and invited some of our German friends to an exhibition match and afternoon tea. In less than no time the Thiergarten became a social centre, and the 'quality' flocked to it in crowds – amongst them, if I remember right, the famous (later) Graf Zeppelin![22]

Very soon, the Thiergarten became too small for the elegant company which moved to Bad Cannstatt on the opposite banks of the River Neckar. There, play was resumed on a court which finally met the requirements after the necessary equipment had arrived from England. On this court, two memorable matches took place, related by Greene with a great deal of gusto.

The tragic hero of the first was an officer of the Blue Uhlans. One day, oblivious to the fact that military men were not permitted to appear in public without their uniform, he arrived in white flannel trousers and a black blazer. He was court-martialled without much ado, but, not willing to give up a game (which was the invention of a military man after all), he decided henceforth to play in his uniform. Going into lawn tennis action one day, one of his spurs caught in his watch chain (!) by which his knee was viciously dislocated. This first known case of tennis knee (as distinct from tennis elbow) put an inglorious end to his lawn tennis career.

The hero of the second match was Conyngham, Greene's brother. One day, he was engaged in what must have been a rather exciting match. At least, some rather amateurish oarsmen found it of sufficient interest to pull up their boat near the shore in order to watch. With their eyes riveted on the goings-on ashore, but heedless to the river, they were surprised by a wave and their boat capsized. Conyngham, a 'Herr Gesandtschaftssekretär', immediately abandoned his game and leapt into the river in order to help them. But when he again emerged from it, his legs, clearly visible through his wet trousers, caused such a shock to the matrons present at the lawn tennis that they fled in panic (it was still the time of the almost proverbial 'unmentionables'). Almost at once a ban was imposed on the game, which was considered to have given rise to the scandal, and this was, at least for the time being, the end of lawn tennis in the Swabian metropolis. Harry Plunket Greene (1865–1936), the chronicler of these amusing lawn tennis events, later became a celebrated singer whose reputation also spread to the European continent.[23] Despite his assertion to the contrary, however, Stuttgart was in this country no more the cradle of lawn tennis than it had been that of the medieval game. While it is true that Greene prepared for his musical career, at least in part, on the continent, he nevertheless took his first lessons in Stuttgart (where he studied under A. Hromada,[24] singer at the Royal Court) no earlier than 1883,[25] and that is why the Scottish Anstruthers, to say nothing of Viscount Petersham, have an advantage over the Irish Greenes of no fewer than seven years. However, with regard to local lawn tennis history, Greene makes a most welcome correction. It has always been thought that the beginnings of lawn tennis in Stuttgart should be set in the summer of 1891, in which year the game is said to have been played on the very same Cannstatter Wasen (Cannstatt Green) where the Greene brothers had conducted their lawn tennis experiments.[26] The first permanent court was that laid out in the summer of 1893 on the so-called Berger Insel (Berg's Island). Strangely enough, it belonged to the Cannstatt FC, a football club founded on 25 March 1890. By this initiative, the soccer players hoped to pass the dull time of inactivity (football being strictly a winter sport) and at the same time to create a suitable diversion for its passive members and the ladies.[27] However, lawn tennis soon ceased to be a mere stopgap. After a new court had been built to the rear of the Veiel'sches Brünnele (Veiel's Little Fountain), near the municipal gasworks (a somewhat unromantic site)[28] in 1896 (it was followed by a second in 1901),[29] the club eventually abandoned football altogether in favour of lawn tennis.[30] The Stuttgarters succumbed to the lures of lawn tennis again in 1894 when the members of seven English families established the Stuttgart LTC (which was later to become the Tennis-Club Weissenhof) in the suburb of Stöckach.[31] By this time, too, the military had ceased to be court-martialled for not wearing a uniform on court. A poem written in 1893 began with the following lines:[32]

> *Das liebe gute Tennisspiel,*
> *Nie wird's genug gepriesen:*
> *Das einz'ge ist's, das in Civil*
> *Der Lieutenant darf geniessen!*

> *(Good old lawn tennis dear*
> *Praise thee would I fain:*
> *The only game the cavalier*
> *Can play in garments plain.)*

THE ALSATIAN BARON AND THE ENGLISH REVEREND: LAWN TENNIS IN BADEN-BADEN

On closer inspection, not only did Viscount Petersham and the Scottish Anstruthers get the better of the Irish Greenes, but a good many other people as well. At about the same time when the Anstruther clan encroached on the lush pastures of Homburg, the new-fangled game also caught on in another German Spa, Bad Pyrmont. In 1877, the very year of the first Wimbledon championships, a certain A. Boursée had laid out, most beautifully situated in the shadow,[33] a public lawn tennis court in the princely gardens. Boursée's court had a very special feature from the start. The man with the French-sounding name does not seem to have had much confidence in the British method of playing lawn tennis, as its name implied, on grass. His court, said to have in the beginning counted among its customers only the most elegant female visitors to the spa, and the inmates of several (girls') boarding-schools and English colleges, was a 'dirt' court, perhaps the very earliest of its kind. That is why Boursée can, with some justification, claim to be the inventor of this type of playing surface. In the years to come, he was to pass on his expertise to other would-be court builders elsewhere in the country, at the moderate rate of six marks a day and against reimbursement of his expenses for a third-class railway ticket. One of the places which profited from Boursée's innovation was Hamburg. It was from there, the venue of the prestigious German lawn tennis championships since 1892, that Boursée's method became known in imperial Germany as a whole.

Very early, presumably towards the end of the 1870s, lawn tennis also began to be played in the most important of German spas, Baden-Baden. Strangely enough, the earliest reference to its existence seems to have escaped the notice of local historians, and it was not even spotted by one of the local lawn tennis matadors and near contemporary, the indefatigable Baron von Fichard. The Baron did mention that an English family played the game in 1880,[34] but he apparently knew nothing about the existence of a fully fledged lawn tennis court 'in the park not far from the archducal palace' by 1880. Two beautiful American girls who played on it in the spring of that year were the reason why the knowledge of its existence has been passed down us. The young ladies so captivated a rather precocious young man from one of the leading families of nineteenth-century Europe that he simply could not help incorporating them in one of his autobiographical works. The young man's name was Alexander Mikhailovich. He was the son of Grand Duke Mikhail of Russia and a grandson of the tsar, and had come to Baden-Baden in the company of his mother to pay a visit to his uncle, Grand Duke Max of Baden.[35]

The honour of having had the first lawn tennis club in Germany must again be conferred to Bad Homburg. There is conclusive evidence that as early as 1879 a lawn tennis club existed in this town. It fulfilled the most essential requirement for a club to deserve that name, that of having a committee (it was referred to by the word Comité).[36] The Homburg club was followed, in 1881, by the Lawn-Tennis-Gesellschaft (lawn tennis company) in Spechten Garten, Strasbourg,[37] then by the Baden-Baden LTC. In Baden-Baden, too, English visitors were the first followers. Attracted by the new *Kurhaus* (put up in 1824), and the casino and the Iffezheim race-course, completed in 1838 and 1858 respectively, they used to come to the archducal summer residence in great numbers. It was therefore only natural that towards the end of the 1870s the new-fangled game should have been much in demand. On 25 June 1881,[38] a clergyman, the Reverend Thomas Starnes White of the Anglican High Church,[39] a Mr Jonstone and a young baron, the 16-year-old Freiherr Robert von Fichard called Baur von Eysseneck, descendant of an old family of the Austrian nobility,[40] founded a lawn tennis club which was able to rally twenty-nine enthusiasts in the first year of its existence. It was called the Baden-Baden LTC. The foundation testifies to the support lawn tennis was given in the early days by the English clergy, and the name implies that the members of the club were predominantly English,[41] some of whom attended the 'French Ecole Forestière in Nancy'.[42] The club does not seem to have differed much from that of Sir Robert Anstruther, and that is why the Bad Homburg LTC has claim to being the first of its kind in Germany. The Baden-Baden LTC continued to play, on two courts on the lawns in front of the 'Alleehaus' which had been placed at the club's disposal by the city authorities,[43] for another year. Then, on

9 July 1883, a second club, the International Lawn Tennis Club, came into being,[44] after the newly created 'Gemeinnütziger Verein Baden-Baden' had obtained a lease for a large plot of ground on the former 'Eiswiese' or 'Schlittschuhweiherwiese' (Skaters' Pond Meadow) where the club set its hand to laying five grass courts (**Figure 85**). These were opened in 1883,[45] the year in which the 25th anniversary of the Iffezheim Races was celebrated, with a splendid lawn tennis tournament in which the Prince of Wales (afterwards Edward VII) competed in the mixed doubles and, gracefully supported by Madame Reynittiens from France, beat Lord and Lady Montagne.[46] In the year following, the pioneering Baden-Baden LTC dissolved, and its former members joined the new club.[47]

In the 1880s, many more clubs were founded, and in most cases British residents were again among the founding members. This sometimes becomes evident from the names adopted by them. The pioneering clubs were, in chronological order: the English Lawn Tennis Club Freiburg im Breisgau (1883);[48] the Cassel Lawn Tennis Club (1883);[49] the Essener Turn- und Fechtklub (i.e. Gymnastics and Fencing Club; 1884);[50] the Strasbourg LTC (1885);[51] the Eisbahn-Verein vor dem Dammthor (i.e. the Skating Rink Club, Hamburg; 23 October 1886);[52] the 1. Nürnberger Lawn-Tennis-Club (*c.* 1887);[53] the Eisbahn-Verein auf der Uhlenhorst (Hamburg; 26 October 1888);[54] the Pöseldorfer Lawn-Tennis-Club (Hamburg; 1888);[55] the Elberfelder Lawn-Tennis-Club (spring 1889);[56] the Duisburger Lawn-Tennis und Croquet-Club

FIGURE 85   The lawn tennis courts and pavilion of Baden-Baden in 1895.

(3 December 1889);[57] the Cannstatter Fussball- und Tennis-Club (25 March 1890);[58] a club in Bad Ems (1 May 1890);[59] and last but not least the Heidelberger LTC (July 1890).[60] Of all these, the Heidelberger LTC has the distinction of being the oldest still in existence. In Cannstatt, as we have seen, lawn tennis was not played prior to 1891, and the Duisburg club was absorbed by a hockey club in 1911 which led to a loss of its original name. It is now the well-known Club Raffelberg.[61] Finally, two institutions also deserve to be mentioned although they were not lawn tennis clubs in the strictest meaning of the term: the recreation ground companies (German *Spielplatz-Gesellschaften*) 'Im Palmengarten' in Frankfurt[62] and in Berlin,[63] founded in 1887 and 1890 respectively. Not unlike the skating clubs of Hamburg, they placed lawn tennis courts at the disposal of customers who had to bring along their own rackets and balls. On their courts, many private clubs constituted themselves almost immediately, although next to nothing is known about the identity of most of them. After the Society had had to move to Barbarossa Strasse in 1896,[64] the most prestigious lawn tennis clubs of modern Berlin, the Lawn Tennis Turnier Club 'Rot Weiss', and the Tennis-Club 1899 e.V. Blau-Weiss came into being on its grounds. The former was founded by Karl von Jecklin, Dr Hans Schultz, and Dr Max Oechelhäuser in 1897, the chief purpose of their club being the organization of a tournament befitting the German capital.[65] The latter owed its existence to three schoolboys who convened the inaugural meeting, on 19 May 1899, in an arbour (*Gartenlaube*) of all places. Their names were Carl Lange, Ernst Zehrmann, and Otto Griebel, and Zehrmann became the Club Secretary.[66] The origin of the somewhat unusual names of the two clubs is connected with a rather funny story. The usual explanation of the name 'Rot Weiss' would relate it to the colours of the metropolis Berlin, but as a matter of fact both the names of 'Rot Weiss' and 'Blau Weiss' go back to the desire of the founding members to adorn their boaters, which had become fashionable around the turn of the century, with two-coloured hatbands.[67] In the first case, red and white bands were purchased by Karl von Jecklin at Steinhart's, a Berlin department store;[68] in the second blue and white ones bought by an unknown representative of 'Blau Weiss' at another department store, Pfingst's.[69]

THE FATHER OF LAWN TENNIS, CARL AUGUST VON DER MEDEN

Since Englishmen had played such a dominating role in the early days of lawn tennis in Germany, we may justifiably ask when and where the Germans took the matter in hand themselves. This happened in Hamburg, and was due to the initiative of a man who has rightly been called the 'Father of lawn tennis in Germany'.[70] His name was Carl August von der Meden (**Figure 86**).

As has previously been said, two skating clubs had been founded in Hamburg in the second half of the 1880s. They were both located on either side of the Alster, 'in the country' outside the former city wall. The fact was mirrored in their very names. The first, the Eisbahnverein vor dem Dammtor (**Figure 87**), owed its name to a city gate, the so-called Dammtor, whereas the name of the other, the Eisbahnverein auf

PLATE 1   One of the earliest illustrations of the *jeu de la paume*, the ballgame played with the palm of the hand (1300). We have before us a tennis lesson in which the cowled instructor advises his pupil to aim his service onto an imaginary slanting roof. The returning party awaits the ball with hands raised above shoulders in a characteristic manner. The intervening ornamental border does not indicate a line or net. Such a device is still long in coming.

PLATE 2   In a miniature from the treatise *Avis aus Roys* (Advice for Kings) (1360) the roof has been supplemented. Apparently, the game has even at this early date a firm hold over the young of noble birth.

PLATE 3　On a fine evening in June. Tennis on the market place of a small town in the north of France (*c.* 1450).

PLATE 4   The first medieval picture to show the roofed gallery of the traditional tennis court
(*c.* 1450) which had its origin in the medieval cloisters. The chess players are Scipio (*Scipion*) and
Laelius (*Lelius*), the ballplayer is Scaevola (*Sceuola*) who in all likelihood is depicted twice, as
server (left) and returner. Note the kid glove he wears on his right hand. It is the precursor of
the racket.

PLATE 5   One of the many magnificent paintings on the David and Bathsheba theme, signed 'R.A. 1559' [Andreas Ruhl]. As late as the middle of the sixteenth century even a royal tennis court such as King David's could be devoid of a line or net.

PLATE 6 One of the many off-shoots of the medieval *jeu de la paume* was the *jeu de tamis* in which a portable sieve mounted on three legs serves as a substitute for the slanting service roof. Here a match is in progress outside the walls of Beaumont Abbey in Hainaut in the south west of Belgium in 1598. Tiles on the pitch mark the chases.

PLATE 7 Around the turn of the seventeenth century (c. 1600). Students at play in a continental covered tennis court (a *Ballhaus* in Germany). There has been of late a primitive net; this is, in fact, the earliest picture showing one.

PLATE 8 The covered court of the Collegium Illustre in Tübingen was the best known *Ballhaus* in Germany and a favourite subject in the so-called *liber amicorum*, a collection of painted or printed sheets presented to fellow students when leaving the college. Curtains are being rigged up in the clerestory in order to prevent the sun from interfering with the young aristocrats' play.

PLATE 9   Another interior view of the Collegium Illustre. Academic discussions by non-competitors on court were apparently tolerated.

PLATE 10   A typical Victorian garden tennis party interrupted by a shower. There was no special lawn tennis outfit. People simply wore their Sunday best. The painting by Edith Hallyar, a still life and genre painter who exhibited at the Royal Academy between 1882 and 1897, was sold at Christie's in July 1970.

PLATE 11 'The Tennis Party' by the Scottish painter Sir John Lavery (1885), perhaps the most acclaimed Victorian tennis painting. Exhibited at the Royal Academy in 1887, it was awarded a gold medal at the Salon des Champs Elysées, and shown at the prestigious Royal Neue Pinakothek, Munich, in 1903, which acquired the painting at that time.

PLATE 12   A tennis party in America (1886).

PLATE 13   Tennis and tea, an opportunity for the Victorian matron to engineer the marriage of a daughter with a promising young man from the neighbourhood.

PLATE 14 The 19th-century private lawn tennis court and the favourite lawn tennis discipline of the time, the mixed doubles.

PLATE 15　Lawn tennis in Bad Homburg, the haunt of European aristocracy and the rich. The attire of the Bad Homburg ballboys – red jacket, blue trousers – was referred to in contemporary sources which are, however, silent about who devised these colours and why.

PLATE 16   Illustration of what in Germany was known as Engagement Tennis (Verlobungstennis) by Th.Th. Heine, a well-known contributor to the satirical journal *Simplicissimus*.

FIGURE 86   Carl August von der Meden, the Father of Lawn Tennis in Germany. For more than a decade he had lived in England, and on his daily journeys to his office in London he had passed by the courts of the All England Club. He may well have witnessed the inaugural tournament in 1877. In 1892 he started the German championship tournaments in Hamburg and in 1902 he became the first President of the German Lawn Tennis Federation.

der Uhlenhorst (**Figure 88**), went back to an ancient field name, literally meaning 'owls' hurst [= coppice, wood]'. The Eisbahnverein vor dem Dammtor – today the venue of the German Open, Hamburg Rothenbaum – had since its foundation in 1885 built a large pavilion (including a restaurant, a ladies' room, a dressing room and a music hall) and a large skating rink (grassland flooded in the winter) which was surrounded by a bicycle track.[71] The Uhlenhorst club had also erected a handsome and spacious pavilion which the visitor approached on a broad gateway leading from the main entrance on Hofweg through the club's ten courts on either side of it.[72] The club house (pavilion) had a 'music temple' in the middle, a dressing room for the skaters to the right, and a restaurant and a ladies' room on the right wing. In the left part of the building, there was the men's dressing room which prided itself on 30 lockers, wash stands and mirrors, and a bathroom (which latter, installed in 1894, was said to meet a long-felt need!). In the building on the left wing, the groundsman resided in a large flat. He was paid an annual salary of 1,200 marks, with lodging, lighting and heating free.[73] There were five additional courts close to the building, a ladies' court (for ladies only) and the so-called 'Paradeplatz' (parade court) to the right of it,[74] and three to the rear: the Love Court and the Veterans' Court (both

FIGURE 87 The courts of the Eisbahnverein vor dem Dammtor in 1907, today the venue for the German Open.

FIGURE 88 The earliest known picture of von der Meden's Eisbahnverein Auf der Uhlenhorst, Hamburg (1894).

property of the Uhlenhorst committee members, all veterans of a club which had adopted the name 'The Love Club'), and the Invalids' Court, so named (according to von Fichard), because it was opened at a time when an illness well known to tennis players had struck them for the first time, tennis elbow.[75]

The club to come into prominence through the activities of Carl August von der Meden was the Uhlenhorst club. The club had been founded at an inaugural meeting which took place in the house of the famous shipbuilder Carl Laeisz on 26 October 1888 (**Figure 89**). The purpose of the new club, formulated in the most lumbering officialese of the time, appeared from the first paragraph of its statutes:[76]

> The purpose of the club is to devote the area belonging to the premises of the orphanage and bordered by Bleicherstrasse, Hofweg, Schulweg and the footpath leading to the street first named to the setting-up of a skating rink and to other sporting and recreational activities.

Strangely enough, there was, at the inaugural meeting under the presidency of Carl Laeisz, no reference to Carl August von der Meden who has always been considered

FIGURE 89 The famous shipbuilder Carl Laeisz, President of the Eisbahnverein Auf der Uhlenhorst, Hamburg, wearing rather exotic lawn tennis garb. Because the brand of tennis shoes he wears were advertised by the 'Gummi-Waaren Fabrik' in Berlin in 1895, the photograph by Benque & Kindermann, Court Photographers, Hamburg, can be dated fairly accurately.

one of the club's founding members. Nor do the statutes say anything about lawn tennis. The name of von der Meden was first mentioned in the minutes of a committee meeting on 14 April 1889, the purpose of which was the adoption of two new sports for which, in turn, a sub-committee for each had to be elected. The new sports sanctioned by the committee were cycling and lawn tennis, and the committee members for the latter were a certain Fawcus and Carl August von der Meden.[77] Fawcus was, without any doubt, an Englishman,[78] and this was no surprise, since lawn tennis in those days was run almost exclusively by Englishmen. The question is how his partner, Herr von der Meden, as truly a German as any and a native of Hamburg, could have passed for a lawn tennis expert. This is a fascinating story.

In the 1920s, Hans Oskar Behrens, one of von der Meden's pupils who in 1913 chaired the inaugural meeting of the International Lawn Tennis Federation, had fond memories of his lawn tennis tutor who, he said, in his youth had lived in England for a long time, 'that vastly superior lawn tennis nation in those days'.[79] If this had been the case, it seems very strange that von der Meden himself should never have been explicit about this early part of his life.

On 12 April 1864, the authorities of the Hanseatic city issued a passport to the then 24-year-old,[80] the offspring of an old family of traders and real estate agents who could trace their origins as far back as the sixteenth century.[81] The passport specified the following destinations: England, East India, China, Russia, and further ('& weiter').[82] Young Carl August, apparently, planned a journey, in the course of which he hoped to visit, one after the other, members of his family which had branches all over the globe. Whether or not the young adventurer carried out his plans we cannot tell. One thing, however, is certain: he must have set course for England. On 9 December 1868, he married Sophie Mathilde Eckhardt, the second daughter of Ferdinand Eckhardt, a merchant from Frankfurt who lived in Bradford.[83] The marriage was celebrated at All Saints Church in Horton. The couple's first child, Sophie Elisabeth Gertrude, was born in nearby Headingley, the headquarters of a famous cricket club as well as a rugby league club. In the directory for Leeds, Carl August was described as a 'manager' in 1870,[84] but then his name disappeared: he was not listed in the census of 1871. Before that, he must have succumbed to the lures of the capital, London, for here he soon appeared again having established himself as a merchant. He first traded in wool and then became a japan merchant,[85] his office first being in St Mary Axe, and later at nearby Jeffrey's Square, a site now occupied by the Baltic Exchange. At the same time, he seems to have lived the life of a country gentleman, first in Teddington, then in Hampton Wick, Middlesex. In Teddington, he had rented a house in Teddington Park Street from a local surgeon named Spencer Clement. It was located very close to a wax factory and its bleaching grounds and bore the fine-sounding name of 'Blenheim House'. In Teddington, his daughters Elsa (1871) and Evelyn Lilian Thekla (1872) were born,[86] and the latter got into trouble the Reverend Hurling Smith of St Mary's Church when it came to entering her name in the register of baptisms. He resolutely spelt it 'Thecklar'.[87] About his sojourn in Hampton Wick, nothing is known except that his son Carl August Walther was born there (1875).[88] By 1881 at the latest, Carl August must have been back in Hamburg, for on 6 May of the same year he was granted citizenship there, his status and profession being stated as house-agent.[89] Carl August von der Meden had spent more than a dozen years in England, and his place of residence had not been 'anywhere in England', but (if we now return to the original question of where he might have become acquainted with lawn tennis) only a stone's throw from the grass roots of the sport, Wimbledon. Teddington is not far from Worple Road where in 1877 the inaugural All England Championships were held. Indeed, on his daily travels on the 'London & South Western Railway' from Waterloo Station to his country home his train passed near the courts of the All England Club, and it was almost inevitable that the German would at least catch a glimpse of the first championships (**Figure 90**). Later, he had every chance of becoming an eye-witness of subsequent ones before he eventually left England for good. However, if that had actually been the case, the question still is why he never cared to mention his extraordinary

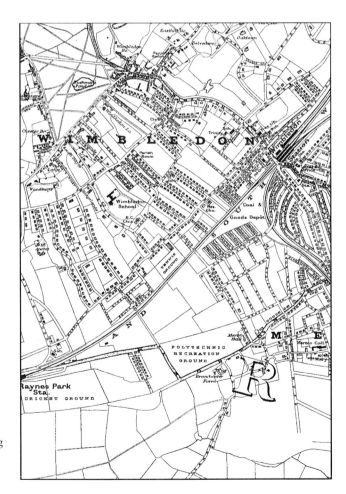

FIGURE 90 A map of Wimbledon in the early 1880s giving a good idea of the site of the courts and illustrating well how a passenger on the London and Southampton Railway like Carl August von der Meden could not help being involved in the goings-on there.

experience, an experience which would not only have aroused the envy of his countrymen, but which in his native country would have raised him high above all others as a lawn tennis authority. The reasons for von der Meden's reticence were, perhaps, not entirely honourable, but very human. The woollen and japan merchant went bankrupt in 1880,[90] a fact nobody would want to tell the whole world about if he intended (as von der Meden did)[91] to set up, in the highly conservative City of Hamburg, a house agent and insurance company. Insistence on his involvement in the Wimbledon tournaments harboured the danger that something about earlier failure might leak out. He therefore decided to let sleeping dogs lie and never said a word about it.

Members of the two Hamburg skating clubs were shareholders who in the so-called *gründerjahre* (foundation years before the turn of the century) had subscribed a hundred marks and more for their memberships. If skating during the winter did not satisfy these gentlemen and their ladies, and they wanted to indulge in the novel pastime of lawn tennis in the summer, they might buy either a day-ticket or a seasonal one, the latter at the price of ten marks for the individual and twenty marks for the whole family (the family's status symbol, the maid, included).[92] During the first years, members of either skating club played their matches without bothering about who played on the court next to theirs. A feeling of solidarity arose, however, when competition-orientated players from both clubs made up their minds to have clubs of their own. As a result, the Pöseldorfer LTC was founded in 1890 on the premises of the Dammtor skating club;[93] it was followed one year later, on 10 June 1891, by the Harvestehuder LTC.[94] The Uhlenhorst club, meanwhile, played competitive lawn tennis without a club within the club,[95] but this did not prevent its players from becoming (according to Hans Oskar Behrens) the arch-enemies of the Harvestehuders.[96]

Behrens also remembered the truly remarkable matches which took place on his home ground every morning from half past six till eight o'clock. They involved Carl August von der Meden who, before office hours, was extremely busy on the lawn tennis court together with distinguished members of the Hamburg society, Herr Schlubach, the Consul General, Laeisz, the shipbuilder and the club's president, and Messrs Gabe, Jochheim, Treusein, Thomsen and Doctor Pinckernelle – very busy Hanseatic traders every one of them.[97] The courts on which these matches were contested were the 'Love Court' and the 'Veterans' Court' of which we have heard earlier and which were labelled 'private courts' in the club regulations.[98] These matches, unimportant though they may have been from a sportsman's point of view, had a side-effect, the importance of which for the development of the sport in Germany can hardly be underestimated. As again Hans Oskar Behrens put it:[99]

> We Uhlenhorst boys, Winzer, Bush, Grobien, André, Wantzelius, myself, later Nirrnheim
> etc., who at first, for one summer at least, had only permission to play 'against the wall',
> but not on court, had our ambition stirred. We were allowed to pick up the old
> gentlemen's balls, and he who could make up a four was infinitely proud and started

thinking about the wise instructions regarding technique and tactics ... Then we realized that Papa Meden had picked us Hamburg youths in order to make us consider such questions as tournament management, regulations, maintenance of courts, etc. At the age of fifteen, sixteen we were allowed to assist in the preparation of printed circulars, to draft letters, to submit handicap lists, to cash small amounts of money, etc. The nights before a tournament in Papa Meden's house where instructions were given and hard work awaited us, belong to the most pleasant memories of my life.

What Behrens described was the deliberate training of young and competent assistants with the help of whom von der Meden could soon contemplate the organization of championship tournaments in Hamburg, to be conducted according to English practice.[100] Without them, von der Meden would hardly have been able to organize the famous Bad Homburg tournaments, the outstanding lawn tennis event on the European continent before and after the turn of the century.[101] Later, he could count on them when the important Hamburg Lawn Tennis Guild, and after it, the German Lawn Tennis Federation (Deutscher Lawn-Tennis-Bund) were founded. Two of von der Meden's pupils, Hans Oskar Behrens,[102] his ball boy and the writer of the above lines, and Otto Nirrnheim were among the founders of the International Lawn Tennis Federation.

By 1895, von der Meden had also become the author of a little manual on the organization of lawn tennis tournaments. Its title was *Leitfaden zur Veranstaltung von Lawn-Tennis-Turnieren* (*Manual for the Organization of Lawn Tennis Tournaments*). In a postscript, the author acknowledged his debt of gratitude to W.H. Collins and Herbert Chipp, who at that time were the Vice President and Honorary Secretary respectively of the LTA. He called both his friends and expressed his thanks for advice he had received in writing and orally.[103] In the book, the duties of officials from the tournament manager to the meanest ball boy were described at some length, and with a great deal of good humour. Players needed ball boys who were well drilled ('gut einexercierte Knaben'); if not available, they could be dispensed with altogether, he continued, for a great error it was to believe that they could be trained during a tournament. Boys who always stood in the way, or who were not ready with the ball, did more harm than good.[104] An umpire should not be short-sighted,[105] and when assembling a Honorary Committee for a tournament one did well to pick personalities who were influential, but not too young. Nor was it necessary that they were themselves lawn tennis players. Indeed, it was ideal if they tried to compensate for their lack of sporting expertise by a timely opening of their purses.[106]

THE GERMAN CHAMPIONSHIPS

The first lawn tennis tournament (for members only) to be held in Hamburg took place on the courts of the Dammtor club in 1887, another in 1888, but both were hardly a success.[107] On the opposite banks of the Alster, the Uhlenhorst club was more fortunate. At the committee meeting of 14 April 1889, it was decided to spend

2,000 marks on the laying of lawn tennis courts ('Lawn-Tennys-Plätze'), and an additional 1,000 marks on lawn tennis tapes ('Lawn-Tennys Bänder').[108] The astonishing expenditure of 1,000 marks only for tapes is in need of some explanation. The German term '*Bänder*' did not refer to tapes, but to sheets of iron. Sunk into a surface which consisted mainly of the black rub-off of imperial cobblestone roads and a finishing cover of fine gravel,[109] and painted white with oil paint at the upper edge, they served as lines. They were the hallmark of the Uhlenhorst championship courts until well after the turn of the century.[110] The reference to the iron lines in 1889 indicates that the Eisbahnverein auf der Uhlenhorst had by that time made a decision to have new all-weather courts built with a view to staging a championship tournament. The first dirt court, presumably designed by the very same A. Boursée from Bad Pyrmont mentioned earlier,[111] was completed and put to use in 1889.[112] By 1893, the year of the second 'lawn tennis championships for Germans', three courts of this type were available.[113]

The Uhlenhorst club organized its first tournament in 1890.[114] A second tournament was held in the autumn of 1891 (from 29 August to 6 September).[115] In the handicap event, not only did von der Meden's 15-year-old son Walther compete (he was soundly beaten 6:1, 6:0 in the second round, after a bye in the first), but 'Papa' von der Meden, at that time almost 50, also entered. Having been matched with Walter Howard, who had won the open event before,[116] he scratched. It was, in fact, the only occasion on which von der Meden is known to have ever taken an active part in any tournament.

The English players who graced the event with their presence had, according to an account given by the journal *Pastime*, followed its advice to make 'a visit to this meeting' given to them in its columns two months previously.[117] It was the first time that Carl August von der Meden had resorted to what he called 'Circulaire' (circular letters), announcements for his tournaments in suitable papers and journals with the help of which he hoped to attract players from all parts of Germany, but, above all, the much admired Britons.[118]

After similar circulars had apparently been sent in the spring of the following year, there appeared, in the journal *Pastime*, regular advertisements in which players from England were invited to enter a tournament set for 27 August and the days following.[119] The advertisements had been placed by a certain A. von der Meden, Esquire, Bellevue, Uhlenhorst, Hamburg, who recommended to the readers of the journal the daily 'direct express steamers from (London) Harwich, Grimsby and other ports' and promised to send, upon application, 'prospectuses and particulars' to those interested. Against payment of an entrance fee of 5s each,[120] the lawn tennis experts from England could make their choice from five different events. They were not eligible, however, for an event labelled 'local event' in the same ad.[121] It was 'open only to Germans and Austrians', and there was a reason why it was (though apparently irrelevant for the British player) nevertheless announced with unconcealed pride. This 'local event' was nothing less than the first singles championship of the country.

Local Hamburg papers were more explicit about this championship. The *Hamburger Fremden-Blatt*, in its issue of 30 June 1892,[122] told its readers that the cup presented by Carl Laeisz, the ship magnate and president of the Uhlenhorst club, had to be won three times (or twice successively; this alternative was soon abandoned)[123] in order to pass into the victor's possession; that the champion had, in the year following, to stay out and to defend his title, in a so-called challenge round, against the winner of the all-comers' event.[124] Clearly, the championship of the Germans was modelled on the All England Championships, and the organizers were entertaining hopes of making Hamburg Uhlenhorst the German Wimbledon. The British journal *Pastime*, and later Baron von Fichard, revealed the monetary value of the championship cup. Whereas Mr Howard, of London, had spent six guineas for the Hamburg cup, the trophy of the main open event in the tournament, the shipbuilder had really dipped into his pocket: his cup was worth £21, or 700 German marks.[125]

AN UNINVITED GUEST

Some 187 competitors had been allured by the prizes offered. Among these, there were 25 from outside Hamburg, although it is not known how many of them were foreigners, and how many had entered for the championship of the Germans.[126] One visitor, however, who came from as far away as Russia and did not fail to make an appearance, had been known well in advance. It was the Asiatic cholera. In the presence of this guest, both uninvited and unpleasant, the number of competitors diminished as rapidly as the Ten Little Indians in the well-known children's song. Six entries were withdrawn even before the unflinching Carl Laeisz had allowed the tournament to begin on 27 August 1892, regardless of the epidemic.[127] Another 25 competitors had beat a hasty retreat by the next day, Sunday, which occasioned the organizers to speak of a 'stampede'. It was decided, however, not to call off the meeting completely, but to resume play on 10 September for the gentlemen, and 16 September for the ladies. It so happened that the last final was played on 20 September. As a result, the first championships of the Germans became the longest ever on record.[128]

What had been heralded as the Championship of Germany was, under these unlucky circumstances, indeed reduced to a 'local event'. With the exception of James von Fichard from Strasbourg,[129] a brother of the chronicler of German tennis, and a certain Dr du Bois-Reymond from Berlin (who thought it wise to scratch after a bye in the first round), all competitors were residents of Hamburg. And it was one of them, Walter Bonne, who was the first to have his name engraved on the shipbuilder's silver cup, and possibly much to von der Meden's chagrin, whose own offspring, Walther, had received a drubbing in the first round. Mr Bonne, a rather uninspired retriever from the baseline whose chief weapon was a heavily undercut forehand stroke,[130] was a Harvestehuder, a member of the Pöseldorfer LTC from the opposite banks of the Alster![131]

In the following year, there were only nine entries, and the all-comers' event was won by Christian Winzer who, the year before, had lost against Bonne, the champion, in the first round. Now he turned the tables on Bonne in the challenge round (played for the first time after the model of the Wimbledon championships), by beating him 'somewhat easily by three sets to one': Bonne played with his usual stamina from the baseline and 'lobbed with accuracy ...', but could not cope with Winzer's volleying, which was good'.[132] There came an enthusiastic report of the match (and one very funny in retrospect) from the German sporting journal *Spiel und Sport*, written at a time when sporting journalism was in its infancy in Germany.[133] In those days, a journalist was obviously unable to draw on any established sporting terminology,[134] and a great uncertainty existed generally as to how to deal with a strange subject such as a lawn tennis match. The epic of the fight itself was, for example, preceded by a description of the venue which, translated into English, read thus:[135]

> A very numerous attendance had come to see the challenge round on the last day. One side of the Veterans' Court, on which the battle was fought out, was at the ropes almost exclusively occupied by ladies, behind them, the gentlemen were standing in three and four rows, at the other side of the [stop]nets, the other players, who had competed in the tournament, had taken their seats, above and below spectators also pressed against the [stop]nets, there were indeed many hundreds present. The expectation, whether the champion would keep his title, or have to surrender it, caused great excitement among the crowd. Above them all, the umpire, Herr Horley, one of the English guests, was enthroned, whereas the referee [von der Meden] and the editor of the German lawn tennis journal 'Spiel und Sport' [John Bloch], who had come from Berlin in order to watch the spectacle, were mounting guard at the other side of the court.

This introduction had a conclusion befitting it as well as the feats of heroism that had occurred on the court:

> Never-ending cheers greeted the victor, his friends surrounded him, even the ladies did not consider it beneath their dignity to press the flushed young man's hand! He seemed to us, like Busch [another successful young player], to be the ladies' darling.

Despite his achievement, the main sensation of the event was not caused by Winzer, but by a young nobleman from Mecklenburg, Count Viktor Voss-Schönau.[136] He had been beaten by Winzer in the semi-final, but by a narrow margin only (6:4, 6:4), and the discerning eye of the reporter from *Spiel und Sport* recognized at once that he had played with 'the best English players' before, who had taught him all those little tricks which were completely absent from the play of even the best Hamburg players. Voss used his head (as Winzer, the champion, had had to admit himself), and the only thing liable to criticism was the fact that he did not move speedily enough about the court.[137]

The following year, Voss took revenge on Winzer in the challenge round, but although he won in three straight sets, it was, despite the premature praises sung on his behalf, by no means an easy victory, and the third and decisive set in particular was hotly contended (6:1, 6:4, 11:9).[138]

After Voss's success, the fickleness of womankind became evident. Those female supporters who, the year before, had hugged the young hero Winzer, and who had again turned up in huge numbers, now, with unending applause and waving their handkerchiefs, celebrated the triumphant Count.[139] Clearly, in imperial Germany, otherwise known for its prudery, lawn tennis matches provided an outlet for eroticism.

The championships of 1895 were bedevilled by a nasty weather on the first few days (a characteristic of Hamburg tournaments to the present day), and saw another success by Voss who scored an easy victory this time against Winzer (6:2, 6:1, 6:2).[140] The latter, who had moved to Paris in the meantime and had had little practice, showed poor form, but had nevertheless fought his way to the final of the all-comers' event, where he beat Hans Oskar Behrens, von der Meden's ball boy. Behrens, in turn, had eliminated the champion of Berlin, the formidable H. von Schneider, a player who, with regard to his powerful drives, hardly had his equal in the whole country, if he was 'in the mood'.

CHARLES ADOLPH VOIGT

The man who had dropped this rather flimsy remark on the play of von Schneider, and later on in his report even recommended him to abandon the volleying game altogether,[141] was a certain Charles Adolph Voigt (**Figure 91**). It was he who, before the turn of the century and in the decade after it, was to become the leading lawn tennis authority on the European continent and who, as we shall see, in all probability became the originator of one of the outstanding competitions the sport has known, the Davis Cup. Voigt, who was here writing for the Berlin-based sporting journal *Sport im Bild*, had in 1895 published a lawn tennis manual titled *Das Lawn-Tennis Spiel und Die Kunst zu spielen* (*The Game of Lawn Tennis and the Art of Playing It*) (**Figure 92**). The most remarkable feature of the booklet were the photographs illustrating it. They showed its author, racket in hand, demonstrating the various strokes the mastery of which he (and, to judge from some rather unusual poses, not infrequently only he) considered would lead to perfection.[142]

Charles Adolph Voigt was born in San Jose, California, on 2 May 1869.[143] He began travelling at a very early age and was educated in France, Germany, Italy, and South Africa, finishing up at a German college.[144] His upbringing was certainly the reason why he was later characterized thus by his compatriot Paret:

> He is the most picturesque and interesting man I have ever known. Combined with the face of a German, the accent of an Englishman, the manners of a Frenchman, and the good-fellowship of an American, he has the experience of a cosmopolitan and the tongue of a linguist.[145]

Besides being multilingual, Voigt was an all-round sportsman, having tried his hand at cricket (he called himself 'a very fair bowler'), long distance running, and, by

FIGURE 91 Charles Adolph Voigt, manager of the famous Bad Homburg tournaments for more than a decade and the man who as early as 1886 advanced the idea of the Davis Cup.

FIGURE 92 One of the pictures which adorned Charles Adolph Voigt's tennis primer in German, titled *Lawn-Tennis, und die Kunst zu spielen* (1895) (Lawn Tennis, and the Art of Playing). Here Voigt demonstrates the overhead service.

1899, golf. An injury to his wrist incurred playing rugby football had handicapped him severely, and this prevented him from doing himself justice in lawn tennis, a sport in which, he said, he had 'never got far beyond garden-party form'.[146] The fact that in 1900, at the age of 31, he still managed to win four games from his excellent countryman Basil Spalding de Garmendia, in the first round of the Olympic tournament,[147] proves that he was speaking with typical British understatement when he said this. When he wrote his tournament report for *Sport im Bild* in 1895, he was an employee of the 'Friedr. Krupp Gruson Werk' in Magdeburg,[148] a branch of the famous Krupp steel-cast factory and weapons manufacturers from Essen (Gruson had specialized in the manufacture of armoured turrets and gun-carriages).[149] But the man who throughout his lifetime as much insisted on the English pronunciation of his name as he was conscious of the fashionable cut of his jacket (the inevitable carnation in his lapel), was at the time obviously on the point of entering upon a new career.[150] Magdeburg, to his truly cosmopolitan taste, soon became much too provincial. In 1896, he took an extended business trip to his country of birth where he at once indulged in his favourite pastime, lawn tennis, attending no fewer than half a dozen of the country's more important tournaments, and soon became very popular with American players who nicknamed him 'the Baron'.[151] After his return, he first moved to Berlin, then to Rotterdam,[152] and later to Paris and London.[153] It was from these metropolitan centres that he began, in 1896, to manage important lawn tennis events on the European continent, producing an extraordinary wealth of correspondence in the process, written, a foible of his well known among players, 'in blue and red pencils'.[154] The most prestigious tournament was that of Bad Homburg vor der Höhe. Here, he started as Honorary Secretary in 1896 and was tournament manager from 1899 to 1910.[155] Residing in the Hotel Metropole, he was 'advance agent, honorary secretary, host to foreign visitors, chief scorer, and "Lord High Everything Else", as Gilbert put it in *The Mikado*.'[156]

In 1904, the 'Baron' had announced, in the columns of the journal *Lawn Tennis and Croquet*, his betrothal, in a way befitting his rank:[157]

> The engagement and approaching marriage at Nice of Baronne Marguerite Bauwens d'Everstein, of Brussels, with Mr. Charles A. Voigt, of Paris, is announced. It will come as a surprise to the latter's numerous friends and acquaintances in all European countries as well as in America. Mr. Voigt, who is a Californian by birth, is certainly well known to all lovers of lawn tennis for the great interest he takes in the game, and for the admirable way in which he manages the Monte Carlo, Homburg, Paris, Lucerne, and other international tournaments. It has been truly said that a tournament abroad without Mr. Voigt, is indeed like Hamlet minus its Prince.

Much later, in 1912, and in a remote corner of the journal *Lawn Tennis and Badminton*,[158] the 'Baron' told the story of his visit to a tournament in Niagara-on-the-Lake, on the Canadian border. It had taken place a long time ago, at the end of July in 1896 and during his stay in the United States, of which we have heard earlier.

During this tournament, in which R.D. Wrenn had put an end to a long streak of successes by E.P. Fischer, 'a terror on hard "dirt" courts', Voigt was talking shop one night with the same 'Eddie' Fischer and the well-known tennis writer, Parmly Paret, when he caught sight of a young tennis player emerging from the ballroom in the company of 'the belle of the place', and disappearing into the moonlit gardens a few moments afterwards. 'Who on earth is this young sport?', Voigt queried. 'Why that's our young multi-millionaire, Dwight Davis, of St Louis', he was told. So rarely had he, to use Voigt's own words, had the good fortune of meeting a millionaire who played lawn tennis and such a young one into the bargain, that his first observation was: 'A millionaire, is he? If so, why don't you people get him to do something for the game? Put up some big prize, or cup?' It is very unlikely that Davis, preoccupied with other thoughts at the time, paid any attention to what the man with the strange-sounding name had suggested, even if he happened to overhear his words. However, the next morning, Voigt's initiative of the evening before, and the discussion following it which centred on the 'possibilities of international visits and matches' was recorded in the daily tournament bulletin *The Lark*. The latter, compiled by Scott Griffin, the tournament manager from Toronto, and Parmly Paret, notoriously spread the news of all goings-on during the tournament including Davis's evening strolls with his girl 'in the shrubberies'. It was therefore almost inevitable that the young man from St Louis, who naturally had a very personal interest in the bulletin's stories, also became acquainted with what Voigt had said about 'the Cup'. Voigt was therefore right when he truly believed that his 'passing remark' had 'laid the foundation of the Davis Cup', and that his was 'the true history of how the Davis Cup originated'. In retrospect, it is understandable that Davis when he, as US Governor-General of the Philippines and at a time less open-minded than ours, wrote about the invention of his Cup, because of the circumstances under which the idea had been born, mentioned neither the tournament at Niagara-on-the-Lake nor indeed the man who had come forward with the idea, Charles Adolph Voigt.[159] Generally speaking, it is at least interesting to note that, by a curious coincidence, Malcolm D. Whitman and Beals Wright, the latter then very young, should also have been present at Niagara. Then Davis's rivals for the beautiful girl's favour, they were to become, in 1899, his teammates on that legendary tour to Monterey in California which, in all the handbooks, is invariably credited with having given rise to the invention of the Davis Cup.

Charles Adolph Voigt was not only an inventor and a tournament manager of note, but also a prolific writer. As an employee of Gruson's, he had not only enlarged on the art of lawn tennis, but also, in the *United Service Magazine*, on subjects such as 'Smokeless Gunpowder', and 'Land and Coast Defence Systems'. A devotee of agriculture, he had even compiled a little treatise on 'Manurial Problems'.[160] His fame, however, rests on contributions he made, with equal linguistic competence, to sporting journals such as *La vie au grand air* (in French), *Sport im Bild* (the prestigious German journal edited by his Scottish friend Andrew Pitcairn-Knowles)[161] as well as *Lawn Tennis and Croquet* (later *Lawn Tennis and Badminton*) in English.

Although Voigt on several occasions expressed the intention of returning to his native country one day,[162] he apparently never did.[163] He died in London on 3 July 1929, one day after the Wimbledon final and at the age of 60.[164] His death remained unnoticed in tennis-playing Germany, the country where he had made such a Herculean effort to promote the game.

UHLENHORST IN 1896 – RAIN AGAIN AND STILL COUNT VOSS

In 1896, the weather at Uhlenhorst was as bad as the prospects of those challenging the champion, Count Voss, in the tournament from 22 to 30 May. From Berlin, von Schneider had brought along young Lieutenant von Gordon (a competent player who was later to succeed Voss as lawn tennis tutor of the Grand Duchess Anastasia), but since the Count had again improved his game by a margin of 15 (in those days, the quality of a player was assessed by means of a handicap), they both stood no chance. Despite their good strokes, they lacked, according to the anonymous writer in von Fichard's lawn tennis annual, the necessary experience in tournament play. At the net, and in placing the ball they had yet to learn a lot.[165]

Von der Meden's youngsters, André (who beat another nobleman from Mecklenburg, Count Grote (6:2, 6:3),[166] Behrens, and above all Wantzelius had also made great progress. Indeed, the latter was said to have caught up with the former champion Winzer (who, for reasons unknown, was absent that year).[167] But all was of little avail. The same Wantzelius, who throughout the tournament had not conceded a single set, was soundly trounced by the irresistible Count and in the three straight sets of the challenge round he only gathered two measly games (1:6, 0:6, 1:6). 'However much interest there was in the championships of the ladies (these were contended for the first time), so disconcerting was the way the gentlemen's championships of Germany took their course,' the anonymous commentator complained.[168] Count Voss cared little for such statements. He had his name engraved on the Laeisz cup for the third time in a row and bagged the trophy for good. Unlike its many successors, this precious relic of German lawn tennis history has by some stroke of good look survived the vicissitudes of the times. It is now kept – a fact little known in the country – in the safe of a bank in Braunschweig.[169]

THE 'COUNT OF MECKLENBURG': VIKTOR FELIX EUGEN VOSS-SCHÖNAU

Count Voss (**Figure 93**), Chamberlain to the Grand Duchess of Mecklenburg-Schwerin,[170] was born at his parents' manor Schorssow on 31 March 1868; his mother was Elise Szápáry, a Hungarian Countess, and his father was descended from Mecklenburg's ancient nobility.[171] Since Voss in Low German meant 'fox', his family used a coat of arms showing (quite contrary to the statuesqueness the Count exhibited on court) Red Reynard on the run.[172] Count Voss had received his first lawn tennis lessons, from 'an American gentleman' who had stayed there for a few months sometime at the beginning of the 1890s, on a private court at his parental manor in

FIGURE 93 Count Voss, Chamberlain to the Great Duchess Anastasia of Mecklenburg-Schwerin, and three times Champion of the Germans before the turn of the century. He had been trained by the Renshaw twins during his annual winter sojourns in Cannes and outshone his countrymen by far.

Mecklenburg.[173] At first, the admiration the young nobleman felt for his American tutor was great, but then he had to see how, at a tournament and much to his disappointment, he was beaten easily by an English player who, he was told, was only third class.[174] Voss made a decision henceforth to take lessons from no one except the very best. The very best, at that time, were William and Ernest Renshaw. The twins, former All England champions and both, as sons of an English industrial magnate, men of means, had given up competitive lawn tennis early and decided to play the game for fun only. This they did, and especially during the winter season, on the excellent courts of the Hotel Beau-Site in Cannes. By a happy coincidence, it was to exactly these courts that young Voss had to go, in his capacity as a member of the household of Frederick Francis III, Grand Duke of Mecklenburg-Schwerin.[175] In the early 1880s, the Grand Duke, suffering from asthma and severe neuralgia accompanying it, had built in Cannes the 'Villa Wenden', a stately Italian-style mansion perched on a steep rock high above the Mediterranean Sea.[176] It was here that the Grand Duke spent the winter months together with his wife and his children. Here, too, Count Viktor Voss diligently performed his duties, as chamberlain to Anastasia, the Grand Duke's wife.

The Count's duties included daily lawn tennis matches with the Grand Duchess, an enthusiastic player herself, and since these took place on the courts of the Hotel

Beau-Site it was inevitable that he should have run into the Renshaws who practised on the same courts. The twins, perhaps a little flattered by a real nobleman's desire to keep them company, genially agreed to become his tutors.[177] Apparently not satisfied with this, Voss later also called upon the services of perhaps the best professional of the time, the Irishman T. Burke. Burke, twice world champion of the professionals, had settled in Paris, but had adopted the habit of coming over to Nice during the winter.[178] In Nice, too, Count Voss would take up quarters, together with Countess Clara von der Schulenburg, his equal socially and also an excellent lawn tennis player. After practising with Burke, he would valiantly cover the short distance to Cannes, right into the barrage of his English tennis foes. As a means of transport, he availed himself of his much admired 'red-coated' automobile: the Count, not only a first-rate lawn tennis player, and an excellent pigeon shot,[179] was also one of the first gentleman drivers in Germany.[180]

From his first appearance at the championships in 1893 until the turn of the century, Count Voss was the chief attraction of both the Hamburg and the Homburg tournaments. In 1899, at the peak of his career, he at last met a demand that had been made in Wilhelmine Germany long before, namely, to beard the lion in his den.[181] His trip to the green courts of the British Isles resembled the quest of Sir Gawain, King Arthur's itinerant knight, to the chapel of the Green Knight. After competing in the Chiswick tournament, he got as far as Dublin, reaping some moderate success against England's and Ireland's second best,[182] which aroused the curiosity of contemporary English sporting journals. *Lawn Tennis*, for instance, found much to commend in his game:[183]

> The great feature of the Count's game, besides his powerful service, varied ever and anon by a most puzzling underhand screw,[184] is his hard and accurate drive into his adversary's backhand corner and his smashing from the service line. When he is in form, it is useless to try and toss, as his great reach enables him to smother even the most perfect lob.

Impartial critics such as Dr J.M. Flavelle, an English physician from London and a tournament player who knew continental lawn tennis well, were less polite in assessing the Count's abilities. Dr Flavelle, while not denying him a capable forehand drive and a sound volleying game, considered his first service (which *Lawn Tennis* had rated powerful) to be easy to return,[185] his smash middling, and his backhand decidedly weak. The praise heaped on him, he said, mostly came from the mouths of professionals who, since they had to earn a living, had every reason to extol their protégé's achievements.[186] Nevertheless, when Slazenger and Sons, the famous manufacturers of lawn tennis equipment, bestowed on one of their rackets the name Voss, this was a fitting tribute to the Count, although the firm may above all have hoped to boost their sales figures in the Fatherland.[187]

The noble champion's hallmark was a white towel slung round his head, turban-like, and his admirers, and above all the fair sex, swore that this towel was wet. In response to an enquiry of a friend, a fair American was once heard to observe at

Homburg: 'Yes, the Count suffers so much from headaches that he wraps a wet bath-towel round his head.'[188] Eventually, the leading imperial sporting journal *Sport im Bild* shed light on a question which had occupied the minds of a whole nation. Even though the *New York Herald* confirmed the wearing of wet towels (turban-fashion) in the United States where, the *Herald* said, this was by no means unusual, it might be of interest to its readers that the Count's white cloth was dry! It was applied, *Sport im Bild* explained, to his forehead solely because of the heavy perspiration of his scalp, and it helped to prevent a misting of his horn-rimmed spectacles (these were another special feature of Germany's tennis hero). In England and in the United States, a great many players wearing spectacles did exactly the same, and the journal named two of them as cases in point, C.B. Neel and E.G. Meers.[189]

Voss left the stage when he realized that in the world of lawn tennis no new territories could be conquered. When, after the turn of the century, the sun of his compatriot Otto Froitzheim began to rise, Voss swore a solemn oath never again to invade the tennis courts.[190] Because the manor where he was born, Schorssow, had been sold in 1891, he retired to another family estate, Ulrichshusen, a moated castle in the gothic style which had possessed a drawbridge and was set on a little lake. From that day, the sporting press (which never ceased to bemourn the timely withdrawal of its former hero) bestowed on him the epithet 'der Ulrichshusener' (the man from Ulrichshusen). In the park of his manor, fragments of a tennis court, laid out, according to local tradition, around the year 1910, are still clearly visible, and older villagers still remember having seen Voss playing on it.[191] This means that the Count, at least from time to time, allowed himself to lapse into old habits, despite his oath.[192]

In Ulrichshusen, the story still persists of a liaison between Count Voss and the Grand Duchess, Anastasia, his partner in many a game of mixed doubles.[193] Yet, the Count was married twice. His first wife (whom he married in New York in 1911) was a divorced Italian marchesa, his second an old acquaintance from the heyday of his lawn tennis career on the Riviera, Countess Clara von der Schulenburg, a divorced ex-commoner and a champion like himself whom he married in Berlin-Grunewald in 1928.[194] Voss, who had no children, died in his villa in Waren on Lake Müritz (which, now a part of Neu-Brandenburg, in those days belonged to Mecklenburg) on 9 August 1936.[195] He had been ill for five months, and his death occurred almost unnoticed because of the Olympic games which at the time were in progress in nearby Berlin.[196] He was buried in the family vault in the chapel of Gross-Gievitz, another family estate and the residence of his elder brother Felix.[197] The fact was long hushed up by the communist authorities of the German Democratic Republic, who were anxious to wipe out even the slightest trace of the hated aristocrats. Of late, however, a cross adorning the Count's grave and bearing his name can again be seen in the vicinity of the chapel.

THE FIRST LADIES' CHAMPIONSHIPS

At the 1896 tournament, the first ladies' championships of the country were also contested. In marked contrast to the men's event, these were 'open' championships. The prize had been presented the year before by an Englishman from London, Walter Howard, and it had been the intention of the donor to attract players from England.[198] The trophy was, according to von Fichard, not a cup, but a silver dish or bowl ('eine silberne Schale') which again testified to the organizers' attempt to make the Hamburg tournament a true copy of the All England championships where the ladies' prize was a rosewater bowl.[199]

Despite such clever stratagems, English ladies were in the first year conspicuous by their absence. The silver dish therefore went to a German, Miss Maren Thomsen, a rank outsider. Miss Lantzius, the favourite, who had in the first round easily eliminated another likely candidate for the victory, Miss Holtz, played 'below her usual form' in the final,[200] resorting to a rather cowardly game from the baseline. Thus the more aggressive play of Miss Thomsen, of youthful appearance who possessed 'a very good overhand service',[201] a rarity at the time, prevailed. Her victory in three straight sets (6:3, 6:2, 7:5) was a very popular one, a fact which became apparent, the correspondent of *Spiel und Sport* wrote, by the many kisses she received from the female supporters, and the handshakes from the gentlemen.[202] Miss Thomsen was at once heralded 'the rising star' on the German lawn tennis scene, but her success was to remain an ephemeral one. Nothing more was ever heard of her. She had only just turned 17 when she won the championship.[203] The only star, if any, German tennis was to produce in the years to come was Countess Clara von der Schulenburg who had in the same event not even survived the first round where she had been soundly beaten – by the very Miss Maren Thomsen, the champion.[204]

The first champion's life does not seem to have been a very happy one. She was at one time engaged to a widower who had two children. He died before the marriage. Afterwards she nursed her ailing parents and then for some time ran the household for her brother-in-law after the death of her elder sister. Failing to play the role of a mother for her sister's only child, a daughter, she rather prematurely succumbed to a fatal disease in 1936.[205] Her death passed unnoticed. Already seven years earlier, in 1929, the official chronicler of the German Tennis Federation, Karl Grauhan, had spoken of the first German ladies' champion, a 'Miss M. Thomson', as of an Englishwoman.[206] This was a truly remarkable example of the uninformedness and lack of interest so very characteristic of tennis officialdom.

OPEN CHAMPIONSHIPS FOR MEN AND WOMEN ALIKE

In 1897, a novelty was introduced at the Uhlenhorst tournament: a new Championship of Germany which was, in marked contrast to the traditional Championship of the Germans (which nevertheless continued to be contended), open to all comers. The donor of the new cup was again the shipbuilder Carl Laeisz, whereas Count Voss, three-time champion of the Germans, generously provided a new cup for future champions of the Germans (**Figures 94 and 95**).[207] It is difficult to tell whether the inauguration of this Championship of Germany was inspired by the initiative of Walter Howard who had created open championships for ladies one year previously, or simply by the fact that the trophy for the championships of the Germans had gone into the possession of Count Voss for good which made the expenditure for a new trophy necessary. There is one circumstance by which the first explanation appears to be the most plausible one.

FIGURE 94   The cup (left) presented by Carl Laeisz in 1891 for the Championship of the Germans. After three successive wins it was given permanently to Count Voss in 1896.

FIGURE 95   The so-called Voss Cup (right), presented by Count Voss himself in 1897 for the Championship of the Germans.

The 'Father of Lawn Tennis in Germany', Carl August von der Meden, had been the driving force not only behind the Hamburg tournaments. Since 1894, he had also been the heart and soul of a tournament which, by the mere splendour of its annual celebration, had put in the shade even his original invention. This was the famous autumn tournament held in Bad Homburg vor der Höhe, a spa not far from Frankfurt at the foot of the Taunus and frequented in equal measure by the representatives of European high aristocracy as well as international high finance. The place was patronized by industrial magnates such as Friedrich Krupp,[208] and counted among its guests the Prince of Wales (later Edward VII) as well as the German Emperor.

The administration of the *Kurort* had, in 1890, taken in hand the eight existing lawn tennis courts. Under its new *Kurdirector*, Ferdinand von Schoeler, their number had been increased to twenty-five by 1893.[209] Apparently, Herr von Schoeler had realized that expansion of that magnitude was a sheer necessity, if he wanted to attract more visitors from abroad as well as from fashionable Germany.[210] That he had soon been successful on both scores appears from an article 'Sketches from the Bad Homburg Sporting Life' in 1896. In an old Bad Homburg tourist guide, its author wrote, I once read that there were among the facilities of the place a few lawn tennis courts for the English. … That this has long changed we are taught by simply looking at one of the tennis courts where not only the red-locked [English] miss, but also the blue-eyed daughter of the Teutons gracefully smacks the tiny ball about (**Figure 96**).[211] However, in order to make visitors perfectly happy, more was needed than the mere facilities. What the sporting gentlemen and their consorts needed was, besides their daily matches, the excitement of first-class competitive tennis. As early as 1892, a tournament had taken place in which no less a personage than William Renshaw had been victorious (he had also contributed to the organization).[212] This may well have whetted von Schoeler's appetite. Looking for somebody in Germany with enough expertise to do a similar job, he, of course, landed up in Hamburg.[213] In the winter of 1893–94, he sent an official in order to have him instructed in the laying of the new-fangled 'gravel courts' without which the staging of a tournament was considered impossible on the continent.[214]

After four new championships courts had been completed in the spring of 1894, Carl August von der Meden had offered to take over the responsibility of tournament manager himself.[215] In order to secure smooth organization, he had conscripted W.H. Collins, vice-president of the LTA, Wimbledon referee, and his personal friend. He had also invited Sir Edward Malet, who at that time held office in Berlin as the English ambassador, to join himself and *Kurdirector* von Schoeler to form the managing committee, and to be its president. The most important prerequisite was a cup which, at a time when a meal in the *Kurort* cost 2 marks, full board between 4 and 5, and lodging 20 marks, was worth 1,200 marks. The cup was presented by the administration of the *Kurort*. The inaugural tournament of 1894 was a huge success at once, not least by the participation of Grand Duchess Anastasia who, partnered by Count Voss, even competed in the tournament, and her brother, the Russian Grand Duke Mikhail Mikhailovich (**Figure 97**).[216] The presence of these two members of

FIGURE 96   Bad Homburg lawn tennis scene (1885) when the game was a society pastime rather than a serious sport.

FIGURE 97   An illustration of the first large-scale Bad Homburg tournament in 1894 on the front page of the Frankfurt daily *Kleine Presse*, clearly an imitation of illustrations in contemporary English society journals (compare FIGURE 72).

the European grand aristocracy provoked much interest. The Grand Duke, exiled by the tsar because of a marriage far below his status,[217] and known as the 'King of Cannes' in society circles,[218] was, perhaps, the man most talked about in contemporary gossip columns. His equally extravagant sister received criticism and praise alike. Her appearance on the Bad Homburg tennis courts – under the pseudonym of 'Mrs. W.'[219] – was frowned upon by her equals such as the Empress Friedrich,[220] but extolled by the liberally-minded Baron von Fichard who wrote:[221]

> We will not fail to point out the praiseworthy example given by her Royal Highness, the Grand Duchess of Mecklenburg-Schwerin, by engaging in the tournament, to Germany's womanhood. If, in order to liberate the latter from the trammels of a narrow-minded prejudice which excluded German women and girls from health-improving games, a special effort was needed: here indeed it was made by the high-minded lady, to whom we most thankfully pay homage.

The Homburg cup was won by a certain D.S.H. Hughes, a doctor of medicine from Australia and a member of the All England Club,[222] but this was less important. The reason for the tremendous success of the tournament, and indeed of those which were to follow, was not so much the excellence of sport exhibited, but the gossip and scandal which the presence of the smart set produced in the press.[223] To the players, the ignorance of these people, and their boisterous and undisciplined behaviour during matches was very often most embarrassing.[224] In addition, as it turned out, conditions for play were far from ideal. Equipment and the organization,[225] and even the courts were not infrequently subjected to severe criticism by experts.[226] But then, lawn tennis was not what the 'snobility' and the rich had come for.

In 1896, the Homburg tournament was highlighted by the presence of the reigning All England champion, the Irishman Harold S. Mahony,[227] and the Doherty brothers who in England were on their way to the top. This fact must have escaped the notice of the untiring chronicler of German lawn tennis, the Alsatian Baron von Fichard. The poor performance of the favourite M.F. Goodbody (who took a beating by Reggie Doherty in the final) aroused the Baron's indignation, and caused his rather scathing comment:[228] 'seldom have we seen an affair lamer than this one, the whole thing was a walk-over for Doherty, and we cannot but regret it. … The only explanation which can be found is that the defeated was decidedly not well!'

Despite the discomfiture of Goodbody, the sensation caused by the presence of the English lawn tennis élite in Bad Homburg had its repercussions elsewhere. The fact had, for instance, been noted in Hamburg where Herr von der Meden must have entertained ideas such as these: If the English stars had come to the continent once, they might be persuaded to do so again. And if they decided to pay another visit to Bad Homburg anyhow, why not invite them to take a little detour to Hamburg before? What was needed was a little tinkering with the tournament calendar, a seasonal shift of the tournament to autumn,[229] and some additional lure, and here, after the precedent set by Walter Howard the year previously, the creation of an 'open' championship for gentlemen virtually suggested itself.

Von der Meden's hopes were fulfilled beyond all expectations in 1897. Although Reggie Doherty, by that time the unrivalled lawn tennis champion, did not put in an appearance despite an earlier announcement that he would,[230] other English players of note did. The first International Championship of Germany was eventually contended by G.W. Hillyard and his Irish doubles partner G.C. Ball-Greene. Hillyard became known in this country because of his curious service for which he used to toss his ball into the air with both hands while at the same time standing bolt upright.[231] Ball-Greene was familiar to contemporaries mainly because his name had given rise to a pun. What is, the question was, the difference between a sour apple and a tennis player? The answer was, of course, that a sour apple was a green ball, and a tennis player Ball-Greene. Being associated with a sour apple may have been of little importance to the Irishman, but the outcome of the Hamburg final is most likely to have left him with a sour smile. After winning the second and the third set by the sheer skill of his play, he from sheer exhaustion went down 0:6, 0:6 to Hillyard's powerful drives in the final sets.[232]

The ladies' championship of Germany was won by another family member, Mrs Hillyard, the four-times All England champion who, as Blanche Bingley, had first won that title in 1886. She outplayed the All England champion of the two previous years, Miss Charlotte Cooper. 'Chatty', despite her defeat, 'captivated the lawn tennis world at Hamburg by her style of play. An occasional volley from middle court', the English journal *Lawn Tennis* wrote, 'the German ladies will venture on, but to see a lady go up to the net volleying and smacking balls has not fallen to the lot of players in the Fatherland before.' 'Certainly,' the journal summarized its report, 'no better lawn tennis has ever before been witnessed in Germany, even the play at last year's Homburg Höhe Tournament, where Mahony, Goodbody, Voss and the Dohertys competed, was not better.'[233]

Count Voss being absent, the championship of the Germans fell to Wantzelius who beat Behrens in five sets after a 'severe struggle'. Wantzelius was one of a number of young players from Hamburg who, again according to the English sporting journal *Lawn Tennis*, all played decently enough:[234] They 'lob very accurately, … and all … place well, but unless they put more severity into their strokes they will do no good'. Sadly, the journal was quite right in its pessimistic outlook. For another decade and until the appearance of the great Otto Froitzheim who beat the four-time Champion of Germany, M.J.G. Ritchie, at Hamburg in 1907, the efforts of German players, at least at an international level, were doomed to failure.

THE BAD HOMBURG INTERLUDE

On the face of it, the International Championships of Hamburg were quite successful, and yet, to everybody's surprise, they were discontinued and transferred to Bad Homburg in the following year (**Figure 98**). Several reasons were given for this exodus. For one, there was the rivalry of the two skating clubs which both hosted international tournaments and, as it were, cut the ground from underneath each other's feet. For another, the two clubs still were skating clubs in the first place, the statutes of which prevented them from giving lawn tennis its due.[235] The result was a 'lack of funds' (as it was aptly described by the organizers afterwards).[236] It looks as if, even in the era of the amateur when cash prizes or 'appearance money' were treated with scorn, championships could not be held without them.[237] However, this does not seem to be the whole story. What really led to the tournament's demise was less its economic collapse, but the fact that, it was said, leading personalities in charge of the organization no longer were willing to take on responsibilities.[238] The truth of this rather vague statement may be that Carl August von der Meden had himself thrown in the towel. The organization of the 1897 event had met with some severe criticism. The correspondent of the journal *Sport im Bild*, writing under the pen-name of 'Volley',[239] had especially found fault with the favours lavished on English competitors. These had been allowed a belated arrival in Hamburg on Tuesday. This meant that a German player arriving on the opening day, Saturday, and pitted against one of them in his first round match, just sat there twiddling his thumbs until the English gentleman deigned to put in an appearance. Apart from tolerating the extravaganzas of his British guests (for which von der Meden had quite a reputation), he also gave a preferential treatment to local competitors. These attended to their various business obligations during the day, and nobody objected if they played their matches in the

FIGURE 98   This photograph from Bad Homburg proves that the Champion of 1898, the Irishman Harold S. Mahony, quite rightly had the reputation of being a ladies' man. Charles Adolph Voigt is sitting on the extreme left and standing, in the uniform of a groundsman, is Friedrich Becker, the inventor of the red clay court, with a group of ball boys.

evening. However, the upshot of it all, at least in the opinion of 'Volley', was the absence of ball boys. This he called a downright outrage ('unerhört'). The excuse brought forward by the organizers, namely that ball boys 'were always standing in the way and therefore more of a hindrance than useful', could well have come from the mouth of von der Meden himself. It echoes almost exactly the words he had used in his lawn tennis primer two years previously. At any rate, it looks as if 'Volley's' volleys hit von der Meden where he was most vulnerable. He had taken pride in being the country's ultimate lawn tennis authority, and the unexpected attack from the leading sporting journal may well have prompted his untimely withdrawal.

Bad Homburg had no reason to deplore the wreck of the country's lawn tennis flagship. Although not entirely without financial difficulties themselves,[240] its tournament managers soon proved that a well-known Irish player was quite right when he insisted on going to 'Homburg without the Bad'. Asked by a railway official at the Hook of Holland whether he wanted to go to *Bad* Homburg, he swore that from all he had heard, Homburg was 'not a bad place at all', but 'in fact, a jolly good one'.[241]

Among the competitors of the first year, 1898, four were exceptional players: the Doherty brothers, Harold S. Mahony, the Irishman and All England champion of 1896, and Dr Joshua Pim, his countryman. As in his ignominious Davis Cup match in 1903, Pim played under a pseudonym, and might have added, as 'Mr J. Wilson', to his MD and his two All England titles of 1893 and 1894 the title of a Champion of Germany, had he not finally succumbed to Mahony.

The two Dohertys, on the point of winning both the Homburg Cup and the Championship of Germany, had decided in favour of the former and, in order not to sweep the board completely, had generously scratched to Pim and Mahony in the semi-finals. This was, at least, the opinion of the German sporting journal *Sport im Bild*.[242] Upon closer examination, however, it looks as if the Dohertys had mainly wanted to circumvent playing against each other. This they never did, and they were quite notorious for it. In the challenge round of the Homburg Cup, as if to prove it, Reggie Doherty, the holder, was given a walk-over by his brother Laurie. In the Championship of Germany, however, the walk-over Mahony received was due to the absence of Hillyard, the holder.[243]

Pim's defeat was somewhat unfortunate. He was rather exhausted from a strenuous Homburg Cup match against Laurie Doherty when he met Mahony in the final, and had then the misfortune of being matched with an opponent who throughout the whole tournament was playing at the very top of his game. On the hard Bad Homburg gravel courts, Mahony's high bounding service proved extremely difficult to return, and whenever Pim managed to pull off a brilliant 'side-liner' all the same, the way the Irishman still reached it to a baffled German crowd was sheer wonder. On this day, the player 'with reputedly the worst forehand in the game' had only one weak spot.[244] According to the anonymous correspondent of *Lawn Tennis*, it was his smash, and he was recommended 'the experiment of jumping off the ground just before making the stroke',[245] a comment which casts an interesting sidelight on contemporary championship tennis. A worthier champion of Germany than Mahony would have been very hard to find. Among German players, he was by far the most popular of the English contingent. Mahony was a rare bird among players from the British Isles past and present: he spoke German fluently! Both the champion of Germany and the runner-up later became members of British Davis Cup teams. But whereas Pim was the scapegoat of the losing side of 1903, Mahony was fortunate enough to belong to the victorious team of 1904, because, by a stroke of good luck, Collins, the British team captain, chose not to let him play. The same good luck vilely forsook him shortly afterwards, though. On 25 June 1905, when indulging in another sporting activity extremely popular at the time, cycling, Harold Sigerson Mahony met his fate (to borrow a phrase from his countryman William Butler Yeats) by Lake Caragh in the county of Kerry, between Glencar and Killorglin, after descending from a steep hill. What may well have been the first fatal accident in mountain-biking made front-page news in the Fatherland where his death was deeply mourned.[246] A fitting tribute to the man and his game was given by a contributor to the German journal *Sport im Bild* writing under the pen-name of Pilot one year later, after Mahony had lost his title to an American, Clarence Hobart, in the challenge round. Commenting on the Irishman's service, Pilot had to say the following:[247]

> The posture he assumes when executing his service is very peculiar and at times even comical to those watching his game. Mahony sometimes keeps this strange posture for a couple of seconds, before actually serving the ball. Indeed, his game is very different from that of other first class players. His style is very beautiful and effective, especially when he uses his backhand or when he plays overhead. His forehand stroke is perhaps the weakest spot in his entire game. Whenever he hits the ball with either a forehand or a backhand stroke, his arm makes a short, jerking movement which, however, does not look unelegant. Mahony's tactics are such as to run up to the net immediately after his service, even if in a given situation a defensive game would seem advisable. In his memorable match against Hobart, in which he had to defend the Championship of Germany, he also adhered to this principle, but, trying to intercept Hobart's shots sent down the lines with extraordinary precision, frequently arrived at the net too late which eventually caused his defeat. During matches Mahony talks to himself a lot which often is the cause of much hilarity among the crowd.

DRURY LANE

The Ladies' Championship of Germany was, as it were, the first act of a piece which might have come straight from contemporary Drury Lane theatre. Appropriately, the heroine of the drama went by the name of Elsie Lane. Miss Lane was a steady and accurate baseliner, equipped with a backhand which the correspondent of *Lawn Tennis*, rather ungentlemanly, chose to call 'a scoop'.[248] She beat the brilliant, albeit erratic Toupée Lowther, who had abandoned her usual play in favour of an uninspired game from the baseline, in two straight sets 7:5, 7:5.[249]

The champion, a resident of Hove (**Figure 99**), was to perform acts two and three in 1904 and 1905 and, after having won the title of Champion of Germany three times, captured Walter Howard's silver dish for good.[250] In 1906, a new trophy was presented by Grand Duke Frederick Francis of Mecklenburg Schwerin.[251]

By 1904, the belief had become firmly established in the Fatherland that, if the National Women's Champion (with the exception of Countess von der Schulenburg) were to play Miss Lane, the outcome would be 'a double bagel',[252] and by 1905, Elsie (in England less well known than her sister Hilda who frequently competed in Wimbledon)[253] had acquired the epithet 'invincible'.[254] Her unfailing retrieving qualities were the terror of her continental opponents who knew that she would emerge victorious even if taken to rallies of 50 to 60 strokes. In 1905, an especially knowledgeable tennis enthusiast, who had heard about her serving a double fault, with broad sarcasm remarked: 'Then she will die shortly!' In the Fatherland, Elsie was the female counterpart of the infallible M.J.G Ritchie, five times Champion of Germany between 1903 and 1908, whose style of playing it safe, however, was not recommended even there. The two were successful only, it was said, as long as they did not meet the 'positive' player, the one going for his or her point and who did not wait for the opponents' errors. Championship honours were therefore denied to them in England.[255]

FIGURE 99   The extremely successful members of the Lane family on their home ground in Brighton around the turn of the century. From right to left: Ernest Wilmot Lane, his sister Hilda, an unidentified brother, Elsie, and the family dog.

The redoubtable Elsie was the daughter of Wilmot Lane (**Figure 100**), a barrister-at-law who had been a civil servant in India for almost a lifetime. He had retired in 1889, on an annuity of £1,000,[256] and it was then that the father of nine children decided to have a look at the brighter side of life. At the age of 56,[257] and despite the handicap of having lost his left arm,[258] 'Little William' was determined to become a lawn tennis great. In 1896, the tennis veteran ventured out onto the European continent and began by scoring, at the age of 63, a minor success against a young player from Hamburg in the handicap B event of Bad Homburg; afterwards he also competed in Baden-Baden.[259] As late as 1902, he won first prize in a handicap event in Spa.[260] During his raids on the continent he apparently kept a watchful eye on his daughter, for Elsie never got married. However, her becoming a very successful player more than compensated for it. As early as 1896, in Bad Homburg and Baden-Baden, she was victorious in every event which she entered with the exception of the mixed doubles. Indeed, despite the fact that she never competed at Wimbledon, an expert such as Charles Adolph Voigt could speak of her as of one of the best-known English tournament players ('die zu den bekanntesten englischen Turnier-Spielerinnen gehört').[261] Her wrenching a first prize from Toupée Lowther in Homburg in 1896 was watched 'with great interest' by the donor of the trophy, the Prince of Wales.[262] Her performance in Baden-Baden shortly afterwards elicited the highest praise imaginable. 'Miss Lane', a correspondent of *Sport im Bild* wrote,[263] 'the successful English player who in Homburg as well as in Baden-Baden defeated all her opponents brilliantly'

FIGURE 100 Elsie's father, Wilmot Lane, an official of the Indian Civil Service in Punjab.

demonstrated 'the best tennis ever seen in the Ladies' game in Germany'. In 1897, when her father entered for the championships of Germany in Hamburg,[264] but then scratched, Elsie caused a mild sensation at once. She reached the semi-finals of the Women's Championships, losing 10:8, 6:0 to no less a player than Chatty Cooper, the All England champion of the previous year. Elsie, as we have heard, then went on to win the title of champion of Germany in Bad Homburg in the year following, at the age of 34,[265] and that she was truly a chip off the old block became evident in 1905 when, of late chaperoned, and hardly less successfully so, by her brother Ernest Wilmot,[266] she reaped her third championship of Germany at the age of 41. Her last major success dated from 1907 when she won the singles, doubles (with a Mrs Anderson) and mixed doubles (with A.C. Holland) championships of Switzerland and the singles championships of the Engadine.[267]

What became of Walter Howard's 'silver dish', the championship trophy which she captured for good after her third win in 1905, or, for that matter, prizes such as the 'Coupe d'Ostende' which she is known to have captured by means of her 'rather ungraceful, though extremely clever style' in 1903,[268] has remained a mystery, although one thing at least is certain: all the prizes she had reaped during her successful career stayed with her. In his will, her father, 'in consideration of her kindness and never wanting attention' not only bequeathed to her part of his shares, but in fact gave her 'the cases in which the prizes won by her are kept'.[269] Elsie's father died, shortly before his 90th birthday, in 1924,[270] and Elsie, unlike her unfortunate sister Hilda who, younger than she by twelve years, died in 1916, at the age of 39,[271] was also long-lived. Aged 81, she died in Hove, a place she never seems to have abandoned after her family's return from India, on 10 August 1948.[272] In her will, she left the residue of her estate to her sister-in-law, Florence Emily, the wife of her tennis-playing brother Ernest Wilmot, who at the time lived in Wimbledon, of all places.[273] No silverware, witnesses of her tennis triumphs of yore, was mentioned, however, and this may mean that after the Second World War she no longer possessed the cups nor the cases in which these had once been enshrined.

That in the year of Elsie's first triumph, 1898, Count Voss would win the championship of the Germans, if only he chose to enter, was a dead certainty. Although he had not played any tennis since his inevitable stay at the Riviera in spring, he dispatched the champion of the previous year, Wantzelius, with ease and, in the final, yet another young player from Hamburg, Hans Oskar Behrens,[274] the very same who was to chair the inaugural meeting of the ITF in 1913.

BRITISH SUPREMACY UPSET BY AN AMERICAN

The 1899 tournament, with Charles Adolph Voigt and W.H. Collins acting as honorary secretary and honorary referee and tournament manager respectively, was a tremendous success. The Dohertys had put in an appearance as well as the very pick of players from the British Isles: A.W. Gore, E.D. Black, the rising star from Yorkshire who had just won the Scottish championship, and H.S. Mahony, the champion of the previous year.[275] There were players from the Low Countries, Belgium, Austria, and Sweden, and from as far away as Canton and Barbados. However, for all of them, including Germany's champion Count Voss, there was little hope of challenging British supremacy. There was nevertheless a minor threat to it, and this was caused by an American, Clarence Hobart (**Figure 101**). He had a reputation mainly as an outstanding doubles player – in fact, he had been US doubles champion three times – but was winner of the all-comers at Newport in 1891, and as the only American to defeat Pim at a tournament at West Newton in 1895, no mean singles player either.[276]

In the championship of Germany, Gore had disposed of Black, after losing the first set mainly because of the Yorkshireman's brilliant backhand crosses, and then profited from yet another withdrawal in the third round by the invincible R.F. Doherty. But when he must have been contemplating what tactics to resort to in the challenge round against 'run-in-on-anything' Mahony, he was beaten in the final by Hobart in three straight sets. It was therefore the American's turn to think of a suitable antidote against Mahony's attacks. The one he finally adopted, magnificent topspin drives which had cleared the way for him in his previous matches, proved to be more than a match for the Irishman. This forehand stroke, which purists such as Charles Adolph Voigt qualified as 'jerky',[277] but which was admired by contemporaries because of 'that wonderful sharp drop, as the ball crossed the net',[278] whizzed past Mahony 'eight times out of ten',[279] despite the latter's formidable reach. The match was a fiercely

FIGURE 101 Clarence Hobart, the American who won the Championship of Germany in 1899, frequently competed in tournaments on the European continent and gave an interesting account of the European lawn tennis scene.

contended five-setter all the same. In the third game, Mahony had to concede a love game after a string of the American's racket (apparently the only racket an American championships player possessed at the time) had snapped, and the Irishman had generously lent his opponent one of his, an E.G.M. racket,[280] the top players' favourite brand in those days.[281]

Hobart's success, and especially his surviving the dramatic suspense of five close sets, caused a great surprise. In the States, he had always been credited with too poor a physique and too nervous a temperament to accomplish such a feat and to become a champion.[282] At least once, at Bad Homburg, where he became Champion of Germany, Hobart was able to belie these prejudices.

It is true that the Yankee had received a walk-over in the semi-final from W.R. Martin, a strong Irishman, and that the fifth set had to be played, after 'the shades of night' had been falling fast during the fifth, the following afternoon,[283] but then Hobart had had only a quarter of an hour's rest before the final,[284] but, unlike Pim the year before, overcame this handicap with ease.

In retrospect, Hobart's success was remarkable in other ways. Victorious in the Bad Homburg challenge round in 1899, he became notorious as the Man Who Refused to Challenge in 1907. In that year he competed in the Longwood tournament and won the All-Comers from a strong field. But then he refused to play his countryman Larned in the challenge round, giving his reasons for doing so later on in a letter. He wrote:[285]

> For many years I have opposed the practice of permitting the holders to stand out in our tournaments, … on the obvious ground that it is unjust to pit a tired man against a fresh one, and equally unjust to give the holder only one chance for defeat while the challenger must necessarily have several.

Hobart's decision contributed a great deal to the eventual abandonment of the old method.[286]

By a tragic coincidence, Hobart, not unlike his opponent in the challenge round, also died an untimely death, and, again like Mahony, while engaging in a sport other than lawn tennis. In the summer of 1930, at the age of 59, he slipped when making a back dive at the Beaver Lake swimming pool in Asheville, NC, and struck his head on a pipe below the surface of the water.[287]

After an extensive tennis tour through Europe, Hobart returned to the United States in the spring of 1900.[288] Afterwards, the Champion of Germany gave an interesting account of Continental European lawn tennis in the American journal *Outing*, in which he graphically described how part of his Homburg success was due to the fact that he had discovered a method of how to come to grips with the indomitable race of German ball boys:[289]

> At all continental tournaments well trained ball-boys are provided for every court. Those at Homburg are very picturesque in scarlet jackets. Each one wears a large figure on his sleeve corresponding to the number of the court to which he is attached. For

every match six balls are given out, with the number of the court stamped on each ball.
The boys are held responsible for these, and a failure after the match to turn in the full
quota entails a reduction of their earnings. This causes them to show almost ludicrous
energy in retrieving balls. In fact their efforts are frequently too violent, when, as often
happens, they seem to develop the football instinct to follow the ball at all hazards.
Their special delight seems to be dashing in between points to recover a ball near the
net, just as the server is making the preliminary motions before serving. As these ball-
boys speak only German, the player who is not acquainted with that language is
frequently in difficulties. I have seen an Englishman with fire in his eye, ready to explode
with wrath, glaring at a boy but realizing his helplessness he boiled inwardly and held
his peace. Everybody knew what he wished to say, and enjoyed the situation intensely.
My own plan, which proved quite effective, was to procure the services of someone
familiar with German before each match, and to call up the boys to receive a lecture
through my interpreter, laying particular stress on the injunction not to invade the court,
particularly the region near the net, except at the end of games.

At a time when the seeded player was unknown, the most interesting matches tended
to occur in the earlier rounds of a tournament. The Ladies' Championship of Germany
well illustrated this fact. The closest match of the event was that between three-time
All England champion Charlotte Cooper and the runner-up of the previous year,
Toupée Lowther. In the second set, the latter was leading by five games to one and
then lost six games in a row and the whole match. 'With her perfect style and thorough
knowledge of the game', commented *Lawn Tennis*, 'it is a pity she does not go in
more for the game'.[290] In the final, Charlotte Cooper beat Germany's number one,
Countess Clara von der Schulenburg who, for reasons unknown,[291] played under the
pseudonym of 'Frau Hartwig' (Hartwig being the first name of her husband). In the
German press, the agility on the court and all-around game of the good-looking
blonde were as much praised as her cheerfulness and happy nature.[292]

   In 1899, the championship of the Germans was for the first time contended at a
different venue, Heiligendamm, the oldest seaside resort on the Baltic. As might have
been expected, again nobody could get the better of Count Voss, who in a literal
sense was playing a home-match. Nevertheless, his opponent in the final, Wantzelius,
this time might have snatched the first set.[293] (There had never been a challenge round
for the Voss cup where, since its inception in 1897, the usual procedure of the
champion's standing out was not adhered to.)[294] A curious thing happened at the
same event. Not only did the Count of Mecklenburg strive for the Championship of
the Germans, but also, under the pseudonym 'Wenden', the Grand Duke of
Mecklenburg, his sovereign. After a walk-over in the first round, the son of Grand
Duchess Anastasia, a pupil of the great professional Burke as well as of Voss and
therefore an able player,[295] succumbed in the second to Otto von Müller.[296] The latter
was to become Champion of Germany in 1912 and lost this title in the last challenge
round before the First World War to Heini Schomburgk.[297]

The wasps and a wayward weather

The championships of 1900 were bedevilled by wasps, bad weather and a certain Mr Sholto Douglas whose Tuesday night dance was 'chiefly responsible for the unpunctuality of most of the players, who are long sleepers as a rule', on Wednesday, 23 August 1900. This was 'a pity', the correspondent of the English journal *Lawn Tennis* complained,[298] because they missed 'the charm of the early morning hours at Homburg', and their knowledge of the place was therefore 'confined to the tennis courts throughout the day and the Kurhaus terrace in the evening.' 'Players are, however, very rarely scratched at Homburg', he continued, 'and their wishes are carefully noted by the referee and the honorary secretary.' And whenever, he concluded, 'a number of ladies' gave 'notice that a picnic or golf competition' claimed their presence, they were 'promptly excused'. The referee and honorary secretary who in such a way heaped happiness and bliss on Homburg's players were the Messrs H.S. Scrivener and, as usual, Charles A. Voigt respectively.

Mr Douglas' dance and its consequences, and 'rain and thunderstorms, which would have done credit to the tropics' and made play impossible on two entire days,[299] not only unduly delayed the tournament, they also led to its being concluded in a helter-skelter fashion. Several players withdrew in the finals of the two open events, the most spectacular being that in the final of the Championship of Germany. Because Mr Hillyard was very much in a hurry having to catch the boat for the Newcastle tournament,[300] he was given a walk-over by H.L. Doherty. Laurie, it was thought, could well afford dallying with a German championship as he had beaten Hillyard in the final of the Homburg Cup,[301] but on closer inspection Laurie's generosity, or lack of interest, again seem to have been part of the Doherty brothers' well-known strategy to avoid playing against one another. In the third round, Reggie had scratched to Cazalet in order to avoid meeting his brother in the next, and in the semi-final of the Homburg Cup which, as we have heard, was eventually captured by his brother, he had cleared the way for Hillyard.[302]

Besides the antics of the Dohertys, there were others of a very different sort. A 'great nuisance on the courts' was caused by wasps. 'It is most annoying to have a wasp buzzing round your nose just as you are going to serve', wrote the correspondent of *Lawn Tennis*, who nevertheless did not fail to note an attractive aspect of the insects' doings. Although many players had been badly stung, 'to the spectator some of the antics and frantic gambols of the player so annoyed' were, to his mind, quite 'amusing'.[303] The player suffering most from waspish attacks was the Champion of Germany, George Hillyard, because they took 'a particular fancy to his M.C.C. hatband' slung around a broad-brimmed white hat (he seldom played 'bareheaded, contrary to the habits of the Dohertys', who wore 'no headgear even in the most tropical weather').[304] The other competitor who did wear a headgear, Count Voss, had been trounced by Hillyard in the fourth round. The wearer of the wet towel had not yet recovered from an illness and his game suffered from a lack of practice. He lost hands down against the man whom he had beaten several winters ago at Monte Carlo.[305]

For the ladies' Championship of Germany it had been ruled that the holder should play through, but unfortunately the holder was absent. This prevented outright another clash of the two Wimbledon heroines of the 1890s who had each bagged a German championship once, Blanche Hillyard and Charlotte Cooper. But this did not do much damage to the quality of the event. A great many other remarkable players had entered. There were Bad Homburg *habituées* such as the Countess von der Schulenburg, and the Misses Toupée Lowther and Gladys Duddell. The last named was an agile and stylish lefthander endowed with such extraordinary good looks that all her matches were keenly watched by large crowds,[306] and those who could not see her at Homburg stood a good chance of catching a glimpse of her at least on a postcard showing her and the German Crown Prince after a mixed doubles match.[307] What also aroused the curiosity of the Germans was the fact that, despite her elegance, youth and aristocratic looks, she was in the habit of knitting socks whenever she was around the Homburg courts and not engaging in a match herself.[308] There also was an excellent player from America, Marion Jones, who had acquitted herself well at the Paris Exhibition tournament, and a young lady from England of whom it was predicted that 'the very highest champion honours should soon be hers'.[309] Her name was Muriel E. Robb, and the prediction soon turned out to have been quite correct: Only two years later, in 1902, Miss Robb was the first to put an end to an uninterrupted series of wins of the Ladies' Championship of England by either Mrs Hillyard or Mrs Sterry (the former Charlotte Cooper), by beating the latter at Wimbledon.[310]

Miss Duddell and Miss Lowther went down to the ferocious drives of Mrs Hillyard, to whose strokes the gravel courts suited 'to a nicety', in the first and second rounds respectively. The unfortunate Miss Lowther was again 'too uncertain' and failed 'to put up the game she usually' played.[311] Miss Robb disposed of Countess von der Schulenburg and, only after losing the first set and having been 4:1 down in the third, of Marion Jones, the young Californian whose 'weak physical condition prevented her from keeping up her effort'.[312]

The fact that Miss Robb had beaten Mrs Hillyard before at Buxton added to the excitement of the final. Miss Robb, as if to prove that her recent victory had been no fluke, won the first set by six games to two and was leading by three games to one in the second (only to lose it by six games to eight), and by five games to three in the third set. But although she was four times within one point of the set and the match, the last set was snatched away from her by seven games to five at last. As in her many struggles on the centre court of Wimbledon, the 'marvellous generalship and pluck' of Mrs Hillyard came out most strongly when her position was almost hopeless. Her second Championship of Germany was, as a consequence, ranked 'among the highest of her many fine achievements'.[313]

Heiligendamm had again been appointed to hold the championships of the Germans, but lethargy and incompetence of local administrators, who exhibited all the slowness and stolidity characteristic of the true Mecklenburger, prevented it.[314] At the very last minute, the Lawn-Tennis-Turnier-Club, Berlin,[315] decided to incorporate them in its club tournament set for 21 September and the days following on the courts in Martin Luther (or Heinrich Kiepert) Street. The Berlin club was the right one to care for the orphaned competition. Founded in 1897, its chief object was the organization of an annual international lawn tennis tournament befitting the capital whose colours it had adopted.[316] Its activities, however, were by no means confined to the Prussian metropolis. For some time, it had lent its expertise to the staging of tournaments on the Baltic, notably those at Heringsdorf and Kolberg. The club did not possess any courts of its own, but availed itself of those of the Berlin Recreation Grounds Company (Berliner Spielplatz-Gesellschaft).[317]

In the absence of Voss, the champion, who, after the disastrous abandonment of the Heiligendamm tournament, sulked in far-away Mecklenburg and was, because of his illness, still 'indisposed' to defend his title,[318] the championship was won by A.W. Schmitz from Frankfurt. He was one of the three players (the others being Baron Kurt von Lersner and Rudolf Schindler) who had competed in the Homburg tournament before and were therefore said to have greatly improved their game on account of it, with the exception of Schindler.[319] It was only natural, therefore, that one of them should prevail in the end. Schmitz, who in Homburg had lost abysmally to Laurie Doherty in three straight sets (2:6, 2:6, 1:6), was still one too many for the 'rest of Germany', for he not only beat 16-year-old von Lersner for the championship of the Germans, but was victorious in every other open event, five in all, including a championship of Prussia. Young von Lersner, the runner-up, who had been treated as the Fatherland's lawn tennis darling throughout the season by the country's sporting press, was for the first time severely taken to task. What the correspondent of the journal *Sport im Wort* noted with displeasure was the fact that the game of this exceptionally talented player was utterly devoid of any powerful strokes. This was the worst that could be said about a member of the warlike Teutonic race.

1901 – THE ABSENCE OF THE BROTHERS IS DEPLORED

At the 1899 Bad Homburg tournament, a young lady had been mystified by a famous English player who, when asked how he was getting on, replied: 'Well, I am out of Europe, but still in Germany, also Homburg.' This was a short way of saying that had been knocked out of the Championship of Europe (which had then only just been inaugurated),[320] but was still in the open singles for the Championship of Germany and the Homburg Cup. The utterance illustrated well the player's dilemma at the time. If today's competitors in major tournaments shirk whenever possible participation in doubles or mixed doubles events, the nineteenth-century ace was expected not only to take part in several concurrent open singles events, but also in a doubles and in various handicaps. And out of sheer gallantry he would never refuse to engage in a mixed doubles. Under such circumstances, not even the wizardry of a Charles Adolph Voigt could safeguard that a tournament was properly concluded, without severe numbers of withdrawals and multiple retirements and walk-overs in the final rounds, and the inevitable injustice of a player having to play a crucial match after having barely finished another.[321] Even if we do not assume manipulation of the kind described above on the part of the Dohertys, it becomes understandable how the unsurpassed lawn tennis champions of the time could have escaped becoming Champions of Germany. By giving a walk-over to Hillyard in 1900, Laurie had, of course inadvertently, squandered his and his brother's last chance. It was the last time the pair competed in a German championship tournament, and they were also never to return to Homburg.[322]

'Time brings about its changes', *Lawn Tennis* began its report of the 1901 tournament full of melancholy:[323]

> it is bound to happen in the case of all foreign tournaments that there will occasionally be seasons when … most of the usual players cannot manage to be present. They will doubtless appear again at the next tournament, but in the meantime their absence is greatly felt by the many friends they have made in Germany. In the recent tournament there were no Dohertys, nor were Mr and Mrs Hillyard upon the scene, and our better known players were represented by F.W. Payn and Miss Lowther.

As for the Dohertys, they did not even compete in the Davis Cup in 1901 which explains their absence from Bad Homburg.[324] The Hillyards had been on the point of embarking for the Continent when the news of the passing away of the Empress Friedrich reached England. In the belief the tournament would under these circumstances be called off,[325] they did not undertake the journey.

The 'better known players' representing the British Isles were, of course, almost unanimously considered the favourites. Of F.W. Payn, a left-hander and a member of the Queens Club and well known on the Continent, and who relied 'almost exclusively on the volleying game', it was said that he was 'capable of giving … the greatest opponent' serious trouble.[326] Nevertheless, a young Frenchman, the 18-year-old Max Decugis, was considered by some experts a serious rival.[327] The Frenchman had accepted an invitation by Charles Adolph Voigt.[328] Miss Lowther's victory was believed to be 'a foregone conclusion'.[329] Having participated in most of the important tournaments in England during the summer,[330] she had acquired the steadiness for which she, having 'played for Walter Howard's cup more regularly than any other player',[331] had hardly been noted up to this point. Her victories over Miss Matthews of the Edgbaston Club and Miss Duddell, in the penultimate round and in the final, were triumphs 'of patience and perseverance', the results being 6:0, 6:0 in both cases![332] That the unfortunate Miss Duddell should have been punished so severely was, perhaps, pardonable. She had been invited to join the tournament committee with a view to looking after the ladies' matches. This was a novelty and imitation of this emancipatory act in England and elsewhere was recommended,[333] but it must have distracted her from her game.

Unlike Miss Lowther, her countryman, F.W. Payn, fell short of expectations. Although he managed to secure for himself the third set 'by dint of well-judged net-play and some splendid cross and stop volleys',[334] he was outplayed by Max Decugis who in the final was clearly the better man in most aspects of the game and excelled in his service (styled severe and often unreturnable) and his smashes.[335] The correspondent of *The Field* likened the Frenchman's game to that of H.L. Doherty, calling it 'wonderfully taking to watch'. It was 'good all round and full of variety', and illustrated well 'the axiom that volleying pure and simple without the capacity for playing a defensive game from the base line' was 'always liable to end in disaster'.[336]

As in the years before, the tournament was graced by the presence of royalty. On several afternoons, King Edward could be seen watching the matches and several players had the honour of being introduced to His Majesty.[337]

The Championship of the Germans was again contended, under the patronage of Her Imperial Highness, the Grand Duchess Anastasia, on the courts of Heiligendamm. The Berlin Lawn-Tennis-Turnier-Club, by extending its activities on the Baltic, had taken over the responsibilities of the organization.[338] Ten players had entered for the championship and their very best were routed one after the other by H. von Schneider who in the final beat another 'von', Lieutenant A. von Gordon, albeit only after a severe four-set tussle.[339] The runner-up was a lieutenant of the Cuirassier Guards and had in 1897 and in 1899 been the winner of the famous Kaiserpokal, a trophy for the military, the last of which was contested for at Bad Homburg at the outbreak of the First World War. A 'kaiserpokal' sold at auction at Sotheby's in December 1994 was the Emperor's cup awarded for the 'Championship of Prussia' at the annual Pentecost tournament in the Grunewald in 1914.[340]

THE RETURN

In its second issue of 1902, the Berlin sporting weekly *Sport im Wort* reported on a meeting which had taken place in Hamburg on the last Sunday of the previous year, 29 December 1901. It had been convened by the two rival skating clubs and resulted in a foundation which its founding members, by adopting a suggestion made by Dr Traun,[341] the Olympic champion, dubbed the Hamburg Lawn Tennis Guild.[342] By this foundation, the two clubs had settled their disputes. Rather than vying with each other for supremacy, by holding international tournaments separately, the clubs had decided to conduct a single international tournament and a local one, and to put the organization of each into the hands of an independent body, the Guild. Members of the Guild were recruited mainly from the two skating clubs, but membership of players from outside was also welcomed. On the average, every member paid an annual fee of 5 marks and these fees, together with substantial allowances from either club, were to form the financial mainstay of the annual tournaments.[343] Significantly, the statutes of the Guild stipulated that the committees of either club should be represented proportionally in the ten-person committee of the Guild.[344] Carl August von der Meden of the Uhlenhorst club was elected the Guild's first president, Oscar Maas of the Dammtor club its vice president (**Figure 102**), and, according to the election, the first international tournament under the auspices of the new organization was to be held on the Uhlenhorst courts, the local

FIGURE 102   Carl August von der Meden (left) and Carl Maas, the outstanding representatives of the Uhlenhorst and Dammtor clubs respectively, on the courts of the latter club in 1909, two years before von der Meden's death.

one on those of the Dammtor club. This order was to be swapped, and swapped again, in the years to come.[345]

The report was silent about the fact that the inaugural meeting of the Guild had in reality been a plot. The two skating clubs had buried the hatchet at last for the sole purpose of wresting from the as yet unsuspecting Bad Homburgers the Championships of Germany. The cat was out of the bag by the end of March when the Guild in its official organ *Sport im Wort* laid open the programme of its international tournament set for 10 August 1902.[346] Not only would Hamburg again host the ladies' and the men's singles Championships of Germany, but also a doubles Championship of Germany for which the prize, two elaborately chased silver pots worth 1,000 marks,[347] was donated by the Guild itself.[348]

What causes surprise today is the matter-of-factness of the announcement. What the citizens of Bad Homburg, their *Kurdirector*, Count Axel von Maltzahn, and above all lawn tennis mogul Voigt thought about this turn of events is nowhere revealed,[349] although the loss of the championships must have caused them a great deal of discomfort. The Bad Homburgers tried, albeit not very successfully, to recover from the inroad on their programme by introducing two events which were completely new: an open singles competition for which the town of Homburg presented a handsome cup worth 500 marks 'in commemoration of the coronation of King Edward VII', and a new doubles competition for which an enthusiastic American, William Rhinelander Stewart, had been willing to finance the neccessary trophy.[350] This latter event was pompously styled the 'Championship of Europe'.[351]

The Championship of the Germans was the only national championship not contended in Hamburg. In 1902, it preceded the others. The Berlin Lawn-Tennis-

Turnier-Club had again offered its help to Heiligendamm where the assistance was gladly accepted. After a two years' absence from tournament play, Count Voss was again competing. Besides him, there was a host of also-rans from Berlin: Bœlling, von Gordon, Carl Lange and Schindler. The Count proved convincingly that he was still the country's best player, but for reasons unknown he scratched to Schindler and his cup was therefore doomed to be captured by an also-ran. Schindler was beaten by Carl Lange,[352] who in the final met Bœlling. Bœlling had in the earlier rounds finished off the runner-up of the previous year, von Gordon, and von Schneider, and beaten his opponent in a different event in two straight sets the day before. However, it was Lange who came out victorious this time. Bœlling, who according to normal practice had entered for almost every other event and in the majority of cases reached the final rounds, was obviously played out and could not hold his own in a best of five sets match.[353]

After a lapse of five years, the championship tournament on the Uhlenhorst courts encountered difficulties. Unlike the organizers in rival Bad Homburg, the Guild had not been able to persuade a fair number of foreigners to undertake the journey to the north. It is true that Max Decugis, the promising young Frenchman, had come together with another able player, his countryman Germôt.[354] But then Decugis had to defend a title which was sufficiently stimulating. In England, in the absence of any such stimulus, nobody seemed excited over the prospect of becoming a champion of Germany. Only a single player of note had accepted their invitation, Dr J.M. Flavelle. At home, the doctor, a member of both the All England and Queens Club,[355] was known as the player who had disproved the assertion that to be a first-class lawn tennis player it was 'essential to start in boyhood'.[356] Educated at Rugby where lawn tennis was frowned upon, he had been broken into the routine of the game comparatively late in life, but by expert professionals. A baseline player in the first place with a decided predilection for the indoor game on wood surfaces, his favourite stroke was a low forehand drive with a lot of top spin. His service was without any distinctive qualities, but he had the reputation of being a player with great endurance.[357] A famous traveller, he had notified the Prague committee in April 1902 that he, at that time on duty as a military surgeon in the South African War, would not be able to compete in their tournament.[358] Luckily for Hamburg officials, the Boers were defeated by May, and the Doctor therefore could present himself in Hamburg, and in top form, when the championships began on 10 August 1902.[359]

For a time, Hans Oskar Behrens of Hamburg, and W.S. Thomson, an American who lived in Bremen, must have entertained hopes of overcoming the favourites for the championship, Decugis, Flavelle, and Germot. Thomson, however, was beaten by Germot in the forth round, and Behrens, after scoring a surprising success against Germot in the fifth,[360] was disastrously routed by Flavelle in the final of the all-comers' event, the score being 6:0, 6:2, 6:0. Thus Dr Flavelle and Decugis, as predicted by many,[361] met in the obligatory challenge round.

This memorable match took place on Sunday at noon, on one of the Uhlenhorst VIP courts, the 'Love Court', and before what was in those days a capacity crowd:

600 to 700 people (**Figure 103**).[362] Reports on what exactly happened are contradictory. It is certain that Flavelle, who had succumbed to Decugis in two other events in the week before, had decided not to be overcome easily this time. Especially by dint of passing shots sent down the lines with incredible pace, he succeeded in taking the first two sets. In the third set, the delicate-looking Frenchman, who against the sturdy Englishman showed traces of fatigue, was again trailing hopelessly behind. According to one account the score was 5:0, 40:30 in the Englishman's favour,[363] according to another, somewhat less dramatic and presumably correct, it was 5:1, then 5:4, 40:30. Flavelle, however, unable to convert his match point, and subsequently another, lost the set 7:5.[364] After five-all in the fourth set, Flavelle had again had his trouble for nothing, losing it 7:5. Flavelle seemed disconcerted, the Frenchman, backed by a 'heavy, albeit sometimes very little justified applause',[365] mostly from the female portion of the crowd,[366] was greatly encouraged. In the fifth set Decugis took five games off the reel, the last of which owing to 'a wrong decision of the umpire'. 'This', according to the correspondent of *Lawn Tennis and Croquet*,[367] 'upset the Doctor so much, that he retired before the commencement of the sixth game, thereby disappointing many of his friends and the public at large.' Otto Nirrnheim reporting to *Sport im Wort* gave a somewhat different account. After the score had been 5:0, thirty-all, the umpire called Flavelle's service a fault, but the linesman declared that it was all right. It was then ruled that the ball should be played again. Flavelle double-faulted, and, facing a match-point and furious, decided he had had enough, and quit.[368] Although not exactly in accordance with the principles of fair play for which English competitors were at the time universally praised on the European continent,[369] the Doctor's reaction

FIGURE 103   A good impression of the German championships in Hamburg after the turn of the century may be gained from this photograph of the men's singles final of 1902, in which the promising young Frenchman Max Decugis (on the attack at the net) defeated the steady baseliner Dr Flavelle in five sets.

becomes understandable if one bears in mind that he had been deprived, after deuce had been called eleven times, of the first game of the final set on account of a linesman's decision which had been blatantly wrong.[370] After a match so dismally concluded, the cheers for the champion were naturally less vociferous. However, when the prizes were finally distributed, a thunderous applause greeted Decugis, and the northerners even raised the Frenchman on their shoulders.[371] His ultimate success was attributed to the fact that he was as good from the baseline as at the net where his opponent proved to be a bungler. In addition, the Frenchman's service was rated greatly superior to the Englishman's who also lacked the former's agility. To the mind of the sub-editor of *Sport im Wort* who at this point could not help adding this personal comment, this was easily explained by the contenders' big difference in age.[372]

Even more so than the men's championships, the ladies', by the total absence of any foreigners, was virtually reduced to a local event. It resulted in the triumph of Miss Mary Ross who, after beating the favourite, Miss Hertha Friederichsen, had the better of Miss Hilda Meyer after trailing behind 5:1 in the first set.[373] The only interesting features of the ladies' championships were two imaginative pseudonyms adopted by two of the competitors, namely 'T. Ennis' and 'G. Olf', but even in this respect the ladies were outwitted by the gentlemen. These featured a 'Dr Zobeltier' (literally 'Dr Sable Beast') from Heidelberg and a certain 'W. Uchtig' ('M. Assive') in the singles, and in the doubles championships an ingeniously funny pair who, with a rare awareness of their competence in misjudging balls, had named themselves 'T. Rüber' and 'B. Lick' ('B. Leary' and 'E. Yed'). The adoption of pseudonyms was a necessity at the time for society people who, for reasons of propriety, did not want their names to be made public in connection with sports: members of the high aristocracy, physicians, officials, military men without a leave of absence or pupils playing truant. Sometimes, it was a downright abuse, as in the case of that ubiquitous and distinguished player 'A. N. Other' who, around the turn of the century, frequently graced continental courts with his presence, and on one occasion even entered for the Championship of Germany.[374] This pseudonym served two purposes. It either helped to eliminate byes, or functioned as a disguise for a top player, or a player who was not sure whether he could come, and who thus was at liberty to arrive at the venue long after the list of entries had been closed. It was, so to speak, the Victorian Wild Card. On one occasion, there had been no fewer than three A.N. Others in a single draw. What would have happened if all three had transmuted into living beings defies belief. Which of the A.N. Others was to play whom? But even the appearance of a single Mr A.N. Other is likely to have baffled the tournament manager who would have been completely at a loss as to which of the A.N. Others this particular A.N. Other was.[375]

The greatest interest of the first championships under the auspices of the Guild was claimed by the newly created doubles championship of Germany. Today, the doubles game has almost lost all of its former popularity. Notable exceptions are the Davis Cup and, of late, the Olympic tennis event, albeit for reasons altogether pedestrian: points, or gold medals, awarded in the doubles count, in the eyes of the statistician, as much as those captured in the singles. In the old days, a great deal of prestige was attached to doubles competitions generally, and so it was that the final in Hamburg attracted the greatest attendance ever seen at a lawn tennis match in Germany.[376] In the lower half of the draw, W.S. Thomson and Jack Bornemann, of Bremen, had had an easy time and on their way to the final had not lost a single set, whereas their opponents, the French pair Max Decugis and M. Germot, had with difficulty survived three close matches.[377] Thomson and Bornemann looked the winners when they managed to snatch the third set after Bornemann, who on court excelled all others, had thrown away the pair's chances of winning the second by serving too many double faults.[378] However, the Frenchmen's excellent net-play and agility, and their coolness and composure prevailed in the end, not least because Decugis's forehand and Germot's backhand combined to excellent effect.[379] On the other hand, Thomson's play disintegrated when it mattered most. Brilliant at times, he showed great weakness overhead, sending many a ball out.[380]

THE FOUNDATION OF THE GERMAN LAWN TENNIS FEDERATION

George W. Hillyard, who in 1888 had been instrumental in founding the famous LTA, also had a hand in the foundation of the German Lawn Tennis Federation (Deutscher Lawn-Tennis-Bund), although neither he nor anybody else in England or in Germany is likely to have ever been aware of this curious coincidence. Attempts at the foundation of a nationwide organization representing German lawn tennis players in their entirety were made as early as the beginning of the 1890s. In 1892, the subject was broached by *Spiel und Sport*, then the country's only sporting journal opening its pages to lawn tennis, significantly in its English language supplement titled 'English Chat'. The initiative, the periodical wrote, should be taken by a distinguished personality, Baron von Fichard, and it went on to suggest that Carl August von der Meden should also be involved as, so to speak, the Baron's adjutant. As a consequence, the two gentlemen did hold consultations in Baden-Baden in August 1893, but instead of getting under way the foundation of a German Association, they were agreed on the 'advisability' of joining the LTA![381] However, no further steps seem to have been taken at the time, even in this direction.

In 1888, the catalyst by which the LTA came into existence had been Hillyard's jealousy. What gave rise to the foundation of the German federation was (strange as it may seem) Hillyard's playing lawn tennis in Portugal. In October 1901, after the end of the tennis season, Mr and Mrs Hillyard had been invited to spend a week in Cascaes, a fashionable seaside resort near Lisbon and very close to Estoril where in recent times the European claycourt season is set in motion. Together with Mr and Mrs Durlacher, Miss Robb and Messrs Cazalet and Mahony, they had competed in a tournament arranged by the country's best player, the Honorary Secretary of Cascaes Sports Club, Mr Guilherme F. Pinto Basto. In so doing they had flattered the vanity of Dom Carlos, the stout King of Portugal, a would-be tennis champion who also competed and gallantly partnered Blanche Hillyard in his favourite game, the mixed doubles. In return for the favour of playing with some of Britain's best, Dom Carlos had entertained his guests most royally.[382]

In faraway Germany, the royal treat given to a British lawn tennis expedition by the King of Portugal had come to the notice of a certain Emil Gramm.[383] Herr Gramm had read about it in the *Vossische Zeitung*, a society journal with next to no knowledge about the game and therefore at liberty to refer to Mr and Mrs Hillyard as 'professionals'. This had reminded Herr Gramm of a rather humiliating experience he had had years ago, in 1880. In that year he had, as a member of Frankfurt Rowing Society, wanted to compete at Henley, but he and his crew had been requested to have their status of gentlemen confirmed by the English Consul. In England, the German oarsman suspected, foreign teams were always welcome as long as they did not, as in the case of soccer, threaten English supremacy. In other sports, however, the situation was different. At Henley, for example, people tended to be rather fussy about the amateur status of guests, and even if it was found without a blemish in the end, the press would take up the subject eagerly, and represent public opinion thus: that Henley was for the English, and that foreigners had no business to be there! Herr Gramm knew well that Mr and Mrs Hillyard had competed successfully for the Championship of Germany (they had, in fact, both been Champions of Germany twice!), and he wondered whether the two representatives of the Empire should be considered professionals or not, namely people who by playing lawn tennis had pecuniary benefits or even earned a living. In order to make sure of it, he wrote a letter to the editor of the weekly *Sport im Wort*,[384] in which he asked for the expert opinion of someone in the know. It was this letter which set the ball rolling.

The ball landed, to continue the metaphor, first in the court of Charles Adolph Voigt. Voigt had himself, in an article submitted to *Sport im Bild*, sung the praises of the Portuguese lawn tennis potentate – possibly because he had himself been regaled most royally. Perhaps peeved a little about Gramm's tactless inquisitiveness, he was only too ready to champion Hillyard's and the other players' cause.[385] He categorically refuted the view that any of them could be considered professional. They were, he said, very well-to-do people all of them, and especially Messrs Cazalet and Durlacher, and they had undertaken the journey to Portugal for fun and because they had not known the country before and had after the close of the season in England not had anything better to do.[386] He had to admit, however, that even in England some had found fault with the fact that the English players, rather than paying all expenses for the journey themselves, had allowed themselves to be entertained. All things related to lawn tennis were, he continued, strictly 'amateur', and although the LTA had paid the travel costs for their Davis Cup representatives the year previously, there were many players of the 'old school' who would protest most vigorously whenever first-class players (as it often happened) were invited by committee members to compete in this or that tournament where they were, of course, the big attraction. Many players grudged the English aces winning so many prizes. He concluded by referring to other sports such as horse racing and rowing, and by quoting the example of a well-known

English tennis player R., invited by a wealthy gentleman H. from Berlin to be his doubles partner. The English player, he said, who refused such an invitation, would act most foolishly, and even the wealthiest player would not. As far as he knew, only the Dohertys never accepted invitations or any hospitality extended to them, and their expenses for the love of the game, according to his own estimate, used to run up to 20,000 marks per annum at least.[387]

Herr Gramm was quick to reply, and he did so with his tongue in his cheek.[388] At first, he seemed to accept without reservation the statement of 'a personality with so great an experience in the sport' that the English players in question had been no professionals. But then he harked back to the 'faultfinders' mentioned by Voigt. He confessed that he, unlike Mr Voigt whom he pertly classed with the 'new school', was a follower of the 'old school' who would, again unlike Mr Voigt, not call an English player refusing an invitation a fool, but a gentleman! From the example of the Dohertys he drew the conclusion that in the case of all others it was the rule to entertain them. And it was not private persons who did so (since these did not organize tournaments), but committees. And even though this was still the private affair of those committees, it was nevertheless desirable for the German ace to know whether such hospitality was also shown by the committee in charge of the German championships. And Mr Voigt, he said, would be the one in a position to clarify this point, since it was he who had been Honorary Secretary of exactly this committee for years. Of course, Herr Gramm knew only too well, and the remainder of his letter to the editor makes this perfectly clear,[389] that the first-class English player who competed in Homburg (and the Honorary Secretary, Herr Voigt, too) had his bill paid by the *Kurdirector*.

The person who, shortly afterwards, had had enough of this hanky panky was an energetic young tennis player and a junior lawyer from Frankfurt, Karl Schmidt-Knatz.[390] For the Germans, the amateur question could not be answered satisfactorily by the method adopted by Herr Gramm, he wrote. A decision could not be reached by having the question thoroughly examined by a host of individuals. A definitive ruling as to who was an amateur and who a professional, and the application of such a ruling to a given situation, could only be safeguarded by a lawn tennis association representing all of Germany.[391] Schmidt-Knatz then drew up a whole list of defects, grievances and irregularities which, he hoped, might be redressed by a governing body: the faulty laying and inadequate keeping of tennis courts; the lack of authoritative rules which would help deciding questions such as qualification for club membership and for participation in tournaments (to which belonged the question of who should be rated a professional); the shortage of well-trained tournament managers, umpires, and linesmen which prevented the smooth running of tournaments, and especially, in view of the vastly growing number of players, a satisfactory handling of the draw (he apparently had in mind the popular handicap-events of the time); and, last but not least, the confused tennis jargon which (with no unified German terminology as yet) existed on the Fatherland's tennis courts.

However, despite this long list, the fact remained that it was George Hillyard and the amateur question which had led to Schmidt-Knatz's decisive move.

Schmidt-Knatz's letter was followed by a postscript in which the foundation of a Southern German lawn tennis association was announced (it actually came into being later),[392] this as a first step towards a governing body for the whole country. It was signed by five clubs, and in it the hope was expressed that similar activities be engaged in by clubs in the north, and that, as a result of these, negotiations should be entered into.[393] The postscript was concluded by a summons to all clubs south and north to make known in writing their approval of an All German Lawn Tennis Association to the journal *Sport im Wort*.[394]

Schmidt-Knatz's initiative met with immediate response not only from the north, but also from the east. From the north, a candidate of the Technical University, Hanover, who at the same time was the first *spielwart* (games superintendent) of the local Deutscher Tennis-Verein (German Tennis Club), made himself heard. His name was C. Schetelig. Two years earlier, Herr Schetelig had already written a letter to John Bloch's *Spiel und Sport* in which he had urged the foundation of an All German lawn tennis association,[395] but he had apparently addressed the wrong paper. He had now sent a similar letter to *Sport im Wort*, into which, incidentally, *Spiel und Sport* had in the meantime been incorporated. Although he doubted that any progress could be made before German lawn tennis clubs emerged from hibernation, he invited private correspondence between clubs and a kind of brainstorming on the paper's pages which would help – after all arguments had been made known – to arrive at conclusions more quickly when it eventually came to the foundation of an association. He raised the question of whether the association, for which he proposed the name 'Bund' (federation), since there existed already a great many 'Verbände' (associations), should include Austria,[396] and whether the organization should represent all lawn tennis players of the country, or only those clubs engaging in competitive tennis. Convinced that an association for the adepts of competitive tennis would be sufficiently prestigious to exert influence on the merely recreational members of Germany's tennis community, he would rather opt for this alternative.[397]

In the east, the Secretary of the East German Lawn Tennis Tournament Association, Lieutenant F. Schlepps, raised his voice. The association, which prided itself on the membership of no fewer than seventeen clubs, some of which had a hundred members and more, had among its objectives, Schlepps wrote, the introduction of the German language into the game, and to take the initiative to found an All German association. By achieving the latter goal, they had hoped to overcome more easily the difficulties presenting themselves in attaining the first. In the east, for that matter, in normal matches German was spoken and the toss conducted in the German language. He advocated an umbrella organization for associations rather than individual clubs to which membership should be denied. He concluded by mentioning earlier negotiations his association had entered into with 'influential personalities' in 1900, and by expressing the hope that the recent summons might soon lead to a tangible result.[398]

More letters were sent in by von der Meden's disciple, Otto Nirrnheim of Hamburg, and Emil Bartels of Braunschweig. Nirrnheim supported the suggestion made by Schlepps to set up an organization on the basis of major associations, saying that, unless a small number of delegates representing important memberships took the matter in hand, the whole procedure of constituting it would become unwieldy.[399] Bartels objected that to found larger associations would take years, and that he therefore was in favour of admitting associations as well as clubs. If something was put to the vote, clubs could decide whether they wanted to exert their rights themselves, or whether they preferred delegating them to the association they belonged to. In the first case, their vote – here Bartels was thinking of one vote for any fifty members – would be deducted from the overall votes of their association.[400]

Already Lieutenant Schlepps' casual remark had shown that there had been goings on behind the scenes for quite some time. One of those apparently *au courant* was the Alsatian Baron, Robert von Fichard. In another letter published in *Sport im Wort*, the Baron took sides with Otto Nirrnheim who had suggested an organization made up of smaller associations, and he objected to the Southern Association announced by Schmidt-Knatz. The reason for this becomes clear later. Negotiations between himself and Carl August von der Meden had made much progress, hence his support for Nirrnheim, von der Meden's *aide-de-camp*. The foundation of an All German organization in which he and von der Meden hoped to play the dominant role was in the offing, hence his objection to Schmidt-Knatz whose powerful Southern League, he feared, might turn into a serious rival. The remainder of von Fichard's letter revealed a rather unpleasant side of his character: his vanity and arrogance, and his unabashed fawning on the LTA and its officials. He tried to assume an air of importance by the cocksure manner with which he declared that Schmidt-Knatz's requests would be met (as if he alone had to decide this), and by being very mysterious about the negotiations in which he was involved and the results of which, he said, would be made public on the pages of *Sport im Wort*.[401] Clearly, the implication was that such was not for the clamorous rabble writing letters to *Sport im Wort*.

That the Baron considered himself to be in lawn tennis affairs in a class of his own also appeared from the way he lectured poor Schmidt-Knatz. Schmidt-Knatz was wrong when he said that there were no authentic rules of the game. The rules of the LTA were being observed most loyally by German tournament committees, and the rules as well as the regulations for tournament play, rendered into the German language and edited by himself (!), had been approved by the same Association. If the sanction of the LTA were followed by that of the German LTA, then they would have to be considered 'authentic' in the way Schmidt-Knatz had meant them to be. The principles of the draw had never been seriously disputed on the continent. Amendments to them, he said, in one of his many attempts to be pally with the much admired LTA, were not in the power of the German LTA, but solely at the discretion of the LTA which was, as he had pointed out repeatedly, a cosmopolitan institution encompassing the whole world with the exception (more apparent than real) of the American LTA. As for the alleged terminological errors and confusion, they were much overrated. It was he who had, first on his own account, then in collaboration with the 'Allgemeiner Deutscher Sprachverein' (General German Language Society),[402] been untiring in recommending for use a code of terms. He was sure that the same recommendation would be made on the part of the German LTA. Nor would the German LTA set itself the task of establishing standards for qualification for membership in a club, or expulsion or leaving it, because interference with the affairs of individual clubs did not not seem practicable to him. Lastly, professionalism was of no significance in Germany, but the question would nevertheless have to be regulated by the German LTA – just in case.[403]

In yet another letter, Schmidt-Knatz evaluated the arguments of Nirrnheim and Bartels, but wisely abstained from quarrelling with the Baron (in fact, he did not even mention his letter). Instead, he made some important points himself. He expressed his satisfaction that his first letter had roused widespread concern in all parts of the country, and that all parties were prepared to set up an association in a joint effort. There was at this point unanimity, he believed, about the fact that a first draft of statutes should be sent to the clubs listed in von Fichard's 1902 lawn tennis annual for examination, and that this should be, after bringing to bear on it the suggestions made by the clubs, turned into a second draft which would then have to be put to the vote at the inaugural meeting of the association. The only problem which still had to be solved was that of who should be entrusted with the twofold job of setting up the rules of the game and the regulations for tournament play, and of laying down the statutes of the organization. The first part of the task, which would be 'a milestone in the development of lawn tennis in Germany', he blandly suggested, should be undertaken by Baron von Fichard, the second by Carl August von der Meden.[404] As for the question of representation in the inaugural assembly, he advocated the subdivision of the 150 to 170 existing clubs into ten regional entities ('Bezirke') by taking into account associations which had already been established. These should be allowed two representatives each, to be elected by their constituencies according to the majority principle, each club with less than fifty members allowed one vote, those under 120 members two, and those with more than 120 members three votes. The All German Association, he concluded, rejecting the view expressed by Nirrnheim, should establish the regional associations, and not vice versa.

Schmidt-Knatz's opinion met with the wholehearted approval of Mr Schetelig who had in the meantime become a graduate engineer and had moved to the Fatherland's lawn tennis metropolis, Hamburg. He welcomed the idea that Baron von Fichard and Carl August von der Meden should attend to the matter, but he could not help contradicting the views expressed by the former which, he said, were, in the opinion of many players at least, arguable.[405] Von Fichard, he wrote, had considered premature the setting up of a programme for the association's activities prior to its coming into being. However, he believed that the foundation of an association would be approved of by many only if its programme appealed to them. He therefore welcomed all the contributions which had been made up to this point, and he invited further discussion on the pages of *Sport im Wort* in order to clarify points and positions. As for the question of official rules and the regulations of tournament play, it was linked to that of the status of the (English) LTA. It was true that up to this point this organization had been the recognized authority, because the Germans, not having regulations of their own, had availed themselves of those of the LTA as translated by Baron von Fichard. That was the reason why, whenever the LTA decided to amend its regulations, the Germans had followed suit 'loyally'. As soon as they possessed an association of their own, however, they would be completely independent, and although the German lawn tennis world had no reason to be at variance with the LTA, it would nevertheless stand on its own feet and should not be looking to England for leadership. From the fact that lawn tennis in its present form had its roots in England, and that the LTA called itself 'cosmopolitan' (Schetelig here expressed his doubts whether it actually was), it did not follow that the Germans should subject themselves to it. They wanted to be equal to it at least, since in Germany (here Schetelig's words became truly prophetic) the fascinating sport was steadily gaining ground, whereas in England it was, rather, on the decline.

While for the time being the rules and the regulations for tournament play of the LTA would be observed without much change, they would be adapted, as soon as the need became felt, to conditions existing in Germany, and without consulting England. As for tournaments held on German soil, foreign players would obey the regulations of an organization representing the German lawn tennis world in much the same way as Germans would recognize foreign statutes when playing abroad.

Finally, confusion and errors in the use of the tennis language were, contrary to what Baron von Fichard had claimed, very considerable. Von Fichard's attempts at setting up a unified German lawn tennis terminology were highly commendable and had won the recognition of many in lawn tennis circles, but they had come to grief because of two large obstacles. For one, countless lawn tennis players, who attached little significance to an adequate terminology, professed no interest in introducing a unified language of the game, and, when it came to the question of which of the many existing rules books they should use when taking up the game, these people showed the same indifference. For another, even in sports-orientated lawn tennis circles, only a few supported the idea of a unified German terminology, because no such universally approved terminology existed; nor was von Fichard's translation, authorized as it was by the LTA, sanctioned by any organization representing German lawn tennis. Official recognition of von Fichard's code had, in addition, been very difficult, because of the international character of the country's big tournaments (Schetelig named Berlin, Hamburg, and Homburg) where it had been no easy job to find umpires, let alone such as could have been pledged to counting the score in German only. Schetelig concluded by expressing the hope that the foundation of the German Lawn Tennis Federation (Deutscher Lawn-Tennis-Bund) would remedy it all![406]

At this point, a personality who had, to the mind of *Sport im Wort*, reputedly taken a vivid interest in continental, and especially in German, lawn tennis, but had chosen to write anonymously, offered his expert advice.[407] The 'personality', no doubt, was Charles Adolph Voigt. Voigt highly commended the enthusiasm which men younger than himself exhibited for a German organization, but he was sceptical about their plans. The inherent 'Englishness' of the sport had for a long time prevented the establishment in Germany of a supreme board, an 'alma mater' he called it, and the difficulties of concerted action were being greatly underestimated. 'A "unified lawn tennis language", and German score cards?', the American queried, and he discarded the idea at once. At Homburg, where the English language would always triumph over all others, there would be hardly any change in the running of the tournament, nor with regard to the rules and regulations, even though the German Lawn Tennis Federation presumed to introduce innovations or to depart from the rules of the LTA. However, a German association might be helpful, he wrote, in order to do away with technical shortcomings on which there was agreement among the best English players: the question of the 'let' in net-balls, the question of foot-faults, etc.[408] Changes of this kind would have to be made after thorough consultation with those personalities who were (like himself) fully acquainted with German tournaments and the sport in general, and by involving the English greats visiting the Homburg tournament who would have to give their approval. It is interesting that he considered the German association alone capable of 'technical' innovations. The LTA, and most other associations in England, he said, were too conservative and mainly composed of old codgers (*'bemooste Häupter'*, literally 'mossy heads'), and no pioneering work could be expected from these quarters. One thing seemed highly desirable to the professional tournament manager: that the German association early in winter should establish a German tournament calendar and see to it that all tournaments were held in an appropriate order and should take into consideration foreign fixtures. Such would enable German as well as foreign players to engage in a series of tournaments without loss of time. He insisted that Hamburg, Heiligendamm and Homburg should, in this order, be set for the month of August (because, of course, he himself profited most from such an arrangement), and that in international tournaments suitable personalities (again he was thinking of himself) should be appointed for the offices of referee and manager. Finally, a single brand of balls should be used, for the purchase of which special conditions could be negotiated with the manufacturer annually. (Perhaps Voigt hoped to be part of such a deal, too.)

According to Voigt, the personalities most suited to be running an All German organization should be sought among the experts of the Hamburg Lawn Tennis Guild, and perhaps the Berliner Lawn-Tennis-Turnier-Club. Herr August von der Meden was considered by him the only person qualified to be its president, and Baron von Fichard the most suitable to be its Secretary. Behrens, Traun and Nirrnheim, of Hamburg, and Count Spee and Herr Brüggemann, of Berlin, would be hard-working assistants. Apart from a few 'corresponding members' in the major cities of the German Empire who might be summoned to an annual general assembly, these people would be enough, and he was thinking of the model of the LTA in London where current business was conducted by Messrs Collins and Mewburn in their capacities as President and Secretary respectively. Von Fichard's yearbooks and

Sport im Wort were equally sufficient as official organs of the Association, although a special journal would not be long in coming and might even pay.

At the bottom of the page which contained Voigt's letter there was printed a brief note about a committee meeting of the Berliner Lawn-Tennis-Turnier-Club on 20 February 1902. The note was concluded by the following statement: 'The negotiations which have been conducted by Messrs von Jecklin and Brüggemann with Mr von der Meden of Hamburg regarding the foundation of a German Lawn Tennis Association were approved of by the club committee.'[409] What these 'negotiations' had been like was revealed by Hans Oskar Behrens, a quarter of a century later when the Federation celebrated its twenty-fifth anniversary. There had been what may in retrospect be called a Hamburg–Berlin Axis, and Behrens, in his capacity as von der Meden's agent had, in evening sessions at the homes of Karl von Jecklin, a lawyer and a senior administrative officer and the president of the influential Berlin Lawn Tennis Tournament Club, and Dr M. Oechelhäuser, another lawyer, negotiated the details of the foundation. Back in Hamburg, he had reported the results of his talks to von der Meden.[410] That is why, when all parties concerned believed that sufficient progress had been made, Carl August von der Meden could spring the following news on the German lawn tennis public, in a note which again appeared in *Sport im Wort*, in its issue of 7 March 1902:[411]

> **On the Foundation of a German Lawn Tennis Association.** After the question of the foundation of a German Lawn Tennis Association has been discussed at length and by private correspondence among the more important lawn tennis clubs of Germany and several personalities who have made a name for themselves in lawn tennis circles, Herr A. von der Meden, Hamburg, fulfilling a wish expressed by all parties concerned, has taken the initiative and has issued a summons to several gentlemen who could be regarded as the main representatives of lawn tennis in the several parts of Germany to submit to him by Easter of the current year suggestions regarding the foundation of an association or a draft of the statutes respectively.

The journal then gave the names of seven persons to which von der Meden's letters had been circulated,[412] adding that, in order to discuss the answers received, a meeting had been convened for Whitsun on the occasion of the Berlin International Tournament.

In mid-April, the foundation of a German Association was among the topics at a meeting of the East German Association in Danzig. Schlepps, after reporting on the state of affairs, had to defend the plans for a German Association against the views of Herr Busenitz, the chairman, and Herr Gelhorn. Busenitz would rather have restricted activities of a national organization, and both gentlemen expressed their doubts as to whether it would be willing to promote the sport in the east. In order to make known the opinion of their association, not only Schlepps, but also Gelhorn decided to attend the inaugural meeting in Berlin.[413]

In its issue of 25 April 1902, *Sport im Wort* published an advertisement in which Baron von Fichard announced his new 1902 annual. One of the yearbook's assets, according to its author, was a carefully revised and up-to-date list of the country's clubs and associations which would soon be joined in an All German Tennis Federation.[414] On 9 May 1902, von der Meden had published in *Sport im Wort* a second note in which he extended his original invitation to another seven personalities, adding that, as a result of the correspondence exchanged between those concerned, the foundation of the 'Federation' could be taken for granted; it would materialize 'shortly', and, by attaining a goal for which so many lawn tennis communities in the country had striven for so long a time, further advance in the sport could be hoped for in Germany.[415]

Then, in its issue of 23 May 1902, *Sport im Wort* hailed the birth of something which, to use the journal's words, was the fulfilment of a long-cherished wish of many German lawn tennis circles: the birth of the German Lawn Tennis Federation. On the evening of Whitsun Monday (19 May 1902), after two days of negotiations in the Berlin Palast-Hotel, the delegates – von der Meden (Hamburg), von Jecklin and Brüggemann (Berlin), Pummerer Sr. and Stahlmann (Munich), Dr Hillig and Gulden (Leipzig), Bartels (Braunschweig), and Schlepps and Gelhorn (Danzig) – signed the minutes testifying to the founding act.[416] The statutes had been drafted by von Jecklin, a tennis player of note and one of the founders of Berlin Lawn-Tennis-Turnier-Club, a most generous promoter of young talent who died prematurely in 1910, after he had had to retire in 1907 owing to severe illness.[417] Von Jecklin's statutes, after having been unanimously accepted as a basis for discussion, were approved of, with minor modifications. Baron von Fichard, who was prevented by official duties, had filed motions in writing and delegated von Jecklin and Brüggemann to take care of them. Following his suggestions, the administrative structure of the Federation was made less complicated, a different subdivision into regional districts (seven in all) agreed upon, and changes made with regard to the right to vote and annual membership fees.[418] Carl August von der Meden, who (according to Bartels, an eye-witness) had chaired the assembly jovially and stolidly,[419] was elected President, whereas von Jecklin, Brüggemann and Dr Oechelhäuser, all residents of Berlin, obtained the posts of First Vice President, Secretary and Treasurer respectively. The statutes provided that the First President of the Federation was entitled to appoint the Second Vice President. As might have been expected, von der Meden's choice was Baron von Fichard.[420] The Presidents of the regional districts, the three Presidents of the Federation, its Secretary and its Treasurer were to form the Federal Committee which would convene once in a year in Berlin. The statutes also provided that a general assembly should be held annually, and that every second one should take place in Berlin.[421]

FREEDOM FROM ENGLISH RULE

Although it was hardly noticed at first, the inauguration of an All German Tennis Federation proved a first step towards the country's emancipation from English dominance. In its statutes, printed in von Fichard's annual of 1903, the goals of the

Federation were formulated. Among these, the creation of a German-language version of the rules of the game and tournament regulations, and the enforcement of a unified language were most prominent.[422] At a special meeting of the committee in Berlin on 11 April 1903, a decision was deferred to the committee's annual meeting at Pentecost.[423] It was then at last that the country's self-appointed Teutonizer-in-chief, the Alsatian Baron von Fichard, was allowed to have his say. In a rather long-winded paper, interspersed at times with specimens of baronial forced humour, the Second Vice-President of the Federation expounded to the committee members the results of his long labours with the German tennis language. For the most part, his suggestions, after having been put to the vote, found favour with his colleagues. The terms and phrases which had been approved were published, together with their English equivalents, in the Baron's yearbook in the following year.[424] In retrospect, the call for a German tennis language was only natural if seen against the background of the development of the German language as a whole. Since the German Empire had been constituted in 1871, a unification of the German language had been attempted in many areas of public life such as the imperial mail and telegraph services, the railways, legislation, education and administration, and especially the German armed forces.[425] It was only natural therefore that sports organizations in their attempt to rally under their leadership the supporters of their sport nationwide should have had similar ambitions.[426] In their joint efforts, government and private organizations gained support from a language and political movement initiated by the highly influential educator Joachim Heinrich Campe who, at the turn of the previous century, had vehemently advocated the Germanization (*Verdeutschung*) of all foreign words in the German language.[427] If in Campe's days it was the words borrowed from French which were discredited by the purists, their role as linguistic bugbears had, when the century drew to its close and imperialism was rampant, been taken over by borrowings from arch-rival England.[428] By this time, Campe's and his followers' cause was championed by an influential journal, the *Zeitschrift des Allgemeinen Deutschen Sprachvereins*, founded in 1885.[429] Significantly, the journal not only published decrees of the German Emperor Wilhelm II on military language,[430] but also discussions by Baron Robert von Fichard and Professor Konrad Koch, a football pioneer from Braunschweig, on the language of lawn tennis and association football.[431] It is hardly surprising that the Baron should have promised to place at the disposal of the Allgemeiner Deutscher Sprachverein (for the purpose of further propaganda) a sufficient number of copies of the Germanized lawn tennis terminology as soon as they were released.[432] It is not known whether this promise was kept. The official German lawn tennis rules were published in 1904.[433]

More important than in the field of tennis language was English domination on the lawn tennis court. After the Championship of Germany had again be captured by an Englishman in 1903, Dr Robert Hessen,[434] the eloquent founding member of the German Lawn Tennis Federation, concluded a eulogy on the Bad Homburg tournaments with a rather sombre note:

There is but one very discordant note in all this that the Germans themselves in whose country the event takes place have not reaped any laurels in competition. Even the Championship of Germany, which was in 1897 held by Hillyard, in 1898 by Mahony, in 1899 by the American Hobart, in 1900 again by Hillyard, had in 1901 and 1902 to be delivered up to the Frenchman M. Decugis who then, owing to his year of service, had to surrender it to Ritchie, and it looks as if in the future our prospects will depend on whether the famous foreigners want to come or not.

As was indicated by the doctor, present English domination on the German court had a name: Major Josiah George Ritchie (**Figure 104**). Ritchie made his first appearance in Hamburg in 1903 where his won the Championship of Germany at once, finishing off the unfortunate Dr Flavelle after the latter had, as in the year before, been leading by two sets to love. The match lasted three hours due to rallies during which the ball had travelled over the net thirty to forty times, but in which points were also won after no fewer than 43 and 65 strokes.[435] Ritchie, who was over 30 when he first went to Hamburg,[436] immediately acquired notoriety for his stonewall tennis which combined calmness,[437] unfailing safety and great retrieving and staying powers.[438] How he had acquired these assets was explained by the sports writer of the *Prager Tagblatt*, Dr Rosenbaum-Jenkins. It was the caution, he said, with which he had picked his parents (the owners of two houseboats on the Thames)[439] which allowed him to do nothing except play lawn tennis and rowing;[440] in fact, before he had come to Germany, he had competed in a regatta in Laleham where he had won the single sculls event, and, together with C.D. Head, the coxless pairs.[441] Dr Rosenbaum-Jenkins might have added that he also was an addict of table tennis, and had as such been elected Secretary of the Table Tennis Association, founded in 1902.[442]

FIGURE 104 A most successful threesome. In 1904, when this photograph was taken, Elsie Lane had won the Championships of Germany whereas her countryman, Major Josiah George Ritchie, became singles and, partnered by Elsie's brother Ernest Wilmot (left), doubles Champion of Germany.

This may have been one of the reasons why his and Dr Flavelle's game in the final of the Championship of Germany was described as 'ping pong' by a knowledgable Hamburger.[443] In 1904, Ritchie defended his title against Curt von Wessely, a young, promising, dark-haired and smart-looking Austrian from Prague, against whose southernly temperament he pitted his thoroughbred Englishness, which tempted an unknown German sports writer to turn poetic:[444]

> It is a fascinating sight, to watch them, fascinating above all because of the strange contrast of styles in which at the same time a difference of the two protagonists in national character seems to find expression. Here you have the fair-haired, coolly pensive Englishman, who places balls with colossal safety, who with an almost – *sit venia verbo* – stiff calmness ponders the little inadequacies and weak spots of the opponent and takes advantage of them. Every stroke a well-considered plan of action, forged calmly and brought to an either lucky or unlucky end with energy. … When he at the end of a rally returns to his place at the baseline in his slow, somewhat pushing gait, his hand goes up mechanically, and with a thoughtful gesture, to his thin lips pressed together after which he strokes the hair of his forehead bleached to a flaxen colour by the tennis sun. There is a summer lightning on the chiselled features of his face. The spirits of future battles are gambolling round there.

In the challenge round, Ritchie beat von Wessely in three straight sets 6:4, 6:0, 10:8; the Austrian had in the fourth round eliminated a young student of law in Bonn, Otto Froitzheim of Strasbourg, who had undertaken the long and expensive journey to Hamburg for the first time and by his plucky game had aroused the curiosity of the correspondent of *Der Lawn-Tennis-Sport*.

In 1905, with still no German candidate in the offing, a young student from Cambridge, Anthony Wilding, tried to wrest the German Championship from Ritchie, but experience triumphed again. As much as the student tried to get the better of Ritchie by rushing to the net, he was outmanoeuvred time and again by Ritchie's passing shots and, above all, his lobs.[445] After his defeat in three straight, albeit fiercely contended sets, the young man took Ritchie to task, decrying his play, for a change, as an 'old wife's game' rather than ping pong.[446] The German sporting press had seen Ritchie's performance in a different light, though. 'The lodestar, better still: the dominant of the event was again M.J.G. Ritchie', it said.[447]

> He was the lion of the day and reaped championships with smug satisfaction; … in the big orchestra of the remainder of players A.F. Wilding played the first violin;[448] he proved a fierce competitor of the primas and was not at all easily convinced of his superiority.

After three consecutive wins, Ritchie could at last claim the cup presented by Carl Laeisz in 1897,[449] and apparently decided to start another series of wins at the championships in the years to come. In 1906, and in the absence of any competitors of note from the British Isles, things promised well. In the challenge round he had to meet a young German who hardly counted even among the Fatherland's very best, F.W. Rahe from Rostock in Mecklenburg. Rahe had reached the final by a lucky draw by which the six best players had been consigned to the upper half. Of course, Ritchie had no difficulty in having his name engraved on the new championship cup which had, incidentally, been presented by Rahe's sovereign, Grand Duchess Anastasia of Mecklenburg Schwerin.[450] An incident had occurred all the same which was considered ominous by some. The most attractive match of the tournament had been played between the invincible Ritchie, and a young German from Frankfurt, Oskar Kreuzer. Not in the least intimidated, Kreuzer had attacked Ritchie courageously and taken the first set from him by 6:4. Of course, Ritchie had then resorted to his usual defensive play, a tired Kreuzer had made all the mistakes,[451] and the Englishman snatched the next two sets. Nevertheless, the correspondent of *Der Lawn-Tennis-Sport* was led to 'scent the morning air'. 'For the first time we have realized that we are on our way to climb the rungs of the ladder leading up to Wimbledon,' he wrote,[452] 'even if we are today on the lowest steps only, such need not deter us. With Kreuzer, we have a first-rate man who has only one defect, his youth.'

Kreuzer's partial success may well have been the reason why, in 1907, German expectations were high.[453] There was, besides Kreuzer, a second candidate believed to be capable of putting an end to British rule on German tennis courts, Otto Froitzheim. Froitzheim was born in Strasbourg on 24 April 1884, the son of a master ('Oberlehrer') at a 'lyceum' (secondary school).[454] As a boy, he had excelled in many sports, and particularly in soccer, a game he regarded as a prep school for tennis.[455] In addition, he was a boy of exceptional intelligence who passed examinations effortlessly. He had picked up a racket at the age of 16,[456] and two years later won the championship of Alsacia. In 1903, he continued his studies of law at the University of Bonn where on the courts of the Bonn Skating Club, the then leading tennis club in the Rhineland, he had excellent training conditions.[457] By the time he entered the 1907 championships he had passed his examination as a junior lawyer. His game was characterized by its fluent, seemingly effortless movement on court, and clean forehand and even better backhand strokes of extraordinary length.[458] Although mainly marshalled from the baseline, it was, despite its elegance, nevertheless highly aggressive, keeping his opponents on the run.[459] The Alsatian's main asset, however, and the terror of his antagonists, was his unperturbedness and unfailing accuracy. In his 'lexicon', it was said, the term 'double fault' simply did not exist.[460]

When Ritchie and Froitzheim met in the challenge round (**Figure 105**), Froitzheim had decided the question of whether he or Kreuzer was the better man by beating Kreuzer in two sets.[461] That is why the Englishman must have had misgivings as to the outcome of the match.[462] This was well brought out by Otto Nirrnheim's report which has become a classic in German tennis literature and was rendered into English verbatim (although with some significant omissions), and published in the English journal *Lawn Tennis and Badminton*:[463]

> These two met on the following Sunday [15 August 1907] before a large and enthusiastic audience, and though Ritchie was looked upon as the ultimate winner, the opinion was that the German would certainly book one, if not two, sets in his favour. It was evident

FIGURE 105   Otto Froitzheim, outstanding German lawn tennis player before the First World War, in 1907, the year of his triumph over Ritchie. In the opinion of many, Froitzheim had even greater potential than Baron Gottfried von Cramm in the 1930s.

at the commencement that Ritchie meant to win the first set, and it was equally evident that Froitzheim was eager that he should not. Both forced the game. The first six games went to the server, then Froitzheim took Ritchie's service game, Ritchie replying in the same way, following with his own, 5/4 Ritchie leads. Froitzheim, however, was not to be denied, and took the next three games, and with it the first set at 7/5. Apparently, this result had disappointed Ritchie. Anyhow, he began the next set very badly, almost throwing the first two games away, but then pulled himself together and playing in good form, he drew level. Then Froitzheim put up a brilliant game, giving Ritchie no chance until the games stood 5/2 – the eighth game Ritchie secured, when Froitzheim ran out with the next game at 6/3. That the excitement now grew intense, everybody who ever visited a Hamburg Tournament, where the audience is almost entirely composed of lawn tennis players, will understand. Having watched Ritchie's play for years, they knew what a stubborn player he was, while they feared Froitzheim could not last a third set, and loss to him of this set meant the loss of the match. Froitzheim, however, knew the danger full well, and in the following set put up his very best and took the first three games; then Ritchie booked the fourth. The fifth was the hottest, and after the umpire had called deuce six times, Froitzheim took this, and stood at 4/1. In the next game he slackened down, and Ritchie, taking advantage of this, drew level at four all. The ninth game fell to Froitzheim, the tenth game was Ritchie's service, and he got to 15/0, 30/0, 40/0, and five games all was expected. Then [Froitzheim scored the next two points and][464] Ritchie served a double fault, and deuce was called. Ritchie again got to advantage, deuce again, and gave Froitzheim the advantage game by serving another double fault. A long rally ended in Froitzheim's favour by a brilliantly played passing shot, and with it the challenger decided the match in his favour.

What the English report wisely withheld from an English readership was the fact that Froitzheim's winning of the first set was greeted by the partisan German crowd with prolonged applause, and this angered Ritchie as much as the fact that his plans had been upset.[465] The jubilant note with which Nirrnheim concluded his account was also suppressed, presumably with regard to national feeling. And so Froitzheim after eleven years won the Championship of Germany, Nirrnheim continued where the English report broke off, and he quoted in a significant way from Friedrich von Schiller's poem 'Der Kampf mit dem Drachen' (The Fight with the Dragon), thus transforming the young Alsatian into the German national hero Siegfried who had just slain the Dragon of England: '"The crowd then burst out with frenzy" – it was one of the finest victories we have seen in Hamburg.'[466]

Nirrnheim's enthusiasm was shared by the whole nation. Immediately after Hamburg, Froitzheim in Bad Homburg beat a champion greater than Ritchie, Anthony Wilding,[467] and among his many triumphs which followed were the Olympic silver medal in 1908,[468] the world championship on hard courts in Paris in 1912, and his five-set match against the Australian 'Wizard' Norman Brookes in the all comers' final of Wimbledon in 1914.[469] It was his Hamburg victory, however, which linguered in the memory of his countrymen until well after the First World War, a war in which Nirrnheim, the writer of the above lines, lost his life,[470] and in which Otto Froitzheim survived as a prisoner-of-war in the country of his opponent.[471] In 1927, when the German Federation celebrated its 25th anniversary, Hans Oskar Simon, the Federation's semi-official historian, called 15 August 1907 the day on which Germany ostensibly joined the ranks of the great lawn tennis nations.[472] A year before, Froitzheim's biographer F.W. Esser, like him a lawyer, had written in the same vein:[473] Froitzheim was the first, he wrote, who in 1907 by his sensational victories over Ritchie, who had seemed unbeatable up to that day, and over the Australian world champion Wilding, conclusively destroyed the false doctrine that only the foreigner, and above all the Anglo-Saxon, was cut out for reaping the most beautiful fruit of healthy sporting activity. It is as if, after the lost war, these writers wanted to capitalize on Froitzheim's victories in an attempt to rally the German nation to a new upsurge of national pride, the consequences of which, of course, they could hardly have anticipated at the time.[474]

Notes

◇

CHAPTER 1

1. In Medieval Latin *idiota* was not necessarily a term of abuse, but merely meant 'ignoramus'. All translations in this work are, if not otherwise stated, the author's.

2. See Strange, vol. 1, p. 36 (ch. XXXII: De conversione Abbatis Morimundi, qui mortuus fuit, et revixit). Because of its importance for the history of tennis, this text deserves to be reproduced in full: 'Daemones ... ordinabant se ex utraque parte vallis; et qui stabant ex una parte, animam miseram ad similitudinem ludi pilae proiiciebant; alii ex parte altera per aera volantem manibus suscipiebant.' An English translation of this story was long ago published by G.C. Coulton, who was correct in interpreting the game described by Caesarius as tennis. Unfortunately, no tennis historian has ever taken notice of this source. See Coulton, vol. 2, p. 227. The anecdote was incorporated in a late Middle English collection of the fifteenth century, where it took on the following form: 'And when he was dead and prestis and clerkis sang salmys aboute hym, devuls tuke his saule, and on the to syde of a vayle all of burnstone thay playd therewith as wha played at the fandyng of the hand-ball our this dale, and on the toder syde of the valley oder fendis clekid it with ther sharpe naylis; & this passid all maner of other paynys.' See Banks, vol. 1, p. 468f. (no. DCXCIX). For an account of Caesarius and his *Dialogus* see the *Lexikon des Mittelalters*, vol. 1, cols. 1363–1366. The author first referred to

Caesarius' story in his study *Os Métodos de Investigação*, p. 4f. There are two English versions of this pamphlet, albeit without illustrations, namely *Modern Methods of Research* (1987), and *Medieval Sport* (this latter being a more explicit version, 1988).

3. Marienstatt literally means 'St Mary's Site'. For an account of the miraculous relocation of the abbey and its consecration in 1324 see Struck, p. xix and pp. 138–40, no. 327: the Virgin Mary had appeared to Abbot Hermann with a blossoming whitethorn twig and had told him to have the monastery built anew where he would find another such twig: hence the name. This must have been some time after 1215.

4. See Manrique, vol. 2, pp. 68–9 (Annus Christi 1178, caput IV, 11–12), and Dubois, p. 154f. and p. 413f. (Series Abbatum Morimundensium): '13. Petrus I, Coepit ann. 1183. ... Abdicat 1193. 16. Petrus I, qui cessarat, iterum eligitur. ... Obiit anno 1198. De eo multa et mira narrat Caesarius'. There is a German translation of this book, translated from the second French edition (Dubois, *Geschichte der Abtei Morimond*, 1855), in which the story of the ball game in hell is referred to on p. 135.

5. It is, perhaps, not altogether out of place to insist at this early point on the distinction made in the French language between the term *jeu de la paume*, which refers to the game, and the term *jeu de paume*, which refers to the tennis court.

6. See Douteil, vol. 1, pp. 30–2.

7. See *Beleth*, ibid., vol. 2, p. 223 (cap. 120a):

Sunt enim quedam ecclesie, ubi in claustris etiam ipsi episcopi uel archiepiscopi cum suis clericis ludunt, ut etiam descendant usque ad ludum pile. Et dicitur hec libertas ideo decembrica, quia antiquitus consuetudo fuit apud gentiles, ut hoc mense pastores et serui et ancille quadam libertate donarentur festa agentes conuiuia post collectas messes. Licet autem magne ecclesie ut Remensis hanc ludendi consuetudinem teneant, tamen non ludere laudabilius esse uidetur.

8. This story has here been retold after Lewis, pp. 64–7. In his edition, Lewis believed that the oldest extant manuscript of the romance was written around 1300 and that the lost original was composed about the middle of the thirteenth century; ibid., p. 224. The portion of the text dealt with here is reprinted (together with an English translation) in my article: 'The Origin of European Ball Games', pp. 39–41.

9. See *Antony and Cleopatra*, II, v, 3–7. All quotations from Shakespeare in this book follow the edition by G. Blakemore Evans; the text quoted here can be found on p. 1358.

10. See Riese, pp. 23–7. On the question of the date of composition see ibid., p. xvi, and Gruber in *Lexikon des Mittelalters*. vol. 1, col. 771 (under the entry *Apollonius von Tyrus*). The extract dealt with here is also reprinted, along with an English translation, in my article: 'The Origin of Ball Games', p. 36f.

11. See Seel, p. 24f., lines 185–90, and the commentary, ibid., p. 100f. On Roman ball games see also Wegner, pp. 15–20 (on *pila trigonalis*), Weiler, pp. 265–8 (on Roman ball games), and Lukas, pp. 88–100 (section 3.4.2 on ball games).

12. See Massingham, pp. 223–7 (The Origin of the Ball).

13. The book by the late Tom Todd, a pioneering study as far as the history of modern lawn tennis goes, may be quoted as a case in point, see Todd, pp. 11–16 (Chapter 1: From Pagan Head to Christian Ball).

14. See Henderson, *passim*. In a short article by the knowledgeable sports historian Erwin Mehl, Henderson's theory is rejected outright, see Mehl, 'Stammen die modernen Ballspiele', pp. 8–12. Henderson's ideas were adopted uncritically by Simri, in his article 'The Religious and Magical Function of Ball Games in Various Cultures', *passim*.

15. The French author de Luze also conceived of the Moors as intermediaries, but the game they transmitted, according to him, was the polo game of the Persians which, in turn, he said gave rise to tennis! This absurdity is rightly dismissed out of hand by Bombin, who represents the Spanish point of view, see Bombin, vol. 1, p. 373f.

16. See Decker, *Annotierte Bibliographie zum Sport im alten Ägypten*, *passim*, and, more recently, *Sport und Spiel im alten Ägypten*, pp. 119–24 (on ball games). On an Egyptian 'ball game' with a completely different function see Borghouts, *passim*.

17. On his Davis Cup career between 1900 and 1902, interrupted by his studies of law, see Whitman himself in an autobiographical note titled 'Net Play', *passim*.

18. See Whitman, *Tennis: Origins and Mysteries*, pp. 22–32 (Chapter II: The Origin of the Word Tennis).

19. See Metzeltin, p. 126. On the linen of Tinnis, which was used for turbans, caps and women's garments, see Gay, vol. 2, p. 393, s.v. *Tinnis*. Gay, who quotes from Arabic sources, also mentions the destruction of Tinnis by Al-Kamel in 1226.

20. In medieval ordinances the manufacturers of tennis balls are enjoined to use (sheep's) leather for the cover of the ball, see the ordinances published in d'Allemagne, p. 186 (Royal Ordinance of 1480 and the Ballmakers' Statutes of 1504). This practice persists in almost all the traditional games which are descended from the medieval game and which will be dealt with in the second chapter of this book.

21. See Hayakawa, p. 96f. (the chapter on 'Directives with Collective Sanction', 6), and the rather inadequate German translation of the book, pp. 130–2 (the chapter 'Weisungen mit kollektiver Sanktion', 6). It should be noted at this point that not only wedding ceremonies, but also the signing of other contracts and treaties was accompanied by equestrian games. This custom is illustrated early by the Strasbourg Oaths which occasioned simulated cavalry battles by the armies of

Charles II the Bald and Louis I the German, see Parisse, p. 179. A real host of examples from medieval literature of how sports and games served as a background for coronation oaths and nuptial vows has only recently been provided by Smithers, p. 168f. (Appendix C).

22. I am quoting from Mills, p. 149 (from the romance of *Sir Gowther*).

23. See Carew, p. 74f., who was quoted by Henderson, p. 86f. The Italian variety of football, Florentine *calcio*, also used to be practised on the occasion of weddings, although here the players were the sons of patricians who belonged to a different social stratum. See on this issue, with numerous examples, Magoun, 'Il gioco del calcio fiorentino', *passim*.

24. See Rambeau, pp. 16–26, and the translation of the passage into modern French by Langlois, *Adam le Bossu*, pp. 93–106. The passage is discussed in my study, 'The Flemish Ancestry of Early English Ball Games', p. 61.

25. See Howlett, vol. 2, p. 423: 'sui (i.e. Ricardus primus) quoque regni milites in propriis finibus exerceri voluit, ut ex bellorum sollemni praeludium verorum addiscerent artem usumque bellorum'.

26. See Molenaer, p. 404, lines 19–25.

27. On the term *tornei* (from the Old French verb *torneier*, 'to turn the horse') which, since about the middle of the twelfth century, not only meant 'warfare on horseback', but also 'sporting competition on horseback', see Mölk, pp. 163–74. English *joust* is a loan from medieval French where *jouste* (compare Latin *juxtare*, 'to position opposite to each other') denoted the clash of two riders.

28. What it meant to 'keep the pass' is well illustrated by the author of the medieval English romance of Richard the Lionheart (*c.* AD 1300) who describes a scene in which the English during the Third Crusade defend, under the command of Sir Fouke, one of the gates of an oriental city against Saracens trying to reconquer it:

Into the toun they wolde agayn.
Sere Ffouke and hys men theroff were fayn
The paas to kepe and to lette [= prevent
them from doing so].

Quoted from Brunner, p. 314, lines 4569–71.

29. See Horák, p. 96.

30. See Gougaud, p. 572, note 4, and the present writer's study 'A Tee for Two', p. 32, note 1.

31. See Schottus, *Itinerario*, after p. 23. A similar representation of football, on which a gate is being attacked, has also survived from Venice. It first appeared in Giacomo Franco's work *Abiti d'Huomeni et Donne Venetiane*, and in the eighteenth century served as a model for a painting by Gabriel Bèlla titled 'Giuoco Del Calzo Che Si Fa Nel Brissaglio a S: Alvise La Quaresima Al Quale Non Giuocavano Se no Li Gentil 'Huomini'. Today it belongs to the collection of the Pinacoteca Querini-Stampalia in Venice. Both pictures are reproduced and discussed in Mazzarotto, pp. 145–54 (chapter IX: Giochi sportivi). It is perhaps worth mentioning here that the famous Florentine game of *calcio*, first recorded in 1490, was played on the so-called 'Prato', a venue which was, significantly, situated in front of the city gate so named, see Artusi and Gabbrielli, p. 28. For a notable instance of medieval *soule à la crosse*, the variety played with a shepherd's crook on a spacious field in front of a city gate, from the last decades of the twelfth century see the present writer's article 'The Language of English Sports', p. 271.

32. The attitude of the medieval church towards sports and games has only recently been aptly described by Jean-Michel Mehl, compare his article 'Les autorités ecclésiastiques', *passim*. For an account of the views of Jewish religious instructors see Hanak, pp. 23–5. An earlier account is that by Simri, 'The Responsa of Rabbi Moses Provencalo (1560)', dealing, among other things, with the question of whether it is allowed to play tennis on Sabbath (ibid., p. 51f.; English abstract), and pp. 19–25 (in Hebrew). Simri writes: 'Rabbi Moses ... concluded that tennis could be played on Sabbath provided that the court was rented not for the Holy Day only, that no racquets were used (which is to say that the French-originated Jeu-de-Paume [*sic*] would be played) and that no heavy betting would take place.' (Ibid., p. 51.) Apparently, any game in which an implement or tool (such as a racket) was used, or a large sum of money was staked,

was liable to being considered work by which the Sabbath would be profaned.

33. See the rules printed in Dahlgren *et al.*, p. 3: 'Vid pärkspel, gammalt gotländskt bollspel, skall bollen slås med handen eller sparkas med foten.'

34. See Loomis, 'Richard Cœur de Lion and the Pas Saladin in Medieval Art', especially p. 526.

35. The story was told in a poem in Old French, see Lodeman, 'Le pas Saladin', columns 21–34; 84–96 (text); 209–29; and 273–81.

36. The Saracens are said to have used the ensign of the dragon as early as in the *Chanson de Roland*; see Schramm, vol. 2, p. 660. The Old French term for it was *vivre* (English *wyvern*).

37. The 'three leopards passant guardant' (in the language of heraldry) in Richard's shield started the tradition of armorial bearings at the end of the twelfth century, see Broughton, p. 420, s.v. *shield*; Richard's leopards were mentioned in the Middle English romance which carried his name, see Brunner, *Der mittelenglische Versroman über Richard Löwenherz*, p. 369, line 5709f.:

> On hys schuldre a scheeld off steel,
> With three lupardes wrought fful weel.

38. See Isaacs, p. xxi. On the etymology of *billiards* (the game did not, of course, originate in Spain), see below note 84.

39. See *Les jeux des jeunes garçons*, Figure XIX.

40. A notable early instance of the term *wicket* is found in the romance of Richard the Lionheart (*c.* AD 1300) dealing with the Third Crusade. Here the Saracens, in an attempt to recapture their lost city of Orglyous, are smuggled into the city through the *wicket* by a conspirator from inside:

> The Sarazynes they were alle withoute,
> And comen armed to the gate;
> ...
> They knokked on the wyket ...

(Quoted, with slight normalization of spelling, from Brunner, p. 302, lines 4258–4261.)

41. This picture is referred to, under the heading 'Games, Sports, and Pastimes', in Randall, who called the game in question handball (p. 105). Only this picture clearly illustrates medieval tennis. The remainder of the pictures listed here show rather unspecific ball games, e.g. British Library MS. Royal 10 E.IV (the so-called 'Smithfield-Decretals'), fol. 98v, and Cambridge Trinity College MS. B 11.22, fol. 11v. The picture from Bodleian Library MS. Douce 6, fol. 135, reproduced as Figure 336, could with equal justification be a pictorial representation of bowls.

42. For a pertinent introduction to the genre of the book of hours see now Plotzek, pp. 9–64 (bibliography on p. 64). Miniatures with sports and games mostly occur in the calendars which precede the book of hours proper. This peculiarity gives us a clue as to where and at what time of the year the games were played. Not infrequently, the names of the saints appearing in the calendar were especially popular in some specific geographical area, and the months under which the pictures appear indicate the time. The competitive game of *soule à la crosse*, for example, from which modern hockey evolved, normally came under the month of January, tennis mostly occurred under the month of June or (as an the indoor variety?) November. Hansen (p. 32) must be credited with having drawn sports historians' attention to the books of hours, but even he underrated the number of sporting pictures contained in them.

43. See Wieck, p. 80.

44. The two players of the second picture from the same source (Figure 11) who, perhaps, belong to the returning side also illustrate team-work.

45. See Mayans y Siscar, vol. 1, p. 387 (from the 'Leges ludi' of Vives' *Exercitatio linguae Latinae*): 'in Francia vero et Belgica luditur super pavimentum lateribus constratum, planum, et aequale'. When, in 1582, the Antwerpers built a tennis court for the Duke of Anjou they saw to it that it was provided with a tiled floor so that the Duke might play in the same way as in the Louvre, ('net als in het Louvre', see van Passen (1989), p. 52.

46. See Pasquier, p. 382 (Chapitre XV): 'en sa jeunesse ... ils ioüoient seulement de la main ... Et finalement de là s'estoit introduite la Raquette telle que nous voyons auiourd'huy, en laissant la sophistiquerie du Gand'. (The first

edition of the *Recherches* appeared 1560–1643.)

47. On the ancient court at Falkland Castle, which celebrated its 450th anniversary in 1989 and can be regarded as the oldest extant tennis court, see Puttfarken and Stuart. The court was built between 1539 and 1541 on the behest of James V after the manner of the variety of French courts called *jeu carré*. Its significant feature was the absence of a *dedans*. Because it was only rarely used, Falkland court hardly underwent any changes. It is therefore a precious relic of tennis history, much more so in fact than the court at Hampton Court.

48. See Guigniaut and de Wailly, *Recueil des Historiens des Gaules et de la France*, vol. 21, p. 663 (from the *Excerpta e memoriali historiarum auctore Johanne Parisiensi, Sancti Victoris Parisiensis canonico regulari*):

Sed dum haec agerentur, circa Pentecostem, rex frater suus (i.e. comitis Pictavensis), valde gravem aegritudinem incurrit in nemore Vicenarum, hoc modo, ut refertur. Cum sicut puer ad jactum pilae diu laborasset admodumque fuisset calefactus, indiscrete sequens sensibilem appetitum, in quamdam frigidissimam caveam est abductus, et sine mensura bibit vinum; frigus eum usque ad viscera penetravit, et statim decumbens in lecto obiit in vigilia Trinitatis.

49. See de Wailly and Delisle, *Recueil des Historiens des Gaules et de la France*, vol. 22, p. 163 (from the *Chronique rimée attribuée à Geffroi de Paris*, ibid., pp. 87–166).

50. See de Wailly and Delisle, op. cit., p. 26 (*E chronico anonymi Cadomensis*): 'mortuus est rex Ludovius, una cum filio suo parvo, per venenum ut dicebatur'.

51. See Shirley, *Here Folowing Begynnythe a Full Lamentable Cronycle of the Dethe … of James Stewarde, Kyng of Scotys*, p. 16:

the privay, that was all of hard stone, and none wyndow … therupon, save a litill square hole, … that at the makyng therof … was levid opyne to clense … the said privay. By the which the Kyng myght well escapid; bot he maid to let stop hit well iii dayes afore hard with stone, bicause that whane he playd there at the pawme, the ballis that he plaid withe oft ranne yn at that fowle hole, for ther was ordenyd withowt a faire playng place for the Kyng.

52. Why the match should have taken place in the moat is not clear; there was a tennis court in the castle itself shown on a print of *c.* 1500 reproduced in de Bondt, *Heeft yemant*, p. 23, Figure 6.

53. See de Mandrot, vol. 2, p. 380f.

54. See Gay, vol. 2, p. 213: 'Pour deux draps lons de Bruxelles achetés pour faire quatre paires de robes fourrees de menu vair, qu'il (le roy) bailla à certaines personnes ausquelles il les avait perdues au jeu de la paume, 144 esc.'. The fur of the grey squirrel was so expensive that the cloistered clergy was forbidden to wear it, see Benson, p. 807, note 194.

55. See Bentley (the items will be listed separately in the notes following). Henry's payments are also referred to by Marshall, *Annals*, p. 60f., who consulted the original records in the Public Record Office rather than Bentley's edition. The Duke of Norfolk was billed in 1464, as appears from *Manners and Household Expenses of England in the Thirteenth and Fifteenth Centuries*, p. 252: 'Item, the sayd day (i.e. the "xxvj. day of Marche") payd that my master lost at tenyse to Syre Robart Chamberley, … iiij.s.iiij.d' (From The Expenses of Sir John Howard, Knight, of Stoke by Neyland, afterwards Duke of Norfolk from November, AD 1462, to July AD 1469.)

56. See Bentley, p. 98.

57. Ibid.

58. Ibid., p. 101.

59. Ibid., p. 102.

60. Ibid., p. 108.

61. Ibid.

62. Ibid.

63. The Spaniard's name seems to have been Petir Malvesy, or Malvesey, who during the reign of Henry VIII (in 1520) was referred to as one of the Grooms of the Chamber, see Marshall, *Annals*, p. 60.

64. This 'Biscayen' is referred to in Arlott, p. 764, s.v. PELOTA. It is unfortunate that in publications of this kind no source should ever be given.

65. Saint-Germain, in his account of Picardian *balle au tamis*, p. 4, even went so far as to claim a Basque origin for it as well as for the majority of other ball games. In his opinion, the game was introduced into Picardy via Flanders by the Basque contingents of the Spanish occupational forces: 'Ce jeu, comme la

plupart des jeux de balle, est d'origine basque. Il a été importé en nos régions lors de l'occupation des Flandres par les Espagnols, par les Basques de l'armée conquérante.'

66. See Colas, p. 204, Figure 711. The inscription reads: CI . GIT . LE . CORPS DE MAISTRE . GVIEEM (Guillaume) . DIRIARTEVI . MOVRVT LE . 27 DE IVIEEET (Juillet) 1629. (Here rests the body of master William Diriart who died on 27 July 1629.)

67. See Charles Lewis, p. 64: 'mais à tous ceulx que il jeuoit il les sourmontait car il estoit en se jonesse apris de si fais (fais) pour luy deporter si qu'il affiert à fil de roy; mais sour tous les aultrez savoit il tant de la cache [= tennis] que il n'avoit sen parel en nul pays'.

68. See Furnivall, *The Three Kings' Sons*, p. 37: 'The kynge, for to assaie him, made Iustis & turneis/& noman did so wele as he yn rennyng, pleyyng at the pame'. For details on this romance see Severs, Fascicule 1, I. Romances, pp. 163–5 (bibliography p. 321b).

69. See Molenaer, p. 219. On the translation of *ludus pili* in the Latin original which became *pelote* in the French version, Molenaer remarks, p. 441: 'If the Latin text *ludus pili* [the genitive of *pilum*, "spear"] is correct, the translation *pelote* [= *pilotta*, diminutive of *pila*, "ball"] is wrong.'

70. See Coopland, vol. 2, p. 212: 'se tu joues a la paume un jeu ou deux; et que ce soit en lieu secret et non pas longuement, la chose se puet passer'.

71. See Bornstein, p. 11f.

72. See Robert Lucas, p. 13: (Les enhortements qu'on doit faire aux enfans des princes):

car dit le philosophe que cellui n'est mie sage qui n'entent des toutes choses; et aussi est bien fait que aucunes foys il exercice son corps en aucun labeur et travaille en aucun jeux si comme a la paulme aux barres et aultres jeux semblables, mais que se soit sans trop et que mesure y soit gardee a celle fin qu'il ne s'avachisse trop et devienge trop pesant et gourt par trop de repos et qu'il n'assemble superflues humeurs.

A late fifteenth-century English translation of this passage can be found in Bornstein, p. 32.

73. See Alston, fols. 98–103 (I, xxvii). The quotation is on fol. 99.

74. This important passage is quoted here from MS Royal 18.B.xv. in the British Library written, around 1598, by James himself. See on this Craigie in his critical edition of the text commissioned by the Scottish Text Society, pp. 186–8.

75. See Weigel, pp. 183–5.

76. See Weigel's preface to his *Abbildung der Gemein-Nützlichen Haupt-Stände* 'nach dem Leben gezeichnet und in Kupfer gebracht'. This holds good primarily for those pictures based on the sketches by his collaborator Georg Christoph Eimmart who had gone to the various Nuremberg craftsmen's shops in order to study their work and methods meticulously. Weigel presumably had first wanted to publish a German version of *Het Menselyk Bedryf* by the Dutch engravers Jan and Caspar Luyken whose plates he either borrowed or copied; but then he decided to give his description of the crafts a typically southern German touch, and employed Eimmart for the purpose, see Michael Bauer, *Christoph Weigel*, cols. 840 and 845f. It is in a way unfortunate that Caspar Luyken had provided Weigel with an engraving of a Dutch ballmaster, and Weigel therefore did not ask Eimmart to pay a visit to the local Nuremberg ballmaster Johann Georg Bender, who will be dealt with in Chapter 5, below. On the biography of Weigel, see Bauer, op. cit., cols. 751–791.

77. The Dutch engraver Caspar Luyken, had, along with his father Jan (1649–1712), brought out a similar work entitled *Het Menselyk Bedryf*. According to van Eeghen, Weigel copied 87 engravings from this work, and used another five from Jan and another eleven from Caspar Luyken which were altogether new. Among the latter, there was the picture of a ballmaster which, although it is not signed C.L. (as is the remainder of Weigel's engravings), must be attributed to Caspar on account of the sieve on which the ball was bounced before the service: this variety of the tennis game has never been played in Germany. For a detailed analysis of which pictures – Jan and Caspar Luyken's (original or copy), Eimmart's – went into the *Abbildung* or, for that matter, the *Etwas für Alle* by

Abraham a Sancta Clara (see the following note), see now Bauer, *Christoph Weigel*, cols. 1142–1158.

78. On the joint venture of the engravers Weigel and Jan and Caspar Luyken (who stayed with Weigel in Nuremberg for a long time around the year 1700), and the authors Hansiz, Faber and Abraham a Sancta Clara see Eybl, pp. 360–383, and especially p. 363. Weigel's co-operation with Abraham a Sancta Clara explains why his picture of the ballmaster should later have been included in a continuation of Abraham a Sancta Clara's book *Etwas für Alle, Das ist: Eine kurtze Beschreibung allerley Stand- Ambts- und Gewerbs- Persohnen (1899)* which appeared in 1711 (ibid., p. 69), see van Eeghen, vol. 2, pp. 407–18, especially p. 411, no. 10, and Bauer, *Christoph Weigel*, cols. 840–842, and 1143, no. 16, Ballmeister. This continuation, however, is not by Abraham, the Capuchin monk who served as a model for the famous preacher in Schiller's *Wallensteins Lager* and died in 1609, see Bauer, op. cit., col. 860f. and Krieg, p. 10.

79. On tossing in a blanket see Moser, pp. 282–4, and Endrei and Zolnay, p. 152 (both with illustrations).

80. See Cawley, p. 113.

81. Literary criticism in which this view is expressed is evaluated in my article, 'The Gift of a Tennis Ball'.

82. On the origin of the *noël* see, for instance, Gastoué, p. 109, 'Un genre, très français, de la poésie et du chant populaires, … sort directement, vers la fin du XVe siècle, des divertissements ou farces pastorales des mystères de la Nativité', and de Smidt, p. 36 'On n'a donc pas eu tort de voir dans de nombreux noëls … un débris ou un prolongement des Nativités dramatiques.'

83. See de Smidt, p. 104 (6th stanza).

84. From as early as the second half of the fourteenth century, there are numerous references, mostly in Royal letters of pardon (*lettres de rémission*), to 'grass billiards', a game owing its name to the curved stick (*billart*) with which it was played. See the excellent collection of original references to medieval games made by Vaultier, pp. 182–209 (Chapitre VI: Les Jeux), especially p. 185f. The oldest (and presumably unique) pictorial

representation of billiards played by shepherds on 'Mother Earth' forms part of a series of eight engravings entitled *Histoire fort plaisante de la vie pastorale et la fin d'icelle* (Bibliothèque Nationale, Cabinet des Estampes, shelf mark: Ed.5.g.rés., fol. 125v). These pictures were edited around 1585 by Jean Leclerc, a member of a dynasty of Paris engravers, of whom at least four went by the first name of Jean. The author would like to thank Madeleine Barbin, Conservateur de la Réserve, for information given on the provenance of this picture. A reproduction of it can be found in the author's article: 'Die mittelalterlichen Ballspiele', p. 87.

85. See Burchfield, vol. 3, p. 1090, s.v. *real*, a.2 4.e. A remarkable illustration of the use of the term occurs in an interview given by the German champion Count Voss in 1900, and printed in the English journal *Lawn Tennis and Croquet*, see 'A Chat', p. 469: [Interviewer] 'I believe you occasionally play tennis, I mean "real" tennis, as Mr. Mahony would say?' Here, not only do the inverted commas indicate that the term is a relatively recent coinage; it is also one of the rare instances in the history of languages where the originator of a word, namely the Irish All England champion of 1896 and Champion of Germany in 1898, Harold Sigerson Mahony, can possibly be pinned down. In the opinion of Baltzell, the inventor of the term *lawn tennis*, which was also meant to distinguish the new game from the old brand of tennis, was Lord Balfour, 'the last aristocratic amateur (unpaid) Prime Minister of Britain', see idem, p. 114, without naming his source. This, however, is very unlikely since the term lawn tennis was used as early as in the first official announcement of the game in the *London Court Journal* on 7 March 1874.

86. See Bouchel (Laurentius Bochellus), p. 1025f. (Book VI, Chapter 19: De aleae lusu, choreis, spectaculis, & aliis prohibitis.)
    Ex Synod. Lingon. 1404 Cap. 1.

Prohibemus Clericis & viris Ecclesiasticis, potissime in sacris ordinibus Constitutis, & maxime sacerdotibus & Curatis, ne omnino ludant ad taxillos, ad aleas, ad trinquetum, quod aliter nominatur ad punctum stacarij, neque ad cartos, neque ad stophum [this seems to be the Latin equivalent of Old French *esteuf*, '(tennis) ball'], dictum à la paulme, neque ad luctam, neque ad iactum lapidis, ad saltum, ad choreas, neque ad clipeum, neque cum fistula vel aliis musicalibus instrumentis, quibus cum ore seu bucha luditur. Non negamus quin cum cithara & organis seu huiusmodi aliis honestis chordarum instrumentis, in officio Ecclesiastico seu secreto in domo coram paucis causa cuiusdam consolationis possint aliquando, licet raro vti. Non ludant etiam ad marellas, ad bolas, ad cursum vel currendum in campo pro lucro, vel pro vino, ad iaculandum vel gladiandum, neque ludant ad quillas, vel torneamenta seu iostos. Summopere caueant sacerdotes & clerici, potissime in sacris ordinibus constituti, ne intersint neque ludant in ludo quod dicitur chareuari, in quo vtuntur laruis in figura daemonum, & horrenda ibidem committuntur: quem ludum non solum clericis, sed generaliter omnibus subditis prohibemus sub excommunicationis poena, & decem librarum Turonen. nobis applicandarum: neque etiam in ludis illis inhonestis, qui solent fieri in aliquibus Ecclesiis in festo fatuorum, quod faciunt in festiuitatibus Natalis Domini. Non ludant etiam ad ludum scatorum [possibly a misreading of *scacorum*, 'chess', owing to the difficulty of distinguishing the graphs *c* and *t* in medieval scripts], nisi forsan raro: quia quamuis sit ludus honestus & proueniat ex subtilitate ingenij, tamen magnam & inutilem requirit occupationem, & prolixitatem temporis.

(Excerpt from the Statuta Synodalia Lingonensis Dioecesis collecta & reformata per Ludouicum Cardinalem de Barro anno Domini 1404. Rege Carolo VI.)

87. See Moore, p. 85f.

88. Ibid., p. 101 (Article V). Whether a similar ban imposed on ball-players within the precincts of St Paul's Cathedral by the Bishop of London, Robert de Braybroke, in 1385 referred to tennis players (this has been claimed by some tennis historians without stating their source of information) is now perhaps impossible to ascertain. The only source, to the present writer's knowledge, is Dugdale, p. 16, who has the following wording: 'that no person whatsoever should defile it, or the church-yard, with piss or other excrements; nor presume to shoot arrows, or throw stones at crows, or any birds making nests therabouts; or to play at ball, either within or without it.' S. Freeth, of The Guildhall Library, kindly informed the author that the 'Liber G' from which Dugdale quoted

is no longer part of the documents transferred to the library from St Paul's. Tennis was also banned from the churchyard in the Instructions for Parish Priests by John Mirk (floruit 1403). In an Oxford manuscript of *c.* 1450 there is, in the margin of the text containing the tennis ban, a scribbled note: 'Danseyng, cotteyng [*quoits*], bollyng [*bowls*], tennessyng, hand ball, fott ball, stoil ball [= *stool ball*] & all manner other games out cherchyard.' See Peacock, p. 11, note 2.

89. See Fink, II 20. Fink could not explain the inscription above Veit Konrad's head which reads 'O mi rubuco zuge'. As a consequence, he marked it with a question mark. In the eighteenth century, Reichard, p. 118, also had difficulties with this text: 'Oben, gerade über dem Haupte des Schwarz, stehen in einiger Entfernung auf einem fliegenden Zettel annoch die, mir etwas unverständlichen, Worte: O – Rebuzo, Zuge. O schlaget doch den Geck zurück!' (Just above the head of Schwarz there are, on a flying banner, the words somewhat difficult for me to understand: O – Rebuzo, Zuge. Oh strike back the fool!)

90. The text is here reproduced from the edition of Dunstan, vol. 3, p. 119f. Later on in the text, Lacy insists on the delinquents receiving a citation to appear before him should their names be discovered: 'inquirentes nichilominus de nominibus et cognominibus huiusmodi delinquencium et in cimeterio predicto ad pilam in ludo huiusmodi vulgariter nominato *Tenys* ludencium, et si quos in hac parte culpabiles seu reos in hac parte reppereritis, citetis seu citari faciatis peremptorie eosdem quod compareant coram nobis'. (Ibid., p. 121.)

91. On the abbey of Marmoutier see Höfer and Rahner, vol. 7, column 100, s.v. *Marmoutier*, and, on the colleges of the University of Paris, idem, vol. 8, column 97, s.v. *Paris*, 3) Kollegien.

92. See Félibien and Lobineau, vol. 3, pp. 395–8 (Statuts du College de Marmoutier, An. 1390).

93. See Article XLIV of its statutes in Félibien and Lobineau, vol. 5, p. 670a/b:

Nullus ludat intra domum ad pilam vel ad crossiam [hockey played with a shepherd's crook after the rules of football] vel ad alios ludos insultuosos, sub pena sex denariorum, nec ad taxillos, vel qualitercumque ad pecuniam imbursandam, vel ad comessationes, sub pena decem solidorum; nisi aliquando & raro ad ludos honestos vel recreativos, pro pinta vel quarta vini seu fructibus, & sine grandi strepita atque mora.

On the foundation of this college see ibid., vol. 5, p. 662a/b:

antecessores nostri qui...collegium scolarium stabiliverunt ... Inter que unum speciale collegium supreme universitatis societate nobile membrum parisius in vico Cithare inter portam Ferri & palatia Termarum, ante cenobium fratrum minorum à parte orientali, in loco qui dicitur collegium Narbone, pro pauperibus scolaribus seu studentibus provincie Narbonensis fundaverunt.

On the date of the foundation see again Höfer and Rahner, vol. 8, column 97, s.v. *Paris*, (3) Kollegien.

94. See Höfer and Rahner, vol. 8, column 96, s.v. *Paris*, (3) Kollegien.

95. See ibid., column 95, s.v. *Paris*, (2) Universität.

96. See on this matter Orme, p. 62. As a rule, it was the second sons (often intended for an ecclesiastical office, although almost as often not entering upon this career later in life) who received their education in a monastery. See on this question Boehm, p. 155.

97. The plan of the monastery in St. Gallen, which became the blueprint for European monastery architecture, envisaged the locutorium – and, therefore, the *grille* – on the Western side of the cloister, see Badstübner, p. 19. Judging from the position of the *grille* in Renaissance tennis courts as well as in modern Real tennis, it was therefore the half adjacent to the Southern confines of the cloisters which was selected for playing purposes. This was a very sensible choice, since at the opposite end the precious stained windows of the monasterial church would have been under the constant threat of stray tennis balls.

CHAPTER 2

1. For a description of the game see Toulet, pp. 97–105.

2. This is a paraphrase of the descriptions given of the *jeu à dedans* and of the *jeu*

carré by de Garsault in his *Art du Paumier-Raquetier, et de la paume* of 1767, reprinted by Hermann, vol. 2, pp. 103–44.

3. See Bender, p. 22: 'man findet es [i.e. the plank] aber selten in einem Ballen=Spiel / dann kein Ballen=Spiel wie das ander gemachet'.

4. Bascetta in his critical edition of selected chapters from the *Trattato*, vol. 2, pp. 271–323 (illustration after p. 292), and the facsimile editions of the *Trattato del Giuoco della Palla di Messer Antonio Scaino da Salo*, p. 164f., and Scaino (1984), pp. 107–9 (part I, chapter XVI, the *Terza Figura*).

5. See Scaino (1984), p. 61f. (part I, chapter XXVII), Mehl, 'Antonio Scaino', p. 445 (on Scaino's chapters 26 and 27); and Bender, p. 25.

6. See Hermann, p. 109: 'Tout l'intérieur de quelque Jeu de Paume que ce soit, est peint en noir: les Maîtres Paumiers composent eux-mêmes ce noir: en voici la recette pour un Jeu de Paume ordinaire. Prenez un demi-muid de sang de bœuf, 14 boisseaux de noir de fumée, 10 amers de bœuf pour délayer le noir de fumée, & un seau d'urine pour donner de lustre à la composition; mêlez tout à froid.' The English translation is that by Catherine W. Leftwich, see Garsault, *The Age of the Tennis-Racket-Maker*, p. 7, § 23. On the question whether one of the ingredients should be urine or wine see ibid., p. iv.

7. That this was the case is suggested by the archaic Frisian *keatsen* and the Saterlandic game in which striking the ball back across the server's baseline (called *boppe*-stroke in *keatsen*) has the same function as the strike into the gallery in medieval tennis.

8. The Saterlandic game as well as Gotlandic *pärkspel* suggest that originally a chase could be laid only in one direction, in the area of the gallery attackers. At a later point in the evolution, chases could be made in both directions, as is demonstrated by modern Real tennis. In the Saterlandic game, the defenders (there was apparently no limit with regard to the number of players on either side) had to serve the ball, one after the other, across the *pork*, that line which marked the beginning of their opponents' playing area (the ball had to land behind the *pork* which was from twenty to thirty steps

from the so-called *steute* depending on the server's skill). In this playing area, every ball stopped after its second bounce was marked (*merk*, compare French *marquer*, English *to mark*). Only the *merk* most advanced into the opponents' territory was regarded as a chase (*katt*). If the *katt* was considered either too good by the defenders, or too poor by the servers, five points were conceded to the opponent. Whenever the quality of a *katt* seemed doubtful, the teams changed ends and contended it. The winner of the *katt* was again awarded five points. A strike beyond the server's baseline was worth ten points. In the West Frisian variant of *keatsen* and in Gotlandic *pärkspel* the park, which originally constituted the whole playing area, has degenerated into a comparatively small rectangle and its original function can therefore no longer be recognized. Yet it is still aimed at by the server. Generally speaking, the chase, in the opinion of the present writer, represents the tackling of the ball-carrying player in ball games such as rugby football and American football in which features of the medieval game are preserved. If this were true, this would be yet another parallel between medieval football and the varieties of medieval tennis.

9. See Roques, p. 52, lines 1712–1714.

10. See Archives Nationales (Paris), Série JJ. 84, fol. 389r:

Johannes dei gratia francorum Rex ... Que come ou temps passe quatre ans a ou enuiron Regnaut ... et fremin de beaumont demourons a corbie Jouassent ensemble a la paume en la dicte Ville de Corbie au quel Jeu eussent vne chasse en debat a Jugier la quelle chasse Jehan hunaut oncle du dit mahieu et cousin au dit pierre et thiebaut juga ... lorament Et pour ce que la dicte chasse fu Jugiee povre le dit fremin de beaumont huc de beaumont fils a Jehan de beaumont et neueu du dit fremin vint ... au dit Jehan Hunaut et li dist plusores laides ... paroles pour les quelles le dit Jehan hunaut ... feri le dit huc le quel huc auec plusores ses complices en ce propre moment et lieu battient ... le dit Jehan Hunaut vilainnement.

This letter, and another dealing with a similar dispute, is referred to by Vaultier, p. 186 (the above quotation is from a microfilm of the Archives Nationales). Vaultier was, of course, misguided when he claimed that the chase mentioned here was in medieval tennis some kind of service ('un document signale une chasse, c'est-à-dire à peu près l'équivalent d'un service de tennis').

11. See Halkin *et al.*, p. 166, line 1315.

12. See Macaulay, *The English Works of John Gower*, vol. 2, p. 490, line 295f.

13. See Champion, vol. 1, p. 144f., XC.

14. See above, Chapter 1, note 73.

15. This episode in Henry's life is referred to by Aberdare, p. 40f., who is quoting from the chronicler Hall for the year 1522.

16. See Mayans y Siscar, vol. 1, p. 388.

17. See Halkin *et al.*, p. 166, line 1310f.: 'Signa terminum testula aut rudere aut, si mauis, pileo tuo.'

18. See Mayans y Siscar, *Vives Opera Omnia*, p. 387: 'SCIN: Pilei sunt æstate leviores, in hyeme autem crassi, profundi, cum offendice sub mente, ne in agitatione vel elabantur ex capite, vel decidant in oculos.'

19. See Roetert Frederikse, p. 14: 'datmen de ... kaetsen teekent / onder tiden met sticx van steenen / of van teghelen / of met spaenderen / ondertiden met spuwe / ondertiden met eenighen anderen dynghen / dat de teekenaers of de kaetsers selve eerst vinden'.

20. This amusing detail of the Tuscan game was noted by Morgan, p. 191, note 11, who quoted from Bambagini, p. 73: 'mentre l'arbitro che segue il gioco con un fiasco di vino in mano, segna con uno sputo in terra il punto preciso ove avviene l'infrazione'.

21. 'Here we see a player just about to strike the ball,... behind him stands the figure of another player, or an instructor, ... seeming to direct him how to play; and, on the opposite side of the page, – separated from these by the upright inter-columnar ornament, of which I cannot but think the designer has taken advantage, to indicate some sort of intervening line, – stand two more players, with uplifted *palms*, ready to receive and return the expected ball.' See Marshall, *Annals*, p. 3f.

22. See Mayans y Siscar, *Vives Opera Omnia*, p. 338: 'habent funem tensum, ... sub funem misisse globulum, vitium est, seu peccatum'.

23. For an account of these paintings see Lugt, p. 86f. (No. 347). Painting E on Lugt's list, said to be in the possession of the Duke of Palmela, Lisbon, is now

owned by the London art dealer Richard Green.

24. This painting from the collection of Professor Carlo Emanuele Restelli della Fratta, Como, has been reproduced in Clerici (centre photograph in the left-hand row of three pictures on the second colour page after p. 40).

25. Besides the painting owned by Professor Restelli there used to be one from the collection of Ernst aus'm Weerth, a professor of the University of Bonn. It was last referred to in an auction catalogue of Lempertz of Cologne in 1913. Nothing is known about its whereabouts. Sales lists at Lempertz were lost during the war. The painting has however been reproduced in two catalogues of Lempertz, mentioned by Lugt, loc. cit., and by Gothein, vol. 2, p. 88.

26. See Marshall, 1895, p. 87: 'It is unfortunate that the third numeral of the date should have disappeared, but there can be little doubt that is was a 3.'

27. See Marc Geerarts' view of Bruges (detail) in his *Brugae Flandorvm vrbs et emporivm mercatv. celebre an a chr. nat. 1562*. The captions relating to the numbers 76 and 77 read: '76 La Cour du Prince.'; '77 La Monnaie' [= The Mint].

28. See Sander, p. 188 (detail). I am indebted to Dr Roger Morgan, Cambridge, for calling to my attention the two views of Bruges.

29. In the caption relating to this picture, number 11 tells us that the building in question is the 'Conchiergerie vant Caetspel', i.e. the one accommodating the personnel responsible for the upkeep of the tennis facilities.

30. Compare the letter of pardon issued by King John of France and referred to above p. 39f., and note 10.

31. Compare here and in what follows van Passen, 1989, p. 61f.

32. For a reference to tennis in Renaissance Hungary see Endrei and Zolnay, pp. 106 and 176.

33. See Mayans y Siscar, vol. 1, p. 388.

34. Quoted from Habenicht, p. 202, note on stanza 1084(B) *Thou hast stricken the ball, vnder the line*. This is the wording in Heywood.

35. This text offers a special problem. It only figures in Rabelais' last version which, corrected by the author himself, appeared in 1542. It is absent in both the first and the second edition of the work of 1534(?) and 1535 respectively. The intriguing question is that of whether the line was known in Lyons, where Rabelais lived, as early as 1534/1535, or whether he introduced it as a remarkable novelty in 1542. See for the text the critical edition by Calder and Screech, p. 314 (*Gargantua*, the end of Chapter LVI; the 1542 variant is printed at the bottom of the page).

36. See *Gargantua*, LVIII, 209.

37. See van Afferden, fol. 45r.

38. The expression is referred to in Blazy, p. 4.

39. See Frederikse, p. 5f.

40. See The Pierpont Morgan Library, p. 40: 'A Game of Hand Ball'. The description of the picture is also rather inadequate.

41. See The Pierpont Morgan Library, M. 456, fol. 68v.

42. See here and for what follows van Passen, 1988, p. 15f. Van Passen is quoting from the Assizes' Registers of the City of Antwerp (S.S. 106, 151v).

43. See ibid., p. 16: 'vanden muerkene teynden der voerss. [= aforementioned] Michils ... *caetspeele* gestrect vorwaert ter straeten waert vute'.

44. Ibid.: 'Wateble mocht voortan aan die muur timmeren, metselen, ankeren'.

45. The name of the proprietor, Wateble, is Northern French (= *wasteblé*, 'waste wheat'; it is a nickname for a miller; the Central French form *Gateble* is instanced in a document of the following year). The name is illuminating in that here a Frenchman seems to have married into a local family and tried to make a living out of a game which was extremely popular at least in his own native country.

46. See the book-length study by Bouissounouse, and the more recent article by Metken.

47. An attempt to locate the MS was made by Meurgy who wrote, p. 97: 'On y voit ... des joueurs de choule; or ce jeu était jadis répandu dans toute la Picardie. Ce sont aussi les saints de cette province, de l'Artois et de la Flandre dont on rencontre le plus souvent les noms dans le calendrier.' To Meurgy's mind, the miniatures were executed after the fashion of the famous miniaturist Jean Fouquet.

48. See Lewillie and Noël, p. 74f.

49. A similar rule has survived in some descendants of the medieval game, e.g. Basque *bote-luzea*, Belgian *kaatsen*, and, most notably, in the Saterlandic ballgame and Frisian *keatsen*. It has completely disappeared from Gotlandic *pärkspel*, and in the French *longue paume* where a strike beyond the camp of the server entails, on the contrary, the loss of fifteen on the part of the returner, see Michel, p. 281, and p. 294, article 1332 of the rules for the so-called 'partie à enlever' (a variant of *longue paume*) reads: 'Il est placé derrière le tiré [= service point] … une troisième lisière … qui se nomme *rapport*. Le rapport limite le jeu, et toute balle venant du rachat [= the returners' camp] dont le premier bond tombe sur cette ligne ou au délà, compte quinze pour le tiré.' Enclosed in the journal which published Buffard's article was a leaflet which contained a paragraph titled 'Principes et Combinaisons'. Here the rule was stated thus: 'Toute balle dépassant le tirer (en partie à terrer), le rapport (en partie à enlever) compte quinze à celui qui l'a envoyée.'

50. The picture is reproduced in Lewillie and Noël, p. 75. On the page preceding it, there are notes on the court at Brussels by Lewillie and, by his co-author Francine Noël, on the artist who had made Antwerp the centre of his activities.

51. Van de Velde's picture is a clear example of historicism: compare the much earlier painting by van Velen who took account of the innovations which time had brought about.

52. For a description of the picture see de Hoop Scheffer, p. 56, no. 168. The picture is reproduced ibid., p. 89.

53. See Noël in Lewillie and Noël, p. 234.

54. See Noël, loc. cit.

55. For an early account of this game see Scaino, pp. 99–102. If the painting really belonged to the sixteenth century it would be one of the earliest pictorial representations of the game. By far the oldest is that on a mid-sixteenth-century (*c.* 1554) fresco in the palace of the Duke of Ferrara, see Größing, p. 93f.

56. See Lewillie and Noël, p. 74. The palace had been built on the so-called Coudenberg in the fifteenth century by Philippe le Bon. In the course of the sixteenth century it was extended and embellished by Charles V and archduke Albert and Isabella. Its rather antiquated tennis court may well go back to the fifteenth century.

57. See Scaino (1984), p. 143f. (part II, chapter XLI), and Erwin Mehl, 'Antonio Scaino', p. 493. Scaino is here advocating the use of adequate tennis wear.

58. See Schulz, p. 63, 105.

59. See Scaino (1984), p. 56 (part I, chapter XXI), and Erwin Mehl, 'Antonio Scaino', p. 444 (on Scaino's chapter 21). A good description of the original *jeu de la longue paume* which still included a roof can be found in *La plus nouvelle académie universelle des jeux* of 1752, vol. 1, pp. 389–392. It proves that the theory which would assign to *longue paume* (without a roof) the role of the ancestor of tennis, and which is often repeated in histories of ball games, is contradicted by the facts. The game in the cloisters (i.e. one with a roof) gave rise to all others. See also the reference in de Bondt to tennis roofs standing in the open on 'public ways' as late as the second half of the seventeenth century, '*Heeft yemant […]*', p. 143, note 17.

60. For an overview of the main centres of the game after the turn of the century (1913) see M. Michel, p. 248f.

61. That the sieve might have served as a substitute for the roof was first suggested by Drost, p. 70: 'Hij, die den bal "opgeeft", laat hem eenige malen op de zeef vallen, om hem dan naar de tegenpartij te slaan. Het schijnt wel, dat men voor de zeef oorspronkelijk een dak of iets dergelijks gebruikte.' It may well be, however, that the sieve is a relatively recent invention (fifteenth century), preceded by solid surfaces such as the trunk of a tree (as in the very archaic Saterlandic ball game), or stone slabs (as in some Southern varieties of medieval tennis).

62. For an apt description of the server's task in the *jeu de tamis* see Mayer, p. 14f.:

Le tamis constitué de crins extensibles contribue à faire rebondir la balle en lui donnant un mouvement rotatoire. Il sert de point de départ au livreur et ajoute de la grâce au jeu. Le tamis effraie presque tous ses adeptes et il est un épouvantail pour les autres. A tort on le croit capricieux et vicieux, alors qu'il ne fait que suivre les règles de la physique élémentaire. ... Les différence dans le poids, dans la conformation, dans le jet des balles, dans le point de contact et l'inclinaison du tamis produisent chez le même livreur des différences de hauteur, de longueur, de vitesse et de la direction qui multiplient les aléas assez faciles à vaincre.

63. See Lecotté, p. 13. This little volume contains off-prints of articles which had previously appeared in the *Bulletin Folklorique d'Ile-de-France* (nos 2, 3 and 4 of 1946, and no. 4 of 1947). It was published in 1946 on the occasion of the Congrès sur les Divertissements et Jeux Régionaux. The reference to the oldest source of the *jeu de tamis* originates in an article by Roger Vaultier in the same volume entitled 'Le Jeu de Tamis (XVe au XXe s.)'.

64. The picture and its history are dealt with by Lewillie and Noël, p. 132f.

65. This picture is to be found in Lecotté's collection of articles, p. 12. See Figure 50 on p. 108.

66. See Hollstein, vol. 3 p. 106. P. van der Borcht IV, 469–472; 4 plates; 'Playing Monkeys', 'Le jeu des Singes'. For a reference to the artist who was born in Malines in 1545, where he was active until 1572, and died in Amsterdam in 1608, see ibid., p. 99.

67. Very typical of Flemish tennis scenes is the inclusion of a band of carousing spectators occupying a bench which is virtually on the court itself. This is well illustrated by the David and Bathsheba paintings which we have been discussing, but also by the picture from the German (?) student's *Stammbuch* (Plate 7). As will be remembered, the motif first occurred in the mid-fifteenth-century book of hours of Adélaïde of Savoy and its Portuguese equivalent (Plate 3 and Figure 27).

68. See de Borger, p. 119: 'Deze opslag moet gebeuren vanuit de opslagrechthoek (De "zeef" of "zift").'

69. See Breuker, *Keatserstaal*, p. 90.

70. Only Kalma, p. 86, included in his account the picture of a wooden chest (called *keats*) which was used for storing provisions by Frisian sailors and had a slanting lid. Since a similar chest is also found on a silver ball awarded as a trophy in *keatsen* contests in 1828, see Kalma, p. 87, the conclusion seems inevitable that it functioned as a service slab. The *keats*

has an intriguing parallel in the so-called *almud*, a wooden chest of very much the same shape used on the island of La Palma (in the Llanos de Aridane) for measuring grains. This serves as a makeshift service surface, see Navarro, p. 119, figure 2.

71. See Breuker, *Belgyska keatsers*, p. 37: 'Al liket it op grûn fan it boppesteande net útsletten, dat yn't foarige ek yn Fryslân it jeu au tamis gongber west hat, it definitive bewiis dêrfoar is net levere'.

72. Bröring, who characterized the game as a national game ('Nationalspiel'), stated in the first part of his work in 1897 that it had been played by young and old with enthusiasm fifty years before, but that it had fallen into disuse because his compatriots had taken to frequenting pubs and playing cards instead. What used to be the national pastime once was now the pastime of schoolboys at best, and Bröring clearly foresaw the day when it would fall into oblivion altogether (p. 132). Unfortunately, Bröring was proved right. When by 1935 the reply sheets for the *Atlas zur deutschen Volkskunde* had been collected, there were negative reports by the informants of Scharrel, Strücklingen and Ramsloh, the places representing the Saterland, relating to question 34 of the questionnaire: 'Are there traditional games?' Only the informant from Scharrel mentioned, and in fact described, a game played with a wooden bowl [*kuse*], and referred to by Bröring under the name of *gåtekaljen* or *Löcherkallen* (Bröring, p. 133). The informant called it *kuseschlon*, adding that it was rather a children's game. The collection of reply cards of the *Atlas* is now housed in the Institut für geschichtliche Landeskunde der Rheinlande in the University of Bonn. Sadly, those relating to traditional games have never been evaluated.

73. See here and in what follows Bröring, p. 128f. In Bröring's sketch of the playing area (ibid., p. 129) the printer apparently misplaced the expressions *buppe*, 'upwards', and *unner*, 'downwards', which ought to occupy each other's position. The error was tacitly corrected by Seitz, p. 402. The *buppe* area is the one nearer to the *steute*.

74. For a description of this game see Galtier, pp. 205–7.
75. See Guarinonius, p. 1210:

Das ander Ballspiel ist eines etwas grössern/lidernen/härten Ballns/wellichen man mit der Hand schlagt vnd wider schlagt/durch gantz Italien/vnd viler Orten Teutschlands/von daselbsten her bräuchig/meistens aber den groben/starcken Handwerckern/als den Edlen gemein/weil sollichem Spiel einer guten/starcken/vnd nicht zarten Hand bedürfftig. Inmassen den Spielern die Händ von solchem Spiel anlauffen/vnd wer sich vnter den empfindlichen vnd zarten hinein läst/der muß heymlich in die Hand vor Schmertzen blasen/oder mit Vnwillen vertuschen/vnd hat den Spott darzu/dann wer darzu den Handschuch brauchen wolte/der möchte nicht so hurtig vnd füglich den Ballen hinwenden/wohin er wolte/vnd durch subtilen Handschuch würde es ihme wenig helffen. Ich hab meines theils offt angebissen vnd versuchen wöllen/aber mir ist sollliches Spiel nicht anderst fürkommen/als da mir vor zeiten meine præceptores mit der hölzern ferula oder Pritschen zuweilen die Hand geraumt. Vnd weil bey sollichem Spiel wegen beyhengendem Handschlagen wenig Kurtzweil/hab ich mich dessen nie viel geachtet/der Anwurff geschicht auff einer stenigen Blatten/darauff man den Balln nider wirfft/vnnd im vberschnellen denselbigen von freyer Hand weit in die Lüften der andern Parthey/vnnd dieselbige widerumb dieser mit vnterschiedlichem lauffen vnd springen auff allen seiten/wie auch bucken vnd vbersich heben/zuschlagen/etc. biß so lang der Balln auff die Erd kompt/daselbst man das Zeichen macht/vnd das Ort oder den Stand verwechßlet/ist sonsten ein gute/starcke vnd frische Vbung/für Studenten aber/Organisten/Lautenschlagern/etc. gar nicht tauglich/dann es grobe/dicke/schwere händ macht/etc.

In this seventeenth-century account, the comparison by which the impact of the ball is likened to a preceptor's rod is highly instructive. It shows that the invention of the racket was simply inevitable. There is a scholarly and very funny discussion of the role of the rod in the schools and monasteries of the Renaissance by Zappert.

76. These games are aptly described by Blazy, pp. 186–99, and Bombin Fernandez and Bozas-Urrutia, vol. 1, pp. 1214–21.
77. See Blazy, p. 171: 'Dans quelques villages, comme aux Aldudes par exemple, le butoir est un plan incliné en pierre sur

maçonnerie adossé à un mur de maison qui forme le fond de la place.'
78. See Bombin Fernandez, p. 1215.
79. Ibid., pp. 1214 and 1218.
80. These games have been described by Millo and, more recently, by López Muños.
81. See Millo, p. 48f.: '*A rebote.* – Esta modalidad se practica más generalmente en las provincias de Castellón y Alicante. … *b)* El saque se realiza desde el centro del trinquete a un metro de la muralla, saltando la pelota en una banqueta inclinada, en el suelo o brazo'. Millo is quoting from the Rules codified for the first time in 1944 by the Secretaría Técnica de la Federación Española de Pelota with the assistance of sport historians and adepts of the game (see ibid., p. 45).
82. Here and in what follows the present writer is indebted to Navarro and Cabrera *et al.*, whose typescript was also made accessible to him by Navarro. In addition, there is now a useful little monograph by Auta, the emphasis of which is on the didactics of the game. It includes the Rules of the Game (ibid., pp. 69–71) as well as a Vocabulary (pp. 75–9).
83. See Navarro, p. 117 and p. 135, note 65.
84. Ibid., p. 117. The original name of the street was *La Carrera*, but eventually *Calle Pelota* was substituted for it, apparently because the street was constantly associated with the game played there.
85. See Cabrera *et al.*, p. 13:

Este [i.e. the service device] ha evolucionado con el paso de los años, en cuanto a su forma. En un principio era muy sencillo y rústico. Constaba únicamente de un paredón (cúmulo de piedras) con una laja encima algo inclinada. Poco después, este se transformó en un aparato de madera que tenía tres patas. … Más adelante apareció otro donde variaba unicamente el no de patas, se le añadía una pata más que proporcionaba mayor estabilidad al bote, siendo el bote más seguro, más fuerte y no campanea tanto.

86. According to Navarro, p. 120, who is here indebted to Auta, p. 17, these are, for one, the villages of Soo, Tiagua und Teguise, and, for another, those of Tinajo, Tao, Tahiche, Haría und Guatiza, names Navarro found in Cabrera, p. 5. The playing area is confined by two parallel lines (each from 60 to 70 paces long), the

distance between them being from 8 to 9
paces. There is no boundary line at either
end, but a middle line (called *raya de
falta*) dividing the area into two camps,
see Auta, p. 18f., and Navarro, p. 120.
The service ball in order to be good has to
be hit beyond it. After the service, it loses
its function altogether and the players of
either team may invade the opposite camp
across it, see Auta, p. 21. Chases are
referred to as *rayas*, the counting is similar
to tennis, namely 15, 30, 40, 50. A game is
called *chico* (an expression also used in
colloquial Spanish to denote a game in
billiards; author's note) and the score is
recorded by means of strokes in the centre
of the middle line (where a stone indicates
the spot). Five *chicos*, enough to win the
match, constitute a *pajero*, literally 'a hay
stack'. A *pajero* is marked by drawing a
semi-circle round the *chicos*, see Auta,
pp. 42–6. In the centre of the *raya de falta*,
too, in earlier days the wagers were
deposited in the form of smaller coins, see
Navarro, p. 127. Points may be scored
either by faulty service (whenever the ball
fails to travel across the *raya de falta*); by
strokes which cross the side boundaries
without having bounced in the playing
area; by strokes which fail to be parried by
the last player; and by chases won, etc.,
see the faults (*faltas*) listed by Auta,
p. 69f., and idem, p. 58f. (Forma de
Ganar la Raya). The returning or
defending side (*equipa que defiende*)
consists of three agile forwards positioned
immediately behind the *raya de falta*. They
are known as *jugadores de vuelta* or
jugadores de falta (right and left) and
jugador de medio. To their rear, there is
the *jugador de tercio* (compare the term
tiers in the French *jeu de la longue
paume*). The last position is occupied by
the most reliable hitter of the team, the
jugador de salto; his antagonist at the far
end of the other camp is the server, called
botador, see Auta, p. 36f., and Navarro,
p. 125, figure 6. The game is played on
late Sunday afternoons, after the
scorching heat of the day, the morning
being the time of the Divine Service, see
Navarro, p. 127. A characteristic beverage
consumed between matches is the so-
called *ponche*, 'punch'; it is made of three
litres of water, one litre of rum, lemon
peel, a package of cinnamon and sugar

(Cabrera, *et al.*, p. 26, and Navarro,
p. 138, note 105).

87. See Bolaños Cacho, p. 11 [Regla IV,
Inciso 5]: '"Botadera" es la piedra plana
en una pequeña rueda aplastada [i.e.,
presumably, a small circle on the bare
ground made level] al efecto, de donde se
hace el 'saque'.' And further on, p. 15
[Regla V, Inciso 2]: 'la botadera que es
una piedra plana que tiene un diámetro
más o menos de treinta centímetros'.

88. See the preface to the Rules of the Game
by Bolaños Cacho, director of physical
education of the State of Oaxaca, p. 5f.:

Las tribus pobladoras del Estado de Oaxaca no
permanecieron ajenas al desenvolvimiento des
esas creaciones [ie. the creation of ball games
which had the roots in the Indians' worship of
the sun], y así, al florecer la gran Cultura
Mixteco Zapoteca, apareció la actividad
deportiva conocida con el nombre de 'PELOTA
MIXTECA' actividad autóctona que hasta la
actualidad viene siendo practicada por nuestra
población indigena … Uno de los errores más
grandes que hemos cometido, radica en que
nos olvidamos de nosotros mismos, en mucho
se desconoce el pasado histórico deportivo de
México, vivimos familiarizados con desportes
extranjeros. Esto es muy conveniente, pero
triste es que conozcamos de Básquetbol,
Fútbol, Volibol, etc.; que es cierto que son muy
buenos, pero no son representativo de nuestro
desenvolvimiento americano.

89. The term *botero* for the place from which
the service is executed is also used in
Ecuador, although the implement itself
does not seem to be known, see Weichert,
p. 224. The situation is here similar to that
in Flemish *kaatsen*.

90. See Stern, p. 74:

The Zapotec dictionary of Córdova [i.e. J. de
Córdova, *Vocabulario Castellano-Zapoteco*,
Mexico, 1942] indicates clearly that a Spanish
ball game was introduced early in post-
Conquest times in the region of Oaxaca and
that it had become known to the Indians.
'Pelota mixteca' in all probability bears strong
traces of that game. In particular, the use of a
wool-stuffed leather ball as an alternative to the
solid rubber ball, the protection of the hand
with a leather gauntlet sometimes reinforced by
a studding of nail heads, the lay-out of the
court and the appearance of what appear to be
chases in play, and the method of scoring,
proclaim European origin. Nonetheless,
aboriginal traits may also be retained. Acosta
and Moedano Koer have indeed pointed to an
analogy between the level disk on which the

server bounces the ball in service and the alley markers of the Maya courts.

91. See Swezey, *passim*. Swezey's sums up his view in the following way: 'As to the antiquity of this game, in this author's opinion, the uniqueness of the equipment, the complexity of the rules, and the evident geographic location, i.e. Oaxaca, strongly indicate Pre-Conquest roots' (p. 471). Swezey describes the service in the following way: 'The ball is placed in motion by a specialist who by dropping the ball against an inclined serving stone smacks it with an underhand motion on its first bounce' (p. 472). He then goes on to detect a similarity between the service disk used in pelota Mixteca and a circular stone discovered in the ball court of Monte Alban: 'A ... similarity ... between the serving stone of the Pelota Mixteca and the circular stone uncovered in the center of the ball court at Monte Alban' (p. 473). Strangely enough, even Taladoire, the French archeologist who might have been better informed about the traditional games of his own country, in a more recent article rules out a European origin of the game: 'Los rasgos de este juego se van entonces muy diferentes de los juegos de origen europea, a pesar de ciertes semejanzas con el Volley-ball (el saque), o el tennis (los tantos). Es necesario, por consiguente buscar una origen local' (Taladoire, p. 433). On the religious ball games of Ancient America see Leyenaar and Parsons, *passim*; on the circular boundary markers (*marcadores*) see ibid., p. 97.

Although Swezey's views on the origin of *pelota mixteca* are misguided, his description of its spread and his characterization of its practitioners (p. 471) is nevertheless quite accurate: 'Pelota Mixteca is played today in the states of Oaxaca, Puebla, Veracruz and the Federal District. The game is played by Oaxaqueños, both of Mixtec and Zapotec speech, who have left their native state and have relocated. Very few, if any, non-Oaxaqueños participate in this strenuous and frequently dangerous sport.'

Professor Malina's comment, in a letter to the author, on Figure 42 was as follows:

The illustration ... is from the Zapotec-speaking community of Santiago Ixtaltepec (population of 495 in 1970). ... The photograph was taken in the summer of 1971 on a Sunday when the village was having a competition with men from another village. The name of the visiting community excapes me, although I think it was San Mateo Macuilxochitl (population of 1796 in 1970) which is across the highway from Santiago Ixtaltepec. I do recall, however, that they were celebrating the village's saint's day, which called for a special celebration, including the competition. The participants are *campesinos* (peasants) who are essentially subsistence farmers. They are not, to the best of my knowledge, formal teams that represents [*sic*] the villages in organized competitions. I have the impression the competitions are situational related to various celebrations. Some wagering among participants and spectators probably occurs. ... I also observed the game in the suburbs (*colonias*) of the city of Oaxaca (I do not recall the field season), and in a community in the Etla wing of the valley (Huizo) in the summer of 1968.

92. In addition, a rubber ball is used, see Bolaños Cacho, p. 9f. [Regla II, Inciso 1]: 'Se usan pelotas de dos clases, las de "forro" y las de "hule". Las primeras están de hilo, lana y estambre, forradas de gamuza [= English *chamois*, 'sheep leather']; las segundas son de hule duro, fibra o hule blando.'

93. According to Bolaños Cacho these gloves were rarely used in games with balls stuffed with wool (*pelotas de 'forro'*), but mostly in games with the rubber ball. This is borne out by Figure 43 where the player clearly holds a rubber ball. See Bolaños Cacho, p. 10 (Regla II, Inciso 3): 'cuando se juega con pelota de "forro" son pocos los jugadores que usan el guante.'

94. For the sake of documentation, the chase rule of *pelota mixteca* will here be quoted in full from the Rules as laid down by Tomás Pérez Bazán and Adulfo Manterola (ibid., p. 6):

Cuando la pelota sea detenida porque haya dado dos botes o venga arrastrando, es decir 'de malas', entonces se pintará una raya como de medio metro, perpendicular a los escases paralelos, lo cual quiere decir que el jugador ha logrado obtener una ventaja para su partido hasta ese lugar, a fin de que al cambiarse los jugadores ... la lucha por dominar a los contrarios tenga el límite de la raya pintada. Cuando durante el juego se hacen dos rayas, o cuando uno de los bandos tiene en su contabilidad cuarenta y se hace una raya, inmediatamente se cambian los jugadores que

esteban en el saque, al campo del resto y
viceversa, para disputarse desde luego las dos
rayas o la raya hecha ... a fin de ganar el tanto.
Al hacerse el cambio, los contendientes tratarán
de dominar a sus adversarios ..., procurando
que la pelota no sea detenida por sus
contrincantes sino después del lugar en donde
está pintada la raya, para poder ganar el tanto.

In addition to the Rules by Bolaños Cacho
there is a third set of regulations (it is, in
fact, the earliest) by a certain Espiridión
Peralta (reprinted in the present writer's
study, 'The Dissemination', pp. 31–3). It is
couched in a rather clumsy Spanish and
very difficult to understand. Its title is
Juego de Pelota. Reglamento, and it is
dated Oajaca de Juarez, Julio 29 de 1903.
It contains 32 articles or rules, printed on
a broadsheet, and deals mainly with the
duties of the so-called *coime*, the players'
wagers and rulings for the more unusual
events during a match: the rules are
clearly meant for the insider who already
knows the game well. The term *coime*, a
Mexicanism, was labelled obsolete in the
dictionary of Icazbalceta as early as 1899
where it refers to the game of billiards, see
Icazbalceta, p. 109: '*Coime. m. Mozo
que en el juego del billar arma los palos y
tantea*', 'servant who in the game of
billiards sharpens the cues and counts'.
Nevertheless, the term is frequently used
in the rules of Bolaños Cacho in
connection with the duties of the umpire
(*chacero*), and it looks as if the task of the
chacero and the *coime* overlapped to a
certain degree. Whereas, generally
speaking, the *chacero* seems to have
functioned as umpire, the *coime* was
somebody who ran a (commercial) ball
court (*patio*), or who was the owner and
whose duty it was to provide the umpire,
see Bolaños Cacho, p. 28 (Regla IX, Inciso
1):

Se llama Chacero a un individuo que a petición
de los jugadores o proporcionado por el coime
o dueño del patio, sirve de Juez o sentenciador
de todas y cada una de las jugadas
comprendidas en el partido, el cual a la vez
llevará la contabilidad de los tantos o 'quinces'
que cada grupo vaya tomando en su juego.

95. See Ortiz, p. 85: 'se marca un punto ...
con una piedra o otra señal y se llama
saque.' The article by Ortiz is conveniently
reproduced in Jaramillo, pp. 77–80. For
an account of the same game as played in

the town of Otavalo (where it is still
played with the palm of the hand), and a
permanent exhibition of pelota by-gones
in the Casa de la Cultura Ecuatoriana in
the town of Latacunga near Quito see
now van Mele, p. 63f., and, on the
varieties of the game played in Ecuador
generally, the article on 'Pelota Nacional'
(!) by Wilson Dalgo and Jorge E. Vinueza
P. (in Weichert, pp. 220–5). Of course, the
statement of these authors ('El señor Luis
G. Tufiño manifiesta que el juego de
pelota, tal como se acostumbra en el
Ecuador, es el deporte clásico que
tenemos, y, al parecer, estrictamente
nacional') is in need of revision.

96. See Ortiz, p. 85: 'Estas lineas paralelas
llamadas *cuerdas* en la jerga de los
jugadores, se marcan en el terreno, ya sea
con una herramienta apropriada para
hacer un surco ligero o por medio de
pedrezuelas a cáscaras que permitan ver
distintamente una línea perfectamente
marcada.' The expression *cuerda* denoting
the lateral boundaries is also instanced in
Peralta's rules of *pelota mixteca* (today
they are normally referred to as *escases
laterales*). This is final proof of the
European origin of this game, if indeed
such a proof were needed.

97. See Diffloth, p. 558.

98. The term *cuerdas* is also used in the
various forms of the ball game of Ecuador,
see Weichert, p. 224.

99. See Windeatt, p. 376 (Book IV, line 460).

100. This meaning of *raket* has been adopted
for the new (second) edition of the
dictionary, see Simpson and Weiner,
vol. 13, p. 80, s.v. +racket. sb.1 ... [Etym.
obscure.] Some game played with dice.
The mistake of the *OED* is noted by
Benson, p. 544, line 460, and p. 1046,
note on line 460: '*raket*: Surely "rackets,"
a form of tennis or handball played off
walls, like squash. ... The *OED* wrongly
deduces from a citation in Lydgate that it
was a dice game.' Benson may well have
made the right guess since the quotation
from Lydgate is printed immediately after
that from Chaucer, but the mistake may as
well have been suggested to the editors of
the *OED* by an entry in Du Cange, vol. 5,
p. 149, s.v. 2. *LUDUS*. The Chaucerian
expression *pleyen raket* was imitated by
his contemporary Adam Rusk in his

Testament of Love, see Skeat, *Chaucerian and Other Pieces*, p. 13 (I, 2, line 166).

101. See Mary, p. 203:

> *Item,... vint à Paris une femme nommée Margot, assez jeune, comme de vingt-huit à trente ans, qi estoit du pays de Hainaut, laquelle jouoit le mieux à la palme que oncques homme eust veu; et avec ce jouoit devant main et derrière main très piussamment, très malicieusement, très habilement, comme povoit faire homme; et pou venoit d'hommes à qui elle ne gagnast, se ce n'estoit les plus puissants joueux [sic]; et estoit le jeu de Paris où le mieux on jouoit en la rue Grenier [this is the contemporary spelling of Garnier, see Franklin, vol. 2, p. 552, s.v. Paumiers]-Saint-Ladre, qui estoit nommé le Petit-Temple.*

102. See Verdon, p. 166. Charles V of France (1338–1380) possessed a court in the Hôtel Saint-Paul and had another built in the Louvre, see Franklin, vol 2, p. 552, s.v. *Paumiers*. Another commercial tennis court in the province is referred to around the middle of the fifteenth century. It was located in Béthune and its owner made such a profit that the Duke of Estampes claimed his share which, in turn, he diverted to one of his favourites, see La Fons, Part 2 (1851), p. 530.

103. For an account of this romance see Severs, p. 58f., and p. 244 (bibliography).

104. The title 'King of Man' does not imply that we have before us the ruler of the Isle of Man. It is purely fictitious, and the king is described as a muslim sultan eager to pick a bone with a bishop called Bodwine who, he says, has overmuch preached on a crown of thorns, see Williams, p. 90, lines 154–7.

105. See Williams, pp. 90–3, lines 151–88, and Furnivall and Hales, vol. 1, p. 96f., lines 151–86. Williams provides a summary in Modern English on pp. 12–21. Of the three final lines of the tennis episode, the last is based on conjecture:

> *The ball of brasse was made for the giants hand*
> *there was noe man in all England*
> *were able to carry it.*

Well before the incident, the Turk (in what may be called an instance of epic prediction) had called attention to the colossal ball, see Williams, p. 90, lines 140–142:

> *thou shalt see a tenisse ball*
> *that never knight in Arthurs hall*

is able to give a lout.

Here *lout*, literally meaning 'inclination', 'bend', must be translated by 'turn (on the ground)'. To judge from the order given by the king ('goe feitch me forth my tenisse ball', see Williams, p. 91, line 173), the tennis ball belongs to him.

106. See Arlott, p. 756, s.v. PELOTA.

107. See Baksh, p. 32.

108. See Halkin *et al.*, p. 164f., lines 1274–6: 'NICOLAVS. Minus sudabitur, si ludamus reticulo. HIERONYMVS. Imo reticulum piscatoribus relinquamus. Elegantius est palma vti.' This edition of the *Colloquia*, printed in Basle by John Froben in March 1522, is the first to contain the tennis dialogue.

109. See Mayans y Siscar, vol. 1, p. 388.

110. See *Much Ado*, III,2,47: 'and the old ornament of his cheek hath already stuff'd tennis-balls'.

111. See Grosart, *The Non-Dramatic Works of Thomas Dekker*, vol. 2, p. 227.

112. See Mayans y Siscar, vol. 1, p. 387: 'SCIN. ... sphaerulas minores vestratibus, et multo duriores, ex corio albo: tometum est, non ut in vestris lanugo e pannis tonsa, sed pili fere canini: eamque ob causam raro luditur palma.'

113. In the sixteenth and seventeenth centuries, six patches of sheep leather seem to have gone into the cover of Dutch tennis balls which were stuffed with calves' hair, see de Bondt, 'De kaatsbanen', p. 94, note 49.

114. See above note 93.

115. See note 112, above. In the earliest statutes of the paumiers' (proprietors of tennis courts's) guild of 1408, it is stipulated that the balls should be made of good leather and good [wool] stuffing and that each should weigh seventeen sterling: 'de bon cuir et de bonne bourre, et chacun d'iceulx peser dix-sept estelins', see Franklin, vol. 2, p. 552, s.v. *Paumiers*. Besides giving tennis lessons, the master paumier's daily routine included the manufacture of balls and later that of rackets.

116. See Charles Lewis, p. 120f.

117. Ibid., p. 64.

118. See Ortiz, p. 86.

119. As for the meaning of the term *chuspilla*, Yolanda Mora de Jaramillo of the Instituto Colombiano de Antropología in Bogotá had to say the following:

En lo que se refiere al significado de la palabra 'chuspilla', estuve consultando con un colega nacido en el Departamento de Nariño. Aunque fué jugador de la chaza durante su juventud, no pudo decirme más que la palabra es el diminutivo de 'chuspa', voz quechua, muy usada actualmente en Colombia, y que quiere decir *bolsa, pequeña talega*. Pero no supo encontrar una relación directa entre el significado estricto de la palabra y su uso en el juego.

The meaning of the term *tranquilla*, which refers to the line dividing the court in two halves, also escapes us. It seems to exist in colloquial Colombian Spanish only where it means 'obstacle', 'hindrance', see the *Wörterbuch der regionalen Umgangssprache in Lateinamerika*, p. 607, s.v. *tranquilla* f.

120. See Champion, vol. 1, p. 114f.

121. See Galtier, p. 206.

122. See Diffloth, p. 558, and de Borger, p. 118f.

123. See Morgan, p. 185, and p. 181, figure 8.

124. See Michel, pp. 287–9. This applies to the so-called *partie terrée* or *partie à terrer*, whereas the so-called *partie enlevée* or *à enlever* is a four-a-side game.

125. See the sketches in the rules book by Dahlgren *et al.*, *Pärkspelet*. However, the number seven seems to have originated in more recent times. In a written challenge (called wagering letter) in the town archives of Visby from the year 1820, reference is made to five players on either side, see the author's article 'Den skriftliga utmaningen', p. 34, letter no. 1.

126. See Bröring, p. 129: 'Die Anzahl der Spieler konnte beliebig groß sein wie bei dem heutigen Kegelspiel.'

127. See Frederikse, p. 2f.: 'drie kaetsspeelders beroupen hebben een spel ende hebben gheseyt te wederstane alle andre wye hem lieden up comen willen in ghelike ghetale'. Here, the emphasis laid on the egality of number mirrors a good old tournament convention. Dividing a tournament gathering in two numerically equal teams was referred to by the French term *partie* (from the Latin feminine participle *partitam*) whence the expression *faire une partie de tennis* (etc.), 'to play a game of tennis'. A very good example of the tournament custom comes from Chaucer's *The Knight's Tale* which culminates in a tournament. Here, under the leadership of Palamon and Arcite

respectively, one hundred knights on either side face each other, and in order to rule out manipulation of any kind the names of the competitors have to be read aloud, see Benson, p. 60, line 2595f.:

[...] *hir names rad were erverichon,*
That in hir nombre gyle were ther noon
[...].

Against this background, the match between Gawain and the giant team of the King of Man, in which the Arthurian knight has to deal with no fewer than seventeen opponents, is therefore decidedly unchivalric and unfair.

128. Quoted from Jusserand, p. 143.

129. See on this the chapter 'Gotländskt våg' in Nyberg, pp. 6–14, and, more generally, the author's article 'Den skriftliga utmaningen', *passim*. On the written challenge in the chivalric tournament see now Barker, p. 97f., and the author's article 'Challenge Letters'.

130. See Ortiz, p. 85: 'Los jugadores entre sí se invitan a jugar un *partido*.' On a similar challenge in the Mixtecan ballgame see below, note 136.

131. See van Torre, p. 180. The author here wishes to express his gratitude to the library of the Rijksuniversiteit Limburg in Maastricht for having provided him with extensive copies from this rare work.

132. See here and in what follows Kalma, pp. 82–5, and, more recently, Lolkama, p. 17. The verb *uitdagen*, 'to challenge', appears for the first time in a work already referred to, Pieter van Afferden's *Tyrocinium*: 'Prouocare aliquem pila palmaria/yemandt wt daghen int caetsen.' See de Tollenaere and Claes, fol. 40v.

133. See Mak, *De Gedichten*, p. 278, note on line 4: 'Den bal to slane te kolven'.

134. Ibid., p. 279f., 5th and 7th stanza (left column).

135. See Kalma, p. 84.

136. This Frisian challenge has a remarkable parallel in the procedure followed as late as around the turn of the century in the Mixtecan game, see article 29 of Peralta's *Reglamento* reprinted in the present writer's article, 'The Dissemination', p. 33: 'Si en algun patio desafiaren algunos partidos de compromiso, le deben participar al coime para que sepa quiénes son los compañeros de uno y de otro, y si le dan á depositar dinero les deben decir,

de á como son los partidos y en qué lugar los van á jugar y á qué hora.'

CHAPTER 3

1. See Molenaer, p. 404f.
2. Ibid., p. 405, lines 9–17 (author's italics):

> Dont il avient que quant *cil de hors* le chastel prennent aucun de *ceus de denz*, il ne les tuent pas, ainces lor coupent aucuns membres par coi il sont non puissanz et neent profitables a *ceus de denz*, et les renvoient a ceus du chastel por cen que il manjucent oveques les autres du chastel, por cen que lor viande lor faille plus tost, et aient plus (et) tost soufrete et mesese.

3. See Vinaver, vol. 2, p. 981, lines 6–16. [Book xvii, Chapter i.] The passage is quoted by Hellenga, p. 78.
4. See ibid., pp. 981–2, lines 31–4.
5. 'In the fifteenth century, … the distinctive form of the sport was the *pas d'armes*, in which individuals or teams proclaimed their intention to defend a given place against all comers.' (Barber and Barker, p. 107.) These fifteenth-century passages of arms are aptly described by Barber, pp. 107–38 (Chapter 5: The Late Medieval and Renaissance Tournament: Spectacles, Pas d'Armes and Challenges).
6. See Hellenga: 'The tournaments in Malory do not reflect the customs and practices of his own day but of the period in tournament history between the pitched battles of the twelfth century and the pageants of the fifteenth.'
7. See on this point the excellent article by Parisse, p. 195f. (with numerous examples from literary sources, including the one here quoted from Chrétien's *Perceval*).
8. In what follows I am quoting from Hilka. There is a good translation of the text into modern French by Foulet.
9. See Jusserand, p. 132: '«Tenir le pas» était le fait des défenseurs ou «tenants», qui repoussaient l'attaque des «venants», de «ceux de dehors»'; and ibid., p. 144: 'Le jour d'ensuite [at Sandricourt], les chevaliers «tiennent le pas» contre tous venants. A la «huitième course», s'est présenté monseigneur de Saint-Vallier de dedans contre Marcillac de dehors'.
10. See Gay, vol. 2, p. 207.
11. On the importance of this work from the historical and lexical viewpoint see the foreword in Henry's critical edition: 'le Roman du Hem est un document historique de tout premier ordre, que certains médiévistes, Ch. v. Langlois entre autres, n'ont pas manqué d'exploiter largement. Enfin, le Roman du Hem offre des vocables dignes de retenir l'attention du lexicographe'. On the date of composition and the personality of the author see Henry, pp. xliv–xlvii. On the contents, see Henry, pp. ix–xiii; Michel, pp. xlv–lj; Gröber, p. 767f., and Barker, p. 88.
12. See Henry, p. xii: 'le mot *roman* n'a d'ailleurs ici que son sens primitif: composition en langue vulgaire. Une seule expression, fort anachronique il est vrai, pourrait, semble-t-il, caractériser avec exactitude le *Roman du Hem*: c'est un «reportage en vers» qui a la valeur d'un document historique.'
13. See Henry, p. lii:

> au XIIIe siècle, les lieux se présentaient de la façon suivante: la rivière, à quelque distance un château et, entre les deux, une petite plaine. N'était-ce pas un endroit tout désigné pour l'organisation d'un tournoi? … Une petite plaine, fermée d'un coté par une forêt ou une rivière, de l'autre par les murs d'une ville ou d'un château; sur les deux derniers cotés, on dressait des barrières de bois et, au dehors, étaient tendus les pavillons des jouteurs. Tout cela, on le trouvait au Hem.

As for the term *château*, the editor quotes the lines *Le bel castel de Hem sour Somme* (469), and *li castiaus et li pars* (4477).
14. See Henry, from whose edition all subsequent quotes have been gleaned, p. 110, line 4009 (Michel, p. 361, line 16): 'Il [Huart de Basentin] vint droit de devant la porte'; and lines 4020–5 (Michel, p. 362, lines 1–5): 'Mesire Kex … et autre … Monsigneur Huon en amaient Devant la porte du castel'. The castle confining the tournament lists at one end could also on occasion be made of canvas as has been pointed out by Barker, in a study based on meticulous evaluation of original source material:

> Castles were a popular piece of scenery since they could be attacked and defended, they could house captured damsels who had to be rescued by jousting in the lists, as at Le Hem, or they could serve as a station at the end of the lists from which the jouster would emerge. It is even possible that the canvas castle was the sort of Round Table house or tent often referred to in romances, in which the feasting after the

hastiludes and other games took place. (Ibid., p. 90.)

15. See Henry, p. 119, lines 4338–40 (Michel, p. 373, lines 22–5). Those from outside and those from inside are dashing past so fast, the poet says, that he did not know how to retain in his memory the name of every one:

Et cil dehors et cil dedens
Couroient si espressement
Que je ne savoie comment
Retenir de cascun le nom.

In the glossary, ibid., p. 147, *cil* or *ciaus dedens* are called 'les jouteurs de pays, opposés à leurs invités étrangers (see dehors, defors)'; *dehors* is described as 'le parti des chevaliers étrangers'.

16. See Henry, p. 122, lines 4458f. (Michel, p. 378, line 7f.):

Lors veïssiés rens commenchier
Par tout et aval et amont.
(Then you might have seen that jousts began everywhere, downwards and upwards.)

Concerning *amont*, Henry, p. 143, rightly observes: 'adv., à l'extrémité des lices'. In connection with the local peculiarities of Le Hem, Henry quotes from a contemporary description of the place: 'Nous avons vu ... une plaine suffisamment étendue et offrant une déclivité douce et régulière vers la rivière.' We thus have before us the classical instance of a castle located *amont*, 'uphill'.

17. A characteristic of this tournament was that all participants impersonated knights of the Round Table.

18. See Henry, p. 123, lines 4474–7 (Michel, p. 378). Another occurrence of the term *parc* is to be found on p. 99, line 3614. Henry, p. 156. The editor explains the term thus: 's.m., enceinte où se font les joutes'.

19. See Greimas, p. 471, on Old French *parc*, 2° Lice; and Verdam, p. 459, on Middle Dutch *Parc, perc, parric*, 2) ... strijdperk, krijt.

20. See von Wartburg, vol. 7, p. 666a, s.v. *parricus*, 3.a. Afr. mfr. 'lice, champ clos pour les joutes, les tournois, etc.' (c. 1200–1559 ...); and p. 667: 'Es handelt sich offenbar um eine spätl. ablt. von **parra*, 'stange', deren bed. etwa war "aus stangen zusammengesetzt".' (We

apparently have before us a late Latin derivation of **parra*, 'stick', the meaning of which was something like 'composed of sticks'.) The German term derived from *parricus* is *Pferch*, 'enclosure for animals'.

21. See Greimas, p. 364, s.v. *lice*, 1° Barrière, palissade; 3° Champ clos pour le tournoi *Les dames qui sont sour les lices Regardent le Fosseu venir* (Sarrazin), and Onions, p. 531, s.v. *list* 1.

22. See Simpson and Weiner, vol. 2, p. 446, s.v. *bourd*, v.² (first instanced c. 1450), and *bourdise*, v. (c. 1320) (the latter is derived from the noun *bourdis*, 'tilting', ibid., first instanced 1303).

23. See von Wartburg, vol. 15 (1969), p. 106, s.v. The word is related to English *hurdle*, 'rectangular wattled framework'. The *burdis* seems to have been a more playful tournament variant designed for the budding knight, the bachelor, or squires, see the present writer's *Service*, p. 77, note 257. Sometimes an enclosure of strings seems to have served as a substitute for the wooden barriers, possibly because Old French *lice*, 'champ clos pour un tournoi' (from Frankish) was confounded with *lice*, 'filet' (from Latin *licia*, a neuter plural conceived as a feminine singular).

24. See Cowper, p. 195.

25. See Hebel *et al.*, vol. 3, p. 29, lines 825–832.

26. See Constans, vol. 2, p. 98f.

27. See Essenwein, and Alwin Schultz, vol. 1, pp. 448–450, and figure 107. Here, the ivory carving is, for a change, a mirror case. It formerly belonged to the collection of the Cistercian abbey of Rein, Austria, but, as the Custodian, Dr Walter Steinmetz, kindly informed the author, is no longer there. Nothing is known about what became of it.

28. The failure to understand the artist's point is apparent from the words of Loomis, p. 259: 'On the casket lids the middle panel is usually occupied by a jousting scene, without any immediate relation to the Siege of the Castle.' Several caskets of this type are described by Koechlin, vol. 2, pp. 449–454 (no. 1281–1286). A specimen in which both the gate and the joust are depicted particularly well is Figure 48 which was reproduced in van Marle, p. 142, figure 128. The storming of the Castle of Love (Minneburg) in medieval art is also dealt with by

Antoniewicz, especially on pp. 248–51. A passage of arms known to have been conceived of as the conquest of the Castle of Love was the *Pas de la joyeuse garde*; it was held near Saumur in the summer of 1446 (according to Crapelet, p. 37, in the winter of 1447) by King René, see Barber and Barker, p. 116. Here, a wooden castle was put up for the purpose. The only author to be aware of the relation between the passage of arms proper and the concept of the Castle of Love is Barber. He mentions a joust 'before a "castle of love"' depicted on an ivory mirror-case, op. cit., p. 110.

29. The picture does not represent, as Eskénazi seems to believe, Yvain's fight with the Knight of the Fountain, see his edition of *Chrétien de Troyes. Yvain ou Le Chevalier au Lion*, illustration on the fly-leaf: 'Combat d'Yvain et du défenseur de la fontaine'. The same mistake is made by Annunziata, p. 155, note 8.

30. See the bilingual edition (Old French–German) by Nolting-Hauff, p. 38, line 508f.:

> *Qu'an mon bois et an mon chastel*
> *M'avez feite tel anvaïe.*
> (That on my wood and on my castle
> you have made a raid.)

It is these lines which the miniaturist of MS. Bibliothèque Nationale FR 1433, folio 65, meant to illustrate. That is why the identification here made is the only possible one, even though the two lines in question read somewhat different in the Paris manuscript:

> *Quen men [sic] bois & en mon chastel*
> *Maues ore fait tel outrage.*
> (That you have against my wood and my castle
> committed such outrage.)

31. See Nolting-Hauff, p. 40, lines 538–41:

> *Et li chevaliers me feri*
> *Si roidement, que del cheval*
> *Parmi la crope contre val*
> *Me mist a la terre tot plat...*
> (And the knight dealt me
> such a heavy blow that he sent me from
> my horse
> down over the croup
> flat onto the ground ...)

32. See Nolting-Hauff, p. 40, line 544:

> *Mon cheval prist et moi laissa.*

> (He took my horse and left me to my own
> devices.)

33. Swords are used later in the novel by the Knight of the Fountain and Yvain.

34. See Blazy, p. 186 (on the oldest known variety of the game, *bote luzea*): 'Dans le bote luzea le fait de dépasser les limites du fond constitue un quinze'; and idem, p. 195 (on the variant of *lachoa* played with gloves, but otherwise identical with *bote luzea*): '1er but refilé par camp O (i.e. that of the returning party) qui dépasse la raie du butoir, soit à la volée, soit en roulant sur le sol. Le compteur crie "paso" et compte quinze pour le gagnant, camp O'. The *raie du butoir* is identical with the line at the *steute* in the archaic Saterlandic game, and the *paso* is an equivalent of the famous *boppeslach*, i.e. a return ball which travels across the servers' base line, in Frisian *keatsen*, see Bröring, p. 130, and Breuker, *Keatserstaal*, p. 130. In Frisian, the term *boppeslach* (Dutch *bovenslag*) has acquired the figurative meaning of 'huge success'.

35. The first record of the game from the south of the Low Countries seems to be that contained in the statutes of the city of Antwerp of 1292, see van Passen, 1989, p. 59: 'Item, dat niement bal en slae op der straten erghens binnen vterster vesten, noch op eenich kerkhof binnen der vriheit van der stat op die peine van X s.' (Item, that nobody may hit the ball anywhere in the street within the Outer Fortification, nor in any churchyard within the liberty of the city, on a fine of 10 shilling.) The phrase *bal slaen*, 'to strike [a] ball', in medieval Dutch (as well as in German) referred to tennis exclusively.

36. See for this characterization of the Frisians' Rohwer, p. 1.

37. In his study 'Medieval Sport', the present writer has tried to determine when and from where *pärkspel* reached the Swedish island (ibid., p. 62f.). The most complete description of the game is that of the Rules drawn up by a commission and published in 1966 (see Dahlgren, *passim*). The commission consisted of Reinhold Dahlgren, Anders Dahlgren, Ivan Jacobson and Allan Nilsson (who was in charge of the variant of *frampärk*). There are the following accounts of the Gotlandic game, some of which contain attempts at explaining the game's history:

Balck, pp. 74–83; Bergman, pp. 214–36 (Om Gotlands folk-lekar); Götland, pp. 45–7; Gustavson *et al.*, 1936–1945, vol. 2, pp. 740–2, s.v. *pärk*; Gustavson, 1948, pp. 13–17; Karlsson, pp. 67–73; Klint, pp. 57–66; Møller, pp. 45–7; *Nordisk Familjeboks Sportlexikon*, cols. 1034–42, s.v. *pärk*; Nyberg, p. 22–34; Överstyrelsen för Svenska Röda Korset, pp. 830–4; Snöbohm, pp. 371–8; and Törngren, pp. 46–52. Törngren also includes, on pp. 87–96, what may well be the first description of lawn tennis in Swedish (with an interesting illustration of a doubles game). An apt description of *pärkspel* in English is contained in the official programme of the Olympic Games of Stockholm (1912), which also featured exhibition matches of *pärkspel*, see Bergvall, pp. 817–20.

38. On the Saterlandic game see the articles by Bröring, vol. 1, pp. 128–33, and Seitz, *passim*.

39. See on this issue Häpke, p. 180.

40. See Markey, p. 255:

> Saterland was settled in the 13th century by, presumably, Emsland Frisians who relocated in what are now the three small villages of Ramsloh, Strücklingen, and Scharrel in an area that is surrounded by moors. Saterland is quite literally an island in the moor. The Frisian community is contained in an area roughly 15 kilometers long and five kilometers wide; it extends from Utende in the North to Sedelberg in the South.

Matuszak, p. 8, even considered the twelfth and thirteenth centuries as the time when the Frisian settlers arrived.

41. See Häpke, p. 185. Conversely, Gotlanders were forbidden to take the opposite route to the West: 'nec — mare occidentale de cetero liceat frequentare'. Frisian seafarers are reported in Gotland as early as 1210. In that year, they are reported to have overpowered Courlandic pirates and to have abducted their booty on four ships to Riga, see Häpke, p. 174. In 1251, Frisians, at least from the city of Stavoren, were among the skilful sailors who managed to reach the Baltic Sea by sailing round Jutland, a feat which led to their being called, admiringly, 'Umlandfahrer', and to their being granted special privileges in Skåne by the Danish king Abel, see Häpke, p. 177, and

Rohwer, p. 98. On the whole issue see Berkenvelder, especially pp. 140–2.

42. See on this question the present writer's article 'The Gameless Country', p. 69.

43. The 'park games' are also unique in the complete absence of the scoring by fifteens ubiquitous in all the remainder of the tennis family. The implication is that they must be older at least than the first occurrence of it shortly after the year 1415. The curious method of scoring by fifteens will be discussed at the end of this chapter.

44. The Eastern Frisian variant *park* referred to by Breuker, *Keatserstaal*, p. 90, even shows the phonology of the underlying French term. *Perk* is first instanced in the Latin–Dutch phrase booklet by Pieter van Afferden, a professor of Latin at the college of the fraternity of St Gregory in Harderwijk and later rector at the Great Latin School in Amsterdam. This booklet, discovered in 1956 and a source of sixteenth-century life and culture the value of which can hardly be overestimated, has never been evaluated by writers on the history of sport. It contains, among other things, a chapter on the terms used in contemporary tennis together with their Latin equivalents. Here we find *scopus ludi*, literally the target aimed at in a game, which is rendered by 'dat perck', see de Tollenaere, fol. 44v (from chapter 23: De Pila palmaria). Van Afferden's *Tyrocinium* appeared in 1552 at the office of Jan de Laet in Antwerp, but the preface, dated 1545, indicates that a printable version had been completed by that time.

45. See Dahlgren, p. 6. The side-lines go by the name of *stång*, the front line is called *framsticka*, 'front stick', that to the rear *baksticka*, literally 'back stick'.

46. An obsolete synonym of *perk*, is *krite*, see Breuker, *Keatserstaal*, p. 90. Frisian *krite* corresponds to Middle Dutch *crijt* , 'lists', see Verdam, p. 313, s.v.; it confirms that the original idea was that of playing at ball after the fashion of the tournament.

47. It is somewhat strange that Matuszak, who in his dissertation attempted to give a complete list of Saterlandic vocabulary, noted *boppe* and *unner*, but failed to include technical terms such as *katt* (the *merk* most advanced on the opponents' territory, masculine gender), *merk* (all

points where the ball had been stopped after its second bounce, neuter gender), *pork* (masculine gender) and *steute* (feminine gender). His bibliography nevertheless features the work of Bröring.

48. See Bender's little treatise of 1680, p. 13f., where he is speaking about the height of the line: 'Es gebühret sich auch / daß man die *Corde* … nicht höher hänge / als daß der Obenstehende … deß Untenstehenden Füsse über das Seil hinsehen könne.' ('It is fitting that the line should not be hung up higher than that the one standing upwards (on the *dedans* side) can see above the line the feet of the one standing downwards'.)

49. In the Tuscan game of *palla*, the terms are *sopra* and *sotto*, see Morgan, p. 188; in the Colombian *juego de la chaza*, they are *arriba* and *abajo*, see Ortiz, p. 85. In the latter, they are applied, from a historical point of view, to the wrong sides.

50. See the present writer's study 'The Dissemination of Traditional Games', p. 36, note 54.

51. See Wallace, *Uppies and Downies*, p. 8f.

52. See Robertson, *Uppies and Doonies*, pp. 3–12. Wallace names no fewer than four other places, apart from Ashbourne, Kirkwall and Workington, where the same distinction is made, e.g. Jedburgh, Chester-le-Street, Witney, and Campton and Hodkirk.

53. See Roetert Frederikse, p. 5f.

54. Ibid., p. 48. An early instance of the custom of swapping the inside and outwards positions after two chases have been made is to be found in Rabelais' *Gargantua* (edition of 1542): 'apres les deux chasses faictes, sort hors le jeu celluy qui y estoyt et l'aultre y entre.' (See Calder and Screech, p. 314, variant reading at the bottom of the page.)

55. See the *Authorized Version*: 'And she smote twice vpon his [Holofernes's] necke with all her might, and she tooke away his head from him.'

56. See van Passen, p. 22. On 5 April 1582, a certain Peeter Hoochstraeten, a former inmate of the abbey who had renounced the old faith, applied for the post of a caretaker of the tennis court. He said that he had long forsworn the godless life in a monastery and had become a follower of the true Christian faith in the service of His Excellency (i.e. the Duke of Orange)

where he had acquitted himself well for many years, and he considered a most important asset that he was able to manufacture large balls (for *pallone*) and small ones (for tennis) with which the said noblemen would be very pleased: 'vermits de supplicant van over langen tijd het goddeloos kloosterleven verlaten heeft om sich te begeven tot de oprechte Christelijke religie in dienst van Z. Exc., in welken dienst hij zich gedurende menige jaren goed heeft gekweten, en daar hij expert is in het maken van "ballons" groote en kleine, waarmede de gezegte edellieden zeer zouden geaccommodeerd zijn, zoo verzoekt hij om de bewaring van het kaatsspel.' See Prims, p. 303.

57. See Mak, *Uyt Ionsten Versaemt*, p. 197f.

58. See van Torre, p. 182.

59. See Bender, p. 9: 'damit man wisse/wer im Spiel oder draussen sey' (in a passage on tossing for ends).

60. See the rulebook for *pärkspel* by Dahlgren, p. 6: 'Bakpärk är ett lagspel med 7 spelare i varje lag. Spelet tar sin början med att lagen lottar om vilket lag som skall bli ute- eller innelag.' (Bakpärk is a team game with seven players on either side. The match begins with the drawing of lots as to which team is going to be the outside or inside team.)

61. See Breuker, *Keatserstaal*, p. 126, 11.2.1.

62. See Gay, vol. 1, p. 201.

63. According to Bardi, the author of the oldest treatise on the Florentine game of football, a point was won whenever the ball was carried over the rear boundary of the football pitch (this is the equivalent of the *paso* in Basque pelota). After each successful attempt, significantly called *caccia*, the teams would change ends, in much the same way as the players did in medieval tennis whenever a chase had to be contended. This again shows the close relationship between these two games. In Florentine *calcio*, he who achieved the greatest number of *cacce* in the time allotted to the game was the winner. See on this point Bardi, *Discorso*, in Bascetta, vol. 1, p. 123: 'Il giuoco … consisteva nel far passare una "palla da vento" piuttosto grossa oltre quella che oggi chiameremmo linea di fondo, ottenendo un punto ("caccia"). Conseguiva la vittoria quella squadra che allo scadere del tempo aveva

accumulato un maggior numero di cacce; ad ogni punto, era d'obbligo scambiare il campo con gli avversari.' According to Scaino, the ball had to be driven, not beyond the rear boundary, but into a rectangle marked there on the ground, see the 1984 edition, p. 176 (Chapter LXXXII: Del Giuoco del Calcio). The action was significantly referred to as *cacciar la Palla*. On the ultimate relationship of tennis and soccer see also the author's articles, 'Linguistics and Sports Historiography', p. 36f., and 'The Dissemination', p. 25f.

64. The Picardian dialect form *cache* (for standard French *chasse*) survived until 1987, the year in which the Picardian *balle au tamis* apparently ceased to be played. The term denoted the chase rather than the game itself.

65. See Charles Lewis, p. 65.

66. Text quoted from Desees, p. 16.

67. See Girvan, p. 35f., lines 1240–1255.

68. Another early reference to tennis in Scotland comes from the account of the Scottish Lord High Treasurer under the date of 7 June 1496. The entry reads: 'To Wat of Lesly that he wan at the cach frae the king. 23 1.8s.' See MacGregor, p. 73.

69. See Kinsley, p. 159, lines 3400–3419.

70. From the point of view of the linguist, it is interesting that *caiche* should rhyme with *preich*, Modern English *preach*. Lindsay's pronunciation of the word is mirrored in the contemporary Scottish spelling *ketch*.

71. See Craigie, vol. 1, p. 189. For other Scotticisms which, despite the King's efforts to weed them out, were allowed to stay in the second edition, see ibid., vol. 2, p. 115.

72. In Spanish, the term *chaza* is first instanced in Juán del Enzina's or Encina's (born in 1469) *Auto de Repelón* which was written around 1500 and of which a printed version appeared in 1509. It is here used in a figurative sense as 'mockery', 'derision', see Macrí, p. 153. As a technical term, it always denotes the spot where the ball has been stopped, but never that where it bounced a second time. The noun *chaza* yielded the verb *chazar* which, in marked contrast to French *chasser*, never refers to driving the ball, but either to the action of stopping the ball, or to that of marking the chase. Of *chazar*, in turn, a noun *chazador* was derived. It denotes the player who manages to stop the ball, or the one in charge of stopping (compare English *stopper*). In his capacity as stopper, the *chazador* occupies an advanced position in the centre of the playing area: 'el qual regularmente se pone en el medio del juego', see Real Academia Española, *Diccionario de Autoridades*, vol. 1, p. 313. The term *chazador* could also refer to the marker of the chases, see again the *Diccionario de Autoridades*, p. 312f., and Corominas and Pascual, vol. 1, p. 348. The term *chaza* (besides the more usual term *raya*) is not unknown in the Basque game of *bote luzea*, see Bombin and Bozas-Urrutia, vol. 1, p. 1216, and in the Mixtecan ball game. In the latter, too, *raya* is the normal word, but Bolaños Cacho in his Rules, at one time and rather inadvertently, lets slip the term *chaza*. The fact that he puts it in quotation marks indicates, however, that he was here using an insider term not normally intelligible to the uninitiated: 'Toda reclamación que hagan los jugadores en la disputa de rayas, será desechada cuando el chacero haya levantado la "chaza"', i.e. 'whenever a chase is disputed, every "How's that?" by the players shall be rejected as soon the umpire has made a decision about the chase' (op. cit., p. 29, Inciso 9). In *pelota mixteca* the umpire is regularly called *chacero*, see Pérez-Bazán and Monterola, p. 7: 'Los partidos serán presididos por uno o dos jueces, que se denominan "chaceros"'; and Bolaños, *passim*. The Colombian *juego de la chaza* can, because of its retention of *chaza* as a technical term, be said to be more closely related to both *bote luzea* and the Mixtecan ball game. The entry *chaza* in the *Diccionario de Autoridades* is mentioned by Navarro Adelantado, p. 137, note 94.

73. The phonological side of this transfer is somewhat problematic. Retention of initial *k* points to the French north whereas *ts* (rather than *ch*) seems to indicate more Central, i.e. Parisian influence. The Dutch stem *caets-* would thus be the reflex of some hybrid dialectal variant. Early instances of *caetsen* (fourteenth century) are listed by Westra, p. 99.

74. See van de Kerckhove, p. 119f.

75. See Cornelis Kiel (Cornelius Kilian), 1599, reimpression of 1972, p. 219: Kaetsen/ketsen. Sectari pilam, ludere pila palmaria, exerceri pila; and the *Etymologicum*, 1632 edition, fol. 123v, s.v. *kaetsen/ketsen*, and fol. 130v, s.v. *ketsen* met den bal. j. kaetsen, sectari pilam, ludere pila. Kilian's *Dictionarium Teutonicolatinum*, a dictionary published by Christophe Plantin in 1574, does not include the variant *ketsen*, see Kiliaan, the 1975 reimpression which also contains a useful introduction to Kiliaan's work as a lexicographer by F. Claes (ibid., pp. v–xii). The Flemish dialect variants *ketsen* and *kitsen* were also noted by van de Kerckhove, p. 123.

76. See August Heinrich Hoffmann von Fallersleben, 1856, p. 49. Hoffmann von Fallersleben's *Horae Belgicae* have recently been reprinted in a three-volume edition, see the *Horae Belgicae. Studio atque opere Hoffmanni Fallerlebensis*, 1968. In sixteenth- and seventeenth-century legal documents from Antwerp there are four instances of the variant *ketspel*, 'tennis court', e.g. 'het vliegen van ballen kommende uit het *ketspel*', sixteenth century; 'huys ende *ketspel* metten toebehoorten', 1590; 'heuren *ketspele* … daer wte nv hangende is de Meereminne' ('of her tennis-court where now the mermaid hangs out'; this refers to the custom of attaching picturesque inn-signs to long horizontal poles, compare the names of English pubs such as 'The Fighting Cocks', 'The Saracen's Head', etc.), 1562; 'wesende een hoeckhuijs ende hebbende eertijden een *ketspel* geweest', 1632 (see van Passen, pp. 7, 14, 20, 21). In all these cases *ketspel* seems to reflect the local dialect as opposed to the standard forms *caetspel/kaetspel* which are by far more frequent even in the corpus of Antwerp legal documents.

77. In historical linguistics, an asterisk indicates that the form is not documented in a text.

78. In Dutch, the term *raket*, 'bat used in tennis', first appeared in van Afferden's *Tyrocinium* (manuscript 1545/printed 1552), see the edition by de Tollenaere and Claes, fol. 44r: 'Reticulum, instrumentum quo pila percutitur, factum ex fidibus crassiunculis/een raket.' This Latin definition is strongly reminiscent of

Vives. Van Afferden does not seem to know a verb *rakaetsen/*raketsen*, 'to return the ball'. He has, instead: 'Repellere pilam/den bal wederom smijten. Remittere pilam, idem.' (Op. cit., fol. 44v.) A plural form *raketten* is instanced in Dutch (Amsterdam) as early as 1531, see de Bondt, 'Heeft yemant', p. 27: ' […] met raketten te caetsen, op straffe van 1 schelling Vlaams …]'. Kilian in his dictionary defines the racket as an 'instrumentum cordis intentum siue maculis, quibus pila excipitur & expellitur', 'an implement strung with cords or meshes with which the ball is received and hit outwards', see Kilian, *Etymologicum*, 3rd ed. of 1599, p. 423, s.v. *racket*. This, if 'hit outwards' is taken literally, seems to contradict the theory that the racket was initially used for striking the ball back after the service.

79. I am indebted for this piece of information from the files of the *Französisches Etymologisches Wörterbuch* to Margaretha Hoffert, Basle.

80. See von Aphelen, *Grand Dictionnaire Royal Danois et François* (1759), p. 852, s.v. *Raquette*: 'en Raket eller ketse i Balhuse at slaae Boldet tilbage med,' a racket or a 'ketse' in the ballhouse with which to hit the ball back. The modern Danish term for racket is *ketscher*.

81. See Onions, p. 167, s.v. *cherry*.

82. This important source is quoted by the knowledgable Julian Marshall, *Annals*, p. 62, from MS. Cotton Vespasian C, xii, p. 281v. It is ignored by the *Oxford English Dictionary*, even in its second edition (1989).

83. In French, by means of *-ette* nouns are dervied from verbs. These nouns typically denote tools as in the case of *pincer*, 'to pinch', which yielded *pincette*, see Meyer-Lübke, pp. 50f. and 69, as well as pp. 116f. and 158. An early instance of *raquette* is to be found in Rabelais' *Gargantua* (editions of 1534 and 1535) where the spelling is *racquestes* (plural), see Calder and Screech, p. 314, Chapter LVI, line 127. A different etymology of *racket* has only recently been offered by Schmitt (see Christian Schmitt, 'Die Araber und der Tennissport', p. 52) who in a learned article considers a Latin root *coactiare*, 'to compress', but, in view of the fact that the derivations of French

chasse (amongst these the verb *rachasser*) are well established in the numerous tennis games the world over, also opts for Latin **captiare*, 'to chase' as the ultimate source of the word.

84. See Bal, 'Sur le vocabulaire du jeu de balle', p. 24. As a term for the return in the Picardian patois of Mesnil-Martinsart *racachier* is also recorded by Flutre, *Le Parler Picard de Mesnil-Martinsart*, p. 217.

85. See Craigie, *Dictionary*, p. 412, s.v. *Cach(e)pell*, 1.b.

86. See Jakob and Wilhelm Grimm, *Deutsches Wörterbuch*, vol. 5, p. 301, s.v. KATZENSPIEL.

87. See Whitman, *Origins*, p. 126f. Whitman is a good example of the inaccuracies which bedevil older works on tennis history. The year ought to have been given as either 1534 or 1535 if Whitman meant to quote from the first or the second edition of *Gargantua*. In these early editions, however, there is no mention of either sheep or goats. The passage in question here reads: 'ces *nerfz et boyaulx de bestes innocentes* sont des racquestes'; only in Rabelais' corrected edition of 1542 do we have the reading 'les chordes des rasquestes sont faictes de boyaux de moutons ou de chevres', see Calder and Screech, p. 314 (*Gargantua*, LVI, line 126f., and the 1542 variant at the bottom of the page).

88. See Buffard in the course of a short history of tennis in a brochure published by the Fédération Française de Longue Paume (after 1970): 'Après l'emploi du battoir en bois et à manche court, l'usage de la raquette à manche plus ou moins long et cordée en boyau de chat ou de mouton se généralise à cette époque.'

89. In his handbook of 1892, he wrote, under the heading 'Das Katzenspiel oder die Katze':

Wie *longue paume* – denn dieses ist gemeint – in den Rheingauen zu diesem humoristischen Namen kommt, ist mir nach dem Stand meiner Nachforschungen unmöglich aufzuklären. ... Es ist ... möglich, dass longue Paume infolge der mit demselben verbundenen heftigen Bewegung bei seiner Einbürgerung von den an ruhigere Ballspiele gewöhnten Deutschen einen Spitznamen erhielt, der dem Spiel nachträglich verblieb.' ('How *longue paume* (for this is here referred to) acquired this humorous name in the Rhineland is, at the present state of my investigations, impossible to explain. It is possible that longue paume, because of the excessive motion characteristic of it, was so nicknamed, after its introduction, by the Germans who had been accustomed to more peaceful ball-games, which name hereafter was retained for the game.')

See the *Handbuch*, 2nd edn, p. 24.

90. See Simpson and Weiner, vol. 2, p. 984, s.v. *catgut*. The first quotation in the *OED* (1599) has the spelling *cats guts*, and all seventeenth-century instances retain the medial *s*. The explanation given by the dictionary of the history of the word is a rare specimen of contradictoriness: 'So far as the *name* can be traced back, it distinctly means guts or intestines of the cat, though it is not known that these were ever used for the purpose.' The meaning of *catgut*, according to the dictionary, is nevertheless: 'The dried and twisted intestines of sheep'.

91. As in French, identification with the Frisian word *kat*, 'cat', may have led to the term *katt* (without final *s*), 'chase', in the Saterlandic game. On Saterlandic *kat*, 'cat', see Matuszak, p. 78.

92. See for instance, Hécart's dialect dictionary, p. 101, s.v. CAT, 'chat'. The term *rouchi* in the title of the dictionary refers to the Walloon dialect. On its origin see the preface by Claude Deparis, p. 6.

93. See Monmerqué and Michel, p. 537.

94. A tax roll for the city of Paris from the time of Loüis' father, Philip the Fair (the Taille of 1292), has been said to contain the names of no fewer than thirteen *paumiers* who have been considered the owners of commercial tennis courts, see Endrei and Zolnay, p. 998, for a more recent statement to this effect. If this were true, it would prove (at least by implication) the existence of the name *jeu de la paume* at the time, see Franklin, vol. 2, p. 552f., s.v. *Paumiers*, and pp. 671–3, s.v. *Tailles* ... . This tax roll was published by Géraud, but it has apparently never been consulted by the tennis historians who make the claim, nor has the existence of the thirteen *paumiers* (which is taken for granted even by more recent writers such as Bonhomme who, in fact, has his book begin with them, ibid., p. 14) ever been questioned. We here give a list of the thirteen entries which, if they could be taken as evidence of owners of

medieval tennis courts, would certainly be an important document:

1. Géraud, p. 1 [La paroisse Saint-Merri.] Paumier Bigot [the brother of a certain Jacques Guy]. Tax: 48 sous.

2. Ibid., p. 2 [La paroisse Saint-Jaque-de-la-Boucherie.] Paumier Garnier; – Jehannin de Brachefort, en compaingnie des Gaaingne-biens [which means that Garnier and Brachefort ran the business together]. Tax: 50 livres [= pounds].

3. Ibid., Paumier Saint, u coing de la rue [i.e. at the corner of the street] Guillaume-Joce. Tax: 10 sous.

4. Ibid., p. 29 [La rue Saint-Germain.] Guillaume, le paumier. Tax: 8 sous.

5. Ibid., p. 30 [La harengerie.] Thomas, le paumier. Tax: 2 sous.

6. Ibid., p. 34 [La septieme queste de la porte, du Chastelet jusques a la Faute de Grant-Pont.] Belon, la paumière. Tax: 16 sous..

7. Ibid., p. 46 [La Grant-Rue.] Symon, le paumier. Tax: 3 sous.

8. Ibid., p. 79 [La rue Giefroi-l'Engevin, i.e. the rue Geoffroi-l'Angevin in 1837, see Géraud, p. 248.] Jehan, le paumier. Tax: 2 sous.

9. Ibid., p. 103 [La queste du bout de la Péleterie, devers le Pont, jusques a la Pièrre-au-Poisson; i.e. all houses located on either side of the Pont au Change, see Géraud, p. 266.] Jehan Paumier, son gendre [i.e. the son-in-law of a certain Jehan Maupas, a money-exchanger mentioned before]. Tax: 70 sous. [Below this entry: Guillot l'Ami-Dieu, vallet Jehan Paumier, i.e. the servant of Jehan Paumier, tax: 16 sous.]

10. Ibid., p. 177 [… queste du Temple dehors les murs, i.e. the residence of the knights of the Templars' Order and their Grand Prior outside the city walls, later a prison of state and a well-known fair in 1837, see Géraud, p. 348.] Jehan, le paumier. Tax: 10 sous.

11. Thomas, le paumier. Tax: 18 sous. [Thomas had a step-daughter, La fillatre Thomas le paumier. Her tax was 5 sous, see ibid., below.]

12. Guiart, le paumier. Tax: 10 sous.

13. Jehan, le paumier, le viel [= 'the Old', this latter the surname given by the tax collectors in order to differentiate him from the Jehan listed previously, i.e. no. 10, above].

The bearers of the surname *(le) paumier* (including the feminine form *la paumière*) were not the proprietors of commercially run tennis courts (which, incidentally, Géraud admits himself, ibid., p. 529). In all probability, they had been so named because they had distinguished themselves as palmers, pilgrims to the Holy Land (Latin *palmarius*; such a derivation is also suspected by Schmitt, 'Die Araber', p. 51)! In order to authenticate their pilgrimage, these would carry with them the branches of the palm tree, hence the name. Géraud tried to substantiate his claim by saying that one of them had a servant, but this is hardly convincing. Why should not a former pilgrim to Jerusalem have had a servant?

95. See Gay, vol. 1, p. 174.

96. See Shirley, *Full Lamentable Cronycle*, p. 16.

97. This reference is from a newspaper clipping, presumably from *The Times*, which aroused the curiosity of Lord Aberdare who made it accessible to the present writer. The text reads thus: 'A scrap of parchment preserved among the Canterbury city records relates to the presentment before the Burghmote, *c.* 1396, of one William Terrey for permitting divers men to play "le Closhe and le Tenesse" in his house. It would be of interest to know if objection to the game was confined to Canterbury. Mrs. G. Gardiner, The Precincts, Canterbury.' Unfortunately, all attempts by the present writer to retrieve the 'scrap of parchment' from the Canterbury city archives have been unsuccessful.

98. Portions from the two ordinances, issued in 1365 and 1388 respectively, are printed in Magoun, *History of Football*, p. 7f. In 1369, Charles V of France enacted a decree in the same vein in which the playing of games was forbidden and in which his subjects were enjoined to practise archery with bow and crossbow instead for the improvement of military skill. This was, at the time of the Hundred Years' War, of vital importance:

defendons par ces presentes, tous geux de Dez, de Tables, de Palmes, de Quilles, de Palet, de Soules, de Billes, & tous autres telz geux, qui ne acheent point à exercer ne habiliter noz diz subgez, à fait & usage d'armes, à la deffense de nostredit Royaume, sur paine de quarante sols

Parisis ... & voulons & ordenons, que noz diz subgez prennent & entendent à prenre leurs geux & esbatement, à eulz exercer & habiliter en fait de trait d'Arc ou d'Arbalestres.

(Quoted from Secousse, vol. 5, p. 172.) In 1397, artisans were allowed to play tennis, skittles, dice and cards on working days by the provost of the merchants of Paris, see de la Fons-Melicocq, p. 527, note 3. As appears from an entry in the Tamworth Court Roll in 1424, tennis players were in danger of imprisonment from which they could be released only after a ransom of twenty pound had been paid: 'Order that no one play at hand-ball [= Tennis] or quoits [ordinatum est quod nullus ludet ad pilam manualem et ad le Koyte] under penalty of imprisonment and that anyone found after the ninth hour at night be arrested and imprisoned until a pledge of £20 is found, payable to the bailiffs; and that pigs be not allowed to wander; but be kept within or given into custody of the swineherd, under penalty of 12d, half to the bailiffs and half to the common chest.' (Court. 6 Staff. 6 Nov. 1424.) The Tamworth Court Roll is preserved in the Library of the University of Keele, Staffordshire.

 99. See del Lungo and Volpi, p. 81.
100. In these words the stress falls on the second syllable. The spelling *z* in the verb indicates voicing of the sibilant which did not occur in final position, hence the voiceless *s* in the noun **teneys*. In both cases, the *y* indicates length of the preceding vowel.
101. See Hitti, p. 98.
102. See al-Sayed, p. 211.
103. See Heathcote *et al.*, p. 12.
104. See an article titled 'Das Tennisspiel' which had previously appeared in the *Allgemeine Sportzeitung*, a Viennese sporting journal edited by Victor Silberer, and was reprinted in the *Deutsche Turn-Zeitung* (1902), p. 584f. Some rather bizarre etymologies of sports terms, and among them one for tennis, are to be found in an article by H. O'Shea: 'Tennis est un terme qui a été probablement emprunté à la grande salle basse appelée *Tinel*, servant de cellier, dans lequel on gardait des vases d'étain ou des cuves, appelés *tines*'. Ibid., p. 43.
105. See his *An Etymological Dictionary* (1882) p. 630, s.v. TENNIS: 'Putting all together,

we have the orig. form as *teneis* or *tenis* or *tenyse*, accented on the latter syllable, and expressed in Low Latin by *tenisia* and *teniludium*. I suspect a derivation from O.F. *tenies*, plural of *tenie*, 'a fillet, head-band, or hair-lace; ... This O.F. *tenie* = Lat. *tænia* ..., a band, ribbon, fillet ... We might imagine *tænia* to be used ... for the band or string over which the balls are played'.
106. See Minshew, p. 486, s.v. *Tennis play*.
107. See Besant, p. 356.
108. See Lecotté, p. 12.
109. See Morgan, p. 185f.
110. See Fink, p. 216: 'Auf dem Spruchband an der Wand: "O mi rebuco [sic] zuge" (?).' Reichard, p. 118, has the following: 'Oben, gerade über dem Haupte des Schwarz, stehen in einiger Entfernung auf einem fliegenden Zettel annoch die, mir etwas unverständlichen, Worte: O – Rebuzo, Zuge. O schlaget doch den Geck zurück!'
111. In sixteenth-century north Italian the phrase is *zu(o)gar alla balla*, 'to play at ball'. A remarkable instance of how it was used comes from an article by Zdekauer, ibid., p. 139f.:

Nel 1567 troviamo certi giovani, che <si hanno fatto lecito di voler per forza e con violentia al despeto delli Frati de S. Zanepolo nel loro convento zuogar alla balla, inzuriando et batendo fra Martino converso portoner, qual d'ordine de suo prior non li voleva lassar zuogar>.

This looks like a typical instance of tennis in the cloisters.
112. See Ortiz, p. 86. This is the 3rd person singular of the future tense, the polite form of address *Usted* being understood.
113. See the *Desiderii Erasmi Opera Omnia*, p. 646. In a similar tennis dialogue by Cordier, printed in 1555, every rally is initiated by a cry *excipe!*, see the *Varij lusus*, pp. 21–6. At one point, the service has to be repeated, because the cry had not been voiced: 'R[enatus]. Frustrà misisti: vtpote nil præfatus. M[atthæus]. Iteretur iactus.' (Ibid., p. 25.)
114. See *King Henry V*, I. ii. 258f. The comment on the term *chases* (I, ii, 266) – 'missed returns' – in a standard edition such as Blakemore Evans's *The Riverside Shakespeare* is a classical example of the literary scholar's disdain for so trivial a matter as sport and games.

115. See Emmerig, 'Dariusbrief', p. 362: 'In meiner schrift [i.e. "The Bataile of Agyncourt" im Lichte geschichtlicher Quellenwerke] … habe ich (p. 22ff.) nachzuweisen versucht, dass die … bekannte spöttische sendung der tennisbälle … jeder historischen grundlage entbehrt'.

116. See Emmerig, *Bataile*, p. 17. The text of the play – *The Famous Victories of Henry the fifth: Containing the Honourable Battell of Agin-court: As it was plaide by the Queenes Majesties Players. London Printed by Thomas Creede, 1598* – is easily accessible in the source material gathered by Bullough, vol. 4 (1962), pp. 299–343. Here, the tennis ball episode can be found on p. 323f. Truly remarkable from the view point of the tennis historian is Henry's rhetorical antithesis in which the tennis balls of the French are contrasted with those of the English proving that as late as the end of the sixteenth century tennis balls were made of leather:

> But tel him [i.e. the Dauphin], that in steed
> of balles of leather,
> We wil tosse him balles of brasse and yron
>   *(line 847f.)*

117. The MS from which Brie printed his text, MS. Un. Libr. Camb, Kk I 12, belongs to the middle of the fifteenth century; it was collated by Brie with two other MSS, MS British Museum Add. 24,859 and British Museum Reg. 17 D XXI which were both written in the second half of the fifteenth century, see Brie, vol. 2, p. vif.

118. See Brie, vol. 2, p. 374.

119. Ibid., p. 374f.

120. See Brie, op. cit., p. 376.

121. See Emmerig, *Bataile*, p. 11.

122. Quoted from Nicolas, p. 302f. On the poem and the surviving manuscripts see the late Dr Robbins in his contribution to Hartung, *Manual*, vol. 5, p. 1426. It is titled *Poems dealing with Contemporary Conditions*. According to Robbins, p. 1665, Manuscript Harley 565 was written between 1440 and 1450. Robbins, loc. cit., also points to yet another version of the poem, hitherto unpublished, i.e. MS Bodleian 11951 (Rawl C.86), fol. 178a–186a (1480–1500). For an account of the ballads see Wylie and Waugh, vol. 1, pp. 425–30; see also Kingsford, 1913, pp. 238–40.

123. British Museum MS. Cotton Vitellius D. xii. (from which we quote) was destroyed in the fire of 1731, but had fortunately been published before by Hearne, *Thomas de Elmham vita & gesta Henrici Quinti*. Oxford, 1727. In the passage reproduced here (Hearne, pp. 362–4), only the abbreviations have been expanded. The same text has also been reproduced in Nicolas, pp. 307–11.

124. See Hearne, p. 363.

125. See Hearne, p. 363f.

126. For the etymology of English *penthouse* see Onions, p. 666, s.v. *penthouse*.

127. In this Italian–English language primer which appeared in 1591 the interlocutors are perhaps taken from life. Sir Henry, one of the elegant tennis-players of high rank, can perhaps be identified with the Earl of Southampton, Henry Wriotheley, and the 'Master John' could well be 'Giovanni' Florio himself, see Yates, p. 125f. Yates points out, however, that Florio was in the Duke's pay no earlier than 1594.

128. See Simonini, p. 25.

129. See Nicolas, p. 309.

130. See Nicolas, p. 72 of the appendix. In the C-version, the French are particularly keen on avenging themselves on the English by winning, as it were, the return match; compare the braggadocio of the Duke of Bourbon whom the poet had swear by God and his national saint, St Denis, most ingeniously, since the latter's name rhymed on tennis (see Nicolas, p. 75):

> The Duke of Burbone answeryd sone
> And swere 'by God and by Saynt Denys,
> We wyll play them euerychone,
> These lordes of Engelande at the tenys.'

131. Another very instructive example illustrating the indifference of men of letters to the terminology of sport is the conjecture 'Bolde felowes, we go to game' placed at the disposal of the Shakespeare scholar by Bullough, p. 414, line 136. Bullough is indebted for it to the edition of the poem by W.C. Hazlitt in 1866.

132. On the life of John Audelay which, in the entourage of Richard Lestrange, a notorious trouble-maker, perhaps was not as innocent as has been thought, see the recent article by Bennett referred to in the bibliography.

133. On the genre of the English carol see Standop and Mertner, pp. 145–8.

134. In the opinion of Richard Leighton Greene, p. 475, the coronation of Henry on 6 November 1429, gave rise to the poem, but the poem itself does not provide a clue as to the date of its composition. Henry V's wooing was not the reason, but the result of the French campaign, see Greene, p. 476.

135. I am quoting from Whiting, pp. 193–5 (39). For an account of the poet see ibid., pp. xiv–xv.

136. The dissemination of cultural phenomena can be said to resemble closely that of linguistic innovations to which latter the 'norm of the lateral area' applies. The following maxim was introduced in the twenties by the Italian dialectological school of the *linguistica spaziale*: 'If, of two linguistic forms, one is found in peripheral areas and the other in central areas, then the former is the older.' Quoted from Chambers and Trudgill, p. 183. See on this issue generally the present writer's study 'The Dissemination of Traditional Games in Europe'.

137. See Ariès, p. 63 (from his chapter 'Petite contribution à l'histoire des jeux'): 'les moulins à vent ont depuis longtemps disparu de nos campagnes, alors que les petits moulinets pour enfants se vendent toujours dans les magasins de jouets … . Les enfants constituent les sociétés humaines les plus conservatrices.' Both the toy and the game are depicted in Stella and Bouzonnet-Stella, pp. 6 and 35. The game, a parody of the medieval joust in which two boys, riding piggyback on the shoulders of a comrade, try to tilt each other over, in Stella's picture has preserved its old name, *jouste*.

138. Svabo's interesting observations are referred to by the knowledgable Erwin Mehl, in his article 'Latinismen im Kinderspiel', p. 77f.

139. The preservation of the name *tennis* in this children's game has an interesting parallel in English. In English, the normal term for the game was *cat* or *tip-cat*, but the *Oxford English Dictionary* also notes the variant *cat's pellet*: 'A game … vsed in the towne of Manchestr called giddye guddye or catts pallet.' (See the *OED*, s.v. *Cat*, sb.1, 19. Quotation for the year 1609.) This is almost certainly an instance

of popular etymology for Dutch *caetsspel*, 'tennis', but, in view of the final *t*, the influence of Scandinavian *spelet*, 'play', cannot be ruled out altogether.

140. See Christmann, vol. 2, col. 210f., s.v. *Tenee-ui*, and the interesting variants listed in Josef Müller, *Rheinisches Wörterbuch*, vol. 8, p. 1135, s.v. *tenee*.

141. An etymology for *soule* (from Popular Latin *cepulla*, 'onion', a slang term for 'ball') has been suggested by the present writer in his article 'The Origin of European Ball Games', p. 29f. Another linguistically acceptable explanation was advanced by Thomas (see the bibliography) who derives *soule* from Old High German *kiulla*, 'leather pouch'. The attempt to relate it to a Germanic root **keula-*, 'bump', by von Wartburg, vol. 16, p. 316f., seems strained and does not carry conviction.

142. See Jodogne, p. 295, line 22083. Here it is the devil Fergalus who speaks.

143. See ibid., lines 22071–22074.

144. See Frederikse, p. 63.

145. Ibid., p. 64.

146. See Halkin *et al.*, p. 166, lines 1321–1327:

> NICOLAVS. … Vicimus triginta, vicimus quadraginta quinque.
> HIERONYMVS. Sestertia?
> NICOLAVS. Non.
> HIERONYMVS. Quid igitur?
> NICOLAVS. Numeros.
> HIERONYMVS. Quo pertinent numeri, si nihil est quod numeres?
> NICOLAVS. Noster hic ludus est.

147. See Scaino, *Trattato del giuoco della palla*, 1984, pp. 36–9 (Chapters V–VI).

148. On the *physis* vs. *nomos* controversy in Plato (Scaino here, absurdly, seems to favour both) see Dinneen, p. 74f. and p. 148. Dinneen also refers to the etymology of Latin *homo*, 'man', which can be traced back to Isidore of Seville.

149. See Scaino, 1984, p. 44.

> (chapter XI: Come il numero quindici e accommodato per chiamar l'acquisto delle Caccie): 'Percio che è cosa da se manifesta, che qualunque giuocatore guadagna cinque caccie l'una dopo l'altra, l'istesso fa anco acquisto de i tre gradi di premio: & chiunque a tal grado d'honore arriuare intende, conuiene, che per l'ardua e difficile strada delle cinque caccie caminando s'affatichi, & sudi. Qual dunque piu accommodato nome, quale piu acconcio numero si potea scieglere dall'arte Arithmetica, che'l numero quindici, in cui sono comprese

tutte l'operationi, tutto l'essere, la forma, & la perfettione dell'artificio, nel quale è ordito il giuoco della Palla?'

150. The various explanations for the scoring method in tennis are surveyed by Erwin Mehl in his article, 'Warum zählt man …?'. On Scaino, whom Mehl does not seem to have understood perfectly, see ibid., p. 25f.

151. See Mehl, p. 26. According to Mehl, the reasoning of those advocating the circle argument was thus: a match consisted of six games, in exactly the same way as the circle can be subdivided into six segments of four times fifteen degrees each. As will be seen, Mehl not only misrepresented Gosselin's sixteenth-century explanation (reprinted in the *Maison Académique*), but also failed to give a complete account of it. The idea of a subdivision of a competition day into twenty-four hours was brought forward, again according to Mehl, by a certain Dr H. Schnell from Hamburg in 1901.

152. See La Marinière, *La Maison Academique*, p. 113: 'Declaration de deux doutes qui se trouuent en contant le Ieu de la Paume, lesquelles meritent d'estre entenduës par les personnes d'esprit.'

153. Ibid., p. 115f.: 'pourquoy on conte le jeu de la Paume en augmentant le nombre par quinzaines, comme quinze, trente, quarante-cinq, & puis vn jeu, qui vaudroit soixante, plûtost que de conter par quelqu'autre nombre plus petit, ou plus grand'.

154. Ibid., p. 116: 'quelle espece de mesure signifient iceux nombres, quinze, trente, & les autres'.

155. Ibid., p. 117:

Or les hommes doctes en Astronomie connoissent bien qu'vn Signe Physic (qui est la sixième partie d'vn cercle) est diuisé … en soixante degrez, chaque degré en soixante secondes: suiuant cette raison sexagenaire peuuent dire, que la maniere de conter le jeu de la Paume a esté instituée suiuant icelle raison sexaginaire; & à l'imitation d'vn signe Physic: Car quinze degrez pris quatre fois valent vn signe Physic: tout ainsi que quatre fois quinze valent vn jeu de la Paume.

156. Ibid.: 'Ioinct aussi que ceux qui jouent à la Paume ne s'amusent pas tant à contempler le Ciel, comme ils trauaillent à frapper & chasser l'estœuf, ou à le renuoyer.'

157. Ibid., p. 120f.:

Il est donc bien manifeste par les raisons cy-dessus declarées, que les nombres du Ieu de la Paume representent les quatre quarts d'un climat, & contant quinze pour chaque quart, & qu'iceux nombres du Ieu de la Paume signifient pieds. Sembla[ble]ment qu'vn Ieu de la Paulme denote vn climat: Pareillement qu'vne partie gaignée à la Paume signifie vn Iugere, en mesurant chacun d'iceux selon la longueur seulement: car les chasses & coups d'esteuf se mesurent selon leur longeur, & non pas selon leur largeur.

158. See Butler and Wordie, p. 76f.

159. See Quarles, *Emblemes*, 1635, p. 40 (Book I, X).

160. See Greene, *The Early English Carols*, p. 231, no. 393 (stanzas 1 and 6).

161. See Roetert-Frederikse, p. 18f.

162. See Simonini, p. 25.

163. See Mehl, 'Warum zählt man … ?', p. 26f.

164. On the history of the *Groschen* (English *groat*) see Suhle, 1968, p. 155.

165. On the *gros tournois* worth fifteen *deniers* in the fourteenth century see von Schrötter, p. 243, s.v. *Gros tournois*.

166. See Fisher, p. 227, Fragment C, line 656. *Bones* has been used ever since in English as a slang term for dice, see Wentworth and Flexner, p. vii.

167. See Spitzer, 1891, p. 16.

168. See Tauber, p. 61: 'nieman niht spilen über sehtzic haller [the *haller* owed its name to the mint where it was coined, the town of Schwäbisch-Hall] noch umbe dehainer slahte ding oder guot über sehtzig pfennige'.

169. Ibid. On the limitations of stakes by law see also Semrau, p. 13.

170. See Tauber, p. 39.

171. See Roetert-Frederikse, p. 50. Initial *t* does not belong to the noun proper (which is *voordeel*, or *voredeel*), but is part of the definite article.

172. See Champion, vol. 1, p. 144f. The implication of the passage is that, after the score had been deuce, Worry by stopping the ball prevents a long chase by which the Poetic I might win one of the 'big points'.

173. See Simonini, p. 25.

174. In French, the use of *quarante* for *quarante-cinq* seems to be attested, at least by implication, for the year 1536. In that year appeared, as has only recently been shown by Christian Schmitt in his article

'Etymologie und Semantik', Maturin Cordier's *De corrupti sermone emendatione*. In this treatise, Cordier finds fault with the use of Latin *quadra* for the correct *quadraginta quinque* by schoolboys: 'Caeterum omnino ineptum est quod pueri dicunt, QUADRA, pro QUADRAGINTA QUINQUE.' See Schmitt, 'Etymologie und Semantik', p. 196.

175. For the historical background against which the poem should be viewed see Pirenne, vol. 2, pp. 349–74 (Book V, Chapter iv: Le Déchirement des Pays-Bas), especially p. 362. The poem is echoed later on, in 1591, in a so-called *geusenlied* (song of the geuzen, the Calvinist Dutch guerillas) titled 'Het Kaetspel van syne Exellentie [i.e. Maurice of Nassau, Prince of Orange]', see de Bondt, *'Heeft yemant'*, p. 82f.

176. See Mak, *Uyt Ionsten Versaemt*, p. 197 (5th stanza).

177. On *blot*, from Middle Dutch *bloot*, 'bare', see Murray, p. 62.

178. See Simpson and Weiner, s.v. *Closh*, sb.1.

179. See my article 'The Flemish Ancestry', pp. 65–7.

180. See now the present writer's study 'A Tee for Two', *passim*.

181. See the present writer's article 'Mit Kind und Kegel'.

182. From Dutch *lukke*, see Toll, p. 52.

183. See Onions, p. 692, s.v. *poker 2*. *Poker* appears to be the Dutch equivalent of the German *Pochspiel*, 'bragging game'.

184. See the author's article 'The Flemish Ancestry', p. 69.

185. See Simonini, p. 25.

186. See now on this issue *Refugees and Emigrants in the Dutch Republic and England*. There were several censuses conducted in sixteenth-century London in order to assess the percentage of foreigners. According to the census of 1567, London had 45 Scottish, 428 French, 45 Spanish and Portuguese, 140 Italian, 44 Burgundian, 2 Danish, one Liègois and no fewer than 2030 Dutch residents. Most of those called 'Dutch' are believed to have been Flemings, see Besant, p. 80: 'There were ... thousands of immigrants from Flanders ..., fleeing from religious persecution ... In the first year [i.e. of the 1567 census] we find a large number of Dutch; they are fugitives.'

On p. 203, Besant has somewhat different figures to offer; they seem to be based on a special census of the same year, 1567: 'There were also a great many "Dutch", among whom were numbered the Flemings. Thus, in 1567, a census was taken of "foreigners" in London. There were found to be 4851 altogether, of whom 3838 were Dutch, and 720 French.'

Chapter 4

1. In what follows, the present writer relies, at least in part, on his study 'Ballspielgedichte des Spätmittelalters'.

2. See Champion, vol. 1, p. 144f.

3. See Bender's account of the German ball-house, which itself is based on earlier French tennis treatises, p. 9f.

4. It is highly questionable whether a critic such as Alice Planche, who considered the chase to be the spot where the ball finishes its first bounce – 'le lieu où la balle finit son premier bond' (p. 266, note 153 – could have grasped the meaning of the poem after all. In the fifteenth century, the chase was marked where the ball, after its first bounce, had been stopped!

5. See Kervyn de Lettenhove, vol. 3, p. 134 (Chapter XXVIII). Philip the Good is referred to by Poirion, *Le lexique de Charles d'Orléans*, p. 116, s.v. *Quarente*. Poirion also mentions the poem by de Viau which will claim our attention next. On Chastellain in general, see Poirion, *Le moyen âge II*, p. 280.

6. See de Viau, in *Le parnasse satyrique*, Bibliothèque Nationale, manuscrit n.a.fr. 4237, fol. 84v.

7. On Théophile's trial, his two-year sentence, and subsequent banning see the exhaustive treatment by Adam, pp. 333–404 (Chapter V: La disgrâce et le procès). There seems to be a parallel for the fifteen in tennis in American baseball terminology, namely *first base*, see Considine, p. 19: 'The preliminary step in a relationship or endeavor (couldn't get to first base with her).' Judging from this early tennis example, *first base* might also have a long tradition which, however, if it existed, has not been recorded.

8. This holds good at least for the tennis officialese of the time. In an intriguing article, Christian Schmitt, professor of

Romance philology at the University of Bonn, has recently referred to Maturin Cordier who as early as 1536 found fault with students who out of sheer neglect would say *quadra* rather than, correctly, *quadraginta quinque*. The implication may be that whenever they used their native French they counted *quarante* rather than *quarante-cinq*:

Habemus quadraginta quinque. vel, tamen per eclipsim dici solent, Quindecim, Triginta, Quadraginta quinque: videlicet suppresso verbo gratia compendii: Id est Brevitatis. Caeterum omnino ineptum est quod pueri dicunt, QUADRA, Pro QUADRAGINTA QUINQUE.

See Cordier, p. 284b, and Schmitt, p. 196.

9. On emblem books and tennis see Bath, *passim*.

10. A rare specimen of these found in the rafters of Westminster Hall is now preserved in the London Museum. The change from a leather cover to cloth was noted by Sir Robert Dallington who in 1598 observed that in France this change had taken place seven years previously, see Aberdare, p. 27.

11. This point was made by Simon and Smart, p. 19.

12. See Horden, *Guillaume de la Perrière*, Emblem V. An original copy of this work is to be found in the Bayerische Staatsbibliothek, Munich, shelf mark 8° Rar. 1686. Bath, p. 47f., based his account on a different version of the poem published in 1540 and showing a text deviating considerably from this one. This variant does contain a motto, namely: 'A chose incertaine ne se doibt l'homme fier', 'man should not trust in a thing uncertain'. Guillaume's poem was rendered into English by Thomas Combe (1593). A single, albeit incomplete, copy of this edition is now in Glasgow, another of an edition of 1613 in the Huntington Library, Pasadena, California, see Bath, pp. 49–52.

13. See Dijkstra, vol. 2, p. 46, s.v. *keatse*, v.: Dy 't keatse wol moat de ballen wachtsje. Breuker, p. 46, proverb no. 36, has the following version: 'Dy't keatse wol, moat de bal(len) (fer)wachtsje'. In a Dutch source of 1835 this is glossed by: 'die een ander de Waarheid wil zeggen die ontvangt het antwoord te rug', 'he who

wants to tell somebody the truth receives back the answer'.

14. See Müller, *Rheinisches Wörterbuch*, vol. 4, p. 268, s.v. *katschen*: Redensart [proverbial saying]: '*Wenn gej k. wellt, moj* (musst du) *den Ball verdrage könne, – mott den B. verwachte* (erwarten) wer das Angenehme einer Sache will, muss auch das Unangenehme derselben vertragen' ('who wants to enjoy the more pleasant aspects of a thing will have to bear its unpleasant aspects as well'). There is an English version by Combe also of this poem, see Bath, p. 52f. Bath's contention that the 'second tennis emblem in La Perrière' did 'not appear to have any proverbial basis', is, of course, erroneous.

15. It is reproduced in Breuker, *Boppe!*, p. 6, whose source is the *Vriesch Almanak, of Tijdwijzer, voor het Schrikkeljaar 1824*. Leeuwarden: M.v.d.Bosch. Here the proverb runs: 'Die kaatst die moet den bal verwagten'.

16. See Horden, *Claude Paradin*, p. 236. For more examples of the *devise* see Praz, p. 16.

17. See Horden, *Henry Peacham*, p. 113.

18. This is yet another instance of the cultural lag by which children's games are separated from the games of adults, the former preserving features which have disappeared from the latter.

19. Among those familiar with this idea were the Latin poet Plautus (*Captivi*, Prol. 22), Montaigne, the dramatist John Webster (*Duchess of Malfi*, V. iv. 63–64), and Solórzano Pereira in his *Emblemata* (Madrid, 1651).

20. See Horden, *George Wither*, p. 16 (Book I, Illustr. XVI).

21. See Horden in the note preceding his edition, and the now again easily accessible work of Rollenhagen, *Nucleus emblematum selectissimorum*, p. 16. According to *The National Union Catalogue*, vol. 444, p. 179, the illustrations in Wither's book are the work of Crispijn van de Passe (the Older) (1565–1637).

22. In Rollenhagen's work the Latin motto is:

CONCVSSVS SVRGO, *Casus me tollit in altum,*
Plaudit vt in medijs Mens cruce pressa malis.

Here the emblematic poem, translated into French by a professor of French from Cologne, has the following wording:

Le ballon boursoufflé, sur la terre tombant,
Par sa cheute leger, reiallit bondißant:
Ainsi l'esprit constant oppreßé de misere,
Se redresse a l'encontre & la tourne a sa
gloire.

23. See Figure 62.
24. This is the expression used by Höltgen, p. 146. The poem, from *Divine Fancies. Digested into Epigrammes, Meditations, and Observations*, London 1632, is here reproduced from Grosart's edition, vol. 2, p. 233.
25. Many of the following examples have been gleaned from the study of Brewster. Of course, the subject was prominent in other literary genres of the age as well, but the numerous instances listed by Huguet from sixteenth-century sermons are for the most part rather dull, see Huguet, chapter VI: 'Les jeux', especially pp. 76–91; see also what is said ibid., p. 162f., on the term *boute-hors* which, as we saw earlier, also referred to the medieval game of tennis.
26. See van Fossen, p. 70.
27. See van Fossen, p. 74.
28. See Herford and Simpson, vol. 5, p. 170 (I, i, 186–189), and vol. 10, p. 10 (note on line 188).
29. See Herford and Simpson, vol. 4, p. 65 (*Cynthias Reuells*, II, i, 63–9).
30. On 'Paul's Walk' (the central aisle of St Paul's Cathedral), 'a promenade, place of business and assignation, and an exchange of gossip' in the sixteenth and seventeenth centuries, see Harvey, p. 625, s.v. *Paul's Cathedral*.
31. See Grosart, *The Non-Dramatic Works*, vol. 2, pp. 238–40.
32. See Greg, [p. 33].
33. See Lucas, vol. 1, p. 128 (*The White Devil*, V, 71–77).
34. According to Millo, p. 54, these inscriptions are still a characteristic of the ball courts (*trinquetes*) of the city of Valencia. In 1857, the owner of the 'Trinquete la Encarnación' submitted to the town authorities the draft of a set of rules one of which required of a player to speak with moderation ('modesto en el hablar'). In the ancient court of Burriana the following lines were inscribed on a tile (Millo, p. 53):

El jugador de pelota tres cosas ha de tener:
hablar poco, jugar mucho y no quedar a
deber.
(*The player at ball has to observe three*
things: speaking little,
playing much and to leave no debt
unpaid.)

35. See *The Duchess of Malfi*, V, 4, 63f. The passage is indebted to Sidney's *Arcadia*, see Lucas, vol. 2, p. 120, and p. 197, commentary on line 63.
36. See Greg, *Porter, Henry. The Two Angry Women of Abington* p. [25f.], lines 834–841.

Chapter 5

1. The story can be found in Nick, p. 37f. In a number of tennis histories this episode is said to be the first reference to tennis in Germany, e.g. in Voigt, *Das Lawn-Tennis Spiel*, p. 1f., Heineken, p. 29, and von Reznicek, p. 9 (Voigt gives the year 1539 rather than 1339). To the mind of all three authors, the unfortunate Weissenburg was the murderer (to Voigt his name was even Weissenstein, and both Heineken and von Reznicek copied the mistake thoughtlessly, thus illustrating perfectly the quality of earlier sport historical research in this country). To von Reznicek, a lost tennis match was the only reason for the murder.
2. See Verdam, *G. van der Schueren's Teuthonista*, p. 169f. On the author see ibid., p. ii.
3. On the manuscript see Menne, pp. 77–9. The manuscript formerly belonged to the Gymnasialbibliothek of Cologne where in former times all manuscripts from local monasterial and college libraries were collected before they were eventually transferred to the City Archives, see Vennebusch, p. xi.
4. See Clemen, p. 214f.
5. Ibid., p. 215.
6. See Stadtarchiv Köln, MS. G.B. 4° 87, fol. 36v: 'nochtan geuelt it dat man spilt mit eynre kaetschen ind niet mee. Ind dat koemt/ want die eyn parthie hait vnderzijden xlv / ind die ander parthie en hait niet dan xxx off [= or] xxxv.'
7. The Flemish term *cache* has not survived in Cologne, but in a street-name of Aachen, Katschhof, which has been

called, and perhaps correctly so, the oldest sports ground of the German Empire, see Reiner Müller, p. 3.

8. Fol. 8v: 'Als die kaetscher haint gekoren eyn goede stede ind sy eyns van hertzen syn wa sy spillen willen, so is in noit zu hain zweyerleye dienre. Die eyne, vmb wail zu zeigen ind getruwelichen die kaetschen / Water ir niet en behoert vntruwelichen zo zeigenen, mee der eynen partien zo baten, dan der anderen.'

9. In modern times, during the city's famous carnival pageants, the windows of Cologne serve as targets for sweets and chocolates. In the Middle Ages, and in much the same as in the French city of Orléans, they apparently were the destination of many a tennis ball.

10. See MS G.B. 4° 87, loc. cit.: 'It is ouch noit, anderkunne dienre zo hain, die die belle holen als sy verre geslagen off vngereit syn: It sy in gossen, in kelren, in vynsteren of anders wae.'

11. Ibid.: 'Ind dese dienre synt schuldich vil belle bi sich zo hainn: Dair vmme als der eyn vnbereit iss / dat sy eynen anderen bal mogen geuen vmb myt zo spillen / die wijl man den anderen bal soekt / vp dat die spilre niet ledich syn en duruen / noch beiden na dem vngereiden balle.'

12. Ibid., fol. 15v: 'dae man sicher spilen wil / so pliet man gelt off pende bi zo lagen', 'in order to play safely, the custom is to deposit money or pledges'.

13. From Low German *bur*, 'neighbour', 'fellow-citizen', and *sprake*, 'speech', 'discussion'.

14. I am grateful to my colleague Rudolf Holbach for bringing this interesting source to my attention. Dr Holbach discovered it in Pauli's nineteenth-century description of medieval Lübeck, ibid., p. 56f., but has been unable to trace Pauli's original source, the 'Ober-Stadtbuch'. The genuineness of the source, however, is beyond doubt.

15. See Streib, p. 378. We shall in what follows profit time and again from Streib's pioneering study.

16. See Historisches Archiv der Stadt Köln [Historical Archive of the City of Cologne], *Libri registrationum Protocollum Senatus*, vol. 21, fol. 9r:

Nachdem vile klagen kommen vber die kaetzbane vff sanct Gereonstrassen neben dem convent Nasareth das der ort vil

Gotslesterungen gebraucht dergleichen allerley Schandtschrifften vber die Maure Int convent, zu argernuss der Geistlicher Personen geworffen werden sollen Ist befolhen [Clas van] Mors [, Euerhart] Suderman vnd beiden Thurnhern vmb sich der sachen zuerkunden auch die gelegenheit zu besichtigen davon zum negsten Relation zuthun.

17. On the convent also see Clemen, pp. 241–3.

18. See the *Libri registrationum*, vol. 21, fol. 12r:

Es haben die hern Liskirchen Renthmeister Clas van Mörse Euerhart Suderman vnd beide Thurnhern referirt wie das ire liebde vff des Paters zu Nazareth vilfeltlige Clage, die gelegenheit der Kaetzbanen besichtigt vnd vil schendtlichs vnraths daselbst befunden zu grossem argernuss der geistlicher Kinder und anders nachtheilgs schadens So ist entlich verdragen das die Thurnhern denn Landskronen sollen alsbalde vorbescheiden vnd ernstlich ansagen die kaetzbaene den negsten Werckdag als Mondag vur Mittag abbrechen zulassen, wae das nit beschieht sollen die Geweldrichter mit vnser hern Werckluiden den naemittag dargaen vnd die kaetsbane niederwerffen vnd zerstoeren Es soll auch den Inwonern bei straff des Thurnses geboten werden die zween feirdage als Morgen und Vbermorgen keine kaetzerei daselbst zuhalten.

19. For a complete account of early tennis in the Low Countries see now de Bondt, *'Heeft yemant lust met bal ...te spelen ...?', passim*.

20. See van Afferden in de Tollenaere and Claes's edition, fol. 44r–45r.

21. See Pieter van Afferden, *Tyrocinium latinae linguae*, Cologne: Johann Gymnich, 1575, pp. 119–21. A copy of this rare book is in the Bayerische Staatsbibliothek, Munich, shelf mark Ling. lat. 51.

22. Mahler, p. 47, note 2, lists the feminine noun *Raggetten* for the year 1561 (Frisius), and *Ragetten* (Maaler) for the year 1561.

23. Von Fichard, in the second edition of his *Handbuch*, p. 24f., refers to a passage from the *Buch Weinsberg*, the famous family chronicle of Cologne (1572), in which Charles IX of France receives the message of Coligny's murder while engaged in a match of *jeu de la paume* in the Louvre, and flies into a rage. The quotation proves that in the Cologne

dialect of the time, the term used for 'to play tennis' was *die Katze [slan]*: 'wie dem Konink diese Zeitung quam, da er den bal und *Katze sloich* [inflected 3rd person past tense], nam er sich grois zorns an.'

24. See the *Libri registrationum*, vol. 45, fol. 236v.

25. In the second half of the sixteenth century the written standard of Cologne was, not least because of the influence of the Counter-Reformation, gradually superseded by the language of the German south. This made itself felt above all in the local book trade, and that is why van Afferden's German translation which appeared in Cologne in 1575 should (despite the terms *khatzen* and *khatzbahn* occurring in it) have been effected in the latter and not in the Cologne dialect. See on this issue in general Hoffmann, 'Zur Geschichte', p. 99f.

26. See Bolland, Part 2, p. 137:

Und dewile sodan speel to verderve der jungen joget utsuhet, so wil ein erbar radt sodan speel gantz afgedan und verbaden hebben. Und ein jeder, de dat gebruket und daraver werdt beslagen, de schal, so ofte dat geschuet, der wedde X Jochimdaler verfallen sin.

For the references to tennis activities in Hamburg, the author is again indebted to his colleague Rudolf Holbach.

27. See ibid., p. 139: 'Dar sik averst jemandt understan wurde, dusdem mandat toweddern solch katspil achter sinen husern oder op den hoven antorichten, datsulvige schal durch de buwhaveslude wedderumme afgebraken und der anrichter wegen sines ungehorsams in vifhundert daler straffe genamen werden.'

28. On the Viennese tennis courts see Erwin Mehl, 'Das Ballhaus-Spiel', p. 171, and 'Prager Erinnerungen', p. 15. Mehl's short descriptions are based on a thesis written at the Institut für Turnlehrerausbildung [Training College for Teachers of German Turnen] in the University of Vienna by Hedwig Kühr, see ibid., pp. 61–137 (see the entry in the bibliography).

29. According to Mehl, 'Prager Erinnerungen', p. 15, it was first mentioned in 1534.

30. This ballhouse was first mentioned in 1542, and turned into a national theatre by Emperor Joseph in 1776. It was here that in 1797, on the birthday of the German Emperor Francis II, the

composer Haydn directed his 'The People's Hymn' (Volkshymne) to the tune of which, in 1841, the poet Hofmann von Fallersleben wrote the text of 'Deutschland, Deutschland über alles', the German national anthem, see Mehl, 'Prager Erinnerungen', p. 15f. There was yet another imperial tennis court, and another four which were privately owned: one in the so-called Ballgasse (of which the streetname is the only reminiscence today), 'Boyer's Ball Court' (das Boyersche Ballhaus) in Himmelpfortgasse, one in Teinfaltstrasse, and that of Prince Auersperg in Lerchenfelder Strasse. Apart from those existing at the time in France, this last named is perhaps the only court in nineteenth-century continental Europe where real tennis was still played (till 1872), see Mehl, 'Prager Erinnerungen', pp. 16–18. As late as 1941, Mehl was still able to see the netting which protected the glass windows, and traces of the old chase lines on the stone floor.

31. See Mehl, 'Prager Erinnerungen', p. 14f. The architecture of the court, a magnificent Renaissance building in the palace gardens, devised by the famous architect Bonifaz Wolmeut, is said to be influenced by that of Upper Italy, and notably that of the famous architect Palladio. There was a second court in Prague (seventeenth century) in Egidigasse (Jilska ulica).

32. See Kühr, p. 64. Other keepers of the imperial courts were Colin Olifir (Oliueer) (1586); Francesco Menrico (1593); Ciasi di Marchio and his son Francisco (1613), Kühr, p. 65.

33. Ibid., p. 71.

34. For details on the Salzburg ballhouse see the articles by Günther Bauer, *passim*.

35. But see below, note 106.

36. See the statistics in Streib, p. 378f., with additional details. The ballhouse in Jena, built in 1671, was praised by Ph. Florini in 1751, and in a Dutch encyclopedia of 1774 because of its exceptional symmetry and the good overall quality of its facilities, see Streib, p. 379, note 94, and de Bondt, '*Heeft yemant*', p. 51. Another was put up in Leipzig during the Thirty Years' War, see Streib, p. 379.

37. The present writer is indebted to Wolfgang Baer of the Augsburg City Archive for having made known to him

the relevant passages from the so-called Welser Chronicle, and the City's Council Minutes.

38.

Im Aprilen ward zu S. Anna neben die Bibliotheca ein Ballhauß der Spanier und anderer Hofleuth halben, auffgericht, mehrerteils aber Antonio dem Bischoffe zu Arras zugefallen: Damit derselbe … durch zusehen bey solchem Spiel sich erlustiren, unnd die Melancholey vertreiben köndte: Da aber solch Spielhauß nun schier gar ausgemacht war, fiele es plötzlichen wider ein und erschluge drei Personen. Wurde aber alsbald widerumb mit einer besseren Grundveste underbauwen, also daß es hernach viel Jar lang zu einem Ballhauß starck gewesen.

This passage was quoted, very imperfectly and without quoting the source, by Voigt, *Das Lawn-Tennis Spiel*, p. 2, and Heineken, p. 28, the latter of which was referred to by Streib, p. 380. The site was redesigned in 1614 by Elias Holl, and on an engraving by Lucas Kilian titled 'Annahof mit Stadtbibliothek und Gymnasium bei St. Anna' there is no trace left of the former ballhouse.

39. 'Nach dem Maister Bernhart Zwitzel das Palhauß bey sannd Anna zumachen bevolhen unnd angedingt worden, daß selbs aber am gestern eingefallen, So ist erkannt, daß ihme soll aufferlegt werden, dasselb wider auff seinen selbs Costen auffzupauen.'

40. See Streib, p. 378, note 65.

41. See Hepp, *Religion und Herrschaft*, p. 389, note 66. This 'old' ballhouse was presumably erected in 1594 by Frederick IV. Another ballhouse for students was put up in 1594 by a certain Hans Caton von Gülich, a Reformist expelled from the Low Countries by the Spaniards and a manufacturer of tiled ovens. It was located at a place in the suburb called 'uff dem Graben', on the corner of Hauptstrasse and Ziegelgasse, see Christ, p. 1, and ibid., note 2.

42. See Hepp, *Matthaeus Merian*, p. 58, and illustrations on pp.17 (Merian's 'großes Panorama' of 1620); 51 (from Zincgref's *Emblemata*; and 87 (Merian's engraving of 1645).

43. See Aberdare, p. 54, and illustration on p. 55, and Marshall, *Annals*, Plate 15 (before p. 65).

44. See Streib, p. 378, note 70. On this ballhouse see now Günther Bauer, 'Das f.e. Salzburger Hofballhaus', p. 116f., who quotes extensively from a thesis from Munich (1971) by Erna Lang entitled *Ballhaus und Reitschule, zwei Bauten im Umkreis der Universität Ingolstadt*.

45. See Streib, p. 379, note 74.

46. The 'Petrarch Master' is so named after a series of illustrations he contributed to a German sixteenth-century edition (1532) of Petrarch's *De remediis utriusque fortunae*.

47. See Streib, p. 379. Another was built during the Thirty Years' War in Rostock.

48. See Decker-Hauff and Setzler, p. 106. On the Knights' Academies in general see Mahler who also refers to the game at ball practised there (p. 47f.). On the institution in Austria see now Strohmeyer, *Beiträge*, pp. 36–42, § 5.3. Die Ritterakademien.

49. See Decker-Hauff and Setzler, loc. cit.

50. See Decker-Hauff and Setzler, loc. cit. In this year, 1559, Duke Christopher of Württemberg gave a grant to a limited number of young aristocrats ('ein anzal Junger vom Adel') who were intended to receive a schooling as ducal administrators after which they would be employed 'for the preservation of good order, acquiescence and peace and the defence of the church and the office of preaching' ('erhaltung guter Policey, rhu und friden … beschirmung der Kirchen und Predigtamts').

51. See 'Die Geschichte eines Deutschen Ballhauses', p. 307.

52. See here, and in what follows Decker-Hauff and Setzler, pp. 106–108.

53. See Decker-Hauff and Setzler, p. 108, and the picture on p. 107. The picture shows the inscription over the southeastern porch of what now constitutes the Wilhelmstift.

54. See Decker-Hauff and Setzler, p. 109.

55. See Saurbier, S. 90f. (4. Leibesübungen an Ritterakademien und Universitäten). John Frederick was the son and successor of Frederick (who died in 1608). He had himself been an inmate of the college and in 1608, in the final session of the local parliament, he had to promise revision of the existing statutes. This marked the beginning of a quarrel over the statutes between the college and the university

which could be settled as late as 1614 only. Whereas students of the university might attend lectures, bodily and courtly exercises (including, of course, tennis) were for the students of the college only. The collegiate statutes were never subjected to more than minor revisions, and remained essentially unchanged until 1817 when the institution was eventually dissolved, see Decker-Hauff and Setzler, p. 114f.

56. A tennis 'professional' (as he would now be called in real tennis) had been in the Duke's pay before, but after a visitation early in the year 1606, in the course of which incredible abuses had come to light, he was sent packing, the reason for his dismissal being stated as selfishness ('wegen Eigennutz'), see Schneider, p. 230.

57. It was published by Beyrer, pp. 86–92. On the two authors of this itinerary ('Reisebeschreibung') see the biographical note, ibid., p. 204. On the college and its ballhouse see also Heineken, pp. 33–6.

58. According to Schneider, p. 220, only the stonework of Einsiedel monastery, after it had been destroyed by fire, went into the building of the college. He confirms, however, that the college was maintained from church property. He also mentions the violet outfit of the inmates which, after a black one had been prescribed before, became obligatory as early as in the statutes of 1594, see idem, p. 224.

59. See Streib, p. 381, note 123.

60. A game called 'Kreisball-Spiel' (circle ball game) is described in Rulemann, p. 103f.

61. See Beyrer, p. 88: the professor of history lectured from 8 to 9, the law professor from 9 to 10, the French language teacher from 1 to 2.

62. See for these details the article 'Die Geschichte eines Deutschen Ballhauses', p. 307. This article is at variance with Streib who says that it was converted into a church in 1790 which was in turn demolished in 1817, op. cit., p. 378, note 69. According to 'Die Geschichte', loc. cit., a new ballhouse had meanwhile been put up in Tübingen at the Lustnauer Tor which, however, became the home of the game of billiards, and never seems to have been used for tennis.

63. See Streib, p. 381, note 121.

64. See Konrad, p. 6.

65. See Decker-Hauff and Setzler, p. 106.

66. Since Jacob von der Heyden's *Speculum Cornelianum* was published in Strasbourg, one is inclined to regard Figure 62 as an illustration of one of the two contemporary ballhouses of that city. The picture is, however, the work of the Dutch engraver Crispijn van de Passe I (the Older), or, possibly, that of one of his pupils, see Konrad, vol. 1, p. 20, no. 30. Before the engraving was incorporated in von der Heyden's collection, it had appeared in van de Passe's *Academia sive speculum vitae scholasticae* of 1612 as well as in his *Nieuwen Jeucht Spieghel* (without year, the Dutch version of the former). Both books contain scenes from contemporary students' life, see Franken, p. 261f., no. 1343; Boon, p. 65, no. 16; and Boon and Verbeek, p. 295f., no. 14. Von der Heyden's *Speculum Cornelianum* had a predecessor, the *Pugillus Facetiarum Iconographicarum in Studiosorum ... gratiam ex propriis eorundem Albis desumptarum*, see Konrad, p. 20, no. 28. To this, the van de Passe engraving was apparently added later when it became the *Speculum*. According to de Bondt, p. 96, caption to figure 5, and idem, 'Kaetsen', p. 78f., some of the pictures in van de Passe's *Academia* show buildings of the university of Leiden, e.g. Leiden university library, the Theatrum Anatomicum and the Hortus, and that is why he ventured to surmise that one of the Leiden tennis courts served van de Passe as a model; either the one located near the so-called Noordeinde, or the one at the Koepoortgracht (the court near the Catharijneklooster, de Bondt's first choice, was discarded by him, since it was built as late as *c.* 1624 only, see de Bondt, 'Kaetsen', p. 85). Presumably because van de Passe lived in Utrecht as from 1612 onwards, his pictures have also been considered illustrations of students' life in that city, see Franken, p. 261 (and indeed many others). In de Bondt's list of Dutch Renaissance tennis courts ('De kaatsbanen in Den Haag', p. 100f.), there is a notable absence of Utrecht tennis courts. Here, a pall mall was built in 1637 to attract students to the new university, but no tennis court, see Perks, p. 3. Since Utrecht university was not founded before 1636, van de Passe's engraving (1612) cannot

show a local court there. It is not impossible that the picture represents the 'katzbaen' of Cologne where van de Passe was active prior to his settling down in Utrecht. Van de Passe's picture also inspired the German engraver Peter Rollos (floruit Berlin 1628–1639) to whom we owe an interior view of a seventeenth-century tennis court. Artistically, it is clearly inferior to its model. It is to be found in Rollos' *Speculum Cornelianum* (there are editions of 1624 and 1639, and a French version titled *Le centre de l'amour*, see Konrad, p. 21, nos 35 and 35a; Rollos picture is reproduced in Bartlett, after p. 48, figure 5(a) and elsewhere; a copy of the book in the Bibliothèque Nationale is missing since 1949). The adjective *cornelianus* in the works above mentioned refers to the type of the profligate student after a character in a comedy by Albrecht Wichgrev (1600), see Konrad, p. 20, no. 27. The type is depicted in von der Heyden's *Speculum Cornelianum*, figure [23], and there is an explanation of the picture in the preface of the same work [Praefatio], see ibid., p. [4]. Among the things which have led to the dissolute student's ruin is, of course, tennis: a racket can be seen at his very feet, and a bill issued by a ballmaster ('ballen meister zedel') adorns his writing desk.

67. The essentials of Guarinonius's biography have been compiled by Grass, pp. 9–17. See also Rapp, *passim*.

68. Quoted from Grass, p. 15.

69. See Guarinonius, pp. 1208–1213 (Book 6., Chapter XV. Von siebenerley vnderschiedlichen Förm vnd Nutzbarrkeit deß Ballenspiels). The merits of Guarinonius were assessed by Mehl, 'Von siebenerley Nutzbarkeit', *passim*.

70. See Guarinonius, p. 1208f.:

Das Ballspiel das Hauptspiel vnter allen Spielen sey/zeigen alle Oerter vnnd namhaffte Stätt/insonderheit alle Potentaten der Christenheit an/welche zu Erhaltung dieser schönen vnnd lustigen Vbung/besonders gelegne vnd ansehenliche grosse Gebäw führen/vnd darzu mit allen Nohtwendigkeit/auch mit darzu bestimpten vnd beywohnenden Ballmeistern versehen/vnd ihre Jugend/meistens die Edle Knaben besonders fleiß darinnen abrichten lassen.

71. See Grass, p. 11.

72. Guarinonius frequently refers to him as 'that worldly prince who for more than half a millennium alone held sway over the whole art of medicine' (den 'über ein halb Jahrtausend die ganze Medizin allein beherrschenden Fürsten der Erde'), see Grass, loc. cit.

73. See Guarinonius, p. 1209.

74. Ibid.:

Gnug ist es/daß solliches Spiel den gantzen Menschen/vnd alle Glieder nach dem besten vbet/sintemal der Kopff vnd Halß sich auff alle Ecken vnd Seiten/vbersich/vntersich/ wie auch die Augen biegen vnd wenden müssen/nachmals die Füß/den Leib/dem fliegenden Balln nach behend hin vnd wider hengen/allda man laufft/springt/an das Gemäwr vnd Wand hinauff schwingt/sich buckt/erhebet/hintersich/für sich/nach allen Seiten trehet/die Hand aber mit Hebung der Ragetten/vnd alle Finger allermassen in Vmbwendung anderst vnd anderst beweget/ da man einmal den Balln ob [= *oberhalb*, 'above'] dem Kopff/dann neben den Füssen/das dritte völlig/das vierdte schnittig [i.e. 'with the flat of the racket, or with cut'] abholen vnd wider schlagen muß.

75. See Gumpelzhaimer, p. 257; the passage is quoted by Mahler, p. 48.

76. See Guarinonius, p. 1209:

Darbey auch das Gemüht mit sehr großem Lust ergötzt wirdt/vnd hierinnen ihr viel dermassen zu denen Zeiten gevbt/daß sie an statt einer Raggeten ein Pantoffel oder Schuch/oder ein Becher oder Glaß in die Hand nemmen/den Balln im Flug fangen/vnd wider hinschlagen oder werffen.

77. Ibid.:

Diß Spiel ist aller Jugend/sonderlich der edlen und zarten erst gewachsnen von 14. Jahr an/biß auff das 31. einlich/weil solliches Alter in Leibs Bewegung zum hurtigsten vnd behendigsten/auch kein Gefahr/al: etwan des zu grossen Eyfers an sich hat/sonderlich wann man vmb viel Gelt spielet/welliches das gantze Spiel verderbt/vnd vnlustig macht.

78. Ibid.: 'Ist ein Spiel für alle junge Fürsten/Potentaten vnd Herren/die sich mit gutem Nutz sanfftlich/vnd ohne grosse Mühe vben wollen.'

79. Ibid.: 'die Ballhäuser [sind] alle mit Zieglen gepflastert/damit der vbenden Füß sicher hafften mögen'.

80. On the *Wappenbuch* of Johann Michael Weckherlin (1547–1610), a Rentkammerrat (paymaster) of the Duke of Württemberg in Stuttgart, see Marks in

his article in the festschrift *150 Jahre Oberösterreichisches Landesmuseum*, p. 245. The author would like to thank the librarian, Margarete Ploch, for calling to his attention the festschrift, and her successor, Waltraud Faißner, for her generous permission to re-use the picture.

81. See Guarinonius, p. 1209. Mehl, 'Von siebenerley' , p. 202, believed that a Protestant was the target of Guarinonius's invective, and the Counter-Reformation its immediate context.

82. Ibid.: 'mit der Raggeten ... auff sein vngewaschene Goschen [literally 'unwashed trap']'.

83. See Guarinonius, p. 1209f.

84. Ibid., p. 1210:

> solte vielleicht dieser Fürst sich mit fressen/sauffen vnd dergleichen Lastern/darin sich etlich andere Fürsten/vnd der ehrvergessne Pasquilant selbsten dapffer an statt des Ballnspiel vben/gevbt haben? ... Wellicher vnerzogne Tropff wissen vnd lernen solle/daß das Ballspiel nicht allein ein offentliches/ehrliches/löbliches vnd edles/sonder auch ihr vielen ein nohtwendiges Spiel ist/...vnd diesen Balln den schlag ich ihme bey dieser Gelegenheit zu/...nicht heymisch/sonder fein offentlich.

85. The author has, in what follows, summarized Herrmann's excellent study *Ballhäuser und die Strassburger Ballhausgasse*.

86. See Herrmann, vol. 2, p. 12, and p. 66, no. 4.

87. See ibid., p. 9f.

88. See ibid., p. 63, no. 1:

> Seindt Bauherrn und [Dreyer vom Pfenningthurn] zu der Statt hin und wider gefahren, und sonderlich, weil Johann Klap ein Springer und dantzer unnd ein Pallenschlager bei Rhat & XXIer angesucht Ime zu gönnen ein Pallenhauss zumachen und daselbst Ime befohlen, sich umb ein gelegenen ortt umbzusehen, Derhalben er in dem Thumherren hoff ... solches anzurichten vorhabens, und vilmal bei den Herrn umb den Augenschein gebetten. Also daselbst hin gefahren, in solchen alten hoff der schir an allen orten infallen will, so vor jaren hertzog Reichert Pfalzgrave ingehabt, und beffunden, da er den alten langen Stall hinweg bricht, das zu solchem Platz genug were & deshalb umbgefragt, ... weil solchs im Thumherren hoff, und da sich bey solchem spiel zwischen graven und herren ein span oder ein todtschlag oder dergleichen zutragen solte, das der Zugriff von den Thumherren nit gut

geheissen, unnd meinen Herrn Vorwurf anrichten würde, derhalben Ihm solches abzuschlagen und an einem ortt der gemeinen Statt zustendig vil ehr zuzulassen were. Jedoch ist dissmal geschlossen, man sollt Ihme willfahren, doch für unsere Herren bringen, da man Ihme Supplikanten als burgeren wol allerhand inbinden kann.

89. Ibid., p. 65, no. 3.

90. See ibid., vol. 1, p. 41f.

91. Ibid., p. 12: 'denn man hie verlige; welches nitt geschehe so einer dergleichen exercitia hätte', 'for people lay idle there; which would not be the case if one had such exercise'. Here, the verb *verligen*, 'to lie idle' (it no longer exists in the German language) is a reminder of medieval German chivalry. It formerly referred to the knight who preferred a life led in idleness to one filled with military campaigns, feats of arms and tournaments.

92. Ibid., p. 66, no. 5.

93. Ibid., p. 67, no. 6.

94. Ibid., vol. 2, p. 18 and p. 69, no. 10, note 2.

95. Ibid., p. 68, no. 8.

96. Ibid., no. 9.

97. Ibid., p. 68f., no. 10.

98. Ibid., p. 69, no. 10.

99. Ibid., p. 71, no. 15.

100. Ibid., p. 71, no. 16.

101. Ibid.

102. Ibid., p. 72, no. 17.

103. Ibid., p. 20. .

104. Ibid., p. 21.

105. See Herrmann, vol. 1, p. 73:

> X: Hats auch ein Ballhouses in dieser Statt?

> Y: Ja freylich / Ja zwei neben einander/wie die Nachen/ so von Basel herab fahren. Lasset uns hingehen ein dutzet ballen zuverschlagen.

Daniel's tennis dialogue was published, after the last edition of 1660, by Herrmann, vol. 1, pp. 73–80. The quotations on the following pages are from this edition. The same text, based on the edition of 1637, was published by von Fichard in his *Handbuch des Lawn-Tennis-Spieles* of 1902, pp. 28–34.

106. Despite Daniel's statement, there existed in Strasbourg, according to Baron Robert von Fichard (in his article 'Lawn-Tennis in Germany') no fewer than five ballhouses!

107. Ibid., p. 73, note 1.

108. Ibid., pp. 75–77.

109. Ibid., p. 74.
110. Ibid., p. 74f.: 'Lass auch ein maass Bier her bringen / vns zu erkühlen / wann wir erhitziget seind. Hernach komme vnd zeichne vnsere schasse auff / vnd gib auff unser Spiel achtung.'
111. See Gumpelzhaimer, p. 257: 'der [i.e. the ball] von Strimpffgarn auff ein bleyen kügelein fein starck gewunden wird, und mit leder überzogen'. The passage is quoted by Mahler, p. 48.
112. See Herrmann, p. 75.
113. Ibid.
114. According to the *Supplement to the Oxford English Dictionary*, the expression *rough or smooth* is hardly older than the 1890s, see Burchfield, vol. 3, p. 1363, s.v. *rough, a.* I, 1.d., and vol. 4, s.v. *smooth, a.* 1.d. In tennis, squash, etc., of one of the two sides of the racket … : used as a call when the racket is spun to decide the right to serve first or to choose ends. 1890 J. MARSHALL in *Tennis, Rackets, Fives* 26 *Smooth*, the front of the racket, which shows no knots. *Spin*, the decision by a racket, thrown spinning up into the air by one player, while the other calls 'rough' or 'smooth'. 1901 *Encycl. Sport II.* 621/2 *Smooth side of racket*, the side from which the twisted gut does not project.
  The method of stringing rackets in this way, and which resulted in the distinction between *rough* and *smooth*, seems to have been abandoned in real tennis around the year 1857, though, see J.M. Heathcote, p. 35f. Since that year, the cross-strings used to be threaded through the main-strings, a fact which makes the late appearance of the expression *rough or smooth* in the English language very difficult to explain. Perhaps it applied to the so-called 'treblings', cross-strings at the upper and lower end of the head which continued to be wound round the main strings, see Kuebler, *Buch der Tennisrackets*, p. 19f.
115. See Herrmann, p. 75.
116. Ibid., p. 80: 'Herr verspieler, was wolt jhr mir bevor geben / ich will mit einem schlägel, einem korb oder blawel mit euch spielen / oder vnderm schenckel.'
117. This tour de force demonstrating the greatest possible superiority of a tennis player has resulted in an idiomatic expression in the French language, namely *jouer quelqu'un par-dessous (la)*

jambe, literally 'to play somebody from underneath one's legs'. It is still used in the slightly modified form *traiter quelqu'un (quelque chose) par-dessous la jambe*, 'to handle somebody (a thing) lightly', see de Coen, p. 45f. Extravagant handicaps apparently were the flavour of the ancient game of tennis. As early as 1582, the German writer Fischart, in his *Geschichtsklitterung*, an adaptation of *Gargantua* by the French poet Rabelais, had the famous Olympic champion of Greek antiquity, the wrestler Milo of Croton, play tennis with an ox (alive) on his shoulders, see von Fichard, *Handbuch*, p. 25. The models for such demonstrations of skill and muscular strength may well have graced contemporary tennis courts. As late as the nineteenth century, the famous French *paume*-player J. Edmond 'Papa' Barre is reported to have engaged in a handicap match, the marker on his shoulders. The French eighteenth-century champion Raymond Masson is known to have excelled in a match in which he had to emerge from a barrel for every stroke, see Aberdare, p. 80 and p. 64. During the first decades of lawn tennis, similar handicaps seem to have been extremely popular, see on this issue Todd, p. 138.
118. See Herrmann, p. 75: 'Er wird mich trillen nach seinem gefallen.'
119. Ibid.: 'dass ist / umb die Ballen / die spielschuhen / den trunck / dess marckiererslohn vnnd umbs fewer'.
120. Ibid.: 'Es kan wol sein, dass die buben / welche gemeiniglich in der Gallerey zu dem end stehen / einen theil haben in jre schieb oder dieb säck gestossen.'
121. See Hönn, p. 31f.
122. For its full title see the bibliography. The complete text is now easily accessible in the form of a facsimile reprint which appeared in volume VI of the journal *Homo ludens* (1996).
123. See Bender, p. 2f.:

Nachdem ich gar oft zu Gemuet gezogen / was massen denen jenigen / die das vortreffliche / von vielen hohen und niedern Stands-Personen beliebte Ballen-Spiel zu lernen guten Lust getragen / wegen vieler Puncten / so alle auf einmal nicht wol zu merken / etwas schwer vorkommen / sonderlich in der Partie, weßwegen auch mancher darvon abgestanden / und die Beliebung zu solchen / allen andern lobwuerdigen Exercitien sinken lassen; So ist es

zwar nicht ohne / daß es Nachdenkens
vonnoethen / aber doch nicht so schwer / wie
es ihm mancher vorsetzt / ergreiffts auch
immer einer eher als der ander.

(After having contemplated fairly often how
those greatly desirous to learn the excellent
ball-game, popular among many persons of
high and low estate, have abstained from it, and
have lessened their interest in such exercise
praiseworthy above all others, because it
appears somewhat difficult to them, because of
the many points hard to remember at once, and
during a match in particular, [at this point the
author loses control over his syntax altogether];
it is yet, although not such as to make thinking
unnecessary, not so difficult as it is put before
him by some, since some will always
understand it sooner than others.)

124. Bender, despite his clumsiness, was not
completely uneducated, though. As is
shown by the many parallels in his
booklet, he at least knew a French treatise
on tennis, i.e. *L'Ordonnance du Royal et
honorable Jeu de la Paume ... contenant
vingt-quatre articles* of 1592, published by
Forbet in 1599 and printed anew by
Hulpeau in 1632. The *Ordonnance* was
printed in Albert de Luze, pp. 246–51.

125. Bender, p. 3f.:

Obwolen nun allerhand Exercitia und Freye
Kuenste in Büchern gedruckt gefunden werden
/ wornach die jenige / welche solche zu
verstehen Lust tragen / sich reguliren koennen
/ so ist doch von dem lobwuerdig=beruehmten
Ballen=Spiel noch niemalen nichts aufgesetzt /
viel weniger in den Druck gegeben worden /
hat auch niemalen keiner / solches zu thun /
sich bemuehen moegen. Derowegen habe mich
fuer gut zu seyn bedunken lassen / die
Beschaffenheit auf das kuerzeste / nicht mit
hohen praechtigen / sondern ganz
verstaendigen und deutlichen Worten / also
zusammen zu richten / daß ein jeder Liebhaber
/ so es lesen / gar leichtlich / ohne geringe
Mühe / fassen und erlernen / auch in kurzer
Zeit begreiffen wird.

126. Ibid., p. 5f.

Die Dedication habe ich / aus schuldig-
dienstgeneigter Affection / an den Ehrnvesten
und Wohlfuernehmen Herrn Georg Winter /
Burgern und Handelsmann allhier / als einen
dieser Kunst und Exercitii hochverstaendigen
Liebhabern / meinen großgeneigten Patron /
stellen wollen / mit hochfleissiger Bitte / dieses
wenige nicht zu verschmaehen / sondern
großguenstig zu acceptiren / und meinen in
unterdienstlicher Geflissenheit geneigten guten
Willen / daraus zu verspuehren. Hiemit

verbleibe / neben Empfehlung Goettlicher
Obhut / Euer Ehrnvest Dienstbereitwilligster
Johann Georg Bender / Ballenmeister in
Nuernberg.

127. Ibid., p. 7.
128. Ibid., p. 7f. As in Daniel Martin's book, a
distinction is made between rough,
French *revers*, and smooth, French *droit*,
the German equivalents being 'Knöpff'
('knots') and 'glatt' (see Herrmann).
129. Ibid.; on *peloter* see also de Coen, p. 47.
130. Ibid., p. 9.
131. Ibid.
132. See Herrmann, vol. 1, p. 76.
133. See Bender, p. 10. According to Bender,
the wager was settled after the first game;
and this is a regulation which can be
traced back to the *Ordonnance du Royal et
honorable Jeu de la Paume* of 1592 printed
in Hulpeau, 1632. See Herrmann, vol. 1,
p. 75, note 9.
134. See Bender, p. 13f.
135. Ibid., p. 14f.
136. Ibid., p. 15.
137. Ibid., p. 16:

soll auch besagter Marquier oder Aufseher /
bey Verlust seines Lohns / und daß wegen
seines Unfleisses / andere ihme zum Spotte an
die Statt gesetzet werden / die Chassen und
andere Spruenge der Ballen fleissig zeichnen /
ferner zum treufleissigsten / welchem Theil
recht oder unrecht gegeben wird / und weme
die Zusehenden am meisten beypflichten /
merken / dann ohne einige Scheu und Ansehen
der Person / sie sey auch wer sie wolle /
anzeigen.

138. Ibid., p. 20: 'wann man zwo Partien
spielet / darff man nicht abtretten / es sey
dann aus erheblichen Ursachen / als daß
einen die anfallende Nacht und das
Ungewitter abtriebe / dann dasselbe Spiel
auf folgende Tage ausgespielet und
vollendet werden muß.'
139. Ibid.
140. Ibid., p. 30.
141. The text has *Biscave*, a misprint for
biscaye.
142. He added a *nota bene* to this effect, ibid.,
p. 31: 'N.B. Dienet gar wol zum
Ausmachen / auch dem Gegentheil zur
Verhinderung der Partie.' (It serves well
the purpose of finishing, or, on the
contrary, of preventing – the loss of – a
match/set.)
143. See Bender, p. 35f.:

Letzlich / ist vor allen anderen sehr
nothwendig wol zu observiren / den jenigen
insonderheit / die um Geld Parti spielen / daß
allezeit ein jeder so viel / als warum man spielet
/ an Parschafft unter die Corde oder Seil lege /
dann es geschicht oft / wann gleich mancher
viel gewonnen / hernach da nicht aufgesetzt
worden / doch wenig / ja wol gar nichts
bekommt / wie manche genug mit Schaden
erfahren müssen. In diesem Stück ist kein
Scheu zu tragen / Weilen das Recht hierinnen
einem so wol als dem andern gebuehret es zu
begehren / so ist man der Bezahlung am
gewissesten versichert.

CHAPTER 6

1. See Aberdare, pp. 61–87, on '18th
   Century Tennis' and '19th Century
   Tennis'.
2. Ibid., p. 72, and Streib, p. 376.
3. See Alexander, *Wingfield*, p. 72.
4. See ibid., p. 151f. Wingfield was a
   member of the Gentlemen-at-Arms, the
   Royal Body Guards, and met the future
   king in the mess of this corps. Wingfield,
   later in life the founder of an English
   gourmet society, was instrumental in
   improving the culinary standards of the
   mess over which he presided for eighteen
   years.
5. See ibid., p. 201, the facsimile of the
   original.
6. See ibid., p. 95.
7. See ibid., p. 201f.
8. See Alexander, *Lawn Tennis*, p. 15f.;
   idem, *Wingfield*, pp. 88f. and 196; and
   Todd, p. 231. Much to the reader's
   bewilderment, Alexander, *Lawn Tennis*,
   p. 109, and *Wingfield*, p. 205, states in an
   introductory note to the facsimile print of
   the *Book of the Game*, that it was
   'published in December, 1873'. This is at
   odds with what he says on the pages
   referred to above, but must be wrong
   since the same author's purpose elsewhere
   (*Wingfield*, p. 194) is to prove wrong his
   countrymen Whitman and Henderson
   who had assumed an earlier publication of
   the book, i.e. in December or November,
   1873, respectively, thus accusing
   Wingfield of an act of dishonesty, namely
   to have claimed the possession of the
   patent at a time when it had not yet been
   granted.
9. See idem, *Wingfield*, p. 205, Appendix B.
10. See ibid., p. 207, Appendix B.
11. See ibid., p. 212f., Appendix B.
12. See Alexander, *Wingfield*, p. 77: 'The
    game of croquet had caused to be built
    thousands of well-rolled, weed-free, level
    lawns which measured at least thirty yards
    by twenty yards.'
13. The lawn mover was invented around the
    middle of the nineteenth century by
    Alexander Shanks, from Arbroath, and
    Thomas Green, from Leeds, see Todd,
    p. 47, and Gibbons, p. 7.
14. See Wilberforce, *Lawn Tennis*, in Bell,
    p. 2.
15. See Alexander, *Wingfield*, p. 86, and
    idem., *Lawn Tennis*, p. 3. The question of
    what German firm exactly supplied the
    first lawn tennis balls to the English major
    has, to my knowledge, never been
    answered. The Ayres ball, used for the
    Wimbledon tournaments for many years,
    as well as the Wright and Ditson ball,
    used for the US championships since
    1887, were also imported from Germany,
    see Sears, in C.G. Heathcote, p. 234. Even
    in their case, the name of the
    manufacturer seems to have been a trade
    secret of the English and American
    companies. This is confirmed by a letter
    signed D.H. and reprinted in von
    Fichard's *Illustriertes Lawn-Tennis-
    Jahrbuch* of 1905, p. 93f. Assessing the
    quality of the ball produced by the
    German manufacturer Franz Clouth,
    Cologne, D.H. claimed to have been told
    by insiders of the trade that two
    prestigious London firms had their balls
    manufactured in Germany.
16. See Alexander, *Wingfield*, pp. 91–3.
    Another publication of this kind has only
    recently been detected by Bob Everitt
    amongst a heap of magazines in a
    bookshop, in a copy of the journal *Land
    and Water* 17 (1874), no. 436, of 30 May
    1874. Here, an article titled 'Lawn Tennis'
    begins with the following words: 'This
    game is one of the best outdoor games,
    especially for ladies, that has ever come
    under our notice.' Next to it, on the left-
    hand side, appears an advertisement of
    French and Co. in which 'The New Game
    of Sphairistikè or Lawn Tennis' is offered
    for five guineas. The ad is, perhaps, the
    earliest of its kind.
17. In this case, Wingfield had prevailed upon
    an acquaintance of his, Sir Gerald D.

Fitzgerald, to write a letter to the editor; it sings the praises of the new game, and in it the wish is expressed of having reproduced, at least in part, the rules which the writer had chosen to enclose, see Todd, p. 55, and Alexander, *Wingfield*, p. 263, Appendix D.

18. The whole correspondence relating to lawn tennis is readily accessible in the appendices of the books by Alexander.

19. See Alexander, *Wingfield*, p. 94. This number appears from the ledger of the firm which covers the period from 6 July 1874 until 26 June 1875. The book was a few years ago acquired by the Wimbledon Lawn Tennis Museum where it is referred to as Wingfield's Day book.

20. See Alexander, *Wingfield*, pp. 273–5, Appendix D, the letter Gem wrote to *The Field*. It has the following conclusion: 'The club [i.e. The Leamington Club] has for its founder Mr Pereira, a gentleman of Spanish family, and well known as a racquet player ... He introduced the game fifteen years ago, and it has recently received the name of Pelota, a Spanish word adopted in compliment to its originator, and signifiying any game played with a ball.'

21. See S.D.R., 'The Late Major Gem. Edgbastonian Origin of Lawn Tennis', p. 126. The earliest account of Harry Gem is an obituary written by an S.D.R., which appeared in 1881 in the December issue of the journal *Edgbastonia*. The most complete accounts of Gem and his friends are to be found in Todd, pp. 39–46 (chapter 4 on 'Harry Gem and his pelota friends'), and in Lerry, pp. 1–3. The two chapters on Harry Gem and Augurio Pereira by Gibbons, ibid., pp. 21–31, are merely paraphrases of Todd, but contain some interesting photographs and inside information since the author as a boy was an eye-witness of the famous Leamington lawn tennis tournaments of the 1920s. These were still played on the premises of the Manor Hotel, the site of Harry Gem's lawn tennis court, and in the nearby Jephson Gardens; see ibid., p. 10f.

22. See S.D.R., loc. cit.

23. See Todd, p. 39.

24. According to Todd, p. 40, Gem had founded the Bath Street Racquet Club in Birmingham, and Pereira, his frequent playing partner there, is said to have been only a little inferior to Samuel Young, who in his day had beaten the best players in England. Aberdare, p. 136f., reports on a championship match between John Charles Mitchell and Samuel Young at the Bath Street court as early as 1846. There must therefore have been a court at Bath Street before Gem's alleged foundation of the racquets club in 1859. Again according to Todd, Mitchell had become champion by defeating the reigning champion John Lamb, and had taken on Young only after that. Aberdare, however, says that Lamb had died of consumption in 1840, after which the title had remained vacant for six years before it was contended by Mitchell and Young. Aberdare, quoting from some of Gem's publications on racquets, gives the initials as 'T.J. [Gem]'.

25. According to Todd, p. 45, Gem became a member of Leamington Tennis Court Club the court of which is shown in Figure 19. No confirmation of this statement has so far come from this club. Of Pereira, neither his place of origin in Spain nor what ultimately became of him and his family is known. He seems himself to have retired to Spain in 1885 at the latest, see Todd, loc. cit.

26. See Todd, p. 42, and Gibbons, p. 2f.

27. See Gibbons, pp. 33–9 (chapters 5 and 6).

28. See Todd, p. 42.

29. There is an original print of 11 pages and a frontispiece titled *Lawn Rackets or Pelota; Rules and Laws of the Game as Played by the Leamington Club.* It was printed by a Leamington printer, D. Sarney. No year is given, but it pre-dates S.D.R.'s article of 1881, since it is reproduced there, on pp. 128f., together with Gem's drawing of the plan of the court. The leaflet, preserved in the Public Library of Birmingham, also contains the 'Rules of the Leamington Pelota Club'.

30. On Gem's lawn tennis club, Gibbons has to say the following, ibid., p. 12: 'It is not certain just how long Gem's original Leamington Club lasted but it would seem that it was less than 15 years.' On Gem's Rules see Todd, p. 42. The two copies were among Gem's papers which his widow bequeathed to the City of Birmingham shortly after his death. They came to light in 1969 after which they became incorporated in the Birmingham

Reference Library. Gem described his game in a letter written to *The Field* on 21 November 1874. It is reproduced in Alexander, *Wingfield*, pp. 273–5, Appendix D.

31. The Birmingham Rifle Volunteer Corps was founded in 1859 when there were fears in England of an invasion by the French, see Todd, p. 41. Gem died in 1881 at the age of 62 as a result of an illness he had contracted during the annual encampment of his military unit, see Todd, p. 45.

32. See Gibbons, p. 10. Renshaw was born in Leamington which explains his frequent participation in this local event. In Gibbons' account, the history of the Leamington lawn tennis clubs does not become sufficiently clear. According to him, the present Leamington Lawn Tennis Club goes back to the Milverton Lawn Tennis and Croquet Club founded in 1902.

33. 'The Wearing of the Green' is a famous Irish street ballad. Composed in 1798, it was a political song in which Paddy (one of the Irishman's traditional nicknames) is made familiar with the (fictitious) laws of the despotic English: the shamrock is no longer allowed to grow on Irish soil, nor may Paddy wear green, see Grigson, pp. 193f. (for the text) and 350 (for the note on p. 193). Against this background, Gem's poem is doubly ironic: winter will make it impossible for himself and his friends to enjoy their green, i.e. their lawn tennis court.

34. That the term *list* in the third stanza might be interpreted in this way appears from a letter Gem wrote to *The Field* in which he described his court in the following manner: 'the division thus formed [i.e. the pitch marked by its outer boundaries] is called "the lists".' See Alexander, *Wingfield*, p. 274, Appendix D. However, the more likely meaning of 'high upon the list' would seem to be 'classed as a top player'.

35. Quoted from a printed leaf, signed THG and dated 19 October 1874, in the Leamington Public Library. The poem was also reproduced by Gibbons, p. 25f., albeit not without errors. I am grateful to my friend Gerald N. Gurney for having made accessible to me copies of the material from Leamington Public Library.

36. See Todd, p. 47f., and Barrett, p. 19: 'On the lawn beside his house [i.e. Rhysnant Hall] Wingfield began experimenting with the height of the net, the size, weight and colour of the ball, the size of the racket and the dimensions of the court.' Rhysnant Hall, which seemed run-down to Todd in 1979, has in the meantime been pulled down, see Alexander, *Wingfield*, pp. 6–8.

37. See Todd, pp. 49–51.

38. On the manor at Nantclwyd, see Alexander, *Wingfield*, p. 79f.

39. Among these sceptics is Todd, p. 53, although he seems reluctant to rule out a lawn tennis demonstration at Nantclwyd altogether.

40. See Alexander, *Wingfield*, p. 79.

41. See ibid., p. 78f.

42. See the detailed account of the goings-on by Alexander, pp. 79–86. In his earlier publication, see his *Lawn Tennis*, p. 4, Alexander had still advocated the Nantclwyd pheasant shoot which enabled Wingfield to enact his lawn tennis shoot-out. Nantclwyd pheasants have ever since graced American lawn tennis histories, e.g. Shannon, p. 1, and Travers, p. 6.

43. See Alexander, *Wingfield*, p. 78.

44. Ibid., pp. 86 and 135, quoting a letter to the *Daily Telegraph* by R.T. Combe, of Earnshill, Curry Rivell, which appeared on 15 May 1881: 'It is now some seven or eight years since Major Walter Wingfield first put up a lawn tennis court here.'

45. See Heathcote *et al.*, p. 129, and, after him, Todd, p. 69, and Alexander, *Wingfield*, pp. 183 and 243 (extract from the *Sporting Gazette*, reprinted in the appendix to the fifth edition of the Rules (1876)): 'You are tired of croquet, come with me and let us try our hands at "Sph-Sph-Sphair-." No! – I don't mind playing it, but I will *not* undergo the torture of pronouncing it; ... I content myself with the last syllables, "Stikè."'

46. See Todd, p. 47, and, for greater detail, Alexander, *Wingfield*, p. 36.

47. Explanations such as the one offered by Cummings, p. 24, show that the Greek of Wingfield's critics is hardly better than the Major's: 'As for "Sphairistike", it was merely the ancient Greek command for "Play ball!".'

48.See Alexander, *Wingfield*, p. 94f. This move has a parallel in the ledger of French and Company in which the merchandise, as from 12 September 1874 onwards, was labeled *sphairistikè* exclusively.

49.Compare, above all, his Preface.

50.See Todd, p. 57f.

51.See Todd, p. 57f.:

a correspondent, who signed himself 'P.T.B.', was writing to the editor of the *Field* to ask the width of the net as it was 'evident by the sketch' that the net was not as wide as the base-lines. This letter was published just before the Easter holiday. Over Easter ... the Major considered the matter. He was quick to realise that here was an unforeseen possibility of giving his game the distinction for which he yearned and which was so necessary if he was to secure protection. Quite by accident he had designed a court that was unlike that used for the ancient game. Thus it was that over the Easter week-end of 1874 Wingfield made up his mind and immediately after the holiday wrote to the *Field* to say that the net was to be 7 yards wide and the base-lines 10 yards. The hour-glass court had been invented!

The wording of the letter (reproduced in Alexander, *Wingfield*, p. 264f.) is: 'The length of the centre net is 7 yards, ...'.

52.See Alexander, *Wingfield*, p. 228f. (from the fifth edition of his book of 1876).

53.See ibid., p. 175.

54.See ibid., p. 201. It is difficult to explain why Alexander, who refutes Todd's theory (albeit without naming him personally), should not have availed himself of this piece of information in order clear Wingfield of this accusation.

55.It is only fair to admit that Wingfield may have seen an hour-glass-shaped badminton court in India. Todd, p. 4, speculates about whether the Major may have seen badminton played in India, and on p. 171 reproduces a photograph showing a badminton court in India in the closing years of the nineteenth century, with marked indentations at the net strongly resembling an hour-glass. On the influence of badminton in the evolution of lawn tennis see also Crawley, *passim*.

56.See his rules of 1876, p. 13 (quoted from Alexander, *Wingfield*, p. 229): 'The whole science of this game for out-of-doors depends on the court being smaller at the net than at the base.'

57.See Alexander, *Wingfield*, p. 2.

58.See Todd, p. 210, and Alexander, loc. cit., note 1. John Wingfield, who is said to have fought in the battles of Crécy and Poitiers and died in 1361, can hardly have been the gaoler of Charles, taken prisoner in 1415, a claim made by Alexander after a rather superficial reading of an article by Richard Haslam in the magazine *Country Life* (quoted by Alexander in the above note). Michael de la Pole, chancellor of England and 1st Earl of Suffolk who died in Paris in 1389, had in 1384 obtained royal permission to enclose his manor by a crenellated wall, see Aldwell, p. 7. He was buried together with Sir John Wingfield, whose daughter Katherine he had married, in the nearby church of St Andrew's, see Champion, *Vie de Charles d'Orléans*, p. 222. His son Michael, the 2nd Earl of Suffolk, died of fever during the siege of Harfleur, and Michael's eldest son, in turn, was killed in the battle of Agincourt. To Michael's second eldest son, William de la Pole, 3rd Earl and 1st Duke of Suffolk, fell the task of guarding the French Duke. The Wingfields had nothing to do with, nor indeed were they involved in the erection of Wingfield Castle which was so named after the nearby hamlet. The famous prisoner was kept, according to Champion, in rooms located in the keeps on either side of the fortified castle gate, and the time he spent there was, according to the itinerary established by the same author, relatively short (from 1434 to 1435), see idem, p. 67. On the Wingfield family and William de la Pole see Aldwell, pp. 4–7 and pp. 12–17 respectively.

59.See Alexander, *Wingfield*, p. 3.

50.See ibid., p. 9, and the extract from the baptismal register, ibid., p. 11. The exact date of birth is, for some unknown reason, not communicated by Alexander, but it is supplied by Shannon, p. 4.

61.See Alexander, *Wingfield*, p. 10.

62.See ibid., p. 32f.

63.See ibid., p. 36.

64.See ibid., p. 56.

65.See ibid., p. 70.

66.See ibid., p. 72.

67.His oldest son Watkin serving as lieutenant on the frigate *Newcastle* was drowned on 3 December 1876 a hundred miles from Singapore in an attempt to rescue a comrade; his second oldest son,

Rowland Penrhyn, died on 16 January 1882 from heart disease which he had contracted in India, where he had only just entered on a promising career; his youngest son, Walter Clopton, called 'Tig', died in Paris on 11 December 1886 as a result of a shot in the head in a gunsmith's shop, from an 'unloaded' revolver.

68. See Alexander, *Wingfield*, p. 105.

69. See ibid., p. 181 and p. 293 (Wingfield's letter dated 5 June 1875).

70. See Alexander, *Wingfield*, p. 149.

71. See ibid., p. 153.

72. See ibid., p. 167.

73. See ibid., p. 172.

74. See the picture 'The author [i.e. Alexander] at Wingfield's unattended grave in Kensal-Green cemetery' in the Appendix of his book *Lawn Tennis*.

75. See Alexander, *Wingfield*, p. 189, and ibid., p. xi (preface by Herbert Warren Wind).

76. See ibid., p. 206 (Appendix B; inner cover of his Rules of December 1873).

77. See Alexander, *Lawn Tennis*, p. 73.

78. See Todd, p. 128.

79. See Hillyard, pp. 1–3. Hillyard, in his recollections, is silent about the fact that he was twice singles champion of Germany.

80. See Burchfield, vol. 3, p. 306, s.v. *pat-ball*, '… Also used as a contemptuous name for lawn tennis, especially when not played vigorously; … 1890 S.W. Gore in *Tennis, Lawn Tennis, Rackets, Fives* (Badminton Libr.) 282. This derisive name of "pat-ball" was applied to lawn tennis by tennis and racket players, who maintained that, from the absence of back- or side-walls, it was impossible to hit hard without sending the ball out of court' (this quotation has been gleaned from a contribution to Heathcote's article on lawn tennis by the first Wimbledon champion Spencer W. Gore; it is titled 'A Reminiscence of Fifteen Years of Lawn Tennis', and printed in Heathcote *et al.*, pp. 279–306); and ibid., p. 316, s.v. *patters*. '*University slang* … A university students' name for tennis. *Patter(s)* had been coined after the pattern of *eccer*, *soccer*, and *rugger* (by applying the characteristic ending -*er*), the slang equivalents of *exercise*, *Association football*, and *Rugby football* in standard English.' In addition, there existed the term *lawners*, see Robertson, p. 12, which seems to have escaped the notice of the compilers of the *Oxford English Dictionary* as well as that of the slang specialist Partridge.

81. Another reason for the reputation of lawn tennis as an effeminate game seems to have been the frequent use of the term *love*, see Todd, p. 104f. As late as 1920 the Americans wanted the ILTF to abolish the word since it gave, they said, the game an effeminate character, but the motion was turned down, see 'Von der Zählweise im Tennissport', p. 172. In the United States, too, lawn tennis was at first considered *sissy*, a game for women, weaklings and cowards, see Lumpkin, p. 1.

82. The remarks of the famous All England Champion Lottie Dod on the subject of lawn tennis balls are highly illuminating:

> Quantities of balls are sold in various shops stamped 'Regulation,' but with which it is not possible to play lawn tennis, they being of all weights and sizes, frequently either too hard or too soft. With a standard ball one learns in time what result can be attained by a certain strength; whereas, without such sound basis, it is impossible to be accurate and precise.

(See L. Dod, in C.G. Heathcote *et al.*, p. 309f.)

83. See on this point Eichberg, an authority in the historiography of modern sport, p. 103:

> Regeln modernen Typs hingegen haben die umgekehrte Funktion: nicht zu differenzieren [here the author's starting-point is the many handicaps which were a characteristic of the varieties of court tennis inherited from the Middle Ages], sondern zu vereinheitlichen, nicht die Möglichkeiten zu vermehren, sondern sie zu beschränken. Im modernen Ballsport ist die Regel der Rahmen, der nicht als solcher wichtig ist, sondern zur überprüfbaren Feststellung von Leistung dient.'

(Rules of the modern type, however, function just the other way round: they do not attempt to differentiate, but to standardize; they do not increase the possibilities, but limit them. In modern ball games a rule is the frame which is of no importance as such, but only serves the assessment of a performance that can be checked.)

84. See Todd, p. 104f.

85. See Beneke, pp. 18–20.

86. The question is whether the 'sportification' of medieval games is a

phenomenon exclusively English, or whether it should be attributed to the nineteenth-century Zeitgeist. A similar development, and one where English influence seems completely absent, took place in the Basque country, where around the middle of the nineteenth century traditional pelota games abandoned most of their medieval features (most notably the chase rule) and evolved into modern varieties such as *pelota a mano* or *la remonta* which are characterized by speed and a high level of athletic performance. See on this point, and the role played by the newly introduced rubber core ball, Toulet, p. 17f.

87. On the biography of Heathcote, see Weaver, p. 246f., and Aberdare, p. 75.

88. See Todd, p. 7.

89. On the history of the All England Club see ibid., pp. 80–93.

90. See Barrett, p. 34. Good railway connections contributed a lot to the rise of Wimbledon. At the time of the first Wimbledon tournament, the All England Club was surrounded by open countryside, see Barrett, p. 26. From Wimbledon station, a dusty path along the railway track led to its site, and access to it could be gained through a small gate in the wire fence running parallel to the railway. In his introductory chapter, Barrett provides a vast amount of background material relating to the early history of Wimbledon. Among this is an old ground plan from a programme of 1889 which makes it clear how the famous centre court acquired its name, see ibid., p. 40. Barrett's description is confirmed by contemporary maps in the Greater London Record Office, located in the London Metropolitan Archives, 40 Northampton Road, London, see Figure 90.

91. It is not clear whether the members of the club adhered to Wingfield's *sphairistikè*, or whether they practised the version devised by J. Hinde Hale, who was a member of the club, see Todd, p. 77, and the group picture ibid., p. 83.

92. See Todd, p. 81.

93. The suggestion was also made by Walsh, and supported by B.C. Evelegh, see Myers, *Fifty Years*, p. 7. Evelegh, a former croquet champion, was not a lawn tennis

player himself, but after 1890 became a famous Wimbledon umpire, see Myers, ibid., p. 31.

94. See C.G. Heathcote, p. 140, on the invention of his namesake:

In the early days of the game, the ball had been almost, if not quite, universally uncovered, but on December 5, 1874, a letter appeared in the 'Field,' signed J.M. Heathcote, stating that the writer had found advantage in covering balls with white flannel, which made them bounce better, while they were also easier to see and to control. One of these balls used at Conington Castle, in Huntingdonshire, in the autumn of 1874, is still in existence, and though rude and archaic in construction is undoubtedly the direct lineal ancestor of the latest and most improved championship ball.

In the course of the same letter, Heathcote suggested the inauguration of the MCC commission. It is reprinted in Alexander, *Wingfield*, p. 278. The advantage of the flannel cover was its air resistance reducing the speed of the ball and the stabilizing effect it had on its trajectory. In addition, it added weight.

95. It is reproduced in Alexander, *Lawn Tennis*, p. [132].

96. See Lee, p. 574. A very personal opinion is given by Wilberforce in his contribution to Hillyard, *Forty Years*, p. 31f.

97. See Alexander, *Wingfield*, p. 93. Jones, who died in 1899, is still referred to as an authority in accounts of the history of bridge.

98. See Hedges, p. 9f.

99. See his letter of 5 December 1874, reprinted in Alexander, *Wingfield*, p. 278: 'My court is rectangular ...'. Of the rules commission of the All England Club, Julian Marshall is said to have advocated this form of the court, see Gore, in C.G. Heathcote, p. 281.

100. See Todd, p. 78.

101. It was subsequently reduced to three feet six inches, see C.G. Heathcote, p. 152.

102. On this development see Todd, p. 78f., and idem, pp. 213–15 (chapter on 'The Evolution of the Court').

103. See C.G. Heathcote, p. 161. Todd, p. 122, has the year 1884.

104. The meeting took place at the Freemason Tavern in Great Queen Street, London, at a short distance from Covent Garden, see Todd, p. 122.

105. According to C.G. Heathcote, the secretary of the All England Club (who at that time was Julian Marshall) had used to chair these meetings, see C.G. Heathcote, p. 161.
106. On the role of Jones, see Todd, pp. 123–5, and Wilberforce, in Hillyard, *Forty Years*, p. 39f. Marshall resigned from his post as secretary of the All England Club in the spring of 1888, see C.G. Heathcote, p. 151.
107. See Todd, p. 125.
108. See here in in what follows Barde, *Fédération*, p. 4, Todd, p. 172f., and Gruber, 65f. Other myths about the origin of the Federation are listed by Hedges, p. 122f., in his not very accurate account of the International Lawn Tennis Federation.
109. In 1963, when the ITF celebrated its fiftieth anniversary, Barde was the last living of the founding members. Barde, who is not always reliable and therefore should be used with care, wrote an account of the history of the Federation from 1913–1963 which was published both in English and in French, see The Kenneth Ritchie Wimbledon Library, p. 77.
110. Wallet was, of course, not the president of the French Lawn Tennis Federation, as was claimed by Barde, and without any qualms repeated by Todd, p. 172. The French Fédération was founded as late as 1920. The address of the Commission at the time, identical with that of Wallet, was Neuilly-sur-Seine, Boulevard Maillot 92.
111. As opposed to the (albeit inofficial) world championships on grass, Wimbledon. This version is that of A.R. de Joannis who was Commissioner General of the world championships on clay, see de Joannis, p. 2.
112. According to an article in the German journal *Lawn-Tennis und Golf* titled 'Gründung einer Internationalen L.T.-Föderation', the Comité International, which, on the initiative of France, had been formed to organize the championships of 1912, had taken the initiative and elaborated for the future organization the draft of conventions (published in the same article), see 'Gründung', p. 31. The president of the Comité was the vice-president of the USFSA, Pierre Roy; he also attended the

inaugural meeting of the ILTF. Of the founder members of the Fédération Internationale de Lawn Tennis, its Honorary Secretary, Robert Gallay, had been the secretary of the Comité before, and the Belgian Chevalier P. de Borman and the German Dr Hans Oskar Behrens had belonged to it, see de Joannis, p. 4. The view of de Joannis is also that of Gruber, p. 65. The German Behrens and the secretary (Bundesleiter) of the German Lawn Tennis Federation (Bartels, of Braunschweig) had attended preparatory meetings preceding the inaugural session of the ILTF, see Nirrnheim, 'Gründung', p. 64.
113. See the letter by the Frenchman R. Gallay printed at the end of the draft of the conventions, 'Gründung einer Internationalen L.T.-Föderation', p. 31f.
114. The unfavourable description of the place ('in den nicht gerade glänzenden Räumen') where, after preliminary talks in the morning, the meeting began at a quarter past two in the afternoon, is that of the German participant Dr Otto Nirrnheim, see his article 'Die Gründung', p. 64.
115. The founder members were Australia, Austria, Belgium, France, Great Britain, Spain (absent at the inaugural meeting on 1 March, but present at a preliminary meeting in October 1912), Switzerland, Denmark, Germany, Holland, Russia, South Africa and Sweden. The representatives of the individual nations were Behrens, Lürman and Nirrnheim for Germany; Inglis for Australia; Zborzil for Austria; de Borman for Belgium; McNair, Monckton, Taylor, Sabelli for Great Britain; Larsen for Denmark; Wallet, Gallay, Gillou, Muhr, Roy for France; Feith for The Netherlands; Gambs for Russia; Clarke for South Africa; Zetterberg for Sweden; and Barde for Switzerland. Australia acted as proxy for New Zealand, the USA were informed about the goings-on by Sabelli. Through an oversight, Japan had not been invited, see Barde, *Fédération*, p. 7.
116. See Barde, *Fédération*, p. 4, and the present writer's *Tennis bei Olympischen Spielen*, p. 221. Duane Williams was the father of the twice American lawn tennis singles champion and Davis Cup player Richard Norris Williams who survived the

shipwreck. On the sinking of the *Titanic*, and Duane Williams, a direct descendant of Benjamin Franklin, see the interesting chapter 'Class Complacency Challenged in 1912: The Sinking of the *Titanic*', in Baltzell, pp. 83–101.

117. Originally the English, following a proposal by the French hosts, were to bag no fewer than eight votes. The Germans, successfully, protested against such generosity in their favour, see Nirrnheim, 'Die Gründung', p. 64.

118. In addition, the right of holding world championships on clay was for three successive years conferred to Paris, whereas Stockholm (1913) and Copenhagen (1914) were to organize world championships (on wood) for covered courts, see Nirrnheim, 'Die Gründung', loc. cit.

119. See Shannon, p. 48. The ILTF at its inaugural meeting nevertheless acknowledged the Davis Cup as the official team world championship, see Barde, *Fédération*, p. 8: 'L'Assemblée de 1913 reconnut la Coupe Davis comme seule rencontre officielle internationale par équipe.' Another reason for not joining the ILTF was the Americans' unwillingness to change the rules as practised in their own country.

120. See Nirrnheim, 'Die Gründung', p. 64:

Auf Vorschlag von McNair, des Präsidenten der letzten Zusammenkunft [there had, therefore, been a preliminary meeting] wurde alsdann Dr H.O. Behrens als Verhandlungsleiter einstimmig gewählt: eine uns sehr sympathisch berührende Wahl, die uns gleichzeitig die Gelegenheit gab, jedweil entscheidend in die Verhandlung eingreifen zu können.

(Following a proposal by McNair, the chairman of the last meeting, Dr H.O. Behrens was afterwards unanimously elected chairperson: a choice which to us was extremely favourable, as it gave us an opportunity of making ourselves heard whenever it was necessary.)

See also Barde, *Fédération*, p. 8: 'Les membres présents à l'assemblée de 1913 désignèrent M. Behrens comme président et M. Gallay comme secrétaire honoraire.'

121. The Paris assembly expressly did not elect a president, but made the Frenchman Gallay Honorary Secretary. From its headquarters, Paris, the Honorary Secretary had to deal with the current affairs of the organization. In addition, the assembly elected a committee of management (*Commission Consultative*, later *Comité de Direction* (Barde); *Comité consultatif de permanence* (Nirrnheim)) of which the Frenchman Wallet, the Englishman McNair, the German Behrens, the Australian Inglis and the Belgian de Borman were members. These five voted for Wallet as president of the Committee of Management, see Barde, *Fédération*, p. 8, Nirrnheim, 'Die Gründung', p. 66, and the extract of the minutes published by the German Lawn Tennis Federation, 'Auszug aus dem Protokoll', p. 290. Barde made a point of the fact that the president of the Committee was not by virtue of his office the president of the ILTF, nor even the chairman of its general assemblies. The chairman had to be elected anew at the beginning of each general assembly.

When, in the spring of 1919, the ILTF had its first meeting after the First World War, Behrens was, in his absence and on the proposal of de Borman, replaced by Barde, see Barde, *Fédération*, p. 9. Only after the general assembly of 13 June 1919 did the procedure become established of proposing the president of the committee for the chairmanship of the general assembly who, after having been elected, then also became the *de facto* president of the whole organization: 'Au début, les assemblées générales nommaient leur président qui était en général le président du Comité de Direction et en fait le président de la Fédération.' (Barde, *Fédération*, p. 21). Officially, however, the ILTF continued to have a president of the management committee only, and in letters written shortly before his retirement in 1924, Wallet always signed in his capacity as 'Le Président de la Commission Consultative de la F.I.'. This custom was also adhered to by his successor, A. Canet, in the late 1920s.

122. See Barde, *Fédération*, p. 10, and Todd, p. 127.

123. See Todd, p. 94.

124. See Barrett, p. 25.

125. See Max Robertson, p. 12f.

126. See Todd, p. 94.

127. See idem, p. 95.

128. Ibid.

129. The average wage-earner at the time earned £1, see Barrett, p. 23. Twenty shillings made one pound, twenty-one = one guinea.

130. A facsimile of the programmes is printed in Alexander, *Lawn Tennis*, p. [139]. It seems to have appeared in print on the final day, i.e. Monday, 16 July 1877, for the results are printed completely with the exception of that of the final which was added by hand together with the note that the final had to be postponed until Thursday, 19 July 1877, 4.30 p.m., on account of the rain.

131. See on this and the following Young, *Olympic Myth*, pp. 19–21.

132. With regard to lawn tennis, these were (theoretically) those who received prize money, but in fact those who were paid by the clubs for their services as coach. In real tennis, they still go by the name of professional.

133. See Young, op. cit., p. 20, note 22.

134. See idem, pp. 44–9.

135. See the statement of the semi-finalist, C.G. Heathcote, in J.M. Heathcote *et al.*, p. 143:

> The All-comers prize and the Championship were won by Mr Spencer Gore, an old Harrovian and racket player; the second and third prizes being secured by Messrs. W.C. Marshall and C.G. Heathcote respectively, who were both tennis players. Mr Gore had previously defeated Mr M. Hankey and Mr F. Langham, who had been proficient as tennis players, and whose style was modelled on that game.

136. Only as late as 1885 was the 'bye' used for the first round and exclusively so; nevertheless, 'byes' were distributed regularly for the whole draw. The modified (so-called) Bagnall Wild system got into effect in 1887, see Myers, *Fifty Years*, p. 23, and Hedges, p. 20. It is made explicit in Baddeley, pp. 133–5 (item 19 of the Regulations for the Management of Lawn Tennis Prize Meetings). The system devised by R.B. Bagnall (1884) is the ingenious solution to the mathematical problem of how to obtain for the second round a number of ties which constitute, since two finalists are required, a power of two (e.g. 2, 4, 8, 16, 32, etc.). According to Bagnall Wild the number of entries is subtracted from the next power of two. In this way the number of the byes necessary

for the first round is ascertained. If, for example, there are nine entries there will be seven byes and one tie (16–9 = 7). There are then eight players to continue in the second round. See C.G. Heathcote, p. 165. Players were seeded as from 1919 onwards, see Wilberforce, in Hillyard, *Forty Years*, p. 57.

137. See Lerry, p. 3.

138. See C.G. Heathcote, p. 144. He is quoted by Myers, p. 10, and Robertson, p. 12.

139. This is what the winner said himself, see C.G. Heathcote, p. 268.

140. See Spencer W. Gore in his contribution to C.G. Heathcote (ibid., p. 284f.: 'A Reminiscence of Fifteen Years of Lawn Tennis'):

> These brothers [i.e. the Renshaw brothers] were the first of the new race of lawn-tennis players. They were among the first to begin learning the game while young enough to be capable of improvement. Their predecessors had taken up the game when too old and too stiff to do more than play at the game in the style in which they had played at other games before lawn tennis was introduced; and they could therefore never get beyond a certain point of excellence before either their loss of activity or their failing eyesight prevented further improvement.

141. This procedure had been taken over from croquet tournaments, see Todd, p. 101.

142. According to Todd, p. 100, Hadow was a coffee planter, whereas Hedges, p. 104, has him cultivate tea.

143. See here and in what follows C.G. Heathcote, p. 147, Myers, *Fifty Years*, p. 11, Max Robertson, p. 13f., and Todd, pp. 100–2.

144. In a letter he wrote, 71 years old, to Wallis Myers, see Myers, *Fifty Years*, p. 11.

145. Hadow's own opinion was this: 'I was told the "lob" had not been introduced before – certainly I had never tried it before.' (See Myers, p. 11.) C.G. Heathcote surmised, p. 147: 'If he did not invent the lob, he was the first to practise it with any great success, and he met and vanquished Mr. Gore's tactics by a free use of this resource.'

146. See Todd, p. 101.

147. See Todd, ibid. Before that, only short sets, allowing the winning result of 6:5, had been played. In advantage sets, as is well known, a difference of two games is

required as soon as the players are at five games all.

148. See Myers, p. 12. There were two competitors of that name in the tournament of 1878, e.g. G.E. Tabor, and A.S. Tabor, see Todd, p. 220.

149. See C.G. Heathcote, p. 148. It deserves notice that Heathcote who wrote a graphic account of the tournament and the tactics adopted competed himself in the tournaments of 1878, 1879 and 1880, and in 1879 had lost against Hartley in the quarter-finals, see Barrett, p. 200. Myers, *Fifty Years*, pp. 13–15, published a letter in which Hartley gave his personal impressions of the match and referred to his opponent as 'the now notorious Goold of Monte Carlo fame'. In 1907, Goold and his French wife were accused of murdering a wealthy Danish widow. Goold died eight months after he had been sent to a prison camp on Devil's Island, see Todd, p. 102, note.

150. See C.G. Heathcote, p. 149.

151. See Gore, in C.G. Heathcote, p. 283:

> A large proportion of the competitors in 1879 adopted the very safe style of play introduced by the champion of 1878; and the winner of the Gold Prize, Mr. J.T. Hartley, was preeminent in that style. It is impossible to say decidedly what would have been the result of a match between Messrs. Hartley and Hadow; but it is quite certain that there would have been a record established in the number of strokes to a rest [synonym of the more usual *rally*] had that match been ever played.

152. See Gore, in C.G. Heathcote, p. 286: 'Indeed, it is little short of marvellous that so light a ball can be hit so hard, in a space of such limited dimensions, without being driven out of court.'

153. See idem, ibid., p. 284: 'The "runner-up" of this year was Mr. H.F. Lawford, who was beginning to develop that wonderful power of hard hitting to which by constant practice he has now attained.'

154. See Gibbons, p. 41f., who gives the address as Brandon Lodge, Brandon Parade, which is now 60 Holly Walk, Leamington Spa; there is a picture of the house in Gibbons, p. 42.

155. For an assessment of the qualities of the brothers see Hedges, p. 198.

156. C.G. Heathcote was showing off his knowledge of classical mythology when, writing of the Irish championships of

1884, he remarked, p. 165: 'Mr. Lawford … had not much difficulty in wrestling the championship from Mr. E. Renshaw, the holder, who had prejudiced his chance of success by dancing into the small hours of the day of the match. Lawn tennis is an exacting mistress and will not brook dalliance with the attractions of Terpsichore.'

157. See Max Robertson, p. 14.

158. Ibid.

159. On the evolution of the overhead service see Gore, in C.G. Heathcote, p. 289f.

160. Gates of the finals from 1877–1880 developed in the following manner: 200 (1877), 700 (1878), 1100 (1879), 1300 (1880), see C.G. Heathcote, p. 153. In 1885, at the peak of the brothers' success, 3500 watched the final, ibid., p. 168.

161. See Myers, *Fifty Years*, p. 17.

162. See Little, p. 47.

163. See C.G. Heathcote, p. 157f.:

> The title of champion thus won in 1881 by Mr. W. Renshaw was retained by him until 1887, when he retired owing to an injury to his arm, now widely known as tennis elbow, of which the first public mention is found in the columns of the 'Field' in 1881. [This first occurrence has escaped the notice of the editors of the *Oxford English Dictionary*, their first instance being from 1883.] It is not impossible that Mr Renshaw, by the increased severity both of service and smash introduced by him at this time, and at once imitated by a host of players, may have contributed to the vastly increased prevalence of the injury which has since, though fortunately only for a time, taken its revenge upon himself. Tennis elbow has generally been attributed to the great and sudden strain thrown upon the muscles of the arm by the overhand service.

164. See Todd, p. 109f.

165. See C.G. Heathcote, p. 161f.

166. See Myers, *Fifty Years*, p. 18, commenting on the year 1882: 'Some concession to the baseliner was made by the M.C.C. and the A.E.C., who, in joint communion, lowered the net at the posts from 4ft. to 3ft. 6in.' See on this issue also C.G. Heathcote, p. 151f., and Alexander, *Lawn Tennis*, p. [135].

167. In his verbal exchanges with Lawford, William Renshaw certainly overshot the mark when he claimed that 'before many years taking the ball off the ground [would] be quite the exception', see C.G. Heathcote, p. 161.

168. This was the opinion of a contemporary, C.G. Heathcote, who said, with much perspicacity: 'His [i.e. Lawford's] long and persistent advocacy in theory and practice of base-line playing received its due reward. He had learned something from the volleyers, but they in turn were forced to resort to his tactics.' Lawford, as time went on, by no means shrank from the volley completely; rather, he, too, allowed himself to be in turn inspired by the Renshaws. When Wimbledon celebrated its fiftieth anniversary, Myers could come to the following conclusion: 'the modern game of today was then in the crucible and, thanks to the Renshaws and Lawford, there was moulded the type of all-court lawn tennis which successive generations, inspired subconsciously by their example, have, under improved conditions, produced today.' See Myers, *Fifty Years*, p. 20.

169. See Myers, p. 13.

170. See C.G. Heathcote, p. 148. Here the champion was Miss M. Langrishe.

171. See Myers, p. 24.

172. See Baddeley, p. 15.

173. According to Baddeley, p. 16, the doubles play in which the two partners advanced to the service line was invented by the Americans Sears and Dwight. The Renshaws are credited with having perfected it. However, the method seems to have been developed independently on either side of the Atlantic, see Sears, in C.G. Heathcote, p. 320f.

174. See Gore, in C.G. Heathcote, p. 291.

175. See Myers, *Fifty Years*, p. 31.

176. See Baddeley, p. 16.

177. See Hillyard, p. 149. When Maud was defeated by Lottie Dod in Wimbledon in 1886, she had been victorious in fifty-five successive matches.

178. Here and in what follows I am indebted to Gibbons, p. 43f.

179. See Wills, p. 285. About the end of her career, Maud stated the following, ibid., p. 287: 'I played from the time I was sixteen until I was about twenty. Then I went swimming off the Jersey coast, and nearly drowned. I was rescued with difficulty and afterwards was ill for three years. It finished my tennis. Now I live in the country and am interested in horses.'

180. It is little known that in 1907, after the early death of William Renshaw, his family presented another cup honouring the memory of its famous member, see Wilberforce, in Hillyard, p. 46. The 'Renshaw Cup' is still awarded, as an additional gift, to the winner of the Wimbledon singles championship, see Todd, p. 107.

181. Gibbons, p. 45, calls it a flower-basket. It is, however, a rosewater dish which served the purpose of cleansing one's fingers after meals, a custom introduced from the east. Together with a ewer it formed a set. One specimen of it is now part of the collection of Gerald Gurney, another was offered for sale at an auction by Phillips, London, where it was described in the following way: 'The Venus Rosewater Dish: A mid-Victorian electrotype after the original Renaissance design of François Briot, in the manner of Elkington & Co., inscribed beneath central medallion: "L. Oudry et Cie, Pres Editeurs", silvered on copper, 44.5cm diameter, the base with detachable medal showing profile portrait of Briot (£4000–6000)'. To this was added: 'The Dish is a similar example to the Wimbledon Ladies Singles Trophy: the central boss shows a repoussé figure of Temperance; encircling that are Venus, Jupiter, Mercury and Salacia, a water goddess, representing the four elements; the rim shows Minerva presiding over the seven liberal arts. The Wimbledon Trophy differs in being hallmarked, in having parcel gilt decoration and listing all the winners since 1884. The dish is one of a limited number.' See *The Tennis Collector*, no. 6, August 1989, p. 7, item 304. The item was not sold.

182. He wrote:

We may not wish to encourage our wives and daughters to emulate Nausicaa, Margot, Mademoiselle Bunel, or Madame Masson, and to compete with us in an exercise fatiguing to all, and to them possibly dangerous, but we accord to them a hearty welcome when they honour the 'dedans' with their presence.

See Heathcote, p. 40. On the famous female real tennis players, Miss Bunel and Madame Masson, see Marshall, *Annals*, p. 62, and on the latter, Aberdare, p. 64.

183. The following points were made by Lottie Dod, the five-times All England champion, who in 1890 contributed a short essay on women's tennis to C.G.

Heathcote, ibid., p. 307f. This essay, written by an 18-year-old girl, is so thoughtful and witty that one easily understands the exceptional role played by its author in contemporary lawn tennis.

184.These are the words of Lottie Dod, in C.G. Heathcote, p. 308.

185.See the descriptions by Lumpkin, p. 7, and von Meister, p. 37f.:

When I think of the clothes convention obliged women to wear – skirts down to the ankles and blouses with high whale-boned collars, to say nothing of the elaborate paraphernalia beneath – I marvel that we were ever able to hit a ball. I look with envy nowadays at the young generation with its freedom of movement, equipped in 'shorts' and very little else, and wonder how many points in handicap this revolution in feminine attire adds to their game.

Some interesting details can also be gleaned from an account in von Fichard's manual of 1887, pp. 27–9.

186.See Baddeley, p. 82 (Chapter XX; Ladies' Chapter; By a Lady Player).

187.See Lumpkin, p. 8.

188.I am quoting from the American edition of 1885, p. 74. The first edition of the book came out in London in 1884. I am indebted to this piece of information to Frank V. Phelps, King of Prussia, USA.

189.See Baddeley, p. 81.

190.This formation was invented by that great American theoretician, Dr James Dwight, who put it to a successful test around the middle of the 1880s with Blanche Bingley (the All England champion and later Mrs Hillyard), against William Renshaw who, partnered by Miss Bracewell, stuck to the baseline, see Hillyard, p. 241, who is, in turn, quoted by Alexander, *Lawn Tennis*, p. 70.

191.See de Coen, p. 60, and the present writer, *Tennis bei Olympischen Spielen*, p. 212, note 193. The role of the female partner in a mixed doubles match was aptly described by a contemporary, Leila von Meister: 'I played in the first class and was sought for as a partner in doubles because I had a good overhand service, which few women in those days affected, … and could run like a hare on the back line when my more brilliant partners let a ball pass them.' See von Meister, p. 37.

192.From 1899–1907, a women's doubles was added to the Wimbledon programme, and a mixed doubles from 1900–1912, but before 1913 neither of them had championship status. These championships were for a long time held in Buxton (doubles, since 1885) and, by turns, in Liverpool and Manchester (mixed doubles, since 1888), see Barrett, p. 34f.

193.See Dod, in C.G. Heathcote, p. 312. To Lieutenant Peile, in 1884, every cloud had a silver lining, although he had, at least in part, to confirm Lottie Dod:

Luckily short dresses are now in fashion, so there is not much difficulty about that point; but if fashion changes, I implore you to beware of long dresses, for two very good reasons:

1. The long dress will spoil your play; and
2. The play will spoil your long dress.

The next point to pay attention to is shoes. Of course you will wear shoes without heels, and equally, of course, will the shoes be of India-rubber. A tight shoe being a disadvantage should be discarded, even though it may offer some attraction in the matter of appearance. A big hat that waggles about is also trying to the wearer, as also are bangles, bracelets, and suchlike ornaments – not to mention five to six rings on one finger. These latter are more liable to cause blisters, by pinching up the skin between the hand and the bat, than anything I know of.

194.See Dod, in C.G. Heathcote, p. 308.

195.See Dod, in C.G. Heathcote, p. 311.

196.Quoted from Todd, p. 129f. The quotation is from Herbert Chipp's *Lawn Tennis Recollections* which were published in London in 1898.

197.See von Fichard, *Deutsches Lawn-Tennis-Handbuch 1896 und 1897*, p. 224f. The same Hermann, gymnastics instructor at the Martino Katharineum Highschool in Brunswick, in 1894 introduced lawn tennis into the games classes he taught to male and female teachers, see von Fichard, *Deutsches Lawn-Tennis-Jahrbuch 1895*, p. 77. Hermann's advocating lawn tennis for women must be viewed against the background of his continued efforts to create for women a substitute for soccer, the preserve of men. That is why, in 1896, he tried to transform the recently invented game of basketball into a women's game (it was, in fact, through him that basketball became known in Germany). Hermann heard about basketball from his son Ernst, the director of the

Massachusetts Hospital for Dipsomanics, on the occasion of one of the latter's visits home, see Hoffmeister, p. 34f., and Eitel, p. 24. Hermann was, in his capacity as sports educationalist, a prolific writer and a committee member of the Zentral-Ausschuß zur Förderung der Volks- und Jugendspiele in Deutschland (Central Committee for the Promotion of Popular and Juvenile Games in Germany), the official body of the 'Recreation Ground Movement' (Spielbewegung) in nineteenth-century Germany, see 'Verzeichnis der Mitglieder des Zentral-Ausschusses', p. 300. (There is a nice picture of the Committee in Hoffmeister, p. 33.) There is an interesting biographical note on Hermann in Hamer, p. 101, note 149, gleaned from a chapter titled 'The playground movement in Germany' in a monograph by an American, F.E. Leonhard, professor at Oberlin College, Ohio (1923), p. 133: 'The teacher of gymnastics (Turnlehrer) at the Gymnasium was August Hermann (1835–1906), whose wife's sister conducted a flourishing private boarding school for girls in Brunswick and in its interest spent several months a year in England. Hermann's own house was a pension which usually contained a number of English boys. ... Hermann ... procured from England a football'. That physical education of German women was Hermann's favourite subject became evident at the First Congress on Popular and Juvenile Games, held in Berlin in 1894, where he read a paper in which he expressed the view that the German woman of the time suffered from nervousness and similar illnesses in an alarming way and that healthy exercise in fresh air as was found in popular and juvenile games was a means and way to remedy this, see Hamer, p. 587.

198. This is the implication of an account of American lawn tennis by the famous Doherty brothers in 1903; it is quoted by Todd, p. 130.

199. Lumpkin, p. 7, quotes a voice from the Ladies Club of Staten Island, significantly a lawn tennis club for women only: 'It has been objected that American ladies would not like the publicity that would attach to their appearance as contestants in an open tournament. This objection, it may safely

be assumed, does not come from the ladies themselves.'

200. See Todd, p. 129.

201. See Dod, in C.G. Heathcote, p. 308.

202. See Lumpkin, p. 7.

203. See Todd, p. 130. This was changed in 1887. From that year, competitions for men and women were held alongside each other, see Wilberforce, in Hillyard, p. 38.

204. See Todd, p. 128.

CHAPTER 7

1. Of the accounts dealing with the beginnings of lawn tennis in the United States, the following deserve to be expressly mentioned: Sears, in C.G. Heathcote, pp. 315–31; Whitman, pp. 112–25; Todd, pp. 140–5; Alexander, *Lawn Tennis*, pp. 53–8; and idem, *Wingfield*, pp. 192–8. Of these, the two last named are, perhaps, the definitive ones.

2. This and the following details are to be found in Baltzell, a mine of information on US family history, p. 46f.

3. The club remained located on this site for forty-six years (where it became the venue for the first Davis Cup match ever in 1900!) after which it moved further out into the country to Chestnut Hill, see Baltzell, loc. cit. It was here that the German doubles team Gottfried von Cramm and Henner Henkel won the US doubles Championship against Budge-Mako in 1937, and where the Davis Cup team of Nazi Germany, which included the Austrian Georg von Metaxa, was defeated by Australia in the Interzone Final of 1938.

4. Tennis clothing evolved from cricket clothing anyway, see the present writer's 'Tennis kam schon früh in Mode', p. 74.

5. See Alexander, *Lawn Tennis*, p. 60.

6. See Sears, in C.G. Heathcote, p. 315: 'it was the end of August in 1874 when the first set was laid out at Nahant, a small seaside resort about ten miles from Boston'. The house in Swallow Cave Road, Nahant, is still there, but another house has been built where the first tennis court must have been marked out, see Alexander, *Wingfield*, p. 198.

7. See Todd, p. 140, referring to a statement by Dwight made in 1895. In an earlier

statement of 1891, Dwight had considered 1875 to be the year of his first experience with lawn tennis, see Todd, ibid., note. It is therefore impossible to ascertain in what year exactly the incident should be set.

8. For the details see Todd, p. 143.

9. My friend, US tennis specialist Frank V. Phelps, suspects that Whitman's research was in reality Henderson's. Henderson, for many years Chief of the Main Reading room at the New York Public Library, was librarian one day a week at the library of the Racquet and Tennis Club, NYC, where Whitman carried out his investigations.

10. See Alexander, *Wingfield*, p. 194.

11. See Todd, p. 144, and Alexander, *Wingfield*, p. 195. Nevertheless, Mary Outerbridge continues to be the Columbus of American lawn tennis, see Travers, p. 6, and, more recently, Baltzell, pp. 40 and 45.

12. According to Frank V. Phelps, it is highly doubtful whether the 'Miss O.' of the passenger list mentioned by Todd was indeed Mary Outerbridge. She is qualified as 'citizen of Bermuda' (not the USA) and was accompanied by 'a male Outerbridge, also a Bermuda citizen, a farmer'.

13. See Alexander, *Wingfield*, p. 196, and Todd, p. 144, who points out her arrival in New York (aboard the steamer *City of Houston*) on 3 May 1875.

14. This was asserted by Sears, in C.G. Heathcote, p. 315f.:

The set in New York was owned by Mr E.H. Outerbridge, who is today one of the Executive Committee of the National Lawn Tennis Association of America. Mr Outerbridge obtained permission from the Staten Island Cricket and Base-ball Club to lay this set out in a corner of their ground, and, naturally, this did more to bring the game into prominence than anything else, as it was the first set laid out in a more or less public place.

However, Sears' assertion that Eugenius rather than A. Emilius Outerbridge was responsible for this is at variance with all other authorities.

15. See idem, p. 316: 'early in the summer of 1880, the Staten Island Cricket and Base-ball Club gave an open tournament on their grounds near New York … Up to that time all the matches were private

affairs held on private grounds, or else club tournaments open to members only.'

16. See Alexander, *Lawn Tennis*, p. 62, and Todd, p. 147f. According to Patricia Barry, who lives in Staten Island and has access to an unpublished autobiography of Outerbridge, the proposal was made to the directors of the club early in the summer of 1880. Outerbridge himself did not compete, because he was a cricketer and not a lawn tennis player. His brother Adolph played in the doubles event.

17. See Barry, in a postscript.

18. See Alexander, *Wingfield*, p. 198.

19. It has been said that there were several American 'championships' in the same year, a view that has been challenged only recently by Barry. According to her, the tournaments of that year were few and without any importance.

20. See Alexander, *Lawn Tennis*, p. 60f., and Todd, p. 148. Alexander quotes from Frank Leslie's *Illustrated Newspaper* of 18 September 1880, Todd from the nearly identical article of *The New York Times*.

21. See the account of the finals by *The Times*, reproduced, in part, by Todd, p. 149, and the postscript in Barry. The *Richmond County Gazette* came up with the results only one week later, on 15 September 1880.

22. See Alexander, *Lawn Tennis*, p. 62. Barry has traced the announcement on the front page of the *Chicago Daily News* of 27 August 1880. Under the heading 'Sporting Miscellany', it says: 'A lawn tennis tournament open to all American players, will open at Staten Island September 1.'

23. See Alexander, *Lawn Tennis*, p. 64f.:

Dr. Dwight was a strict constructionist of rules and while not playing he circulated about courts seeing that officials were enforcing the rules, especially the foot-fault rule. He also was a stickler for proper balls, perhaps caused by his experience at the 1880 Staten Island tournament. Knowing this propensity, Willie Renshaw, when umpiring a match of Dwight's, boxed up the worst of the old balls, and when Dwight called for new balls he gave them those. The anticipated violent reaction caused great mirth among the knowing spectators.

24. See Sears, in C.G. Heathcote, p. 316f. According to a statement made by E.H. Outerbridge in a letter to his brother, the Staten Island club had circulated among

clubs that might be interested the rules under which the tournament was to be conducted and, among these, the assertion that the Ayres ball would be used. Such, however, was apparently not the case.

25. See Baltzell, p. 48. In her postscript, Barry quotes from the *Richmond County Gazette* of 15 September 1880. 'The Lawn Tennis Champion Tournament', the journal wrote triumphantly, 'which began at Camp Washington on September 1st, under the auspices of the Staten Island Cricket Club, was concluded last Wednesday by a brilliant victory for Staten Island's representatives'.

26. See Alexander, *Lawn Tennis*, p. 62; according to Baltzell, p. 48, the note appeared on 8 May. Outerbridge claimed to have started the founding campaign immediately after the Staten Island tournament, see Todd, p. 150. A statement by Barry is to the same effect: 'It was Mr Outerbridge who spearheaded the drive for the organization.' Whether also in this case Mr Outerbridge's memory was failing is difficult to tell. Sears, for that matter, conferred the honor on Dr Dwight, see idem, in C.G. Heathcote, p. 318.

27. The hotel is still in Fifth Avenue, on the corner of Ninth Street, see Todd, p. 150, note.

28. The number of participants in this gathering, thirty-six, was magnified as time went on. Alexander, *Lawn Tennis*, p. 62, who is probably correct, said: 'Nineteen clubs were represented by thirty-six men, and sixteen clubs were represented by proxy.' Sears, in C.G. Heathcote, p. 318, spoke of thirty-six clubs represented which was basically correct, if less precise. In 1930, the assembly had, in the reminiscences of E.H. Outerbridge, been honoured by the presence of more than a hundred club representatives: 'According to my recollection', Outerbridge wrote in a letter to his brother, Sir Joseph, in Bermuda, 'we had over hundred present.' The Bermuda *Royal Gazette* of 26 February 1930 printed the letter in full, see Todd, p. 150, and ibid., note. Baltzell, p. 48, had thirty-three clubs (!) come to New York, and Dwight noted the presence of 'close to one hundred people … in the room'.

29. See Sears, in C.G. Heathcote, p. 318f.
30. Idem, p. 319f.
31. Idem, p. 320.
32. Idem, p. 321.
33. See Sears, 'The First National Championship', p. 22f.
34. See Hedges, p. 91.
35. On Newport Casino, and its notorious builder, James Gordon Bennett Junior, a millionaire who had inherited from his father the *New York Herald*, see Baltzell, pp. 48–51.
36. See Burchfield, vol. 3, p. 1371, s.v. *Round Robin*. b. orig. U.S. A tournament in which every player or team competes with each of the others. The term is first instanced in 1895 in the Official Lawn Tennis Bulletin where it says, significantly: 'The so-called round-robin tournament, where each man plays every other, furnishes the best possible test of tennis skill.' In British English, the term *round robin* referred to a circular arrangement of signatures. This was meant to prevent identification (e.g. in the case of a mutiny) of a ringleader. How the term came to be used in tennis is unknown. The competitive spirit underlying both the round robin tournament and the Davis Cup playing mode is also conspicuous in rankings, an American invention like these others.
37. See Nanteuil *et al.*, p. 211.
38. See Alexander, *Lawn Tennis*, p. 60.
39. Ibid.
40. Ibid., p. 63f. The Clarks apparently had intended to go to England anyway for a cycling tour, see Baltzell, p. 52 (with further details).
41. Dwight held the presidency of the USNLTA from 1882 to 1885 and from 1894 to 1912, see Shannon, p. 83.
42. This was the first covered court, see Todd, p. 98f. It was located in Portdown Road, London, and was the home court of the Renshaws as well as of Lawford who were all members of the Maida Vale LTC.
43. See Alexander, *Lawn Tennis*, p. 64.
44. Ibid., p. 59f.
45. Statements as to where exactly the Renshaws stayed in Cannes are rather contradictory. According to Nanteuil, who was a Frenchman and closest to them chronologically since his book appeared in 1898, it was the Club Réunion which disposed of three courts in the 'Redoute'.

Founded by Captain Clifton Perceval in 1886, it is said to have been the meeting place of an international tennis following, hence the name. After Perceval's death in 1892, the illustrious gathering dissolved and activities were transferred to the facilities of the Hotel Beau-Site, see Nanteuil *et al.*, p. 211f. In the course of the 1890s, Dwight gave up lawn tennis completely in favour of golf. Neither his daughter Elizabeth nor his son, Dr Richard W. Dwight, remembered having seen their father playing lawn tennis, see Alexander, *Lawn Tennis*, p. 68. Both von Reznicek, p. 167, and Cochet and Feuillet, p. 250, have the Renshaws lay the first two clay courts in the park of the Hotel Beau-Site in 1881. These were used by them for practice matches. Baltzell, p. 52, also calls the courts of Beau Site the venue where Dwight played with the Renshaws in 1884.

46. See Alexander, *Lawn Tennis*, p. 64.
47. See Todd, p. 156f. This was the result of a council meeting on 1 July 1897. With regard to an allowance for travelling expenses, Dwight did have his qualms: 'I own I have always had great doubts of the propriety of paying expenses of players.' The LTA, at the same Council meeting, nevertheless resolved on sending an unofficial team of the second category which did quite well. The LTA, therefore, had no reason to be in any way disturbed. See Trengove, p. 18.
48. See Todd, p. 157.
49. Ibid., p. 158. The letter has been reprinted in full by Trengove, p. 20.
50. See Davis, p. 70.
51. An original picture is reproduced in Cummings, p. 73; see Figure 80.
52. The present writer had the opportunity of a close inspection on the occasion of the Stuttgart Davis Cup final in 1989.
53. In the description of the cup, the author has been following Trengove, p. 19f.
54. See Trengove, p. 23.
55. See Macaulay, p. 62, stanza XXXVII.
56. See W.A.B., 'The Dauntless Three', in *Lawn Tennis*, 25 July 1900, p. 242. Trengove apparently was not aware of the literary allusion and splendid joke when he wrote, p. 24: '"The Dauntless Three", as they [i.e. Gore, Roper Barrett and Black] were called by the LTA'.

57. W.A.B., at the time when he wrote his poem, did not know that the venue for the match would not be Newport.
58. See Trengove, p. 19, whose account is based on an article by a certain A. Nanias (this apparently a pen-name) in *Lawn Tennis and Croquet*, titled 'The Departure of the English Team for America'.
59. Roper Barrett commented upon this reception with ill-concealed sarcasm: 'We appreciated Mr. Stevens' kindness in sending down his man; it seemed so friendly and kind and much better than coming himself', see Trengove, p. 23. Stevens was himself a tennis-player who, between 1892 and 1905, was eight times ranked among the American top ten, see von Reznicek, p. 317. He was descended from the prestigious Stevens family the most famous of which was the inventor John Stevens. There is a picture of Stevens together with other contemporary top ten US players in Cummings, p. 67.
60. Trengove, p. 24, says that they visited the falls because they lacked facilities to practise.
61. Ibid.
62. Ibid., p. 25.
63. Ibid., p. 24f. The seven minute rest was envisaged by American rules, see Cummings, p. 74.
64. The article, 'by an "Onlooker"', was reprinted in *Lawn Tennis and Croquet*, 22 August 1900, p. 309f.
65. See Trengove, p. 24f.
66. See *Lawn Tennis and Croquet*, 22 August 1900, p. 308.
67. Only after Whitman's retirement could William A. Larned, the older of the two, win the US championship in 1901, 1902, and 1907–1911.
68. *To bant*, a synonym of *to string* in the dialect of Yorkshire.
69. See the article on lawn tennis professionals, 'Lawn-Tennis-Berufsspieler' in *Sport im Bild*, no. 13 (1900), p. 102.
70. This is what Harold S. Mahony, his countryman and opponent in 1898 for the Championship of Germany in Bad Homburg, wrote about him in his contribution to Wallis Myers' *Lawn Tennis at Home and Abroad*, p. 22. Mahony also gave a full description of Pim's game, ibid., p. 22f.
71. See Todd, p. 159, and Trengove, p. 29. Trengove, p. 27f., made a good joke when

he said: 'Once known as "The Ghost" because of his thinness, he had played little top-class tennis for some years and now his ample silhouette was certainly visible.' However, it was not Pim who was nicknamed 'The Ghost', but his countryman Willoughby James Hamilton who (as has been said) in 1890 put an end to the victories of the Renshaw brothers, see Hedges, p. 104, and Myers, *Fifty Years*, pp. 28 and 31.

72. The choice of pseudonyms was not unusual until well after the turn of the century, either for reasons of propriety as when a member of the high aristocracy wanted to keep his name secret, or if, as in the case of Pim, a doctor of medicine, his social status and the participation in a public tournament seemed incompatible, see Trengove, p. 28. In the Bad Homburg tournament of 1898, Pim had played under the pseudonym of Wilson, see Grauhan, p. 75. Also in the Homburg tournaments, the Grand Duchess of Mecklenburg Schwerin, Anastasia, competed as 'Mrs. W.', the letter W standing for (Countess) Wenden. Most frequently, employers were by means of pseudonyms kept ignorant about the activities of their employees, or, for that matter, school headmasters about those of their pupils playing truant.

73. See Todd, p. 159f.

74. See Cummings, p. 75, and Trengove, p. 29. Todd, p. 160, believed that the venue was still the Longwood Cricket Club, Boston.

75. See Todd, p. 160.

76. The Dohertys won against Davis and Ward in four sets.

77. See Trengove, p. 30.

78. See Cummings, pp. 75–78, Todd, p. 160, and Trengove, p. 30.

79. See Trengove, p. 30, and Shannon, p. 481. Whitman, the number two, had retired from competitive tennis and Beals Wright and Holcombe Ward, the numbers three and four of the year 1902, had not been invited.

80. See Cummings, p. 77f., and Trengove, p. 31.

81. See Trengove, p. 21f.

82. When competitors other than the British Isles and the USA began to enter, preliminary rounds were established. Of these, until the First World War, the victor challenged the champion of the previous year.

CHAPTER 8

1. See Nanteuil *et al.*, p. 205: 'Il ne pouvait en être autrement dans le pays d'origine du vieux jeu de Paume, hélas! maintenant si delaissé, et détrôné par son propre enfant, bâtard il est vrai, mais de belle venue, nous arrivant de l'étranger.'

2. See on this issue in general Mangan, *The Games Ethic and Imperialism.*

3. The museum, with its fine and historically important collection of tradecards, is owned by Charles Hoey who is also the curator of the institution. Besides sections on table tennis and badminton, the museum has a remarkable section devoted to early lawn tennis.

4. The French text on the reverse of the tradecard is the following:

   Le filet partage le terrain en deux carrés égaux. Au centre de l'un d'eux on en place un plus petit de 1m. et demi à 2 mètres de coté. Quant à l'autre on le partage en deux parties égales parallelement au filet, et le rectangle extérieur est lui-même partagé en deux parties égales.

5. See Fieschi, p. 14.

6. Cochet and Feuillet, p. 229, ventured the date 1875 for the privately owned courts of Bel-Sito and La Cruz in Bordeaux, the owners of which were Edouard Lawton and Daniel Guestier. Later the famous club of the Société de la Villa Primerose, founded in 1897, traced its existence back to these facilities. Among the founding members of the club were, besides Lawton, the later French champion and tennis journalist J. Samazeuilh as well as the tennis historian Albert de Luze who later also served as the club's president.

7. The clubs' very names betray the fact that their founders were English, compare, despite their French spelling, the English position of the adjectives before the nouns.

8. See Cochet and Feuillet, p. 240f.:

   Il avait été fondé en 1872 (deux ans avant que le major Wingfield déposât son brevet pour la sphairistikè), mais, bien que dans les statuts de l'époque on puisse relever que la société avait pour objet l'encouragement et le développement des exercices du corps et spécialement des jeux de football, cricket et lawn-tennis, ce n'est que plusieurs années après que le tennis y prit une réelle importance.

9. See idem, p. 241.

10. See Nanteuil *et al.*, pp. 206 and 211, and the present writer's *Olympisches Tennis*, p. 3. The club was located in Neuilly-sur-Seine, its full and correct name being 'Decimal Lawn Tennis and Boating Society'. For this piece of information, the present writer is indebted to Ture Widlund, Stockholm.

11. See Bonhomme, pp. 112–14.

12. See Nanteuil *et al.*, p. 206.

13. See Fieschi, p. 14, and Cochet and Feuillet, p. 244.

14. See Fieschi, p. 14.

15. For these details see Fieschi, p. 14f. The addition 'de France' to the club's name was made later in order to avoid confusion between the Paris and Brussels based Racing clubs, see Fieschi, p. 14, note 1.

16. See Fieschi, p. 15: 'le football, le lawn-tennis, le jeu de paume, l'escrime, le patinage, etc'.

17. To this effect Nanteuil *et al.*, p. 207. Cochet and Feuillet, p. 245, call 9 April the date when the City of Paris granted the plot, but Nanteuil *et al.* seem to be more reliable, since Saint-Clair, the secretary of the Racing Club, co-authored the book. The lawn tennis courts were in the centre of the running track and surrounded by trees which in 1900 obstructed the view of Kurt Doerry, journalist and participant in the 1896 Athens Games, watching the track and field contests of the World Exhibition later raised to the rank of Games of the IInd Olympiad, see Doerry, 'Die Weltmeisterschaften', p. 285.

18. See Cochet and Feuillet, p. 248. Indoor lawn tennis was also the hallmark of the Tennis-club de Paris (T.C.P.) which opened with a tournament in November 1895. The Club, located in the Rue de Civry in the XVI Arrondissement (according to Cochet and Feuillet; on the Boulevard Exelmans, according to Bonhomme near the Gare d'Auteuil), consisted of two courts, two large wardrobes, showers, a reading and a dining room, see Bonhomme, p. 69 (with further details). The club was transferred to the Porte de Saint-Cloud before the First World War. On its extremely fast oak parquet courts French champions acquired their much admired fast reflexes, see Cochet and Feuillet, p. 246f.

19. See Cochet and Feuillet, p. 248f.

20. Ibid., p. 242.

21. See Nanteuil *et al.*, p. 207.

22. See Cochet and Feuillet, p. 243f.

23. See Fieschi, p. 15f.

24. See Fieschi, p. 19, and Cochet and Feuillet, p. 245. According to Cochet and Feuillet, the first commission convened in June 1889 when it approved of holding a first international tournament on the occasion of the World Fair of the same year. The tournament took place from 17 to 22 June 1889 and was won by Hetley, a member of the Decimal Club. Nanteuil remembers having seen the first version of the French rules in a book titled *Jeux et Exercices en plein air*. This was published by Arnould and came out in 1887. Again according to Nanteuil, a lawn tennis commission was nominated by the committee of the Union in November 1890. Its object was to examine the rules, to rework them and to organize championships. The members of this commission were C. Heywood, Viscount de Janzè, Count Jacques de Pourtalès, G. Raymond and L.H. Sandford. They published the rules (which had scarcely undergone any revision) in 1891. A new commission undertook some revisions in 1893, see Nanteuil *et al.*, p. 217f.

25. See Nanteuil *et al.*, p. 212, and Cochet and Feuillet, p. 248.

26. See Nanteuil *et al.*, p. 213. The champions were Des Joyaux and Legrand of the Cercle des Sports de l'Ile de Puteaux.

27. Ibid., p. 214. It was won by Seyrig-Mortier of the Ecole Monge.

28. Ibid., p. 215. It is a curiosity that in 1891 and 1892 the doubles champions had to fight for the singles championship. In 1891, Seyrig emerged victorious from the match of the doubles champions Seyrig–Mortier.

29. Ibid., p. 216.

30. See Fieschi, p. 16.

31. See the present writer's *Olympisches Tennis*, p. 1f.

32. See Fieschi, p. 22. It has been suggested that Davis, when creating the Davis Cup, was influenced by the example of the Athens games, see Cummings, p. 72.

33. See the present writer's *Olympisches Tennis*, p. 2.

34. In his invitations, Coubertin had declared that the main purpose of the congress would be a discussion of the amateur question. The re-introduction of the Olympic Games had been very low on the agenda, but it had become the main topic when the congress opened.

35. For an assessment of his personality see Young, 'Demetrios Vikelas', *passim*.

36. See de Coubertin, p. [2]. The name given under no. 26 of the list of delegates is Decimal L.T. et B. Society where, as has been said, the letter B stood for 'Boating'. There were, of course, other clubs which had lawn tennis sections, e.g. the Racing Club de Paris (no. 3), the Cercle des Sports de l'Ile de Puteaux (no. 4), the Stade Français (no. 13), the New York Athletic Club (no. 29) the president of which, G.A. Adee, belonged to the honorary members of the congress. Apart from these clubs, other participants of the congress had a definite interest in lawn tennis, e.g. Viscount Léon de Janzé and Georges de Saint-Clair, and Count Jacques de Pourtalès who, like Coubertin himself, acted as a commissioner of the congregation. De Janzé and de Pourtalès, as will be remembered, belonged to the lawn tennis commission of the Union of 1890. Le Cocq, of the Decimal Club, was later to be found on the amateur commission, see de Coubertin, p. [4].

37. See de Coubertin, p. [4]: 'XII Que les Sports suivants soient, autant que possible, représentés aux Jeux Olympiques. ... Jeux Athlétiques (Football, Lawn-tennis, paume, etc.).' During the congress, the delegates witnessed a demonstration of *paume*, i.e. the French championships held in the Jardin de Luxembourg. The championship was won by the team of Valenciennes against opponents from Compiègne, Paris, and Amiens, see de Coubertin, p. [2].

38. See Bonhomme, p. 69, and the present writer's *Olympisches Tennis*, p. 2. Coubertin was a member of the prestigious Cercle des Sports de l'Ile de Puteaux, and a picture, reproduced in the present writer's monograph, loc. cit., shows him and three other players, on the premises of this club, and with a racket in his hands.

39. See Young, 'Demetrios Vikelas', p. 91.

40. The Programme, signed C.T. Mano, Honorary Secretary of the Hellenic Committee, Balliol College, was put up, together with a notice, in the Union lobby at Oxford on 14 February 1895, see Boland, in the present writer's *Olympisches Tennis*, p. 148, and in an article by him which appeared in *The Oxford Magazine* on 13 May 1896 when it gave rise to a controversy between him and G.S. Robertson, of New College, Oxford, on the pages of the journal about whether or not the English sporting world had been properly invited by the Greek organizing committee.

41. There was only one institution which could be called advocate of the rules, the LTA (since 1888). The two clubs had been lawn tennis pioneers before that date.

42. See the present writer's *Olympisches Tennis*, p. 3.

43. See ibid., p. 6, for a photograph of the velodrome and its three courts, two of which, as Boland informs us in his diary, p. 103, were marked out as singles courts, one as a doubles court. The governing German body at the time, the 'Komitee für die Beteiligung Deutschlands an den Olympischen Spielen' (Committee for the Participation of Germany in the Olympic Games) had formed a sub-commission for lawn tennis, but it does not seem to have ever become active, see the present writer's *Olympisches Tennis*, p. 5f.

44. See ibid., p. 4.

45. Ibid. Besides Defert, A. Vacherot, the outstanding player of the club, had entered. This becomes evident from a report sent to the Parisian daily paper *Le Vélo* by the track and field athlete and journalist Frantz Reichel. Reichel is a reliable source, since he was himself a member of the Racing Club and therefore must have had inside knowledge. The author is indebted for this interesting detail to his friend Ture Widlund, Stockholm. Of course, Vacherot did not put in an appearance. French champion in 1894, 1895 and 1896, he would have carried off an easy victory, see Nanteuil *et al.*, p. 212f.

46. See the present writer's *Olympisches Tennis*, p. 4.

47. This anecdote goes back to Carl Galle, a team-mate of Traun and, like him, a track-and-field athlete. Without having ever been questioned, it has been repeated over and over again, above all in German accounts of the Games.

48. The present writer is indebted to his friend Don Anthony of the British Olympic Association for having brought the diary to his attention and for providing him with a copy of the entire text. The story of the discovery of the diary is also Don Anthony's.

49. For a comprehensive biography of Boland see the present writer's *Olympisches Tennis*, pp. 9–12.

50. See Boland, *Bonn and Athens Diary*, p. 1: 'A desire to acquire a knowledge of the German language + to make acquaintance with German University life has led me to fix upon Bonn as a suitable University town for spending the winter months.'

51. See Boland, op. cit., p. 32.

52. Boland had an essay on the subject titled 'Auf der Kneipe' published in the March issue of *The Oratory School Magazine*, 1896.

53. See Boland, *Bonn and Athens Diary*, p. 33: 'I attended Professor Loersch on Handels + Seerecht.' Later on Boland gives a charming description of an interview he had with Professor Loersch at 21 Lennéstrasse in Bonn, ibid., p. 57, whom he believed to have been 'the tutor of the kaiser', ibid., p. 79. Before his departure for Athens, Loersch provided him with a letter of recommendation for Giorgios Streit, Secretary of the Greek Organizing Committee, later in life a professor of law like Loersch, and a holder of important positions; from 1910–1914 that of a Foreign Secretary of Greece, see Lennartz, p.156. In Athens, Streit saw to it that Boland received tickets for the Games, see Boland, *Bonn and Athens Diary*, p. 96: 'Streit, the German-speaking Secretary, to whom Prof. Loersch in Bonn had given me an introduction, was very kind + got them [the tickets] for us.'

54. One on the Arndtplatz, see ibid., p. 62; another 'on the Exercir Platz on Cassels Ruhe, with a terrible wind + and no side lines so that the game extended practically indefinitely on one side. It was about the funniest game I ever played in, but I hope our return match on Saturday will be still more so. I expect we shall have quite a gallery.' Ibid., pp. 81f., and 84.

55. Ibid., p. 80: 'On Saturday [7 March 1896] morning I went to Wiesbaden, had a game of Golf on the Exercir Platz'.

56. Boland, when discussing local sports facilities, op. cit., p. 9, once mentioned tennis:

Football is here played by the schoolboys ... In the summer tennis goes on at the 'Sports platz' [allowance must be made throughout the whole diary for Boland's German] + in winter there is football, cycling etc, except when the frost permits its being entirely flooded for skating.

In Bonn as well as elsewhere in Germany, and most notably in Hamburg, lawn tennis clubs had their roots in skating clubs whose grounds, deliberately flooded in winter, were transformed into grass courts in the summer.

57. Boland mentioned costume balls in the restaurant 'Zur Lese', Bonn, p. 70, and in the famous Gürzenich, Cologne, p. 73, and a visit to the Cologne carnival procession on Monday before Lent, p. 71: 'At 12.30 on Monday a party of 8 of us went to Köln to see the famous procession.' Ibid., p. 71

58. Boland, *Bonn and Athens Diary*, p. 84: 'I was unlucky enough to get a cut over the eye through a charge ..., but fortunately the eye has not been affected.'

59. Ibid. Professor Theodor Sämisch was the director of the University eye hospital.

60. 'Having failed to secure Brambeer, Holland, Digby or Spender as a companion for the Grecian trip, + Patrick [Boland's brother Patrick Joseph, 1869–1940] not being keen, I have asked young Pazolt.' Ibid., p. 80.

61. Ibid., p. 84.

62. Where they celebrated St Patrick's Day by a glass of beer at the Hofbräuhaus, ibid., p. 85.

63. At the 'Hofburg theatre' Boland saw (and very much enjoyed) *Much Ado about Nothing* performed in German, ibid., p. 87.

64. Ibid., p. 88.

65. Here Boland again went to the theatre to see 'Wilhelm Tell ... acted ... with not much attempt at dramatic skill + entire absence of stage management.' Ibid., p. 89.

66. Ibid.
67. Ibid., p. 90.
68. Ibid., p. 92.
69. Ibid., p. 93.
70. Ibid., p. 102. Boland had himself taken the initiative several days before, on Thursday, 2 April 1896, and offered Manos and Merkatis, 'the latter the Cricket + Tennis Secretary', to 'play in anything if they were a man short, but neither made any attempt or even suggested my going in for the tennis'. Boland, p. 103. Even without Greek nationality, Greeks from Smyrna, Cyprus and Egypt were allowed to compete for Greece, see Lennartz, p. 139.
71. Boland, *Bonn and Athens Diary*, p. 102f.
72. On Broughton see Lennartz *et al.*, p. 152.
73. See the *Bonn and Athens Diary*, p. 103f. The journal *The Field* in its report spoke of a 'bitterly cold day, with a biting north wind', see the present writer's *Olympisches Tennis*, p. 157, note 63. The weather apparently was too much for the American Charles Waldstein who presumably umpired the match. Waldstein also left a diary in which, under Wednesday, 8 April 1896, he wrote: 'Then [after the military rifle event in which he competed] had to rush to Phaleron to umpire the bicycle race. It was cold + windy, + after this had to stay as ump. in lawn tennis. Chilled through.' The next day he had to stay in bed, see Lennartz *et al.*, p. 151, where a facsimile of the passage is printed. On Waldstein, who became a British citizen in 1899 and in 1918 changed his name to [Sir Charles] Walston, see the short biography by Don Anthony, in Lennartz *et al.*, loc. cit. A reader in archaeology at first, he became fellow at Kings College in 1894 and director of the Fitzwilliam Museum.
74. Ibid., p. 104. Besides the result of the finals, this seems to be the only one to have been passed down to posterity.
75. Ibid., p. 110. On Tapavica, see the present writer's *Olympisches Tennis*, p. 156, note 38.
76. Boland, *Bonn and Athens Diary*, p. 113, states that their opponents were 'Kasdaglis + Akratopoulos', but this must be a mistake: only two Akratopouloses, Aristides and Konstantinos, are known to have been members of the Greek team, see Lennartz, p. 139, and Boland had

himself asserted that he and Traun beat two Akratopouloses in an earlier round of the doubles event.
77. See Boland's *Bonn and Athens Diary*, p. 113.
78. Ibid., 113f.
79. The fact that the doubles final was played before the singles even in those early days was not according to normal tournament practice, above all, if, as in this case, two players, Kasdaglis and Boland, were involved in both matches, see for instance on this point Behrens, *Leitung*, p. 40. By adopting this procedure, the committee certainly revealed a lack of experience.
80. The Spanish *Enciclopedia Mundial del Tenis* (which does not state its source) has the following results for the singles and doubles. Boland, who after the two first sets had officially won the match, is said to have offered to play the Greek in a third set in which Kasdaglis, who had totally lost his nerve, was routed completely, the final score being 7:5, 6:4, 6:1. In the doubles, the Greeks had, according to the same source, declined to play the third set offered to them. Here the final score is said to have been 6:2, 6:4. The French daily *Le Vélo* came forward with different results. According to this source, Boland won in two straight sets in the singles final (6:3, 6:1). In the doubles final, Boland and Traun was said to have, after losing the first set 5:7 (which is correct), won the next two sets 6:4, 6:1 (which Boland now proves to be wrong again). See the present writer's *Olympisches Tennis*, pp. 4, and 158, notes 65–67. In marked contrast with the playing mode observed in Wimbledon, the Athens tournament was a best of three competition. Naturally, the present writer in his *Olympisches Tennis*, p. 7, had not the slightest doubt that the French journal had been reporting the correct results. Only Boland's diary was to set him right.
81. Ibid., p. 114.
82. Ibid.
83. Ibid., p. 104:

the courts were of earth + fairly good, they only want some weeks of playing on to be really good, for up to now no one has played on them + they have only been rolled. All the arrangements were excellent, large high nets at either end to stop the balls, half a dozen boys rigged out in light grey uniform + plenty of committee men to umpire for lines + nearly all of them spoke English + decided points very well.

84. Boland's *Bonn and Athens Diary*, pp. 122–4. This famous ode, printed in *The Oxford Magazine* in its issue of 6 May 1896, had been written by George Robertson, an Oxford student like Boland, on his outward journey to Athens where it somehow had got into the hands of the King. He had induced him to read it at the Stadium. 'Robertson,' Boland said, 'manfully tried the modern Greek pronunciation + with fair success. Though the "Εοδια" in the evening was very rough on him saying that he had read a long poem in the Erasmian pronunciation + one which hardly any one could understand.' (*Bonn and Athens Diary*, p. 123.)

85. See the present writer's, *Olympisches Tennis*, pp. 5, and 148, where the relevant passage from Boland's Oxford diary titled 'An Oxford Breakfast' is printed in full. Boland's brother Patrick had been present at the meeting. When in Bonn, Boland overheard a discussion between his host, Borgass, and Herr Füchtjohann, a colleague of his, on the Olympic Games, see *Bonn and Athens Diary*, p. 62f.:

A propos the Olympic Games in which both Borgass + Fücht Johann display considerable interest, there was an account in today's papers of a projected 'Kampfspiel' in all manner of games, confined to Germans, to take place at Leipzig in 1900. It appears that the Germans were not invited to the first meeting held about the Olympic Games [here Boland is talking about the notorious 'Gil Blas affair', see Lennartz *et al.*, p. 97f.], + being hurt thereat are not going to contest. This account differs from what Mano told me at Oxford, for he said that though all nations were invited to send representatives to Paris, Germany was the only one of any importance which failed to do so.

86. When Pereira died in 1939, Boland wrote an obituary for *The Oratory School Magazine* ('Obituary for Fr Edward Pereira') in which he described Pereira's share in his Athens victory thus:

But it was in lawn tennis that I was fortunate to have his coaching. It was my last year at school, reading for the London B.A. There was one half-hour in the week when I was given free time whilst the other boys were in class. Then it was that Eduard played singles with me, coached me, and laid the foundation which was

so useful for my game when, later, I played lawn tennis for Ireland in the first Olympic Games at Athens in 1896.

In a tribute to his brother Patrick, also in *The Oratory School Magazine*, speaking of the latter's marriage in St Jean de Luz in the summer of 1895, he mentioned frequently made excursions over the frontier to San Sebastian where he played 'on the hard courts of the Club … there were games of tennis, in which we had excellent practice with Eddie O'Byrne [the brother of Partick's wife Norah], Ramon and Jose Joachim Olazabal', see Boland, 'Patrick Joseph Boland (1869–1940)', p. 10. The present writer is indebted to the archivist of the Oratory School, A.J. Tinkel, for bringing these articles to his attention.

87. See the present writer's *Olympisches Tennis*, p. 159, note 12.

88. See ibid., p. 7. Boland's victory by two sets to one is one of the few pieces of information we have about the preliminary stages of the tournament.

89. See von Fichard's report on the tournament, reprinted in his 1894 annual, pp. 100–3. The passage relating to Traun is on p. 100f. This remarkable source is not included in the present writer's *Olympisches Tennis*, because it came to his notice only after the recent dicovery of von Fichard's first lawn annual which had seemed lost, like the 1893 volume of *Spiel und Sport* of which latter no copy seems to exist.

90. See von Fichard, *Deutsches Lawn-Tennis-Jahrbuch 1896/1897*, p. 132, where Traun appears in the same draw together with the three Doherty brothers and Count Voss-Schönau (he was eliminated in the second round by Scudder, an American); and, ibid., p. 134, on the handicap event in which Traun lost to the victor André (from the same Hamburg club) after a fierce battle only.

91. See 'Le Congrès', p. [4]: 'IX. Que, sauf en ce qui concerne l'escrime, il ne soit organisé de concours olympiques que pour les amateurs.'

92. On the other hand, the assembly considered undemocratic the attitude of those associations which (like the British Amateur Rowing Association) excluded from membership the working classes, see de Coubertin, p. [4].

93. The headquarters of the firm was Dublin. The name 'Boland's Limited', in gilt letters, can still be seen on the front of the original plant at 135 Capel Street, see White, p. 41, whose account of Boland's sporting activities is rather inadequate. Even today, Boland's biscuits are well known to every Irishman.

94. The name of the company was Dr Heinrich Traun & Söhne, formerly known as Hamburger Gummi Kamm KG. A comprehensive biography of Traun is contained in the present writer's *Olympisches Tennis*, pp. 13–21.

95. Boland was a student of Christ Church, Oxford, where he studied law, whereas Traun was on the point of moving from Dresden Technical University (Technische Hochschule) to Heidelberg where he obtained the degree of a doctor in chemistry at the age of 23!

96. See the present writer's, *Olympisches Tennis*, p. 21.

97. This was, perhaps, possible only because Coubertin had previously been ousted from the organization of his own invention. At that time, the idea of allowing women to compete would to the Baron have been out of the question.

98. On the whole issue see chapters 7 and 10 of the author's monograph *Olympisches Tennis*.

CHAPTER 9

1. See Todd, p. 63. At about the same time, an order for another set came from the Neues Palais, Potsdam. It was put in by Her Royal Highness, the Crown Princess. The author wishes to thank Alan Little for a copy of the original entry in Wingfield's Day book.

2. See *Lawn Tennis and Croquet*, September 7, 1898, p. 306.

3. See Municipal Archive 'Gotisches Haus', *Homburger Fremden-Liste*, no. 30, 3 July 1874, Angekommene Fremden vom 30. Juni bis 2. Juli 1874, and ibid., no. 31, 5 July 1874, p. 142.

4. See *Homburger Fremden-Liste*, no. 36, 17 July 1874, Angekommene Fremden vom 14. bis 16. Juli. B. In Privathäusern. Obere Promenade. It is interesting that while Viscount Petersham and Herbert Hankey were trying their hands at lawn tennis, Mr Vikelas from London, the first president of the International Olympic Committee, and his wife were also present at Bad Homburg where they stayed at the Russischer Hof, see *Homburger Fremden-Liste* no. 36, 17 July 1874; [Angekommene Fremden vom 14. bis 16. Juli], p. 192: 'Bikelas u. Mrs. u. Bdg., London 15. Juli.' From the age of 17 to that of 42, Vikelas, born in 1835, lived in London, see Young, 'Demetrios Vikelas', p. 87f.

5. See the *India Office List of 1898*, p. 433.

6. Charles Augustus Stanhope was born in 1844; he died in 1917. In 1869, he married the Hon. Eva Elizabeth Carington, daughter of the 2nd Baron Carrington (Baron Carrington, for reasons unknown, had his name spelt with two r's, whereas the remainder of the family opted for one). Eva Elizabeth Carington died in 1919. For information on the identity of Viscount Petersham and his family, and the correct use of his title, the present writer is indebted to Lord Aberdare.

7. The photograph was apparently discovered in 1927, after the celebration of the fiftieth anniversary of the Bad Homburg tennis courts, in the house archive of Th. Voigt, Court Photographers, according to an article in the local daily newspaper *Taunusbote* of 28 August 1951. It is titled '75 Jahre Bad Homburger Tennis', and was written by a certain Fritz Storch. The firm of Th. Voigt is known for its frequent coverage of early Bad Homburg lawn tennis events. Barret, p. 20, claims to have reproduced what he calls the 'first known photograph of lawn tennis on a Sphairistikè court.' However, like the one from Bad Homburg, it is not an instance of *sphairistikè* – there is, in fact, not a single photograph of Wingfield's original version of the game. It shows, in much the same way as the Bad Homburg picture, an hour-glass-shaped court, but identically marked halves and no service diamond in one of them. It therefore follows the rules as laid down by the MCC commission in 1875, and can be said to have originated at any time between the spring of 1875 and the first Wimbledon tournament in 1877 (and even later, if the private owner of the set was of a conservative temperament). A very old photograph has only recently

been acquired by the well-known tennis collector Gerald N. Gurney. It is unique in displaying the Wingfieldian 'wing nets' the function of which has not yet been determined, but its age is nevertheless difficult to assess. Here, too, we have the hour-glass shape and no service crease, but the height of the net seems much too low for the picture to be really early. On the earliest lawn tennis photographs see the article by Gurney, 'Tennis ging ganz heimlich los'.

8. See *Homburger Fremden-Liste*, Angekommene Fremden vom 13 Mai bis 20. Mai 1876, Ferdinandstrasse bei J. Fuchs (Albionhouse): Anstruther, Sir Robert, Baronet, Parlamentsmitglied; Anstruther, Lady; Anstruther, Arthur u. Bdg. [= Bedienung], Schottland.

9. See *Homburger Fremden-Liste* 1876, p. 101, 21 June 1876: 'Bei J. Fuchs (Albionhouse) ... Im Hause Nr. 1 Trelawny, Clarence u. Fam. u. Dschft. [= Dienerschaft], England'. (The address of the Anstruthers is Ferdinandstr. 4, that of the Trelawnys Ferdinandstr. 1.) The personality of Trelawny is an excellent example of the quality of German sports historiography. For many decades German lawn tennis history has been beset by the phantom of an American called Frelawney. Simon, semi-official historian of the German Lawn Tennis Federation, stated ('Von unseres Sportes Werdegang', p. 38): 'Ein Amerikaner *Frelawney*, Mitglied des englischen Klubs in Bad Homburg vor der Höhe, führte dort das Spiel – vermutlich in der Wingfieldschen oder einer ähnlichen Prägung – ein und hielt ein Wettspiel ab – das erste verbürgte überhaupt.' (An American, Frelawney, a member of the English club in Bad Homburg ... introduced the game there – presumably in a Wingfieldian or some similar version – and staged a competition – the first on record of any.) Neuendorf, in his account of lawn tennis, vol. 4, p. 364, depends on him. At the turn of the century, Heineken, p. 205, had written: 'In Deutschland wurde Lawn-Tennis unseres Wissens nach schon 1877 zuerst in Homburg von einem Mr. Trelawney eingeführt.' (As far as we know, lawn tennis was first introduced in Homburg by a Mr Trelawney as early as 1877.) The festschrift *100 Jahre Tennis in Bad Homburg*, after reproducing the photograph, has the following: 'Englische Kurgäste, angeregt durch einen Mr Trelawney, führen erstmalig auf dem Kontinent das Tennisspiel ... in Homburg ein.' (English visitors, on the instigation of a Mr Trelawney, introduced for the first time on the continent the game of tennis in Homburg.) All these testimonies go back to von Fichard, who was closest to the event and eventually at least got the name right. In his first annual of 1894, p. 63, he had stated the following: 'Der Lawn-Tennisplatz zu Homburg [...] wurde im Jahre 1877 von Mr. Trelawney, einem Mitgliede des englischen Clubs z.H.v.d.H. gegründet, und hatte der Platz anfänglich nur 8 Courts.' (The Bad Homburg lawn tennis court was founded in the year 1877 by Mr Trelawney, a member of the Bad Homburg v.d.H. English Club, and there were in the beginning in that place only eight courts.) In his *Deutsches Lawn-Tennis-Jahrbuch 1896 und 1897*, p. 175, he said: 'Homburg v.d.H. ... Die ersten Courts wurden 1877 von Mr. Trelawny angelegt.' (Homburg ... The first courts were laid in 1877 by Mr. Trelawny.) In the former GDR, the following belief was adhered to, see Eichel, p. 303:

Zu den sogenannten exklusiven Sportarten zählte besonders das Tennisspiel ... Ein Amerikaner führte 1876/77 zum ersten Mal in Deutschland den 'weißen Sport' vor ... Die Entstehung von Tennisklubs in bekannten deutschen Kurorten geht vorwiegend auf englischen Einfluß zurück. Das Tennisspiel war ein Sport der 'Reichen'.

(The game of lawn tennis was above all counted among the so-called exclusive sports ... In 1876/77, an American for the first time put on an exhibition of the 'white sport' ... The foundation of tennis clubs in the spas was due to English influence ... Lawn tennis was a sport of 'the rich'.)

The only person giving 1876 as the first year of lawn tennis in Bad Homburg is Crawley who wrote, in 1913, but without stating a source: 'This summer [the reference is to 1876] the game was played at Homburg.' See Crawley, p. 198.

10. See *Homburger Fremden-Liste* 1876, p. 129, Zugangsliste 28. Juni-1. Juli 1876 ... Hotel de France ... Johnstone, J.S. u. Bdg., Ranleigh-House, Falham, London.

Johnstone moved to H. Eifert's boarding house at Kisselefstr. 5 between 9 and 12 August 1876. At Albion House, the address of the Anstruthers, a Mrs Johnston from Dublin and her family are also listed, but the note on the margin of the photograph clearly speaks of a Mr Johnstone, and his name exhibits a final 'e' twice.

11. Sir Robert was born in Heriot Row, Edinburgh, on 28 August 1834. He was educated at Harrow. These and other pieces of information have been gleaned from the family history compiled by his son Arthur Wellesley. see Anstruther, p. 136f., Gen. 23, no. 237, Table 6, s.v. Sir Robert Anstruther; compare also the biographical work of Boase, vol. 4, p. 142. The author owes a debt of gratitude to the late Peter R. Anstruther, Arthur Wellesley's son, for kindly supplementing his knowledge about the family. He died in Hanover, New Hampshire, shortly after having given the present writer a most detailed account of his father's life in a letter.

12. For what follows the present writer is indebted to Sir John Trelawny of Saltwood, Kent, who called to his attention the relevant entries in the *Bibliotheca Cornubiensis*, and Hofrat Dr Rainer Egger, Director of the Austrian Military Archive (Kriegsarchiv), Vienna, who made accessible of him a copy of the relevant entry in the 'Grundbuch' Husaren-Reg. Nr. 7, AbgKL II, 1841–60, fol. 63 (Kt. 1248). The entry seems to confirm a statement made by Simon (see note 13, below) that Trelawny was from Southampton, but in the Southampton city archives there is no reference to the Trelawny family. The registers of St Mary, Southampton, include an entry for the baptism of Caroline Agnes Trelawny, daughter of Harry Brereton and Caroline Estcourt Trelawny of Lottery Hall, 5 March 1827. Lottery Hall was situated on the corner of Orchard Place and Briton Street, St Mary's parish, and so named because the proprietor gained £20,000 in the state lottery. By 1851, Lottery Hall was, according to the census of that year, occupied by the family of Joseph Croskey, an American Consul. I am indebted to Mrs P. Floyd of the Hampshire Record Office, Winchester, and Joanne Smith of

the Archive Services of the Southampton City Council for these interesting pieces of information.

13. Later, in his *Beiträge*, p. 120f., Simon supplemented, and, in part, corrected his earlier statements [author's translation]:

1876 has at times been called the year in which lawn tennis was played in Homburg v.d.H. for the first time, and a tournament – the first tournament on the continent – was held. Yet our tennis historians, Freiherr von Fichard and Philipp Heineken, place these events in the summer of 1877, and, since nothing has been found to the contrary, this statement will have to be considered as representing the facts. That to Homburg v.d.H. belongs the glory of having been, chronologically, the first venue for lawn tennis and a tournament, cannot be doubtful. A visitor for many years, Mr. C. Trelawney [*sic*] from Southampton, was the pioneer who introduced it; the spelling of his name has now been authenticized**) [here Simon is silent about by whom and how]. Mr. Trelawney belonged to the English club which laid out the first courts – on grass, of course – these are said to have numbered eight, a rather impressive number for a beginning, which were transferred to the *kurverwaltung* of the town in 1880 [this ought to be 1890]. The first clay courts in Homburg followed in 1894 only.

To this Simon appended the following note [author's translation]: '**) In my introduction dealing with lawn tennis history (to Kreuzer's *Buch vom Tennis*), I wrote **Frelawney** and called him an American on the basis of communications from Bad Homburg which have been put right only recently.'

The name Trelawny, at any rate, points to the English Southwest, Cornwall, or to Wales, in much the same way as the name Anstruther originates from Scotland, or, more precisely, the county of Fife. See Harrison, vol. 1, pp. vi and 234, and vol. 1, p. 10, respectively.

14. See von Reznicek, p. 19.

15. See Anstruther, p. 156f., Gen. 24. no. 282. Table 6, s.v. *Arthur Wellesley Anstruther*; and *Who Was Who*. vol. III. – *Who Was Who 1929–1940*, p. 30, s.v. ANSTRUTHER, Arthur Wellesley. Arthur Wellesley Anstruther was born 5 March 1864 at 24 Onslow Square, London. Educated in Eton, he became Captain of the Fife Artillery Militia. He was married twice, his second wife being Louise Adèle Rose Trapman[n] who was the daughter of a German-American from Frankfurt, W.H.

Trapman, owner of rice and cotton plantations in Charlestown, South Carolina, USA. The above mentioned Peter was a son by his second wife. Later in life, Arthur Wellesley Anstruther held several positions at the Board of Agriculture. He died on 20 October 1938. Rose Trapman's sister Leila, born in Sunbury-on-Thames in 1871, in 1900 married the Bad Homburg district president Wilhelm von Meister and was connected to the court of Emperor William II who was the godfather of her son Friederick Wilhelm (the author is again indebted to Peter Anstruther for this piece of information). Leila is the author of *Gathered Yesterdays*, an autobiography published by Geoffrey Bles in London posthumously after she had died in the United States in 1957. In this book, the author (who was herself an able player and even participated in the Bad Homburg tournaments) also enlarged on lawn tennis, ibid., p. 37f.

16. This is what he wrote in his letter to the present writer: 'I immediately recognized the handwriting on the margins of the photo as that of my father, Arthur Wellesley Anstruther … Interesting that his style had already formed at the age of 12.' It looks as if Arthur Wellesley, who later even became the author of a family history, was a born chronicler. On the sporting activities of his father, Peter Anstruther had to say the following: 'Although he played tennis rather well, he was much keener about golf, being one of the founders of the golf club at Hook Heath, Woking, Surrey, where I was born in 1907.' Unfortunately, the golf club in question has been unable to confirm this statement. As to the picture, the 'lady' is clearly wearing a pair of trousers which at the time would have been an unpardonable breach of etiquette.

17. See Todd, p. 74. If Todd's assumption, op. cit., p. 76, is correct that only a few matches were played according to these rules the Bad Homburg photograph would not only be the earliest lawn tennis document on the European continent, but also the only testimony of how the MCC code was put into practice there.

18. On the whole issue see Grosche, p. 241, whose account contains other details of interest. Grosche is correct in pointing

out, op. cit., p. 242, that there was a wide divide between the wealth of most of the visitors to German spas and the modest means of most *Kurdirectors*, a fact likely to produce irregularities of the kind Schultz-Leitershofen had been guilty of. The fact also sheds an interesting sidelight on contemporary lawn tennis and the world in which the game flourished. Schultz-Leitershofen had been engaged on 7 November 1872 as one of 32 candidates for the position. Born in Berlin and a lawyer by profession, he was fluent in several languages and had been able to produce letters of recommendation from abroad (including some from foreign health resorts) which were very much to his credit. He had been at the head of the König-Wilhelm-Verein Viktoria-National-Invaliden-Stiftung (a charitable foundation) when he took up his office on 1 January 1873. Before the irregularities became known in 1890, he had acquired the reputation of highly cultivated officer of considerable merits. In the summer of 1891, a note in his files stated that he had left Bad Homburg on 5 June after having made a payment of 5,000 marks, apparently the last instalment of the sum he had taken from the public purse. The author wishes to thank *Kurdirector* Peter P. Bruckmaier for information relating to his predecessor.

19. That there existed a lawn tennis club in Bad Homburg as early as 1876 is the conviction of Cicely Hamilton, an English author of the 1930s: 'It [lawn tennis] was played at Homburg in the year 1876; Sir Robert Anstruther founded a local tennis club and the accompanying photograph shews [*sic*] one of the early games in progress.' See Hamilton, p. 78. It does not become clear whether Hamilton drew on sources other than the photograph which she also published. Hamilton's book was brought to the attention of the Bad Homburg municipal archive at the Gotisches Haus by a Mrs Angelika Baeumerth.

20. See the obituary note in *The Times*, 22 July 1886, p. 7. He was laid to rest at Abercrombie Church, see Anstruther, p. 137. Sir Robert had abandoned his parliamentary career four years earlier on account of bad health. Perhaps his visits

to Bad Homburg, too, had been necessitated by deteriorating health.

21. See Greene, p. 51f. The author is indebted to E.J.W. McCann, Belfast, for calling this source to his attention, and he gratefully acknowleges the help of Christa Scholz of the Württembergische Landesbibliothek Stuttgart for placing at his disposal material relating to the history of lawn tennis in Stuttgart.

22. Count Marcel von Zeppelin is said to have been one of the founding members of the Baden-Baden LTC in 1881, see Grauhan, 'Geschichte des Homburger Pokals', p. 92, whereas Countess von Zeppelin seems to have made an appearence at Baden-Baden tournaments in the early 1880s, see Ertl, p. 414.

23. On Greene see Legg, p. 360f., and Sadie, p. 687.

24. Hromada, born in 1841 in Kladno, Bohemia, had his first engagement in Stuttgart in 1866; he died in 1900 with all his manly vigour ('in voller Manneskraft'), see a note in the journal *Vom Fels zum Meer*, vol. 20 (1900–1901), part 2, p. 678 (this is a commentary on a photograph which appears on p. 670). In the Stuttgart directories of 1883 and 1884 there are the entries 'Hromada, A., K. Hofsänger. Neckarstr. 72, 1. [= first floor]'.

25. See the entry by J.A. Fuller Maitland, H.C. Colles and Desmond Shawe-Taylor in Sadie, p. 687, and the *Adress- und Geschäftshandbuch der königlichen Haupt- und Residenzstadt Stuttgart* of 1884, p. 78. The latter contains the names of a 'Rentier' Harry Greene and a certain W.C. (= Conyngham) Greene, referred to as 'engl. Gesandtschaftssekretär'; here, the term *Rentier* relates to somebody receiving money from elsewhere regularly, and not to a pensioner as modern German usage might suggest. The residence of both Greenes is in 'Kronenstraße 48, zweite Etage' (second floor). Since there are no entries in the 1883 and 1885 directories, the Greenes would seem to have lived in Stuttgart in 1883 and 1884.

26. See Maur, 'Rasenspiele auf dem Cannstatter Wasen', pp. 11 and 14. In those days, the Cannstatter Wasen was a drill ground, and the story of the beginnings of lawn tennis there was told by a well-known sports author of the time, Phillip Heineken, who was the secretary of Cannstatt football club (a photograph of Heineken showing him in 1930 can be seen in the article quoted above, p. 12).

27. Ibid., p. 18: 'Das Lawn-Tennis hatte einen guten Besuch, speziell auch von Angehörigen unserer passiven Mitglieder. … Besonders möchten wir auch unsere verehrten Damen wiederholt auf diesen unterhaltsamen und gesunden Sport aufmerksam machen' (from the annual report of 1893/4).

28. Ibid., p. 20.

29. Ibid., p. 21. In 1901, the club called itself 'Cannstatter Fußball- und Tennis-Club'.

30. Its successor is the Cannstatter Tennisclub e.V., a lawn tennis club pure and simple which celebrated its 100th anniversary in 1990. The references to this club in von Fichard's *Illustriertes Lawn-Tennis-Jahrbuch 1903*, p. 82, are very inaccurate.

31. See the article by R.V. 'Eine neue Tennisanlage in Württemberg', p. 182; and von Fichard, annual of 1895, p. 114. According to the latter, the Stuttgart Lawn Tennis Club was founded in the spring of 1894 and opened its courts (seven doubles and one singles court!) on 24 May 1894. Its members were 13 families and 16 single persons, and von Fichard also names the club's honorary treasurer, a Colonel Borto. Nearby, and apparently located on the same 'Stöckacher Eisbahn' (= Stöckach skating rink), the First Stuttgart Football Club also owned a court (since 1894), see von Fichard, op. cit., p. 113.

32. It apparently appeared in the Berlin sporting journal *Spiel und Sport* on 15 April 1893 and was meant to comment on a *tableau vivant* (very popular among the well-to-do in those days) highlighting an eve-of-the-wedding party in Strasbourg. The poem was reprinted in full in von Fichard's first lawn tennis annual of 1894, p. 136, and, in part, by Voigt, *Das Lawn-Tennis-Spiel*, p. vif. [Preface].

33. This and the following details are reported in von Fichard's second lawn tennis annual of 1895, p. 106. In 1895, according to von Fichard in his annual of 1896/1897, p. 182, the facilities having formerly belonged to Boursée came under the control of Baron von Hundelshausen, the director of the spring water (*Brunnendirector*), who also saw to their reconstruction. Local authorities are

completely ignorant about the existence of these lawn tennis courts and the personality of A. Boursée.

34. See the statement by Baron von Fichard, in a letter to the editor of the English journal *Pastime*, dated 27 September 1889: 'Lawn-tennis was first played at Baden-Baden in 1880 by an English family'. For the reference see the bibliography under von Fichard, 'Continental Correspondence'. Von Fichard is confirmed by a notice apparently gleaned from the contemporary *Badeblatt*, a newsletter published by the authorities of the spa and reprinted in a tournament programme in 1992:

Als ein schlichter Gast zog Lawn Tennis im Jahre 1880 in unser liebliches Oostal ein. Eine englische Familie spielte dasselbe auf einer Wiese in der Allee, und dies regte besonders in der englischen Kolonie die Frage an, ob es nicht möglich wäre, für das folgende Jahr einen Club zustande zu bringen. Am 25. Juni 1881 wurde eine Versammlung behufs Gründung eines Lawn-Tennis-Clubs abgehalten, in welcher einstimmig der hiesige englische Geistliche, Rev. A.T.S. White, zum Ehrenpräsidenten, und Mr. Jonstone zum Ehrensekretär gewählt wurden. Der Club selbst erhielt den Namen: 'Lawn-Tennis-Club Baden-Baden'.

See 'Tennis im 19. Jahrhundert in Baden-Baden', p. 47.

35. See Alexander von Rußland, p. 51. Alexander, born on 1 April 1866, was 14 years old at the time.

36. There is in the town archives of Bad Homburg a letter issued by the local authorities (the 'Städtische Kur- und Badeverwaltung') and signed by Schultz Leitershofen, the *Kurdirector*. It bears the date of 12 September 1879 and refers, in its initial sentence, to a petition by a lawn tennis club founded earlier that year (the implication may be that there had been another before) to be allotted a larger and more suitable area within the *Kurpark* where to put up 10 nets and to level the ground even before the beginning of winter. For this detail, the author is indebted to research carried out by Dr Eugen Kisselmann, of Bad Homburg, put down in writing in 1987 in the form of a typescript. This contains a copy of the letter.

37. See von Fichard, *Jahrbuch 1895*, p. 113, who points out the fact that this lawn tennis club had its roots in the former real tennis club; there was, he said, a certain amount of continuity between this club and the former real tennis association: 'eine gewisse Continuität mit der früheren "Société de Paume"'.

38. The most reliable accounts of the beginnings of lawn tennis in Baden-Baden is that of one of the founders of the Baden-Baden LTC, Baron von Fichard, in his lawn tennis annual of 1894, p. 44f. Ertl's article, despite some interesting details, is rather inaccurate and should be used with caution.

39. The Reverend A.T.S. White was born on 1 September 1843 in Wateringbury, Kent, and baptized there on 16 October 1843; he was the son of a farmer, Thomas White, and his wife Louisa (see I.P., 'The Reverend T. Archibald S. White', and Guildhall Library, London, Ms. 10, 326/285; ordination papers and letters testimonial, 1869). He was one of the founders of the 'Kentish Star Cricket Club', of which the famous cricketer Lord Harris was a member. He attended St Paul's School in London and was a member of their first cricket team which played its matches at Kennington Oval. After studying at Christ Church College, Oxford, where he successfully competed in rowing competitions, he was ordained priest on 23 May 1869. He became a preacher in the West End of London from 1868–1871 in which year he was appointed curate of English visitors to Baden-Baden (on 12 May 1871; see Guildhall Library, Ms. 9532A/6 Diocese of London; Bishop's act book 1864–72). In Baden-Baden, he held the Chaplaincy of the Anglican High Church for more than forty years, from 1871 to 1911, see Schniewind, p. 7. In 1895, he became Rural Dean of the 'Deanery B' in Northern and Central Europe, see Schniewind, p. 66. In 1892, the name of the popular clergyman was mentioned in *The Anglican Church Magazine* in connection with the introduction of golf in Baden-Baden; on 3 June 1893, when the Süddeutsche Fussball-Union (South-West German Soccer Association) was founded, he became the provisional chairman of this body, only to be

unanimously elected its president on 6 October of the same year, see Schniewind, loc. cit., who again quotes from the October issue of *The Anglican Church Magazine*, and I.P. in the article quoted above. Reverend White also founded the Baden-Baden Football Club. It hosted an athletic sports event in 1895 which gave rise to the following comment in the tourists' newspaper *The Swiss & Nice Times* (see the entry Baden-Baden in the bibliography):

We can remember the times when it was a matter of common complaint that English chaplaincies abroad were too often served by ecclesiastics of broken health and indifferent energy. How Baden-Baden has fared in the past in such a respect is not within our knowledge, but we are very sure that there is no post in the English church, whether at home or abroad, that has for its incumbent at this moment a more vigorous or devoted gentleman (in the true sense of that much abused word) than the present chaplain, the Rev. T. Archibald White, who in the face of many difficulties has won for himself a host of friends.

In the Anglican All Saints' Church in Bertholdstrasse near Gausplatz, which was dedicated in 1867 – this is the present Protestant Lutheran St Johannis Church – two commemorative tablets in the rear part of the nave bear witness to Reverend Thomas White and Mrs White, née Baroness de Seutter-Loetzen, and to his two sons who died at the age of 26, see Schniewind, p. 69f. The author is much indebted to the Reverend J.K. Newsome, Bonn, for referring him to the useful work of Schniewind which contains a lot of information about English visitors to German spas in the nineteenth century. For an assessment of White see also Perkow, pp. 262–74.

40. See Overlack, p. 1, Simon, 'Beiträge', p. 120, Perkow, p. 240 and p. 354, and the anonymous article 'Robert von Fichard. Ein Gedenkwort zu seinem 60. Geburtstag', p. 490. On Robert, an anglophile whose father was a well-known artist and who had an English mother – Georgina [von] Greaves – , and his brother, J[ames]. von Fichard, who both at the time attended a Baden-Baden school, see Simon, 'Beiträge', p. 120. Von Fichard's statement in his annual of 1894, p. 44, which was repeated by Simon, loc. cit., that he himself became the Club's

honorary secretary and treasurer is at variance with the clipping from the Baden-Baden *Badeblatt* quoted above in which this position is assigned to an Englishman, Mr Jonstone. Here it looks as if the Baron, never tiring of extolling his own merits and position, had been tinkering with his text. Again according to Simon, another brother of von Fichard, a certain A. von Fichard, also attending a gymnasium (presumably the same one as his brothers), was also a founding member. In 1931, A. von Fichard was the last living founder and lived, a retired lieutenant colonel, in Karlsruhe, see Simon, 'Aus der Tennisgeschichte', p. 526. Robert von Fichard was born on 11 November 1864; was married in Stockholm in the winter of 1905 – see a note in *Der Lawn-Tennis-Sport* 2 (1905), no. 30, 7 December 1905, p. 445 – died in Metz in March, 1918, and was buried in Baden-Baden. A tournament on his home ground, Baden-Baden, in 1911, the staging of which had not been sanctioned by the German Tennis Federation, led to a boycott of leading German players who had competed in it, and an estrangement of the Federation and the Baron who resigned from his office as its second vice-president. Another founding member of the Baden-Baden LTC was Count Marcel von Zeppelin-Aschhausen, who became the club's secretary; he died in 1894, see the article by I.P.

41. According to Grauhan, 'Geschichte des Homburger Pokals', p. 92, there was, besides the von Fichard brothers and Count Marcel von Zeppelin, also a Swiss, Robert-Tissot, among its founding members.

42. This detail is from von Fichard's letter to the editor of *Pastime*, see von Fichard, 'Continental Correspondence'.

43. The initial two courts are mentioned by von Fichard in his letter to *Pastime*, see von Fichard, 'Continental Correspondence'.

44. Von Fichard, 'Continental Correspondence', calls it a public club: the implication being that the club founded in 1881 was a private one.

45. Von Fichard, in his annual of 1894, p. 45, got the year of the inaugural tournament wrong which, he says, was in 1884.

46. See Ertl, p. 414, and von Fichard, 1894 annual, p. 45.
47. See von Fichard, loc. cit. The Lawn Tennis Club 'Rot-Weiss', credited in most handbooks with being Germany's oldest club, is the continuator of the International LTC, and was founded only on 8 April 1910, see Ertl, p. 415.
48. See von Fichard, *Deutsches Lawn-Tennis Jahrbuch 1896/1897*, p. 171.
49. See M-i., 'Ein Stück Tennisgeschichte aus Kassel', p. 238. Von Fichard, in his 1894 annual, p. 49, did not state the exact year of the foundation when he wrote that the club had existed for more than ten years ('über zehn Jahre'), nor was he sure in his 1895 annual, p. 78, where he set the foundation for about 1884 (gegründet etwa 1884'). At the time the club, the creation of members of the English colony, had one hard and one grass court and a small pavilion in Parkstrasse. Its secretary and treasurer was a certain W.H. Kirwan Ward. A Deutscher Lawn-Tennis-Club was founded in 1891 for army officers and their friends; its three courts were 'im Hof-Bleichplatz in der Karl's Aue', see von Fichard, 1895 annual, loc. cit.
50. See *Lawn-Tennis-Handbuch. Amtliches Jahrbuch des Deutschen Lawn-Tennis-Bundes*, Ausgabe 1909/10, p. 15; the date, however, is uncertain, and there is no evidence as to when exactly lawn tennis began to be played in this club. Lawn tennis was included in the activities of the Essener Sportverein (founded on 22 March 1899) according to von Fichard's *Deutsches Lawn-Tennis-Jahrbuch 1902*, p. 61. In 1903, the club owned two courts 'an der Chaussee (Hubertusburg)' and was a member of the Rheinisch-Westfälischer Spielverband, see von Fichard, *Illustriertes Jahrbuch 1903*, p. 90f.
51. See von Fichard, *Deutsches Lawn-Tennis-Jahrbuch 1901*, p. 72, and *Illustriertes Jahrbuch 1903*, p. 105. According to the former, the 'Tennis-Club von Strassburg' was founded in 1885 and had a court in the 'Spittelgarten (jardin Specht)': according to the latter, it went, in 1903, by the name of LTC Contades, and had its first court laid out to the rear of the 'Volksgarten am Zornstaden'.
52. See Urselmann, *Chronik des Harvestehuder Tennis- und Hockey-Clubs 1891–1991*, p. 9, and von Fichard, *Illustriertes Jahrbuch 1903*, p. 93. In his annual of 1894, p. 55, von Fichard had stated that the club was founded in 1885 and owed its success to its long-time secretary F.F. Eiffe, a track and field enthusiast. It is not known when exactly lawn tennis was first played by the members of this club. Von Fichard, loc. cit., says that again English residents ('dort domicilierte Engländer') had been the initiators. For details of the beginnings of sports competitions – track and field, soccer, and skating – in the early 1880s on the Moorweide in front of the Dammtor and the foundation of two sports clubs there, the Hamburger Sportclub, and the Anglo-American Football Club, see above all Koppehel, p. 55f. One of the founders, besides Eiffe, of the former was Carl Jochheim who later came into prominence as a member of the Uhlenhorst Club, see below note 78.
53. On this club, initiated by a Nuremberg physician, a Dr R. Cnopf and having a court in the local park, and a second club, founded in 1890, with a court on the left bank of the River Pegnitz close to the rear of the Kleinweidemühle and in the vicinity of the rowing club, see von Fichard, *Jahrbuch 1895*, pp. 96–8.
54. See von Fichard, in his 1894 annual, p. 59, and Mendel, 'Aus der Chronik', May 1929, p. 3. Again, it is not known whether prior to the election of a special lawn tennis committee (on 14 April 1889) lawn tennis belonged to the activities of the club.
55. See von Fichard, illustrated annual of 1903, loc. cit. and idem, *Deutsches Lawn-Tennis-Jahrbuch 1900*, p. 33; according to Mendel, *Aus der Geschichte*, p. 4, and Urselmann, p. 13, the club was founded in 1890. The club's homeground were the courts of the Eisbahnverein vor dem Dammtor.
56. See von Fichard, annual of 1896/1897, p. 170, and idem., *Deutsches Lawn-Tennis-Jahrbuch 1901*, p. 60, where von Fichard refers to two courts of this club on the Victoriaplatz. In his 1895 annual, p. 83, the Baron has the following to say on this club:

In der gewerbsfleissigen Industriestadt besteht ein Lawn-Tennis-Club, der 'Elberfelder Lawn-Tennis-Club' mit 70 activen, spielenden Mitgliedern, Herren und Damen der ersten Stände, welche in der besseren Jahreszeit auf 2 Spielfeldern dicht am Rande der Stadt, an der Rheinischen Strasse spielen.

57. This is the present Club Raffelberg e.V. Duisburg. According to von Fichard, *Illustriertes Jahrbuch 1903*, p. 90, the club was founded on 8 July 1891. However, from the statutes of 1911 it appears that the club came into being as early as 3 December 1889; the club's chairman at that time being a certain Arthur Böninger who, together with other members of the the so-called 'Societät', had brought the new games with him from England (A.B., who 'die neuen Spiele mit anderen Mitgliedern der Gesellschaft Societät aus England mitgebracht hatte'). In the beginning, there was only one court on the premises of Curtius near the police headquarters ('nur einen Platz auf dem Curtiusgelände neben dem heutigen Polizeipräsidium'), see *77 Jahre*, p. [4]. In 1900, play continued in the Speldorfer Solbad Raffelberg and on Hochfelder Friedenstrasse (three courts), see ibid., and *100 Jahre*, p. 15. According to Sting, p. [14], a 'Major Hartmann' is said to have returned with the game from a journey to England. According to *77 Jahre*, loc. cit., the same Major Hartmann (then retired) in his capacity as representative of the *Kurhaus* Raffelberg founded a hockey club in 1911 in order to draw Duisburg families to the *Kurhaus*. In the same year, the lawn tennis and the hockey club merged and adopted the name Club Raffelberg. In 1914, it had eight tennis courts and a hockey ground on Lotharstrasse.

58. The first official reference to this club comes from von Fichard, *Illustriertes Jahrbuch 1903*, p. 82. The Cannstatter Tennisclub apparently had availed itself of this early date when it celebrated the 100th anniversary of its foundation in 1990. Nevertheless, the date relates to the foundation of the Cannstadt Soccer Club, and that is why it is in need of qualification with regard to the adoption of lawn tennis into the club's activities. According to Phillip Heineken, a well-known sports writer at the turn of the

century and at the same time a member of the Cannstatt Club, it was not before the summer of 1891 that lawn tennis began to be played on Cannstatt Green by the members of the club. Indeed, Heineken's recollections seem to be the only source for these early days, see Maur, p. 18, and more recently Pfisteren, p. 10. The first permanent court – on the so-called Berger Insel – was built in 1893 only, see Pfisteren, p. 13. The name 'Cannstatter Fussball und Tennisclub' (including tennis) was adopted at a committee meeting on 23 February 1901.

59. See von Fichard, *Illustriertes Jahrbuch 1903*, p. 90.

60. See Novak *et al.*, *100 Jahre Heidelberger Tennis-Club 1890 e.V.*, p. 14.

61. Von Fichard, in his article 'Lawn-Tennis in Germany', writing in the spring of 1890, has a few additions to the list:

Among the first lawn-tennis clubs in Germany were those of Homburg, Baden-Baden, Hamburg, and Munich, those towns ... which continually come into connection with English people. ... I know of clubs at Berlin, Göttingen, Strassburg (Elsass), Colmar (Elsass), Zabern (Elsass), Freiburg, Nürnberg, Stuttgart, Vienna, and of public grounds at Frankfurt A.M. (in the Palmengarten) and Rippoldsau (Black Forest).

The Baron's first annual of 1894, a rarity of the first order, a copy of which the present writer has after many years of searching discovered, does not confirm the existence of clubs in all the places named. For one, the Alsatian and the Viennese clubs do not count, if one considers the question from a modern perspective. For another, although lawn tennis was certainly played in Berlin, Frankfurt, Freiburg and Rippoldsau, there do not seem to have been any clubs at the time. The Berliner Spielplatz-Gesellschaft (under the patronage of His Excellency the minister of state Dr von Gossler) was not a lawn tennis club in the strict sense of the term. It came into being in 1890 when it had three courts (von Fichard, annual of 1894, p. 45). In Vienna, a club, the I. Wiener LTC, had been founded as early as 1883 (it enjoyed the patronage of Princess Esterházy-Croy); it had two asphalt courts in the old Vienna zoo (Thiergarten), and later, under the presidency of Baron Gudenus, moved to the Prater. In 1890, the English Vienna LTC became the Wiener Lawn-Tennis-Club after the acceptance of 30 new members, all gentlemen from the Austrian capital, see von Fichard, op. cit., p. 77f. The Baron is altogether silent about Göttingen and Munich where, according to the Nuremberg physician Dr R. Cnopf, lawn tennis was played in the American Club as early as 1885, see von Fichard, annual of 1895, p. 96.

62. The courts, rolled sand with iron lines as in Hamburg in 1892, were in the so-called Neugarten (new garden) to the rear of Körnerstrasse and in Sachsenhausen ('hinter der Körnerstraße und in Sachsenhausen'), see 'Vom Lawn-Tennis und Cricket-Platz im Frankfurter Palmengarten', and 'Lawn-Tennis im Palmengarten'.

63. See von Fichard, in his lawn tennis annual of 1894, pp. 45f. and 141. The Berliner Spielplatz-Gesellschaft, under the patronage of Dr von Gossler, a minister of state, owned three gravel courts on the corner of Motzstrasse and Lutherstrasse in 1890 (four in 1891 and ten in 1893). An anonymous writer in 1914 paid tribute to the late Messrs Ernst Zehrmann and Erdtmann said to have been at the head of the Recreation Ground Society and at the same time remembered the green lawn tennis courts in Martin Luther and Barbarossa Strasse:

Wer entsinnt sich nicht noch der grünen Rasenflächen, des Barlaufplatzes, der in der Martin Luther und Barbarossastrasse gelegenen Tennisplätze, auf denen die ersten Turniere ausgefochten wurden? ... Hier wurzelten die beiden ältesten Tennisvereine Berlins, Rot-weiss und Blau-weiss. Der Anglo-American-Club existiert nicht mehr, und der Akademische Sport-Club auch nicht.

Accounts of the foundation of the Spielplatz-Gesellschaft are rather contradictory. According to one, the initiative was taken by a school headmaster (Schulvorsteher) named Vogler and a professor named Wüllenweber who approached Emil Zehrmann, a banker, who saw to it that a spacious lawn for the play of boys and girls, and a playground for small children were set up on a part of the dump of a Berlin coal-dealer named Urlaub. In order to raise additional funds for the Society

running the playground, lawn tennis courts were laid which were rented to the public. On these courts, Berlin youngsters were initiated to lawn tennis by the Secretary of the British Embassy, Herbert C. Dering; see Blömeke, p. 5f. According to another account, the Society was founded by Dr Max Oechelhäuser, a different banker, Otto von Mendelson-Bartholdy, and Dr Hans Schultz, Syndic of the Deutsche Bank, see Hofer, p. 20. On the Anglo-American Club and the Akademischer Sportclub and their founder Andrew Pitcairn-Knowles see the present writer's article 'English Editors', pp. 42–4.

64. Owing to building activity, the Society had to move to the outskirts as time went on, to Potsdamer Strasse (Botanic Gardens) in 1904, and to Leibnizstrasse (Hosemannsche Plätze) in 1907, see Blömeke, p. 6. It was then that the LTTC was able to acquire, on the initiative of Dr Max Oechelhäuser and with the assistance of the club's patron, Her Royal Highness Princess Friedrich Leopold of Prussia, the Kaiser's sister, its present site on Hundekehlesee, the venue of the German ladies' Open tournament, see Hofer, pp. 21 and 23f.

65. See Hofer, p. 16.

66. See Blömeke and Huber, p. 6.

67. In the German language, these hats were referred to as 'Kreissäge', literally circular saw, because of their indented brims, the result of using rather crude straw blades for their manufacture. On German lawn tennis courts around the turn of the century, the boater was simply ubiquitous.

68. See Hofer, p. 17, quoting from an article (1963) by Rudolf Ullstein, a founding member of the club. According to Daisy Uhl, the daughter of Dr Hans Schultz, it was her mother who bought the bands.

69. The original bands were green and white, but because one of them got lost at an early date, blue and white ones had to be substituted because the former colours were no longer available, see Blömeke and Huber, p. 6f.

70. So-called as early as 1896 in a note from the English journal *Lawn Tennis*, 9 September 1896, p. 192.

71. See the description given by von Fichard. In his annual of 1895, p. 87, the Baron enlarged again on the site of the club and

its 15 courts located beautifully in the open fields and by their romantic ambience inviting every sport-loving passer-by to linger and watch ('auf freiem Felde reizend gelegen und locken jeden sportliebenden Spaziergänger durch ihre romantische Lage zum Zuschauen ein'). There is another description from the 1890s by the journalist Kurt Doerry in the journal *Sport im Bild* 1 (1895), p. 240.

72. The 'broad gateway' ('breiter Weg') mentioned by von Fichard seems to be a rather narrow passage through the courts, to judge from a front view on the title page of the championships programme of 1904, preserved in the Hamburg State Archives.

73. These details were reported by von Fichard, in his 1894 annual, p. 56. The groundsman's salary for 1894 is confirmed by the statistical overview of income and expenditures for the years 1888–1902 contained in the Uhlenhorst annual report for the season 1901–1902 preserved in the Hamburg State Archives.

74. This court was, according to the club regulations, reserved for players whom the club's committee considered qualified, see von Fichard's annual of 1894, p. 61.

75. See von Fichard, loc. cit.

76. See Mendel, 'Aus der Chronik', p. 3: 'Zweck des Vereins ist die Ausnutzung des zum Waisenhaus-Gebiet gehörigen, von der Bleicherstraße, dem Hofwege, Schulwege und dem nach der erstgenannten Straße führenden Fußsteige begrenzten Platzes zu einer Eisbahn und sonstigen Sport- und Vergnügungszwecken.' The minutes of these inaugural meetings, still accessible to Mendel in 1929, later fell prey to a great fire in 1943. The passage is quoted by Kerkhoff, p. 20. The evolution of the Uhlenhorst venue also becomes evident from old maps in the Hamburg State Archives, e.g. Plankammer P 3932, scale 1:4000, of 1884; P 3931, with additions of 1891 and 1892; and P 3930, with additions of July 1907.

77. See Mendel, 'Aus der Chronik', p. 4.

78. A few months later, Carl Ferdinand, the shipbuilder's son, was substituted in Fawcus's place. At the same time, another member was added to the lawn tennis committee, Carl Jochheim.

79. See Behrens, 'Aus guten alten Tennis-Zeiten', p. 323.

80. Von der Meden was born on 6 December 1841; he died in Hamburg on 11 May 1911. A conspicuous feature of the funeral service in Ohlsdorf cemetery was a funeral wreath, made, according to the season, of lilies of the valley, and sent by Anastasia, the Grand Duchess of Mecklenburg-Schwerin. There were, of course, funeral wreaths by the Hamburg Lawn Tennis Guild, the German Lawn Tennis Federation, the Uhlenhorst, Bremen and Lübeck-Travemünde Clubs.

81. On the von der Meden family see generally the monograph by Möring, *Nic. von der Meden & Co. 125 Jahre Hausmakler*, passim. On the origin of the family, see ibid., p. 5.

82. This was kindly communicated to the author by Heino Rose, of the Hamburg State Archive, who placed at his disposal the copy of his passport, issued on 12 April 1864, and carrying the number 556/1864. It contains the following personal data: 'Stand: Kfm.; ... Statur: gem[ein]; Haare: Augenbrauen: d[unkel]blond; Bart: [no entry]; Stirn: frei; Augen: blau; Nase: Mund: groß; Kinn: Gesicht: oval; Gesichtsfarbe: gesund; Besondere Kennzeichen: keine'. (Occupation: merchant; ... Stature: normal; Hair: Eyebrows: dark-blond; Beard: no entry; Forehead: free; Eyes: blue; Nose: Mouth: large; Chin: Face: oval; Complexion: healthy; Distinctive Features: none.)

83. For particulars relating to Carl's presence in the Bradford area I am indebted to Alan Longbottom, Anglo-German Family History Services, Pudsey, West Yorkshire. See also Meyer, p. 227, whose data were completed and corrected by Heino Rose, of the Hamburg State Archives. Sophie was born in Frankfurt on 15 May 1846 and died in Hamburg on 16 February 1921. Her middle name also appears in the 1837–1883 Register of Baptisms of St Mary's in Teddington, Middlesex, p. 137, entry no. 1095, relating to the baptism of Thekla von der Meden.

84. His address at the time is given as Ashwood Villas, Headingley Lane.

85. His being a woollen merchant may have something to do with his earlier activities in Bradford. There was a small colony of

several hundred Germans in that area who were mainly merchants in the textile trade.

86. Elsa was later to marry Franz F. Mutzenbecher, an insurance magnate from Hamburg. There are many interesting references to, and several photographs of her, in a book by her grandson, Geert-Ulrich Mutzenbecher (see the entry in the bibliography). A particularly charming portrait showing her in 1905 is on p. 31.

87. See St Mary's Church, Register of Baptisms, 1837–1883, p. 137, no. 1095.

88. See Meyer and Tesdorpf, p. 229, who has 'Middlesea' and 'Hampton Wiek' respectively. Carl August Walther's application for citizenship, no. 533 of 18 July 1906 in the Hamburg State Archives and apparently based on a London birth certificate, has, correctly, 'Hampton Wick'. One branch of the von der Medens, the family of the merchant Otto von der Meden (born on 14 October 1828 and married to the daughter of a London merchant named Coad), lived in London. Otto von der Meden had five children three of whom were sons who were all London merchants, see Meyer, p. 227. The youngest, Edward Otto, was born on 1 October 1863. Otto was the son of Daniel von der Meden, an uncle of Carl August von der Meden, Sr, the lawn tennis pioneer's father. The Post Office Directory of the Home Counties Kent, Surrey and Sussex, 8th ed. of 1874, p. 2337, lists (under Court Directory Surrey) one 'Vondermedan [*sic*] Otto, Balham Hill, s.w.'; The London branch of the family may have been responsible for Carl August's pitching his tent in Middlesex. Walther, in family circles referred to as (uncle) Wally, in Hamburg society was later to grow a reputation as a philanderer and someone who did not take his profession as a merchant seriously, see again Mutzenbecher, p. 66f. There is a photograph of him showing him in tennis outfit, with a tennis racket in his hands, at Ruhleben, a Mutzenbecher estate, in 1922.

89. This appears from the registration form in the Hamburg State Archives, a copy of which was kindly placed at the author's disposal by Heino Rose.

90. See the entry in *The London Gazette* of 17 August 1880, [p.] 4533[a], referring to 'the Matter of Proceedings for Liquidation by Arrangement or Composition with Creditors, instituted by Carl August von der Meden, of 4, Jeffrey's-square, Saint Mary Axe, in the city of London, Japan Merchant, trading under the style of A. von der Meden, and residing at Hayne-road, Beckenham, in the country of Kent.' The entry proves at the same time that von der Meden had in the meantime moved to Beckenham in Kent.

91. He actually founded, together with his son Walther, a firm of this denomination, 'C.A. & W. von der Meden', as late as 1899, see Möring, p. 18 (the precise date of the foundation was, according to Heino Rose, 1 June 1899). One wonders how he earned a living for a whole decade before that date.

92. See Mendel, 'Aus der Chronik', p. 3. The prices were those to be paid by shareholders; others paid 15 and 30 marks respectively, sums confirmed by advertisements in local daily newspapers, e.g. the *Hamburgischer Correspondent*, morning issue of 9 October 1892, p. 6. Those applying for a seasonal family ticket had to state the names of all family members separately. The prices paid entitled one to an hour of play per day on one of the courts of the skating club. The court had to be booked one day in advance, see Mendel, *Aus der Geschichte*, p. 4, where the prices given differ from those in his earlier account.

93. On the foundation of this club see above, note 55. The club, about which little is known, dissolved in 1905 (according to Mendel, *Aus der Geschichte*, p. 4) or 1906 (according to Urselmann, p. 13), and the remainder of its members joined the Harvestehuder LTC.

94. See von Fichard, annual of 1895, p. 87. Urselmann, p. 13, gives particulars about the foundation which took place in the guests room of the hotel in 50 Magdalenenstrasse, Hamburg, due to an initiative of a local merchant, Otto H. Becker. The meeting is said to have been attended by ten members of whom the names of six are listed by Urselmann, and black and yellow was adopted as the club's colours for the simple reason that

the founders liked the colours of the royal house of Habsburg.

95. Nevertheless, the club regulations issued in April 1894 encouraged the formation of clubs on its premises provided the applicants could name at least eight players who knew how to play the game, and were willing to adopt the club colours (light blue) along with those of their own club, see von Fichard, annual of 1894, p. 62. One of the clubs to take up headquarters on the Uhlenhorst ground was the so-called Lawn-Tennis Club Howard (so named after Walter Howard, a Londoner who in the 1880s played for the London Athletic Club and then became a member of the Cumberland Lawn Tennis Club founded in 1880 by the residents of Cumberland Terrace on the east side of Regents Park, hence the name; the club, one of the oldest clubs in England, moved to its present site at 25, Alvanley Gardens, NW6, in 1908). The Hamburg LTC Howard, founded on 1 April 1892, was quite successful, and one of its players, Christian Winzer, became German champion in 1893. On this club see von Fichard's annual of 1895, p. 86f.

96. 'In Hamburg aber war ein herrlicher Lokal-Wetteifer zwischen Uhlenhorst und Harvestehude. Man hasste sich wie England und Deutschland im August 1914' (In Hamburg, however, there was a magnificent local rivalry between Uhlenhorst and Harvestehude. They hated each other like England and Germany in August 1914), see Behrens, p. 324.

97. See Behrens, 'Aus guten alten Tennis-Zeiten', p. 323f. Of these, Emil Thomsen was the father of Maren Thomsen who, in 1896, won the first German ladies' championship. He was a dealer in paints and lost his fortune and his business before the First World War as a result of the shellac slump.

98. See von Fichard, lawn tennis annual of 1894, p. 61.

99. See Behrens, p. 324:

Wir Uhlenhorster Jungens Winzer, Bush, Grobien, André, Wantzelius, ich, später Nirrnheim usw., die wir zunächst mindestens einen Sommer erst 'gegen die Wand', nicht auf dem Platz spielen durften, wurden beim Ehrgeiz gepackt. Wir durften bei den alten Herren Bälle aufheben, und wer als Vierter aushelfen durfte, war unendlich stolz und fing an, über die weisen Belehrungen in Technik und Taktik nachzudenken. ... Dann erkannten wir, wie 'Papa Meden' uns Hamburger Jungens ausersah, um Fragen von Turnierveranstaltung, von Bestimmungen, von Platzpflege usw. in uns fortleben zu lassen. Wir durften mit 15, 16 Jahren die Drucksachen mit vorbereiten, Briefe entwerfen, Vorgabelisten vorlegen, kleine Kassen führen usw. Die Abende vor einem Turnier bei 'Papa Meden' im Hause, wo Order pariert und scharf gearbeitet wurde, gehören zu den schönsten Erinnerungen meines Lebens.

100. See Behrens, p. 323: 'C.A.v.d.Meden ..., der in jungen Jahren lange in England ... lebte, der seit den 80er Jahren eine Tradition für die Hamburg-Uhlenhorster Turniere (mit englischem Einschlag) geschafffen hatte'.

101. See the praises sung of von der Meden by the English journal *Pastime* and by Charles Adolph Voigt in von Fichard's annual of 1896/1897. *Pastime* wrote:

Seven young Hamburg players went to Homburg to take part in the International Tournament ... earning general congratulation. Their sportsmanlike conduct gained for them much popularity, and it would have been difficult for the tournament manager to have got through his work in six days at his disposal without their valuable and willing help as umpires.

See *Pastime,* 5 September 1894, p. 298, under 'Varia', and von Fichard, op. cit., p. 22 (von der Meden proudly quoted this passage in his lawn tennis manual, p. 39). These services of Hamburg umpires continued to be called upon when in 1898 the German championships moved to Bad Homburg, see Mendel, *Aus der Geschichte*, p. 2.

102. The following details about Hans Oskar Behrens have been gleaned from Eberl *et al.*, p. 75, the *Gesamtverzeichnis des deutschsprachigen Schrifttums*, p. 463, and the *Jahres-Berichte der Hamburger Lawn-Tennis-Gilde 1904–1914*: Hans Oskar Behrens was born in Hamburg-Hohenfelde on 28 October 1880 as the son of a banker. He died on 25 February 1953 in Doorn, the Netherlands. After attending the Dr Lieben's private middle school (Realschule) in Hamburg (where he graduated in 1896), he became a commercial apprentice (1896–1899) and then studied for three terms at the commercial colleges of Cologne (Bachelor

of Commerce, 1903) and, for another
term, Leipzig. He then, after three terms
at the department of political sciences of
Tübingen university, earned a doctor's
degree, by writing a dissertation on the
development of German merchant
shipping to the South Americas (1904).
He afterwards worked as a merchant in
Hamburg and Antwerp (where his second
place of residence was at Place de Meir 21
at least as early as 1908). Antwerp became
his main residence from 1912 to 1914
when he returned to Hamburg. During
his stay in Antwerp, he was the president
of the lawn tennis section ('Beerschot
Tennis-Club') of the New Beerschot
Athletic Club on the courts of which in
1920 the Olympic tennis event was
contested, see *Lawn-Tennis und Golf*,
vol. 11 (1914), no. 11, of 9 June 1914,
p. 278. During the First World War he is
said to have been in the diplomatic service
in Brussels; according to the *Jahres-Bericht
der Hamburger Lawn-Tennis-Gilde für das
Jahr 1914*, p. [8], he was promoted to the
rank of lieutenant (reserve: *Oberleutnant
der Reserve*), and became, as from mid-
November 1914, the head of the central
passport office to the Governor-General
in Brussels. After the war, he took up
residence in the Netherlands where he
became the director of the Hollandsche
Transport en Handels Mij., The Hague
(1922–1934), as well as the N.V. Handel
Mij. Behrens & Co. (China-Import)
(1921–1932). After the First World War
he was in charge of foreign affairs on
behalf of the German Tennis Federation.
In 1933, when the ITF celebrated the
30th anniversary of its foundation, he was
awarded a gold medal by the organization.
It is now in the possession of Hilde
Hoffmann-Lesten, Wedel. At the annual
ITF conference of 1937 in Paris he was
elected chairman of their executive
committee for the period of 1937–1938,
see 'Jahres-Tagung des Internationalen
Tennis-Verbandes', p. 87. There are
photographs of Behrens in *Lawn-Tennis
und Golf*, vol. 10 (1913), no. 3, mid-
March 1913, p. 72, Eberl, op. cit., p. 631,
and Gruber's *Amtliches Handbuch of
1927*, p. 19, two of which are reproduced
in the present writer's *Olympisches Tennis*,
pp. 57 and 95. Behrens also was the
author of a richly illustrated manual on

the organization of tennis tournaments
entitled *Leitung grosser Lawn-Tennis-
Turniere* (1904) which he wrote in
deliberate imitation of that of his great
predecessor, Carl August von der Meden
(1895).

103. See von der Meden, *Leitfaden*, p. 54f.

104. Ibid., p. 15.

105. Ibid., p. 41.

106. Ibid., p. 10f.

107. See von Fichard in his annual of 1894,
p. 55.

108. See Mendel, 'Aus der Chronik', p. 3.

109. See Mendel, 'Die Geschichte des Stamm
Vereins', p. 2. There is, in the archive of
the Friedrich Krupp GmbH, Essen,
Germany, file no. FAH 21/417m-s,
pp. 7–9, a remarkable letter (dated 5 May
1897) by the Bad Homburg groundsman
Wilhelm Noss on the construction of
these courts. In all likelihood, Noss had
been the 'inspector' who in 1894 had been
sent to Hamburg in order to be initiated
to the method, see Mendel, 'Aus der
Chronik', p. 6, quoting from the annual
report of 1894 by the Uhlenhorst
treasurer, Johannes Gabe.

110. As late as 1903, G.W. Hillyard (champion
of Germany on the very same courts
in 1897) commended the Hamburg courts
highly: 'The Hamburg tournament … is
held on the excellent sand courts of the
Uhlenhorst Club …'), see Myers, *Lawn
Tennis at Home and Abroad*, p. 102. His
countryman, Dr J.M. Flavelle (runner-up
in 1902 and 1903) also praised the surface
of the courts, but found fault with the
lines: 'The surface is perfect, but
unfortunately the lines are of iron', see
Myers, op. cit., p. 232. From von der
Meden's tennis manual it appears that it
was less the iron tapes themselves than the
the iron staples used to fasten them in the
ground which caused many an erratic
bounce of the ball and therefore gave rise
to criticism, ibid., p. 16f. Von der Meden
himself may well have been the inventor
of this curious device which was only
abandoned as late as 1906, see *Der Lawn-
Tennis-Sport* 3 (1906), p. 317.

111. That Boursée had been in charge of laying
the Hamburg courts was stated by Hans
Oskar Simon in his article 'Beiträge zur
Tennis-Geschichte', p. 120.

112. See Mendel, 'Aus der Chronik', p. 4:

Bereits für den Winter 1889 wird ein neuer Tennisplatz hinter dem Gebäude, also dem Platze, wo jetzt [i.e. 1929] unsere Tennishalle steht, 'eingerichtet'. Die Benutzer müssen eine Extra-Abgabe von M 20.- für Person und Winter erlegen. 'Einführung je einer Dame ist denselben frei gestattet'.

This seems to imply that this court was used even during the winter! The annual report of the Eisbahnverein auf der Uhlenhorst of the season 1901–1902 issued in December 1902, a copy of which is preserved in the Hamburg State Archive, contains statistics of the club's income and expenditures for the years 1888–1902. The shares bought by the club's founders yielded 42,100 marks in the first year, subscription tickets 15,319 marks, and the total income was 57,565 marks. What I take to be the costs for the purchase of the estate (termed 'Anlage') amounted to 39,522.18 marks, various expenditures (not specified) to 13,043.77 marks, the total of expenditures (exceeding the total income somewhat) being 59,358.66 marks.

113. See Mendel, 'Aus der Chronik', p. 4f., and *Aus der Geschichte*, p. [10f.]. The special feature of these courts was that they were permanent ones as opposed to those located in front of the club pavilion, on a large area which during the winter was used by the skaters. The location of these permanent courts, to the rear of the club house, is well illustrated on contemporary Uhlenhorst maps in the Hamburg state archives, e.g. 'Plankammer P3930 Uhlenhorst 1884 1:4000 … ergänzt … Sept. 1902'.

114. See von Fichard, lawn tennis annual of 1894, p. 60. This is confirmed by Simon, 'Von unseres Sportes Werdegang', p. 40, and the British journal *Pastime* in its account of the 1894 championships (issue of 18 July 1894, p. 185): 'This year's meeting was certainly the most enjoyable since Hamburg's first yearly lawn-tennis week in 1890.'

115. This 'trial run' for the first championship tournament in 1892 has never been mentioned even by local tennis historians. There is an extensive report on it in the English journal *Pastime* of 16 September 1891, p. 208f. It could well have been written by Carl August von der Meden himself.

116. The same Walter Howard, partnered by J.G. Howard, his brother, also won the gentlemen's open doubles event. Their prize, a glass decanter having an engraved silver lid, has recently been bought at auction in Lewes by an antique dealer from Munich. It has in the meantime passed into the possession of the successor of the Uhlenhorst club, the Klipper Tennis- und Hockey-Club auf der Uhlenhorst e.V. and constitutes one of the earliest (if it is not, in fact, the earliest) known tennis prizes in this country. Four fine early (1890–1910) lawn tennis rackets from the same lot, two of which each bear the name 'W. Howard', and the initials 'J.G.H[oward]' respectively, have in the meantime been acquired by the present writer.

117. See 'Hamburg', in *Pastime*, 16 September 1891, p. 208.

118. See von der Meden, *Leitfaden*, p. 12f. Apart from English journals such as *Pastime* and *The Field*, he recommended the first German sporting journal of note, *Spiel und Sport*, and, tentatively, the reading of the elegant world, the journals *Illustrierte Zeitung*, *Ueber Land und Meer*, *Moderne Kunst* and *Vom Fels zum Meer*.

119. The first hint to the tournament is to be found in a calendar of events in the issue of 4 May 1892, p. 277: '[FIXTURES OPEN TOURNAMENTS – 1892] Aug. 23, etc., – St. Andrews[;] 27, etc. – Uhlenhorst, Hamburg [;] … 29, etc. – Brighton …'. Sizable advertisements followed in the issues of 6 and 20 July, and were repeated every week in the month of August, i.e. on 3, 10 and 17. A quarrel between the lawn tennis sub-committees and committees of the two skating clubs had preceded the advertising campaign, because the latter were unwilling to face the estimated costs for two lawn tennis tournaments. That is why a different type of circular was dispatched by the lawn tennis committees in which sponsors were asked to subsidize the organizers by paying a certain sum to a fund ('Garantie-Fonds') set up for the purpose, see Mendel, 'Aus der Chronik', p. 4, and idem, *Aus der Geschichte*, p. 2. It looks as if from the very beginning the two skating clubs contributed to the financing of the tournaments, although it should be emphasized at this point that the initial

championship tournaments from
1892–1897 and again, after the Bad
Homburg interlude, the one of 1902, were
held on the Uhlenhorst courts, a fact
which has never been brought out
properly by local tennis historians, and
not even by the only chronicler to have
had access to the original Uhlenhorst
sources, Paul Mendel. Only after 1902
was there an annual change between the
Dammtor and the Uhlenhorst venues, the
former being that of the modern German
Open. In 1991, when the 100th
anniversary of this event was celebrated at
Hamburg Rothenbaum, the celebration
was not only premature, but took place on
the wrong site.

120. The entrance fee for Germans was 3
marks for members of the two skating
clubs and 5 marks for non-locals,
according to the newspaper article
referred to in note 122, below.

121. A more explicit note appeared in *Pastime*,
17 August 1892, p. 102 (under 'Varia'); it
read:

Five of the six events at Hamburg are open,
three of them being handicaps. The other event
is open to Germans and Austrians only. All
entries must be sent to A. Von der Meden, the
hon. sec., by Saturday next. The courts, about
twelve in number, are of gravel [as we have
heard, there were, by this time, only two gravel
courts available, but it was on these that the
matches were contested], and the grounds are
situated at Uhlenhorst, a very pretty suburb of
Hamburg, easily accessible from the town by
rail or steamboat. The members of the
committee are renowned for their hospitality,
and the residents in the neighbourhood take a
great interest in the game. The best route from
London is via Flushing, and the hotels
recommended are the Hotel de l'Europe and
the Hotel Viev [*sic* = Vier] Jahreszeiten.

122. See *Hamburger Fremden-Blatt*, no. 151, 30
June 1892, 3rd supplement ('Dritte
Beilage'), under the heading 'Jagd und
Sport'. This important source has never
been mentioned by local historians of
sport.

123. See the tournament account in *Pastime*,
28 September 1892, p. 201: 'the Cup has
to be won three times, not necessarily in
succession'; and von Fichard, in his
annual of 1894, p. 60, who stated that it
had to be won three times, though,
perhaps, not in a row ('eventuell ohne
Reihenfolge').

124. As opposed to modern practice, the All
England champion stayed out of the
competition, a procedure continued in
Wimbledon until 1921, in the United
States until 1911. In 1913, at the last
German championships before the First
World War, Heini Schomburgk was the
last to defeat the champion of the
preceding year, Otto von Müller, in a
challenge round. An important initiative
against the institution of the challenge
round was taken by the American
Clarence Hobart, incidentally German
champion in 1899, see the article 'When
Hobart Refused to Play', and, below, the
account given of the 1899 championships
in Bad Homburg.

125. See the tournament account in *Pastime*,
28 September 1892, p. 201f., and von
Fichard, in his lawn tennis annual of 1894,
p. 60: 'ca. Mk. 700'.

126. These figures are given in the extensive
account of the tournament given by the
Berlin-based sporting journal *Spiel und
Sport* in its issue of 1 October 1892. The
initial volume of this journal (and also that
of 1893) do not seem to have survived,
but its report on the Hamburg
tournament was fortunately reprinted in
the (extremely rare) 1894 annual of Baron
von Fichard, pp. 83–93. The English
journal *Pastime*, in its issue of 28
September 1892, p. 201, has a completely
different figure, i.e. 149. Both reports
could nevertheless have the same author,
Baron Robert von Fichard, the former
being an extended version of the latter.

127. The cholera, which caused more than
5,000 casualties, was at its peak on 27
August 1892, see the interview given by
the Hamburg medical officer Dr Kraus to
the *Hamburger Fremden-Blatt*, a daily
newspaper, ibid., no. 211, Friday, 9
September 1892, third supplement, and
the diagram in another daily, the
Hamburgischer Correspondent, no. 717, 11
October 1892, on its title page:
'Graphische Darstellung der revidirten
Cholera-Statistik'. One of the two highest
incidences of newly infected and deaths is
on 27 August 1892. All schools had been
closed down, see the *Hamburger Fremden-
Blatt*, first supplement to no. 201,
Saturday, 27 August 1892, under
'Tagesbericht'; dances were not to be held
either, and sporting events to be

postponed until after the epidemic, see the daily *Hamburgischer Correspondent*, no. 691, evening issue, Friday, 30 September 1892, p. 4, under 'Sport', where a rowing event is announced for 2 October 1892 which had been set for 4 September 1892. For another example see the same daily, 7 October 1892, no. 709, p. 4.

128. See von Fichard, annual of 1894, p. 83, and 'Hamburg', *Pastime*, 28 September 1892, p. 201. The English journal is not quite accurate as to the date. According to von Fichard, the final of the championship of Germany was contested on Sunday, 18 September, that of the ladies' singles only on 20 September, see also von Reznicek, p. 174, who had access to either von Fichard's yearbook, or the Baron's original contribution to *Spiel und Sport*.

129. *Pastime*, loc. cit., has T. von Fichard which may mean that its report was based on a letter written by hand.

130. We are informed about this detail by Dr Wilhelm Schomburgk almost exactly half a century later, in 1942, in an article contributed to the journal *Der Tennissport*, see Schomburgk, 'Hamburger Tenniserinnerungen', p. 54. In this article, Schomburgk mentioned a ledger formerly owned by Baron von Fichard in which the pioneer of German lawn tennis had scrupulously collected tournament programmes and newspaper clippings from the dawn of German lawn tennis history. Sadly, this collection of most valuable information about tennis in this country in the early days fell prey to a fire in Dr Schomburgk's library in Leipzig during the Second World War.

131. See *Pastime*, loc. cit., where his play is characterized thus:

The champion's play, as far as style goes, is rather clumsy. He plays a good deal from the base line, and does not often go to the net, but has a knack of picking up difficult returns. Accurate lobbing appears to be his strongest point. Altogether he plays a defensive game, and relies on his great endurance. As he is still very young he will very likely have plenty of opportunities to get rid of his faults. He has certainly the making of a good lawn tennis player in him.

This is an English paraphrase of the description in von Fichard's annual of 1894, p. 84.

132. See 'Hamburg', *Pastime*, 20 September 1893, p. 184.

133. It was reprinted in von Fichard's lawn tennis annual of 1894; the whole article on the Hamburg tournament ran to twenty (!) printed pages. In 1893, *Spiel und Sport*, published by the Jewish entrepreneur John Bloch, was in the third year of its existence. On the role of English editors of German sporting journals at the turn of the century, John Bloch (*Spiel und Sport*), Andrew Pitcairn-Knowles, a Scotsman (*Sport im Bild*), and Fred Manning (*Der Lawn-Tennis-Sport*, the first journal devoted to lawn tennis in the country from 1904–1916), see now the present writer's article 'English Editors'.

134. Trying to characterize the future German champion, Count Voss, the anonymous writer, speaking of the advantages of his height, and his colossal reach, had to admit that there was no German word for *reach*: 'Dabei gereicht ihm noch zum besonderen Vorteil seine grosse Gestalt, sein reach (es fehlt uns hier das passende deutsche Wort) ist kolossal.' See von Fichard, lawn tennis annual of 1894, p. 110.

135. See von Fichard, op. cit., p. 111.

136. See von Fichard, in his 1894 annual, p. 110: 'von allen deutschen Spielern … hat uns sein Spiel am meisten gefallen'.

137. Ibid.

138. See the accounts of the final given by the English journal *Pastime*, 18 July 1894, p. 185, and by von Fichard, in his 1895 annual, p. 34f., quoting from a report in the Hamburg daily newspaper *Hamburgischer Correspondent*. Voss, said to have competed in other events before on the same day, and who throughout his career seems to have been lacking in fitness, only won with a last effort, knowing that he would have lost had the match lasted longer. Voss's lack of staying power was also pointed out by Clarence Hobart, who as late as in 1901 wrote: 'Count Voss, whose game is distinctly first class, but who, unfortunately, lacks endurance, and is unable to do himself justice in a long match.' See Hobart, p. 685. The year before, in 1900, Voss had

himself given an explanation of this major weakness, see 'A Chat', p. 469f.:

I was very ill a couple of years ago, and I have never been my former self since; I can't last well now, and am played out after the second set ... I should like nothing better than a couple of weeks' play in England every year, if I could stand the strain, but when it comes to a five-set match I cannot bear the strain.

The final match was also aptly summarized in *English Chat*, the English language supplement of *Spiel und Sport* (quoted from von Fichard, lawn tennis annual of 1895, p. 135):

The Championship of Germany, open to Germans only, was the principal event on the card and the victory of Graf Voss-Schönau was both well earned and popular. The loser was last year's holder, Herr C. Winzer, and though he showed excellent knowledge of the volleying game, the winner was superior in his placing tactics. Herr C. Winzer might have again been the winner had he not persistently rushed up to the net after every service.

139. See von Fichard's 1895 annual, p. 34f.: 'Besonders die zahlreich erschienenen Damen konnten kein Ende finden im Beifallklatschen und Tücherschwenken.'

140. Details of the 1895 championships have been gleaned from C[harles].A[dolph].V[oigt], 'Das grosse internationale Hamburger Turnier', in von Fichard, *Deutsches Lawn-Tennis Jahrbuch 1896*, pp. 20–34.

141. Whether or not von Schneider took to heart Voigt's advice, he became champion of the Germans (as distinct from champion of Germany) at Heiligendamm in 1901.

142. See Voigt, *Das Lawn-Tennis Spiel,* especially those after p. 32, Fig. IX, and after p. 54, Fig. XII, which, from a modern point of view, are very funny indeed. The book is an adaptation of a manual by Wilberforce, as Voigt admitted himself, who called himself guilty of inaccuracies and mistakes at the same time, see 'Mr. C.A. Voigt', p. 42.

143. See the bibliographical entry in the 1929 *Ayres' Lawn Tennis Almanack*, p. 603. The author wishes to thank Frank V. Phelps for making accessible to him this source. The most detailed account of Voigt is to be found in the interview published by *Lawn Tennis and Croquet*, mentioned in the preceding note, where,

on p. 43 and apparently affecting, contrary to his habit, broad American English, he confirmed his American origin: 'Wal, I guess I'm a Yankee! I come from San José in California, a part of the world with which you may be familiar from Bret Harte's tales, and I daresay I shall return there one day.'

144. See his own testimony in 'Mr. C.A. Voigt', p. 42.

145. See Paret, 'Lawn Tennis on the European Continent', p. 470.

146. See 'Mr. C.A. Voigt', p. 42.

147. See the present writer's *Olympisches Tennis*, p. 27.

148. Voigt is called a 'Beamter' (a term today used to refer to government and municipal officers only) of the Gruson factories in local directories of 1895 and 1896 as was kindly communicated to the present writer by the state archivist (Landeshauptarchiv Sachsen-Anhalt) in Magdeburg, his address being 'Anhaltstr. 3' and 'Breite Weg 270' for 1895 and 1896 respectively; despite his own testimony ('For six years I was in the famous Krupp-Gruson works ...', 'Mr. C.A. Voigt', p. 42), his name does not appear in the directories before 1895. According to the archivist, Dr Köhne-Lindenlaub, there is no reference to the nature of his activities in the Historical Archives of Friedr. Krupp AG in Essen. For an account of lawn tennis in Magdeburg, and a special reference to the private court of the factory owner, Dr jur. H. Gruson, see von Fichard in his 1895 annual, p. 95. It could well be that the photographs in Voigt's manual were taken on this court.

149. On the former Gruson factories, now SKET Vereinigte Maschinen- und Anlagenbau GmbH, see Kraft, *Die geschichtliche Entwicklung der Friedr. Krupp Grusonwerk Aktiengesellschaft in Magdeburg*. The factory, founded by Hermann Gruson (1821–1895), was taken over by Friedrich Krupp on 1 May 1893 and continued under the name of 'Friedrich Krupp Grusonwerk', see Kraft, p. 8.

150. This is how he was characterized by von Reznicek, p. 44, who considered him to be a predecessor of the modern sports promoter, and in the article 'Mr. C.A. Voigt', p. 41: 'that crowning triumph of art – the buttonhole – with which his

immaculate sartorial taste will assuredly decorate his manly breast'.

151. See Paret, p. 470.

152. Here he lived in 1899, when the interview appeared in *Lawn Tennis and Croquet*, see 'Mr. A.C. Voigt', p. 43: 'my present home in Rotterdam'.

153. See Paret, p. 469. In the programme of the Hamburg championship tournament of 1906, where his name appears on the list of the honorary committee, Paris is given as his place of residence. In 1929, according to *Ayres' Almanack*, p. 603, his address was 3, Cursitor Street, Chancery Lane, [London] EC.

154. See the funny anecdote told by Wallis Myers, *Captain Anthony Wilding*, p. 249f.

155. See *Ayres' Almanack*, loc. cit., and a note from the German journal *Lawn-Tennis und Golf*, vol. 7 (1910), no. 23, 1 September 1910, p. 473, where he is said to have been presented, in recognition of his merits and on behalf of the *Kurdirector*, von Maltzahn, a valuable cup by Prince Albert zu Schleswig-Holstein. However, Voigt was again in charge of the Bad Homburg tournament in 1914 which, owing to the outbreak of the war, was not held, though, see a note in the journal *Lawn-Tennis und Golf* 11 (1914), no. 18, 28 July 1914, p. 482.

156. See Paret, p. 470.

157. See 'The Approaching Marriage of Mr. Charles A. Voigt', in *Lawn Tennis and Croquet* 8 (1904), no. 214, 3 February 1904, p. 569.

158. See Voigt, 'The Origin'.

159. The truth of what Voigt wrote in 1912 is in a way confirmed in the interview given in 1899, see 'Mr. C.A. Voigt', p. 41: 'Mr. Voigt's dream probably takes the form of a meeting or tournament at which teams or individuals representative of every country under heaven shall appear to uphold the honour and renown of their native land.'

160. On his writings see 'Mr. C.A. Voigt', p. 42f. *The British Library Catalogue of Printed Books* lists the following writings: *Riviera Rambles and Gambols* (1905); *Parisiana Summer Annual*, a journal started in 1911; *Famous Gentleman Riders at Home and Abroad*, London 1925; and *Wimbledon Lawn Tennis Championships*, London 1925. None of these seems to have found its way into Germany.

161. On Pitcairn-Knowles, see now the present writer's article 'English Editors', pp. 40–9.

162. See the note which appeared in the German journal *Der Lawn-Tennis-Sport* 2 (1905), no. 21, 17 August 1905, p. 327: 'Wie uns aus Homburg v. d. Höhe mitgeteilt wird, dürfte das diesjährige Turnier das letzte sein, welches von Herrn C.A. Voigt geleitet wird, da letzterer beabsichtigt, definitiv nach den Vereinigten Staaten von Amerika zurückzukehren.'

163. According to Jack Douglas of the San Jose State University archives, he at least never returned to San Jose. There was nevertheless evidence that a Dr C.B.F. Voight lived there in the 1870s who may have been his father.

164. The Entry of Death of the Registration District Shoreditch, Sub-district of Shoreditch South West, county of London, bearing the date of 8 July 1929 states that he died of endocarditis at 1a Shepherdess Walk, the informant being a certain H.G. Goodman, who is called the 'occupier' of the flat. The physician certifying his death was a certain R.T. Taylor. Voigt's address and occupation are given as 15? Burgskull, St Giles, Bloomsbury, which is at odds with what was said in *Ayres' Almanack*, see above, note 153. His occupation was given as that of a journalist.

165. See 'Das internationale Turnier zu Hamburg-Uhlenhorst' in von Fichard, *Deutsches Lawn-Tennis-Jahrbuch ... 1896*, p. 85.

166. Ibid., and loc. cit., p. 90.

167. See von Fichard, op. cit., p. 85. Von Fichard's correspondent was confirmed by the anonymous writer of the English journal *Pastime* who wrote, in its issue of 24 June 1896, p. 26:

The chief interest lay in the play for the Championships of Germany. In the Gentlemen's Championship Count Voss-Schönau, the holder, had no difficulty in maintaining his right to the title for the second [this ought to be 'third'] year in succession. He has greatly improved his game since last year. ... Of the other German players who have improved their game of late may be mentioned G. Wantzelius, H.O. Behrens, and J. André.

168. See von Fichard, op. cit., p. 87: 'So interessant sich nun das Meisterschaftsspiel der Damen gestaltete,

so nüchtern entwickelte sich das Herren-Meisterschaftsspiel von Deutschland.'

169. On the first Laeisz cup, see Kirchner, *passim*. The second Laeisz cup, presented in 1897, was captured by Major Josiah George Ritchie in 1905, see Grauhan, 'Geschichte der deutschen Meisterschaften im Herren-Einzelspiel', p. 557. His son, R.J. Ritchie, who lives in England, had no idea about what happened to it. It is one of the ironies of history that it may well have been destroyed by German bombers, for when he returned from Africa (where he had been a prisoner of war) after the Second World War, the house of his father had been bombed in a German air raid. The third championship cup, presented in 1906 by the Grand Duchess Anastasia of Mecklenburg and again decorated with Ritchie's name in that year, was won by Otto Froitzheim in 1910, see Grauhan, .op. cit., p. 557f., and the *Jahres-Bericht der Hamburger Lawn-Tennis-Gilde für das Jahr 1910*, p. [2]: '1. Herren-Einzelspiel um die Meisterschaft von Deutschland. Herausforderungspreis Ihrer Kaiserlichen Hoheit der Frau Grossherzogin Anastasia von Mecklenburg-Schwerin: *O. Froitzheim, Strassburg*. Froitzheim gewann diesen Preis in diesem Jahre zum 3. Mal und damit endgültig.' The Grand Duchess also donated the fourth championship cup on which again Froitzheim's name was engraved in 1911. Froitzheim (after winning his sixth championship after the First World War, in 1922, see Grauhan, p. 559) could again lay claim to this trophy. Sadly, the two Froitzheim cups hardly fared better than Ritchie's. Froitzheim's son Rainer had to confess that after the Second World War (which left Froitzheim's wife penniless after Froitzheim himself had been put into an internment camp by the Allied Forces), both had to be turned into cash: they were sold to members of the Jewish community in Wiesbaden, Froitzheim's place of residence, who shortly afterwards emigrated to Israel. Froitzheim's son believes that the cups were soon melted down by their new owners who were, of course, completely ignorant of their value. It looks as if only a miracle could restore these precious trophies. The cup presented by Voss in 1897 for the future champions of the Germans, now also in Braunschweig, was kept, after the temporary dissolution of the German Tennis Federation under the Nazis, at the office of their 'Fachamt Tennis' in Berlin Charlottenburg in 1936, see Gruber, 'Graf Voss', p. 528.

170. See von Huck, p. 444, and Baroness von Reibnitz-Maltzan, p. 15. There is a great deal of confusion in contemporary newspapers as to whose chamberlain the Count was. Sometimes he was said to be attached to the Grand Duke of Mecklenburg, at times he was considered to render services to the Russian Grand Duke Mikhail Mikhailovich.

171. See von Huck, p. 444. On the family estates see Kneschke, vol. 9, p. 420, and Sieber, *Schlösser und Herrensitze in Mecklenburg*, p. 91f. (No. 60: Schorssow) and pp. 92–4 (No. 61: Ulrichshusen), and the nice pictures from old engravings in the latter, pp. 208 and 209 respectively. Schorssow, on the western bank of the Malchiner See, was sold in 1891 to one Lieutenant Colonel von Tiele-Winckler.

172. See von Huck, loc. cit. ('Herzschild, darin ein links aufspringender r[oter] Fuchs'); and Kneschke, p. 419: 'Voss, Grafen (Erhebung von 1800: Schild geviert, mit Mittelschilde, … . Im silbernen Mittelschilde ein linksgekehrter, in vollem Lauf begriffener, rother Fuchs.)'

173. See 'A Chat', p. 468, and 'Kleine Plauderei', a translation into German from the former, p. 49. The interview, in the course of which Voss made this statement, was given in the winter 1899/1900, at the Hotel Beau-Site in Cannes.

174. See 'A Chat', loc. cit.

175. Details about Voss's relationship to the Grand Duke and the Grand Duchess, and his frequent stays at Cannes have been gleaned from the highly informative typescript by Baroness Louise von Reibnitz-Maltzan who belonged to the retinue of the Grand Duchess Anastasia. The present writer is greatly indebted to his Highness, the Grand Duke of Mecklenburg-Schwerin, for his kindness in placing this important document, 99 pages in all, at his disposal for evaluation. The typescript is titled *Grossherzogin Anastasia von Mecklenburg*, and was completed in 1922.

176. There is a picture of the house in *Erinnerungen*, an autobiographical account by the Grand Duke's daughter, Crown Princess Cecily (Cecilie) which appeared in 1932, see ibid., after p. 128.

177. In 'A Chat', loc. cit., Voss said himself that in his early days he 'learnt most from the Renshaws'. In 1896, Baron von Fichard confirmed this, comparing his style with that of the best English players, and especially with that of William Renshaw against whom he had, as far as he knew, played many a friendly practice match on the Riviera: 'sein Stil kommt dem der besten englischen Spieler gleich, besonders hat die Art und Ausführung seines Schlages grosse Aehnlichkeit mit derjenigen William Renshaw's, dem er, wenn wir nicht irren, schon oft im friedlichen Uebungsspiel an der Riviera gegenüber gestanden hat.' See the Baron's 1896/1897 annual, p. 21.

178. During the winter, Burke was employed as a professional by the Nice lawn tennis club, according to Clarence Hobart, the American, who toured Europe in the late 1890s and has left an interesting account of continental European lawn tennis at the turn of the century, see idem, 'Lawn Tennis in Continental Europe', p. 689. On Burke, 'a player inferior only to the Dohertys; […] also an excellent teacher', see Hough in his contribution 'Play in France and Switzerland', in Myers, *Lawn Tennis*, p. 258f. (photograph on p. 258). Burke regularly accepted invitations by the Grand Duchess Anastasia to her country seat of Gelbensande near Rostock which had been provided with a private tennis court. There, the Irishman instructed both the Grand Duchess and her children, see Cecilie, op. cit., p. 56:

Meine Mutter war eine leidenschaftliche Tennisspielerin. Sie ließ daher unweit des Jagdhauses einen Tennisplatz anlegen und lud auch öfter berühmte Tennisspieler ein. So wohnten z.B. mehrere Male die Brüder Doherty bei uns, die mit Mama und ihrem Kammerherrn Grafen Voß sowie der Gräfin Clara Schulenburg manch scharfes Spiel ausfochten. Der berühmte Professional Burke, der Vater [?] der beiden bekannten Brüder, kam regelmäßig jeden Sommer auf einige Wochen nach Gelbensande, übte viel mit Mama und gab auch uns Kindern Unterricht.

179. See 'A Chat', p. 468: 'As a pigeon shot he has few equals, and has won, among numerous other prizes, the Triennial Championship at Monte Carlo, the Grand Prix de Paris, French Championship, and the Grand Prix de Spa.' See also the note with which 'A Chat' is concluded. In 1904, the journal *Sport im Bild* deeply regretted that the Count, the best shot ever to represent Germany in Monte Carlo and once considered to be the coming man, had given up pigeon shooting two years earlier: 'Der beste Schütze, der Deutschland jemals in Monte Carlo repräsentierte, war Graf Voss, der bekannte Lawn-Tennis-Spieler. Seit zwei Jahren hat er jedoch nicht mehr geschossen, obwohl er einst als der 'kommende Mann' galt.' See 'Taubenschiessen in Monte Carlo', p. 107. Count Voss also played real tennis during his frequent visits to Paris in the company of Grand Duchess Anastasia, who used to stay there (according to von Reibnitz-Maltzan, p. 56) every year from May until mid-June: [Interviewer] 'I believe you occasionally play tennis, I mean "real" tennis, as Mr. Mahony would say?' 'Yes, I do occasionally when passing through Paris. I find it so convenient to run across from my hotel to the tennis courts in the Tuileries Gardens, when I have a game with one of the markers, but I have never taken to tennis seriously.' See 'A Chat', p. 469f. When in Paris, the Grand Duchess used to stay at the Hotel Campbell near the Arc de Triomphe and not far from the Bois de Boulogne, and the sports she and her company engaged in were tennis, pigeon shooting, horse races (at Longchamps) and bicycle races, see von Reibnitz-Maltzan, pp. 49, 51, and 53.

180. See the testimony of Hobart, p. 688:

By way of illustrating the quality of entries at these tournaments there were at Cannes, at the time of my visit R.F. and H.L. Doherty, J.M. Flavelle, E.S. Wills and C.B. Weir, all English players – while from the other side of Nice, Count Voss and Countess Schulenburg came almost daily, the former in his magnificent great red-coated automobile. It is on account of this yearly winter practice with some of the best English players that these two Germans have so far outstripped all their compatriots.

Cecilie, the German Crown Princess, reported that Count Voss, who, she said, also was a great lover of horses, had learnt to drive in 1897, op. cit., p. 79. In the same year, he accomplished a remarkable feat for any beginner, by covering in his car the distance from Mecklenburg to the Riviera. In 1936, the year of his death, he was reported to have still made, in the company of his wife, the same trip to Cannes and Alassio for the past eight years, and one of his last grand tours was said to have been to the Engadine in 1935, see Gruber, 'Graf Voss', p. 528. However, the same 'gentleman driver' had, according to Crown Princess Cecilie, p. 89, also been guilty of a rather serious accident when his car, on a downhill course in Cannes, drove off the road and turned over. Cecilie's sister Alexandrine ('Adini') and her husband, the future king Christian X of Denmark, had also been victims of the accident.

181. See the daring comparison made by Baron von Fichard, in his lawn tennis annual of 1896/1897, p. 20f.:

> der deutsche Meisterspieler ... wird bald wie Alexander der Grosse nach neuen Eroberungen lechzen und es wird ihm schliesslich nichts mehr übrig bleiben, als nach England zu reisen, um, im Kampfe mit den dortigen Grössen, sich wieder einmal schlagen zu lassen! ... und trotzdem der Graf vorläufig noch nichts von einer englischen Reise wissen will, wird er bald einsehen, dass, um weitere Fortschritte zu machen, ihm sonst kein anderer Weg offen bleibt. (The German champion will soon, like Alexander the Great, thirst for new conquests, and he cannot help going to England at last, in order to be, battling against the greats there, again beaten once in a while. ... And although the Count, for the time being, does not want to have anything to do with it, he will soon realize that, in order to improve his game, this is the only way to do so.)

182. See 'A Chat', p. 469. In Chiswick, he managed to beat one of the Allen twins, E.R., and lost to Greville in the final. In Dublin he was defeated by the formidable Frank Risely (who afterwards had the better of H.L. Doherty), albeit in five sets only, see von Reznicek, p. 28.

183. See 'A Chat', p. 470.

184. This second service was described by Charles Voigt, in von Fichard's lawn tennis annual of 1896/1897, p. 21:

sein zweiter Schlag, ohne viel Kraft zu verlieren, ist gewöhnlich gut plaziert, ... Ein dann und wann ganz plötzlich zur Abwechslung angewandter sogenannter 'underhand twist' Servierschlag, der im feindlichen court ganz sachte aufschlägt, aber beim Aufsprunge durch das dem Ball mit dem Schläger gegebene 'effet' nach der Seite 'bricht', bringt den in aller Eile nach vorne laufenden Rückschläger gar oft ausser Fassung und gewinnt den betreffenden Gang. (His second service is well placed, without losing much power, ... a so-called 'underhand twist', used for a change once in a while, which comes down softly in the opponent's court, but then, after the impact and as a result of the spin imparted to it with the racket, 'breaks', upsetting the opponent who has come forward in great haste, thus winning the rally in question.)

185. Charles Voigt, here advocating the German cause, was of a very different opinion; his remarks are, in addition, an interesting testimony of how players in those days tried to cope with a high-speed service: 'Sein erster starker Servierschlag – wenn derselbe gelingt – wird selten zurückgegeben und dann nur als Lob ...'. (His first service, when successful, is seldom returned and, if at all, only as a lob.) See von Fichard, lawn tennis annual of 1896/1897, p. 21.

186. Vgl. Flavelle, 'The Game in Northern Europe', in Myers, *Lawn Tennis at Home and Abroad*, p. 228f.

187. This name appears in a catalogue issued by Slazengers in 1906, see Gurney, *The Racket*, pp. 22 and 27. The name is absent, however, from advertisements the firm had published in German periodicals of the time.

188. See 'A Chat', p. 470.

189. See *Sport im Bild* 2 (1896), No 44, p. 700: '[es möge zur] Information ... [der] Leser ... dienen, dass das weisse Tuch trocken' [sei] 'und lediglich der heftigen Transpiration der Kopfhaut wegen um die Stirn gelegt' [werde], 'um somit eine Trübung der Brillengläser zu verhindern. In England und Amerika' [pflegten] 'viele brillentragende Spieler dasselbe zu tun.' Voss's white headdress was also remembered by the Grand Duchess's lady-in-waiting, von Reibnitz-Maltzan, p. 59: 'Ihr [Anastasia's] Partner war meistens Graf Vicco Voss. Beide waren von weitem leicht zu erkennen. Die Grossherzogin in kurzem schwarzem

Rock trug gewöhnlich eine hochgeschlossene weisse Hemdbluse und einen kleinen Matrosenhut, Graf Voss überragend gross mit einer Hornbrille band sich stets ein weisses Tuch um die Stirn.'

190. See on this the anonymous article titled 'Der Voss-Pokal und seine neue Heimat', p. 283. The anonymous writer of the article is explicit neither about the precise date of Voss's oath, nor indeed about the circumstances which led to it.

191. This is what Wilhelm Frank, local historian and head of the Building and Environment Department of the municipality of nearby Grabowhöfe, told the present writer in a letter. Voss was also remembered by Gideon-Ernst Loudon. Voss was his great-uncle, i.e. the youngest brother of his grandmother on the paternal side, and he met him as a boy at the beginning of the 1930s, much impressed by his tall and upright figure and his old age ('der mit seiner schlanken, aufrechten Figur und seines hohen Alters wegen einen nachhaltigen Eindruck gemacht hat.'). (Quoted from a letter to the present writer.) His family knew that Voss was an enthusiastic tennis player, but was not aware of the fact that he had been Germany's first champion, enjoying an international reputation.

192. A private photograph reproduced in Gruber, 'Graf Voss', p. 528, showed Voss and his wife wearing tennis dress in Alassio as late as 1934.

193. The story of this affair was known to the vicar of Groß-Gievitz whose wife had heard it from her mother who lived in Dahmen-Rothenmoor on the Malchiner See.

194. See *Gothaisches Genealogisches Taschenbuch der Gräflichen Häuser*, p. 606. Clara von der Schulenburg died on 10 February 1951 in Berlin, her address presumably being Berlin-Schlachtensee, Schoenerer Zeile 15, see ibid., loc. cit., and p. 496, s.v. Schulenburg 2. Haus Angern; see also von Huck, *Genealogisches Handbuch der gräflichen Häuser* (Gräfliche Häuser Band VIII) (Genealogisches Handbuch des Adels, vol. 63), p. 444, 2. Clara's lawn tennis expertise is easily explained by the fact that her first husband, Count Hartwig von der Schulenburg-Angern, Councillor at a

Prussian inferior court, had as early as 1891 seen to the laying of the first lawn tennis court in Magdeburg, in the velodrome 'Werder', see von Fichard, lawn tennis annual of 1895, p. 95.

195. He died at Kaiser-Wilhelm-Allee 3 (today G.-Hauptmann-Allee 3), according to a letter the author received from the honorary archivist of the town, Joachim Frank.

196. See Gruber, 'Graf Voss', p. 528.

197. According to Werner Bollmann, the vicar of Gross-Gievitz, Felix sold the manor in 1929 and moved to Ludwigslust. This may have been the reason for his brother's settling down in Waren.

198. See Voigt, 'Das große internationale Turnier', p. 22: 'Herr Walter Howard … hat nun … eine silberne Vase, als Herausforderungs-Preis für Damen-Einzelspiel ohne Vorgabe, open to all comers, gestiftet, was hoffentlich Veranlassung geben wird, künftighin auch englische Damen zum Hamburger Turnier herüberzulocken.'

199. See the report by an anonymous writer 'Das internationale Turnier zu Hamburg-Uhlenhorst', in von Fichard, annual of 1896/1897, p. 86. The trophy, now lost with apparently no clues to its possible whereabouts, presents many mysteries. Only recently, a small silver cup clearly awarded to the first year's winner of the Ladies' Championship has been re-discovered by the present writer (it is now owned by Mrs Monika Melcher, the winner's grand-niece, who lives in Ammersbek near Hamburg). However, although the journal *Pastime*, 24 June 1896, p. 26, mentioned a 'Challenge Cup', Mrs Melcher's cup can hardly have been the championship trophy, but in all likelihood is an additional commemorative piece of silverware. As late as 1902, when after a lapse of four years the Ladies' Championships were again contended in Hamburg, Otto Nirrnheim, an Uhlenhorst insider and a lawn tennis expert of the first order, unmistakably spoke of one competitor as the one with the best prospects of winning the silver dish ('Frl. Friedrichsen, der man die meisten Aussichten für die Silberschale zusprach'), see Internationales Lawn-Tennis-Turnier Hamburg Uhlenhorst [1902], p. 461.

200.See the report in *Pastime*, loc. cit.

201.See 'Hamburg 1894', p. 185. Miss Thomsen was certainly no beginner, having taken part in tournament tennis even before 1892, see 'Hamburg 1892', p. 201: 'Miss Thomsen, though still very young, has played in tournaments before'.

202.See von Fichard, annual of 1896/1897 p. 87.

203.She was born in the month of April, 1879. Personal communication by a relative.

204.See the results in von Fichard, op. cit., p. 91. The score had been 4:6, 6:4, 6:1 in Miss Thomsen's favour.

205.See Steffen, p. 57, and personal communication by a relative. Maren Thomsen died of skin cancer.

206.See Grauhan, 'Zur Geschichte', p. 603:

Dem damaligen Stand des deutschen Damen-Tennissports entsprechend, war es selbstverständlich eine Engländerin, die zum ersten Male die deutsche Damen-Meisterschaft gewann und zwar Miss M. Thomson [*sic*]. Unter den Spielerinnen, die der neuen deutschen Meisterin jedoch besonders erbitterten Widerstand leisteten, war schon im ersten Jahre der Austragung unsere langjährige beste deutsche Spielerin, Gräfin Klara von der Schulenburg, die sich von Miss Thomson erst nach einem Dreisatzkampf mit 4:6, 6:4, 6:1 geschlagen gab.

207.The regulations governing this competition provided that the Voss cup remained the property of the Uhlenhorst club and they left at the discretion of C.A. von der Meden to decide during his lifetime when and where the cup would be contended. The name of the winner would be engraved on it, and there was to be no challenge round. The club entrusted with the organization of the championships of the Germans was obliged to provide a first and a second prize. The matches had to be best of three matches with the exception of the final which was a best of five one. See 'Voss-Pokal', p. 180.

208.According to a note which appeared in the weekly *Sport im Wort* shortly after Krupp's death in December 1902, Krupp was an ardent admirer of lawn tennis and had private courts built in Essen, on the island of Capri and elsewhere. He used to rent a court of the Baden-Baden lawn tennis club whenever he stayed there and attended a match between Mahony and the professional Burke in Homburg in the 1890s which was discontinued after each player had won two sets. To Voigt he is said to have on this occasion remarked that he had had no idea that the game might present itself in such perfection, and that the energy and motion exhibited in it should be so great and manifold.

209.Von Schoeler had obtained a five-year contract from the town authorities (1892–1897), but did not stay in office for the whole period, presumably because of constant quarrels with the mayor, a Dr Tettenborn, see Grosche, p. 242. The Homburg tournament of 1897 was conducted under the auspices of a new *Kurdirector*, Baron Axel von Maltzahn, see Simon, 'Beiträge', p. 167. Von Maltzahn resigned from his office on 1 April 1911, see Grosche, loc. cit. He died in 1912, and was succeeded by Count Eberhard Zeppelin who shortly before the First World War was in charge of the organization of the Bad Homburg officers' tournament, an invention of von Schoeler for which the Kaiser had annually donated a prize called 'Kaiserpokal', which had been held there since 1895. By that time, a new groundsman, Burghardt, had also been appointed. He was the successor of Friedrich Becker, the inventor of the red clay court who had obtained the post in 1898 after 'Professor' Noss, his predecessor, had passed away. On von Zeppelin and Burghardt see a note in *Lawn-Tennis und Golf* 11 (1914), no. 18, 28 July 1914, p. 484f.

210.In 1902, the general secretary of the Bad Homburg tournament, Charles Adolph Voigt, could claim of the tournament of the previous year that 70 per cent of those present were Englishmen or Americans, and 98 per cent capable of understanding the English language, see Voigt, 'Etwas über die Turniersprache', p. 227.

211.See Baer, p. 248.

212.See the report in the English journal *Pastime* in its issue of 17 August 1892, p. 112.

213.It is not quite clear whether the initiative was taken by von Schoeler or by von der Meden. In August 1893, von der Meden wrote a letter to the editor of the Berlin-based sporting journal *Spiel und Sport*, John Bloch. It read thus:

Whilst our friends of the pen are fighting out whether the thing should be called a racket or a Schläger, ... I have been arranging with Mr. Julian Robinson of London to hold an annual international tournament at Homburg. The Homburg authorities look kindly on the scheme, and the Cur-Director, Baron von Schoeler, is doing his best to bring the thing about. Baron von Fichard (Baden-Baden), Mr. J. Robinson (London), Baron von Schoeler (Homburg), Herr R. Runge and myself (Hamburg) together with some American gentlemen, and some of the best English players, will be asked to join the committee. We cannot have tournaments enough to raise the standard of our play, and we want to be thoroughly beaten by our cousins year after year before we can aspire to be decent players. We think Homburg the most convenient place, where north, south, east and west can meet. Of course this is only to take place for the first time in 1894.

Von der Meden's letter was reprinted by von Fichard, *Erstes deutsches Lawn-Tennis-Jahrbuch*, p. 147.

214. See von Fichard in his lawn tennis yearbook of 1895, p. 46f. This is confirmed by the treasurer of the Uhlenhorst Club, Gabe, in his 1894 cash report quoted by Mendel, 'Aus der Chronik', p. 6.

Ich darf erwähnen, daß alle Fremden voll des Lobes über die vorzüglichen und practischen Einrichtungen auf unserer Bahn waren, und daß unsere Lawn-Tennis-Plätze, nach dem übereinstimmenden Ausspruch von Sachverständigen, für die besten in ganz Deutschland erklärt werden. So hat sich die Kurdirection in Homburg v/d Höhe s. Zt. veranlaßt gesehen, ihren Inspector nach Hamburg zu senden, um sich unsere Einrichtungen anzusehen, wodurch die neuen Grandplätze in Homburg v/d Höhe, auf denen das große Internationale Lawn-Tennis-Turnier im August a.c. [= anni currentis] abgehalten wurde, genau nach dem Vorbild unserer Plätze angelegt worden sind.

The 'inspector' may well have been Wilhelm Noss, the Bad Homburg groundsman, nicknamed the 'Professor' (i.e. the schoolmaster) and the dread of the local ball-boys. Noss has left an authentic description in his own hand of how to construct a gravel court. It is preserved, under the file number FAH 21/417m-s, pp. 1–9 and 17–20, in the historical archive of the Friedrich Krupp GmbH in Essen, Germany. The court

surface consisted of the black dust abraded from cobble stone (basalt) roads, slaked lime, cinders, salt, iron cuttings which, turned into a kind of mortar, were put in a thin layer (1.5 centimetres) onto 12–15 centimetres of gravel and decayed brick. The surface had to undergo frequent watering and rolling with a heavy roller. The lines were made of fir planks the upper edges of which (breadth 5 centimetres) were painted white, first, with a mixture of chalk and milk, finally, with a mixture of white lead, distemper and turpentine oil. The lines were a Bad Homburg speciality criticized by Dr Flavelle, an Englishman from Hamburg, as late as 1903, see Myers, *Lawn Tennis,* p. 238.

215. See von Fichard, *Deutsches Lawn-Tennis-Jahrbuch 1895*, p. 46.

216. In 1906, both also attended the All England Championships in Wimbledon, see Little, *The Changing Face of Wimbledon*, p. 8.

217. He had married, in San Remo in 1891, a well-known contemporary beauty, Countess Sophie von Merenburg, who in society circles was referred to as 'le rhume de Wiesbaden' to which the male members of the European aristocracy succumbed in great numbers. The Countess was a daughter of Prince Nicolas of Nassau and a bourgeois, a daughter of the Russian poet Pushkin.

218. This epithet was passed on to posterity by von Reibnitz-Maltzan, p. 19.

219. The 'W.' was an abbreviation of one of her hereditary titles, that of 'Countess Wenden'.

220. See the graphic account by von Reibnitz-Maltzan, pp. 59–62, of a visit of the Empress, who had stayed in one of her residences near Bad Homburg, to Anastasia's headquarters in Bad Homburg, the Parkhotel Ritter, at a time when the Grand Duchess was engaged in a tournament match and absent from home.

221. See von Fichard, *Deutsches Lawn-Tennis-Jahrbuch 1895*, p. 92, and also, in a similar vein, the anonymous account 'Das internationale Lawn-Tennis-Turnier zu Homburg', p. 548: 'Nicht minderen [*sic*] Dank gebührt Ihrer Königlichen Hoheit, der Frau Grossherzogin von Mecklenburg-Schwerin, welche –

bekanntlich selbst eine vorzügliche Spielerin – für die Entwickelung des Tennissports in Deutschland unendlich viel gethan hat und überall als gütige Protektorin des Tennissports verehrt wird.'

222. Hughes, an M.D., shortly afterwards returned to Australia, see von Fichard, *Deutsches Lawn-Tennis-Jahrbuch 1895*, p. 49, and nothing was heard of him any more. At the All England Club he is, according to Alan Little, completely unknown.

223. See Grauhan, 'Geschichte des Homburger Pokals', p. 93: 'Wenn damals in führenden deutschen Tageszeitungen bereits regelmäßig über das Homburger Turnier berichtet wurde, so war der Grund hierzu wohl kaum das sportliche Interesse des Verlages oder der Leser am Tennissport, sondern die einzigartige Ansammlung von Fürstlichkeiten in Homburg.' A complete list of society people attending the 1894 tournament is given by the prestigious society journal *Vom Fels zum Meer*, vol. 14,1 (1894–1895), p. 20f., one containing the names of those attending the 1896 event, which included the Prince of Wales, can be found in von Fichard, *Deutsches Lawn-Tennis-Jahrbuch 1896/1897*, p. 235.

224. See von Fichard, *Deutsches Lawn-Tennis Jahrbuch 1896/1897*, p. 127 (report on the 1896 event).

225. See von Fichard, loc. cit.

226. Understandably, an expert such as Dr J.M. Flavelle (in Myers, *Lawn Tennis at Home*, p. 237f.) was not over-enthusiastic in his assessment of Bad Homburg society tennis:

The courts are ideally situated from the spectator's point of view, but leave much to be desired from the player's. The tournament is usually played on six courts. ... Very fine trees are very close to the base lines ..., giving delightful shade to the spectators who lounge in basket chairs and watch the play. ... At the other base-line amongst the trees is a tea house, and quite a feature here are the groups at little tables taking tea and chattering. From the player's point of view the courts might be much better. The great mistake is the wood lines, they should be tape. In the composition of the courts there is probably not enough clay, as there is too much loose material on the surface. The trees are too close, casting both in the

morning and late afternoon most perplexing shadows.

227. Collins credited himself with persuading him to undertake the trip to the continent, see von Reznicek, p. 41.

228. See von Fichard, lawn tennis annual of 1896/1897, p. 128.

229. See *Volley*, 'Vom Hamburger Turnier', p. 602: 'Zum ersten Mal fand das Turnier im Herbst statt. Dadurch ist es gelungen, eine Menge guter englischer Spieler und Spielerinnen, die in Homburg und Baden spielen wollten, vorher nach Hamburg zu ziehen.'

230. See *Sport im Bild* 3 (1897), no. 32, p. 534.

231. See Hessen, *Technik and Taktik*, p. 17.

232. See Volley, 'Vom Hamburger Turnier'.

233. See 'Hamburg' [1897], p. 299f.

234. See the article 'Hamburg', p. 300.

235. See von Fichard, *Deutsches Lawn-Tennis-Jahrbuch 1902*, p. 62.

236. See *Eisbahn-Verein auf der Uhlenhorst. Bericht über die Saison 1901/1902*, p. [1]: 'Es wurden zum ersten Male wieder nach manchen Jahren die Meisterschaften von Deutschland ... in Hamburg gespielt, welche s.Z. für die Uhlenhorst gestiftet waren, wegen Mangel an Fonds aber zeitweilig von hier nach Homburg v.d. Höhe verlegt werden mußten.' (The report is contained in the papers of Alexander Kähler in the Hamburg State Archives; Kähler, a senator of the city, was a member of the Hamburg Lawn Tennis Guild under the auspices of which the championships were again held in Hamburg from 1902 onwards.)

237. Nevertheless von der Meden is said to have, according to von Fichard, *Erstes deutsches Lawn-Tennis-Jahrbuch*, p. 146, in a conversation in Baden-Baden as early as 1893, been toying with the idea of transferring the Championships to Bad Homburg.

238. See Grauhan, 'Die Geschichte der deutschen Meisterschaften im Herreneinzelspiel', p. 75, who is silent about who these 'personalities' were.

239. See *Volley*, 'Vom Hamburger Turnier', loc. cit.

240. In October 1898, the new *Kurdirector* von Maltzahn wrote a letter to the Bad Homburg magistrate in which he emphasized the importance of the annual lawn tennis tournament for the town's economy and expressed his satisfaction

that, owing to a grant by local hotel owners, the administration of the *Kurbad* and sponsors, he was in a position to cover the costs for the 1899 event. He nevertheless requested the sum of 1,500 marks for a new, attractive Bad Homburg cup, because Reggie Doherty had bagged for good its predecessor after three consecutive wins, pointing out that the 1898 tournament had produced a deficit. (Bad Homburg, municipal archives, inventory no. 1965; date of letter 20 October 1898; the stamp of local authorities acknowledging receipt also bears the date 20 October 1898, and has the inventory no. 2896 I.)

241. See the note in the column 'Ins and Outs' of the journal *Pastime*, 7 September 1898, p. 306.

242. See 'Das Internationale Lawn-Tennis-Turnier zu Homburg', p. 564: 'Um nicht die beiden offenen Konkurrenzen davonzutragen, gaben die Brüder Doherty ihren Gegnern Mahony und "Wilson" Walkover.'

243. See the article 'Homburg v.d. Höhe', p. 308: 'The semi-final round ... resulted in two walk overs, the players being also engaged in the Homburg Cup Singles, and Mahony consequently had to meet "Wilson" in the finals, which proved to be the cup-round, as G.W. Hillyard did not defend.'

244. See Guiney, p. 13, who quotes a certain Tony Buckley of Carrigtwohill, a resident of the County of Cork where Mahony lived most of his short life: 'Harold S. Mahony was a lively Irishman with reputedly the worst forehand in the game. With a tremendous reach he volleyed his way to victory in most of his games.'

245. See 'Homburg v.d. Höhe', loc. cit.

246. See the obituary article H.S. Mahony on the title page of the journal *Der Lawn-Tennis-Sport* in its issue no. 15 of 6 July 1905, p. 217, and Guiney, p. 12. From Guiney, who has a short biography of the man about whom, he admits, 'very little is now known', it appears that Mahony was born at Dromore Castle, Co. Kerry, at the time the ancestral home of the Mahony family, on 13 February 1867.

247. See Pilot, 'Homburger Skizzen', p. 390 (translated from the German original).

248. Her backhand was frequently commented upon in Germany. In 1901, when Elsie won the Championships of Bohemia and Vienna, and in 1902, when she won the Championships of Berlin – at the Pentecost tournament at which, incidentally, the German Lawn Tennis Federation was founded – and Austria and Bohemia in Prague, the correspondents of the journal *Sport im Wort* wrote:

Von den Damen sind Miss Lane und Miss Attfield den Wienerinnen bedeutend überlegen. In der Endrunde siegte die erstere sicher. Sie hat einen schönen glatten Forehandschlag und gute Länge, wodurch sie langsam aber sicher ans Netz kommt. Auch plaziert sie besser als Miss Attfield, die einen ausgezeichneten Drive spielt. Die Backhandstellung von Miss Lane (ein Überdrehen des Unterarmes ohne Griffwechsel) widerspricht allen Begriffen eines eleganten Stils. (The backhand position of Miss Lane (a contortion of the underarm without change of grip) contradicts all concepts of an elegant style.)

And 'Miss Lane spielt sicher, ohne jedoch graziös zu sein; ihr Backhand-Schlag ist aber unschön und durch eine sonderbare Haltung des Armes hervorgebracht.' See 'V. Internationales Lawn-Tennis-Turnier in Wien', p. 307, and 'VIII. Internationales Lawn-Tennis-Turnier zu Berlin', p. 287. As late as 1906, when she competed successfully in the Marienbad tournament in which she was partnered by Anthony Wilding, the following 'epilogue' was written on her continental career: 'Von den Damen gilt als die stärkste die altberühmte Miss Lane. Ihr Spiel ist gleich unscheinbar und totsicher geblieben, auch ihr hässlicher Rückhandschlag. Bewundernswert ist ihre Zähigkeit.' (Among the ladies, Miss Lane, famous of old, is considered the strongest. Her game is as plain as it is deadly safe, and so is her ugly backhand stroke. Her staying power is admirable.) See Kauder, p. 264. A photograph showing the players Oskar Kreuzer, Anthony Wilding, Elsie Lane and Miss Salusbury appeared in the journal *Der Lawn-Tennis-Sport* one year later, in 1907 (ibid., p. 425), where it was wrongly attributed to the Karlsbad tournament of the same year.

249. See 'Homburg v.d. Höhe', p. 309. This result was less unexpected than it appeared at the time. Elsie Lane had literally trounced the very same Toupée

Lowther the year previously, the scores in the ladies singles and in the ladies singles handicap where both players owed 30 were 6:0, 6:2, and 7:5, 6:1 respectively in Elsie Lane's favour, see Voigt, 'Lawn-Tennis. Das grosse Turnier zu Homburg', p. 585. In the Fatherland, Miss Lowther had a reputation not only as a tennis player, but also as an outstanding fencer and, rather shockingly, boxer as well as a pianist who had been awarded prizes at the conservatories of London, Paris and Berlin, see 'Lawntennis-Turnier in Homburg', Nos 196 and 197, pp. 3 and 2 respectively, and Myers, *Lawn Tennis at Home*, p. 180f. A title page in *Sport im Bild* showed her performing a 'grand salut' with an excellent gentleman fencer of the day, and one of Britain's best, Mr Egerton Castle, and in an explanatory note it was said that the skill and grace with which she handled the foil at a fencing academy in Oxford had met with undivided applause. Her father, it was said, had on her behalf sent a challenge to all (male) amateur fencers of England. See *Sport im Bild* 5 (1899), no. 3, 20 January 1899, title page and p. 40f.

250. See a note which appeared in *Der Lawn-Tennis-Sport* 3 (1906), no. 19, 2 August 1906, p. 267f. This is confirmed by a programme in the English language of the Hamburg tournament of 1906, preserved in the Wimbledon Lawn Tennis Museum which states that the 'silver bowl' had been 'won outright by Miss E. Lane in 1905', ibid. p. [2].

251. Ibid. This is again confirmed by yet another programme, an original copy of which is to be found in the papers of Senator Dr Fr. Sthamer in the State Archives, Hamburg. It is interesting that in the same year the name of the donator of the original trophy, Walter Howard, should have appeared on the front page among the names of the honorary committee.

252. See Robert Hessen, who in an article titled 'Deutsche Nationalmeisterschaften' contributed to *Der Lawn-Tennis-Sport*, assessed the quality of German players in comparison with leading English players (p. 25):

Vielleicht sind auch wirklich die deutschen Handgelenke nicht so begabt für Tennis. ... Und wie steht es mit der Meisterin? Gesetzt, sie würde in Abwesenheit der Gräfin Schulenburg erkoren, der Lokalpatriotismus schwelgte sich satt in Beschreibung ihrer Vorderhand- und Rückhandschläge, fände nicht Worte genug, um zu schildern, was alles sie dazugelernt habe, und bei der nächsten Gelegenheit käme der melancholische Nachsatz: Miss Lane 6–0, 6–0?

Even the knowledgeable Doctor apparently was not aware of the fact that in 1897, her first appearance at the Hamburg championships, Elsie had defeated the very same Countess Schulenburg 6:1, 6:1.

253. For a short note on Hilda and a photograph see Myers, *Lawn Tennis at Home*, p. 182f. There was a brother, Ernest Wilmot Lane, with whom Elsie competed successfully in the mixed doubles event of Hamburg as late as 1906. Elsie's as well as her brother's address was, according to the Brighton directory of the same year, 3 Eaton Gardens, Hove. A picture of Elsie's brother (showing him during the Hamburg championships of 1907) appeared in von Fichard's annual of 1908, p. 28.

254. See here and in what follows Nirrnheim, 'Hamburg 1905', p. 376.

255. For an analysis of their game, and indeed a graphic account of Wimbledon and all its players at the turn of the century from the continental sports journalist's point of view see Rosenbaum-Jenkins, 'Beobachtungen bei den englischen Lawn-Tennis-Meisterschaften in Wimbledon 1903', p. 477, and *passim*.

256. Lane, a barrister-at-law, had, after attending Haileybury College, started his career in India in 1855, see *The India Office List for 1923*, p. 558, the *History of Services of Gazetted Officers*, p. 3, and The British Library, Oriental and India Office Collections, Ref L/AG/23/5/2. For these pieces of information, the present writer owes a debt of gratitude to H. Aumeerally, Reader Services, Oriental and India Office Collections.

257. Wilmot Lane was born on 19 September 1833, see The British Library, Oriental and India Office Collections, Ref. L/AG/23/5/2.

258. When in 1903 he competed in the Ostend tournament, a photograph showing him together with his daughter Elsie and Clarence Hobart and his wife was published in *Sport im Bild*. It had been

taken by the journal's former proprietor, Andrew Pitcairn-Knowles, and the caption underneath it revealed the fact of Lane's one-armedness and of his having won, in the previous year, a handicap event at Spa. See 'Interessantes aus dem Lawn-Tennis-Sport', p. 566.

259. See von Fichard's lawn tennis annual 1896/7, pp. 134 and 140. In Homburg, where he engaged in the singles handicap B., Lane took the promising young Hamburg player André to three sets ('André ... musste ... 3 Sätze fechten ... gegen den Veteranen Lane'), and in Baden-Baden he lost 6:2, 6:2 against the oldest of the Doherty brothers, W.V. Doherty, in the first round of the handicap event, see von Fichard, op. cit., pp. 131 and 140.

260. See 'Interessantes aus dem Lawn-Tennis Sport', p. 566, caption to a photograph taken by Andrew Pitcairn-Knowles and showing him and Elsie at Ostend. In his will, a 'silver goblet' is mentioned which he 'won at Scarborough'; this, together with 'one of my best tiger skins' was bequeathed to one of the executors of his will, Sir Aleyne Alfred Boxall, the second executor being his son Ernest Wilmot.

261. See Voigt, 'Lawn-Tennis. Das grosse Turnier zu Homburg', p. 584.

262. See Voigt, 'Das grosse internationale Turnier zu Homburg', p. 569: 'Seine Königliche Hoheit, der den ersten Preis für die offene Damen-Einzelspiel-Konkurrenz gestiftet hatte und besonders das Spiel der Damen Lowther und Lane mit grossem Interesse verfolgte.' A photograph by a certain Ehrhardt, Homburg, apparently taken shortly after the victory ceremony shows Elsie Lane sitting next to Count Voss with the prize, a cup, at her feet, see *Sport im Bild* 2 (1896), no. 38, p. 598.

263. See 'Lawn-Tennis. Das internationale Lawn-Tennis-Turnier in Baden-Baden', in *Sport im Bild* 2 (1896), no. 39, p. 618.

264. The organizers had on the occasion raised him, albeit wrongly, to the rank of Colonel. This mistake was repeated by Charles Adolph Voigt in an article on the subsequent Homburg event when he wrote: 'Oberst Lane, Mr. Lloyd und Dr Pollen waren die Veteranen und obwohl alle weit über das fünfzigste Jahr hinaus sind [Lane was, in fact, well over 60],

spielten sie ebenso eifrig wie die Jüngsten.' (Colonel Lane, Mr Lloyd and Dr Pollen were the veterans and although they were all well past their fifties they played as enthusiastically as the youngest.) See Voigt, 'Das grosse Turnier', p. 584.

265. Elsie was born on 22 June 1864, presumably at Lucknow in India where her father served at the time. See The British Library, Oriental and India Office Collections, Ref L/AG/23/5/2.

266. Ernest Wilmot Lane was a capable player himself who in 1904, partnered by M.J.G. Ritchie, even became doubles champion of Germany.

267. See 'St. Moritz', p. 541, and p. 557f. Apparently on the same tour, she won the singles and mixed doubles (with E.M. Hall) championship of Ragaz, see 'Das Ragazer Turnier', p. 558f. The tournament report of St Moritz pointed out the superiority of Elsie Lane, significantly despite a non-existent backhand stroke ('trotz nicht vorhandenen Rückhandschlags'), ibid., p. 541.

268. 'Es sei zum Schluss noch erwähnt', wrote Andrew Pitcairn-Knowles, the correspondent of the German sporting journal *Sport im Bild*, 'dass Miss Lane mit ihrer wenig graziösen, jedoch äusserst geschickten Spielweise ihre sämtlichen Gegnerinnen im 'Coupe d'Ostende' glänzend bezwang.' See 'Interessantes aus dem Lawn-Tennis-Sport', p. 567.

269. I am quoting from his will, proved and registered in the Principal Probate Registry of Her Majesty's High Court of Justice on 8 May 1924. A copy of it was placed at my disposal by Judith Joseph, Edgbaston. According to Wilmot Lane's certificate of death, Elsie was indeed present at his death.

270. Wilmot Lane died at his home in Hove on 24 February 1924.

271. On 14 November 1916, see again Ref L/AG/23/5/2 of the Oriental and India Office of the British Library.

272. See the Certified Copy of an Entry of Death Given at the General Register Office on 4 March 1996 DXZ 328136. Elsie died at 19 Lansdowne Place, Hove, apparently the home of her sister Mabel, her own residence being 6 Lansdowne Place.

273. See His Majesty's High Court of Justice, The Principal Probate Registry, dated 23

September 1948 (office copy). The will, drawn up on 24 December 1947, was signed by Elsie and two witnesses, Estelle and Lilian Hersee who, like Elsie, lived at 6 Lansdowne Place, Hove. In it, the address of Florence Emily Lane is given as 14, Grosvenor Court, Wimbledon, London, SW19. Ernest Wilmot, it seems, was no longer alive.

274. See 'Homburg v.d. Höhe', loc. cit., and 'Das Internationale Lawn-Tennis-Turnier zu Homburg', p. 564, where the writer is guilty of a glaring anglicism: 'Der Sieg des Grafen Voss war eine tote Gewissheit [dead certainty]'. The result of the final was 6:0, 6:2, 6:4.

275. See Voigt, 'Homburg v.d. Höhe [1899]', p. 289.

276. See 'Clarence Hobart: a Great Figure', p. 584, and Voigt, 'Homburg v.d. Höhe', p. 313.

277. See Voigt, 'Homburg v.d. Höhe', p. 289.

278. See the testimony of Henry W. Slocum in 'Clarence Hobart', p. 584.

279. See Voigt, 'Homburg', p. 313.

280. Ibid.

281. The E.G.M. racket was so called after its inventor E.G. Meers, and later manufactured and marketed by Slazengers and Sons, see this manufacturer's advertisement in von Fichard, *Illustriertes Lawn-Tennis-Jahrbuch ... 1903*, p. II: 'Der E.G.M.-Schläger ... nach den Angaben des wohlbekannten Sachverständigen Herrn E.G. Meers'; and Kuebler in his pioneering work on tennis rackets, p. 239. From 1893 to 1898 (with the exception of 1895) all Wimbledon championships had been won with it, see Heineken, *Lawn-Tennis. Seine Geschichte und Taktik*, p. [229], another advertisement of Slazengers & Sons, and in 1896 Baron von Fichard revealed, in an article on the Bad Homburg tournament published in *Sport im Bild* 2 (1896), no. 37, p. 584f., that Mahony, the Dohertys and Count Voss all played with this 'Wunderwaffe'. The E.G.M. at the time was at 21 marks (25 shillings) and the most expensive of all, the cheapest being Slazengers' 'Renshaw' at 8.75 marks, see von Fichard, *Deutsches Lawn-Tennis-Jahrbuch ... 1896*, p. I (advert by wholesale dealers Benetfink & Co., Cheapside, London, who offered five different Slazengers rackets); prices in shillings are contained in von Fichard, *Illustriertes Lawn-Tennis Jahrbuch ... 1903*, p. I. The E.G.M., in addition, was a highly valued tournament prize for umpires. From a notebook of Otto Nirrnheim in the Hamburg State Archives it appears that he was awarded one in 1899 for his umpire's services at Bad Homburg, and another for his services as a handicapper in 1900.

282. See 'Clarence Hobart: a Great Figure', p. 584, where statements to this effect are made by Oliver S. Campbell and Hobart's doubles partner Fred S. Hovey: 'his physique and nervous temperament counted very much against him and prevented his winning our National Championship' (Campbell); 'Of a naturally nervous temperament, he pulled out many a match on sheer nerve. Possibly his lack of endurance may have cost him the singles championship, as I have seen him play many wonderful "two sets out of three" matches' (Hovey). Both players, however, praised Hobart's powerful forehand drive: 'His forehand stroke I do not think has been equalled by any player since his day – especially in severity and accuracy' (Campbell); 'His [forehand] stroke, while not so ferocious as McLoughlin's, had a world of top and plenty of speed' (Hovey). In the same article, loc. cit., O.M. Bostwick stated: 'I thought at the time [1893, when Hobart beat Larned in a five-set match] that Hobart's forearm drive was the best that I had ever seen ... the most effective in America.'

283. See the flowery account by Voigt, 'Homburg', p. 313.

284. See Pilot, [Part] II, p. 165.

285. See 'When Hobart Refused'; Longwood at the time was the most important US tournament next to the US championships at Newport. On Longwood in general, see Chapter 7, 'Lawn Tennis in America', note 3.

286. In the United States the challenge round was abolished in 1912, the first playthrough winner of the US championship being the Californian Maurice McLoughlin, but in Wimbledon it was adhered to until 1922 when the first championship was held at the new Wimbledon on Church Road. For an account of the whole issue see now

Baltzell, p. 105f., who does not mention Hobart's role in the process, though.

287. See 'Clarence Hobart: a Great Figure', p. 584. Hobart was born at Waltham, Mass., on 27 June 1870, and died on 2 August 1930.

288. See a note which appeared in the German sporting journal *Spiel und Sport* 10 (1900), no. 19, 12 May 1900, p. 365: 'Clarence Hobart, der amerikanische Spieler, ist nach den Vereinigten Staaten zurückgekehrt, nachdem er fast alle europäischen Tennis-Centren aufgesucht hat.'

289. See Hobart, 'Lawn-Tennis in Continental Europe', p. 687.

290. See 'Homburg v.d. Höhe', p. 289.

291. She had never done so since her participation in the first Championship in 1896, nor did she adopt a pseudonym afterwards.

292. See Pilot, 'Homburger Skizzen', p. 391, and Rosenbaum-Jenkins, p. 476, commenting on the non-appearance of Mrs Hillyard and Mrs Sterry at the 1903 All England Championships owing to their having each given birth to future lawn tennis champions, of whom little Rex (Sterry) had a very distinguished godfather, Prince Batthany-Strattmann. In 1903, the young mother, Mrs Sterry, was characterized as 'as blonde, rosy and amiable as ever' by Dr Rosenbaum-Jenkins.

293. See 'Heiligendamm', p. 295.

294. See the tournament regulations for the Championship of the Germans printed in an advertising note of the 1900 tournament in *Sport im Wort*, no. 35, Thursday, 30 August 1900, p. 361: '2) der Pokal bleibt Eigentum des Hamburg-Uhlenhorster Lawn-Tennis-Turnier-Ausschusses. Eine Herausforderung bezw. eine Verteidigung findet deshalb nicht statt, und hat der jedesmalige Sieger – dessen Name auf dem Pokal eingraviert wird – durchzuspielen.' (The Cup remains the property of the Hamburg Uhlenhorst Lawn Tennis Tournament Committee. There will therefore be no challenge or defence respectively, and the winner, whose name will be engraved on the Cup, has to play through.)

295. According to a note in *Lawn Tennis*, issue of 23 August 1899, p. 288, under 'Ins and Outs'.

296. See 'Heiligen Damm', p. 296.

297. Incidentally, Heini Schomburgk was the first German to compete in Wimbledon in 1906. His brother Wilhelm, who after the First World War was to become Secretary (Bundesleiter) of the German Lawn Tennis Federation (1920–1937) until the Nazis ousted him from his position, wrote in the same year an interesting account of his and his brother's visit to England in which he with a lot of perspicacity analysed the state of the art in England and Germany, see W. Schomburgk, 'Englisches und deutsches Tennis', *passim*.

298. See 'Homburg. Some Notes', p. 348.

299. See 'Homburg International Tournament', p. 362.

300. See 'Das Homburger Turnier', p. 370. In Newcastle, Hillyard after the championship of Germany also reaped that of Northumberland, see *Sport im Wort*, no. 38 (1900), Thursday, 20 September 1900, p. 396.

301. See 'Homburg International Tournament', p. 362: 'In the final Mr Hillyard was given a bye by Mr Doherty who had already beaten him in a five-set match for the Homburg Cup, and as Mr Hobart was not present, Mr Hillyard becomes his successor as the holder of the championship of Germany.'

302. Laurie reciprocated by giving R.F. a walk-over in the final of the handicap event: 'This actually brought the brothers into the final of the handicap, a unique occurrence. R.F. Doherty received a "walk-over" from his brother, and consequently had the satisfaction of winning H.I.H. the Grand Duchess of Mecklenburg-Schwerin's lovely first prize – a large silver cup.' See 'Homburg', p. 351. The correspondent of *Lawn Tennis* apparently did not see through these machinations when he wrote (Homburg, p. 350):

This last occurrence [i.e. R.F.'s retirement in favour of Hillyard for the Homburg Cup] was very regrettable, as R.F. Doherty has held the Homburg Cup (winning the last cup outright in 1898). If he had won it this year, it would have required but one more victory next year for the handsome new 1,500–mark cup to become his property.

In retrospect, it is significant that in 1898, when H.L. was left 'to challenge R.F. Doherty for the [Homburg] cup', 'the former was not feeling well' and 'scratched, so that the champion [R.F.]' won 'the cup outright after victories in three successive years.' See Homburg v.d. Höhe, p. 309. The Dohertys not playing against each other also was a feature of the Olympic tennis event in Paris in 1900. Nothing is known about what became of the trophies won by the Dohertys in Bad Homburg.

303. See Homburg, p. 349.

304. Ibid., p. 350. Hillyard's hat can be seen on a photograph included in the account of *Sport im Bild*, Das Homburger Lawn-Tennis-Turnier, p. 481.

305. See 'Das Homburger Turnier', p. 370, and 'Homburg', p. 349. That Voss had not given up wearing a towel appears from a picture in 'Das Homburger Turnier', loc. cit. It showed him engaged in a doubles match and partnered by R.F. Doherty.

306. See 'Homburg v.d. Höhe [1899]', p. 314, and 'Homburg', p. 348.

307. The picture in J.M. Flavelle's account of 'The Game in Northern Europe', in Myers, *Lawn Tennis at Home and Abroad*, p. 227, was available as a postcard and a specimen of it is part of the collection of Robert Lebeck (Hamburg). The postcard is reproduced in Lebeck's *Auf- und Rückschläge*, p. 100. For a biographical account of Gladys Duddell see the present writer's article 'Das Geheimnis der Miss Duddell', *passim*.

308. See Pilot, 'Homburger Skizzen', p. 391.

309. See 'Homburg', p. 351. The correspondent of *The Field* predicted the same: 'one might do worse than hazard the prophecy that in her we have the lady champion of the future'. 'Homburg International', p. 362.

310. See Myers, *Lawn Tennis at Home*, p. 172.

311. See 'Homburg', p. 348.

312. Ibid., p. 349, and 'Homburg International', p. 362. There is a most interesting account of this match by Toupée Lowther in an article she had published in *The Badminton Magazine of Sports and Games*, see Lowther, 'Lawn Tennis', p. 356f. In this article, she emphasized the importance of staying power (a quality which women posessed more than men, a fact illustrated by the 'plucky' Jones vs. Robb match) and that

of having nerve (a quality she apparently never possessed herself).

313. See 'Homburg International', loc. cit.

314. The inglorious history of the cancellation of the tournament is dealt with at some length in various contributions to the Berlin sporting weekly *Sport im Wort*, e.g. Voigt, 'Das Heiligendammer Turnier'; and 'Eingesandt' (reprint of a letter by the 'Kurverwaltung'), ibid., p. 347f.; and no. 36 (1900), Thursday, 6 September 1900, p. 372, an extract reprinted from the daily newspaper *Rostocker Anzeiger*. Voigt, who had in vain tried to steer the course of events from faraway Paris, eventually decided not to have anything to do with Heiligendamm tournament organization either in word or writing ever again. The turmoil had involved the Counts Voss and Grote, an ailing 'Syndikus' (syndic) Dahlmann from Rostock, in charge of the organization in 1899, and an ailing leaseholder of the resort, Otto von Kahlden, a retired Captain of the Horse (Rittmeister a.D.), who died in the process aged 72.

315. The Berlin club had been asked by the committee of Hamburg Uhlenhorst whether they would be willing to do the job, and the Berliner Spielplatz-Gesellschaft had placed their courts at the disposal of the club, see 'Lawn-Tennis-Turnier-Club, Berlin', p. 250f.

316. This annual tournament in which the championships of Berlin and Prussia were contended was held at Pentecost. It was inaugurated in 1896 and in the year following appropriated by the newly founded Berlin Lawn-Tennis-Turnier-Club. In addition, this club organized a club tournament every fall. It was into the latter that the Championships of the Germans were sandwiched in. The Whitsun tournament was to form the background of the founding of the German Lawn Tennis Federation in 1902. On the beginnings of the Lawn-Tennis-Turnier-Club see above, p. 244, and von Reznicek, '40 Jahre Rot-Weiss', *passim*; on the tournament of 1896 see the account in von Fichard's lawn tennis annual of 1896/97, pp. 105–13.

317. See von Fichard, *Deutsches Lawn-Tennis-Jahrbuch 1901*, p. 54f.

318. See the article from the *Rostocker Anzeiger* quoted in note 314, above: 'Graf

Voss ist, … zur Zeit indisponiert, seine bisher ruhmvoll bestandene deutsche Meisterschaft zur abermaligen Entscheidung zu bringen.'

319. See the article 'Das Berliner Herbst-Turnier', to which I am indebted for the remainder of this paragraph, p. 417.

320. The cup was presented by the English journal *Lawn Tennis*, and in its first year captured by Mahony. It was contended in Ostend (winner M.J.G. Ritchie), Paris (Max Decugis) and on the covered courts of Queens (H.L. Doherty) in the years following.

321. See 'Homburg v.d. Höhe', p. 350: 'In the Championship of Germany event, H.L. Doherty retired in favour of Hillyard, who was not challenged in the championship round by last year's winner, Mr. Clarence Hobart, of New York, absent. Another good final match not played, but this is unavoidable with two open Singles at one tournament!'

322. See Hessen *Technik and Taktik*, p. 90, expressing his misgivings in 1904: '1900 waren sie zum letztenmal dort'. (In 1900, they – the Dohertys – were there for the last time.)

323. See 'Homburg [1901]', p. 397.

324. R.F. Doherty's poor health, which caused his loss of the All England Championship to Gore in that year, is given as a reason for their not playing.

325. See 'Das internationale Turnier zu Homburg v.d. Höhe', p. 453.

326. This was the opinion of Wallis Myers in his *Lawn Tennis at Home*, p. 161f.

327. See 'Zum Internationalen Lawn-Tennis-Turnier', where both Payn and Decugis were declared favourites, ibid., p. 427. The correspondent of *Lawn Tennis* wrote: 'it was thought highly probable that one of the Frenchmen [in addition to Decugis, his countryman Jacques Worth competed] would carry off at least one of the cups for the two Open Singles', ibid., p. 397 (in fact, Decugis carried off both). The correspondent of *The Field* wrote about Payn: 'It was generally expected that Mr Payn would win both cups …' (i.e. that of the Championship of Germany and the Homburg Cup), see 'Homburg International', p. 368.

328. See Voigt, 'Etwas über die Turniersprache', p. 227.

329. See 'Homburg International Tournament [1901]', p. 368.

330. See 'Homburg [1901]', p. 397.

331. See 'Homburg International [1901]', p. 368.

332. Ibid. The title of a ladies' Champion of Germany was won by a most versatile sportswoman who was not only an excellent lawn tennis player, but had a reputation as a fencer and a boxer. She also was said to be a musical artist. See above, note 249.

333. See 'Homburg International [1901]', p. 368, and 'Homburg [1901]', p. 397: 'The committee made an innovation which might perhaps be followed with advantage in England and elsewhere; they invited a lady to join their number with the special mission of looking after the ladies' matches. The lady member of the committee was Miss Duddell, who is highly popular in Germany.'

334. See 'Homburg [1901]', p. 397.

335. Ibid.

336. See 'Homburg International', p. 368.

337. Ibid., p. 368.

338. See 'Internationales Lawn-Tennis-Turnier zu Heiligendamm', p. 427.

339. Ibid., p. 428.

340. The Homburg 'kaiserpokal' was won by a certain Lieutenant E. Kraeusel of the Infantry Regiment 51. As for the championship cup of Prussia, German newspapers said that this cup had never been contended on account of the outbreak of the First World War. This, however, is blatantly untrue. The Grunewald tournament did take place, and the cup was won by Otto Froitzheim. A very different question is how it found its way into the collections of Sotheby's. The firm, at any rate, has been unable to shed any light on this question. The cup has now been acquired by one of the prestigious Berlin lawn tennis clubs, Blau Weiss.

341. See Behrens, 'Aus guten alten Tennis-Zeiten', p. 324.

342. See Behrens, 'Gründung', p. 21.

343. The first annual balance sheet available of the Guild is that of the year 1904 published in the Jahres-Bericht der Hamburger Lawn-Tennis-Gilde für das Jahr 1904. In that year, the fees of 454 members totalled the sum of 2,347 marks, and the Uhlenhorst and the Dammtor

clubs contributed 3,000 and 2,500 marks respectively, the greater share of the former presumably owing to the fact that in the first year the courts of this club were the venue for the international tournament. (In later years, every club paid 3,000 marks irrespective of where the tournament was held.) Expenditures for the tournament of 1904 ran up to 4,305 marks. According to a note in *Sport im Wort*, the Guild counted 150 members by the middle of March 1902, in 1904 it had 454, and in 1914 it could, according to the last annual report before the First World War, pride itself on 711.

344. Thus the founding committee of the Guild consisted of the following officials: 1) Carl August von der Meden (president), 2) Carl Maas (vice-president); 3) Hans Oskar Behrens, 4) Dr F.A. Traun (secretaries); 5) Johannes Gabe, 6) Oscar Delaval (treasurers); 7) Dr L. Pinckernelle, 8) Dr W. Bonne, 9) Otto Nirrnheim, and 10) K. Grossmann, Jr. Of these, those with uneven numbers were members of the Uhlenhorst club. See Behrens, 'Gründung', loc. cit. Seeing that such an ideal parity would be difficult to maintain in the future, the founders of the Guild, in § 4 of the Statutes, were less strict about the composition of their committee. Very wisely, they laid down that of the ten committee members to be elected annually by the general assembly no fewer than three and no more than five should be eligible from either club, and that each club should be represented by one of its committee members.

345. See Behrens, 'Gründung', loc. cit.:

nicht die E.-V. werden getrennt weiterhin ihre Turniere veranstalten, sondern die Leitung letzterer wird der Gilde übertragen werden, und zwar derart, dass 1902 auf der Uhlenhorst das grosse internationale, in Pöseldorf ein lokales Turnier stattfindet, 1903 in Pöseldorf das internationale und auf der Uhlenhorst das lokale, und in dieser jährlich wechselnden Folge weiter. (The skating clubs will no longer hold their tournaments separately; rather, the organization of the latter will be entrusted to the Guild, and in such a way that in 1902 the great international tournament will take place at Uhlenhorst, and a local one in Pöseldorf [local name of the suburb in which the Dammthor club had its headquarters], in 1903 the international in Pöseldorf and the local one

in Uhlenhorst, and so on with the same annual change of venue.)

346. See Nirrnheim, 'Die Hamburger Lawn-Tennis-Gilde', p. 158f. So surprising was this *coup d'état* that even the editors of *Sport im Wort* needed some time to adapt themselves to the new situation. As late as the end of April, they still credited Bad Homburg with the championships in their tournament calendar, correcting their mistake in the issue of 2 May 1902, pp. 226 and 228 respectively.

347. See Nirrnheim, 'Internationales Lawn-Tennis-Turnier Hamburg Uhlenhorst', p. 461.

348. See Nirrnheim, 'Die Hamburger Lawn-Tennis-Gilde', p. 158f. Not only Nirrnheim, its committee member, claimed that the donor of the two pieces worth 1,000 marks had been the Guild. The claim was repeated in the Guild's annual reports. In reality, the High Senate of the Hanseatic City had been willing to foot the bill. There is a petition dated 14 February 1902 in the Hamburg State Archives filed by the Guild and apparently drawn up by its secretary, Dr Traun, in which the Guild asked for the Senate's support for the sport of lawn tennis by donating a two-piece challenge cup for an international doubles championship. The petition sheds an interesting light on the beginnings of lawn tennis in Hamburg and the sport in Germany at large. It begins by saying that lawn tennis had obtained a status equalling that of equestrian sports, sailing and rowing; it comprised more portions of society than these, and it enhanced, as one of the few sports also suited for the female sex, the physical as well as the mental development of numerous members of the nation.

Appealing to the senators' patriotism, it emphasized the pioneering role of Hamburg and of citizens such as the late Carl and Ferdinand Laeisz, deplored the exodus of the championships to Bad Homburg, called to the senators' attention the newly founded Guild, and then tried to enlist them to help. In so doing, it did not forget to mention the examples set in this respect by His Majesty the Emperor, His Majesty King Edward VII, the Grand Duke and Duchess of Mecklenburg-Schwerin, and a host of others including the magistrate of the rival town of Bad Homburg.

349. That the change was a rather one-sided decision on the part of the Hamburg clubs appears from the account of the championships in the English journal *Lawn Tennis and Croquet* where it is stated laconically: 'At the end of last year the chief clubs at Hamburg decided to hold the championships again at Homburg. For this purpose they founded a new association solely for the purpose of holding tournaments.' See 'Hamburg (Elbe)', p. 391. The addition 'Elbe' in the headline is interesting. It indicates that it took the ordinary Briton some time before he realized that the famous continental tournament was no longer held in his beloved Bad Homburg.

350. See Pilot, 'Das Homburger Lawn-Tennis-Turnier', p. 368, where a picture of the Coronation Cup (eventually won by M.J.G. Ritchie) is shown. According to a note in *Sport im Wort* both the coronation cup and Mr Stewart's cup, a mighty tankard worth 500 dollars, were exhibited in the *Kurhaus* well before the tournament. The latter can today be viewed in the Bad Homburg 'Museum im Gotischen Haus'; it bears the following inscription: 'Challenge Cup For The International Lawn Tennis Doubles Team Championship of Europe Presented To The Lawn Tennis Tournament Committee of Homburg Vor Der Hohe Germany By William Rhinelander Stewart of New York 1902'.

351. It was meant to encourage the entries of representative pairs from different nations. The trophy was to be kept by the winners of the first prize for one year should they be of the same nationality. The cup was in its first year won by the English pair Hillyard/Ball-Greene. See 'Homburg Open Tournament [1902]', p. 390f. According to Pilot, loc. cit., the cup had to be won three times in order to be owned for good which, however, it never was. G.W. Hillyard and G.C. Ball-Greene who won the event a second time in 1905, came closest to winning it for good. The other victors inscribed on it are: Wylie C. Grant/Robert LeRoy, USA (1903); Wylie C. Grant/J.C. Wright, USA (1904); A.F. Wilding/G.M. Simond, England [*sic*] (1906); O.

Froitzheim/Freiherr K.v.Lersner, Germany (1907); A.F. Wilding/C. von Wessely, 'Australien' [*sic*]-Austria (1908); H.A. Parker/L.O.S. Poidevin, 'New Seeland' [*sic*] Australia (1909); O. Froitzheim/O. Kreuzer, Germany (1910). Of these, Robert LeRoy won two silver medals at the Olympic tennis event of St Louis in 1904, see the present writer's *Olympisches Tennis*, p. 33. In later years, it seems, it became more and more difficult to adhere to the original scheme, pairs representing a single country. After 1910 the event was apparently discontinued due to the absence of foreign pairs as a result of the withdrawal of Charles Adolph Voigt.

352. See 'Heiligendamm', p. 448.

353. Ibid., p. 449.

354. According to Voigt, by that time a resident of Paris and an expert on tennis in France, Decugis together with P. Aymé, A. and M. Vacherot, P. Lebreton, J. Worth, and P. Verdé-Delisle represented the French first class at the beginning of 1902, whereas M. Germot, together with seven other players, was rated second class by him. See 'Le lawn-tennis en France', p. 36.

355. Dr Flavelle, who originated from Dublin, but is referred to as an Englishman in contemporary reports, had competed for the championship of Germany before, at Bad Homburg in 1899, and with considerable success, succumbing in the penultimate round only to A.W. Gore. After the drama of 1902, he returned to Hamburg in 1903, only to be beaten by Ritchie, again in the final and again under most unfortunate circumstances. As in 1902, he had again been leading by two sets to love.

356. See Myers, *Lawn Tennis At Home*, p. 159.

357. Ibid., p. 159f.

358. This piece of information was given in a note in the first May issue of the Berlin weekly *Sport im Wort*.

359. While on medical duty in South Africa, he had not failed 'to engage in his favourite pastime both at Pretoria and Standerton', see Myers, op. cit., p. 159. This had apparently prevented him from getting out of shape.

360. See 'Hamburg (Elbe)', p. 391: 'The other rounds of the championship called for no remarks, except that Germot (Paris) beat

Thomson unexpectedly, only to succumb easily to Behrens in the next round.'

361. See Nirrnheim, 'Internationales', p. 460: 'Der Hauptheld des Turniers war Decugis, ... Der einzige Gegner, der ihm gefährlich werden konnte, war Dr Flavelle.' ('The chief hero of the tournament was Decugis, the only opponent who might have become a danger to him was Dr Flavelle.')

362. See Nirrnheim, p. 460.

363. See 'Hamburg (Elbe)', p. 391: 'In the third set he stood 5:0 and 40:30, so that one ace was wanting to get him the title'.

364. See Nirrnheim, 'Internationales', p. 461:

Nachdem Decugis auch noch das nächste Spiel gewonnen hat [after an initial score of 5:1 in Flavelle's favour], führt Flavelle im 10. Spiel mit 30–0. Decugis spielt sehr gewagte Bälle, die ihm aber meist gelingen. Flavelle hat 40–30; ... 'deuce'. Nächster Ball für Flavelle. Wieder letzter Ball. [Decugis again scores this point.] Die beiden nächsten Bälle gehen an Decugis, es folgen die beiden nächsten Spiele, Satz 7–5 für Decugis. (After Decugis has also won this game, Flavelle is leading 30:0 in the tenth game. Decugis tries very daring shots, but is successful most times. Flavelle has 40:30; ... 'deuce'. Next point to Flavelle. Last point again. The next two points go to Decugis, and so do the next two games, 7:5, set to Decugis.)

365. See Nirrnheim, 'Internationales', p. 461: 'Als Flavelle dann das nächste Spiel verliert, wächst die Spannung im Publikum, das den Franzosen schon verloren gab, nun aber seine Erfolge mit heftigem, allerdings manchmal sehr wenig gerechtfertigtem Beifall begrüsst.'

366. See 'Hamburg (Elbe)', p. 391: 'The crowd was very excited, applauding both men frequently, the ladies seeming to be more in favour of the delicate-looking Frenchman than the robust Englishman.'

367. Ibid., p. 391.

368. See Nirrnheim, 'Internationales', p. 461.

369. Dr Hessen, in his book *Technik und Taktik*, devoted a whole noteworthy chapter to the question of 'What is Fair?', see ibid., pp. 82–7. The greatest obstacle to a player's technical perfection and to sportsmanlike behaviour, the Doctor said, were 'Lady Greed' and her daughter 'Fear of Losing' who was, to his mind, a great deal uglier than even her mother (p. 83). Comparing the ways in which sporting competitions were conducted in Germany and in England, he discovered the following. Whereas in England the smooth running of a match was the rule, in Germany an atmosphere of protest usually arose after ten minutes. Suspicions full of rancour were muttered, players looked daggers at each other, a lack of discipline was exhibited and finally even rude words might be resorted to. The reason for this, he said, was to be sought in the different development of the two nations. Young Germans behaved excellently as long as they were in rank and file or standing sentry, in a word, whenever some superior was giving orders, or they knew they were being supervised, or liable to being court-martialled. If, however, some effort was required of them out of their own free will, they usually failed. In the Anglo-American world, sport with its inherent idea of subjecting oneself freely to a cause had for many centuries held the place of Prussian military drill. That was the reason why those educated from childhood to self-commitment and fairness never believed they had accomplished something extraordinary or a work of merit when in the course of a tournament they showed model behaviour, whereas in Germany the young gentleman with his special wishes, whims and obstinacy annoyed the tournament management intolerably (p. 85f.). Dr Hessen concluded by referring to the example of Girdlestone, a well-known English resident of Heidelberg, who, whenever an umpire had credited him with a point which, in his own opinion, he did not deserve, would, rather than hit the next ball with his racket, catch it with his hand. H.L. Doherty had done likewise in the challenge round against Clothier at Newport, and in the case of H.L. such fairness was based not only on his organic equanimity, but on one strengthened and refined by self-education. Never did he show excitement, rejoicing or a flagging spirit, but always, in all vicissitudes, favourable or not, the same smile. (p. 86)

370. See Nirrnheim, 'Internationales', p. 461.

371. Ibid., pp. 461 and 470.

372. Ibid., p. 461:

Decugis gewann hauptsächlich dadurch, dass er guter Baseline- und Netzspieler ist, während Flavelle am Netz nicht viel ausrichtet, ... ferner ist Decugis' Aufschlag dem Flavelle's stark überlegen, und er besitzt eine grössere Beweglichkeit als der Engländer (was in dem grossen Altersunterschied seine Erklärung findet. Die Red.)

373. See Nirrnheim, 'Internationales', p. 461.

374. At Bad Homburg in 1899. On the use of pseudonyms see also above, Chapter VII, note 72.

375. There is a very illuminating article on this subject by an anonymous writer in *Sport im Wort* entitled 'Zum Kapitel der Pseudonyme' from which the information contained in this paragraph has been gleaned.

376. See Nirrnheim, 'Internationales', p. 461: 'Bei diesem Kampf war eine so grosse Zuschauermenge versammelt, wie wir sie unseres Wissens [Nirrnheim, perhaps the most knowledgeable man in the whole country, knew what he was talking about] noch bei keinem Wettspiel in Deutschland gesehen haben.'

377. See Nirrnheim, loc. cit.

378. See 'Hamburg (Elbe)', p. 391.

379. See Nirrnheim, loc. cit.

380. See 'Hamburg (Elbe)', loc. cit.

381. See Simon, '25 Jahre', p. 25f. In its issue of 10 September 1892, the journal, discussing the 'strong hold Tennis has taken upon the highest classes' in Germany, finished by saying that, although the game was in its infancy, it did 'not need a prophet … to predict a very big future for the infant, especially as a Tennis Association for Germany' was 'on the tapis'. Two weeks later, in its issue of 24 September 1892, the paper reported on a letter in the English language which it had received from Baron Robert von Fichard and which reflected 'the highest possible credit upon his scholastic attainments'. In reply to the paper's suggestion, von Fichard had written that he was 'fully' of its opinion, and that to hear more from him on this subject might be expected shortly. The paper went on,

No-one has done more for Lawn Tennis in this country than Baron von Fichard, and no-one is more fitted than he, to call such an organization into life. Herr von der Meden, the energetic and assiduous hon. sec. of the Hamburg Lawn-Tennis Club has always been very keen on the subject of an Association, and in this gentleman Baron von Fichard would find a most capable and efficient co-worker.

About one year later, in its issue of 12 August 1893, the foundation of a German Association, contrary to what is said on this point by Simon, was no longer the question. A meeting between von Fichard and von der Meden had taken place on 24 July 1893, but in the course of their discussion both gentlemen had been 'agreed upon the advisability of adhering to the English L.T.A.'(!) Not a single copy of the 1892 and 1893 volumes of *Spiel und Sport* seems to have survived, but the relevant passages are quoted in the appendix of von Fichard's *Erstes deutsches Lawn-Tennis-Jahrbuch* of 1894, pp. 143 and 145. In all likelihood, even Simon quoted from the yearbook and had no access to the original. It is interesting, in view of what will be said about the foundation of the German Federation on the following pages, that Lawn-Tennis-Turnier-Club Berlin, perhaps the most prestigious club in the country at the turn of the century, should have been a member of the LTA, but dropped its membership after the foundation in 1902, see Hofer, p. 23.

382. For an account of the 'Days at Cascaes' see Voigt, 'Der König von Portugal als Lawn-Tennis-Spieler', and no. 496 of the *Vossische Zeitung* referred to by Gramm, p. 643. Hillyard himself gave an account of this tennis party in Portugal, in his contribution to Myers' *Lawn Tennis at Home and Abroad*, pp. 104–6, which also contains some very interesting photographs, one of which at least was taken by H.S. Mahony.

383. Gramm was the chairman of the Lawn-Tennis-Club Frankfurt, successor of an earlier club called the Spiel-Vereinigung-Körnerwiese and founded in 1897, see von Fichard's lawn tennis annuals of 1901 and 1903, pp. 61, and 91 respectively.

384. See Gramm, 'Eingesandt', November 1901, p. 643f., a letter to the editor which has been summarized here.

385. See Voigt, 'Lawn-Tennis "Berufsspieler"', p. 660f. In the course of his reply, Voigt mentioned the English journal *Lawn Tennis* which in its November issue had dealt with the Portugal episode.

386. Hillyard, in Myers' *Lawn Tennis at Home and Abroad*, p. 104, indicates that the boat trip to Portugal had in fact been sponsored by the owner of a certain

steamship line: 'Satisfactory arrangements were made, largely owing to the generous and most sporting manner in which the owner of a certain steamship line placed one of his boats at the disposal of the visiting side.'

387. This is an interesting figure in itself. From a note in *Sport im Wort* in February 1902 it appears that the equivalent of 40,000 marks was £2,000. This sum had been the stake in a table tennis match in London between Messrs. Durham Stokes and Eugene Corri.

388. See Gramm, 'Eingesandt [II]', p. 675.

389. See Gramm's reference, loc. cit., to the coupons by the clipping of which 'Aces' eked out a living: 'Ob jene Cracks ihr Dasein durch Couponsabschneiden fristen oder durch Handhabung einer Schreibmaschine, kann höchstens für die Hotelbesitzer Interesse haben'. The reference to the typewriter aims at those tennis players who worked as reporters for sporting journals, another notorious activity at variance with the principles of amateurism.

390. Carl Schmidt-Knatz was the games superintendent (Spielwart) of the Lawn-Tennis-Club Frankfurt, the club of which Emil Gramm was the chairman, see von Fichard, lawn tennis annual of 1903, p. 91.

391. See Schmidt-Knatz, 'Eingesandt', p. 686, and Simon, '25 Jahre', p. 28f.

392. It was founded in Frankfurt on Easter Monday by representatives of six Clubs: Darmstädter Lawn-Tennis-Verband; English Lawn Tennis Club, Freiburg; Mannheimer Lawn-Tennis-Club; Münchener Lawn-Tennis-Club Phoenix; Lawn-Tennis-Club Frankfurt a.M.; Frankfurter Lawn-Tennis-Vereinigung. According to its statutes, its objects were (among other things) the promotion of lawn tennis in Southern Germany, especially tuition of the beginner in writing and by word of mouth, and the foundation of an All German Association. Schmidt-Knatz was elected chairman, and a future founding member of the German Lawn Tennis Federation, Dr Robert Hessen, was elected treasurer. Würzburger Universitäts-Lawn-Tennis-club joined the Association shortly afterwards, see Schmidt-Knatz, 'Der Süddeutsche Lawn-Tennis-Verband', *passim.*

393. The wording here was deliberately vague, as the author of the letter later explained in a second letter. He had wanted to leave to the northern clubs the decision as to whether they preferred a northern association to precede the All German organization, or whether they chose a short-cut leading to an All German association directly.

394. See Schmidt-Knatz, p. 687.

395. See Schetelig, 'Eingesandt', *passim*. In his earlier letter, Schetelig, by suggesting the foundation of a German association, above all strove for German independence from the LTA. He had paid a visit to Bad Homburg in 1899 and competed (as had Karl Schmidt-Knatz, though more successfully) in the Gentlemen's Singles Handicap (Class B), see 'Homburg v.d. Höhe [1899]', p. 314. That is why in his letter he could mention the fact that, although several Germans were on the committee, all announcements had been in English. Even allowing for the presence of a great percentage of Englishmen, he wrote, and the obligation of the local administration to be as polite as possible to foreign guests, such procedure was somewhat difficult to swallow. Schetelig's early letter is referred to by Simon, '25 Jahre', p. 26.

396. The Austrians, however, stole the march on the Germans by founding, on the initiative of Baron Meyern-Hohenberg, an association of their own, on 25 January 1902, see Y.M., 'Die Gründung der Oesterreichischen Lawn-Tennis-Association'.

397. See Schetelig, p. 697.

398. See Schlepps, p. 22.

399. See Nirrnheim, 'Zur Gründung', p. 34.

400. See Bartels, 'Zur Gründung', p. 46.

401. See von Fichard, 'Zur Gründung', p. 56: 'Es ist mir zur Zeit versagt, näheres mitzuteilen, ich kann aber die Interessenten, insbesondere die Unterzeichner des 'Antrages zur Gründung eines D.L.T.-Verbandes' versichern, dass der Anregung entsprochen werden wird. Die nötigen Verhandlungen sind bereits eingeleitet; das Ergebnis derselben wird in dieser Zeitschrift zur öffentlichen Kenntnis gebracht werden.'

402. As a matter of fact, he had been taken to task by the Society, the representatives of which, as true German chauvinists, had seethed with indignation when the English LTA had presumed to judge the competence of von Fichard's renderings. On the Society, founded in 1885 by the art historian Herman Riegel, and its journal see Wells, pp. 225–8.

403. See von Fichard, 'Zur Gründung', p. 57.

404. See Schmidt-Knatz, 'Zur Gründung', p. 73.

405. See Schetelig, 'Zur Gründung [1902]', p. 83.

406. See Schetelig, 'Zur Gründung', p. 84.

407. In what follows the present writer is paraphrasing Voigt, 'Zur Gründung', p. 109.

408. See Voigt, 'Zur Gründung', p. 109.

409. 'Die bisher von den Herren von Jecklin und Brüggemann bezüglich der Frage der Gründung eines Deutschen Lawn-Tennis-Verbandes mit Herrn von der Meden-Hamburg geführten Verhandlungen fanden die Billigung des Club-Ausschusses.' See 'Der Berliner Lawn-Tennis-Turnier-Club', p. 109.

410. See Behrens, 'Aus guten alten Tennis-Zeiten', p. 324.

411. See 'Zur Gründung', p. 122, and Simon, '25 Jahre Deutscher Tennis-Bund', p. 32f.

412. See 'Zur Gründung', loc. cit. The list contained the names of von Jecklin and Brüggemann, Berlin; Schlepps, Danzig; Bartning, Sr, Karlsruhe; Pummerer, Sr, Munich; von Schleich, Nuremberg; Baron von Fichard, Strasbourg.

413. See 'Ostdeutscher Lawn-Tennis-Turnier-Verband', p. 192.

414. See von Fichard, *Deutsches Lawn-Tennis-Jahrbuch 1902*, p. 220.

415. These were Bartels, Brunswick; Gulden, Dr Hillig, Leipzig; Dr Hessen, Mannheim; Baron von Maltzahn, Bad Homburg; Schmidt-Knatz, Frankfurt; and Stahlmann, Munich; see 'Zur Gründung eines Deutschen Lawn-Tennis-Bundes', p. 242. Simon, '25 Jahre', p. 34f., who did not state his source of information, was wrong when he wrote that von der Meden's second invitation was made in the week following the first.

416. The wording of the minutes is printed in Simon, '25 Jahre', p. 35f.

417. Von Jecklin, a Geheimer Regierungsrat, died on 15 April 1910, see the two obituary notices in *Lawn-Tennis und Golf*, 7 (1910), no. 5, 21 April 1910, pp. 61 and 62; and the obituary by G.S. For an account of his work see also 'Aus den Anfängen des Tennissports in Berlin':

Die Herren Dering [an Englishman, member of the English Embassy], v. Jecklin und Oechelhäuser, häufige Preisstifter, wurden zu Ehrenmitgliedern [of the second oldest Berlin club, Blau-Weiss, founded in 1899] ernannt. Von Jecklin war der eifrigste Förderer der Jugend. Er nahm sich besonders junger Tennistalente an und scheute nicht die grossen Mühen ihrer Ausbildung. Ihm und Herrn von der Meden in Hamburg verdanken wir am meisten hinsichtlich der organisatorischen Entwicklung unseres schönen Sports.

418. See 'Gründung des Deutschen Lawn-Tennis-Bundes', p. 272.

419. See Bartels, 'Bundeserinnerungen', p. 320. Bartels was to become von der Meden's successor as president of the Federation after von der Meden had died on 23 May 1911, see Simon, '25 Jahre', p. 40.

420. See 'Gründung', loc. cit.

421. Ibid.

422. See von Fichard's annual of 1903, p. 4, I. Zweck § 2.2.4: '[Der Zweck des Bundes ist eine]… anerkannte praktisch brauchbare deutsche Uebertragung der beim Spiele selbst notwendigen und gebräuchlichen englischen Ausdrücke und Redewendungen … aufzustellen.' ('It is the purpose of the Federation to make sure of an approved and efficient German translation of the English terms and expressions necessary and in common use in the game itself.')

423. See von Fichard, lawn tennis annual of 1903, p. xiv.

424. See von Fichard, annual of 1904, pp. xiv–xvi.

425. See Wells, p. 423. Uniform pronunciation (of the German language) was achieved in 1898 at a conference convened in Berlin and initiated by Theodor Siebs, see Wells, p. 378, and the introduction of a uniform orthography by Konrad Duden, see Wells, p. 376, practically coincided with the unification of the German tennis language. On the complex issue of linguistic imperialism, see Phillipson, *passim*.

426. The German Football Federation (DFB) was founded in 1900, the German Golf Federation in 1907.

427. See Wells, p. 420.

428. Ibid., p. 423.

429. On the Allgemeiner Deutscher Sprachverein, founded by the art historian Herman Riegel in 1885, see Wells, pp. 425–8. It is interesting that not only Baron von Fichard, the Teutonizer-in-chief of the German Lawn Tennis Federation, but also one of the pioneers of German Association football, Professor Konrad Koch of Brunswick, should have contributed articles to its journal.

430. See Wells, p. 423f.

431. See von Fichard, 'Deutsche Lawn-Tennis-Ausdrücke', and Koch, 'Deutsche Kunstausdrücke des Fußballspiels'.

432. See von Fichard, lawn tennis annual of 1904, p. 126.

433. In a yearbook published by the German Lawn Tennis Federation, see von Fichard, annual of 1905, p. xiv. Of this yearbook, not a single copy seems to have survived. The rules were also published separately by Emil Sommermeyer, von Fichard's publisher from Baden-Baden, in 1904, but again no specimen of this separate edition has come down to us. The Deutscher Tennis Bund, Hamburg, has the yearbook of 1906 where the rules are printed (with amendments of §§ 25 and 26) on pp. 81–111. The present writer owns a 1907 edition of the Rules which once belonged to the library of the Realgymnasium in Einbeck.

434. See Hessen, *Technik und Taktik*, p. 90. The predominance of foreigners on German lawn tennis courts was deeply deplored elsewhere, see a report which appeared in the *Leipziger Tagblatt* and was duly reprinted in *Der Lawn-Tennis-Sport* 2 (1905), no. 30, 7 December 1905, p. 446f., note.

435. See 'Hamburg, August 1903', p. 463.

436. See Hedges, p. 202, who has October 1870 and 1955 as dates of his birth and death respectively.

437. A keen observer of Ritchie's match entertained a view which was very different from popular opinion on the Englishman's alleged calmness:

Ritchie's tennis vices and assets are known. He will hardly doublefault fewer than five times in any match, but then whips balls from left and right down the lines with deadly certainty, and I cannot tell whether a smash by him was ever badly placed or weak. You will, however, no longer believe in the unshakable composure with which he is said to have met Wilding, if you do for a moment disregard the court completely and direct your attention to the man. Then Ritchie will remind you of a whirling dervish or an electric eel, so agitated is his body, so incessantly he changes position. His eyes are flashing because of his lust for the ball, he trembles to give it a hell of a knock. It is the height of his tension which is admirable.

See 'Ueber das Vorlaufen im Doppelspiel', p. 371 (author's translation).

438. Ritchie's dictum 'Precision is more important than power' ('Genauigkeit ist wichtiger als Kraftaufwand.') was reported as late as 1931 by the journal *Tennis und Golf* 8 (1931), no. 28, 4 September 1931, p. 717, under a note titled 'Aussprüche berühmter Meister' (dicta of famous champions).

439. See Rosenbaum-Jenkins, 'Beobachtungen', p. 477.

440. Ibid., p. 476.

441. See *Sport im Wort* (1903), no. 37, Thursday, 10 September 1903, p. 459, note.

442. See Gurney, *Table Tennis*, p. 2.

443. See 'Hamburg, August 1903', p. 463. See also the report in *Lawn Tennis and Croquet*, 'Hamburg', p. 472: 'Both players simply sent the ball flying 20 to 30 times from one base-line to the other; and a gentleman was not far from the mark in saying that Ritchie's and Flavelle's game was "not tennis but ping pong".'

444. See 'Vom Internationalen Turnier in Hamburg. Ein Stimmungsbild', p. 251.

445. See Nirrnheim, 'Hamburg 1905', p. 347.

446. Ibid., p. 375.

447. Ibid., p. 346.

448. It is curious that the knowledgable Otto Nirrnheim should have detected so many flaws in the play of the future Wimbledon Champion from New Zealand, 'Hamburg 1905', p. 375 (author's translation):

Wilding's best stroke is his cross-court drive which has a fabulous speed and flatness of trajectory [Rasanz]. The backhand stroke is his weakness; if by any means possible, he tries to to avoid it. His smashes are, in view of of his tallness and muscles, almost childlike, his volley stops, however, are brilliant, … Of the 'reverse twist service' of his countrymen [Wilding apparently passed for a Briton] and the Americans he scarcely has an inkling, his experiments with it looked dangerous, but proved completely harmless. His varied and daring game won him the sympathy of many; personally, he proved to be the 'jolly good fellow' which he reputedly is.

449. Ibid., p. 347. Unlike its predecessor, this cup is in all probability lost forever. R.J. Ritchie, the champion's son, found his father's house destroyed by German bombers when he returned from the war.

450. This cup was won, after three successes, by Otto Froitzheim in 1910. Rainer Froitzheim, Froitzheim's son, remembers having seen it among his father's collection which, unfortunately, was lost completely after the Second World War.

451. See Pepi, p. 373.

452. Ibid., p. 375.

453. See the correspondent of the English journal *Lawn Tennis and Badminton* at the beginning of his report 'Hamburg (Elbe) Aug. 10', p. 388: 'This was the first year since the event became an open one [1897] that the Germans fancied there might be a chance of a native success, either through O. Kreuzer or O. Froitzheim. The whole meeting was peculiarly influenced by these expectations, and whether Kreuzer *or* Froitzheim would prove to be the better man.'

454. See Esser, p. 9. His father was said to be an excellent fencer in the Bonn students' corporation 'Teutonia' of which he had been, like his son after him, a member in the 1860s.

455. Ibid., p. 11.

456. This was on the courts of the 'Lawn Tennis Club Platz Lenôtre' of which at the time the Secretary was Baron von Fichard, see Esser, p. 43, and von Fichard, in his lawn tennis annual of 1895, p. 112f.

457. See Esser, p. 11f.

458. Ibid., p. 24. Several English dailies characterizing Foitzheim's game were quoted in the German lawn tennis journal *Lawn-Tennis und Golf*, see 'Froitzheim in englischer Betrachtung'.

459. See Esser, p. 34.

460. Ibid., p. 20.

461. See Otto Nirrnheim, 'Hamburger Internationales 1907', p. 517.

462. Ritchie had played Froitzheim before, and twice beaten him: in 1904 , in the fifth round of the Hamburg Cup (8:6, 6:1), see H.B.H., 'Internationales Turnier Hamburg', p. 257, and in 1907, also in the fifth round of the Championship of

Hamburg (2:6, 6:4, 6:2), see 'Hamburg (Elbe) Aug. 10', loc. cit.

463. Loc. cit. The original report, in the German language, is by Otto Nirrnheim, 'Hamburger Internationales 1907', pp. 513–18. This was reprinted in Esser, *Otto Froitzheim*, p. 51f, and in Simon, *Berühmte Tennis-Wettkämpfe*, pp. 5–7.

464. The phrase in brackets is missing in the English translation and has been supplemented on the basis of Nirrnheim's text.

465. See Nirrnheim, 'Hamburger Internationales 1907', p. 514: 'Langanhaltender Beifall belohnte ihn. Sei es nun, dass dieser Beifall den Unterlegenen ärgerte, sei es dass er über das Fehlschlagen seines Planes unwillig war, jedenfalls "verkachelte" er ostentativ die zwei ersten Spiele des zweiten Satzes'.

466. Ibid.: 'und hat damit seit 11 Jahren die Meisterschaft für Deutschland gewonnen. "Da bricht die Menge tobend aus" – es war einer der schönsten Siege, die wir in Hamburg erlebt haben.' The quotation is from the first line of the last stanza ('Der Kampf mit dem Drachen', line 289). The poem is about a young dragon-slayer, a member of the order of the Knights Hospitallers of St John of Jerusalem, who, having killed the monster, returns to his monastery only to be reprimanded by his Master for his violation of monastic discipline.

467. See Esser, p. 53.

468. Where he lost the final against no other than Ritchie whom he tried to beat 'at his own game' from the baseline, see the present writer's *Olympisches Tennis*, p. 37.

469. For details see ibid., p. 58.

470. Ibid., p. 59.

471. Ibid.

472. See Simon, *Berühmte Tennis-Wettkämpfe*, p. 5 (in this source this text was spaced out): 'Der 15. August 1907 ist der sportgeschichtliche Tag, an dem Deutschland sichtbar in die Reihe der Tennis-Großstaaten eintrat.'

473. See Esser, p. 7:

Darüber hinaus ist Froitzheim der erste, der durch seine sensationellen Siege über den bis dahin unbesieglich scheinenden Ritchie 1907 ... sowie über den australischen [*sic*] Weltmeister Wilding zum erstenmal und endgültig den die deutsche Sportentwicklung lähmenden Irrglauben zerstörte, daß nur der

Ausländer, vor allem der Angelsachse dazu geschaffen sei, die schönsten Früchte gesunder Sportbetätigung zu pflücken.

474. It is interesting that after the Nazis had assumed power in 1933 Froitzheim, who was ousted from his job as Chief Constable of Wiesbaden because he had refused to become a member of either the SA or the SS, was reinstalled in the provinces, as Deputy District President of Aachen, by the intervention of Hermann Göring who told Froitzheim that he deserved it for he had done enough for the Deutsches Reich. Froitzheim nevertheless had to join the National Socialist German Workers' Party. Personal communication by Rainer Froitzheim, Froitzheim's son.

Bibliography

'A Chat with Count Victor Voss', in *Lawn Tennis and Croquet*, 7 February 1900, pp. 468–70.

'Aus den Anfängen des Tennissports in Berlin', in *Lawn-Tennis und Golf*, 8 (1914), no. 8, 19 May 1914, p. 198.

'Auszug aus dem Protokoll der gründenden Versammlung der Internationalen Sportbehörde für Lawn-Tennis', in *Lawn-Tennis und Golf*, 10 (1913), no. 12, 17 June 1913, pp. 288–90.

'Baden-Baden', in *The Swiss & Nice Times*, Sunday, 15 September 1895.

'Clarence Hobart: A Great Figure', in *American Lawn Tennis*, 24 (1930), no. 356, 20 November 1930, pp. 584f.

'Das Berliner Herbst-Turnier', in *Sport im Wort*, no. 40 (1900), Thursday, 4 October 1900, pp. 417–20.

'Das Homburger Turnier', in *Sport im Wort*, no. 36 (1900), Thursday, 6 September 1900, p. 369f.

'Das Internationale Lawn-Tennis-Turnier zu Homburg', in *Sport im Bild*, 4 (1898), no. 35, 2 September 1898, p. 564.

'Das internationale Turnier zu Homburg v.d. Höhe', in *Sport im Wort*, no. 36 (1901), Thursday, 5 September 1901, pp. 453–5.

'Das Ragazer Turnier', in *Der Lawn-Tennis-Sport*, 4 (1907), no. 25, 5 September 1907, p. 558f.

'Das Tennisspiel', in *Deutsche Turn-Zeitung. Amtliches Blatt der Deutschen Turnerschaft*, 47 (1902), p. 584f.

'Der Berliner Lawn-Tennis-Turnier-Club', in *Sport im Wort*, no. 9 (1902), Friday, 28 February 1902, p. 109.

'Der Voss-Pokal und seine neue Heimat', in *Lawn-Tennis und Golf*, 10 (1913), no. 10, 3 June 1913, pp. 283.

'Die Geschichte eines Deutschen Ballhauses', in *Sport im Bild*, 4 (1898), no. 19, Friday 13 May 1898, p. 307.

'Die Hamburger Lawn-Tennis-Gilde', in *Sport im Wort*, no. 28 (1902), Thursday, 10 July 1902, pp. 376f.

'Eine Plauderei mit dem deutschen Meisterspieler [Graf Voss-Schönau] [translated from *Lawn-Tennis*]', in *Sport im Wort*, no. 7 (1900), Friday, 16 February 1900, p. 49f.

'Froitzheim in englischer Betrachtung', in *Lawn-Tennis und Golf*, 11 (1914), no. 15, 7 July 1914, p. 376f.

'Gründung des Deutschen Lawn-Tennis-Bundes', in *Sport im Wort*, no. 20 (1902), Friday, 23 May 1902, p. 272.

'Gründung einer Internationalen L.T.-Föderation', in *Lawn-Tennis und Golf*, 10 (1913), no. 2, mid-February 1913, p. 31f.

'H.S. Mahony', in *Der Lawn-Tennis-Sport*, 2 (1905), no. 15, 6 July 1905, p. 217.

'Hamburg (Elbe) (Championships of Germany)', in *Lawn Tennis and Croquet*, 27 August 1902, p. 391f.

'Hamburg (Elbe) Aug. 10', in *Lawn Tennis and Badminton*, 4 September 1907, p. 388f.

'Hamburg', in *Lawn Tennis*, 8 September 1897, pp. 299–301.

'Hamburg', in *Pastime*, 16 September 1891, p. 208f.

'Hamburg', in *Pastime*, 28 September 1892, p. 201f.

'Hamburg', in *Pastime*, 20 September 1893, p. 184f.

'Hamburg', in *Pastime*, 18 July 1894, p. 185f.

'Hamburg, August 1903', in *Sport im Wort*, no. 37 (1903), Thursday, 10 September 1903, pp. 461–5.

'Heiligen Damm', in *Lawn Tennis*, 23 August 1899, p. 295f.

'Heiligendamm', in *Sport im Wort*, no. 34 (1902), Thursday, 21 August 1902, p. 448f.

'Homburg International Tournament', in *The Field. The Country Gentleman's Newspaper*, 96 (1900), 1 September 1900, p. 362.

'Homburg International Tournament', in *The Field. The Country Gentleman's Newspaper*, 98 (1901), 31 August 1901, p. 368f.

'Homburg Open Tournament', in *The Field. The Country Gentleman's Newspaper*, 100 (1902), 30 August 1902, p. 390f.

'Homburg v.d. Höhe', in *Lawn Tennis*, 7 September 1898, pp. 308–11.

'Homburg: Some Notes', in *Lawn Tennis*, 5 September 1900, pp. 348–53.

'Homburg', in *Lawn Tennis*, 11 September 1901, pp. 397–9.

'Interessantes aus dem Lawn-Tennis-Sport', in *Sport im Bild*, 9 (1903), no. 36, 4 September 1903, p. 566f.

'Internationales Lawn-Tennis-Turnier zu Heiligendamm', in *Sport im Wort*, no. 34, (1901), Thursday, 22 August 1901, p. 427f.

'Jahres-Tagung des Internationalen Tennis-Verbandes', in *Der Tennissport*, 14 (1937), no. 7, 1 April 1937, p. 86f.

'Lawn-Tennis im Palmengarten', in *Kleine Presse. Stadtanzeiger and Fremdenblatt* [Frankfurt], 24 April 1892.

'Lawn-Tennis-Turnier-Club, Berlin. Jahresbericht 1900', in *Sport im Wort*, nos 20 and 21 (1900), Thursday, 16 and 23 May 1900, pp. 233–5, and 250–2.

'Lawn-Tennis in Homburg', in *Kleine Presse*, nos 196 and 197, 23 and 24 August 1894, pp. 3 and 1f.

'Lawn-Tennis. Das internationale Lawn-Tennis-Turnier in Baden-Baden', in *Sport im Bild*, 2 (1896), no. 39, p. 618f.

'Mr. C.A. Voigt', in *Lawn Tennis and Croquet*, May 10, 1899, pp. 41–3.

'Ostdeutscher Lawn-Tennis-Turnier-Verband', in *Sport im Wort*, no. 16, (1902), Friday, 18 April 1902, p. 192.

'St. Moritz', in *Der Lawn-Tennis-Sport*, 4 (1907), no. 24, 5 September 1907, p. 541, and no. 25, 12 September 1907, p. 557f.

'Taubenschiessen in Monte Carlo', in *Sport im Bild*, 10 (1904), no. 7, p. 107.

'Tennis im 19. Jahrhundert in Baden-Baden', in *2. Internationales Jugend-Tennis-Turnier Baden-Baden* [tournament programme] August 1992, pp. 47–9.

'Ueber das Vorlaufen im Doppelspiel ...', in *Der Lawn-Tennis-Sport*, 2 (1905), no. 24, 7 September 1905, p. 371f.

'V. internationales Lawn-Tennis-Turnier in Wien', in *Sport im Wort*, no. 25 (1901), Thursday, 20 June 1901, p. 307.

'Varia', in *Pastime*, 17 August 1892, p. 102f.

'Verzeichnis der Mitglieder des Zentral-Ausschusses', in E. von Schenkendorff and F.A. Schmidt (eds), *Jahrbuch für Volks- und Jugendspiele*, vol. 6, Leipzig: R. Voigtländer's Verlag, 1897, p. 300.

'Vom Internationalen Turnier in Hamburg. Ein Stimmungsbild', in *Der Lawn-Tennis-Sport*, 1 (1904), no. 19, 1 September 1904, p. 250f.

'Vom Lawn-Tennis und Cricket-Platz im Frankfurter Palmengarten', in *Kleine Presse. Stadtanzeiger und Fremdenblatt*, no. 229, 30 September 1887 [comment on title page of the same issue].

'Von der Zählweise im Tennissport', in *Tennis und Golf*, 4 (1927), p. 171f.

'Voss-Pokal', in *Der Lawn-Tennis-Sport*, 1 (1904), no. 12, 14 July 1904, p. 160.

'When Hobart Refused to Play', in *American Lawn Tennis*, 20 November (1930), p. 586.

'Zum Internationalen Lawn-Tennis-Turnier in Homburg v.d. Höhe', in *Sport im Wort*, no. 34 (1901), Thursday, 22 August 1901, p. 427.

'Zum Kapitel der Pseudonyme', in *Sport im Wort*, no. 48 (1902), Thursday, 27 November 1902, p. 622.

'Zur Gründung einer Deutschen Lawn-Tennis-Association', in *Sport im Wort*, no. 10 (1902), Friday, 7 March 1902, p. 122.

'Zur Gründung eines Deutschen Lawn-Tennis-Bundes', in *Sport im Wort*, no. 19 (1902), Friday, 9 May 1902, p. 241f.

77 Jahre Club Raffelberg [1966], Duisburg: waz-Druck [1966].

100 Jahre Cannstatter Tennisclub, Bad Cannstatt: Dr. Crantz'sche Druckerei, 1990.

100 Jahre Club Raffelberg e.V. 1889–1989 [Duisburg]: Edel-Druck, [1989].

100 Jahre Tennis in Bad Homburg. 1876–1976. Eine Dokumentation, jubilee publication of the Tennis-Club Bad Homburg v.d.H.e.V., Frankfurt a.M.: Kristandt KG, Grafische Betriebe, 1976.

Aberdare, The Right Honourable The Lord, *The Willis Faber Book of Tennis and Rackets*, London: Stanley Paul, 1980.

Adam, A., *Théophile de Viau et la libre pensée française en 1620*, Paris: Librairie E. Droz, 1935.

Adress- und Geschäfts-Handbuch der königlichen Haupt- und Residenzstadt

Stuttgart für das Jahr 1884, Bearbeitet durch Registrator Beck, Erster Theil, Stuttgart: Gebrüder Kröner, 1884.

Afferden, Pieter van (Petrus Apherdianus), *Tyrocinium latinae linguae ... Nunc primum ... accessit ... germanica interpretatio*, Cologne: Johann Gymnich, 1575.

Aldwell, S.W.H., *Wingfield. Its Church, Castle and College*, Ipswich: W.E. Harrison, 1925.

Alexander von Russland [Aleksandr Mikhailovich], *Einst war ich ein Grossfürst*, translated from the English original by Herberth E. Herlitschka, 11th–15th edn, Leipzig: Paul List Verlag, 1933 [1. edn 1932].

Alexander, George E., *Lawn Tennis. Its Founders and Its Early Days*, Lynn, Massachusetts: H.O. Zimman Inc., 1974.

Alexander, George E., *Wingfield, Edwardian Gentleman*, Portsmouth, NH: Peter E. Randall Publisher, 1986.

al-Sayed, Sahira Abdul Hamid, *A Lexicon and Analysis of English Words of Arabic Origin*, PhD thesis, University of Colorado, 1973.

Alston, R.C. (ed.), *Thomas Elyot. The Book Named the Governor. 1531*, English Linguistics 1500–1800. A Collection of Facsimile Reprints, no. 246, Menston: The Scolar Press Ltd., 1970.

Annunziata, Anthony W., 'The *Pas d'Armes* and its occurrences in Malory', in *Studies in Medieval Culture*, 14 (1980), pp. 39–48 and pp. 154–6.

Anstruther, A.W., *History of The Family of Anstruther*, Edinburgh: William Blackwood and Sons, 1923.

Antoniewicz, J., 'Ikonographisches zu Chrestien de Troyes', in *Romanische Forschungen,* 5 (1889), pp. 241–68.

Aphelen, H. von, *Grand Dictionnaire Royal Danois et François*, Première partie. Copenhagen, without publisher's name, 1759.

Ariès, P., *L'enfant et la vie familiale sous l'ancien régime*, [Civilisations d'hier et d'aujourd'hui], Paris: Librairie Plon, 1960.

Arlott, J. (ed.), *The Oxford Companion to Sport & Games*, Oxford: Oxford University Press, 1975.

Artusi, L. and S. Gabbrielli, *L'antico gioco del calcio in Firenze*, Florence: Edizioni della Meridiana, 1971.

Auta, J.M.H., *Un ancestral juego Canario. La pelotamano*, Las Palmas de Gran Canaria: San Nicolás, S.A., 1989.

Baddeley, W., *Lawn Tennis*, London: George Routledge & Sons, Ltd., 1895; 4th edn with corrections 1910.

Badstübner, E., *Klosterkirchen im Mittelalter. Die Baukunst der Reformorden*, 2nd edn with corrections, Munich: Verlag C.H. Beck, 1985.

Baer, L., 'Skizzen vom Bad Homburger Sportsleben', in *Sport im Bild,* 2 (1896), no. 16, p. 248.

Baksh, T., 'Jai Alai of the Basques', in: *Proceedings of the IX International Hispa Congress*, Lisbon: Ponticor, Lda., 1982, pp. 27–34.

Bal, W., 'Sur le vocabulaire du jeu de balle dans l'Ouest-Wallon', in *Mélanges de linguistique romane offerts à M. Jean Haust*, Liège: H. Vaillant-Carmanne, S.A., 1939, pp. 21–9.

Balck, V., *Illustrerad Idrottsbok. Handledning olika grenar af idrott och lekar*, Stockholm: C.E. Fritze's K. Hofbokhandel, 1886.

Baltzell, E.D., *Sporting Gentlemen. Men's Tennis from the Age of Honor to the Cult of the Superstar*, New York: The Free Press, 1996.

Bambagini, M., *Vetulonia-Colonna*, Grosseto, 1979.

Banks, M. Macleod, (ed.), *An Alphabet of Tales. An English Translation of the Alphabetum Narrationum of Etienne de Besançon. From Additional MS. 25,719 of the British Museum*, Early English Text Society, o.s. 126 and 127, 2 vols, London: K. Paul, Trench, Trübner & Co., 1904–1905.

Barber, R. and J. Barker, *Tournaments, Jousts, Chivalry and Pageants in the Middle Ages*, Woodbridge: The Boydell Press, 1989.

Barde, C., *Fédération Internationale de Lawn Tennis 1913–1963. Histoire d'un demi-siècle*, [without place and year of publication; presumably 1963].

Barde, C., 'The International Lawn Tennis Federation', in Deutscher Tennis Bund (ed.), *Amtliches Tennis-Jahrbuch 1964/65 des Deutschen Tennis Bundes*, Göttingen: Martin Sass & Co., pp. 12–17.

Bardi, G.M., *Discorso sopra il giuoco del calcio fiorentino (1580)*, in Carlo Bascetta (ed.), *Sport e giuochi. Trattati e scritti dal XV al XVIII secolo*, 2 vols, Milan: Edizioni Il Polifilo, 1978, vol. 1, pp. 119–62.

Barker, J.R.V., *The Tournament in England 1100–1400*, Woodbridge: Boydell & Brewer Ltd., 1986.

Barrett, J., *100 Wimbledon Championships. A Celebration*, London: Willow Books; William Collins Sons & Co. Ltd, 1986.

Barry, P.M., 'The First National "Open" Lawn Tennis Tournament in America', in *The Tennis Collector,* 4 (December 1988), pp. [10–12].

Bartels, E., 'Bundeserinnerungen aus der Vorkriegszeit', in *Tennis und Golf,* 4 (1927), pp. 320–3.

Bartels, E., 'Zur Gründung eines deutschen Lawn-Tennisverbandes', in *Sport im Wort,* no. 4 (1902), Friday, 24 January 1902, p. 46.

Bartlett, V., *The Past of Pastimes*, London: Chatto & Windus, 1969.

Bascetta, C. (ed.), *Sport e Giuochi. Trattati e Scritti dal XV al XVIII Secolo,* 2 vols, Milan: Edizioni Il Polifilo, 1978.

Bath, M., 'Tennis in the Emblem Books', in Butler and Wordie, op. cit., pp. 44–67.

Bauer, G.G., 'Das f.e. Salzburger Hofballhaus 1620/25–1775', in *Homo Ludens,* 6, Ball- und Kugelspiele, Internationale Beiträge des Institutes für Spielforschung und Spielpädagogik an der Hochschule 'Mozarteum' Salzburg, 1996, pp. 107–48.

Bauer, G.G., 'Das Salzburger Ballhaus 1625(?)-1775', in *Salzburg Archiv. Schriften des Vereines Freunde der Salzburger Geschichte,* 16 (1993) pp. 107–24.

Bauer, M., *Christoph Weigel (1654–1725), Kupferstecher und Kunsthändler in Augsburg und Nürnberg*, PhD thesis, in *Archiv für Geschichte des Buchwesens,* 23 (1982), col. 693–1186.

Behrens, H.O., 'Gründung einer Hamburger Lawn-Tennis-Gilde', in *Sport im Wort,* no. 2 (1902), Friday, 10 January 1902, p. 21f.

Behrens, H.O., *Leitung grosser Lawn-Tennis-Turniere*, Baden-Baden: Verlag von Emil Sommermeyer, 1904.

Behrens, H.O., 'Aus guten alten Tennis-Zeiten', in *Tennis und Golf,* 4 (1927), pp. 323–5.

Bell, E. (ed.), *Handbook of Athletic Sports*, vol. 1: *Cricket - Lawn Tennis - etc.*, London: George Bell & Sons, 1890.

Bender, J.G., *Kurzer Unterricht dess lobwürdigen, von vielen hohen Stands-Personen beliebten Exercitii des Ballen-Spiels*, Nuremberg: Andreas Knorzen, 1680. [Facsimile reprint with an introduction by Manfred Zollinger in: *Homo Ludens,* 6, Ball- und Kugelspiele, Internationale Beiträge des Institutes für Spielforschung

und Spielpädagogik an der Hochschule 'Mozarteum' Salzburg, 1996, pp. 271–90.]

Beneke, L., *Lawn Tennis. Anleitung und Beschreibung*, 2nd edn, Dresden: Verlag von Johannes Henkler, 1892.

Bennett, M., 'John Audeley: Some New Evidence on his Life and Work', in *The Chaucer Review,* 16 (1981), pp. 344–55.

Benson, L.D. (ed.), *The Riverside Chaucer*, 3rd edn, New York: Houghton Mifflin Company, 1987.

Bentley, S. (ed.), *Excerpta Historica, or, Illustrations of English History*, London: Richard Bentley, 1833.

Bergman, C.J., *Gotländska Skildringar och Minnen*, Visby: Gotlands Allehandas Tryckeri, 1882.

Bergvall, E. (ed.), *The Fifth Olympiad. The Official Report of the Olympic Games of Stockholm 1912*, Issued by the Swedish Olympic Committee. Translated by Edward Adams-Ray, Stockholm: Wahlström & Widstrand, 1912.

Berkenvelder, F.C., 'Frieslands Handel in de Late Middeleeuwen', in *Economisch-Historisch Jaarboek,* 29 (1963), pp. 136–87.

Besant, Sir Walter, *London in the Time of the Tudors*, London: Adam & Charles Black, 1904.

Beyrer, K. (ed.), *Die Reise nach Tübingen. Stadtansichten zwischen 1700 und 1850*, Tübingen: Gunter Narr Verlag, 1987.

Blazy, E., *La Pelote Basque*, Bayonne: Imprimerie S. Sordes, 1929.

Blömeke, B.L. and R. Huber, *Festschrift zum 75jährigen Jubiläum. Tennis-Club 1899 e.V. Blau-Weiss Berlin*, Berlin: Brüder Hartmann, 1974.

Boehm, L., 'Das mittelalterliche Erziehungs- und Bildungswesen', in *Propyläen Geschichte der Literatur,* vol. 2, *Die mittelalterliche Welt*, Berlin: Ullstein, 1982, pp. 143–81.

Boland, J.P.M., *Bonn and Athens Diary* [1896]. Original manuscript in the possession of the IOC, Lausanne.

Boland, J.P.M., 'Obituary for Fr Edward Pereira', in *The Oratory School Magazine,* 153 (1993), p. 24.

Boland, J.P.M., 'Patrick Joseph Boland (1869–1940)', in *The Oratory School Magazine,* 153 (1993), pp. 6–16.

Bolaños Cacho, R., *Reglamento de Pelota Mixteca*, Oaxaca: Talleres Graficos del Gobierno del Estado, 1946.

Bolland, J., *Hamburgische Burspraken 1346 bis 1594*, Veröffentlichungen aus dem Staatsarchiv der Freien und Hansestadt Hamburg, 6, 2 Parts, Hamburg: Christians, 1960.

Bombin Fernandez, L. and R. Bozas-Urrutia, *El Gran libro de la pelota*, Federación Internacional de Pelota, 2 vols, Madrid: Tipografia Artistica, 1976.

Bondt, C. de, 'De kaatsbanen in Den Haag. Een onderzoek naar de orsprong van het tennisspel', in *Holland. Regionaal-historisch tijdschrift,* 22 (1990), pp. 83–101.

Bondt, C. de, 'Kaetsen met den Raquette. Een onderzoek naar het tennisspel in Leiden in de 17de en 18de eeuw', in *Leids Jaarboekje* (1993), pp. 67–86.

Bondt, C. de, *'Heeft yemant lust met bal, of met reket te spelen ...?' Tennis in Nederland tussen 1500 en 1800*, Hilversum: Uitgeverij Verloren, 1993.

Bonhomme, G., *De la paume au tennis*, Paris: Gallimard, 1991.

Boon, K.G. de (ed.), *Hollstein's Dutch and Flemish Etchings, Engravings and Woodcuts ca. 1450–1700*, vol. XVI. *De Passe*, Amsterdam: Van Gendt & Co., 1974.

Boon, K.G. de and J. Verbeek (eds), *Dutch and Flemish Etchings, Engravings and Woodcuts ca. 1450–1700*, vol. XV. *Van Ostade-de Passe*, Amsterdam: Menno Hertzberger & Co., no year.

Borger, D. de, *Kaatsport in Vlaanderen*, Serie der Vlaamse Volkssport Dossiers no. 2, Brussels: BLOSO, 1981.

Borghouts, J.J., 'The Evil Eye of Apopis', in *Journal of Egyptian Archaeology,* 59 (1973), pp. 114–51.

Bornstein, D. (ed.), *The Middle English Translation of Christine de Pisan's Livre du corps de policie*, Heidelberg: Carl Winter, 1977.

Bouchel, L. [Laurentius Bochellus], *Decretorum Ecclesiæ gallicanæ ... libri VIII*, Paris: apud B. Maceum, 1609.

Bouissounouse, J., *Jeux et travaux d'après un livre d'heures du XVᵉ siècle*, Paris: G. Jeanbin, 1925.

Breuker, P., *Keatserstaal*, Estrikken - Teksten en stúdzjes op it méd fan de Fryske taal en skriftekennisse - númer LXII, Groningen: Frysk Ynstitut oan de Ryksuniversiteit te Grins, 1983.

Breuker, P., *Boppe! In blomlêzing út de Fryske keatsliteratuer*, Drachten: A.J. Osinga Uitgeverij, 1987.

Breuker, P., 'Belgyske keatsers op de PC fan 1888', in *Wis-In*, 3 (July 1988), pp. 35–9.

Brewster, P.G., *Games and Sports in Shakespeare*, Helsinki: Helsingin Liikekirjapaino OY, 1959.

Brie, F.W.D. (ed.), *The Brut or The Chronicles of England*, EETS, o.s., 131 and 135, 2 vols, London: Kegan Paul, Trench, Trübner & Co., Ltd., 1906–1908.

Bröring, J., *Das Saterland. Eine Darstellung von Land, Leben, Leuten in Wort und Bild*, Schriften des Oldenburger Landesvereins für Altertumskunde und Landesgeschichte. XV, 2 vols, Oldenburg: Gerhard Stalling, 1897–1901.

Broughton, B.B., *Dictionary of Medieval Knighthood and Chivalry*, New York: Greenwood Press, 1986.

Brunner, K. (ed.), *Der mittelenglische Versroman über Richard Löwenherz*, Vienna: Wilhelm Braumüller, 1913.

Buffard, L., 'Le choix d'un sport', in *La longue paume. Bulletin trimestriel officiel de la Fédération Française de Longue Paume,* 2 (1939–1947), special edition, pp. 52–6.

Buffard, P., *Notions historiques sur la longue paume*, Fédération Française de Longue Paume [after 1970].

Bullough, G. (ed.), *Narrative and Dramatic Sources of Shakespeare*, 8 vols, London: Routledge and Kegan Paul, 1957–1975.

Burchfield, R.W. (ed.), *A Supplement to the Oxford English Dictionary*, 4 vols, Oxford: Clarendon Press, 1972–1986.

Butler, L. St John and P. Wordie (eds), *The Royal Game*, Edinburgh: Bookworm Typesetting Ltd, 1989.

Cabrera Ruiz, P., O.T. Bonilla and J. Perdomo, *El juego de la pelotamano en Lanzarote*, thesis; typescript of the Instituto de Educación Física de Canarias, Universidad Politécnica de Canarias, 1987–1988.

Calder, R. and M.A. Screech (eds), *François Rabelais. Gargantua*, Textes Littéraires Français, Geneva: Librairie Droz, 1970.

Caretti, L., 'Noterelle tennistiche', in *Lingua Nostra,* 12, 3 (1951), pp. 77–80.

Carew, R., *The Survey of Cornwall*, London: John Jaggard, 1602.

Cawley, A.C. (ed.), *The Wakefield Pageants in the Towneley Cycle*, Old and Middle English Texts, Manchester: Manchester University Press, 1958.

Cecilie, Crown Princess, *Erinnerungen*, Leipzig: Verlag K. F. Koehler, 1932.

Chambers, J.K. and P. Trudgill, *Dialectology*, Cambridge Textbooks in Linguistics, Cambridge: Cambridge University Press, 1980.

Champion, P. (ed.), *Charles d'Orléans. Poésies*, Les Classiques français du Moyen Age, 34, 56, 2 vols, Paris: Champion, 1923–1927; reprinted 1982.

Champion, P., *Vie de Charles d'Orléans (1394–1465)*, Paris: Honoré Champion, Editeur, 1911.

Chevalier, C. (ed.), *Dom Edmond Martène. Histoire de l'Abbaye de Marmoutier*, 2 vols, Tours: Guilland-Verger; Goerget-Joubert, 1874–1875.

Christ, K., 'Altheidelberger Ballspiele und Ballenhäuser', in *Alt-Heidelberg*, weekly supplement to the daily *Heidelberger Tageblatt*, no. 8, 23 April 1921, p. 1f.

Christmann, E., *Pfälzisches Wörterbuch*, Wiesbaden, Steiner, 1965.

Clemen, P. (ed.), *Die Kunstdenkmäler der Stadt Köln. Ergänzungsband: Die ehemaligen Kirchen, Klöster, Hospitäler und Schulbauten der Stadt Köln*, edited by L. Arntz, H. Neu and H. Vogts, Die Kunstdenkmäler der Rheinprovinz, vol. 7, Part III, Düsseldorf: L. Schwann, 1937.

Clerici, G., *500 Jahre Tennis*, Berlin: Ullstein, 1979; reprinted 1987.

Cochet, H. and J. Feuillet, *Tennis. Du jeu mondain au sport athlétique*, Paris: Stock, 1980.

Coen, B. de, *La langue actuelle du tennis. Influences réciproques de la langue technique et de la langue commune*, thesis for the degree of a licentiate of Romance Philology at the Catholic University of Louvain, Faculty of Letters and Philosophy, 1988.

Colas, L., *La tombe Basque. Recueil d'inscriptions funéraires et domestiques du Pays Basque Français*, Paris: Honoré Champion, Éditeur, 1923.

Considine, T., *The Language of Sport*, New York: World Almanac Publications, 1982.

Constans, L. (ed.), *Le roman de Troie par Benoit de Sainte-Maure*, 6 vols, Paris: Firmin Didot, 1904–1912.

Coopland, G.W. (ed.), *Philippe de Mézières, Chancellor of Cyprus: Le songe du vieil pelerin*, 2 vols, Cambridge: Cambridge University Press, 1969.

Cordier, M., [*Maturini Corderii*] *de corrupti sermonis emendatione, & Latinè loquendi ratione liber unus*, 3rd edn, Paris: ex officiis Roberti Stephani, 1536.

Corominas, J. and J.A. Pascual, *Diccionario Crítico Etimológico Castellano e Hispánico*, 5 vols, Madrid: Editorial Gredos, S.A., 1984–1986.

Coubertin, P. de, 'Le Congrès [Olympique] à Paris', in *Bulletin du Comité International des Jeux Olympiques* 1 (1896), pp. [1–4].

Coulton, G.G. (ed.), *Life in the Middle Ages*, 2nd edn, Cambridge: Cambridge University Press, 1928; new edition in 2 vols, 1967.

Cowper, F.A.G. (ed.), *Ille et Galeron par Gautier d'Arras*, Paris: Picard, 1956.

Craigie, J. (ed.), *The Basilicon Doron of King James VI*, Edinburgh: William Blackwood & Sons Ltd., 1944.

Craigie, W.A., *A Dictionary of the Older Scottish Tongue*, vol. 1 Chicago, 1937.

Crapelet, G.-A., *Le Pas d'Armes de la Bergère*, 2nd edn, Paris: Imprimerie de Crapelet, 1835.

Crawley, A.E., 'The Invention of Lawn Tennis. An Historical Account', in *Lawn Tennis and Badminton*, April 10 (1913), pp. 176–8; and April 17 (1913), pp. 195–8.

Cummings, P., *American Tennis. The Story of a Game and Its People*, Boston: Little, Brown & Company, 1957.

Dahlgren, R. *et al.* (eds), *Pärkspelet*, Visby: Gotlandstryck, 1975.

d'Allemagne, H. R., *Sports et jeux d'adresse*, Paris: Hachette & Cie, 1903.

Davis, D.F., 'The Establishment of an International Trophy', in *Fifty Years of Lawn Tennis in the United States*, Norwood, MA: Plimpton Press, 1931, pp. 69–72.

Decker, W., *Annotierte Bibliographie zum Sport im alten Ägypten*, St. Augustin: Verlag Hans Richarz, 1978.

Decker, W., *Sport und Spiel im Alten Ägypten*, Munich: Verlag C.H. Beck, 1987.

Decker-Hauff, H. and W. Setzler (eds), *Die Universität Tübingen von 1477 bis 1977 in Bildern und Dokumenten*, 500 Jahre Eberhard-Karls-Universität Tübingen 3, Tübingen: Attempto Verlag GmbH, 1977.

del Lungo, I. and G. Volpi (eds), *La cronica domestica di messer Donato Velluti*, Biblioteca di opere inedite o rare di ogni secolo della letteratura Italiana 2, Florence: G. C. Sansoni, 1914.

Desees, J., *Les jeux sportifs de pelote-paume en Belgique du XIVᵉ au XIXᵉ siècle*, Brussels: Imprimerie du Centenaire, 1967.

Desiderii Erasmi Roterodami Opera Omnia, Leiden: Petrus van der Aa, 1703; rpt. in 10 vols, Hildesheim: G. Olm, 1961.

Diffloth, P., 'La balle au tamis', in *La Vie au Grand Air,* 205 (1902), p. 557f.

Dijkstra, W., *Friesch Woordenboek,* 3 vols, Leeuwarden: Meijer & Schaafsma, 1900–1911.

Dinneen, F.P., S. J., *An Introduction to General Linguistics,* Washington, DC: Georgetown University Press, 1967.

Dodt van Flensburg, J. J. (ed.), *Archief voor Kerkelijke en Wereldsche Geschiedenissen, inzonderheit van Utrecht,* 5th Part, Utrecht: N. van der Monde, 1846.

Doerry, K., 'Die Rennen des Sport-Club "Germania" in Hamburg', in *Sport im Bild* 1 (1895), p. 240.

Doerry, K., 'Die Weltmeisterschaften in Paris', in *Sport im Wort,* no. 29, (1900), Thursday, 19 July 1900, pp. 285–8.

Douteil, H., C.S.SP. (ed.), *Iohannis Beleth. Summa de ecclesiasticis officiis,* Corpus christianorum. Continuatio mediaevalis, vols XLI and XLIA, 2 vols, Turnhout: Brepols, 1976.

Drost, J.W.P., *Het Nederlandsch Kinderspel vóór de Zeventiende Eeuw,* 's-Gravenhage: Martinus Nijhoff, 1914.

Dubois, L'abbé Louis, *Histoire de l'Abbaye de Morimond,* Paris: Sagnier et Bray, 1851.

Dubois, L'abbé Louis, *Geschichte der Abtei Morimond ... Nach der zweiten Auflage aus dem Französischen übersetzt von Dr. K.,* Münster: Aschendorffsche Buchhandlung, 1855.

Du Cange (Charles du Fresne) (ed.), *Glossarium Mediae et Infimae Latinitatis,* 10 vols, Niort: L. Favre, 1883–1887; reprint Graz: Akademische Druck- und Verlagsanstalt, 1954.

Dugdale, W., *The History of St. Paul's Cathedral, in London, from its Foundation,* London: Hughes, Harding, Mavor, and Jones, 1818.

Dunstan, G.R. (ed.), *The Register of Edmund Lacy Bishop of Exeter 1420–1455,* Canterbury and York Society, 3 vols, Torquay: Devonshire Press, 1963–1967.

Eberl, I. *et al., 150 Jahre Promotion an der Wirtschaftswissenschaftlichen Fakultät der Universität Tübingen. 1830–1980,* Stuttgart: Konrad Theiss Verlag, 1984.

Ebhardt, C., 'Karl v. Jecklin', in *Tennis und Golf,* 4 (1927), p. 326f.

Eeghen, P. van and J.Ph. van der Kellen, *Het Werk van Jan en Casper Luyken,* 2 vols, Amsterdam: Frederik Muller & Cº., 1905.

Eichberg, H., *Leistung, Spannung, Geschwindigkeit. Sport und Tanz im gesellschaftlichen Wandel des 18./19. Jahrhunderts,* Stuttgarter Beiträge zur Geschichte und Politik, Band 12, Stuttgart: Klett-Cotta, 1978.

Eichel, W. *et al., Geschichte der Körperkultur in Deutschland von 1789 bis 1917,* Geschichte der Körperkultur, vol. II, Berlin: Sportverlag, 1973.

Einhundertfünfzig Jahre Oberösterreichisches Landesmuseum, edited by Oberösterreichisches Landesmuseum, Linz, 1983.

Eitel, R., 'Mit Frauen fing alles an', in L. Cremer *et al.* (eds), *Faszination Basketball,* Bremerhaven: Nordwestdeutsche Verlagsgesellschaft, 1991, p. 24.

Emmerig, O., 'The Bataile of Agyncourt' im Lichte geschichtlicher Quellenwerke, doctoral thesis Munich, Nuremberg: R. Wieser, 1906.

Emmerig, O., 'Dariusbrief und Tennisballgeschichte', in *Englische Studien,* 39 (1908), pp. 362–401.

Endrei, W. and L. Zolnay, *Fun and Games in Old Europe,* Budapest: Corvina Kiadó, 1986.

Ertl, H., 'Der Lawn-Tennis-Club "Rot-Weiss" Baden-Baden', in Roderich Menzel, *Deutsches Tennis,* 2 vols, Gräfelfing near Munich: Aeneas-Verlag, 1955–1961, vol. 1, pp. 413–20.

Eskénazi, A. (ed.), *Chrétien de Troyes. Yvain ou Le Chevalier au Lion,* Paris: Librairie Larousse, 1970.

Essenwein, A., 'Über einige mittelalterliche Elfenbeinschnitzwerke und besonders über ein Spiegelgehäuse im Cistercienser-Stifte Reun in Steiermark', in *Anzeiger für Kunde der deutschen Vorzeit,* new series, 13 (1866), pp. 202–6.

Esser, F.W., *Otto Froitzheim. Ein Tennisleben,* Heidelberg: Verlag Hermann Meister, 1926.

Evans, G. Blakemore *et al.* (eds), *The Riverside Shakespeare,* Boston: Houghton Mifflin Company, 1974.

Eybl, F.M., *Abraham a Sancta Clara. Vom Prediger zum Schriftsteller,* Tübingen: Max Niemeyer Verlag, 1992.

Félibien, M. and G.-A. Lobineau, *Histoire de la Ville de Paris,* 5 vols, Paris: Guillaume Desprez et Jean Desessartz, 1725.

Fichard, R. Baron von, 'Continental Correspondence', in *Pastime,* 2 October 1899, p. 228.

Fichard, R. Baron von, 'Deutsche Lawn-Tennis-Ausdrücke', in *Zeitschrift des Allgemeinen Deutschen Sprachvereins,* 12 (1897), cols 1–7.

Fichard, R. Baron von, 'Deutsche Spielausdrücke und Redewendungen', in idem (ed.), *Illustriertes Lawn-Tennis-Jahrbuch für das Deutsche Reich, Österreich-Ungarn und die Schweiz,* vol. 10, Baden-Baden: Verlag Emil Sommermeyer, 1904, pp. 117–26.

Fichard, R. Baron von, 'Deutsches Lawn-Tennis-Jahrbuch 1902', in *Sport im Wort,* no. 17 (1902), Friday, 25 April 1902, p. 220f.

Fichard, R. Baron von, 'Lawn-Tennis in Germany', in *Pastime,* 16 April 1890, p. 245.

Fichard, R. Baron von, 'Zur Gründung einer Deutschen Lawn-Tennis Association', in *Sport im Wort,* no. 5 (1902), Friday, 31 January 1902, p. 56f.

Fichard, R. Baron von, *Deutsches Lawn-Tennis-Jahrbuch nebst den officiellen Turnierregeln,* vol. 2, Berlin: Verlag der Redaction von '*Spiel und Sport*', 1895.

Fichard, R. Baron von (ed.), *Deutsches Lawn-Tennis-Jahrbuch,* vols 3 and 4 (1896 and 1897), Berlin: Verlag der Redaction von '*Spiel und Sport*', 1897.

Fichard, R. Baron von (ed.), *Deutsches Lawn-Tennis Jahrbuch 1900. Der Jahrbücher fünfter und sechster Jahrgang,* Baden-Baden: Verlag Emil Sommermeyer, 1900.

Fichard, R. Baron von (ed.), *Deutsches Lawn-Tennis Jahrbuch 1901. Der Jahrbücher siebenter Jahrgang,* Baden-Baden: Verlag Emil Sommermeyer, 1901.

Fichard, R. Baron von (ed.), *Deutsches Lawn-Tennis Jahrbuch 1902. Der Jahrbücher achter Jahrgang,* Baden-Baden: Verlag Emil Sommermeyer, 1902.

Fichard, R. Baron von (ed.), *Erstes deutsches Lawn-Tennis-Jahrbuch nebst den officiellen Spielregeln,* Charlottenburg: Redaktion von '*Spiel und Sport*', 1894.

Fichard, R. Baron von, *Handbuch des Lawn Tennis Spieles,* Baden-Baden: Emil Sommermeyer, 1887 [with supplement 1889].

Fichard, R. Baron von, *Handbuch des Lawn-Tennis Spieles,* 2nd revised edn, Baden-Baden: Emil Sommermeyer, 1892; 4th rev. edn 1902.

Fichard, R. Baron von (ed.), *Illustriertes Lawn-Tennis-Jahrbuch für das Deutsche Reich,* *Österreich-Ungarn und die Schweiz auf das Jahr 1903,* Der Deutschen Lawn-Tennis-Jahrbücher IX. Jahrgang, Baden-Baden: Emil Sommermeyer, 1903.

Fichard, R. Baron von (ed.), *Illustriertes Lawn-Tennis Jahrbuch 1905,* Baden-Baden: Verlag Emil Sommermeyer, 1905.

Fichard, R. Baron von, *Lawn-Tennis,* 3rd improved and augmented edn, Leipzig: Grethlein & Co., 1911.

Fieschi, J.T., *Histoire du sport français de 1870 à nos jours,* Paris: PAC Editions, 1983.

Fifty Years of Lawn Tennis in the United States, Norwood, Massachusetts: Plimpton Press, 1931.

Fink, A., *Die Schwarzschen Trachtenbücher,* Berlin: Deutscher Verein für Kunstwissenschaft, 1963.

Fisher, J.H. (ed.), *The Complete Poetry and Prose of Geoffrey Chaucer,* 2nd edn, New York: Holt, Rinehart and Winston, 1988.

Fleckenstein, J. (ed.), *Das ritterliche Turnier im Mittelalter,* Veröffentlichungen des Max-Planck-Instituts für Geschichte, 80, Göttingen: Vandenhoeck & Ruprecht, 1985.

Flutre, L.-F., *Le parler picard de Mesnil-Martinsart (Somme),* Société de Publications Romanes et Françaises, 51, Geneva: Droz, 1955.

Fossen, R.W. van (ed.), *Eastward Ho. George Chapman, Ben Jonson, John Marston (The Revels Plays),* Manchester: Manchester University Press, 1979.

Foulet, L., *Chrétien de Troyes. Perceval le Gallois ou Le Conte du Graal,* Paris: A.G. Nizet, without year of publication; reprint 1984.

Franco, G., *Habiti d'Huomeni et Donne Venetiane,* Venice: G. Franco, 1610.

Franken, D., *L'œuvre gravé de Van de Passe,* Amsterdam: F. Muller, 1881.

Franklin, A., *Dictionnaire historique des arts, métiers et professions dans Paris depuis le XIIIᵉ siècle,* 2 vols, Paris-Leipzig, 1905–1906; reprint Marseilles: Laffitte Reprints, 1987.

Frederikse, J.A. Roetert. (ed.), *Dat Kaetspel Ghemoralizeert,* Bibliotheek van Middelnederlandsche Letterkunde, Leiden: A.W. Sijthoff's Uitg.-Mij., 1915.

Furnivall, F.J. and J.W. Hales (eds), *The Percy Folio Manuscript,* 4 vols, London: N. Trübner & Co., 1868–1869, new edn by Israel Gollancz, The King's Library. London: De la More Press, 1905–1910.

Furnivall, F.J. (ed.), *The Three Kings' Sons*, Early English Text Society, e.s. 67, London: Kegan Paul, Trench, Trübner & Co., 1895.

Galtier, C., *Le trésor des jeux provençaux*, Collection de Culture Provençale, Vaison-la-Romaine: Imprimerie Macabet Frères, 1952.

Garsault, F.A. de, 'Die Kunst der Ball- und Raquettenmacher und vom Ballspiele. Übersetzt durch Daniel Gottfried Schreiber', in *Schauplatz der Künste und Handwerke*, vol. 7., Leipzig, 1768, pp. 227–76.

Garsault, F.A. de, *The Art of the Tennis-Racket-Maker and of Tennis.*, translated into English by Catherine W. Leftwich, Baltimore, MD: Racquet Sport Information Service, 1977; reprint of the first edition privately printed by Raven Printers Ltd, 1938.

Gastoué, A., *Le Cantique Populaire en France, ses Sources, son Histoire*, Bibliothèque de l'Art Musical Religieux, Lyons: Janin, Frères éditeurs, 1924.

Gay, V., *Glossaire archéologique du moyen âge*, 2 vols, Paris: A. Picard, 1887–1928.

Geerarts, M., *Brugae Flandorum urbs et emporium mercatu, celebre an a chr. nat. 1562*, Bruges: without name of printer, 1562.

Géraud, H., *Paris sous Philippe-le-Bel, d'après des documents originaux et notamment d'après un manuscrit contenant Le Rôle de la Taille imposée sur les habitants de Paris en 1292*, Paris: Imprimerie de Crapelet, 1837.

Gesamtverzeichnis des deutschsprachigen Schrifttums 1700–1910, vol. 10, Munich: K.G. Saur, 1979.

Gibbons, W.G., *The Seeds of Lawn Tennis*, Royal Leamington Spa: Jones-Sands Publishers, 1987.

Gillmeister, H., 'A Tee for Two. On the Origins of Golf', in *Homo Ludens,* 6 (1996), pp. 17–37.

Gillmeister, H., 'Ballspielgedichte des Spätmittelalters und der Renaissance', in Nanda Fischer (ed.), *Sport und Literatur*, dvs-protokolle, no. 23, Clausthal-Zellerfeld: H. Greinert, 1986, pp. 100–25.

Gillmeister, H., 'Challenge Letters from a Medieval Tournament and the Ball-Game of Gotland. A Typological Comparison', in *Stadion,* 16 (1990), pp. 184–222.

Gillmeister, H., 'Das Geheimnis der Miss Duddell', in *Tennis Magazin,* no. 6, June 1994, pp. 112–16.

Gillmeister, H., 'Den skriftliga utmaningen i de gotländska bollspelen. Dess kulturella och historiska innebörd', in *Idrott Historia och Samhälle. Svenska idrottshistoriska föreningens årsskrift 1988*, Helsingborg: Schmidts Boktryckeri AB, 1988, pp. 21–41.

Gillmeister, H., 'Die mittelalterlichen Ballspiele: eine Chronologie ihrer Entwicklung', in *Stadion,* 10 (1984), pp. 77–94.

Gillmeister, H., 'English Editors of German Sporting Journals at the Turn of the Century', in *The Sports Historian. The Journal of the British Society of Sports History*, no. 13 (May 1993), pp. 38–65.

Gillmeister, H., 'Linguistics and Sports Historiography', in *Stadion,* 11 (1985), pp. 31–40.

Gillmeister, H., 'Medieval Sport: Modern Methods of Research, Recent Results and Perspectives', in *The International Journal of the History of Sport,* 5 (1988), pp. 53–68.

Gillmeister, H., 'Mit Kind und Kegel. Eine kleine Wortgeschichte des Kegelns', in *Kegel und Kugel. Ausstellungskatalog des Schweizerischen Sportmuseums*, Basel: Gissler Druck AG, Allschwil, 1985, pp. 10–13.

Gillmeister, H., 'Modern Methods of Research and Medieval Sport, Recent Results and Perspectives', in S. Shimizu (ed.), *Civilization in Sport History. ICOSH Seminar 1986. Report*, Kobe: Nakamura Printing Co., 1987, pp. 32–53.

Gillmeister, H., *Olympisches Tennis. Die Geschichte der olympischen Tennisturniere (1896–1992)*, St. Augustin: Academia Verlag Richarz, 1993.

Gillmeister, H., *Os Métodos de Investigação e o Desporto Medieval: Resultados Recentes e Perspectivas*, Desporto e Sociedade. Antologia de Textos 39, Lisbon: Tip. Minerva do Comércio, 1987.

Gillmeister, H., *Service. Kleine Geschichte der englischen Sprache*, Sprache und Sprachenlernen, vol. 306, Bonn: Ferd. Dümmlers Verlag, 1993.

Gillmeister, H., 'Tennis kam schon früh in Mode. Zur Geschichte der Tenniskleidung', in B. Tietzel (ed.), *Sportswear: zur Geschichte und Entwicklung der Sportkleidung*, Krefeld: Joh. van Acken GmbH u. Co KG, Druckerei und Verlag, 1992, pp. 72–7.

Gillmeister, H., 'The Dissemination of Traditional Games in Europe', in

Committee for the Development of Sport (ed.), *Seminar on Traditional Games*, Vila Real, Portugal, 7–10 November 1988, Lisbon: Direcção-Geral dos Desportos, 1990, pp. 23–37. [French version: 'La dissémination géographique des jeux traditionnels; l'unité et la diversité des jeux traditionnels en Europe', pp. 23–35 of the French part.]

Gillmeister, H., 'The Flemish Ancestry of Early English Ball Games: the Cumulative Evidence', in N. Müller und J.K. Rühl (eds), *Olympic Scientific Congress 1984*, *Sport History. Official Report*, Niederhausen: Schors-Verlag, 1985, pp. 54–74.

Gillmeister, H., 'The Gameless Country Had the Ultimate Game. The Ballgame in Germany's Saterland', in G. Pfister *et al.* (eds), *Spiele der Welt im Spannungsfeld von Tradition und Moderne*, ISHPES-Studies, vol. 1, Part 1, Sankt Augustin: Academia Verlag, 1996, pp. 69–75.

Gillmeister, H., 'The Gift of a Tennis Ball in the Secunda Pastorum: a Sport Historian's View', in *Arete: The Journal of Sport Literature*, 4 (1986), pp. 105–19.

Gillmeister, H., 'The Language of English Sports Medieval and Modern', in *Archiv für das Studium der neueren Sprachen und Literaturen*, 233 (1996), pp. 268–85.

Gillmeister, H., 'The Origin of European Ball Games: a Re-Evaluation and Linguistic Analysis', in *Stadion*, 7 (1981), pp. 19–51.

Gillmeister, H., 'Über Tennis und Tennispunkte. Ein Beitrag der Sprachwissenschaft zur Sportgeschichte', in *Stadion*, 3 (1977), pp. 187–229.

Girvan, R. (ed.), *Ratis Raving*, Edinburgh: Scottish Text Society Publications, 1939.

Gothaisches Genealogisches Taschenbuch der Gräflichen Häuser. Zugleich Adelsmatrikel der Deutschen Adelsgenossenschaft, Teil A, 115. Jahrgang, 1942, Gotha: Justus Perthes, 1942.

Gothein, M.L., *Geschichte der Gartenkunst*, 2 vols, Jena: Eugen Diederichs, 1914.

Götland, J. (ed.), *Idrott och Lek*, Nordisk Kultur, vol. 24, Oslo: Det Mallingske Bogtrykkeri, 1933.

Gougaud, L., 'La soule en Bretagne et les jeux similaires du Cornwall et du Pays de Galles', in *Annales de Bretagne*, 27 (1912), pp. 571–604.

Gramm, E., 'Eingesandt', in *Sport im Wort*, no. 48 (1901), Thursday, 28 November 1901, p. 643f.

Gramm, E., 'Eingesandt', in *Sport im Wort*, no. 50 (1901), Thursday, 12 December 1901, p. 674f.

Grass, F., 'Dr. Hippolytus Guarinonius zu Hoffberg und Volderthurn 1571–1654', in A. Dörrer *et al.* (eds), *Hippolytus Guarinonius (1571–1654). Zur 300. Wiederkehr seines Todestages*, Innsbruck: Universitätsverlag Wagner, 1954, pp. 9–17.

Grauhan, K., 'Geschichte der deutschen Meisterschaften im Herren-Einzelspiel, in *Tennis und Golf*, 3 (1926), no. 24, pp. 556–60.

Grauhan, K., 'Die Geschichte der deutschen Meisterschaften im Herreneinzelspiel', in Gruber, *Amtliches Tennis-Hand- und Jahrbuch*, 1927, pp. 72–86.

Grauhan, K., 'Die Geschichte des Homburger Pokals', in Gruber, *Amtliches Tennis-Hand-und Jahrbuch*, 1927, pp. 92–100.

Grauhan, K., 'Zur Geschichte der deutschen Damenmeisterschaft', in *Tennis und Golf*, 6 (1929), no. 23, 2 August 1929, p. 603f.

Greene, H. Plunket, *Where the Bright Waters Meet*, London: P. Allan & Co., 1924; reprinted 1946.

Greene, R. Leighton (ed.), *The Early English Carols*, 2nd edn, Oxford: Clarendon Press, 1977.

Greg, W.W. (ed.), *Porter, Henry. The Two Angry Women of Abington 1599*, The Malone Society Reprints, London: Oxford University Press, 1912.

Greg, W.W. (ed.), *Chapman, George. An Humorous Day's Mirth 1599*, The Malone Society Reprints, Oxford: Oxford University Press, 1937.

Greimas, A.J., *Dictionnaire de l'ancien français jusqu'au milieu du XIVᵉ siècle*, 2nd edn, Paris: Librairie Larousse, 1968.

Grigson, G. (ed.), *The Faber Book of Popular Verse*, London: Faber and Faber, 1971.

Grimm, J. and Grimm, W., *Deutsches Wörterbuch*, 16 vols, Leipzig: Hirzel, 1854–1960.

Gröber, G., *Grundriss der Romanischen Philologie*, vol. 2, 1st Part, Strasbourg: Karl J. Trübner, 1902.

Grosart, A.B. (ed.), *The Complete Works in Prose and Verse of Francis Quarles*, 3 vols, Edinburgh: T. and A. Constable, 1880–1881.

Grosart, A.B. (ed.), *The Non-Dramatic Works of Thomas Dekker*, 5 vols, New York: Russell & Russell Inc, 1884–1886, reprinted 1963.

Grosche, H., *Geschichte der Stadt Bad Homburg vor der Höhe*, vol. 3. *Die Kaiserzeit*, Frankfurt a.M.: Verlag Waldemar Kramer, 1986.

Grössing, S., 'Pallone - ein aristokratisches Spiel', in *Homo Ludens,* 6 (1996), pp. 79–106.

Gruber, F. (ed.), *Amtliches Tennis-Hand- und Jahrbuch 1927 zum Jubiläum 1902–1927 des Deutschen Tennis Bundes*, Heidelberg: Verlag Hermann Meister, 1927.

Gruber, F., 'Graf Victor Voss †', in *Tennis und Golf,* 13 (1936), no. 33, 1 December 1936, p. 528f.

Guarinonius, H., *Die Grewel der Verwüstung Menschlichen Geschlechts*, Ingolstadt: Andreas Angermayr, 1610.

Guigniaut, J.D. and J. Natalis de Wailly (eds), *Recueil des Historiens des Gaules et de la France*, vol. 21, Paris: Imprimerie Impériale, 1855.

Guiney, D., *Gold, Silver, Bronze*, Dublin: Sportsworld, no year of publication.

Gumpelzhaimer, G., *Gymnasma de exercitiis academicorum*, Argentinae: E. Zetznerus, 1621.

Gurney, G.N., *The Racket*, Great Bromley, (privately printed), 1991.

Gurney, G.N., 'Tennis ging ganz heimlich los', in *Tennis Magazin*, no. 10, October 1992, pp. 84–7.

Gurney, G.N., *Table Tennis. The Early Years*, London: The International Table Tennis Federation, no year of publication.

Gustavson, H. (ed.), *Svenska Lekar, 1. Gotländska Lekar*, Kungl. Gustav Adolfs Akademien, Uppsala: Almquist & Wiksells, 1948.

Gustavson, H. *et al.* (eds), *Gotländsk Ordbok*, Uppsala: A.-B. Lundequistska Bokhandeln, 1936–1945.

Habenicht, R.E. (ed.), *John Heywood's A Dialogue of Proverbs. 1546*, Berkeley: University of California Press, 1963.

Halkin, L.-E. *et al.* (eds), *Colloquia*, [*Desiderii Erasmi*]', in *Opera Omnia Desiderii Erasmi Roterodami*, I.3.D., After the edition by Jean Froben. Basle, 1522, Amsterdam: North-Holland Publishing Company, 1972, pp. 121–222.

Hamer, E.U., *Die Anfänge der 'Spielbewegung' in Deutschland*, Beiträge und Quellen zu Sport and Gesellschaft, vol. 3., London: Arena Publications 1989.

Hamilton, C., *Modern Germanies. As Seen by an Englishwoman*, London: J.M. Dent & Sons, 1931.

Hanak, A., *Leibesübungen der Juden im Mittelalter und in der frühen Neuzeit*, Tel Aviv: Hauser, 1986.

Hansen, W., *Kalenderminiaturen der Stundenbücher. Mittelalterliches Leben im Jahreslauf*, Munich: Verlag Georg D.W. Callwey, 1984.

Häpke, R., 'Friesen and Sachsen im Ostseeverkehr des 13. Jahrhunderts', in *Hansische Geschichtsblätter,* 19 (1913), pp. 163–94.

Harrison, H., *Surnames of the United Kingdom. A Concise Etymological Dictionary*, 2 vols, London, 1912–1918; reprinted in one volume, Baltimore, MD: Genealogical Publishing Company, 1969.

Harvey, P., *The Oxford Companion to English Literature*, 4th edn, Oxford: Clarendon Press, 1967.

Haslam, R., 'Wingfield College, Suffolk', in *Country Life,* 171 (1982), no. 4403, 7 January 1982, pp. 18–21.

Hayakawa, S.I., *Language in Thought and Action*, 4th edn, New York: Harcourt Brace Jovanovich, Inc., 1978.

Hayakawa, S.I., *Semantik. Sprache im Denken and Handeln*, 2nd edn, Darmstadt: Verlag Darmstädter Blätter, no year of publication.

Hearne, T., *Thomas de Elmham vita & gesta Henrici Quinti*, Oxford: E. Theatro Sheldoniano, 1727.

Heathcote, C.G. *et al.*, 'Lawn Tennis', in Heathcote, J.M. *et al.*, *Tennis, Lawn Tennis, Rackets, Fives*, London: Longmans, Green & Co, 1903, pp. 125–349.

Heathcote, J.M. *et al.*, *Tennis, Lawn Tennis, Rackets, Fives*, London: Longmans, Green & Co, 1903.

Hebel, J.W. *et al.* (eds), *The Works of Michael Drayton*, 5 vols, Oxford: Basil Blackwell, 1931–1941.

Hécart, G.-A., *Dictionnaire Rouchi-Français*, 5th edn, Valenciennes: Lemaître, 1854, new imprint Geneva: Slatkine, 1978.

Hedges, M., *The Concise Dictionary of Tennis*, London: Bison Books Limited, 1978.

Heineken, Ph., *Lawn-Tennis. Seine Geschichte and Taktik*, Der Sportspiele im Freien III. Band, Stuttgart: Verlag von Gustav Weise, 1900.

Hellenga, R.R., 'The Tournaments in Malory's Morte D'Arthur', in *Forum for Modern Language Studies,* 10 (1974), pp. 67–78.

Henderson, R.W., *Ball, Bat and Bishop. The Origin of Ball Games*, New York: Rockport Press, 1947; reprinted Detroit: Gale Research Co., 1974.

Henry, A. (ed.), *Sarrasin. Le roman du Hem*, Travaux de la Faculté de Philosophie et Lettres de l'Université de Bruxelles, vol. IX, Brussels: Editions de la Revue de l'Université de Bruxelles, 1939.

Hepp, F., *Religion und Herrschaft in der Kurpfalz um 1660 aus der Sicht des Heidelberger Kirchenrates Dr. Marcus zum Lamm (1544–1606)*, doctoral thesis (educational sciences) at the Pädagogische Hochschule Heidelberg, 1992.

Hepp, F., *Matthaeus Merian in Heidelberg. Ansichten einer Stadt*, Heidelberg: HVA 1993.

Herford, C.H. and P. Simpson (eds), *Ben Jonson*, 11 vols, Oxford: Clarendon Press, 1925–1952.

Herrmann, A., *Ballhäuser and die Strassburger Ballhausgasse*, Collection d'études économiques, médicales et sociales, 2 vols, Strasbourg: Imprimerie O. Boehm, 1939.

Hessen, R., 'Deutsche Nationalmeisterschaften', in *Der Lawn-Tennis-Sport,* 1 (1904), no. 3, 12 May 1904, p. 25.

Hessen, R., *Technik and Taktik. Ein Anleitungsbuch für Lawn-Tennis-Spieler*, Baden-Baden: Emil Sommermeyer, 1904.

Heyden, J. von der, *Speculum Cornelianum … Jetzt auffs newe … An Tag geben …,* Strasbourg, 1618; photolithographic facsimile edition by Edmond Stribeck, Neudorf-Strasbourg: Hagemann & Co., 1879.

Hilka, A. (ed.), *Der Percevalroman (Li contes del Graal) von Christian von Troyes*, (Christian von Troyes sämtliche Werke V.), Halle a.d. Saale: Max Niemeyer Verlag, 1932.

Hillyard, G.W., *Forty Years of First-Class Lawn Tennis*, London: Williams & Norgate, Ltd, 1924.

History of Services of Gazetted Officers employed under the Government of the North-West Provinces and Oudh, 6th edn, Allahabad: North Western Provinces and Oudh Government Press, 1887.

Hitti, P.K., *The Arabs: A Short History*, London: Macmillan & Co., 1948.

Hobart, C., 'Lawn-Tennis in Continental Europe', in *Outing. An Illustrated Magazine of Sport, Travel, Adventure and Country Life*, 38 (1901), no. 6, pp. 685–9.

Höfer, J. and K. Rahner (eds), *Lexikon für Theologie and Kirche*, 14 vols, 2nd edn, Freiburg im Breisgau: Verlag Herder, 1957–1968; special edition 1986.

Hofer, W.A., *Ein Jahrhundert Tennis in Berlin. 100 Jahre Lawn-Tennis-Turnier-Club Rot-Weiss Berlin*, Berlin: Nicolaische Verlagsbuchhandlung Beuermann GmbH, 1996.

Hoffmann von Fallersleben, A.H. (ed.), *Horae Belgicae. Glossarium Belgicum*, Pars Septima, 2nd edn, Hanover: Rümpler, 1856.

Hoffmann von Fallersleben, A.H., *Horae Belgicae. Studio atque opere Hoffmanni Fallerslebensis. 1836–1862*, XII Partes. 3 vols, Amsterdam: Editions Rodopi, 1968.

Hoffmann, W., 'Zur Geschichte der Kölner Stadtsprache: Was man weiss, was man wissen möchte', in G. Bauer (ed.), *Stadtsprachenforschung unter besonderer Berücksichtigung der Verhältnisse der Stadt Straßburg im Spätmittelalter und früher Neuzeit*, Göppinger Arbeiten zur Germanistik, no. 488, Göppingen: Kümmerle, 1988, pp. 95–121.

Hoffmeister, K., *August Hermann 1835–1906. Pionier des Mädchenturnens und braunschweigischer Schriftsteller*, Braunschweig: Stadtbibliothek, 1986.

Hollstein, F.W.H., *Dutch and Flemish Etchings, Engravings and Woodcuts ca. 1450–1700*, vol. 3, *Boekhorst-Brueghel*, Amsterdam: Herzberger, 1949.

Höltgen, K.J., *Francis Quarles. 1592–1644. Meditativer Dichter, Emblematiker, Royalist. Eine biographische and kritische Studie*, Anglia Buchreihe, vol. 19, Tübingen: Niemeyer, 1978.

Hönn, G.P., *Kurtzeingerichtetes Betrugs-Lexicon, Worinnen die meisten Betruegereyen in allen Staenden, Nebst denen darwider mehrentheils dienenden guten Mitteln entdecket werden*, new and improved edn, Leipzig: Christian Samuel Krug, 1743.

Hoop Scheffer, D. de (ed.), *Hollstein's Dutch and Flemish Etchings, Engravings and Woodcuts ca. 1450–1700*, vol. XXXIV, *Jan van de Velde II*, Rosendaal/The Netherlands: Koninklijke van Poll, 1989.

Horák, W. (ed.), 'Lai von Melion', in *Zeitschrift für romanische Philologie,* 6 (1882), pp. 94–106.

Horden, J. (ed.), *George Wither. A Collection of Emblemes. 1635*, English Emblem Books no. 12, Menston: The Scolar Press Ltd, 1968.

Horden, J. (ed.), *Henry Peacham: Minerva Britanna. 1612*, English Emblem Books no. 5, Menston: The Scolar Press Ltd, 1969.

Horden, J. (ed.), *Claude Paradin: Devises Heroïques. 1557*, Continental Emblem Books no. 16, Menston: The Scolar Press Ltd, 1971.

Horden, J. (ed.), *Guillaume de la Perrière, Le Théâtre des Bons Engins. 1539*, Continental Emblem Books no. 17, Menston: The Scolar Press Ltd, 1973.

Howlett, R. (ed.), *Chronicles of the Reigns of Stephen, Henry II, and Richard I*, 4 vols, London: Longman & Co., 1884–1889.

Huck, W. von, *Genealogisches Handbuch der gräflichen Häuser*, Gräfliche Häuser, vol. VIII; Genealogisches Handbuch des Adels, vol. 63, Limburg: C.A. Starke Verlag, 1976.

Huguet, E., *Le langage figuré au seizième siècle*, Études de philologie française, Paris: Hachette, 1933.

Icazbalceta, Don Joaquín García, *Vocabulario de Mexicanismos*, Mexico: Tip. y Lit. 'La Europea', de J. Aguilar Vera y Cª, 1899; reprinted 1975.

The India Office List for 1898, London: Harrison and Sons Ltd, 1928 (compiled from official records by direction of the Secretary of State for India in Council).

Isaacs, J. (ed.), *Games and Gamesters of the Restoration*, The English Library, London: George Routledge and Sons, Ltd, 1930.

Jahres-Bericht der Hamburger Lawn-Tennis-Gilde für das Jahr 1904, until 1914, annual report published in the month of January of the following year in Hamburg.

Jaramillo, H.A., *El deporte indigena de America (desde antes de la conquista)*, Pereira: Universidad Tecnológica, Departamento de Bibliotecas, 1977.

Joannis, A.R. de, 'Erinnerungen an die Weltmeisterschaften (auf Hartplätzen) 1912', in *Lawn-Tennis und Golf*, 10 (1913), no. 1, mid-January 1913, pp. 2–6.

Jodogne, O. (ed.), *Le Mystère de la Passion d'Arnoul Gréban*, Académie Royale de Belgique. Classe des Lettres. Mémoires, vol. XII, Brussels: Palais des Académies, 1965.

Jusserand, J.-J., *Les sports et jeux d'exercice dans l'ancienne France*, Paris: Plon-Nourrit

et Cⁱᵉ, 1901, reprinted Geneva: Slatkine, 1986.

Kalma, J.J., *Kaatsen in Friesland. Het spel met de kleine bal door de eeuwen heen*, Franeker: Uitgeverij T. Wever, 1972.

Karlsson, A.A., *Större Friluftslekar. Regler utgivna av Svenska Lekförbandets Arbetsutskott*, 3rd edn, Stockholm: Björck & Dörjesson, 1931.

Kauder, G., 'Turnier in Marienbad', in *Der Lawn-Tennis-Sport*, 3 (1906), no. 19, 2 August 1906, pp. 263–5.

Kerckhove, L. van de, '"Captiare" in de Zuidnederlandse dialecten', in *Handelingen van de Koninklijke Commissie voor Toponymie & Dialectologie*, 20 (1946), pp. 109–46 (with 4 maps).

Kerkhoff, H., 'Die Geschichte der Klipper', in *100 Jahre Klipper Tennis- and Hockey-Club auf der Uhlenhorst e.V. 1888–1988*, Hamburg: Bergedorfer Buchdruckerei von Ed. Wagner, 1988, pp. 20–37.

Kervyn de Lettenhove, J.M.B.C. (ed.), *Œuvres de Georges Chastellain*, vol. 3, Brussels: Heussner, 1864.

Kiel, Cornelis/Cornelius Kilian, *Etymologicum teutonicæ linguæ sive Dictionarium teutonico-latinum*, 3rd edn, Antwerp: Plantin-Moretus, 1599; reprinted Amsterdam: Adolf M. Hakkert, 1972.

Kiel, Cornelis, *Etymologicum teutonicæ linguæ sive dictionarium teutonicolatinum*, Amsterdam: Apud Henricum Laurentium, 1632.

Kiliaan, Cornelius, *Dictionarium Teutonicolatinum*, Documenta Linguistica. Quellen zur Geschichte der deutschen Sprache des 15. bis 20. Jahrhunderts, Hildesheim: Georg Olms Verlag, 1975.

Kingsford, C. Lethbridge, *English Historical Literature in the Fifteenth Century*, Oxford: Clarendon Press, 1913.

Kinsley, J. (ed.), *Ane Satyre of the Thrie Estaits*, [Sir David Lindsay], London: Cassell, 1954.

Kirchner, H.-H., 'Die Nationalen Deutschen Tennismeisterschaften zum 49. Mal im Bürgerpark zu Braunschweig', in *77. Nationale Tennismeisterschaften von Deutschland 1990*, Brunswick 1990, pp. 9–15.

Klint, A., 'Det gottländska pärkspelet', in *Almanack för Ungdom*, 2 (1907), pp. 57–66.

Kneschke, E.H. (ed.), *Neues allgemeines Deutsches Adels-Lexicon*, 9 vols, Leipzig: Friedrich Voigt's Buchhandlung, 1859–1870.

Koch, K., 'Deutsche Kunstausdrücke des Fussballspiels', in *Zeitschrift des Allgemeinen Deutschen Sprachvereins*, 18 (1903), no. 6, columns 169–172.

Koechlin, R., *Les ivoires gothiques français*, 3 vols, Paris: Auguste Picard, 1924.

Koerner, B. (ed.), *Hamburger Geschlechterbuch*, vol. 2, Görlitz: Druck and Verlag von C.A. Starke, 1911.

Konrad, K., *Bilderkunde des deutschen Studentenwesens. Ein Beitrag zur Entwicklungsgeschichte des deutschen Studententums*, 2nd edn, completely revised, 2 vols, Breslau: Akademischer Verlag W. Finsterbusch, 1931–1935.

Koppehel, C., *Geschichte des Deutschen Fussballsports*, Frankfurt am Main: Wilhelm Limpert-Verlag, 1954.

Kraft, F.G., *Die geschichtliche Entwicklung der Friedr. Krupp Grusonwerk Aktiengesellschaft in Magdeburg*, Berlin: Verlag für Sozialpolitik, Wirtschaft und Statistik, 1943.

Krieg, M.O. (ed.),[*Karl Bertsche*] *Die Werke Abraham a Sancta Clara in ihren Frühdrucken*, 2nd edn, revised and enlarged, Vienna: Walter Krieg Verlag, 1961.

Kuebler, S., *Buch der Tennisrackets von den Anfängen im 16. Jahrhundert bis etwa 1990*, Singen: Kuebler GmbH, 1995.

Kühr, H., *Die Geschichte der Ballhäuser in Frankreich and Österreich*, typescript; thesis at the Institut für Turnlehrerausbildung of the University of Vienna, 1938.

La Fons, A. de, Baron de Mélicocq, 'Police municipale des villes du nord de la France, mœurs au XVe et XVIe Siècles', in *Archives historiques et littéraires du nord de la France et du Midi de la Belgique*, third series 2 (1851), pp. 526–34, and 3 (1852), pp. 170–5.

La Marinière, *La Mayson académique, contenant un recueil général de tous les jeux divertissans, pour se réjouyr agréablement dans les bonnes compagnies, par le sieur D.L.M.*, Paris, 1654, reprinted unchanged 1667.

Langlois, E., *Adam le Bossu, Trouvère du XIIIe siècle. Le Jeu de la Feuillée et Le Jeu de Robin et Marion*, Poèmes et récits de la Vielle France 1, Paris: de Boccard, 1923.

La plus nouvelle academie universelle des jeux, 3 vols, Amsterdam: Arkste'e & Merkus, 1752.

Lawn Rackets, or Pelota; Rules and Laws of the Game, as Played by the Leamington Club, Leamington: D. Sarney, no year of publication [pre-1881].

Lawn-Tennis-Handbuch. Amtliches Jahrbuch des Deutschen Lawn-Tennis-Bundes, 1909/10 edition, Berlin: F. Manning, 1910.

Lawn-Tennis-Handbuch. Amtliches Jahrbuch des Deutschen Lawn-Tennis-Bundes, 1911/12 edition, Berlin: Verlag 'Lawn-Tennis & Golf', 1911.

Lebeck, R., *Auf- and Rückschläge. Aus den Kindertagen des Tennis*, Die bibliophilen Taschenbücher no. 318, Dortmund: Harenberg Kommunikation, 1982.

Lecotté, R. (ed.), *Le jeu de tamis en Ile-de-France*, Meaux: Imprimerie André-Pouyé, 1947.

Lee, S. (ed.), *The Dictionary of National Biography*, Second supplement 1901–1911, vol. 1, London: Oxford University Press, 1920.

Legg, L.G.W. (ed.), *The Dictionary of National Biography*, vol. 26, Supplement 1931–1940, London: Oxford University Press, 1949.

Lennartz, K. *et al.*, *Die Olympischen Spiele 1896 in Athen. Erläuterungen zum Neudruck des Offiziellen Berichtes*, Kassel: Agon-Sportverlag, 1996.

Le parnasse satyrique, Paris: Bibliothèque Nationale, Manuscrit n.a.fr. 4237.

Lerry, R., *Cradle of Lawn Tennis. The Story of Warwickshire and Its Clubs*, Birmingham: Stanford & Mann Ltd, 1946.

Les jeux des jeunes garçons avec une explication et une devise morale, 2nd edn (with corrections), Paris: Chez les Frères Noël, Graveurs-Editeurs; Imprimerie d'A. Egron, 1807.

Lewillie, L. and F. Noël, *Le sport dans l'art belge de l'époque romaine à nos jours*, Borgerhout-Antwerp: Imprimerie N.V. Roels, 1982.

Lewis, C.B. (ed.), 'Die altfranzösischen Prosaversionen des Appollonius-Romans', in *Romanische Forschungen*, 34 (1915), pp. 1–277.

Lewis, R.E. (ed.), *Middle English Dictionary*, Ann Arbor: The University of Michigan Press, 1952– [in progress].

Lexikon des Mittelalters, Munich: Artemis Verlag, 1981–.

Leyenaar, T.J.J. and L.A. Parsons, *Ulama. The Ballgame of the Mayas and Aztecs 2000 BC–AD 2000. From Human Sacrifice to Sport*, Leiden: Spruyt, Van Mantgem & De Does, 1988.

Little, A., *The Changing Face of Wimbledon*, 3rd edn, London: Wimbledon Lawn Tennis Museum, 1987.

Little, A., *This is Wimbledon. The Official Guide of the Championships*, 9th edn, Wimbledon: The All England Lawn Tennis and Croquet Club, 1989.

Lodeman, F.E. (ed.), 'Le pas Saladin (I., II., III.)', in *Modern Language Notes,* 12 (1897), columns 21–34; 84–96 (Text); 209–229; and 273–281.

Lolkama, J., *Perken, Parturen en Koningen. Honderddertig jaar georganiseerde kaatssport in Friesland*, Akkrum: Uitgeverij 'Victoria', 1983.

Loomis, R.S., 'Richard Coeur de Lion and the Pas Saladin in Medieval Art', in *Publications of the Modern Language Association,* 30 (1915), pp. 509–28.

Loomis, R.S., 'The Allegorical Siege in the Art of the Middle Ages', in *American Journal of Archaeology,* 23 (1919), pp. 255–69.

López Muños, A., *La Pilota valenciana*, Valencia: author's edition, Avda. Blasco Ibañez, 36. Paterna, 1984.

Lowther, T., 'Lawn Tennis', in *The Badminton Magazine of Sports and Games,* 16 (1903), pp. 355–66.

Lucas, F.L. (ed.), *The Complete Works of John Webster*, 4 vols, London: Chatto & Windus, 1927.

Lucas, R.H. (ed.), *Christine de Pisan. Le livre du corps de policie*, Geneva: Librairie Droz, 1967.

Lugt, F., *Musée du Louvre. Inventaire Général des Dessins des Écoles du Nord. Maîtres des Anciens Pays-Bas nés avant 1550*, Paris: Musées Nationaux Palais du Louvre, 1968.

Lukas, G., *Sport im alten Rom*, Berlin: Sportverlag Berlin, 1982.

Lumpkin, A., *Women's Tennis: A Historical Documentary of the Players and Their Game*, Troy, New York: The Whitston Publishing Company, 1981.

Luze, A. de, *La magnifique histoire du jeu de paume*, Bordeaux: Delmas/Bossard, 1928.

Macaulay, G.C., *The English Works of John Gower*, Early English Text Society, e.s., 81 and 82, 2 vols, London: Oxford University Press, 1900–1901; new imprint 1957.

Macaulay, Th. B., *Lays of Ancient Rome*, Collection of English Authors, vol. CXCVIII, Leipzig: Bernhard Tauchnitz, 1851.

MacGregor, R.R., 'Tennis in Britain', in *Belgravia,* 37 (1878), pp. 68–74.

Macrí, O., 'Alcune aggiunte al Dizionario di Joan Corominas', in *Revista de Filología Española,* 40 (1956), pp. 127–70.

Magoun, Jr., F.P., *History of Football from the Beginnings to 1871*, Kölner Anglistische Arbeiten, vol. 31, Bochum-Langendreer: Verlag Heinrich Pöppinghaus O.H.-G., 1938.

Magoun, Jr., F.P., 'Il gioco del calcio fiorentino', in *Italica,* 19 (1942), pp. 1–21.

Mahler, B., *Die Leibesübungen in den Ritterakademien*, doctoral thesis Erlangen, Neuruppin: E. Buchbinder (H. Duske), 1921.

Mak, J.J. (ed.), *De Gedichten van Anthonis de Roovere*, Zwolle: N.V. Uitgevers-Maatschappij W.E.J. Tjeenk Willink, 1955.

Mak, J.J., *Uyt Ionsten Versaemt. Retoricale Studiën 1946–1956*, Zwolse Reeks van Taal-en Letterkundige Studies, Zwolle: W.E.J. Tjeenk Willink, 1957.

Mandrot, B. de (ed.), *Mémoires de Philippe de Commynes*, new edn, 2 vols, Paris: Alphonse Picard, 1903.

Mangan, J.A., *The Games Ethic and Imperialism*, Harmondsworth, Middlesex: Penguin Books, 1986.

Manners and Household Expenses of England in the thirteenth and fifteenth centuries, The Roxburghe Club, London: William Nicol, 1841.

Manrique, A., *Cisterciensium seu verius ecclesiasticorum annalium a condito cistercio*, 3 vols, Lyons: G. Boissat & Laurent Anison, 1642–1649.

Markey, T.L., *Frisian*, Trends in Linguistics. State of the Art Report 13, The Hague: Mouton Publishers, 1981.

Marle, R. van, *Iconographie de l'art profane au Moyen-Age et à la Renaissance. La vie quotidienne*, The Hague: Martinus Nijhoff, 1931; reprinted New York: Hacker Art Books, 1971.

Marshall, J., 'Tennis. A German Court, *c.* 1540', in *The Field. The Country Gentleman's Newspaper*, 19 January 1895, no. 2195, p. 87.

Marshall, J., *The Annals of Tennis*, London: The Field Office, 1878: facsimile reprint Baltimore, Maryland: Racquet Sports Information & Services, Inc., 1973.

Martin, E. (ed.), *Le roman de Renart*, 3 vols, Strasbourg 1882–1887.

Mary, A. (ed.), *Journal d'un Bourgeois de Paris sous Charles VI et Charles VII*, Paris: Henri Jonquières, 1929.

Massingham, H.J., *The Heritage of Man*, London: J. Cape, 1929.

Matuszak, H., *Die saterfriesischen Mandarten von Ramsloh, Strücklingen and Scharrel inmitten des niederdeutschen Sprachraums*, typescript of doctoral thesis, Bonn, 1951.

Maur, G., 'Rasenspiele auf dem Cannstatter Wasen 1865–1890 [and other articles]', in *75 Jahre Cannstatter Tennisclub*, Stuttgart-Münster: Theodor Glauner, 1965, pp. 10–24.

Mayans y Siscar, G. (ed.), *Joannis Ludovici Vivis Opera Omnia*, 8 vols, Valencia: Benedict Monfort, 1782–1790.

Mayer, A., *Le jeu de balle et sa technique*, Luttre: Office International d'Éditions, 1922.

Mazzarotto, B.T., *Le feste veneziane, i giochi popolari, le cerimonie religiose e di governo illustrate da Gabriel Bella*, 2nd edn, Florence: G.C. Sansoni, 1980.

Mehl, E., 'Antonio Scaino "Trattato de giuoco della Palla" (Venedig 1555)', in *Leibesübungen and körperliche Erziehung*, 19/20 (1937), pp. 437–45, and 21 (1937), pp. 490–6.

Mehl, E., 'Das Ballhaus-Spiel, für Vieth (1795) eine vergessene "Antiquität der Gymnastik"', in *Die Leibeserziehung*, no. 6 (June 1957), pp. 169–71.

Mehl, E., 'Kulturgeschichte in der Fachsprache des Tennisspiels', in *Muttersprache. Zeitschrift zur Pflege and Erforschung der deutschen Sprache,* 77 (1967), pp. 308–11.

Mehl, E., 'Latinismen im Kinderspiel. "Gesunkenes Kulturgut" aus dem Lateinunterricht der Humanistenschule', in *Rastloses Schaffen. Festschrift für Dr. Friedrich Lammert*, Stuttgart: Kohlhammer, 1954, pp. 74–81.

Mehl, E., 'Prager und Wiener Erinnerungen an das Ballhausspiel. Vom "Spiel der Könige" und vom "König der Spiele", French: Souvenirs des salles de jeu de paume à Prague et à Vienne. Quelques mots sur le «jeu des rois» et le «roi des jeux»', in *Olympische Randschau*, 12 (1941), no. 15, October 1941, pp. 12–23, [18–23].

Mehl, E., 'Stammen die modernen Ballspiele von einem altägyptischen Fruchtbarkeits-Brauch ab?', in *Die Leibeserziehung*, 2,6 (1953), pp. 8–12.

Mehl, E., 'Von siebenerley underschiedlichen Förm and Nutzbarkeit dess Ballenspiels', in *Die Leibeserziehung*, 6 (1957), pp. 200–7.

Mehl, E., 'Warum zählt man beim Tennisspiel "15, 30, 40, 60"?', in *Olympische Rundschau*, 7 (1936), pp. 25–8.

Mehl, J.-M., 'Les autorités ecclesiastiques face aux jeux sportifs dans la France médiévale', in Louis Burgener *et al.* (eds), *Sport and Kultur*, Europäische Hochschulschriften, series XXXV, vol. 5, Bern: Peter Lang, 1986, pp. 61–7.

Mehl, J.-M., *Les jeux au royaume de France du XIIIe au début du XVIe siècle*, Paris: Librairie Arthème Fayard, 1990.

Meister, L. von, *Gathered Yesterdays*, London: Geoffrey Bles, 1963.

Mele, V. van, 'Volkssporten in Ecuador', in *Nieuwsbrief van de Vlaamse Volkssport Centrale,* 8 (1988), p. 63f.

Mendel, P., 'Aus der Chronik des Eisbahn-and Tennis-Vereins auf der Uhlenhorst', in *Mitteilungsblätter*, des Klipper and Eisbahnverein auf der Uhlenhorst 1888 e.V., May 1929, pp. 3–6; June 1929, pp. 2–6; July 1929, pp. 2–6.

Mendel, P., *Aus der Geschichte des Sports in Hamburg*, no place or year [1970]. Hamburg State Archives: E.J. No 337/1970; shelf mark A 509/419 K1.

Mendel, P., 'Die Geschichte des Stamm Vereins', in festschrift celebrating the seventy-fifth anniversary of the foundation of 'Klipper' Tennis- und Hockey-Club 1963, pp. [1–6].

Menne, K., *Deutsche und niederländische Handschriften*, Mitteilungen aus dem Stadtarchiv von Köln: Die Handschriften des Archivs, Heft X, Abt. 1, Part I u. II, Cologne: Verlag von Paul Neubner, 1937.

Metken, S., 'Der immerwährende Kalender. Spiele and Zeremonien in einem französischen Stundenbuch des 15. Jahrhunderts', in *Kunst und Antiquitäten*, no. 6 (1983), pp. 20–31.

Metzeltin, M., *Altspanisches Elementarbuch*, Sammlung romanischer Elementar- und Handbücher. 1st series, vol. 9, Heidelberg: Carl Winter, 1979.

Meurgy, J., *Les principaux manuscrits à peintures du Musée Condé à Chantilly*, Paris: Société Française de Reproduction de Manuscrits à Peintures, 1930.

Meyer, E.L. and O. Tesdorpf, *Hamburgische Wappen and Genealogien*, Hamburg: authors' edition, 1890.

Meyer-Lübke, W., *Historische Grammatik der französischen Sprache*, Second part, Word Formation, 2nd edn, Heidelberg: Carl Winter, 1966.

M-i., 'Ein Stück Tennisgeschichte aus Kassel', in *Tennis und Golf,* 8 (1931), no. 9, 24 April 1931, pp. 238–40.

Michel, F., *Histoire des Ducs de Normandie et des Rois d'Angleterre ... suivie de la Relation du Tournoi de Ham, par Sarrazin, Trouvère du XIIIe siècle*, Paris: Jules Renouard et Cie, 1840; reprinted New York: Johnson Reprint Corporation, 1965.

Michel, M., 'La Longue Paume', in Max Decugis *et al., Tennis, Hockey, Paumes, Balles et Boules*, Sports-Bibliothèque, Paris: Pierre Lafitte & Cie, 1913; reprinted Geneva: Slatkine, 1980, pp. 237–307.

Millo, L., *El 'trinquet'*, Valencia: Prometeo, 1976.

Mills, M. (ed.), *Six Middle English Romances*, London: J.M. Dent & Sons, 1973; reprinted 1982.

Minshew, J., *Hegemon eis tas glossas, id est, Ductor in Linguas, The Guide into Tongues*, London: John Browne, 1617.

Molenaer, S. P. (ed.), *Li livres du gouvernemant des rois. A XIIIth century French version of Egidio Colonna's treatise De regimine principum*, New York: Macmillan, 1899.

Mölk, U., 'Philologische Aspekte des Turniers', in Fleckenstein, *Das ritterliche Turnier im Mittelalter*, pp. 163–74.

Møller, J., *So i Hul - og 99 andre gamle boldspil og kastelege*, Gamle idrætslege i Danmark - Legebog 1., Kolding: Reklame & Tryk as, 1990.

Monmerqué, L.J.N. and F. Michel (eds), *Théâtre français au moyen-âge (XIe-XIVe siècles)*, Paris: Firmin Didot, 1839.

Montanus, *Winke und Spielregeln für Tennisspieler*, Munich: Eduard Pohl's Verlag, 1895.

Moore, S.A. (ed.), *Letters and Papers of John Shillingford, Mayor of Exeter 1447–50*, Camden Society Publications, n.s. no. 2, Westminter: printed for the Camden Society, 1871; reprinted New York: Johnson Reprint Corp., 1965.

Morgan, R., 'The Tuscan Game of Palla. A Descendant of the Medieval Game of Tennis', in *Stadion,* 11 (1985), pp. 176–92.

Möring, M., *Nic. von der Meden & Co. 125 Jahre Hausmakler*, Hamburg: Krüger & Nienstedt, 1955.

Moser, D.-R., *Fastnacht - Fasching - Karneval. Das Fest der «Verkehrten Welt»*, Graz: Edition Kaleidoskop, 1986.

Müller, J., *Rheinisches Wörterbuch*, 9 vols, Berlin: Fritz Klopp-Verlag, 1928–1971.

Müller, R., 'Der älteste Sportplatz des Reiches? Der Katschhof in Aachen and das niederländische Katschspiel', in *Leibesübungen and körperliche Erziehung,* 56 (1937), p. 3.

Murray, H.J.R., 'The Medieval Games of Tables', in *Medium Ævum,* 10 (1941), pp. 57–69.

Mutzenbecher, G.-U., *Die Versicherer. Geschichte einer Hamburger Kaufmannsfamilie*, Hamburg: Verlag Geert-Ulrich Mutzenbecher, 1993.

Myers, A.W., *Captain Anthony Wilding*, London: Hodder and Stoughton, 1916.

Myers, A.W., *Fifty Years of Wimbledon. The Story of the Lawn Tennis Championships*, London: The Field, 1926.

Myers, A.W., *Lawn Tennis at Home and Abroad*, London: George Newnes Ltd, 1903.

Myers, A.W. (ed.), *1929 Ayres' Lawn Tennis Almanack and Tournament Guide*, London: F.H. Ayres Ltd, 1929.

N., H.B., 'Internationales Turnier Hamburg', in *Der Lawn-Tennis-Sport,* 1 (1904), nos 17–19, 28, 25 August, 1 September 1904, pp. 228–30, 238–41, 256–9.

Nanias, A., 'The Departure of the English Team for America', in *Lawn Tennis and Croquet,* 5 (1900), no. 111, 1 August 1900, p. 258.

Nanteuil, E. de, G. de Saint-Clair and C. Delahaye, *La paume et le Lawn-Tennis*, Paris: Librairie Hachette et Cie, 1898.

Navarro Adelantado, V., 'El Mantenimiento de un Juego: la Pelotamano de Lanzarote', in *Stadion,* 15 (1989), pp. 111–38.

Neuendorf, E., *Geschichte der neueren deutschen Leibesübung vom Beginn des 18. Jahrhunderts bis zur Gegenwart*, 4 vols, Dresden: Wilhelm Limpert-Verlag, 1931–[1932], vol. IV, Die Zeit von 1860 bis 1932.

Nick, F., *Stuttgarter Chronik and Sagenbuch. Eine Sammlung denkwürdiger Begebenheiten, Geschichten and Sagen der Stadt Stuttgart and ihrer Gemarkung*, Stuttgart: Gutzkow, 1875.

Nicolas, H., *History of the Battle of Agincourt and of the Expedition of Henry the Fifth into France, in 1415*, 2nd edn, London: W.

Pickering, 1832, reprinted London: H. Pordes, 1971.

Nirrnheim, O., 'Die Gründung der Fédération internationale de Lawn-Tennis', in *Lawn-Tennis und Golf*, 10 (1913), no. 3, mid-March 1913, pp. 64–6.

Nirrnheim, O., 'Die Hamburger Lawn-Tennis-Gilde', in *Sport im Wort*, no. 13 (1902), Thursday, 27 March 1902, pp. 158f.

Nirrnheim, O., 'Hamburg 1905', in *Der Lawn-Tennis-Sport*, 2 (1905), no. 22, 24 August 1905, p. 346f., no. 23, 31 August 1905, p. 359f. and no. 24, 7 September 1905, p. 375f.

Nirrnheim, O., 'Hamburger Internationales 1907. Die Meisterschaften von Deutschland', in *Der Lawn-Tennis-Sport*, 4 (1907), no. 23, 29 August 1907, pp. 513–18.

Nirrnheim, O., 'Internationales Lawn-Tennis-Turnier Hamburg Uhlenhorst', in *Sport im Wort*, no. 35 (1902), Thursday, 28 August 1902, p. 460f. and no. 36, Thursday, 4 September 1902, p. 469f.

Nirrnheim, O., 'Zur Gründung einer deutschen Lawn-Tennis-Association', in *Sport im Wort*, no. 3 (1902), Friday, 17 January 1902, p. 34 (precedes p. 33).

Nolting-Hauff, I., *Chrestien de Troyes. Yvain*, Klassische Texte des romanischen Mittelalters, Munich: Eidos Verlag, 1962.

Nordisk Familjeboks Sportlexikon, 7 vols, Stockholm: Nordisk familjeboks förlag, 1938–1949.

Novak, I. (ed.), *100 Jahre Heidelberger Tennis-Club 1890 e.V.*, Heidelberg: Brausdruck GmbH, 1990.

Nyberg, E., *Några Gotländska Folklekar*, Visby: Gotlänningens Boktryckeri, 1922.

Onions, C.T., *The Oxford Dictionary of English Etymology*, Oxford: Clarendon Press, 1966; reprinted 1976.

Orme, N., *From Childhood to Chivalry: The Education of the English Kings and Aristocracy 1066–1530*, London: Methuen, 1984.

Ortiz, S.E., 'Tres modos de jugar a la pelota en Colombia', in *Revista Colombiana de Folklor*, 3 (1963), pp. 81–8.

O'Shea, H., 'Des mots golf, tennis, trinquet, pelote, etc.', in *Bulletin Mensuel de 'Biarritz-Association'. Société des Sciences, lettres et arts*, I. 3 (1896–1898), pp. 43–5.

Overlack, J., 'Diesseits und Jenseits der Lichtentaler Allee', in *Tennis-Club 'Rot-Weiss' Baden-Baden. Club-Nachrichten*, 23, part 5/6 (1971), pp. 1–14.

Överstyrelsen för Svenska Röda Korset (ed.), *Hälsa och Friluftsliv*, Stockholm: A.-B. Svensk Litteratur, 1934.

Paret, J.P., 'Lawn Tennis on the European Continent', in *Outing. An Illustrated Monthly Magazine of Sport, Travel and Recreation*, 34 (1899), August 1899, pp. 465–72.

Parisse, M., 'Le tournoi en France, des origines à la fin du XIIIe siècle', in Fleckenstein, *Das ritterliche Turnier im Mittelalter*, pp. 175–211.

Partridge, E., *Slang To-Day and Yesterday*, 4th corrected edn, London: Routledge & Kegan Paul Ltd, 1970; reprinted 1972.

Pasquier, E., *Les Recherches de la France*, Paris: Toussaint Quinet, 1633.

Passen, R. van, 'Kaatsspelen te Antwerp in de 15de-18de eeuw', in *Naamkunde*, 20 (1988), pp. 5–23; and 21 (1989), pp. 47–64.

Pauli, C.W., *Lübeckische Zustände im Mittelalter. III. Recht und Kultur. Nebst einem Urkundenbuch*, Leipzig: Verlag von Duncker & Humboldt, 1878.

Peacock, E. (ed.), *Instructions for Parish Priests. By John Myrc*, Early English Text Society, o.s., 31, 2nd edn, London: Kegan Paul, Trench, Trübner & Co., 1902.

Peile, S.C.F., *Lawn Tennis as a Game of Skill*, New York: Charles Scribner's Sons, 1885.

Pepi, 'Das Meisterschaftsturnier in Hamburg IV', in *Der Lawn-Tennis-Sport*, 3 (1906), no. 25, 13 September 1906, pp. 373–6.

Peralta, E., *Juego de Pelota. Reglamento*, Oajaca de Juarez: no publisher, Julio 29 de 1903, [reprinted in Gillmeister, 'The Dissemination', pp. 31–3].

Pérez Bazán, T. and A. Manterola, *Disposiciones y reglamento para el juego con el nombre de 'Pelota Mixteca'*, Oaxaca de Juarez: Departamento de Educación Física, Dirección General en el Estado, 1936.

Perkow, U., *Die englisch-amerikanische Gemeinde in Baden-Baden. 'Residents and Visitors'*, Arbeitskreis für Stadtgeschichte der Stadt Baden-Baden e.V., Kuppenheim: Fortuna-Druck 1990.

Perks, W.A.G., *Geschiedenis van de Maliebaan*, Utrecht: N.V. Drukkerij en Uitgeverij V/H Kemink en Zoon, 1970.

Pfisterer, H.G., *100 Jahre Cannstatter Tennisclub 1890–1990*, Stuttgart: Dr. Cantz'sche Druckerei, 1990.

Phelps, F.V., 'Manliffe Francis Goodbody', in *The Tennis Collector*, 8 (April 1990), p. 4.

Phillipson, R., *Linguistic Imperialism*, Oxford: Oxford University Press, 1992.

P., I., 'The Reverend T. Archibald S. White', in *Spiel und Sport,* 4 (1894), 14 July 1894, p. 712.

Pilot, 'Das Homburger Lawn-Tennis-Turnier', in *Sport im Bild,* 8 (1902), no. 36, p. 368.

Pilot, 'Die Homburger Turniertage [I und II]', in *Sport im Wort*, no. 20 (1899), 18 August 1899, p. 157, and no. 21, 25 August 1899, p. 165.

Pilot, 'Homburger Skizzen', in *Sport im Bild*, 5 (1899), no. 36, Friday, 8 September 1899, p. 390f.

Pilot, 'VIII. Internationales Lawn-Tennis-Turnier zu Berlin. II', in *Sport im Wort*, no. 22 (1902), Friday, 30 May 1902, pp. 286–9.

Pirenne, H., *Histoire de Belgique des origines à nos jours*, 4 vols, Brussels: La Renaissance du Livre, 1948–1952.

Planche, A., *Charles d'Orléans ou la recherche d'un langage*, Paris: Editions Honoré Champion, 1975.

Plotzek, J.M., *Andachtsbücher des Mittelalters aus Privatbesitz. Katalog zur Ausstellung im Schnütgen-Museum*, Cologne: Locher GmbH, 1987.

Poirion, D., *Le lexique de Charles d'Orléans dans les ballades*, Publications romanes et françaises 91, Geneva: Droz, 1967.

Poirion, D., *Le moyen âge II. 1300–1480*, Collection Littérature française, Grenoble: Arthaut, 1971.

Praz, M., *Mnemosyne. The Parallel between Literature and the Visual Arts*, Bollingen Series 35,16, Washington: Princeton University Press, 1970.

Prims, F., 'Apostaten uit de rangen der geestelijkheid', in *Beelden uit den Cultuurstrijd der jaren 1577–1585. Antwerpiensia*, 15 (1941), pp. 299–307.

Puttfarken, T. and M. Crichton Stuart, 'The Royal Tennis Court at Falkland', in Butler and Wordie, *The Royal Game*, pp. 26–35.

Quarles, F., *Emblemes*, London: G. Miller, 1635.

R., S.D., 'The Late Major Gem. Edgbastonian Origin of Lawn Tennis', in *Edgbastonia*, December 1881, pp. 126–131.

Rambeau, A. (ed.), *Die dem Trouvère Adam de la Hale zugeschriebenen Dramen*, Marburg: N.G. Elwert, 1886.

Randall, L.M.C., *Images in the Margins of Gothic Manuscripts*, Berkeley, CA: University of California Press, 1966.

Rapp, L., *Hippolytus Guarinoni, Stiftsarzt in Hall. Ein tirolisches Kulturbild aus dem 17. Jahrhundert*, Brixen: Verlag von A. Weger's Buchhandlung, 1903.

Real Academia Española (ed.), *Diccionario de Autoridades, [1726]*, Edición Facsímil, 3 vols, Madrid: Editorial Gredos, S.A., 1969.

Refugees and Emigrants in the Dutch Republic and England. Papers of the Fourth Annual Symposium of the Sir Thomas Browne Institute, Leiden: Werkgroep Engels Nederlandse Betrekkingen, 1986.

Reibnitz-Maltzan, L. Baroness von, *Grossherzogin Anastasia von Mecklenburg* (typescript privately owned, *c.* 1922).

Reichard, E.C., *Matthäus und Veit Konrad Schwarz nach ihren ... abwechselnden Kleidertrachten ... ausführlich beschrieben ...*, Magdeburg, 1786.

Reznicek, B. von, '40 Jahre Rot-Weiss. Der Berliner Lawn-Tennis-Turnier-Club begeht sein 40jähriges Jubiläum', in *Der Tennissport,* 14 (1937), no. 9, 5 May 1937, pp. 109–12.

Reznicek, B. von, *Tennis. Das Spiel der Völker*, Marburg: Johann Grüneberg Verlag, 1932.

Riese, A. (ed.), *Historia Apollonii regis Tyri*, 2nd edn, Stuttgart: B.G. Teubner, 1893, reprinted 1973.

Robbins, R.H., 'Poems Dealing with Contemporary Conditions', in Albert E. Hartung (ed.), *A Manual of the Writings in Middle English 1050–1500*, vol. 5, New Haven, Connecticut, 1975, pp. 1384–1536 and 1632–1725 (bibliography).

Robertson, J., *Uppies and Doonies. The Story of the Kirkwall Ba' Game*, Aberdeen: Aberdeen University Press, 1967.

Robertson, M., *Wimbledon 1877–1977*, Old Woking: Unwin Brothers Ltd; The Gresham Press, 1977; reprinted 1979.

Robi, 'Das "Tennis" in der Wortforschung', in *Lawn-Tennis und Golf,* 7 (1910), no. 23, 1 September 1910, p. 463.

Rohrbach, P. *et al.* (eds), *F[erdinand] L[aeisz]. Die Geschichte einer Reederei*, Hamburg: Hans Dulk, 1954.

Rohwer, B., *Der friesische Handel im frühen Mittelalter*, (doctoral thesis of the Christian-Albrechts-Universität, Kiel), Borna-Leipzig: Robert Noske, 1937.

Rollenhagen, G., *Nucleus emblematum selectissimorum*, Hildesheim: Georg Olms Verlag, 1985, (reprinted from the Cologne edition of 1611).

Roques, M. (ed.), *Jehan Mayllart. Le Roman du Comte d'Anjou*, Les Classiques Français du Moyen Age 67, Paris: Honoré Champion, 1931.

Rosenbaum-Jenkins, [S.], [= Dr. S. Rabe-Jenkins, husband of Hedwig Rosenbaum], 'Beobachtungen bei den englischen Lawn-Tennis-Meisterschaften in Wimbledon 1903', in *Sport im Wort*, no. 38 (1903), Thursday, 17 September 1903, pp. 476–8.

Rulemann, T. (ed.), *Das grosse illustrierte Sportbuch*, Berlin: Verlagsdruckerei 'Merkur', 1909.

S., G., 'Karl von Jecklin', in *Lawn-Tennis und Golf*, 7 (1910), no. 6, 5 May 1910, p. 83f.

Sadie, S. (ed.), *The New Grove Dictionary of Music and Musicians*, vol. 7, London: Macmillan Publishers Ltd., 1980.

Saint-Germain, J., *Le jeu de balle au tamis*, no place of publication: Fédération Picarde du Jeu de Balle au Tamis, 1932.

Sander, A. [Antonius Sanderus], *Flandria Illustrata*, Cologne: Cornelius ab Egmondt et Socii, 1641.

Satzungen der Hamburger Lawn-Tennis-Gilde, Hamburg 1901.

Saurbier, B., *Geschichte der Leibesübungen*, 10th edn, Frankfurt a.M.: Wilhelm Limpert Verlag, 1978.

Scaino, A., *Trattato del giuoco della palla*, Venice: Gabriel Giolito de Ferrari, 1555; facsimile reprint together with a translation into English by W.W. Kershaw and P.A. Negretti, London: Raquetier Productions Ltd, 1984.

Schetelig, C., 'Eingesandt', in *Spiel und Sport*, 17 January 1900, p. 125.

Schetelig, C., 'Zur Gründung eines deutschen Lawn-Tennis-Verbandes', in *Sport im Wort*, no. 52 (1901), Thursday, 26 December 1901, p. 697f.

Schetelig, C., 'Zur Gründung eines deutschen Lawn-Tennis-Verbandes', in *Sport im Wort*, no. 7 (1902), Friday, 14 February 1902, p. 83f.

Schlepps, F., 'Zur Gründung eines deutschen Lawn-Tennis-Verbandes', in *Sport im Wort*, no. 2 (1902), Friday, 10 January 1902, p. 22.

Schmidt-Knatz, K., 'Der Süddeutsche Lawn-Tennis-Verband', in *Sport im Wort*, no. 15 (1902), Friday, 11 April 1902, p. 188f.

Schmidt-Knatz, K., 'Eingesandt', in *Sport im Wort*, no. 51 (1901), Thursday, 19 December 1901, p. 686f.

Schmidt-Knatz, K., 'Zur Gründung eines Deutschen Lawn-Tennis-Verbandes', in *Sport im Wort*, no. 6 (1902), Friday, 7 February 1902, pp. 72–4.

Schmitt, C., 'Etymologie und Semantik – Zur Entstehung der Zählweise beim Tennissport', in J. Schmidt-Radefeldt and A. Harder (eds), *Sprachwandel und Sprachgeschichte. Festschrift für Helmut Lüdtke zum 65. Geburtstag*, Tübingen: Gunter Narr Verlag, 1993, pp. 191–201.

Schmitt, C., 'Die Araber und der Tennissport', in J. Lüdtke (ed.), *Romania Arabica*, Festschrift für Reinhold Kontzi zum 70. Geburtstag, Tübingen: Gunter Narr Verlag 1996, pp. 47–55.

Schneider, E., 'Das Tübinger Collegium Illustre', in *Württembergische Vierteljahrshefte für Landesgeschichte*, new series, 7 (1898), pp. 217–45.

Schniewind, P.W., *Anglicans in Germany. A History of Anglican Chaplaincies in Germany until 1945*, Darmstadt: Weihert-Druck GmbH, 1988.

Schomburgk, W., 'Englisches und deutsches Lawn-Tennis', in *Der Lawn-Tennis-Sport*, 3 (1906), no. 29, 9 November 1906, pp. 429–32.

Schomburgk, W., 'Hamburger Tenniserinnerungen', in *Der Tennissport*, 19 (1942), no. 7, 4 June 1942, p. 54f.

Schottus, A., SJ [Andrea Scoto], *Itinerario overo nova descrittione de' viaggi d'Italia principali … Illustrato […] da F[rancesco] Bertelli*, Padua: F. Bolzetta, 1642.

Schrader, C. R., *Handlist of Extant Manuscripts containing the De Re Militari of Flavius Vegetius Renatus*, complete edition: *The Ownership and Distribution of Manuscripts of the 'De Re militari' of Flavius Vegetius Renatus Before the Year 1300*, Columbia University, 1976.

Schramm, P.E., *Herrschaftszeichen und Staatssymbolik*, Schriften der Monumenta Germaniae Historica, vol. 13, I–III, 3 vols, Stuttgart: Hiersemann Verlag, 1954–1956.

Schrötter, F. Baron von (ed.), *Wörterbuch der Münzkunde*, Berlin: de Gruyter, 1930.

Schultz, A., *Das höfische Leben zur Zeit der Minnesänger*, 2 vols, Leipzig: Verlag S. Hirzel, 1879–1880.

Schulz, W., *Lambert Doomer. Sämtliche Zeichnungen*, Berlin: Walter de Gruyter, 1974.

Sears, R.D., 'The First National Championship', in *Fifty Years of Lawn Tennis in the United States*, Norwood, MA: Plimpton Press, pp. 21–9.

Secousse, D.-F., *Ordonnances des Roys de France*, vol. 5, Paris: Imprimerie Royale, 1736.

Seel, A., *Laus Pisonis, Text, Übersetzung, Kommentar*, doctoral thesis of the University of Erlangen-Nürnberg, Erlangen: Hogl, 1969.

Seitz, K.L., 'Ein oldenburgisches Ballspiel', in *Körper und Geist*, 11 (1902–1903), p. 402f.

Semrau, F., *Würfel und Würfelspiel im alten Frankreich*, Beihefte zur Zeitschrift für romanische Philologie, no. XXIII, Halle a.d. Saale: Max Niemeyer Verlag, 1910.

Severs, J. Burke (ed.), *A Manual of the Writings in Middle English 1050–1500*, Fascicule 1, I. Romances, New Haven, CN: Connecticut Academy of Arts and Sciences, 1967.

Shannon, Bill (ed.), *United States Tennis Association. Official Encyclopedia of Tennis. Centennial Edition*, New York: Harper & Row, Publishers, 1980.

Shirley, J., *Here Folowing Begynnythe a Full Lamentable Cronycle of the Dethe ... of James Stewarde, Kyng of Scotys*, Miscellanea Scotica. v. 2, Glasgow: J. Wylie & Co., 1818.

Sieber, H., *Schlösser und Herrensitze in Mecklenburg*, Frankfurt am Main: Wolfgang Weidlich, 1960.

Simon, H.O., '25 Jahre Deutscher Tennis-Bund', in F. Gruber, *Amtliches Tennis-Hand-und Jahrbuch 1927 zum Jubiläum 1902–1927 des Deutschen Tennis Bundes*, Heidelberg: Verlag Hermann Meister, 1927, pp. 25–71.

Simon, H.O., 'Aus der Tennisgeschichte', in *Tennis und Golf*, 8 (1931), no. 19, 3 July 1931, p. 526

Simon, H.O., 'Beiträge zur Tennis-Geschichte', in *Tennis und Golf*, 4 (1927), pp. 120f., 167f., 197, 365f.

Simon, H.O., *Berühmte Tennis-Wettkämpfe*, Kleine Tennis-Bücherei, no. 1, Heidelberg: Verlag Hermann Meister, 1927.

Simon, H.O., 'Von unseres Sportes Werdegang', in O. Kreuzer, *Das Buch vom Tennis*, Leipzig: B.G. Teubner, 1926, pp. 1–75.

Simon, R. and Smart, A., *The Art of Cricket*, London: Secker & Warburg, 1983.

Simonini Jr., R.C. (ed.), *Second Frutes by John Florio*, Scholars' Facsimiles and Reprints: Gainsville, Florida, 1953.

Simpson, J.A. and E.S.C. Weiner (eds), *The Oxford English Dictionary*, 2nd edn, 20 vols, Oxford: Clarendon Press, 1989.

Simri, U., 'The Religious and Magical Function of Ball Games in Various Cultures', in *Proceedings of the First International Seminar on the History of Physical Education and Sport*, 1968, Netanya, Israel: Wingate Institute for Physical Education, 1969, lecture no. 2, pp. 1–20.

Simri, U., 'The Responsa of Rabbi Moses Provencalo (1560) about the Game of Tennis on Sabbath', in idem (ed.), *Physical Education and Sports in the Jewish History and Culture. Proceedings of an International Seminar at Wingate Institute*, July 1973. The Wingate Institute for Physical Education and Sport, 1973, pp. 15–29 und 51f.

Skeat, W.W., *An Etymological Dictionary of the English Language*, Oxford: Clarendon Press, 1882.

Skeat, W.W. (ed.), *Chaucerian and Other Pieces. Being a Supplement to the Complete Works of Geoffrey Chaucer*, vol. 7, Oxford: Clarendon Press, 1897.

Skinner, S., *Etymologicon Linguæ Anglicanæ*, London: T. Roycroft, 1671.

Smidt, J.R.H. de, *Les noëls et la tradition populaire*, Amsterdam: H.J. Paris, 1932.

Smithers, G.V. (ed.), *Havelok*, Oxford: Clarendon Press, 1987.

Snöbohm, A.T., *Gotlands Land och Folk*, Visby: Gotlänningens Tryckeri, 1897.

Spitzer, R., *Französische Kulturstudien. I. Beiträge zur Geschichte des Spieles in Alt-Frankreich*, Heidelberg: Carl Winter, 1891.

Standop, E. and E. Mertner, *Englische Literaturgeschichte*, Heidelberg: Quelle & Meyer, 1967.

Steffen, W., *Chronik der Familie Walter Steffen*, typescript owned by the family, September 1944.

Stella, J. and C. Bouzonnet-Stella, *Les jeux et plaisirs de l'enfance*, Paris: aux Galleries du Louvre, 1667; reprinted Geneva: Slatkine, 1981.

Stern, T., *The Rubber-Ball Games of the Americas*, Monographs of the American Ethnological Society 17, Seattle: University of Washington Press, 1949, reprinted 1966.

Sting, H. *et al.*, *90 Jahre Club Raffelberg. Tradition und Gegenwart*, Duisburg: K. Edel, 1979.

Strange, J. (ed.), *Caesarii heisterbacensis monachi ordinis Cisterciensis Dialogus Miraculorum*, 2 vols, Cologne: H. Lempertz & Comp., 1851.

Streib, W., 'Geschichte des Ballhauses', in *Leibesübungen und körperliche Erziehung*, (1935), no. 18, pp. 373–82, and no. 19 (1935), pp. 419–32.

Strohmeyer, H., *Beiträge zur Geschichte von Leibeserziehung und Sport in Österreich*, Wiener Beiträge zur Sportwissenschaft, vol. 6, Vienna: Wissenschaftliche Gesellschaft für Leibeserziehung und Sport, 1980.

Struck, W.H., *Das Cistercienserkloster Marienstatt im Mittelalter*, Wiesbaden: Selbstverlag der historischen Kommission für Nassau, 1965.

Suhle, A., *Deutsche Münz- und Geldgeschichte von den Anfängen bis zum 15. Jahrhundert*, 3rd edn, East Berlin: Deutscher Verlag der Wissenschaften, 1968.

Swezey, W.R., 'La pelota mixteca', in J. Litvak King and N. Castillo (eds), *Religión en Mesoamérica*, XII Mesa Redonda de la Sociedad Mexicana de Antropologia, Mexico, 1972, pp. 471–7.

Taladoire, E., 'La pelota mixteca: un juego contemporaneo con origines complejas', in *Los Procesos de Cambio* (*en Mesoamérica y areas circunvecinas*), XV Mesa Redonda de la Sociedad Mexicana de Antropologia, Universidad de Guanjuato, 1977, vol. 1, pp. 431–7.

Tauber, W., *Das Würfelspiel im Mittelalter und in der frühen Neuzeit. Eine kultur- und sprachgeschichtliche Darstellung*, Europäische Hochschulschriften. Reihe I. Deutsche Sprache und Literatur, vol. 959, Frankfurt am Main: Peter Lang, 1987.

The India Office List for 1923, 37th edn, London: Harrison and Sons, Ltd, 1923.

The Kenneth Ritchie Wimbledon Library Catalogue, 4th edn, London: The Wimbledon Lawn Tennis Museum, 1989.

The National Union Catalogue, vol. 444, London: Mansell Information/Publishing Limited, 1976.

The Pierpont Morgan Library. Sports and Pastimes from the Fourteenth through the Eighteenth Century. Illustrated Guide to an Exhibition March 25, 1946–June 29, 1946, New York, 1946.

Thomas, A., 'Le jeu de la soule', in *Annuaire pratique des Hautes Études. Section des sciences historiques et philologiques*, (1919–1920), pp. 5–8.

Todd, T., *The Tennis Players from Pagan Rites to Strawberries and Cream*, Guernsey: Vallancey Press, 1979.

Toll, J.M., *Niederländisches Lehngut im Mittelenglischen*, Halle a.d. Saale: Max Niemeyer Verlag, 1926.

Tollenaere, F. de and F. Claes, SJ (eds), *Het Tyrocinium van Petrus Apherdianus*, Monumenta Lexicographica Neerlandica. Series II: Saeculum XVI. Volumen 4, 's-Gravenhage: Martinus Nijhoff, 1976.

Törngren, L.M., *Fria Lekar. Anvisning till Skolans Tjenst*, 2nd edn with illustrations, Stockholm: P.A. Norstedt & Söners Förlag, 1880.

Torre, A. van, SJ, *Dialogi familiares*, new edn, Antwerp: Martinus Verdussen, 1657.

Toulet, L., *La pelota vasqua*, Barcelona: Editorial De Vecchi, S.A., 1988.

Trattato del Giuoco della Palla di Messer Antonio Scaino da Salo, Venice: Gabriel Giolito de' Ferrari, 1555; facsimile edn by Libraria Antiquaria W. Casari - Testaferrata, Rome: Soc. Multigrafica Editrice, 1968.

Travers, B. (ed.), *Official MTC 1989 Media Guide*, Raleigh, NC: Schuetz Typesetting Service, 1989.

Trengove, A., *The Story of the Davis Cup*, London: Stanley Paul, 1985.

Urselmann, R., *Chronik des Harvestehuder Tennis- und Hockey-Clubs 1891–1991*, Hamburg: LN-Druck, Lübeck, 1991.

V., R., 'Eine neue Tennisanlage in Württemberg', in *Tennis und Golf*, 4 (1927), p. 182.

van Eeghen, P. and J.Ph. van der Kellen, *Het Werk van Jan en Casper Luyken*, 2 vols, Amsterdam: Frederik Muller & C°., 1905.

Varij lusus pueriles ex D. Eras[mo,] M. Corderio, & L. Vive separati in gratiam puerorum, Paris: Matthaeus David, 1555.

Vaultier, R., *Le Folklore pendant la guerre de Cent Ans d'après les Lettres de Rémission du Trésor des Chartes*, Paris: Librairie Guénégaud, Marc Pénau & Cⁱᵉ, 1965.

Vennebusch, J., *Die theologischen Handschriften des Stadtarchivs Köln*, Mitteilungen aus dem Stadtarchiv von Köln, Sonderreihe: Die Handschriften des Archivs, no. 1: Part 1, Cologne: Böhlau-Verlag, 1976.

Verdam, J. (ed.), *G. van der Schueren's Teuthonista of Duytschlender*, Leiden: E.J. Brill, 1896.

Verdam, J. and C.H. Ebbinge Wubben, *Middelnederlandsch Handwoordenboek*, 's-Gravenhage: Martinus Nijhoff, 1932; reprinted 1976.

Verdon, J., *Les Loisirs en France au Moyen Age*, Paris: Librairie Jules Tallandier, 1980.

Vinaver, E. (ed.), *The Works of Sir Thomas Malory*, 2nd edn, 3 vols, Oxford: Clarendon Press, 1967.

Voigt, C.A., 'Das grosse internationale Turnier zu Homburg', in *Sport im Bild,* 2 (1896), no. 36, p. 569.

Voigt, C.A. 'Das grosse Turnier zu Homburg', in *Sport im Bild*, 2 (1896), no. 37, p. 384f.

Voigt, C.A., 'Das Heiligendammer Turnier', in *Sport im Wort*, no. 35 (1900), Thursday, 30 August 1900, pp. 362–4.

Voigt, C.A., *Das Lawn-Tennis Spiel und Die Kunst zu spielen*, Magdeburg: Verlag von Albert Rathke, 1895.

Voigt, C.A., 'Der König von Portugal als Lawn-Tennis-Spieler', in *Sport im Bild,* 7 (1901), no. 50, p. 792.

Voigt, C.A., 'Etwas über die Turniersprache', in *Sport im Wort*, no. 18 (1902), Friday, 2 May 1902, p. 227.

Voigt, C.A., 'Homburg v.d. Höhe [Part I and Part II]', in *Lawn Tennis*, 23 August 1899, pp. 289–91 and 313–15.

Voigt, C.A., 'Lawn-Tennis "Berufsspieler"', in *Sport im Wort*, no. 49 (1901), Thursday, 5 December 1901, p. 660f.

Voigt, C.A., 'Lawn-Tennis. Das grosse Turnier zu Homburg', in *Sport im Bild,* 2 (1896), no. 37, p. 584f.

Voigt, C.A., 'Le lawn-tennis en France', in *La vie au grand air*, (1902), no. 173, 5 January 1902, pp. 34–6.

Voigt, C.A., 'The Origin of the Davis Cup', in *Lawn Tennis and Badminton,* 5 (1912), no. 23, 11 July 1912, p. 485.

Voigt, C.A., 'Zur Gründung eines Deutschen Lawn-Tennis-Verbandes', in *Sport im Wort*, no. 9 (1902), Friday, 28 February 1902, p. 109.

Volley, 'Vom Hamburger Turnier', in *Sport im Bild,* 3 (1897), no. 36, p. 602.

von der Meden, C.A., *Leitfaden zur Veranstaltung von Lawn-Tennis-Turnieren*, Berlin: Verlag von 'Spiel und Sport', 1895.

Wailly, J.N. de and L.V. Delisle, *Recueil des Historiens des Gaules et de la France*, vol. 22, Paris: Imprimerie Impériale, 1865.

Wallace, K., *The Barbarians of Workington: Uppies v Downies*, Ulverston: The Reminder Printing Company, 1991.

Warner, G.F., *British Museum. Catalogue of Western Manuscripts in the Old Royal and King's Collections*, 4 vols, London: British Museum, 1921.

Wartburg, W. von, *Französisches Etymologisches Wörterbuch*, Bonn und

Basel: F. Klopp Verlag GmbH und R.G. Zbinden Druck und Verlag AG, 1928–.

Weaver, J.R.H. (ed.), *The Dictionary of National Biography 1912–1921*, London: Oxford University Press, 1927.

Wegner, E., *Das Ballspiel der Römer*, doctoral thesis of the University of Rostock, Würzburg: Buchdruckerei R. Mayr, 1938.

Weichert, W. (ed.), *Convenio Ecuatoriano Alemán 'Mejoriamento y difusión de la educación física y el deporte en el nivel primario'*, Memorias I Congreso Nacional de Cultura Física, Quito 1989, Quito: Ministerio de Educación y Cultura, 1990.

Weigel, C., *Abbildung der Gemein-Nützlichen Haupt-Stände ... nach dem Leben gezeichnet und in Kupfer gebracht*, Regensburg, 1698.

Weigel, C., *Abbildung der Gemein-Nützlichen Haupt-Stände ...*, reprint (of the engravings and poems accompanying them), Dortmund: Harenberg Kommunikation, 1977.

Weiler, I., *Der Sport bei den Völkern der alten Welt*, Darmstadt: Wissenschaftliche Buchgesellschaft, 1981.

Wells, C.J., *Deutsch: eine Sprachgeschichte bis 1945*, Reihe Germanistische Linguistik, Tübingen: Max Niemeyer Verlag, 1990.

Wentworth, H. and S. Berg Flexner (eds), *Dictionary of American Slang*, 2nd edn, New York: Thomas Y. Crowell, 1975.

Westra, W., 'Kaatsen', in *De Revue der Sporten,* 1 (1907), pp. 99–101.

White, C.M., 'John Pius Boland (O.S. 1881–90). Scholar–Athlete–Statesman and The Establishment of The National University of Ireland', in *The Oratory School Magazine*, 146 (1986), pp. 40–5.

Whitham, J.A., *The Church of St. Mary of Ottery in the County of Devon*, 8th edn, Gloucester: The British Publishing Company Ltd, 1982.

Whiting, E.K., *The Poems of John Audelay*, Early English Text Society, o.s., 184, Yale doctoral thesis, London: H. Milford, Oxford University Press, 1931.

Whitman, M.D., 'Net Play: A Determining Factor', in *Fifty Years of Lawn Tennis in the United States*, Norwood, MA: Plimpton Press, 1931, pp. 73–81.

Whitman, M.D., *Tennis: Origins and Mysteries*, New York: The Derrydale Press, 1932; reprinted Detroit: Singing Tree Press, 1968.

Who Was Who, vol. III., *Who Was Who 1929–1940*, London: Adam & Charles Black, 1947.

Wickham, L.G. (ed.), *The Dictionary of National Biography 1931–1940*, Oxford: Oxford University Press, 1949.

Wieck, R.S., *Time Sanctified: The Book of Hours in Medieval Art and Life*, New York: Braziller, 1988.

Williams, J.M.W. (ed.), *A Critical Edition of The Turke & Gowin*, Ann Arbor, Michigan: A. Bell & Howard Information Company, 1990.

Wills, H., *Fifteen-Thirty: The Story of a Tennis Player*, New York: Charles Scribner's Sons, 1937.

Windeatt, B.A. (ed.), *Geoffrey Chaucer. Troilus & Criseyde*, London: Longman, 1984.

Wörterbuch der regionalen Umgangssprache in Lateinamerika. Amerikaspanisch Deutsch, Leipzig: VEB Verlag Enzyklopädie, 1977.

Wylie, J.H. and W. Templeton Waugh, *The Reign of Henry the Fifth*, 3 vols, Cambridge: Cambridge University Press, 1914–1929.

Y., M., 'Die Gründung der Oesterreichischen Lawn-Tennis-Association', in *Sport im Wort*, 5 (1902), 31 January 1902, p. 57.

Yates, F.A., *John Florio. The Life of an Italian in Shakespeare's England*, Cambridge: Cambridge University Press, 1934; reprinted New York: Octagon Books, Inc., 1968.

Young, D.C., 'Demetrios Vikelas: First President of the IOC', in *Stadion,* 14 (1988), pp. 85–102.

Young, D.C., *The Olympic Myth of Greek Amateur Athletics*, Chicago: Ares Publishers, Inc., 1984.

Zappert, G., 'Über Stab und Ruthe im Mittelalter', in *Sitzungsberichte der Kaiserlichen Akademie der Wissenschaften. Philosophisch-historische Classe,* 9 (1852), pp. 173–221.

Zdekauer, L., 'Il giuoco a Venezia sulla fine del secolo XVI', in *Archivio Veneto,* 28 (1884), pp. 132–46.

Notes on the illustrations

◇

PLATE 1   The prose novel of Lancelot du Lac, French, from the beginning of the fourteenth century. British Library, MS. Royal 20.d.IV, fol. 207. London.

PLATE 2   *Avis aus Roys*, French, court workshop of Charles V. Pierpont Morgan Library, M.456, fol. 68v. New York.

PLATE 3   Book of hours of the Duchess of Burgundy (month of June, detail), northern French. Institut de France, Musée Condé, MS. 76, fol. 6v. Chantilly Cedex.

PLATE 4   French version of Valerius Maximus by Simon de Hesdin and Nicolas de Gonesse, fifteenth century. British Library, MS. Harley 4375, fol. 151v. London.

PLATE 5   'The letter given to Uriah' (2 Samuel, 11:14), Flemish. The Rt. Hon. The Lord Aberdare. London.

PLATE 6   Abbey of Beaumont in Belgium; gouache by Adrien de Montigny of Valenciennes in *Description particulaire de tout le Pais et Comté . . . de Hainaut*, 1598. Österreichische Nationalbibliothek, Cod.min.50, vol. 12, fol. 42v. Vienna.

PLATE 7   From the *Stammbuch* of a German student who studied in Padua or Siena (*c.* 1610), watercolour. P.J. Wordie, Dunblane, Scotland.

PLATE 8   From the *Stammbuch* of Duke August the Younger of Brunswick Luneburg. Herzog August Bibliothek Wolfenbüttel, Cod. Guelf.84.6 Aug .40: Ballhouse of the Collegium Illustre, Tübingen. Wolfenbüttel, Germany.

PLATE 9   From the *Stammbuch* of Johann Heinrich von Offenburg, 1598. Städtische Sammlungen Tübingen, Germany.

PLATE 10   Edith Hayllar, 'A Summer Shower', 1883. The Forbes Magazine Collection, New York.

PLATE 11   Sir John Lavery, 'The Tennis Party', 1885. City of Aberdeen Art Gallery and Museums Collections, Scotland.

PLATE 12   'Tennis Party in America', from *Shoppell's Homes Catalogue*, 1886, frontispiece. Racket Sports Heritage Collection, Elizabeth, Pennsylvania.

PLATE 13   'Tea and Tennis', *c.* 1890–1900. The Wimbledon Lawn Tennis Museum, London.

PLATE 14   Charles March Gere (1869–1941). Tennis party in a garden owned by residents of Willes Terrace in Leamington Spa (1900). Cheltenham Art Gallery and Museum Service, Cheltenham.

PLATE 15   'Bad Homburg impressions', 1895. Colour wood engraving after a drawing by Fritz Gehrke. Museum im Gotischen Haus, Tannenwaldweg. Photograph by Bernhard Langendorf, Bad Homburg v.d. Höhe.

PLATE 16   'Dur und Moll' by Th. Th. Heine, published in *Vom Fels zum Meer* 14 (1894–5), p.24. Museum im Gotischen Haus, Tannenwaldweg. Photograph by Bernhard Langendorf, Bad Homburg v.d. Höhe.

FIGURE 1   From Andreas Schottus SJ (Andrea Scoto), *Itinerario overo nova descrittione de viaggi principali d'Italia . . . Illustrato . . . da*

F[rancesco] Bertelli, Padua, 1642. The British Library, London.

FIGURE 2   The Porte d'Ardon, photograph by Jan Lou Girard, Laon, France.

FIGURE 3   The cloisters of Moissac, twelfth century. Photograph by Paul Elek Ltd, London.

FIGURE 4   From Viktor Balck, *Illustrerad Idrottsbok*, Stockholm: C.E. Fritze's Hofbokhandel, 1886, p.78.

FIGURE 5   From Viktor Balck, *Illustrerad Idrottsbok*, Stockholm: C.E. Fritze's Hofbokhandel, 1886, p.79.

FIGURE 6   Chest of the 'Pas Saladin' (side view), nineteenth-century copy. Musée National du Moyen Age, Paris. Agence Photographique de la Réunion des Musées Nationaux, Paris.

FIGURE 7   Chest of the 'Pas Saladin' (front view), nineteenth-century copy. Musée National du Moyen Age, Paris. Agence Photographique de la Réunion des Musées Nationaux, Paris.

FIGURE 8   From Charles Cotton, *The Complete Gamester*, 1674. The British Library, London.

FIGURE 9   From *Les jeux des jeunes garçons*, 1807. Schweizerisches Sportmuseum, Basle.

FIGURE 10   Book of hours, Franco-Flemish (? Cambrai), *c.* 1300. The Walters Art Gallery, MS.W.88, fol. 59v. Baltimore, Maryland.

FIGURE 11   Book of hours, Franco-Flemish (? Cambrai), *c.* 1300. The Walters Art Gallery, MS.W.88, fol. 70r. Baltimore, Maryland.

FIGURE 12   Simon Vostre, *Hore beate marie virginis secundum Vsum Romanum*, Paris, *c.* 1510. Bayerische Staatsbibliothek, Munich.

FIGURE 13   Book of hours, French, sixteenth century. Bodleian Library, MS. Douce 135, fol. 7r. Oxford.

FIGURE 14   The National Trust for Scotland for Places of Historic Interest or Natural Beauty, Edinburgh.

FIGURE 15   From Lance St John Butler and Peter Wordie (eds), *The Royal Game*, Edinburgh: Bookworm Typesetting Ltd, 1989, p.32.

FIGURE 16   Tombstone of the Basque pelotari, Guillaume Diriart. Drawing by Louis Colas. From *La Tombe Basque. Recueil d'inscriptions funéraires et domestiques du Pays Basque Français*, Paris: Honoré Champion, 1923, pp.204, 711.

FIGURE 17   Christoff Weigel, *Abbildung der Gemein-Nützlichen Haupt-Stände*, Regensburg, 1698. Universitäts- und Landesbibliothek, Bonn.

FIGURE 18   The *Schwarzsches Trachtenbuch* II, 1561. Herzog Anton Ulrich-Museum, Brunswick. Photograph by B.P. Keiser.

FIGURE 19   Photograph by Wright Color, Warwick.

FIGURE 20   Charles Hulpeau, *Le leu Royal de la pavlme*, Paris, 1632. Bibliothèque Nationale de France, Paris.

FIGURE 21   Washed pen-and-ink drawing, Flemish School, mid-sixteenth century. Musée du Louvre, Paris. Agence Photographique de la Réunion des Musées Nationaux, Paris.

FIGURE 22   Lucas Gassel, 'Courtly Grounds with scenes from the story of David and Bathsheba' (detail). Wadsworth Atheneum, Hartford, Connecticut.

FIGURE 23   Marc Gheerarts, *Brugae Flandorum, urbs et emporium*, Bruges, 1562. Bibliothèque Royale Albert ler, Brussels.

FIGURE 24   Anton Sander [Antonius Sanderus], *Flandria Illustrata*, Cologne, 1641. Universitäts- und Landesbibliothek, Bonn.

FIGURE 25   Johannes Sambucus, *Emblemata*, Antwerp, 1564, p.133. Akadémiai Kladó, Budapest.

FIGURE 26   Johannes Amos Comenius, *Orbis sensualium pictus*. Facsimile reprint of the edition Noribergae, M. Endter, 1658, Osnabrück: Otto Zeller, 1964, p.270.

FIGURE 27   Book of hours, northern French, 1450–60. Fundação Calouste Gulbenkian, Museu MS. L.A.135, fol. 7v. Lisbon.

FIGURE 28   Book of hours, School of Tours, *c.* 1450. Biblioteca Nacional, MS. Vit. 25–3, fol. 8. Madrid.

FIGURE 29   Copper engraving from a series 'Children's Games', French, sixteenth century.

Cabinet des Estampes, Cliché No. 63A 12662. Bibliothèque Nationale, Paris.

FIGURE 30   Barthélemy de Momper, 'Le Koert de Brvxselles', dry-point etching, sixteenth century. Musée de la Ville de Bruxelles–Maison du Roi, Brussels.

FIGURE 31   Jean van de Velde, 'The Court in Brussels', c. 1645, engraver Corneille-J. Visscher. Bibliothèque Royale Albert ler, Brussels.

FIGURE 32   Lucas van Velen, 'L'ancienne Cour de Brabant à Bruxelles', oil on wood, 1635. Musée de la Ville de Bruxelles–Maison du Roi, Brussels.

FIGURE 33   Jacques Stella and Claudine Bouzonnet-Stella, *Les jeux et les plaisirs de l'enfance*, Paris, 1667. Editions Slatkine, Geneva.

FIGURE 34   Lambert Doomer, 'De veste van Samuers', 1646. Fondation Custodia (Collection Frits Lugt), Institut Néerlandais, Paris.

FIGURE 35   Gabriel Perelle, 'Une Partie de Paume jouée avec des Battoirs'. Bibliothèque Nationale de France, Paris.

FIGURE 36   Coloured pen-and-ink drawing from a sketch by Jan Wouters titled 'In universam Aristotelis logicam', 1650. Stedelijke Musea, Louvain.

FIGURE 37   Peter van der Borcht, 'Playing Monkeys', sixteenth century, engraver Justus Sadeler, number 13 of a series of 16 engravings. Rijksmuseum, Amsterdam.

FIGURE 38   Photograph: Sportmuseum Vlaanderen v.z.w., Louvain.

FIGURE 39   *Leeuwarder Courant*, Leeuwarden.

FIGURE 40   *Leeuwarder Courant*, Leeuwarden.

FIGURE 41   Photograph by Dr Vicente Navarro Adelantado, Las Palmas de Gran Canaria.

FIGURE 42   Santiago Ixtaltepec, on the Tlacolula side of the Rio Salado Valley, Oaxaca de Juarez, Mexico, 1971. Photograph by Robert M. Malina, Austin, Texas. Sportmuseum Vlaanderen v.z.w., Louvain.

FIGURE 43   Mixtecan ball game, c. 1950. Schweizerisches Sportmuseum, Basle.

FIGURE 44   Photograph by Veerle van Mele. Sportmuseum Vlaanderen v.z.w., Louvain.

FIGURE 45   KNKB-Kaatsmuseum, Franeker. Photograph by Hommema, Franehof.

FIGURE 46   From the *Vriesch Almanak, of Tijdwijzer, voor het Schrikkeljaar 1824*. Provincjale Biblioteek fan Fryslân, Leeuwarden.

FIGURE 47   Ivory carving, lid of a jewel case. Museo Nazionale di Ravenna.

FIGURE 48   Ivory mirror case, formerly among the collections of the Cistercian abbey of Rein, Austria. From Alwin Schultz, *Das höfische Leben zur Zeit der Minnesänger*, 2 vols. Leipzig: Verlag S. Hirzel, 1879–80, vol. 1, p.450.

FIGURE 49   Chrétien de Troyes, *Yvain*, thirteenth century. Bibliothèque Nationale de France, Paris.

FIGURE 50   Diagram designed by Heiner Gillmeister.

FIGURE 51   Photograph by Heiner Gillmeister.

FIGURE 52   From Roger Lecotté (ed.), *Le jeu de tamis en Ile-de-France*, Meaux: Imprimerie André-Pouyé, 1947, p.12.

FIGURE 53   Photograph by Roger Morgan, Cambridge.

FIGURE 54   From Master [?Johannes] Ingold, OP, *Das guldine spil*, c. 1432. After the edition Augsburg: Günther Zeiner, 1472. Bayerische Staatsbibliothek, Munich.

FIGURE 55   Guillaume de la Perrière, *Le Théâtre des bons engins*, Paris, 1539. Bayerische Staatsbibliothek, Munich.

FIGURE 56   Guillaume de la Perrière, *Le Théâtre des bons engins*, Paris, 1539. Bayerische Staatsbibliothek, Munich.

FIGURE 57   Crispijn van de Passe, '*Kaatsen* in a Dutch town'. From George Wither, *A Collection of Emblemes*, London, 1635.

FIGURE 58   Copper engraving by M. Merian, text by M. Zeiller, from *Topographia*

Palatinatus Rheni et Vicinarum Regionis, 1645. Kurpfälzisches Museum, Heidelberg.

FIGURE 59   The 'Petrarch Master', woodcut illustrating the chapter on 'Von Kurtzweyl des Palwerffens' (the pastime of play at ball). Franciscus Petrarcha, *Von der Artzney Bayder Glueck des Guten vnd Widerwertigen*, Augsburg: Heinrich Steiner, 1532. Municipal Library, Brunswick, Shelf mark C527. Facsimile reprint by Friedrich Wittig Verlag, Hamburg, 1984.

FIGURE 60   From a series of copper engravings by Johann Christoph Neyffer, titled *Illustrissimi Wirtembergici Ducalis novi Collegii . . . delineatio*, 1606–8, engraver Ludwig Ditzinger. Württembergische Landesbibliothek, Stuttgart.

FIGURE 61   From a series of copper engravings by Johann Christoph Neyffer, titled *Illustrissimi Wirtembergici Ducalis novi Collegii . . . delineatio*, 1606–8, engraver Ludwig Ditzinger. Württembergische Landesbibliothek, Stuttgart.

FIGURE 62   Crispijn van de Passe, *Academia, sive Speculum vitae scolasticae . . . Traiecti Batavorum. Ex officina chalcogr. Crispiani Passaei, prostant apud Joannem Jansonium bibliopol Arnhemii*, 1612. Re-used by Jacob von der Heyden in *Speculum Cornelianum . . . Jetzt auffs newe mit vielen . . . Kupferstücken . . . an Tag geben*, Strasbourg, 1618. Deutsche Staatsbibliothek, Berlin.

FIGURE 63   Engraving by Peter Aubry. Formerly part of the Margrave's Collection transferred from Ansbach to Erlangen in 1806. Universitätsbibliothek Erlangen-Nürnberg, Erlangen.

FIGURE 64   Wolfgang Birkner, *Des Durchlauchtigen . . . Fürsten . . . Herrn Johann Casimirs Hertzogen zue Sachsen . . . New erbautes Ballnhaus zu Coburgk*, 1632, engraver Johann Dürr. Kunstsammlungen der Veste Coburg, Coburg.

FIGURE 65   Oberösterreichisches Landesmuseum, MS 10, 737, fol. 352r. Linz.

FIGURE 66   Wingfield, *The Major's Game of Lawn Tennis*, London: Harrison and Sons, 1874. The Racquet & Tennis Club, New York.

FIGURE 67   From Wingfield, *The Major's Game of Lawn Tennis*, p. [5]. The Racquet & Tennis Club, New York.

FIGURE 68   The Wimbledon Lawn Tennis Museum, London.

FIGURE 69   Heiner Gillmeister after Tom Todd, *The Tennis Players from Pagan Rites to Strawberries and Cream*, Guernsey: Vallancey Press, 1979, p. 214f.

FIGURE 70   From *Lawn-Tennis und Golf* 10, (1913), no. 5, 18 April 1913, p.108.

FIGURE 71   The Wimbledon Lawn Tennis Museum, London.

FIGURE 72   From *Illustrated and Dramatic News*, 20 July 1878. The Gurney Collection, Colchester, Essex.

FIGURE 73   From N.L. Jackson (ed.), *The Lawn Tennis Magazine* no. 1 (June 1885). The Gurney Collection, Colchester, Essex.

FIGURE 74   From N.L. Jackson (ed.), *The Lawn Tennis Magazine* no. 1 (June 1885). The Gurney Collection, Colchester, Essex.

FIGURE 75   Leicestershire County Council Museum.

FIGURE 76   Engraving from *Harper's Weekly*, vol. 30, no. 1551, 11 September 1886. Racket Sports Heritage Collection, Elizabeth, Pennsylvania.

FIGURE 77   Engraving from *Harper's Weekly*, vol. 30, no. 1551, 11 September 1886. Racket Sports Heritage Collection, Elizabeth, Pennsylvania.

FIGURE 78   The Racquet & Tennis Club, New York.

FIGURE 79   The Racquet & Tennis Club, New York.

FIGURE 80   From Parke Cummings, *American Tennis: The Story of the Game and its People*, Boston: Little, Brown & Company, 1957, p.73.

FIGURE 81   From a series of photographs by Albert Meyer, Court Photographer, Berlin. Carl und Lieselott Diem-Archiv, Cologne.

FIGURE 82   The Oratory School Archive. Reading, Berkshire.

FIGURE 83   Municipal Archive, Gotisches Haus, Bad Homburg v.d. Höhe.

FIGURE 84   From the private collection of Sir Ralph Anstruther, Fife, Scotland.

FIGURE 85   Original postcard, Municipal Archive, Baden-Baden.

FIGURE 86   From Hans Oskar Behrens, *Leitung grosser Lawn-Tennis-Turniere*, Baden-Baden: Verlag von Emil Sommermeyer, 1904.

FIGURE 87   Bestandsname Senat, file no. Cl VII. Lit. Rf No. 195 b Vol. 2, Staatsarchiv, Hamburg.

FIGURE 88   Robert, Baron von Fichard (ed.), *Erstes deutshes Lawn-Tennis-Jahrbuch nebst den officiellen Spielregeln*, Charlottenburg: Redaktion von 'Spiel und Sport', 1894, p.57.

FIGURE 89   Original photograph from the collection of Jörg von Mitzlaff-Laeisz, Hamburg.

FIGURE 90   London Metropolitan Archives, London.

FIGURE 91   From 'Mr. C.A. Voigt', in *Lawn Tennis and Croquet*, 10 May, 1899, p.41. British Library, London.

FIGURE 92   From Charles Adolph Voigt, *Das Lawn-Tennis Spiel und Die Kunst zu Spielen*, Magdeburg: Verlag von Albert Rathke, 1895, p.16.

FIGURE 93   From 'A Chat with Count Voss', in *Lawn Tennis and Croquet*, 7 February, 1900, pp. 468–70. British Library, London.

FIGURE 94   Braunschweiger Tennis- und Hockey-Club e.V., Brunswick.

FIGURE 95   Braunschweiger Tennis- und Hockey-Club e.V., Brunswick.

FIGURE 96   *Kleine Presse. Stadtanzeiger und Fremdenblatt*, no.108, Frankfurt, Friday, 6 August 1885. Frankfurter Sportmuseum, Frankfurt am Main.

FIGURE 97   *Kleine Presse. Stadtanzeiger und Fremdenblatt*, no.197, Frankfurt, Friday, 24 August 1894. Frankfurter Sportmuseum, Frankfurt am Main.

FIGURE 98   From the private collection of Heinz Becker, Taunusstein-Hahn.

FIGURE 99   From the private collection of the Lane family.

FIGURE 100   Photograph by J. Burke, Punjab. From the private collection of the Lane family.

FIGURE 101   *The Official Lawn Tennis Bulletin*, 1 (1894), no. 4, 1 August 1894.

FIGURE 102   From *Sport im Bild*, 15 (1909), no. 30, p.980.

FIGURE 103   Photograph by O.C. Gehrckens, Hamburg. From Robert, Baron von Fichard (ed.), *Illustriertes Lawn-Tennis-Jahrbuch für das Deutsche Reich, Österreich-Ungarn und die Schweiz*, vol. 10, Baden-Baden: Verlag Emil Sommermeyer, 1904, p.63.

FIGURE 104   From an unidentified German journal, in the private collection of the Lane family.

FIGURE 105   From *Sport im Bild*, 13 (1907), no. 25, p.759.

Index

$\diamond$

Numbers refer to pages unless they are preceded by Roman numerals, or the letters P and F. In these cases, they refer to *notes* of the chapters indicated by the Roman numeral, or to Plates and Figures respectively. If names in the index differ from those appearing in a source quoted, the former will have to be considered the correct and more complete ones ascertained by subsequent research.